Questioning the Media
SECOND EDITION

Questioning the Media
A CRITICAL INTRODUCTION

Editors
JOHN DOWNING
ALI MOHAMMADI
ANNABELLE SREBERNY-MOHAMMADI

SECOND EDITION

SAGE Publications
International Educational and Professional Publisher
Thousand Oaks   London   New Delhi

For information address:

SAGE Publications, Inc.
2455 Teller Road
Thousand Oaks, California 91320

SAGE Publications Ltd.
6 Bonhill Street
London EC2A 4PU
United Kingdom

SAGE Publications India Pvt. Ltd.
M-32 Market
Greater Kailash I
New Delhi 110 048 India

Printed in the United States of America

Library of Congress Cataloging-in-Publication Data

Main entry under title:

Questioning the media: A critical introduction / edited by John
   Downing, Ali Mohammadi, Annabelle Sreberny-Mohammadi.—2nd ed.
      p.   cm.
   Includes bibliographical references.
   ISBN 0-8039-7196-6 (alk. paper).—ISBN 0-8039-7197-4 (pbk.)
   1. Mass media. I. Downing, John. II. Mohammadi, Ali.
   III. Sreberny-Mohammadi, Annabelle.
   P90.Q48   1995
   302.23—dc20   94-48241

95 96 97 98 99 10 9 8 7 6 5 4 3 2 1

Sage Production Editor: Astrid Virding
Sage Typesetter: Andrea D. Swanson

Contents

Chronology of Communications Media

This chronology lists the dates of major technological breakthroughs in communications, first media applications, and establishment of major media institutions. Such a list seems to reproduce the "great men" syndrome; for a critique of this, see Chapter 4. Toward the end of the list, the focus is very much on the United States. (Sources used in the compilation of this list include Wilbur Schramm's *The Story of Human Communications*, 1988, and Frederick Williams's *The Communications Revolution*, 1982.)

35000 B.C.	Cro-Magnon period; speculation that language existed
22000	prehistoric cave paintings
4000	Sumerian writing on clay tablets
3000	early Egyptian hieroglyphics
1800	Phoenician alphabet
130	Library of Alexandria built in Egypt
350 A.D.	handwritten books replace scrolls
600	book printing in China
676	paper and ink used by Arabs and Persians
1200	paper and ink art in Europe
1453	Gutenberg Bible printed
1535	first press in the Americas set up in Mexico
1555	Della Porta projects light
1639	first printing press in North American British colonies

1640   *The Whole Book of Psalmes* is first book printed in North American British Colonies

1665   newspapers first published in England

1690   *Publick Occurrences Both Forreign and Domestick* is first North American newspaper

1741   *American Magazine* and Ben Franklin's *General Magazine* start

1760s   Samuel and John Adams publish *Boston Gazette*

1776   Tom Paine publishes revolutionary pamphlet *Common Sense*

1783   *Pennsylvania Evening Post* is America's first daily newspaper

1790   first federal copyright statute passed by Congress

1791   First Amendment to the Constitution

1817   Harper Brothers establish publishing company

1828   *Freedom's Journal* is first Black newspaper in United States

1833   *New York Sun* ushers in the penny press

1836   Samuel Morse develops the telegraph

1837   Niepce and Daguerre create the daguerreotype

1848   first news agency/wire service, *Associated Press*, formed

1861   *New York Times* established

1866   *The Nation* magazine founded

1866   first transatlantic cable completed

1876   Alexander Graham Bell completes telephone

1888   Eastman produces the Kodak camera

1892   Edison develops kinetoscope

1895   Guglielmo Marconi develops radio telegraphy

1896   Lumière Brothers develop motion picture camera

1910   first alternative movie produced (*The Pullman Porter*, by African American William Foster)

1923   Zworykin demonstrates iconoscope, patents television camera tube

1927   British Broadcasting Corporation founded—model of public service broadcasting authority

1929   Zworykin invents kinescope

1929   Motion Picture Authority formed; Hays Office founded to vet movie content

1931   Workers Film and Photo League established

1933   FM radio demonstrated for RCA executives

1939	paperback books start publishing revolution
1941	FCC authorizes commercial television; WNBT first on the air
1942	first electronic computer in the United States
1943	wire audio recorders used in World War II by Nazi military
1943	duopoly ruling forces NBC to sell a network; start of ABC
1947	transistor invented; Bell Laboratories established
1947	Hollywood Ten jailed for defying communist witch-hunt
1948	*TV Guide* founded
1949	Pacifica radio begins broadcasting
1950	CATV developed; cable TV begins, to boost microwave signal
1954	McCarthy hearings on television
1954	first color television sets; color broadcasting begins
1956	Ampex demonstrates videotape recording
1957	Soviets launch first earth satellite, *Sputnik*
1960	Nixon-Kennedy debates televised
1962	*Telstar* television satellite launched by United States
1965	International Telecommunications Satellite Organization (INTELSAT) begins to relay transatlantic communications
1967	Public Broadcasting Act passed by Congress
1968	portable video recorders introduced
1968	MPAA ratings replace Hays Office
1970	Public Broadcasting Service (PBS) established
1975	HBO starts satellite-based pay network
1975	*Wall Street Journal* publishes via satellite
1977	AT&T tests fiber-optic transmission
1977	Qube interactive cable television starts in Ohio
1980	home computer available for less than $500
1981	videodisc systems marketed
1982	cable television grows at varying speeds; 13% of British households have it
1983	FCC allows broadcasters to offer teletext
1985	cellular mobile telephones marketed
1985	PeaceNet established—first alternative national computer network in United States

1986   Deep Dish TV Satellite Network established; first alternative satellite network

1989   first private satellite launched in the United States

1989   camcorders used in popular movements in Poland and Hungary

1989   fax machines used in the Chinese student revolt to communicate internationally

1989   the Internet begins to be widely available for public use

1991   experiments in interactive television begin to gather momentum

1991   African American Rodney King's savage beating by Los Angeles police is documented by a witness with a camcorder

1992   Star TV begins satellite broadcasts to South and East Asia

1993   digital format dominates global production plans for high definition television (HDTV)

1993   Rupert Murdoch buys controlling stake in Star TV

1994   CD-ROM becomes a standard feature on personal computers

1994   rapid growth of mergers and near mergers under way among telephone, cable, cinema, and computer companies

1994   Japanese and American researchers accelerate development of three-dimensional silicon superchip

Acknowledgments

We would like to thank all those who have made possible the first and second editions of this book, which to our pleasure has made its mark in North America, Europe, and Australia. First and foremost, we thank the authors, who have patiently gone through a series of revisions, aiming for lucidity in the explanation of sometimes difficult material. Second, we are grateful to Bob White, who early on saw the importance of the original project and provided sympathetic critical input at intervals throughout. Third, for this edition, our thanks especially to Sophy Craze, our editor at Sage; Myrna Reagons, her assistant; and Astrid Virding, Tricia Bennett, and Judy Selhorst, who saw the manuscript through production. These individuals have developed to a fine art the precise blend of prodding and cajoling necessary to get the second edition finalized with the coeditors spread across two continents separated by a very large pond, rather than two boroughs of New York City, as was the case for the first edition. Fourth are the students of our respective institutions, and some instructors there and at other institutions, who gave us feedback on the first edition; we hope they see useful advances in the present, sharply revised, edition. Fifth, we thank Liora Schor-Kalish, who hunted down a number of visual images in the public domain for the first edition, most of which appear in this edition as well. Finally, for providing the supportive and stimulating environments that sustain endeavors such as this, we thank very warmly our teaching and staff colleagues in the Department of Radio-Television-Film at the University of Texas; in the Department of English and Media Studies, Nottingham Trent

University; and in the Centre for Mass Communication Research, Leicester University.

We dedicate this edition, as we did the previous one, to our children and to our students.

John Downing
Ali Mohammadi
Annabelle Sreberny-Mohammadi

Preface
A Letter From the Editors to the Beginning Student

This preface provides a way for us to explain to you the thinking behind this book, the issues and perspectives that are introduced, and why we think a **critical** approach is vital for the study of **communication.** It thus orients you as to what to expect, how to read and think about the material, the central issues in certain critical approaches, and how you might integrate a critical orientation into your own work and lives.

This book presents some new ways of looking at the **media** and provides some new tools to help you understand your media environment. So, before you start reading, we want to draw your attention to an especially useful part of this book that you may want to refer to often: the glossary. All the terms highlighted in **bold** in this preface, and many other, sometimes new, sometimes difficult, terms used throughout the book can be found in the glossary. There you will find a definition—often many definitions—for each term, and in many cases cross-references to the chapters in which you can find lengthier discussions and illustrative examples.

Why Media Studies?

Communications media are everywhere. Video screens, car radios, Walkman-type personal stereos and televisions, audio and video recording, compact discs and CD-ROM, photographs, advertising billboards, newspapers, magazines, newsletters—all play a major part in the way people live in industrially advanced countries. Their role in so many people's lives is why they have often been called **mass media** (although many scholars now criticize work that defines people as masses). Behind the media we see and hear are **satellites** thousands of miles above the earth's surface, ocean **cables** carrying optic fibers deep beneath the waters of the planet, computers both simple and sophisticated, and increasingly complex cable systems that can carry telephone and broadcast signals. Aside from visual images and the human voice, huge volumes of data can now travel immense distances in the twinkling of an eye, making possible such things as electronic transfers of funds between banks and scientific and military information gathering from observation satellites. We could describe these media collectively as a global central nervous system.

Communications media make increasing demands on our time, help to define our patterns of leisure, and play a role in our social lives. These media present us with often overwhelming amounts of information and images, about ourselves and about other people. They serve to define what is of political concern, of economic importance, of cultural interest to us. In short, we live in what is often described as a media culture.

A media culture is the product of an industrialized society in which much of the culture is mass-produced in a way quite similar to boots and shoes. Whereas footwear is produced in factories, based upon supplies such as leather, glue, and eyelets, media culture is produced by large organizations who depend on trained personnel with journalistic, entertainment, and business skills, technical know-how, and career commitment.

In the case of fashion footwear, there are, of course, many different manufacturers and many different styles, and by the time we are adults we have developed tastes, know what suits us and what is appropriate wear, and are able to discriminate among the great variety. It is much harder to learn to discriminate about media and their contents, although that is clearly a far more important process than deciding what color shoes to buy.

The purpose of this book is to encourage you to ask some basic questions about the media, to criticize their content, and to become a more discriminating and critical viewer, listener, and reader. Of course, people make many kinds of critical comments about the media—for example, that there are too many reruns, or that the formats are repetitive, merely repackaging old themes. People are concerned that programs with "adult" content are scheduled too early in the evening; parents worry about the effects of "antisocial values" and images of violence on their children. Many are concerned about whether the media reflect and help foster a tolerant multiracial, multicultural society, whereas others worry about the lack of real debate about politics and social issues.

Each of these problems raises a host of further questions about how media are organized and controlled, how they maintain and change our culture, how they alter our way of life in numerous ways. Take the images of women in advertising, for example, a topic of considerable concern to many. Advertising has long shown women mainly in domestic situations, the "traditional" role of women in Western society, or has represented them sexually, as tools to sell products. The first depiction tends to ignore the millions of women in the workplace at many levels of responsibility and decision making. The second reduces women to objects, sometimes just to legs or torsos to be consumed in the same way that the beer or the clothing or the car is to be consumed. We could ask, What do such images do to the self-esteem of women? How do girls, continually surrounded by such images, think of themselves and their future place in society? What does it mean when working women are represented in programming yet omitted from advertising? What effects do such omnipresent images have on men and how they think of women?

We could further examine the kinds of images of women and the definitions of beauty, slenderness, age, and ethnicity that are shown; the limited range of images suggests a culture that values women only if they conform to a limited range of types and roles, hardly the "open society" that our culture prides itself on being. It is little wonder that women get angry, but what can they do? There are far fewer women than men working as advertising executives, few "alternative" images; no wonder women sometimes deface sexist advertising (see the accompanying photo). But the increasing use of men in advertising is no great triumph, as male models are subjected to indignities similar to those that women have long endured. We also need to step further back to examine the purpose and function of advertising as a whole in our society, and again to ask critical questions about the **consumer society** we so often take for granted (see Kellner, Chapter 19).

Given the plethora of criticisms, many people ask, Is this really the best media system that we could have? Is this really media for the

© Jill Posener, The Women's Press, London

people, by the people? Although at first glance there is an abundance of mediated culture, an early lesson in critical media studies is that for television, with the system of **networks**, for example, there are a few major producers who **determine** what most of us can watch, at what times. This volume will help you to ask even more questions, and will suggest that the best ways of answering these questions are by examining the ways in which media are owned and controlled and by linking the media to other social institutions, such as the political system or broader cultural values.

Critical Traditions
in Western Industrial Societies

A critical tradition is nothing new for the United States. Rebelling against the English autocracy in 1776, its citizens were already prepared 200 years ago to defy authority and change a whole system of government. A certain diversity of opinions was tolerated, largely because of the different waves of European settlement up to 1776—first Puritans, then refugees from England's civil war, then Quakers, then poor farmers from

Scotland and Ireland, not to mention the Dutch. The federal structure of government, inspired in part by the Iroquois Confederacy of six Indian nations, also enshrined the importance of debate, criticism, and openness to new perspectives. Open and participatory communication, therefore, was early on understood to be the lifeblood of democracy.

At the same time, from the very beginning there were limitations, not so readily noticed then, when the struggle against the English took center stage. There were the obvious early limitations to the notion of "the people" in whose name the Constitution was written. The people did not include the Native Americans who occupied the territory before the English settlers. The people did not include Africans, imported by force to labor as slaves on the plantations. Nor did the definition of the people really include women; there were no women among the Founding Fathers. Thus from the start, exclusion and struggles to rectify it have been part of the fabric of American political life, with the numerous amendments to the Constitution reflecting changing circumstances and changing awareness of needs and rights.

Similarly, there were powerful ideals established early on in public communication, in the media—most obviously in the First Amendment—that have become embattled ideals. The comparative ease of printing a leaflet or pamphlet in the revolutionary period, or of maintaining a workers' newspaper, was already disappearing by the 1840s. The clamor of numerous voices gave way to the market-oriented newspapers of those select entrepreneurs who could afford to buy the expensive new presses. Although there were brief periods of locally based experimentation with radio and television, both media were very quickly organized into big national networks, and again the potential clamor of many voices was muted.

Political controls have also operated, especially in the limits on reporting the events of the various wars in which the United States has been involved, from the War of 1812 to the Central American conflicts of the 1980s and the 1991 Persian Gulf War. Thus, from the beginning, the noble ideals of the "right to know" and the right to free expression have been embattled ones, pressured by big business and big government, and thus always in need of defense. Communication for the people and by the people gave way to media dominated increasingly by the drives for profit and for power.

In Britain, as in much of Western Europe, broadcasting in the **public service** was for a long time a policy alternative to powerful private media, although that has changed a lot since the 1980s (see McQuail,

Chapter 9). European print media have also often reflected a broader spectrum of political opinion than the U.S. press, with papers owned by left-wing political parties and trade unions. But at the same time, a right to free speech has not been so clearly enshrined in law as in the United States. Various mechanisms have been developed in Great Britain to limit radical or critical voices, such as laws concerning official secrets and libel. There are thus different traditions of public criticism in Western countries and different ways that regimes have devised for muting such criticism. Each system generally has positive points as well as drawbacks, and thus a comparative orientation is always valuable in thinking about media issues.

As we have pointed out, however, being critical is a long-standing, if contested, tradition in Western cultures as well as a healthy strand in American history. It is this tradition that we want to encourage you to call upon and maintain as your own in regard to the media.

Critical Approaches to the Media

Being critical clearly involves posing questions, including awkward and unpopular ones. It means not merely taking information for granted, at face value, but asking how and why these things came to be, why they have the shape and organization they do, how they work and for whose benefit. Thus thinking about something in a careful, reflective way is the start of a critical orientation. In regard to the media, there are already some well-developed critical frameworks that have names and histories.

Let's take television as an instance. Harold Lasswell, a political scientist and one of the "founding fathers" of communication research, constructed a basic formula of the process of mediated communication that is quoted in many textbooks: "Who says what to whom through which channel and to what effect?" Clearly this compound question raises some basic issues, and it can be a useful starting point, but in Lasswell's formulation the communication media are examined in isolation. Other spheres of society, such as the economic, the political, and the cultural, are not included. Thus we might expand on Lasswell's list by adding some broader questions. The perspectives that pose many of these broader questions fall under the general label of *critical perspectives*.

Among the most widely used critical perspectives in media studies are **political economy analysis, cultural studies,** the **critical theory** of the Frankfurt school, and **feminism, semiotics,** and **discourse** analysis. **Reception theory** and **myth** analysis are other significant approaches. What do these approaches entail, and what makes them "critical"?

From an economic perspective, we might ask questions such as, Who owns the media? Do financial assets control access to various media and/or media output? How do people make money through the media? How effective is advertising—does it persuade us to buy things we otherwise would not? And who benefits? Such issues are typical concerns of individuals who use the framework of political economy to examine how the media function in society. And, of course, as the media, like many other businesses, become more and more **transnational** in operations, these kinds of questions come to have more of an international flavor. How large a part of media **corporate** profit stems from exporting programming and advertising? How are media exports priced? Do media help to open up new international markets for both cultural products (e.g., television shows, magazines, records, music videos) and consumer products (e.g., television sets, VCRs, cars, refrigerators, fashion styles)? From this perspective, media in the United States are seen as economic organizations designed to create profit as well as to foster a cultural climate in which profit making is honored. Most of its concerns stem from this orientation.

Karl Marx was one of the earliest critical political economists, although he had little to say specifically about media except for a famous dissection of **censorship.** Herbert Schiller and Dallas Smythe have pioneered U.S. and Canadian studies of media and political economy, although this is a perspective more commonly employed in Europe, Latin America, and elsewhere. The perspective of political economy is broadly reflected in this volume in the contributions by Edward Herman (Chapter 5), Cedric Robinson (Chapter 6), Oscar Gandy (Chapter 13), and Cees Hamelink (Chapter 17). As the label applied to this orientation suggests, its proponents refuse to examine the economic dynamics of media separate from their political dynamics.

The basic issue underlying political questions is power, and critical scholars are all concerned about the relation between power and communications. Here we should think about *political* in both narrow and broad terms. In the narrow sense, politics is the familiar terrain of political parties, elections, the presidency, and so on, in all of which the media play an increasingly influential role. The media package not only individual politicians, but policies as well, yet, at the same time, skilled politicians can use the media to their own interests. Critical approaches ask, How much can and do the media affect the democratic process? When they set the **agenda** of political concerns for us to think about, how much are the media influenced by clever political public relations? In their concern for good television images and sound bites, are the media constructing political celebrities rather than allowing candidates to articulate issues and helping the public to become informed? In Chapter 6 of this volume, Robinson explores the complicated web of relationships between the media and government—both of them elements of the power structure—particularly the U.S. presidency. But often the electoral process does not provide a sufficient arena for certain issues to be debated adequately and acted on. People not only join parties and vote; they also create movements, protest, demonstrate, and agitate. There is a long and rich history of such popular social movements, and in Chapter 14, Downing explores the alternative media that such movements have used.

In broader terms, the "political" also has to do with some basic values and attitudes toward the societies we live in. Thus, for example, in the United States we tend to think that "freedom" is a good thing and that this is a country where "freedom" is valued. Closely linked to the notion of "freedom" is "individualism," valuing the right of each individual to hold opinions and do his or her "own thing." In other countries, different values are held and different priorities are valued. In the former Soviet Union the merit of economic equality was widely accepted; that idea was perhaps taken to greatest lengths by the "stylistic equality" of the Cultural Revolution in China from 1965 to 1975, when men and women, young and old, professionals and workers, all wore the same blue suits in a very particular attempt to erase social distinctions that are often visible through clothing. (Indeed, in Chapter 19, Kellner argues that the U.S. fashion industry deliberately promotes **class** distinction through style.) In Japan, by comparison with the United States, the group has been and still is of far greater importance than the individual. For example, people are concerned with the reputations of their families and their employers, and are used to the lengthy and wide-ranging consultations that take place before any major business decisions are made.

Thus the basic political values of different societies, or their underlying **ideology**, might be quite different. However, it is also important to be critical, to ask whether the **rhetoric** about basic values is actually supported by the reality of people's lives. In the United States, women and minority groups still do not possess the same life possibilities and sense of freedom as do white males, and homelessness and poverty severely limit the personal freedoms of many. In the then Soviet Union, high party officials used to enjoy country houses on the Black Sea while city dwellers stood in lines for poor-quality meat—a situation that mocked the notion of equality. China has recently been rushing full tilt into economic modernization, with an explosion of "style," yet Chinese leaders still resist opening up the country's political structure. Some Japanese complain that the group mentality can hinder creativity and ambition. It is clear that there can often be deep contradictions and value conflicts within systems.

Nonetheless, the dominant social forces in each and every society try to encourage certain sets of values in citizens that fit the particular frameworks of political and economic structures in which they live. Because these values seem so fundamental, they are often taken for granted; thus it is very hard for people to become aware that these values are not simply the obvious truth, but the elements of an ideology. It is very difficult to get people to think about, let alone be critical of, the values and attitudes they hold. We can criticize the values of others easily—as when we look at other societies and wonder, How can these people believe all that?—but we can be amazingly blind to our own assumptions and values.

The process of socialization, or the learning of basic values, particularly as they are reinforced by family, school, religion, the political system, and the media, is often called **hegemony.** Here we can begin to see how the perspective of political economy enables us to make connections between the issue of media ownership and control and the kinds of values, and the diversity (or lack of diversity) of ideas, that the media deliver. Economics affects politics in this broad sense. The sometimes difficult and abstract concepts of ideology and hegemony are explored further in this volume by Alan O'Connor and John Downing (Chapter 1) and Douglas Kellner (Chapter 19); they also appear in the glossary. In Chapter 26, Sari Thomas argues that the media audience is being educated even as it is being entertained; she explores some of the basic **myths** about economic life in the United States that are part of the standard stock of television stories.

Critically examining basic values, or ideology, also leads us in another direction, into the territory of culture and thus cultural studies. An anthropologist would say that culture includes, among many other things, the basic values and attitudes in society, so culture and ideology must have some relation to each other and to the media. What kinds of values do the media carry, and in what kinds of programming, or genres, can we find these values? Do the media carry exactly the same values as the other major agencies of socialization, such as schooling and religion, and are these the same as the values of families? What is the impact of these values on the viewing publics? And so on.

There are and have been many other definitions of culture, however, and other implications for the media. If culture includes the various forms of expression that people use—whether through language, physical movement, music, or pictures—the media act as carriers of some of the cultural material that already exists, but they are also new forms in themselves and create culture in new and different ways. Cultural studies provides an important perspective in the critical analysis of communication. People who use this approach set the mass media within their broad historical and social contexts; they tend to see cultural expression as an arena of competing social and political perspectives, an area where ordinary people can reinterpret and "resist" the dominant values and definitions of reality in society and perhaps create their own culture and meanings. In Chapter 1, O'Connor and Downing examine the many different meanings that have been given to the term *culture* and elaborate on many of these critical perspectives.

One perspective actually bears the label *critical:* critical theory. A group of researchers in Frankfurt, Germany, before World War II tried to link **Marxist** ideas with Freudian ones to develop a better understanding of many dynamics of modern society. These researchers, who came to be known as the founders of the Frankfurt school, included Max Horkheimer, Theodor Adorno, Herbert Marcuse, Walter Benjamin, and, much later, Jürgen Habermas. Among the topics they examined was the problem of **mass culture**, which from their perspective was a bland, commercialized soup of mass-produced and superficial forms, none of which had lasting artistic or intellectual value. Their perspective was a rather pessimistic one; they were concerned not only about the loss of artistic and aesthetic values brought about by mass media, but also, more significant, about the increasing isolation and manipulation of people in modern society through the mass media. In Chapter 19, Douglas Kellner uses this perspective to talk about the creation of needs and desires that supposedly can be satisfied by consumption in a **capitalist** society; Keith Negus (Chapter 22) criticizes this perspective in his examination of popular music. Considerable controversy can be generated when people who hold rather pessimistic critical theory perspectives about the blandness of mass culture argue with people who hold rather optimistic cultural studies perspectives about the creation of meaning in popular culture. Some of that debate can be sampled through a comparison of the arguments in Kellner's chapter with those in Negus's chapter.

Thus already from this overview of critical approaches you can see that the study of communication media intersects with many older disciplines. Sociologists, anthropologists, historians, literature scholars, media critics, film specialists, quality journalists, economists, psychologists, political scientists, legal scholars, **telecommunications** experts, linguists—all can make important contributions to a better understanding of the interrelations among media, culture, and society. This makes communication research at once a very dynamic field, a place where all these interested specialists can try to communicate with one another across the frontiers of their own disciplines, and a difficult one for the beginning student, who may wonder which discipline he or she is really studying. It is also not always easy to get all these specialists to communicate clearly, even with each other.

A news story that was just breaking when we finished the writing for the first edition of this book, in the fall of 1989, was the purchase of Columbia Pictures by the Japanese Sony Corporation, which had already bought the giant CBS Records Division in 1988. We showed a variety of approaches that communications scholars might use to explore that event further. For example, the economist might be interested in the story as yet another sign of the **globalization** of media ownership, a theme explored here by Edward Herman (Chapter 5) and Denis McQuail (Chapter 9). The film scholar might be interested in whether the new owners would favor one or another type of movie, such as megamillion-dollar spectaculars or lower-budget innovative films. The sociologist might be interested in exploring the experience of American cultural producers when employed by a foreign business corporation, or in examining the process of making decisions about which movies will be produced. The cultural studies scholar might be interested in whether the national culture of Japan began to exert any influence over U.S. culture, or indeed whether a new, hybrid, international film culture evolved. The political scientist might be interested in public debate in Congress and the media about potential Japanese domination over mass communication and corporate investment in the United States, and how far, after half a century, U.S. resentment over the Pearl Harbor attack was still an active ingredient in the debate. The telecommunications specialist would be interested in relating this **software** acquisition to Japan's leadership in communication **hardware** production of all kinds, and its technological and economic implications. The serious journalist might pick up on any of these angles, or evaluate to what extent this story was part of the news agenda and how well various news media covered it. Ideally, communication scholars should be interested in all these issues and more, although achieving such multiple competencies is not easy. In this book we try to reflect the spectrum of concerns and critical approaches current in the field of media studies.

Media and Other People: An International Perspective

Because many media now have such global reach, linking the far corners of the world together at a moment's notice, we think an international perspective is vital. Major media corporations are multinational in scope. Their television programs, films, and music flow around the world, often delighting **audiences** but creating concern about national cultural **identity.** These rapidly developing technical communication processes go hand in hand with this century's major changes in the economic, political, and cultural relations among nations and within nations. Communications media both respond to and wield influence over these changes, in ways we can easily see in our everyday lives and in other ways that are not so immediately obvious. Communications media hold many fascinating implications for human relationships and for world development that demand study, reflection, and debate.

It is often through comparison that we learn about ourselves. Study of other media systems helps to highlight what is special about the system we know best and shows how media systems take on the coloring of the economic and political environments in which they function. European media systems have a tradition of public service, Soviet media went through many more changes than most Westerners realize, and **Third World** cultures import a great many Western cultural products and are concerned about their possible impacts. An international perspective is vital if we are to understand ourselves adequately, comprehend the current dynamics of media systems as a whole, and understand others better. The contributors to this volume come from Australia, Britain, Canada, India, Iran, Ireland, the Netherlands, Taiwan, and the United States, demonstrating that communication research is also international in scope and that similar issues and approaches are used in many countries. These specialist scholars offer a variety of orientations to some of the liveliest contemporary thinking about communications media. All of the chapters are original contributions, written especially for this volume, that try to introduce abstract **theories** and complex problems in a manner accessible to the beginning student. The chapters are intended to introduce you to the tasks of analysis, comparison and, above all, critical thinking. All of these contributions utilize some kind of critical perspective in the way they approach the analysis and understanding of the media.

Criticism as a Positive Activity

There are many different ways of being critical. One obvious way of actually being a critic is to publish one's opinions in a newspaper column, as do those who are paid to be television or film critics. What does the critic do? He or she evaluates cultural products from different perspectives, expresses opinions, and develops arguments. The critic can help to steer audiences toward or away from particular films or books, and so can have considerable influence on cultural trends and even on economic results. The more the critic knows about the genre he or she is analyzing—its history, the background and aims of the creator, and so on—the clearer his or her own particular point of view can be, and the more illuminating the commentary.

It is important to move away from the idea of being critical as being something bad. "Being critical" often carries the implication of just being negative, of being hostile, of putting something or someone down, of angry reactions. Sometimes balance is proffered as an alternative—"being in the middle" is recommended as the sound, safe position to adopt. We are arguing that "being critical" is positive and constructive, and that "being in the middle" is often the easy way out—a way to avoid thinking hard or taking a stand. Criticism is necessary for knowledge to advance, because posing questions and trying to understand the world better and from different viewpoints are what create the dynamic of science and rational knowledge in the first place. The pages of history are full of critics who were spurned by their societies, often suffering ostracism, exile, or even death, only to be proven correct later on. Socrates faced a public trial for supposedly corrupting Greek youth. Galileo suffered dearly when he dared to question church teachings that held the earth to be the center of the universe. Women heretics such as America's Anne Hutchinson, who was banished with her children from the Massachusetts Colony, suffered terribly for daring to question received opinion. Criticism may well offend established authority, pose challenges to accepted knowledge, even question cherished values. But in pointing out problems and raising debates, it can also help to spark new solutions, policies, and ethical positions.

All of the perspectives presented here differ from what is often called mainstream, **empiricist** communications research because they are concerned more with questions, problems, and perspectives than with the mere recitation of detailed facts. Indeed, critical scholars would argue that facts by themselves are impossible to interpret if they are not placed into some model or theory about how the media and society work. Critical researchers are also not content with describing what exists, the status quo of the media, but seek to explain how they came to be, which makes history a key element in understanding our current media maps and cultural environments.

We ask, How do the media function and for whose benefits, and indeed how might they be improved, for women, for minorities, for the poor, for the mass of ordinary people? From the critical standpoint, all knowledge assumes some point of view; there is no such thing as neutral information. In particular, certain critical points of view about the media have not had the forum for expression we think they deserve, nor have they been introduced into academic programs in the way we feel is necessary. People holding these various critical perspectives would also agree that the kind of information we get about the media is governed by the questions we ask. That is why this book does not try to bombard you with a great amount of detailed "facts." A chronology is supplied (immediately after the table of contents), and of course each chapter contains relevant "information." More important, we think, is that each chapter introduces you to a certain way of thinking about the media and offers different frameworks that you might not otherwise hear about until graduate school. We believe it is important that these questions be introduced to you early on in your studies, because they will direct you to further relevant and stimulating work.

There are many different ways of being critical, and each poses somewhat different questions, considers some issues more important than others, and may even collide with the others. There are numerous areas of disagreement, and one indication of how well you have read and understood this book will be your ability to pinpoint the differences of outlook among different critical points of view, such as political economy, cultural studies, and feminism. This book does not wrap up "all you need to think" about the media between its covers, so that all you have to do is swallow it and the process is over. You will be invited to be, even pushed into being, an active participant in the process of trying to understand the importance of media today.

Thus, to emphasize the point, in this book we are not proposing a critical perspective that we want you to adopt. We do not wish to market a new critical media orthodoxy. We want you to understand the ongoing process of being critical through learning about some of the major critical perspectives that exist. We also want to stimulate a sense of excitement and to pique your interest in media studies by showing how important media are in contemporary society and that many significant and interesting questions about the media remain to be explored.

Knowledge moves through argument. If democracy is vibrant, it is because of the voicing of dissenting opinions, especially the different voices and points of view of groups that have not been heard before and whose perspectives and interests have not been considered. We anticipate that you will have many discussions with your teachers and professors, argue among yourselves, even become motivated to write to us. If you finish this book with more questions about the media than when you started, we will be more than happy. If you discover the richness of the field and find a further role for yourself as student, researcher, critic, or creative producer, we will be delighted. Being critical means being alert and open to change and new developments. Nothing more positive can be offered you.

PART I

Introductory Perspectives: Culture, History, Technology

As you sit reading this volume, you are probably surrounded by a variety of mass-produced material artifacts, such as furniture, interior design products, consumer electronics, and other cultural objects—posters, magazines and books, cassette tapes, compact discs, and so on. Most of the time we pay such objects little attention, yet we could examine them from a design perspective, asking about their stylistic and aesthetic qualities and how these have changed over time. We could ask about their social uses and impacts and explore their histories, asking how such artifacts came to be developed and the processes of manufacture and the technologies required to bring them into being. We could ask what needs such objects were designed to fulfill, and whether or not they did so, or what interests propelled their development. Such questions focus on the kinds of applied knowledge that have created the material environment we inhabit so "naturally" that we forget it has a history, and a fascinating and complicated history at that.

The chapters in Part I place contemporary concerns about communication in broad historical and cultural frameworks. We are not so much concerned that you learn the specific dates of inventions—indeed, it is actually quite unclear which are the relevant dates to know, as Winston explains in Chapter 4. Rather, we are concerned that you think about the kinds of historical processes, events, and changes that play a part in shaping contemporary communications. That is, "history" is much more than dates, names, and places; it is about long-term fundamental developments in technologies, changing forms of media, and new cultural patterns and values.

This section also pays a great deal of attention to language, to the terms that we use in developing models and theories about communications and media, terms such as **technology** and **culture**. The contributors point out that language use changes over time, and that a single word can take on very different meanings when used within different theoretical frameworks. Unlike Humpty Dumpty in *Alice in Wonderland*, who wanted words to mean what *he* wanted them to mean, we want you to become sensitive to language, to the terms that are used in analyzing communications, and to the shifts and nuances of meaning that these terms acquire.

Throughout this book we present contending perspectives, arguments that challenge received opinion by questioning the meanings and implications of certain terms. An essential part of "being critical" is thinking about the language used to make arguments and to frame theories, whether that language—often called **discourse**—is found in the media or used by scientists or media academics.

1 Culture and Communication

ALAN O'CONNOR

JOHN DOWNING

Until the 1800s, the word culture usually connoted "growing," the way we might speak about growing a mold culture in a biology experiment. But as the use of the word was extended to social processes, it took on a fascinating, even bewildering, array of definitions, until today we have to be very careful when we hear the word culture to be sure that we know what meaning we and others are taking for granted. Not only are there many definitions of the term, but these definitions, like cultures themselves, change over time.

Most definitions of culture share a tendency to focus our attention on (a) activities and (b) their products—for example, journalism and news programs, or architecture and temples. Culture, then, is seen both as a product and as the social process that brings that product into being.

From the perspective of the anthropologist, culture is everything we do in our lives—brushing our teeth, erecting buildings, watching television coverage of the Olympics, participating in marriage ceremonies. Others use the word in the sense of "high culture": opera, ballet, theater, classical music, sculpture, painting. Still others use culture to mean the essence of a people's way of life, as in American culture,

Irish culture, Native American culture, or Gypsy culture: cultural identity. These national and ethnic definitions emphasize the contrasting ways that varying peoples define life. In other words, a culture in this sense is the way we interpret and understand the world in certain ways and exclude other ways of doing so.

Some Australian Aborigines, for instance, may see themselves living in sacred union with nature, whereas European cultural perspectives tend to see nature as something neutral or even hostile, to be exploited and profited from. So culture in this sense acts to cement a sense of priorities, to hold steady our understanding of who we are and where we are headed. Thus culture reinforces a particular social order—but also often the political power of an elite as well.

The intimate connection between culture and power is never far beneath the surface. Take, for instance, the question of personal appearance and dress. During centuries of the Chinese Ming dynasty, the Manchu conquerors who created the dynasty forced all Chinese men to wear their hair in a pigtail as a cultural symbol of their conquered status. Or consider the demand of Muslim fundamentalists in some countries that women should wear veils, although the veil is found nowhere in the Koran, the holy book of Islam, and is not worn by Muslim women in a number of other countries. This seems a case of traditional masculine power over everyday culture and communication, controlling women and signifying their subordinate status.

Depending on what we understand culture to be, we perceive different, even contradictory, roles for the media. From some critical perspectives, the media are viewed as conservative and primarily supportive of existing political and economic power. Others, especially those with a "high culture" perspective, see the mass media as a corrosive force on traditional culture, as producing trash culture instead. Still others would argue that the media are a great eye-opening and leveling force that enables people to see and communicate beyond the boundaries of their own in-groups and cultures.

Whatever meaning we give the word culture, concepts of communication and culture are important because, in the end, we always communicate with each other inside cultural codes. Indeed, the very self-understandings of individuals are tenuous outside of the societies and cultures in which they are embedded. Because cultures give life shape and meaning, understanding culture is central to understanding human communication.

This chapter explores the history and evolution of the term culture, looks at some of the fascinating technical meanings of the word, and asks us to consider culture and communications in relation to the related terms hegemony, ideology, class, semiotics, cultural capital, popular culture, and mass culture. Because this book is dedicated to opening up questions that are never or rarely thought about, considering the multiple interconnections among power, culture, and communication is not only central to questioning the media, it has much to do with our becoming aware of the hidden assumptions that drive our lives.

Culture is one of the most complex words in the English language. Often people think that culture means the arts, sometimes termed *high culture:* opera, ballet, theater, sculpture. A "cultured" person, by this definition, is a highly educated person who is closely aware of these arts, who goes out to enjoy them often, who reads poetry, and perhaps buys paintings. For anthropologists and others, the concept of culture is much broader. Culture is everything we do in our lives, from brushing our teeth with toothpaste to putting up a building, and from watching the Olympics on TV to taking part in a marriage ceremony. Others may think of culture as encompassing characteristic qualities of a nation or people (as in American culture, Canadian culture, or Irish culture) or of an ethnic group (such as Native American culture, French-Canadian culture, or Gypsy culture).

Although the "high culture" and anthropological definitions of the term are narrow and broad, respectively, they share two features. They focus our attention on both products, such as paintings or pieces of music, and creative activities, such as using paint or making music. In the national and ethnic definitions, by contrast, *culture* refers to ways of understanding the world, perspectives on the meaning of life. For example, Native Americans and First Nation Canadians have generally held "Mother Earth" in great reverence. That is their cultural perspective (though it is not universal among them). By contrast, most Europeans, whether in Europe or settlers in the Americas, have tended to see nature as something to be exploited for economic gain, from logging to strip mining to oil-based or nuclear energy sources. Theirs is a different cultural perspective.

However, even these three different ways of using the term *culture*—to indicate a product, the activity that generates the product, and a perspective on the meanings of life—do not exhaust its meanings. At this point you may feel irritated and wonder why academics cannot simply get together, agree on a set meaning, and stick to it. Apart from the fact that no agreement would ever emerge from such a meeting, that a disagreement exists can be taken as a sign that there may be more going on than simple confusion about the sense of a particular word. We need to probe further to find out what is at stake in the divergent meanings of culture, what underlies the clash of definitions. At the very least, we need to be aware that when we meet the term, we must ask ourselves at once, In what way is this writer or speaker using the word *culture*?

In this chapter we will discuss the following uses of *culture* (new technical terms will be explained when we get to them): the history of the use of the term, culture as an interactive process humans engage in and change, the different meanings of "popular" culture and "mass" culture, culture and hegemony, culture and ideology, semiology (semiotics), and cultural "capital." Before setting out on this mapping exercise, however, let us just note in principle why the study of communication and the concepts of culture are important to each other. There is one sense in which the terms *communication* and *information* are both used, namely, to denote the "on/off" digital code to which all computers reduce communication, whether the information is text, image, sound, color, or moving pictures. Yet in and of themselves, these on/off signals communicate nothing at all, absolutely nothing. Unless they themselves are recoded through a computer program within language (itself a central aspect of culture) and within images and sounds that are recognizable in our culture, their elementary communication is null and void for us. We signal to each other, we inform each other, we communicate with each other, in cultural codes, not in electronic impulses or any equivalent of them—although we do communicate through such electronic means if we use computers. Thus culture is central to understanding communication.

Sources of the Word Culture

Some modern meanings of the word *culture* first emerged in Britain a little before 1800. Up until then, the word had been used mainly to describe agricultural processes, such as the culture of wheat or corn (rather as the expression *growing a culture* is used in medicine or biology today). But then the word came to be extended to social processes (see R. Williams, 1977, on whose account much of this section is based).

As some conservative-minded observers reflected on the rapid spread of industrialization that was pushing and pulling farmers off the land into factories in bigger and bigger cities, and in the process uprooting many traditional ways of life, they began to worry deeply. They feared that the old order was in terminal decay, an order they often viewed through very rosy spectacles, where (as they saw it) the "well-bred" aristocrats ran everything for everyone else's benefit and the poorest pig herdsman was humbly grateful, along with his wife and children, for this enlightened oversight. In its place they saw the rise of a new class of factory worker, disconnected from the land and these traditional ties, surly and aggressive, a "dangerous class." They lamented and feared the disappearance of the old "culture," under threat of being trodden under foot by the new, truculent working class. They believed the arts would be destroyed by the extension of democracy to these lower orders—and thus was developed the notion of "high" culture as the arts. English writer Matthew Arnold's use of *culture* more or less reflects these concerns.

The word *civilization* was closely connected with *culture* in these debates. There were others who welcomed the new industrial developments, seeing them as part of a continual evolutionary advance in civilization, and in that sense as changing culture for the better, not leaving it stagnant and stuck in the past. These observers were as optimistic as the conservatives were pessimistic.

Still other, more radical, observers of these changes took yet a third view. They focused on the appalling conditions that the new class of factory worker was experiencing, with 12-hour workdays and 6-day workweeks, with children slaving away as well as adults, living in unsanitary and disease-ridden slum housing, with low life expectancy, and all for a pittance of a wage. Yet at the same time this set of observers envisioned a future in which the members of this class would become more educated, both in the sense of learning to read, write, and do mathematics and in the sense of becoming much more aware of their own importance to the economy and their potential power in society. For these observers, the growth of power from below, a truly democratic civilization and culture, was a goal to be struggled for despite the harsh circumstances.

We have referred to Britain, but similar developments can be traced in the United States. In the period up to the beginning of the 1900s, culture was something the dominant social classes considered that they alone possessed. The term signified intelligence and idealism, and those classes took this to prove their own consequent natural right to exercise leadership in U.S. society (DiMaggio & Useem, 1978). They believed that such idealism and intelligence were not qualities to be found among factory workers, farmers, domestic servants, or slaves. Thus culture replaced the former religious doctrine of many European societies, of the monarch's "divine right" to rule, with a this-worldly claim that sought to justify the superior authority and wealth of the upper classes. As Lewis Perry (1984) writes, "The term culture indicated continuing faith in a hierarchy of merit that distinguished the truly 'noble' person from the herd" (p. 264). Despite the supposedly powerful democratic traditions of the United States, the "herd" was how those in dominant circles saw the general American public, Joe (and Josephine) Six-Pack. Putting this together, we can see how the term *culture* has been used on both sides of the Atlantic to justify politically the rule of the dominant social classes, rather than as a detached, analytic concept.

At the same time, other contradictory definitions of *culture* were beginning to come to the fore. The influential eighteenth-century German writer Johann Gottfried Herder identified culture with nation, in the sense that each nation possesses its own unique national spirit, or culture; eventually this basic notion found its way into the emergent discipline of anthropology in the late nineteenth century. Over time, anthropologists took this notion a step further and identified all artifacts (such as clothing, buildings, and music) as well as beliefs and rituals as culture. In one sense, this was a little more democratic in spirit. Anthropologists at least identified culture with something belonging to everyone, not just to the elite. In principle, they created the possibility that one culture could be considered superior to other cultures in certain respects and not in others.

However, in practice, cultures were identified with civilizations, which in turn were ranked, with white Europeans at the pinnacle and people of color at the bottom. In turn, this definition of culture served to justify invasion for colonial powers—whether the United States in the war against Mexico in 1847-1848 or against the Philippines in 1898 or the British against India in 1857, or white Canadians and Americans against Indian nations throughout the period of settlement. The British spoke of their "civilizing mission" to excuse the plunder of their colonies, the white Americans of their "Manifest Destiny" to impose their culture all the way to the Pacific and the Rio Grande and on to Hawaii and the Philippines.

A very challenging Brazilian film titled *My Frenchman Was Really Delicious*[1] (Nelson Pereira dos Santos, 1971) addresses the issue of cultural superiority. The film, which begins and ends with shots of the Brazilian shoreline, is set in the sixteenth century, when France and Portugal were vying for control of the riches of South America. At the end of the film, a voice-over tells us that the bodies of the Indians massacred by the Europeans were piled high for three miles along this shore, but before that, the film has shown us the fate of a captured Frenchman at the hands of one of the tribes. They give him eight months to live, after which they will kill and eat him, each piece of his body being assigned to a particular tribe member by the chief. In the meantime, however, they treat him well, even giving him as temporary wife the widow of a slain warrior, so he can have normal sexual relations. They also teach him to hunt, though he seems more skilled at hunting humans than at hunting animals. In turn, he teaches them certain agricultural and building techniques. But at the end of the eight months, his time is up, and we last see his assigned wife as she eats his cooked neck (her promised piece) with evident enjoyment.

Strange, indeed; but the film forces us to face the question of which culture was the more barbaric, the cannibalistic culture that allowed one man to be devoured even after he had become personally known to the tribe or the European culture that heaped myriad slaughtered corpses for three miles along the beach, and wiped out the entire tribe. Thus, once more, we find culture being used in situations of power and conflict to support the claims of one side. The term is clearly not just an "academic" one, but one that can be used to gloss over social struggles. Let us move now to other senses of the term, where again we will see issues of power and conflict inextricably interwoven with it.

Culture as an Interactive, Changing Process

Let us begin by criticizing another common way of thinking about culture. We sometimes think of culture as a thing, such as an oil painting, or as a quality, such as a great oil painting. But we would argue that it is better to think of culture principally as an active process or processes. Who paints? What do they paint? For whom do they paint? Culture is simultaneously an ongoing process and an active process of communication and understanding. The study of culture involves the study of activities and interactions, not just the study of cultural products such as paintings.

Let us look at painting as an example of cultural production and ask some important questions. Are painters defined, do they usually define themselves, as "artists"? If so, we usually expect them to have studios and to exhibit their paintings from time to time. We expect them to sell their paintings to try to make a living, which is an important reason for exhibiting their work. Are they mired in poverty, as so many fine painters appear to have been throughout history? Do they have to wait tables to get by? Do they know the people who will buy their paintings, as artists once used to do, or do they sell them mostly to buyers they have never met before and will never meet again? Do they paint how they wish or—to make a living—what they know people will buy? Does their need to earn a living take energy away from their more imaginative, innovative work? How dependent are they on being "in" with the "right" people in the art world's cliques, on positive reviews by influential art critics? If they have all those pieces in place, does that mean their artistic work is important? And last of all, but truly significant in the process, how much impact does interaction with other artists, learning from them, have on their work? We see at once from these questions that "culture" is only in part the painting itself, the piece of music, the T-shirt, the cultural product. Even the painter, the prototype "high-culture" artist, is engaged with economic reality, with the opinions of wealthy collectors, with the judgments of key art critics. Even such an artist, then, is not the solitary genius of popular portrayals, but learns from the work of other artists. Culture is an interactive process, saturated in everyday realities, not just the abstract, spiritual product of the lonely, lofty artist.

If we consider the many art school graduates who work in the advertising industry, we can see even more easily how economics, power, and cultural activity interact. The incomes and creative activities of such artists are guaranteed—so long as their work continues to please their employers. Admittedly, "high-culture" enthusiasts will likely scoff at this example and deny that people who work for ad agencies can be creative artists. In so doing, however, such individuals reduce cultural activity to their own artistic judgments.

How, in turn, should we define modern mural painters, who have set out to create cultural products to be seen at no charge by passersby and that often contain direct attacks on the powers that be, such as property developers or the police? How should we define schoolchildren's paintings, or the work of psychiatric patients in art therapy classes? Or graffiti? Or the act of painting the walls of the room you live in? In fact, the distinctions between grades of cultural producer become less interesting with each example, and it becomes more and more intriguing to explore the process, the context, and the reception of artistic cultural production, for these artists are producing culture for very different audiences, under very different conditions, from those of the supposedly "true" artists. Thus the cultural process is not only ongoing and active, it takes multiple forms even within the seemingly straightforward activity of painting.

We have taken painting as an example because it is so frequently thought of as a cultural activity that brings forth cultural products. Let us change focus a moment and look at some other cultural producers, namely, the people who wear clothes in order to create particular messages. Throughout history, humans have worn particular styles of dress to communicate particular signals. A three-piece suit is a cultural communication of respectability, affluence, status, career. Vividly colored hair, specially shaven scalps, and baseball caps worn backward signify the opposite. Doctors and nurses wear white coats to signify their knowledge about and authority over the human body or mind. Police officers wear uniforms to communicate their rights of arrest and public control.

The power of ongoing cultural activities to communicate can also be seen in an example—a frightening and extreme one—of what can happen when they are canceled or absent. In a horrific period in Argentina between 1976 and 1983, upward of 25,000 political dissidents vanished forever—imprisoned, tortured, killed, and their bodies disposed of without trace. The police who seized them on the streets or in their homes in the middle of the night came without uniforms, in unmarked cars without license plates. When their relatives sought information, from the police or from members of the military government, all knowledge of them was denied. In this case, the absence of uniforms, of cultural signals, communicated that the rule of law had been hijacked by a government whose officials acted like gangsters, that there was no protection in law anymore. It generated what some writers have described as a "culture of fear" in which many people were afraid even to admit that a family member had disappeared. A similar case arose in the tiny Central American country of El Salvador during the 1980s, where more than 50,000 political dissidents or suspects "were disappeared"[2] or ended up as corpses left on the street with their eyes gouged out, their throats cut, and their genitals mutilated, as a terrible warning to instill terror in the public.

The instances recounted above may seem not only grisly, but also a sharp departure from our discussion of the meaning of *culture*. In fact, they are not. They illustrate from the experience of a culture of fear the reality that culture changes, is produced, and is an interactive process—in the cases cited, interactive between a military government and the general public. If the word *culture* normally sounds harmless, perhaps it is because we have not thought about it deeply enough. How deeply racist and sexist, for example, are the historical cultures of Europe and North America? As we have noted, the question of culture and communication cannot be separated from the dilemmas of conflict and power in society and made remote and sanitized, as in "Let's communicate better!" or "What an exotic culture!" The other lesson to be learned from the topics raised in this section concerns the continuous movement and change of culture. Raymond Williams (1977), in a section of his book *Marxism and Literature* titled "Structures of Feeling" (pp. 128-135), provides a finely written account of the ways in which cultural developments contain numerous, almost daily eddies and crosscurrents, tensions between what we have taken for granted so far and what may be on the verge of altering it. Thus it is a gross error to see culture as something static, frozen in time. It is in the very process of social communication that cultures change and mutate.

Popular Culture and Mass Culture

Another debate about culture centers on definitions of *popular culture* and *mass culture*. At first sight, these two terms look as though they should mean the same thing, and, depending on who uses them, they indeed can. In communication research, however, different meanings have been attached to the two terms; the distinction between them may be a useful one. Both terms are often used in opposition to *high culture*, to signify the cultural preferences of the general public, who, as we have seen, are often disdainfully presumed by the elite on both sides of the Atlantic to be not only less formally educated than the elite but also less intelligent, less "cultured." But in the view of leading members of the Frankfurt school—a school of thought devoted to critical cultural research that began at Frankfurt University in Germany in the early 1920s—there is a sharp difference between mass and popular culture, even though both are enjoyed by ordinary citizens.

Examples of popular culture in the United States include several musical forms: jazz, soul, gospel, and blues. These are the products of several centuries of African musical cultures forged anew through the crucibles of Black Americans' experiences of slavery, legalized segregation after the Civil War, existence on the very margins of survival as migrant workers in northern U.S. cities, and sustained resistance to institutionalized racism. Jazz and the blues are among the most distinctive and vibrant features of popular music in the United States. Much rock music has its origins in them, although in practice it sometimes offers a much blander, less focused version than the original. Whether directly or in watered-down versions, this music has had an immense international impact.

Other examples of popular culture include Irish reels and jigs, many of them used at one time as part of preparation for battle, and the intense blend of Canadian and Black Louisianian music known as zydeco, developed by Canadian refugees from the British who relocated in the then French colony of Louisiana. Nonmusical expressions of popular culture include Texan boots, Yorkshire pudding, Mexican Day of the Dead ceremonies and artifacts, Russian fairy tales, Balinese puppet theater, and West African kente cloth.

In contrast, in the view of Frankfurt school critics such as Theodor Adorno and Max Horkheimer (1947/1972), *mass* culture consists of cultural expressions generated by big business simply and solely to advance the bottom line. Such cultural products are generated to fit consumer surveys that chop up the audience into segments according to differential purchasing power (see Gandy, Chapter 13) and are as synthetic as a tube of toothpaste. Examples of mass culture include formula dramas, on U.S. television in particular; for instance, the plot where a giggling psychopath traps a defenseless woman, or the hero, or a child, in a place where no one can find that person, and the suspense comes from waiting to see whether by some new miracle the good guys can find the place in time and blow the monstrous sadist away before the victim is killed. Or the kill-or-be-killed animated video game, or the cop-buddies movie, or easy-listening radio, or any other series of repetitive formulas. Fashion provides many examples; clothing and accessories that are supposed to make us feel as though we are expressing our individuality or that we are ahead of the game actually put us in temporary mass uniforms until the next trend emerges (see Kellner, Chapter 19, for further commentary on this theme).

In other words, from the Frankfurt school perspective mass culture does not emerge from the needs and wishes and hopes of the general public, but is fed to them on the basis of what will sell. There are, of course, questions raised by this analysis. One issue is whether popular culture is being romanticized as a positive force simply because it is an authentic product of "the people." Another is whether mass culture really is the hollow, mindless product these critics claim it to be. A number of audience studies, for example, have found that Harlequin Romances and television soap operas may stimulate women viewers to visualize more satisfying, mutually respectful, and affectionate relationships between men and women (see Ang, Chapter 12). This does not fit with the charge that such mass cultural products are empty and superficial.

Even if the distinction between mass culture and popular culture has problems, we may still see some merit in it for certain purposes. For instance, our comments above about how mainstream rock music has at times taken Black American popular musical forms and made them bland illustrates a distinction that can fairly be drawn between popular culture and mass culture. The question still remains as to how absolutely we can separate the two.

Culture and Hegemony

Interestingly and surprisingly, earlier in the twentieth century some conservative and some radical scholars developed a very similar analysis of mass communication. In the 1940s and 1950s, the left-wing Frankfurt school and conservative Spanish commentator José Ortega y Gasset both took the view that modern societies were being submerged under an ocean of commercially driven, soulless mass culture that met none of the deep needs of human beings. Newspapers, radio, and popular film—and eventually television, when it began to spread—were assumed to act in mechanical ways on the public, destroying meaningful culture and replacing it with mass culture, a pseudoculture. This view was almost a revival of the conservative nineteenth-century attitude described earlier, which lamented the passing of old truths and sniffed suspiciously and disdainfully at new cultural developments. However, when researchers armed with these concepts began to investigate the media, it soon became clear that mass communication did not work in this mechanical way. The mechanical model of mass media as a metaphorical hypodermic syringe capable of injecting beliefs into the public had to be replaced by a much more careful and complex model of how media actually work.

To begin with, a number of U.S. studies in the late 1940s and the 1950s went almost to the opposite extreme, suggesting that mass media had practically no impact at all (see Klapper, 1960, for a summary of this research). However, at a later point, in the early 1970s, with the translation into English of the work of Italian writer Antonio Gramsci, a new term used rather intensively by Gramsci came to be used quite widely: *hegemony* (see, e.g., Forgacs, 1989; Gramsci, 1971; R. Williams, 1977). Derived originally from a Greek word meaning "rule," in Gramsci's writings it took on a fuller meaning: the combined dominance over and leadership of a society by its ruling classes. By definition, we would expect dominance of governing classes, for otherwise they would not rule. Gramsci, however, was intrigued not so much by the fact that dominant classes existed, but by the mechanisms of how they ruled. In particular, he was interested in the extent to which large sections of the public seemed to accept their rule willingly, without any kind of active forced compliance.

Gramsci essentially saw the formula for rule by these classes as an amalgam of force and consent. Force is socially organized, in his view, in the shape of police, courts, prisons, and, in a major crisis, the military and related bodies such as the U.S. National Guard or the British S.A.S. But sheer force by itself does not, and quite possibly cannot, keep people stably in line over long periods. It is effective only in short periods of unrest or organized challenge to the status quo. Over the longer term, the public needs to feel, either gladly or at least passively, that the country is being run by the most competent, farsighted, experienced sectors of the society. By "run" we do not mean only the actions of presidents, prime ministers, and their cabinets, but also the actions of major business executives, leading bankers, top civil servants and military leaders, the scientific and engineering establishment, and, in some countries, even religious leaders—the whole constellation of power at the top, in other words.

The question then arises, How is it that the general public comes to this degree of confidence in the leadership of the society? Why are people not more suspicious, more skeptical, more feisty? For Gramsci, the process of cultural hegemony is at the heart of the answer. In the present context, this process is important for four reasons. First, it suggests we should study mass media, education, the arts, religion, and everyday culture not as spontaneous public expression, but as processes of persuasion in which we are invited to understand the world in certain ways but not in others. Second, it argues that customarily accepted ways of understanding and experiencing the everyday world have important political consequences; they are not simply neutral, charming, or obvious. Third, it suggests that to be successful, cultural hegemony must be flexible, responsive to changing conditions, adaptive—that the same old ideas and procedures, in a situation of change, will fail to wield the same hegemony. Fourth, it implies the possibility of counterhegemonic cultural activity, disruption of the existing hegemony.

The first point proposes that there is normally an intimate connection between culture and power. Communication and cultural processes do not take place on a level playing field where everyone gets to contribute as he or she will and each contribution carries the same value and weight. On the contrary, in the hegemonic view the media are dominated by those sectors of society that also wield considerable economic and political power. Thus what normally gets communicated through mainstream media will rarely challenge the foundations of that economic and political power, even though the media may voice criticism of some particular policies or issues (for further examples, see Herman, Chapter 5; Robinson, Chapter 6; Rodríguez, Chapter 8).

The second point challenges some of our most basic, taken-for-granted assumptions, notions that are sometimes so buried in ourselves that we have never even noticed they are there, let alone examined or questioned them. A quick example can be drawn from our school experience. Along with the subjects we learn, we also—without being especially conscious of it—learn that we are supposed to be on time for things, such as classes; that some people (instructors) have authority over us, which means that others set the pace and content and subject order of the class, and not us; that human knowledge is chopped up into different subjects (e.g., sociology, history, communication, psychology, anthropology, economics, government), even though all have to do with human society; and, not least, that our fellow students in different tracks (in the United States) or streams (in the United Kingdom) are "less" or "more" than us, that humans supposedly have marked differences in "intelligence." Most of us take these things for granted; they are obvious not because they are explicitly taught, but because they are continuously expressed by the daily rituals and organization of schooling. But they do have consequences, not least because we usually do not think about them. This book is dedicated to opening up questions you have never or rarely thought about.

The third and fourth points above concerning hegemony directly challenge the Frankfurt school's and Ortega y Gasset's implied pessimism and dismissal of the public's capacity to have alternative visions of life to those it is fed by mass media. If we acknowledge, as Gramsci does, that cultural hegemony exercised through mass media, education, and other channels is not automatically going to be valid in the same versions for long periods, then we are also acknowledging that the public changes as times change. Especially in periods of social and economic crisis, people's settled ways of thinking and ingrained acceptance of things as they are tend to crumble. At such times, thoughts and visions of life as it might be can arise to challenge convention. People open up in ways they used to think of as pointless or a waste of time. If all this is true, then definitions of mass culture as a lead weight that squashes creative thinking are arguably defective.

Furthermore, if groups of people become substantially detached from the reigning cultural hegemony and begin not only to question the assumptions of their media, their schooling, their religious authorities, but to communicate with each other about such issues, then they are creating counterhegemonic processes and institutions. In other words, the cultural situation is not locked in, as at least some of the founders of the Frankfurt school seem to argue—there are spaces for dissonant communication (for further discussion, see Downing, Chapter 14).

However, all these considerations combine to emphasize the reality that the concept of hegemony directly addresses (or argues for, if you disagree with the proposition) the multiple interconnections among power, culture, and communication in all societies, whether the power is that of dominant social groups or dissident social groups. The concept of cultural hegemony is directly at odds, therefore, with the assumptions that mass communication takes place on a level playing field or that we are victims of a mass culture imposed from above.

Ideology

Another chapter could be written on competing definitions of the word *ideology*, but here we will summarize some of them. *Ideology* is a term the use of which sometimes overlaps *culture* in the sense of a worldview. One common use of *ideology* is to describe a systematic set of ideas, but quite often one that the person doing the labeling does not like and considers dangerous to human well-being. For most of the twentieth century the word was hurled back and forth between the United States and the Soviet Union, with U.S. commentators describing Marxism as an ideology and Soviet commentators describing American celebration of free enterprise as an ideology. Americans would describe Marxism as underpinning the power of the Kremlin; the Soviets would describe the discipline of economics as underpinning the power of Wall Street. Much heat, less light. Sometimes the word *ideology* is used to suggest a strong emotional or psychological attachment to biased ideas, such as the fierce passion of religious fundamentalists, that are generally beyond reach of any reasoned challenge.

One assumption written into these definitions is that ideology needs to be unmasked, stripped away, cleared like a fog, so that its victims can see the truth, "the facts" as they really are. In other words, the term implies that there is reality and there is ideology, truth versus lies, persuasion versus propaganda, honesty versus deception, freedom fighters versus terrorists, devout Christians versus Muslim fanatics, a free press versus government-sponsored TV. But once you pin down some of these seemingly obvious simple oppositions to specifics, especially as in the last three examples, "reality" becomes a whole lot fuzzier.

So far, we have seen how the word *ideology* can be used to denote a stupid set of ideas, a wrong set of ideas, and/or a ferociously believed-in set of ideas. Its first use, by French writer Condorcet in the late eighteenth century, was quite neutral; the word was coined to denote the systematic study of ideas among human beings, as part of the larger project of zoology.

A different meaning of *ideology* is similar to the "wrong set of ideas" definition. Classical Marxist analysis argues that the ruling social class transmits its preferred ideas and views of reality to the general public and that, through this successful communication of its own ideas, the general public learns to think and act in ways that do not challenge—

indeed, that support—the continued rule of that class. There are at least two problems with this argument. One is that it assumes there is a single and homogeneous set of ideas swimming around in the skulls of the members of a ruling class. The other is that it presupposes some surefire way of projecting these ideas into everyone else's skulls and getting them accepted, as in Aldous Huxley's *Brave New World*.

This was a crude and clumsy early form, as you may recognize, of Gramsci's concept of hegemony and of the Frankfurt school's notion of mass culture. Gramsci, however, developed a far more supple and complex analysis of power, culture, and communication than this A + B = C formula, and so did the Frankfurt school researchers. All of them, whatever their other merits or shortcomings, were able to build the shifting and contradictory flows of culture and communication into their analyses, which are quite missing from the crude version.

Our purpose in presenting this analysis, and that of all the terms discussed in this chapter, is to help you recognize the need to ask yourself at once, when you see these words in something you are reading, how the writer is using them. We also hope to encourage you to be precise in the way you use these terms and to hone your ability to analyze culture and communication.

Semiology

Semiology, also known as semiotics, is the study of signs. There are different national traditions of semiology/semiotics—American, Russian, French and Italian—some of which have influenced each other, some of which have not. "Signs" in this context means a whole range of things, from film to architecture, from clothes to gestures, all of which have particular meanings in particular cultures. Originally, semiology examined underlying patterns in culture and communication rather than specific content or messages, much in the same way a specialist in linguistics might study the grammar and structure of languages without focusing on the meaning of a given sentence or word (see Desjardins, Chapter 23).

For example, one very influential early writer in this tradition of cultural analysis is the Russian Vladimir Propp (1928/1968), who argues that all folktales and fairy tales, which number in the thousands, can be reduced to a few basic story lines. Apart from being intriguing, Propp's work is important because it suggests that what is communicated in a folktale—and thus, evidently, in a soap opera or a sports report—is not just the contents, the specific details. If he and other semioticians are correct, then the form, the underlying structure of the tale, is also attractive and important to the audience. This is the basis of the classical semiological technique of analyzing culture, the detection of the underlying structure (sometimes called the "deep" structure). The basic technique can be used in many different situations. For example, one could try to show that Hollywood's countless western movies all had a deep structure of bad:good = Indians:cowboys.

Semiology set out to become an exact science. Its founders thought they were mapping nothing less than the underlying structure of the human mind. It soon became obvious, however, that semiology could not avoid dealing with the specifics of human values and history. It may be true, for example, that all cultures have a fundamental structure of bad:good, but the identification of cowboys with the good and the Indians with the bad rests upon a particular value system, namely, White racism. Most analysts would agree that the deep structure in western movies tells us more about a particular history and culture—racial subjugation in the United States—than about the fundamental structure of the human mind.

As a result of this kind of criticism, semiology began to revise its goals. It is now often seen as only one tool of analysis that must be supplemented by the study of historical and political issues. Many semioticians have come to acknowledge the importance of placing signs in their cultural contexts (see, e.g., Barthes, 1973; Berger, 1991).

Cultural Capital

Cultural capital is a term coined by French sociologist Pierre Bourdieu (1984) that picks up on the notion of "high" culture and takes it in a different direction. It is designed to capture a certain reality of professional middle-class life, namely, the way families in that social class use certain kinds of cultural awareness and information both to maintain their own socioeconomic status and to pass it on to their children. Extra time spent by parents with their children, reading them stories or dragging them around museums and cathedrals; the development of interest in music and the arts; simply being surrounded by "high" culture in the forms of books and CD-lined shelves; exposure to adult discussions of art and politics; the use of home computers as active instruments rather than as relatively passive video games—all these represent the endowment of cultural capital in children. This investment is one that parents hope will pay off for their children in the ability to capture and keep professional or executive careers—and hence to acquire economic capital. Bourdieu argues that this cultural communication is more important for some purposes than is formal education in schools. Because such valued skills take a long time to develop, the chances are great that children from the dominated classes will never catch up.

This manipulation of "high" culture legitimates the high social status and income of the middle and professional classes (DiMaggio, 1982). Possession of this culture pays off in everything from job interviews to professional contacts and "networking." Members of the lower-middle and working classes may aspire to acquire cultural capital, but they find it hard to achieve. They have not imbibed the background. They do not have the time it takes. The tickets are too expensive, whether to the opera or to the "right" university. The working classes are left with what Bourdieu calls "the choice of the necessary." They tend to feel uneducated, lacking in confidence in "those" circles, and know they are left out. Some individuals may even blame themselves, though others may criticize what counts as "high" culture, its pretentiousness, its jargon, and its long-windedness.

Conclusions

We have examined many different definitions of *culture* and related terms (*hegemony, ideology, cultural capital, semiology,* and *mass, high,* and *popular culture*). We have argued that culture should be seen as an interactive and ongoing process, not simply as the products that process brings into being. We have stressed the close interactions among culture, communication, and power, whether economic or political. We have emphasized the conflicts that express themselves in cultural terms as well as in economic or social terms, and the way the very term *culture* has been interpreted differently depending on people's positions in relation to those conflicts. We have looked at culture in the sense of outlook on life or understanding of the world— in other words, as the source from which we begin to make sense of an otherwise bewildering social reality.

The chapters in Part V of this volume deal with what are termed *cultural studies* issues. We have no space to map out here the multiple ways in which cultural studies approaches are used. There are British (e.g., Hall, 1980; R. Williams, 1977), North American (Grossberg, Nelson, & Treichler, 1992), South American (O'Connor, 1991; Rêgo, 1993), and Australian (Bennett, 1992) variants. Nonetheless, you should be aware that this is a rich and significant contemporary movement within communication research; the chapters in Part V will introduce you to some of its insights.

Further Questions

1. How would you describe and identify the main characteristics of your country's culture? Is it very difficult to do so?

2. How would you apply notions of culture, hegemony, interactive process, and the rest to ethnic majority/minority situations in your country?

3. What do you see as the cultural functions of a library or a museum? How important is the memory of past culture to present-day culture?

Notes

1. The film's title in Portuguese is *Como Era Gostoso O Meu Frances.* It is available in the United States, in subtitled format for classroom use, under the title *How Tasty Was My Little Frenchman* (New Yorker Films, Manhattan).

2. The verb came to be used in this form as a way of saying that the government's claim that all these people had simply "disappeared" had to be a lie. The military governments in both Argentina and El Salvador, it should be noted, received extensive aid from the U.S. government.

2 Forms of Media as Ways of Knowing

ANNABELLE SREBERNY-MOHAMMADI

If we are to understand how contemporary society and our communication media have taken on the shapes and roles that they have, a historical sense is vital. History does not have to be a dry and narrow catalog of dead men and dusty dates. Historical epochs can also be defined by different communications technologies, as in the "age of print" or the "television epoch." Sreberny-Mohammadi presents a very broad historical perspective about the rise of three major forms of communication—speech, print, and electronic media—and the social and political impacts of these forms. She argues that the forms, in and of themselves, are important. They can affect how many people can be addressed, the persuasive elements that can be used, and the kinds of communication and interactions that can take place. She argues that traditional political leadership and social authority were altered by the development of these different forms of communication, and examines their impacts at different moments in human history: oral communication in Ancient Greece, print in preindustrial England, and television in the contemporary United States.

The focus here is not so much on the development of technology, but on how the technology has been adopted and institutionalized, and by whom. Sreberny-Mohammadi connects the communications questions to broader sociological and political issues, and shows how different kinds of social groups and different kinds of authority have maintained themselves using these different forms of communication. Thus technology helps to define the kinds of communication that can occur, and, in turn, the pattern of communication plays a central role in structuring the culture. All these terms are intimately linked.

Just as O'Connor and Downing emphasize the links among power, culture, and communication in Chapter 1, Sreberny-Mohammadi explores these connections historically in relation to communication technologies. It may be surprising for readers who instinctively think of communication as a democratic process—"people talking to each other"—to find that people with power have dominated the communication process in the same way they have historically held sway over economic life. Yet from the very word papyrus, the name of an early form of paper made of crushed reeds, we know how far back this combination goes. The word means, literally, "the king's (pharaoh's) thing," signifying that only the ruler had the power to say who could use it to communicate. Although power over communication is not nearly so absolute now, later contributions to this volume by Herman (Chapter 5), Robinson (Chapter 6), Downing (Chapter 11), and Gandy (Chapter 13) all address the issue of how undemocratic some media systems may be.

In industrialized societies most of us now live in such media-saturated environments that we can hardly imagine a time when such obvious, necessary, and pleasurable parts of our daily lives as television, radio, cinema, newspapers, books, and audio- and videocassettes did not exist. But we could indeed trace out one strand of the history of human development as a history of the spread of particular forms of communication.

Looking at forms of communication is somewhat different from examining the technologies of communication, which is the focus of Chapter 4 of this volume, by Brian Winston. Many theorists would agree with a division of communications history into three main epochs: the earliest period, when orality dominated; the epoch of print; and the advent of electronic media. In each period, those communicating took on different roles. In orality, speaking and listening are the central activities. Print requires writers and readers. Electronic media demand organized production and audiences. Now, development does

not mean that one form replaces another; clearly, in contemporary industrial societies we may use all three forms of media on a daily basis, even simultaneously.

Let us look at each of these three forms in turn. We shall pay attention to the basic features of each form, no matter in what time period we examine them. But we shall also look at the kinds of societies within which these forms came to dominate and examine the relationship between the form of media and the form of society. There is not enough space here to describe the social history of each epoch in great detail, so I will present some brief idealized portraits of societies that correspond to the three major media forms; that is, I will highlight their typical features at the expense of omitting the details that make each historical situation different from others. We shall also examine the extent to which each form has provided opportunities for ordinary people to participate in public life, and how much each has been dominated by wealthy and powerful elites to shore up their own positions. Later we will explore the question of whether there is only a single path of communications development and the implications of studying forms of media.

The Nature of Oral Communication

Oral communication, whether in historical or contemporary context, has a number of formal, or necessary, features. These include the fact that oral communication is face-to-face or public communication in which speaker and audience are copresent, there in the same place. Thus the communication is very space bound; only those actually present will hear the message. It is also highly time bound, because sound dies as it is spoken, and speaking is a performance that ends and can be recalled only by those who were present, and we all know how fallible human memory can be. In oral/aural communication the mouth and the ear are the dominant organs and hearing the dominant sense, although all sorts of nonverbal cues, such as clothing styles, facial expressions, and body posture, can also be picked up visually and given meaning by the participants.

Oral communication is one of the oldest and certainly one of the most enduring forms of human communication. The study of oral communication is called *rhetoric*, which is also the name for its skillful application. The roots of the study of rhetoric lie in ancient Greece. By exploring how social life and political life were organized in ancient Greece, we can begin to understand why the practice of rhetoric was important, and thus how its study also grew.

ORALITY: RHETORIC IN ANCIENT GREECE

Ancient Greece was made up of city-states, the most important being Athens and Sparta. In comparison with the enormous nation-states of today, these city-states covered very limited territory—Athens was only about 1,000 square miles—and held small populations. The numbers of citizens active in the politics of the city-states were even more limited, because political life excluded all women and all men who were not taxpayers, mainly slaves. For the minority, the taxpaying male citizens, the political structure of the city-states provided considerable opportunities for participation, both political and legal. Ordinary people acted as jurors in public trials, but juries were made up of hundreds, not just 12 individuals.

There were elections of senators to the Assembly, as well as appointments of ambassadors to deal with foreign states. The practice and study of rhetoric, oral performance, reached their peak in the fourth and fifth centuries B.C. Oral presentation was widely respected, and people admired those who spoke effectively in legal settings, to political bodies, and on ceremonial occasions. The Greek educational system provided instruction in the art of rhetoric and aimed to produce great orators. All education—in contrast to education currently in the United States, which is very text(book) based—had to be conducted orally, because not until the fifth century B.C. were there any kinds of textbooks or other volumes on business management or agriculture, or any written codes of law (Havelock, 1963, 1986). Education thus took place through the close daily association between adolescent boys and their elders, who served as philosophers, guides, and friends. Most of Greek literature up to the time of Plato was poetic, because poetry's purpose was to preserve tradition through memorization and oral recitation.

Thus, for the ancient Greeks, all forms of communication clearly had a purpose and intention. They would have found the contemporary notion of "objective" news coverage quite odd (this concept is indeed critiqued in many places in this volume), because they felt, like Aristotle, who wrote an early and very influential book about the process, that rhetoric is "the effective use of all the available means of persuasion" (see Aristotle, 1967). Aristotle identified three main forms of persuasive proof: *logos,* or the use of evidence in rational argument; *ethos,* or the use of personal characteristics to claim credibility and authority; and *pathos,* or the use of emotion, such as hatred, to move people. There were correspondingly three main purposes of persuasive communication: *forensic,* or informative, used mainly in the court of law (hence our forensic science); *deliberative,* or mobilizing, used predominantly in political contexts to try to get people to vote; and *epideictic,* or entertaining or celebratory, used most frequently at funerals of great men, on feast days, and during other national festivities.

Oral cultures developed many different kinds of mnemonic devices, from poetic rhythms and rhymes to repeated formulas such as daily prayers, as ways of preserving their traditions. Even today there are many cultures that are still predominantly oral. For example, the Hmong people of Vietnam had no written language until some Hmong came to the United States as refugees and became concerned about their cultural heritage. In Western Africa, still, the *griot* is an inherited position of great authority; this is the man who carries the cultural memory of the tribe and chants out the news to the rhythm of a large drum (Niane, 1965).

The audience for oral communication was (and is) comparatively homogeneous in comparison with the huge television audiences of today. The audience and the speaker had a certain amount of social contact. The events were collective, meaningful for everyone involved, and provided plenty of opportunity for instant feedback, such as applause and hoorahs, stony silences or rotten tomatoes. The speaker could adjust his or her language, tone, even content, according to the reception.

Of course, oral communication has played an important role in modern political life (e.g., in the stump speeches of politicians and dissidents in nineteenth-century America) and has even provided opportunities for the general public to express opinions. Black Americans' African roots can be traced through their patterns and rhythms of speech, their delight in the "man of words," usually a preacher, and the Black audience's vocal repetition of and support for the preacher's words. This strong oral tradition has also produced preachers who have become national political leaders, able to mobilize the trust and affection of congregations across the country for change. Most notable in this respect was the Reverend Martin Luther King, Jr., whose "I Have a Dream" speech helped galvanize the civil rights movement. Even in contemporary society, public speaking at political rallies provides some of the best opportunities there are for political figures to make their ideas known and for the public to question, argue, and criticize them in a dynamic, instant-feedback situation.

Thus oral communication bound the community together, maintained a select group of experts with knowledge committed to memory, and endowed old men with authority over the young. It supported a social hierarchy based on gender, age, and the control of collective wisdom.

Oral cultures all develop certain formal linguistic devices, such as poetry, legends and myths, prayers, and strong theatrical and dance narratives, that help in the process of memorizing long and complex stories and human records. Many cultures possess men of knowledge, such as American Indian shamans, African healers, and Polynesian rememberers. In oral cultures, as Fabre (1963), a social historian of language, notes, history is the remembered word.

While Socrates *spoke* his ideas, Plato was already *writing*, for by the fifth century B.C. a shift in communication was evident. The use of language shifted from a concentration on the acoustic flow of sounds pleasurable to the ear to visual patterns that demand the concentration of the eye.

If oral communication is universal, the development of writing can perhaps be claimed as one phylogenetic development of the human species. Not all cultures develop alphabets, and some do not to this day possess written culture, whereas others developed written cultures only after the arrival of missionaries or anthropologists in the eighteenth and nineteenth centuries. But we do know that in very diverse parts of the world, such as Sumeria, Babylonia, and China, alphabetic systems were independently devised and refined, and a totally different form of communication came to prevail.

The shift to writing depended, of course, on the development of writing systems, alphabets. Allow me to digress briefly, simply to underline the fact that the history of the development of writing systems is fascinating in and of itself. We can trace the transformations of pictorial systems, hieroglyphics, into more abstract systems, such as cuneiform, into phonetic alphabet systems such as the Greek, on which ours is based. Other writing systems are based on syllabaries, and still others use ideograms, such as the Japanese and Chinese use today. Some systems are read from left to right, others from right to left (the Greeks even experimented for a while with a system that ran left to right for one line and then right to left—as one would plow a field); still others are read vertically, as is Chinese. There is also an interesting argument that the development of a phonetic alphabet, with its totally abstract way of depicting sounds using a relatively limited number of letters with enormous possibilities of combination, was the essential basis for the further development of Western abstract thought and analytic and classificatory systems (see Logan, 1986).

It is also important to note that sophisticated calendars such as those used by the Egyptians and the Mayans were developed before writing systems, so quite complex knowledge was possible without such systems, but limited. But let us get back to the invention of writing, and the changes it brought about.

The Nature of Written Communication

Written communication can be divided into two epochs: the epoch of chirographic, written culture (*chirography* meaning "handwriting" in Greek) and the epoch of typographic culture, the era of print.

Writing was the first extensive form of information storage. (Lascaux cave paintings and Egyptian hieroglyphics were also ways of presenting information, but they were limited in capacity.) What writing provided was a better and more reliable form of record keeping, about property ownership, about taxes due, about agricultural cycles and volumes of harvest. The numbers of those who could read or write under chirographic culture were limited, so writing was closely associated with power. Royal powers required scribes for accounting and tax collection and for preparing decrees to send across empires. Religious authorities used monks to copy Bibles by hand, creating multiple but authoritative copies, as well as to copy other important texts and to make translations. It took considerable time to copy an entire Bible, and books were often embellished with decorative frontispieces and gold leaf, so handwritten volumes commanded high prices. Still, the number of people who could read and write was quite limited.

How do the formal features of writing/print differ from those of oral communication? First, there is a major shift in physiological orientation from the ear to the eye, which becomes the dominant organ. As noted above, writing depends on a wholly other form of linguistic development, the development of a symbolic language with written syntax and punctuation. Writing is space oriented because it involves the linear organization of words in lines on a page (no matter in which direction those lines run). It is also space oriented in a very different way, because for the first time a message as a material object could be produced that was transportable far away from its producer. Unlike oral communication, written communication does not require the writer and the reader to be copresent—and they rarely are—either in space or in time.

What this implies is that because of the separation of the message from the producer, and the producer from the audience, the context or situation can no longer be as significant for the interpretation of the message. It also means that the writer, compared with the speaker, has much less control over the way her or his message is understood or used. A tragic example of precisely this process can be found in the massive outrage in 1989 among Muslims around the world against Salman Rushdie's fantastical novel, *The Satanic Verses*, with the Ayatollah Khomeini of the Islamic Republic of Iran putting millions of dollars on Rushdie's head for blasphemous writing. Writers write for absent and unknown audiences; they may have certain audiences in mind, but there is no guarantee that authors will reach those audiences. Thus print creates decontextualized communication in which, unlike in oral communication, the *ethos*, the personal charisma or social role of the speaker, is no longer key to interpreting the text. Certainly one might react in a certain way to a particular sonnet if one knows it is the last sonnet that Shakespeare wrote, but one can also read Shakespeare on the subway, at home, or in a class and discover different interpretations and inflections.

Written communication also began to allow for flexibility of use. The writing of a text, as well as its reading, clearly takes considerable time, but there is choice as to when this can occur, because neither writing nor reading is bound by a particular social event. Writing is also the most individualized form of communication, because almost all writing and a great deal of reading—both of which require quiet concentration—occur when writers and readers are alone. Of course, there are many contexts in different cultures in which material is read aloud, particularly where universal literacy does not exist, such as the reading of newspapers in teahouses in the Middle East. But the ideal-typical features of writing promote an extreme individualism, a far cry from the interpersonal nature of oral communication. Writing is essentially linear, logical, progressive, and thus helped to promote abstract thought that was very different from the concreteness of oral memory.

The process of book production was limited by another crucial technical factor, the fact that the West did not know how to make paper until the mid-twelfth century, and the preparation of parchment or vellum was slow and laborious. The Arabs had learned how to make paper after their single and successful military encounter with the Chinese in the eighth century. By the end of that century, paper was being produced in Samarkand and in Baghdad, now the capital of Iraq. The advent of paper so lowered the price of books that private and public libraries became common throughout the Islamic world. Perhaps the world's first library was started by Alexander the Great in Alexandria, Egypt, in 130 B.C. From the eighth century, collections were established by the Abbasid Caliph in the House of Wisdom in Baghdad. There international scholars translated from and into Arabic, Greek, Persian, and Indian works on mathematics, logic, astronomy, philosophy, and biology; they also wrote commentaries on the works and added original works of their own. In addition, the library housed Korans and book collections on Islamic law and theology; books of poetry, proverbs, fables, and witty anecdotes; and works of genealogy, history, geography, and grammar. Similar collections were built up in Cordoba in Spain, Cairo in Egypt, Shiraz in current Iran, and Bokhara in what is now Uzbekistan. The library of the Caliph al-Hakam in Cordoba in the tenth century is said to have contained more than 400,000 volumes, with a 44-volume catalog. Many of the Muslim collections were open to the public, to anyone who had the education to benefit, so that a general level of scholarship and learning was more widely disseminated through the Islamic world than anywhere in Christian Europe until the early Middle Ages, when the West acquired paper-making techniques from the Arabs via Spain. It is important to note that the history of communications developments is very much a global, cross-cultural history, with techniques learned through conquest, with different civilizations enduring periods of dynamism and decline, and with shifting centers of cultural power.

It was another technical breakthrough in written communication, the development and utilization of the printing press, that brought intellectual and cultural dynamism to Northern Europe. The print breakthrough is associated with Gutenberg, who produced the first printing-press Bible in 1453 in Mainz, Germany. Although printing techniques were begun much earlier in the Far East, they remained undeveloped. The age of chirography gave way to the age of typography, the age of print. These two are clearly part of one form of communication, writing, but the social and political consequences of the printing press were dramatic enough to demand our attention.

Printing technique and its products spread rapidly through Europe. Life in sixteenth-century Britain was greatly altered by print. Only about 35,000 books had been printed, mainly in Latin, in the whole of Europe by 1500. However, between 1500 and 1640 more than 20,000 items in English were printed. These ranged from pamphlets and broadsheets to folios and Bibles. By 1600, nearly half the populations in English towns had some minimal literacy. The vernacular spread rapidly, for certainly, outside the universities, people preferred to read in their own languages rather than in Latin or Greek.

Print immediately had powerful economic effects. It created new jobs—printers, typesetters, proofreaders, editors, stationers, publishers, booksellers, librarians, and eventually reporters and journalists. Perhaps most important was the new role of author, someone who could sell his or her words and ideas to a reading public and make a living from royalties paid through this public consumption of cultural products, and who was thus no longer dependent on the patronage of the wealthy. Of course, many of those in the new occupations that arose from the advent of print became new "gatekeepers," people who could decide what should and should not be published, the new arbiters of public tastes and opinions.

Centers of business and banking welcomed the new technique of printing, for merchants depended upon navigation books and almanacs for safe sea-bound trading, ways of keeping accurate accounts, and reports on prices and sales in foreign markets. The economics of increased cross-cultural contact through trade and travel created demands for current information, so by the early seventeenth century, newspapers had begun to develop in northern Europe.

Not all print material was serious or clearly useful. Prose fiction developed as a powerful new form, because poetic rhyme was no longer necessary as a mnemonic device, and newspapers serialized novels. One vivid example of the popularity of the new fiction form, as well as an indication of the size of the reading public in the 1800s, is the story of Charles Dickens's being mobbed on his tour of the United States in 1848, much as a contemporary pop star would be today (Postman, 1984).

There were now both more books and more copies of single books, which helped to foster religious debate and schisms and to spread new secular ideologies, such as liberalism, nationalism, and, later, socialism. Although John Wycliff had been considered a heretic for translating the Bible into English in the 1360s, various editions of English Bibles became the runaway best-sellers of the fifteenth century and began to spread English across the world. One of the earliest uses of the printing press was to produce papal indulgences, which had brisk sales, but the more long-term effect of print was found in the publication of vernacular Bibles, which heralded the demise of papal control over religious interpretation. Luther's criticisms of the church in 1517 sold all over Europe, and Luther himself said, "Print is the best of God's inventions!" (Lenin argued 400 years later that "film is the most important art"; see Downing, Chapter 11.) Religious authorities lost their monopoly on the production of texts, and thus over the control of knowledge and interpretation.

New forms of knowledge and new social authorities began to develop. The new middle class and secular intellectuals began to vie with the aristocracy and the clergy for authority and influence. Secular education helped this process. Universities such as Paris, Oxford, and Bologna had been founded much earlier in the thirteenth century, but the growing recognition of the power of the printed word gradually produced social movements for universal education and universal literacy. Literacy rates were high among the Puritan settlers in America, and for a long time a great deal of print material was imported from Britain.

The new intellectuals possessed neither the traditional authority of religious figures nor the political inheritance of royalty and nobility, but claimed their authority through logical argument, critical analysis, and persuasive language, both oral and written, but primarily written. They found an audience in the literate working class and growing educated middle class, who read and discussed their pamphlets and tracts in what has been called the "public sphere" of bourgeois society, the coffeehouses, pubs, and salons where free debate could circulate without state control (Habermas, 1979).

Print had strengthened the power of states, which could now more easily inform their populaces of new laws, gather taxes, print stamps with royal faces, and require written oaths of loyalty. Print even served to promote nationalism, because it helped the spread of vernacular languages such as English, French, and German in preference to Latin, which promoted the spread of national identity and led to the demise of the multinational empires that had dominated Europe (Anderson, 1983).

At the same time, however, print created new opportunities for dissident opinion to be heard. For political and religious nonconformists, print allowed the production of pamphlets and broadsheets criticizing the authorities, putting forward alternative ideas, and mobilizing a new "public opinion" (see Downing, Chapter 14). Throughout Europe and indeed America, revolutionary movements depended on print to disseminate popular demands for political democracy and social justice. In the United States, Tom Paine published pamphlets; in Britain, William Cobbett sold his penny Chartist paper; and debate in the salons of Madame de Stael in Paris centered on the now readily available books of such Enlightenment thinkers as Rousseau and Montesquieu. Thus print helped the development of ideological politics, fostered the revolutionary ferment of eighteenth-century Europe, and aided the self-conscious rise of the new middle class, or bourgeoisie, and the new working class of the industrial towns (Gouldner, 1976). Governments tried to limit and quash such political activity by imposing fines, arresting writers, and, in extreme cases, smashing the printing presses.

Thus we can catalog important economic, social, political, and cultural aspects of the impact of print, all of which combined to create the new dynamic and conflict-ridden Western industrial society. The third, and last, form we must look at, which is a product of that new economic structure, is electronic media, most particularly television.

Electronic Media

Although the technological breakthroughs had taken place by the end of the nineteenth century, electronic media were not developed as public media in the United States until the 1920s, when radio was established, with television spreading rapidly after World War II. I will use the highly televisual society of the 1980s United States as the ideal-typical example here.

Television, of course, recombines the visual and the aural, the eye and the ear. As a new medium, it again created new orientations to both time and space. Up until the development of audio recording and the VCR, electronic media were extremely time bound, from the precise and regular scheduling of programs to the definition of *prime time*, to the length of individual programs, to the pacing within each program. Whereas the reading of a book is totally flexible in terms of time, so that one can sit up all night reading a good book or dip into it over a period of time, finish it, abandon it, return to it, television makes stringent time demands on the audience. The VCR functions as a kind of storage capacity, allowing the audience to time shift, but it has not caused any visible change in the basic television time schedule, which supports the daily division of work and leisure in highly developed postindustrial societies and reinforces patterns of family life, gender interests, and subcultural tastes. Indeed, if television schedules are designed to offer up the biggest viewing audiences to advertisers, then little flexibility is possible.

Not only are electronic media powerful timekeepers, they also have voracious appetites; daily, they consume huge amounts of programming, continually demanding new cultural production and keeping audiences in a continuously unfolding present of "and now this." In terms of space, the early large television receiver was given pride of place in the family living room, with the remaining furniture rearranged around it; now televisions have shrunk in size, come in a variety of colors, and have crept into the bedroom, the kitchen, and the subway.

If the ethos of the speaker was of great importance in oral societies, and logical argument became the most important rhetorical factor in print communication, how do we analyze television? Ong (1982) describes both radio and television as forms of "secondary orality," forms that reinforce the power of the ear and listening once more. Television appears to bring back the power of ethos, of the credibility and credentials of media figures such as newscasters, whose ability to create trust among the audience is perhaps their biggest asset. Television also seems to undermine the power of logos, the slow development of rational understanding and analysis, in favor of rapid and fragmented bits of information; instead of abstract conceptual language, it provides vivid, particularist images; instead of intellectuals, it creates celebrities. This was powerfully shown in recent U.S. presidential races of 1980, 1984, and 1988, where the photo opportunity and the sound bite worked to undermine any deep discussion of the issues or critical assessment of political positions. Metonymic images—Clinton playing the saxophone or a photo of a convicted rapist—could be used to stand for huge areas of social policy that should have received careful explanation and analysis.

Electronic media voices have from the beginning been far less plentiful than print voices. Monopolistic tendencies mean the media have enormous control over what the U.S. viewing public will watch, become interested in, and be invited to think about; media gatekeepers can really set the social, cultural, and political agendas of modern society. It is interesting and important to ask who the people are who now potentially wield such control in American life. They are not the philosopher-kings that Plato desired, or the traditional religious and aristocratic authorities of oral culture, or the intellectuals or political activists of print. Rather, they tend to be invisible business moguls with conservative agendas, for whom television provides both profit and influence. Of course, technically, there are avenues for popular participation in electronic media; local community and ethnic broadcasting has been established in most big cities, and cable channels have helped.

Yet it is also probably correct to say that most "liberal" and "critical" intellectuals, academics, community workers, and so forth are still more attuned to print and putting out pamphlets, newsletters, and journal articles than to talking on the radio or appearing on television. The gatekeepers of television are even stronger than the gatekeepers of print, and the lack of federal support for public stations in the United States has not allowed these stations to sustain a more invigorating type of television. It is ironic to note that in the United States the public television stations carry more imported programming than do any other stations.

If religious figures held greatest authority during the period of oral communication, and vied with secular intellectuals during the epoch of print, the electronic period is the epoch of the Hollywood celebrity and entertainer—for example, Ronald Reagan or Johnny Carson—and the televangelist—such as Jim Bakker and Oral Roberts.

Conclusion

As this chapter itself shows, it is almost impossible to separate the impacts of a medium from the effects of the particular way in which that medium has been institutionalized in a particular society. I have tried to identify some of the necessary formal features of three basic forms of communication—orality, print, and electronic media—but have also placed these in specific historical contexts to examine the impacts they had and the opportunities they created. History has shown that one communications medium does not replace another; rather, the new one is added on and often comes to dominate as the older forms take on different functions. It is important to note also that since the 1960s electronic media have been developed rapidly in Third World societies in very different patterns, and that the stages of media development described here are not necessarily universal. One very different Third World experience is examined by Mohammadi in Chapter 21 of this volume.

In the West, at least, the three different forms of communication examined here have tended to privilege different social groups and to provide varied kinds of opportunities for ordinary people to participate. It may be one of the greatest ironies of our modern communication times that we are surrounded by big media that speak to us but that give us comparatively little opportunity to speak back. The existence of more media seems to have resulted in less diversity, not more.

Further Questions

1. Monitor the debates about literacy and electronic media in the United States. What are the arguments for and against literacy in the media age?

2. Has the "television age" really turned people away from books?

3. Keep a daily log of all your media-related activities. With which medium do you spend the most time? For what purposes do you use each medium? Log your media-related expenses: What do you buy? How do you use the cultural products you buy? How does a cultural product differ from other material consumer products?

4. New technologies challenge the model presented here. The telephone provides us with a process of oral communication at a distance. The modem provides us with a form of written togetherness. Think of other examples that alter the forms of communication discussed in this chapter.

3 Mediating Communication
What Happens?

JOSHUA MEYROWITZ

No one needs to be told that television is the dominant medium of our age—but what is its real nature, and what does it really communicate? In this chapter Meyrowitz explores television as a new form of human experience that has already had revolutionary effects and may have consequences significantly at odds with the desires of those who control it.

Some 98% of U.S. households have at least one television set, and television is increasingly widespread in the industrialized world and beyond. Television's visual nature and universal presence have destroyed the age-old links connecting where we are, what we see, and what we know. Regardless of explicit content, television by its very nature breaks down many traditional distinctions between adult and child, male and female, public and private. In the same way that the rapid spread of printing and literacy in sixteenth-century Europe had consequences antithetical to the powers of church and crown, fundamental changes in modern society have been accelerated by the advent of television. For instance, for centuries adults used literacy to control children. But television, by exposing children to the very topics that adults are trying to keep from them, dilutes the authority of grown-ups and limits this traditional system of adult control. It even lets children in on the biggest secret of all, the secret of secrecy: that adults are conspiring to censor their knowledge.

The behind-the-scenes view that television affords applies equally to relations between the sexes. Through television, even the most home-bound women can experience parts of our culture once considered primarily male—sports, war, business, medicine, law, politics. This demystification of the masculine has directly contributed to our culture's notion of sexism. On the other hand, because television emphasizes traits traditionally considered feminine—feelings, appearance, emotions—it has helped men to become more aware of their emotions. Through the shared experience of television, the expectations of both sexes have become more similar, as illustrated by the trends toward more career-oriented women and more family-oriented men.

Television also mutes differences between levels of social status. By showing us our political and cultural leaders "warts and all," television decreases distance and awe. Not only have our leaders lost much of their mystique, they have lost a great deal of the control they used to have over the flow of information. By bringing us closer to our leaders and events as they happen and giving us more knowledge about politics and politicians, television has led us toward less blind faith in authority.

The perspective presented here contradicts in part the views of some of the other contributors to this book, who argue that what mainstream media do not tell us, or what they distort, is more typical of the way they work than any form of empowerment they may offer us. It also contradicts in part Sreberny-Mohammadi's position on electronic media presented in the preceding chapter. As elsewhere in this text, readers need to discuss and decide for themselves what their conclusions are.

Although more egalitarian access to information and experience may lead to a broadening of knowledge, for many segments of our society television has raised expectations without providing new opportunities. Its underlying dynamic, however, remains one of more similar expectations for members of different social categories. Meyrowitz suggests this may be the first step toward a more egalitarian society.

The content of television is limited by numerous economic, political, and ideological forces. Nevertheless, for the average person, the net change from the pretelevision era is a widening of sensory experience. Wider experience through television may actually create new social tensions and make people more dissatisfied with what they have and experience locally, but it also makes many people feel wiser and more "aware."

More Than a Message Conduit

In order to perceive and evaluate the consequences of the changes brought about by the spread of television, we need to think of television as more than a passive conduit for ideological and commercial "messages." We need to look at television as a new form of human experience that has consequences apart from the particular desires of those who try to control it (Meyrowitz, 1985).

A look to the past supports the plausibility of this alternative perspective. Consider the impact of the rapid spread of printing and literacy during the sixteenth century in Europe. A focus on only the content and institutional control of the printing industry would suggest that this new medium would strengthen religion and enhance the power of monarchs. Most books, after all, were of a religious nature, and their content was regulated by the church and crown. The consequences for printing the "wrong" material could be severe. William Carter printed a pro-Catholic pamphlet in Protestant-dominated England in 1584, for example, and was hanged. Yet it is now widely believed that printing—by making possible new patterns of knowledge development, storage, and distribution—ultimately helped foster the Scientific Revolution and the development of constitutional systems, thereby advancing the secularization of life and undermining, not strengthening, the power of royalty (Eisenstein, 1979). Even the widespread distribution of the Bible had a revolutionary impact, because it decreased the power of the Catholic Church as prime possessor and interpreter of God's word. These consequences grew out of a number of social forces apart from printing, but they would have been virtually impossible without the structural features of printing technology that made it different from oral communication and from handwritten manuscripts.

Similarly, I argue that we need to look beyond the common concerns about media content and control in order to see the full range of television's influence. To watch a wide array of TV shows, one does not need to travel anywhere, interact with anyone, "pass" as a member of any group, buy or borrow anything, or make any public gesture of affiliation with a group, activity, performance, or publication. One does not even need to know how to read. Because of its imagistic nature, U.S. television has relatively few exclusionary "vocabularies." Viewers can easily graze from channel to channel, watching segments on issues and behaviors they would not read about or go to see a movie or play on, such as those traditionally associated with another sex, age group, social class, race, subculture, or religion. Television is mostly about gazing at people. The "topics"—as they might be categorized by the Dewey decimal system—are much less relevant than they are in print.

Television's visual form and wide pattern of dissemination have broken the age-old link between where we are and what we can see with our own eyes. Television offers us a variety of distant perspectives from which to judge our local experiences. Television close-ups place us at intimate distance from a wide range of "electronic friends"—actors, musicians, talk-show hosts, newscasters, national politicians, foreign leaders—and these relationships compete and interact with the influences of local relationships with family members, real-life friends, coworkers, teachers, and religious and political leaders.

Television's unique features have been encouraging new social relationships by shifting the old balance of "who knows what about whom" and "who knows what compared with whom." Three dimensions of this shift that most of us have experienced firsthand are changes in the relative roles of children and adults, men and women, and national political leaders and average citizens.

New Experiences and New Social Identities

CHANGED CHILDHOOD

For young children, television is a secret-exposing machine. Television undermines several centuries of adults' use of literacy as a tool of control. As printing and literacy began to spread rapidly through Western culture in the sixteenth and seventeenth centuries, literate adults discovered they could increasingly keep secrets from preliterate and semiliterate children. Adults used books to communicate among themselves without children "overhearing." Clerics argued for the development of expurgated versions of the classics, and the notion of the innocence and isolation of childhood slowly began to take hold (Ariès, 1952/1962).

Among the literate classes, adults were able to maintain a private, "backstage" area. Children were kept in the dark about many of the behind-the-scenes realities of adult life (birth, death, sex, adult anxieties, violence, addictions, and so on). Very young children, who were unable to read, had no access to the information available in books. As they grew a bit older, young readers were presented with an idealized, "onstage" version of adult life (including, for instance, knowledgeable and responsible parents who know best). Children were slowly walked up a ladder of literacy, with a new, somewhat less idealized view of adult life presented to them at each step of reading ability. (Even today, many U.S. children's books carry codes on their back covers, such as 5.2, which means "fifth grade, second month.")

Television dilutes the innocence of childhood and the authority of adults by undermining the system of information control that supported them. Television bypasses the year-by-year slices of knowledge given to children. It presents the same general experiences to adults and to children of all ages. Children may not understand everything they see on television (do adults?), but they are exposed to many aspects of adult life from which their parents (and traditional children's books) would have once shielded them.

Books put control over much of children's knowledge in the hands of adults. Adults can decide what to read to very young children. Even with older children, parents, schools, and libraries select some books for them and restricting access to others. But television programs have no physical existence apart from the television set. With television, the decision is usually whether or not to have a receiver in the first place—and 98% of American households have decided to own at least one television, up from only 9% in 1950.

A parent can read a newspaper without sharing its content with children in the same room, but television is accessible to everyone in the same space. Even when future technologies allow parents to block out programs that carry certain ratings, parents will continue to find that they cannot censor their children's television experiences without censoring their own—or separating family members from each other. For most families, neither is a viable choice.

A parent can flip through a book to see what lies ahead for a child, but we can rarely anticipate what will happen on television. I thought

I was giving my young daughter a lesson in science as we watched the space shuttle *Challenger* take off, only to discover that I had exposed her instead to adult failure and tragedy.

A book is like a guest in the house: It makes a social entrance, it is subject to at least nominal adult authority, and it has to be placed somewhere—whether on a coffee table or under a mattress. A television, in contrast, is like a new doorway to the home, and through it rush many welcome and unwelcome visitors. Television and its visitors take children across the globe before parents even give them permission to cross the street.

There was a small hint of these changes in childhood earlier in this century, with the advent of movies and radio. But movies were not in the home (even young children who were "regular" moviegoers saw only an average of two movies a month), and radio had no pictures beyond what the listeners themselves could imagine based on their own experiences (leaving the relatively inexperienced child at a severe disadvantage). Neither movies nor radio, then, challenged the dominance of print communication in controlling the speed and content of children's learning in the way that television does.

Parental advice books allow adults to discuss privately what to tell or not tell children. With the help of such books, adults in a pretelevision culture were once able to keep many secrets from children, and they could keep their secret keeping secret. But the same content on a television talk show has quite a different effect: Thousands of children are exposed to the very topics that adults are trying to keep from them. Such discussions on television also expose children to the biggest secret of all: the secret of secrecy—the fact that adults conspire to censor children's knowledge. Similarly, parental guidance warnings on television are as accessible to children as to adults and generally have a boomerang effect, increasing children's interest in what follows.

Even seemingly innocent programs reveal significant secrets to children. When the first TV generation watched programs such as *Father Knows Best* and *Leave It to Beaver*, for example, they learned that parents behaved one way in front of children and another way when they were alone. In front of their children the TV parents were calm, cool, and collected, but away from their kids they were anxious and concerned about their parental behavior. Because we often reduce the effects of television to imitation, we forget that although the fictional child characters on such programs were innocent and sheltered, the real children watching the program saw how adults manipulated their behaviors to make it appear to their children that they knew best. This is a view that undermines traditional parental authority by making children less willing to take adult behavior at face value. It is no wonder, perhaps, that the generation who grew up watching *Father Knows Best* became concerned with the "credibility gap," that is, the difference between what people proclaim publicly and what they say and feel privately. Television's exposure of many adult secrets may be one reason the current generation of children seems less childlike, and why many parents and teachers have abandoned traditional styles of imposing adult authority over children.

In short, children may love television for reasons that have nothing to do with the sinister desires of corporate owners and advertisers. Children may love television because it extends their horizons of experience, because it expands their awareness of adult behavior and adult roles, and because it keeps them abreast of the latest adult attempts to control them. Of course, this is also one likely source of much adult anger about television, which has focused on what it is doing to children. Relatively few adults, however, are angry enough about television to remove it from their homes. Two other dimensions of social change fostered by television may explain why.

BLENDED GENDERS

Just as the adult world was once a mystery to children, so men and women were once relative mysteries to each other. Until recently, our society assumed that the ideal was for men and women to live in two relatively separate worlds. This was especially true for the literate middle and upper classes. The Victorians, for example, spoke of the "two spheres": a public male world of brutal competition, rationality, and accomplishments; and a private, female world of home, intuition, and child rearing. Men were to suppress their emotions and women were to suppress their competitiveness and personal ambition. Men and women were socialized into these separate roles with the help of different etiquette books written for each sex. The ideal of separate spheres was quite strong in our society when television became the newest home appliance.

Yet even as television situation comedies and other programs featured very traditional gender roles in the two separate spheres, television itself—as a shared arena experienced by both sexes—was beginning to break down the distinction between the male and the female, between the public and the private realms. Television close-ups reveal the personal side of public figures and events (we see tears well up in the eyes of a president; we hear male voices crack with emotion), and many public events are now played out in the privacy of our kitchens, living rooms, and bedrooms. Television has exposed even homebound women to most of the parts of the culture that were once considered primarily male domains—sports, war, business, medicine, law, politics—and it has made men more aware of the personal and emotional dimensions and consequences of public actions.

When Betty Friedan (1963/1977) wrote in *The Feminine Mystique* that women in 1960 felt a "schizophrenic split" between the frilly, carefree image of women in women's magazines and the important events occurring in "the world beyond the home," most of her examples of the latter were unwittingly drawn from the top television news stories of the year. By 1960, television was present in nearly 90% of U.S. homes. Similarly, other feminist writers have described changes in the 1960s by writing metaphorically of the "breaking of boundaries" (Steinem, 1980, p. 19), "a sudden enlargement of our world" (Janeway, 1974, p. 12), and of women having "seen beyond the bucolic peacefulness of the suburbs to the war zone at the perimeter" (Ehrenreich & English, 1978, p. 283). But these writers seem unaware of how closely their metaphors describe the literal experience of adding a television to a suburban household.

The fact that early (and many later) TV programs generally portrayed active men and passive, obedient women did not necessarily have more of an imitative effect on female viewers than the innocent child characters on *Father Knows Best* had on child viewers (who become the members of the rebellious generation of the 1960s). Television, it is true, suggested to women how society thought they should behave, just as etiquette books for women had for centuries. But television did something else as well: It allowed women to observe and experience aspects of the larger world, including all-male interactions and behaviors. Indeed, there is nothing more enraging than being exposed constantly to adventures, activities, and places that you are told are reserved for someone else. Television also demystified the male realm, making it and its inhabitants seem neither very special nor very intimidating. From this perspective, sexist content had a boomerang effect when funneled through the medium of television, encouraging women to demand to integrate the public "male" realm. This analysis does not make sexist content on television any more pleasant for women to watch, but it offers one reason that we as a culture have become aware of the notion of sexism.

The impact of television's new form of experience has been greatest on women because they have traditionally been more isolated than men. But men are affected as well, partly because women have demanded changes in their behavior in public and private spheres, and partly because television emphasizes those traits traditionally ascribed to women: feelings, appearance, emotion. Television is an intimate, personal medium that deals poorly with issues and problems that cannot be pictured. On television, "glorious victories" and "crushing defeats" are now conveyed through images of blood and limp bodies and the howls of survivors. Television has helped men to become more aware of their feelings and of the fact that emotions cannot be completely buried. Even at televised public hearings, it is hard to ignore the rich range of expressions—the yawns, the grimaces, the fatigue.

The inherent intimacy of television makes it one of the few public arenas in our culture where men routinely wear makeup and are judged as much on their personal appearance and "style" as on their "accomplishments." If it was once thought that women communicated and men accomplished, it is telling that President Reagan was praised for being the "Great Communicator" and was admired for his gentle voice and manner and his moist-eyed emotional appeals. Similarly, President Bush promised a "kinder, gentler nation," and President Clinton embodies a "soft" style and a distaste for confrontation that once were thought of as "feminine" traits.

With television, boys and girls and men and women tend to share a great deal of similar information about themselves and the "other," including many aspects of the other sex's behind-the-scenes strategies of how to behave with—and manipulate—them. Through television close-ups, men and women see in a matter of days many more members of the opposite sex at "intimate distance" than members of earlier generations saw in a lifetime. Further, unlike face-to-face interactions, in which the holding of a gaze may be construed as insulting or as an invitation to further intimacy, television allows one to stare at and carefully examine the face, body, and movements of the other sex.

In spite of its often sexist content, therefore, television—as an environment shared by both sexes—has helped to make the experiences and expectations of real men and women more similar. This aspect of television has contributed to, rather than opposed, recent trends toward more career-oriented women and more family-oriented men, toward more work-oriented homes and more family-oriented workplaces.

DEMYSTIFIED LEADERS

Just as television tends to mute differences between people of different ages and sexes, so it tends to mute differences between levels of social status. Although television is certainly an important weapon in the arsenal of leaders, it often functions as a double-edged sword. Unlike other media, television not only allows leaders to reach followers, it also allows followers to gain unprecedented access to the close-up appearance and gestures of leaders.

"Leadership" and "authority" are unlike mere "power" in that they depend on performance and appeal. One cannot lead or be looked up to if one's presence is unknown, yet authority is weakened by excess familiarity. Awe thrives on "distant visibility" and "mystified presence." One of the peculiar ironies of our age is that most people who step forward into the television limelight and attempt to gain national visibility become too visible, too exposed, and are thereby demystified. The more we see them, the more ordinary they appear.

The speaker's platform once lifted politicians up and away from average citizens, both literally and symbolically. In newspaper quotes and reports, the politician—as flesh-and-blood person—was completely absent. And on radio, politicians were disembodied voices. But the television camera now lowers politicians to the level of the common citizen and brings them close for our inspection. In recent years, we have seen our presidents sweat, stammer, and stumble—all in living color.

Presidential images were once much more protected. Before television coverage of press conferences, newspapers were not even allowed to quote a president without his explicit permission. As late as the start of the Eisenhower administration, the *New York Times* and other publications had to paraphrase the president's answers to questions. In earlier administrations, journalists had to submit their questions in advance and were forbidden to mention which questions the president refused to answer. Presidential advisers frequently corrected presidents' answers during meetings with the press, and such assistance went unreported. In the face of a "crisis," our presidents once had many hours, sometimes even weeks or months, to consult with aides and to formulate policy statements to be printed in newspapers. Now, standing before the nation, a president is expected to have all relevant information in his head—without notes and without consultation. A president must often start a sentence before the end of the sentence is fully formed in his mind. Even a 5-second pause for thought can seriously damage a leader's credibility. The apparent inarticulateness of all our recent presidents may be related more to the immediacy of television than to a decline in our leaders' mental or leadership abilities.

In language, the titles *president, governor,* and *senator* still call forth respect. But the close-up TV pictures of the persons filling those offices are rarely as impressive. We cannot help but notice the sweat on the brow, the nervous twitch, the bags under the eyes.

Television not only reduces our awe of politicians, it increases politicians' self-doubt and lowers their self-esteem. A speaker's nervousness and mistakes usually are politely ignored by live audiences and therefore soon forgotten by the speaker as well. But with videotape, politicians have permanent records of themselves misspeaking or anxiously licking their lips. For all these reasons, television may be a prime cause of the complaints of indecisive leadership and hesitant "followership" that we have heard since the mid-1960s.

In the 1950s, many people were shocked that a genuine hero, Dwight Eisenhower, felt the need to hire a Hollywood actor to help him with his television appearances. But now we are much more sophisticated—and more cynical. We know that one cannot simply be the president, but that one has to perform the role of "President." The new communication arena demands more control on the part of politicians, but it also makes attempts at control more visible. Many U.S. citizens lived through 12 years of Franklin Roosevelt's presidency without being aware that his legs were crippled and that he often needed help to stand. But we are now constantly exposed to the ways in which our presidents and presidential candidates attempt to manipulate their images to create certain impressions and effects.

The result is that we no longer experience political performances as naive audiences. We have the perspective of stagehands who are aware of the constructed nature of the drama. We have what might be called a "sidestage" view; that is, we see politicians move from backstage to onstage to backstage. Certainly, we prefer a good show to a bad show, but we are not fully taken in even by a great performance. Rather than being fooled, we are willingly entertained, charmed, courted, and seduced. Ironically, all the recent discussions of how we are being manipulated may only point out how relatively visible and exposed the machinations now are.

I am not suggesting that television has made us a fully informed and aware electorate. Indeed, relatively few Americans realize how selective the image of the world is that we receive through television news. When the same sort of occurrences have taken place in El Salvador and in Nicaragua, or in Iraq and Kuwait, they have been covered in completely different ways—or they are not reported on at all—generally in keeping with "official views" and preexisting news narratives concerning each country. Regardless of the circumstances, U.S. military actions are never described as acts of aggression; and rarely are the human consequences of the "defensive" military actions of the United States given much attention. But regardless of the ways in which the content of television news is often molded, television's immediacy and visual nature are affecting our perception of our leaders.

Most of our information about other countries once came through the president and the State Department, often after careful planning about how to present the information to the public. This allowed the government to appear to be in control of events and always to have a ready response. But today, in many instances, we experience events at the same moment as our leaders, sometimes before them. The dramatic images of the 1989 fall of the Berlin Wall, horrible images from Bosnia, images of the body of a U.S. serviceman being mutilated by Somalis, have been watched by the president, the secretary of state, and millions of other Americans at the same moment. The immediacy of television often makes leaders appear to be standing on the sidelines rather than taking charge or reacting quickly.

Leaders' authority is also diminished by television's accessible, visual nature. Average citizens gain the feeling that they can form their own impressions of televised people and events without depending on official interpretations. Once formed, the mass perceptions constrain our leaders' characterizations of countries and events. President Reagan found he needed to temper his talk of the "Evil Empire" as the public formed a positive perception of Gorbachev. And the televising of Filipinos facing down Marcos's tanks made it difficult for Americans to accept our president's suggestion that the reported results of that country's election should stand because "there was cheating on both sides." President Reagan might have changed his rhetoric on these topics in any case, but the public's direct access to the television images made it appear that Reagan was following rather than leading the nation. More recently, the U.S. public's split reactions to images from Bosnia—a hunger to do something to stop the slaughter and fear of U.S. entanglement—have made it difficult for President Clinton to present the public with a convincing case for either path.

As our leaders have lost much control over the flow of information—both about themselves and political events—they have mostly given up trying to behave like the imperial leaders of the past. We now have politicians who strive to act more like the person next door, just as our real neighbors seem more worldly and demand to have a greater say in national and international affairs. Ironically, we use television as a means of getting close to greatness, yet the closer we come to leaders and the more we know about politics and politicians, the less faith we have in them and in the process.

Changed, but Unchanged

Television's influence extends beyond the shifts in child/adult, male/female, and leader/follower experiences. Other reorientations include the relative blurring of experiences for urban and rural, rich and poor, minority and majority, one nation and another. Again, the experiences available through mainstream television are highly selective, what remains invisible at any moment is as significant as what is visible, and tremendous differences remain—but the net change is a relative broadening of experience for most people.

Does this analysis of television as an empowering medium override concerns about the current institutional patterns of control over mass media? Certainly not. But it adds another dimension to the study of the influence of modern media, and it explains why our attitudes toward television are often ambivalent.

Patterns of control of media content reduce the significance of the role shifts analyzed above. It may now be much more difficult to separate the information available to children from the information available to adults, but the "adult information" to which children now have access includes distorted war stories with heroes and villains as one-dimensional as those found in a child's bedtime tale. So manipulation, secret keeping, and propaganda persist.

Similarly, whereas television may foster more "democratic" access by women to "male experiences," and thereby support women's movement into once all-male professions, the bulk of available jobs are in companies that are not themselves run democratically. And although both men and women now expect to work outside the home, most jobs still involve temporal and spatial demands that seem to assume there is a spouse at home full-time—cooking, cleaning, and watching the kids. The result is often incredible stress in family and work life.

Although television demystifies visible authorities, invisible elites retain enormous power. Further, even as the mainstream national news media dutifully report on the public's disenchantment with "the system" and with "political insiders," they rarely give the public any information about alternative forms of democracy or alternatives to the so-called major candidates who are running for office (Meyrowitz, in press). As a result, we may feel smugly superior to the political leaders we see on television, but we are often left with a powerless sense of dependence on those leaders in whom we have little trust. From one perspective, then, television completely changes the game; from another perspective, it merely reshuffles the cards in the same deck.

More egalitarian access to information and experience through television may lead to a raising of consciousness about one's own life and the lives of others, but it does not lead to instant physical integration or to social harmony. Indeed, the initial effect is often increased social tension. Television makes it seem possible to have integration, but the social mechanisms are not always in place. The potential for gaining access to the male realm, for example, is much greater for some women than for others. The feminist movement has primarily advanced upper- and middle-class women—often in part through the hiring of lower-class women to clean house and mind children.

Ironically, in being exposed to a wider world, many viewers gain a sense of being unfairly isolated in some pocket of it. Members of earlier generations have often reported that it was once possible to grow up poor without fully realizing one was poor; one looked around in one's neighborhood, and saw simply that one's family was "normal." But today, ghetto children see their poverty in every TV show and commercial. For many of us, television enhances our awareness of all the people we cannot be, the places we cannot go, the things we cannot possess.

The old divisions are no longer taken for granted, but for many segments of our society, television has raised expectations without providing many new opportunities. Raised expectations may have led to the angry tone of the late 1960s and 1970s as the first television generation in the United States reached maturity, and to the continuing sense of divisiveness witnessed in the 1992 Los Angeles riots. On the positive side, however, the underlying dynamic remains one of more egalitarian experiences and more similar expectations for members of different social categories, and, ultimately, that is the first necessary step toward reaching a more egalitarian society.

Further Questions

1. In these arguments about television, how much of the influence do you think can be attributed to the "technology" itself and how much to the "cultural" and "social" factors? Could the trends in roles described above have occurred without TV?

2. How has the content of newspapers and books changed to compete with the new sensory experiences available through television?

3. If sixteenth-century monarchs and leaders of the Catholic Church had fully understood the potential of printing to undermine their bases of power, could they have devised methods that would have stopped these trends? How well do you think current elites understand the "threats" from television? Can you think of some recent examples of attempts to counteract television's potential influence?

4 How Are Media Born and Developed?

BRIAN WINSTON

Technologies are not neutral. They embody ideas, needs, imagination, and possibilities from specific periods and places. They are particular solutions to certain problems, usually not the only possible solutions. The same problem identified in another cultural context might find a quite different solution; for example, different architectural styles based on a variety of building materials have developed in different climatic and geographic regions, but all satisfy the basic need for shelter.

Yet technologies can often have such profound impacts that we even define historical epochs on the basis of technological distinctions, from the "iron age" to the "industrial age" and even "postindustrial society." Technologies also have histories, usually a number of histories. Think of the compact disc sound system that may be playing even while you read this. It embodies at least the histories of electricity, of sound recording, of the development of plastics, of the microchip, of interior design, and of consumer electronics design—and we haven't begun to talk about the economics of the music recording industry, its integration with other culture industries, let alone your own particular musical tastes, listening habits, cultural spending, and so on. Thus issues about the development of technologies are complex, and very different kinds of explanations have been proposed to account for technological change.

*Winston focuses here on technological change, specifically in the
sphere of communications, and the kinds of theories that try to
account for such change. He explores the notion of causality, that one
phenomenon inevitably follows another, by comparing two broad
approaches, technological determinism and cultural determinism.
The first suggests that technologies, specifically media technologies,
develop through their own momentum, following an inevitable logic
of their own, bringing about other kinds of change. The second approach argues that social and economic factors are the dominant
factors in supporting or blocking the utilization of technology, and
making human action the prime mover of change. Using a case study
approach, Winston investigates the logics of technological and cultural
determinism and makes a strong case for the cultural perspective.
Through asking questions concerning the logic of technological development, we can also address the issues of whose interests are being
pursued and what social and economic benefits (and losses) might
accrue from these developments. The implications of this chapter, and
of those by Sinha and Stone (Chapter 15), Hamelink (Chapter 17), and
others in this book, include the need for critical examination of, and
ultimately public debate about, the application of science in technological development, an area too often consigned to the experts and
too often omitted from the study of the media.*

This chapter addresses two related questions: (a) How does technological change occur in mass communication? (b) What effect, if any,
does the technology have on the content, the output, of mass communication? These questions are related in that they both deal with the
historical relationship of technology to communication processes.

The first question is clearly historical. There are various accounts
available to explain the nature of these changes. In some, technological
developments are isolated: The technology is the dominant, *determining* factor in the process. I will be calling such accounts of change
technological determinist. Other accounts place a greater emphasis on
socioeconomic factors. In these accounts, technology is but one of
many forces, influenced by and influencing social, economic, and
cultural developments. I will be calling accounts of this sort *cultural
determinist.*

The second question, about the effects of technology on communication, can also be thought of as historical. The only way we can make

Film Projector, c. 1870

a judgment as to the effect of a technology on the content of communications is by comparing the content before and after the technology
is introduced. Thus the second question, which seems to address only
the issue of effects, is also really addressing the issue of change and,
in so doing, is historical.

These two questions are linked in another way. Technological
determinist accounts of media history tend to stress the role of media
technology in governing the content of communication. Conversely,
cultural determinist accounts tend to deny technology this determining role. So the answer to the first question above is likely to condition
the answer given to the second.

This chapter presents four successive accounts of the genesis of
communications technology. It is not, clearly, a full-blown history of
media technology, although you may well find some new information

on the subject. It is designed to encourage you to think more carefully about that history, to learn how to evaluate the problems in historical explanations and not just accept them because a scholar has published them.

Technological Determinist Account A

Technological determinism, notes Raymond Williams (1974),

> is an immensely powerful and now largely orthodox view of the nature of social change. New technologies are discovered by an essentially internal process of research and development, which then sets the conditions of social change and progress. Progress, in particular, is the history of these inventions which "created the modern world." The effects of the technologies, whether direct or indirect, foreseen or unforeseen, are as it were the rest of history. (p. 13)

In its simplest form, this dominant theory explains the "essentially internal process of research and development" as nothing more than the biographies of the scientists and technologists involved, arranged chronologically. This account sees the development and impact of technology as "the progress of great men" (women and people of nonwhite cultures tend not to figure).

Here, presented as a case study, is a short history of the cinema written as "the progress of great men," based on a classic history of film (Ramsaye, 1926).

Case 1: Cinematic Projection

One essential element of the cinema is the idea of projection. The line that leads to projection begins with Della Porta, an Italian, who put a lens on the front of the earliest camera—a simple box. An image was produced on a glass screen set in the back wall of the box. Della Porta made this device in 1555. Next, Athanasius Kircher, a German, produced a magic lantern that projected an image onto a screen (1649).

Peter Roget, an Englishman, theorized in 1824 that the retina of the eye retains an image for a fraction of a second after the image is removed or changed. This "persistence of vision" can be used to fool the eye into believing a succession of separate and slightly different images to be actually one moving image. Toys to exploit "persistence of vision" by animating drawings were then "invented" by men like Paris (English, 1824), Plateau (Belgian, early 1830s), and von Stampfer (German, 1832). In 1852, von Uchatius, another German, put an animated strip of drawing (done on glass) into a magic lantern and projected the resulting moving image onto a screen.

A substitute for glass now had to be found. The line leading to this part of the cinematographic apparatus goes back to early experiments with substances that change their color, essentially by darkening, in response to light. More research, such as that of Wedgewood (English, 1802), led to the first photograms—images made by laying objects, such as leaves, directly onto materials, such as paper or leather, that had been treated with light-sensitive substances. But these images were not "fixed" and would disappear into black if further exposed to light.

Scientists undertook the discovery of a chemical that would halt the darkening process. In 1837 a Frenchman, Nicephore Niepce, found a way of doing this and, with his partner Daguerre, produced a type of photograph known as the daguerreotype. Meanwhile, an Englishman, Fox-Talbot, invented a photographic process that produced first a negative, made of chemically treated paper oiled to transparency, and then a positive copy. This, the essence of modern photography, was then refined. A wood pulp extract called cellulose was used instead of paper. Celluloid film finally allowed George Eastman to "invent," in 1888, a camera that anybody could use.

Back to the cinema. It was Edison who took photography and melded it with the developments in animated drawing and magic lanterns to produce the kinetoscope in 1892. There were British, French, and other claimants for the honor of "inventing" the first motion picture device. Two Frenchmen, the Lumière Brothers, gave the first public cinema (their term) show, using a projector to throw a moving image onto a screen, before an audience, arranged as in a live theater, in 1895.

So was the cinema invented.

There are numerous problems with this account. In its eagerness to create "great men," the story becomes highly selective. For instance, Roget's explanation of why we see apparent motion, "persistence of vision," is not really physiologically accurate (Nichols & Liderman, cited in De Lauretis & Heath, 1980, pp. 97ff.), but even very recent histories still begin with Roget and his idea (see, e.g., Beaver, 1983; Mast, 1981).

Real contributions are seen as coming solely from the genius of a single figure, when, in fact, they were the products of collective inventiveness. For instance, it took more than 30 years to go from the development of celluloid, which was originally produced during the U.S. Civil War as a dressing for wounds, to the Kodak. The full story of those years reveals a number of innovations and dead ends. It involves many, many more people than just George Eastman, who successfully marketed a technology to which a lot of hands had contributed.

Edison's role in this process needs to be revised. Edison was running one of the earliest modern industrial laboratories at Menlo Park, California, and pursuing a range of experiments, including investigations into the moving image. His method was to delegate much of the work to his assistants. In the case of the cinema, the work was actually done by a man named Dickson (Hendricks, 1961). Edison knew this full well, but that never prevented him from accepting credit for the "invention" of the kinetoscope.

The poverty, or "thinness," of great-man histories is not based simply on the desire to create heroes. Another crucial factor is the implicit insistence on the primacy of the West. For instance, the camera did not begin with Della Porta, but with Arab astronomers at least 300 years earlier. There is even a reference to projected images in China in 121 B.C. It has been suggested that the first magic lantern lecture in Europe was given by a Jesuit who had learned the technique while a missionary in China, and that Kircher had nothing to do with it (Temple, 1986, p. 86). Even without this, it is possible that the camera was in existence in Italy for more than a century before Della Porta (B. Winston, 1987, p. 199).

You might also have wondered why, in this account, such emphasis has been placed on nationality. In part, it has to do with national pride. But establishing who did something first has more to it than that. Modern patent rights depend on registering an invention first, and that implies financial advantages.

The failure of the great-man style of technological determinism cannot be corrected simply by writing more comprehensive histories. This sort of history really cannot answer the question of *how* technological change occurs; instead, it simply tells us *when*. The only explanation offered as to *how* is that great men, out of their genius, think of them.

Technological Determinist Account B

There is a more sophisticated version of the technological determinist approach that we need to explore in order to see if these "how/why" questions can be better answered. Here, the changes listed in Case 1 would be treated as a sequence of developments causally related to each other. The "inventors" would be left out, or their parts downplayed. Such a history of the cinema would view its technological development as the inevitable result of scientific progress, part of the never-ending advancement of human knowledge in Western culture. Such an account would suggest that the independent existence of the camera, the lantern, and the lens had to combine to produce the magic lantern. In turn, this development inevitably merged with the development of photography to create cinematography.

The arrival of sound in film provides us with a case study in this more sophisticated mode. This account is based on the work of Ogle (1977).

Case 2: Sound in Film

Sound recording developed using wax cylinders, disks, and wire before the end of the nineteenth century at the same time as the cinema itself was being perfected. However, these were mechanical recording devices without amplification that would not, therefore, work well in a theatrical environment.

Electronic devices that enabled sound to be amplified evolved out of experiments on the nature of electricity itself, then at the cutting edge of physics. By 1906, a number of independent researchers had produced a tube rather like the electric light bulb then being generally manufactured, but this specialized version could reproduce and amplify electrical signals.

The application of this technology to silent cinema was interrupted by World War I, but experiments continued using various systems. Running film projectors synchronously with phonographs was one. Another, more complicated, converted sound waves, via a microphone linked to a light bulb, into light waves to which the film could be exposed.

The technology was therefore awaiting its moment. That came in 1926, when the industry finally realized that the public would accept sound. Earlier attempts had failed because the technology was not quite developed and because there was inertia about changing over from the commercially successful method of having live music at each screening.

The introduction of sound also made easier the introduction of faster (i.e., more light-sensitive) film stocks. The very bright arc lights used in the silent studios used to hiss. This was acceptable in silent shooting but bothersome if sound was being recorded. Incandescent lights were then introduced because they made no noise, but they were also less powerful, so the industry needed faster stocks. More sensitive film had been available but unused since before World War I.

This new stock was black-and-white but panchromatic—equally sensitive to all colors, unlike the slower orthochromatic stock it replaced. "Ortho" was blind to red, which it therefore photographed as black. The introduction of panchromatic film affected makeup, costumes, and set design. It also helped, therefore, to put in place production procedures that would facilitate the next major technical advance—color.

Such an account presents a seamless sequence of technical events, each automatically triggering its successor. Each can be delayed by external factors, such as World War I and industrial inertia. But in the end the technology triumphs.

Yet important clues as to *how* technical change occurs can be gained by thinking of *why* a change occurs at a particular time. This is a more complicated issue than it might seem to be at first. Changes do not occur simply because the materials and the scientific knowledge necessary for advance are at hand. The history of the cinema is a good illustration of this.

The great-man account in Case 1 revealed that there was nothing to prevent Kircher from doing, two centuries earlier, what Uchatius did. Kircher could draw and he had glass. And he had just "invented," or borrowed from the Chinese, the lantern that Uchatius was to use.

Such questions can be extended. Why did Della Porta not place a light where he had put his ground-glass screen? Had he done so, he could have created the magic lantern a century before Kircher. And why did the Arab astronomers not pursue these developments centuries before that? Or the Chinese even earlier?

The great-man style of technological determinism cannot help us to answer such questions. It is equally clear that the sophisticated technological determinism of Case 2 is no better. We do not know from Case 2 why early films did not have sound; after all, sound-recording techniques and motion picture devices developed simultaneously (Hendricks, 1961, p. 111). And we are no nearer to understanding why the Arabs failed to exploit the camera, why Kircher did not invent the camera, and so on.

A better way we can begin to answer these questions is, however, hinted at in Case 2. There we started to hear about forces other than the technological, such as World War I and attitudes in the film industry. In a technological determinist account these are treated as incidentals, but cultural determinists will take these external factors as significant.

Cultural Determinist Account A

To take a cultural determinist view, it becomes necessary to examine the social context of the technology. This implies an examination of the circumstances into which the technology is introduced and diffused through society. In turn, then, a cultural determinist would need to look at the circumstances preceding the development of a technology. Note that the word *development* is preferred to the word *invention* because invention implies a single moment—but these single moments always obscure long-term developments involving many hands. Thus the cultural determinist will at least be an economic historian.

Let us take an economic history type of account of the introduction of sound in film and see how it compares with the technological determinist account offered in Case 2. Here, in Case 3, the key player becomes a corporation (Warner Brothers), but this key player is not a corporate great man. Rather, the struggle to introduce sound is located within corporate competition (Allen & Gomery, 1985, pp. 105ff).

Case 3: The Economics of Sound in Film

In the mid-1920s Warner Brothers was a small studio. It obtained from a New York bank, Goldman Sachs, a line of credit to expand its operations and used this money primarily to acquire movie theaters. Warner's biggest rivals were vertically integrated in this way; that is, studios owned chains of theaters and thus had ready markets for their products. Studios that did not own theaters were at a considerable disadvantage in marketing their films.

Warner also used the money to buy into the new radio industry by acquiring a radio station. This was done because radio was increasingly being used to promote movies. Through this acquisition the company gained familiarity with sound-recording techniques.

It was this changing capital infrastructure in the movie industry that constituted the enabling ground for the introduction of sound. Warner, smaller than the five major Hollywood studios, decided after much internal debate to gamble that sound in its newly acquired theaters would give it an edge. The introduction of sound was thus an attempt to improve market share. Acquisition of a chain of theaters alone was not enough to do this; the chain had to attract audiences by offering something different.

It was the potential disruption to their profitable silent film business, reinforced by their experience of failed experiments with sound dating back to the period before 1914, that "caused" Warner's rivals, the Big Five, not to exploit sound. The technology was available, but the commercial desire and need were not.

Warner successfully demonstrated that sound could be popular with audiences by making a series of variety shorts. Fox, another company struggling to catch up with the Big Five, then demonstrated that sound news films could also be popular.

As a result of this challenge, the Big Five agreed to introduce sound film using a common system. The technology they agreed upon, sound on film, was the most complex and expensive, but, because the Big Five had agreed on it, it was well placed to become the industry standard. It was thus also designed to prevent Fox and Warner, who were using slightly different versions, from continuing to make gains. Warner and Fox fell into line.

The Big Five sound system is the one in use to the present day.

There are a number of differences between the accounts in Case 3 and Case 2. In Case 3 the development of sound film critically depends on the period before its introduction. In Case 2 this period is seen as a lull, a pause before the inevitable triumph of the technology. In Case 3 it becomes instead a period of struggle of the sort that determines not only the pace at which the technology is introduced, but also its form. It is a struggle waged first within Warner, then between Warner and its rivals, to maximize profits and to have a particular technical solution dominate.

The explanation given in Case 3 is not a substitute for the information in Case 2. It is not that we are writing economic history instead of technological history. Rather, we are attempting to combine the "thinness" of the account in Case 2 by trying to write a "thicker" history, one that describes both. Economic historians, in effect, would add a mass of new information about Warner as a business.

However, economics is a crucial element, but not the end of the matter. Case 3 assumes that the main engines of technical change are the corporation and the market, and that the corporation's motivation will always be to increase the "bottom line." There are two problems with this. One is that technical innovation has not always depended upon the existence of corporations seeking profits. Case 3 is good at explaining sound, but it still does not help us understand why the Arabs, Della Porta, Kircher, and the others did not create the cinema.

Second, much innovation is designed to protect corporations and preserve existing markets, rather than to produce new goods and services for profit. Bell Laboratories is a good case in point. Often considered the most effective industrial innovator in history, Bell Labs was actually established to protect AT&T, the telephone monopoly, from new technologies, specifically radio. By 1878 Bell himself had built a good telephone receiver, but his transmitter was terrible. Edison, by contrast, had patented a superior transmitter, but his receiver was not as effective as Bell's. In this patent standoff, Bell and his business partners hired Emile Berliner to get the infant phone company out of trouble. Berliner, who later built the first device for playing records (the phonograph), did just this. In six weeks' time, he produced a good transmitter without infringing on Edison's patents. Thereafter, this pattern of threat averted by patentable innovation was repeated often, until, in the radio era, AT&T's research programs were finally organized into Bell Labs.

The result of Bell's research program is that every telecommunications innovation has relied to some extent on Bell patents. This includes radio, television, sound film, fax systems, and space communications. No innovation has occurred in the telecommunications field without Bell both agreeing to it and profiting from it. The expenditures lavished on Bell Labs were not therefore simply to maximize profit. They were designed to suppress the disruptive—to Bell—possibilities of innovation.

Thus we need to go beyond the economic historian's version of cultural determinism to something "thicker" still. Central to my argument is that *all* technological communication innovation can be thought of as a series of events taking place in the realm of technology, but influenced by and reacting to events taking place (a) in the realm of pure science and (b) in society in general. This model has to be rendered even more complex, because society also influences science, which in turn influences the technology. However, for present purposes I will include society's influences on science as part of science itself.

Cultural Determinist Account B

Let us take another case—television—to illustrate this "thicker" cultural determinism.

Case 4: Television

As industrial capitalism, from the end of the eighteenth century onward, began to stimulate scientists' inquiries into more practical and profitable applications, so substances were discovered that responded to light in various ways. The basic chemistry of photography emerged, as Case 1 showed, because it was known that some substances darken when exposed to light. Here we will be concerned with the fact that a group of substances alter their resistance to electric current according to the amount of light that falls on them.

Selenium was noted as such a substance by 1839, but no theoretical understanding of why this occurs was offered and no immediate applications suggested themselves for about 40 years. Then it became possible to theorize a device that would translate an optical image (light waves) into a variable electric current, using selenium as a sensor. This idea was prompted by parallel developments that used the variable resistance of carbon to electricity to construct a device that translated sound waves into a variable electric current—a telephone.

The problem for "seeing by telephone," as it was called, was that it had no practical application except perhaps as a facsimile device. But facsimile devices, which allowed for images to be sent by telegraph, were already in existence and worked better, because with the selenium versions there was no apparent way of creating a hard copy. Nevertheless, a device for turning images into an electrical wave analogue using a selenium sensor was patented in Berlin in 1884. Use of the word *television* as a description of this process dates from 1903.

Various researchers all over the world realized that television could transmit moving pictures. But what use would that be? The live theater had been industrialized in the nineteenth century by the creation of theatrical circuits that brought entertainment to the masses. Film had partially mechanized theater and would eventually largely substitute for it. There was no social need for television at that time.

Nor did any researcher think money could be made by delivering entertainment to the home. The masses, given the long hours they worked and the poor pay they received, had not yet the means to use it. The consumerist economy, about which Kellner writes in Chapter 17 of this volume, was still around the corner.

Thus by the turn of this century television existed as a technical possibility. It was grounded in scientific research but seemingly had no practical application. By 1908 the actual electronic system used to produce TV images had been outlined. The first image was transmitted in 1911 to a cathode ray tube in St. Petersburg, Russia. Major firms were interested because the technology could potentially be used as an alternative to radio and film, and because of its possible threat to established facsimile systems. Research programs were set up, but they were underfunded. Nevertheless, by 1923 an RCA team, led by Vladimir Zworykin, patented the basic TV camera tube of today.

Further development during the 1920s and 1930s was confused because the major radio industry players were not interested and because solutions other than a purely electronic TV system were also under consideration. These mechanical/electronic systems, which dated back to the 1884 patent, were being explored by a group of researchers largely outside the radio industry.

The confusion persisted because the capital necessary to diffuse TV was then being applied to the movies—by now the talkies—and to radio. The very same firms were interested in all three areas, and judged that TV would be a threat to current business but had interesting future possibilities. Nevertheless, in both Britain and Nazi Germany public television, using a fully electronic system, began in 1936. In Germany it was seen only rarely for theatrical purposes, for the regime continued to focus more on radio, film, and the press to get across its propaganda. In Britain the economic difficulties of the Depression decade prevented its widespread use.

A major factor in the delay in the United States was that RCA so controlled the patents that the Federal Communications Commission was worried about the survival of the other firms that could make TV equipment. It therefore stood in the path of RCA's development of TV from 1936 to 1941. The FCC was trying to prevent the AT&T telephone monopoly from being reproduced by RCA in this area. By 1941 the necessary agreements had been struck, but U.S. entry into World War II that year halted further development.

At the end of the war the situation was quite different. The radio industry was looking for a new technology to exploit, having saturated the market with radio sets. In general, the war had greatly expanded the electronic manufacturing capacity of the country, and if that capacity were not to be lost, the public would have to begin to "need" a range of domestic electrical appliances that it had lived without previously. Further, the opportunities for advertising these and other products through television seemed wide open. The Depression decade seemed to have fixed in policy makers' minds that if consumer demand is flat, no economic growth is possible, and after the many sacrifices of the war, a return to depression would have been political dynamite.

However, it was not an overnight process. The FCC again suppressed the free development of TV by limiting the number of stations that could be built, even instituting a "freeze" on new construction from 1948 to 1952. There were technical reasons for doing this, including the decision as to which color system was to be used, the power and location of TV masts, and the question of VHF and UHF wave bands. But the reasons were not simply technical.

It is often suggested that TV destroyed Hollywood. The great studios are a thing of the past. But where does most TV production still take place? Hollywood. The FCC freeze also allowed Hollywood to maintain its position as supplier to the new TV industry, for it was during that period that the terms of this trade were worked out.

Case 4 attempts to blend all the elements used in the other cases—the individual contribution, the triggering effects of increasing knowledge in science, and the application of other technologies, economic forces, political considerations, social policy, and general cultural factors. These various elements can be thought of as relating in the following way. Imagine the realm of science as a line going from the past to the future:

past_____ future
     science

Now imagine a parallel line, which we will call *technology*:

     _____
     technology
past_____ future
     science

These two lines are connected in the mind of the technologist, the person who has an idea for an application:

The idea is triggered by the understanding of science but is expressed "in the metal" as a technological device. History shows the technologist is likely to build a whole series of devices, some slightly, some radically, different from one another. The device we commonly call the "invention" does not differ from the others because it works and they do not. Often the "preinventions" work just as well. What makes the difference is that a point is reached where one of these contrivances is seen to have a real use. After that recognition of the *application* the device is considered an "invention"; before, it is a "prototype." We will call the emergence of an application *supervening social necessity*:

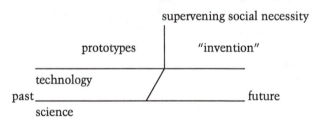

Supervening social necessities are the accelerators that push the development of media and other technology.

In Case 4 the supervening social necessities that influenced the development of television include the rise of the home, the dominance of the nuclear family, and the political and economic need to maintain full employment after World War II. Because of these, the device finally moved out of the limbo of being an experiment to being a widely diffused consumer product.

Supervening social necessities are at the interface between society and technology. They can exist because of the needs of corporations, as when Kodak introduced Super 8 film because ordinary 8mm film had saturated the market. Or they can become a force because of another technology. Railroad development required instant signaling systems, and so enabled the telegraph to develop. Or, as in Case 4, general social forces can act as supervening social necessities. Telephones emerged in the late 1870s because the modern corporation was emerging, and with it the modern office. Not only telephones but elevators, typewriters, and adding machines were all "invented" during this period, although the first typewriter was patented 150 years earlier, the adding machine dated back some 250 years, and the modern hydraulic elevator had been available for more than 20 years.

But if there are accelerators, there are also brakes. These work to slow the disruptive impact of new technology. I describe the operation of these brakes as the *"law" of the suppression of radical potential,* using "law" in its standard social science sense to denote a regular and powerful general tendency.

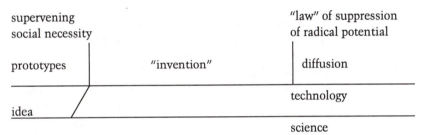

The brakes in Case 4, which caused television to be nearly a century in development, show its radical potential being suppressed, and are thus an instance of this "law." The brakes ensure that a technology's introduction does not disrupt the social or corporate status quo. Thus in the case of TV, the existence of facsimile systems, the rise of radio, the dominance of RCA, and the need not to destroy the film industry all acted to suppress the speed at which the new medium was introduced, to minimize disruption. The result is that all the main film and radio interests of the 1930s are still in business today, and television can be found in practically every house in the nation, sometimes in almost every room.

This concept of supervening social necessities and the "law" of the suppression of radical potential represents one way in which a cultural determinist would seek to understand the nature of change in media technology. I would argue it to be a more effective, more *powerful* way of explaining these matters than any that the technological determinists can produce. For instance, we can now, using this model, answer the questions posed above about the Arabs and the Chinese. The Arab astronomers who pioneered the camera did so for astronomical reasons, which were their supervening social necessity. Furthermore, their Islamic faith by then forbade the making of realistic images of living beings, so that culturally they would have been prohibited from exploring the camera's image-making potential. That was how the "law" of the suppression of radical potential operated on their research agenda. The Chinese produced these technologies in the context of an imperial system that used them as marks of distinction for the court. The culture made the technologies elite and limited and therefore suppressed their further development. It is these sorts of factors, not scientific knowledge or technological know-how, that condition technological developments.

Effects of Technology on Communication Content

We can now begin to address our second question. All communication modes except face-to-face speech depend on technology. Mass communication requires technologies of a sophisticated kind. The question is whether any such technologies determine what gets communicated.

Answers come in weaker and stronger forms. The weakest form is also the easiest to agree with, namely, that it is obvious that not all technologies can do the same thing. A typewriter cannot convey the same information as a photo. But can we go further?

In his essay in this volume on cultural imperialism, Mohammadi (Chapter 21) reviews a well-known study by Daniel Lerner (1958) that argued, based upon research in the Near East, that when modern media were suddenly injected into a traditional village environment in the Third World, they had the effect of expanding many villagers' horizons and expectations quite dramatically. This is a stronger version of the claim that media technology determines the communication that takes place. Mohammadi notes the highly questionable assumptions also carried with this theory, but we might agree that the theory's basic assertion is plausible, even if we might want to rein it in with further "buts" and "if sos." Similarly, Sreberny-Mohammadi's argument about forms of media in Chapter 2 is an intermediate version of the argument that media technologies must be incorporated into the analysis of media effects. So far there may be room for dispute on individual points, but not on the basic position.

However, the stronger versions are quite frequently to be met with in the generalized pronouncements about media influence in the world today that commentators and editorial writers reproduce from time to time. The most renowned exponent of the strong position was Canadian media theorist Marshall McLuhan, who—even though I am now about to attack his arguments—has the distinction of having first encouraged the general public to think seriously about the impact of media technology on society. He was one of a group of Canadian historians, anthropologists, and literary critics who developed a body of ideas suggesting that in communications, technology is the determining influence. His most frequently quoted aphorism is that "the *medium* is the message" (McLuhan, 1964). He meant by this that media content (the explicit message) explains far less about communication than the communicative impact of the technical medium as such, viewed in terms of its effects on whole societies and cultures over centuries of their development. Actual media output therefore was of comparatively little interest to McLuhan. Here is how he describes the impact of printing-press technology:

> Socially, the typographic extension of man brought in nationalism, industrialism, mass markets, and universal literacy and education. For print presented an image of repeatable precision that inspired totally new forms of extending social energies. . . . The same spirit of private enterprise that emboldened authors and artists to cultivate self-expression led other men to create giant corporations, both military and commercial. (p. 157)

The key words here are that "print *presented an image* of repeatable precision that *inspired*. . . . " It is a claim not merely that the printing press determined the content of books or pamphlets, but that leading aspects of our communicative culture (literacy, education, self-expression by authors and artists), our institutions (industrialism, giant corporations, mass markets), and our political self-understanding (nationalism) were summoned into being by this media technology. It goes beyond a technical explanation of how media technology developed to provide a media-technological explanation of modern society.

But McLuhan's approach, although grounded in his reading of history, is difficult to sustain on the basis of the historical evidence. All the effects of the printing press he outlines took centuries to manifest themselves. Nationalism, in its modern form, dates from after the American and French revolutions. How then can a device introduced nearly 300 years earlier have "caused" nationalism? Similarly, universal literacy and the rise of great corporations date from the second half of the nineteenth century, some 400 years after the printing press had been introduced into the West.

McLuhan's technological determinism depends upon a very loose idea of historical causality. "Perhaps the most significant of the gifts of typography to man is that of detachment and non-involvement," he asserts (p. 157). This assertion is built upon his prior claim that the printing press gave birth to the individual author and artist. But his position is untenable. In what sense are modern people more communicatively uninvolved and detached than they were in the past, specifically the medieval European past? Certainly our sensitivity to human cruelty toward other people and animals is vastly increased, although we can be just as brutal, and now on an industrial scale, as our ancestors. How could it be shown that before print there were no authors, artists, or ordinary people who thought of themselves as individuals in the way we think of ourselves today?

Furthermore, McLuhan's basic mode of reasoning may have important ideological effects. If technology is an external force, like nature, it cannot easily be subjected to social control. It implies we are helpless in the face of such a force, rather than that we can adapt and use technology for our own freely determined purposes. The chapters on broadcasting in Western Europe (McQuail, Chapter 9), on Soviet media (Downing, Chapter 11), on alternative media (Downing, Chapter 14), on the audience (Gandy, Chapter 13), and on popular music (Negus, Chapter 22) are only some of the contributions to this volume that point in quite the opposite direction to McLuhan's position.

One last example: For the technological determinist, the fact that color film does not easily photograph Black skin tones is the result of the technical properties of the dyes used in those films. The cultural determinist will want to explore this matter a little more thoroughly. I would begin with the fact that color film was largely created by white scientists to photograph white skin tones. These products do not simply reproduce nature. Each color film stock the chemists designed contained a different solution to the basic problem of representing—or, better, re-presenting—natural colors. Each produces a slightly but noticeably different result.

In doing the creative work involved, the chemists are forced to make choices as to which colors their film will respond to best. For reasons grounded in the fundamental physiology of color perception within the human eye, any one set of choices will result in a film that cannot represent Black skin tones as well as it represents white. Color film stocks in general tend to give Black people a greenish hue. Indeed, the research literature on the development of such stocks reveals that the chemists were primarily interested in getting so-called white (i.e., Caucasian) skin tones as acceptable as possible. They simply did not concern themselves with how Black people would be photographed (B. Winston, 1985, pp. 195ff.). In this way we see once again that it is the social context, not the technology, that determines the content of communication forms.

Conclusions

At the outset, I noted that the answers given to the question concerning how media technologies develop will in turn condition the answers given to the parallel question of what impact technology has on the content of communication. The technological determinist, who wants to see the technology as all-powerful, operating as though in a historical vacuum, will tend to see the influence of media technology on content as overwhelming. The cultural determinist, who wants to place the technology firmly in its social context, will also want to see that context as the primary factor determining both media technology and media content.

Technological determinism tends to present us as comparatively impotent, as malleable consumers, unthinking and unprotesting, in the face of media technology power. The cultural determinist view, by contrast, is empowering. By drawing attention to the ways in which society constantly conditions technological developments, this view gives us the power to evaluate media technologies and to understand that we are not in the grip of forces totally beyond our control. These implications also show us why theories in general are important. Theories can help or hinder us in coming to an understanding of the world. Without that understanding we cannot act. Thus theory is critical to action.

Further Questions

1. Can the pattern described above—of supervening social necessities and the "law" of the suppression of radical potential (B. Winston, 1986)—be applied to the history of any mass medium (e.g., radio)?

2. How do media technologies affect one another? What has been the impact of the compact disc on recorded music? Has television changed as a result of the VCR?

PART II

Media, Power, and Control

In this section we introduce you to the key linkages between communications media and power, both political and economic. More than any other factor, power determines what happens; it is a central issue for anyone interested in understanding human society, whether the concern is with power in relationships in the family, in the classroom, in the economy, or in international relations. However, how power actually works, what the ingredients are in a power relationship, is very hotly debated.

Defining power is not straightforward, but we can make some basic statements. Governments have power to make laws and policies. The armed forces, the judicial system, and the police have power to enforce laws, just or unjust. Major social movements, such as the U.S. civil rights movement of the 1950s and 1960s or the ecological movement, also have power—the power to press for change. Big corporations have power, too: to hire and fire workers, sometimes thousands at a time; to close plants and move elsewhere; to decide what to produce, and how, and what prices to charge; and to influence government, as in the case of defense contractors and their multibillion-dollar dealings with defense ministries. The study of how these centers of power in government and the economy interact with one another is often called political economy.

One important approach to the critical study of communications focuses on the political economy of the media: their relation to the state and to the domination of the economy by giant corporations. (The state as used here does not refer to one of the states of the Union;

75

see the glossary.) Some basic questions are as follows: Are the media free and independent to present views, news, and entertainment just as they want? Are they free to be diverse from each other, not just in format, but in the expression of opinion? Does it matter if increasing numbers of both national and global media channels are owned and operated by large transnational corporations? Are journalists and cultural workers in the media industries empowered to write and screen what they themselves feel they should? Although no one would expect unlimited freedom for every media employee, a basic assumption of many U.S. and Western European citizens is that "our" media are indeed free, diverse, and abundantly opinionated. This freedom is guaranteed by the First Amendment to the Constitution in the United States, by the absence of direct government control over media, and by the fact that the media are owned by many different firms, not just one. U.S. media are proudly claimed to be the best and freest in the world, holding up a torch of liberty to less fortunate countries. Some of the following chapters ask if that is an adequate or indeed useful perspective for understanding the operation of U.S. media.

Other chapters in this section address the use of media power and control in a non-U.S. context, helping us to understand that there are diverse patterns of media ownership, control, and financing, and that comparisons of the benefits and drawbacks of each kind of system can be instructive and sobering. In Chapter 9, Denis McQuail looks at the market challenges to public service broadcasting traditions in Western Europe. In Chapter 10, Andrew Jakubowicz examines mass media in multicultural nations, usefully comparing the different kinds of commitment to multiculturalism and media structures developed by Americans, the British, and Australians. In Chapter 11, John Downing examines media in the change from dictatorship to democracy after the collapse of the Soviet Union.

Once again, it is important to note that a sign of the rapid changes taking place in the world we live in is that some of the language we used until recently to denote international political and economic geography—referents such as *Eastern Europe, Western Europe, Communist bloc,* and even *Third World*—has changed with the dramatic changes in the real world since 1989. Pay attention to the new terms and discourses that now circulate, and think about how they construct different conceptual maps of the world, perhaps even suggesting—to use one new, very popular, and very problematic term—a **global** political, economic, and cultural environment.

5 Media in the U.S. Political Economy

EDWARD HERMAN

In this chapter Edward Herman responds to those who celebrate the freedom of the U.S. media by suggesting that there are five tests or "filters" that information has to pass through before it can become acceptable for presentation in the mainstream media. The five conditions that "news" must fulfill before it becomes "big news"—major media news campaigns for mass consumption—in effect determine what information becomes available to the public.

Herman argues that in a system such as that found in the United States, where wealth and power control access to a privately owned media, government and business interests penetrate the media through either direct control or indirect influence. The process by which this determines which news is fit for most of us to consider fixes the boundaries of public and media discussion.

Herman's five filters are (a) the size, ownership, wealth, and profit orientation of the major media firms; (b) the primacy of advertising as an income source for the mass media; (c) the dependence of the media on information provided by government and business (and by their hired "experts"); (d) "flak"—orchestrated attacks on media programs or coverage by conservative organizations, designed specifically to whip any critical media voices into line; and (e) "anticommunism," a political and ideological control mechanism. Although it may seem strange in the mid-1990s to speak of anticommunism as a powerful determinant of media discourse, Herman uses anticommunism and its ideological analogues to draw convincing examples of successful media propaganda campaigns.

Of course, "propaganda" itself is something most Americans think of as characteristic of dictator-style media; even the word sounds foreign. Herman counters with examples from U.S. history that force us to reconsider what we mean by propaganda. These include the Red scare of 1919-1920, a time when big business was alarmed by increasingly active labor movements; the Red scare associated with McCarthyism in the late 1940s and early 1950s, which weakened the New Deal reform coalition and helped replace it with a Cold War/arms race/probusiness/labor-control policy; the coverage of the highly question-able Bulgarian/KGB involvement in the assassination attempt on Pope John Paul II, at a time when the Western powers wished to revivify the communist specter; and the relative blackout of news concerning hundreds of religious workers brutally murdered by agents of U.S. client regimes in Central America, compared with the highly publi-cized murder of one priest—Solidarity priest Father Popieluszko—in then-communist Poland in 1984.

Herman points out that the seeming reasonableness of the U.S. media process, which allows inconvenient facts to appear sparingly within the framework of official assumptions, effectively excludes fundamen-tal dissent from "big news." This process, combined with quasi-official harassment of small-scale alternative media that stops just short of squelching them entirely, creates a propaganda system far more cred-ible and effective than one with official censorship. In fact, the scat-tered presentation of dissident topics within official frameworks en-hances the credibility of the dominant ideology and perspectives.

As a fitting beginning to this section on media, power, and control, Herman's essay challenges Americans to rethink some of their most cherished and secure assumptions about U.S. society and prods them to be cautious about claiming that the U.S. media are independent and politically diverse. Herman's approach could be adapted to the examination of the dynamics of other media as well.

Three Alternative Perspectives

It is widely agreed among media analysts that the mass media play an important role in the political economy of the United States, managing the flow of entertainment, news, and political opinion. But there is sharp disagreement on the nature and character of media influence and on the degree to which they are an independent force or merely reflect and transmit the views of other important power interests in the country. For example, there is a neoconservative school that points its finger at the centralization of the media in a top tier of "East Coast Establishment" newspapers and television networks, and also at the elevated status of star journalists and TV interviewers—their high salaries, their alleged power, liberal background, and bias. In this view, the very high status of the media stars and their ability to command large audiences gives the liberal culture considerable freedom of action in the mass media. Its representatives are therefore said to be able to push views hostile to business and the government's foreign policy and at odds with the majority attitudes of the working class and middle America (Lichter, Rothman, & Lichter, 1986).

Representatives of the liberal/"gatekeeper" and propaganda analyses (discussed below) deny both that the stars can do as they like and that the mass media have any kind of bias against the status quo. They stress three types of evidence against the neoconservative view: the checks built into the way media operate, how unlikely it is that institutions so firmly embedded in the corporate government world could display systematic antiestablishment bias, and the evidence of actual media output. Both consider the neoconservatives to be speaking for just one wing of opinion inside the national power structure, attacking representatives of the liberal wing of elite opinion as though its members were dangerous enemies of the American way of life.

The most prominent analyses in the United States of how the media came to be as they are come from liberal newsroom and "gatekeeper" studies, as exemplified by the works of Leon Sigal (1973), Edward J. Epstein (1973), Gaye Tuchman (1978), Herbert Gans (1979), and Todd Gitlin (1983). Although there are differences among them, they all focus on journalists and media organizations rather than on the system at large or government and major advertisers. These latter are brought into the picture only as sources, pressure groups, regulators,

Wall Street, New York

or commercial clients. "Gatekeeper" researchers interview media personnel and watch them working to see how they decide on output, with little emphasis on examining and comparing actual outputs and their results. They stress how practical organizational needs shape news media choices directly or indirectly. Let us explore this view a little further.

News organizations seek sources of authoritative and credible news on a regular basis. These requirements are interconnected: If a highly placed person makes some statement, this is newsworthy in itself. The more authoritative and credible the source, the easier it is to accept statements without checking, and the less expensive is news making.

Hence the paradox that even if untrue, such statements may be broadcast without commentary, as "objective" news.

The most highly placed news source is, of course, the government. An oft-cited statistic, based on Leon Sigal's (1973) examination of 2,850 stories in the *New York Times* and *Washington Post*, is that 46% of the stories originated with U.S. federal government officials or agencies and 78% with government officials in general, domestic or foreign. Second only to the government as a news source is business, which also showers the media with a vast array of press releases from individual firms, trade associations, and public relations offshoots.

It is also the case that internal media rules and professional codes help powerful board members or media owners not to have to intervene all the time in editorial decisions. For the most part, journalists reproduce the standard choices of the powerful by a process of self-censorship (see Rodríguez, Chapter 8). Those on the lower rungs of the news ladder need to be alert to the news values at the top in order to produce acceptable copy.

Newsroom gatekeeper studies have added a great deal to the understanding of media processes. Nevertheless, they focus too heavily on organizational criteria of choice, often illustrated by struggles within the media as told by media personnel. They suffer from a lack of theory and measurement of actual media output. As a result, they tend to exaggerate the potential media professionals have for dissent and "space," and to neglect how the usual news choices reinforce the status quo.

A third way of looking at the workings of the mass media stresses their role as part of the national power structure. This approach, which will be examined below, shares a number of features with gatekeeper analyses, but pulls the threads together into an integrated whole and gives more attention to the real interplay between the media and their sources, and to the purposes and effects of news choices and propaganda campaigns. I will call it the *propaganda* model.

The Political-Economic Filters of Mass Media Messages

The basic proposition of this chapter is as follows. In a system of concentrated wealth and power, the inequality in command of resources inevitably affects access to, and the performance of, a private media system. Money and power will penetrate the media by direct control or indirect influence, and will filter out the news thought unfit for most of us to consider. We may trace out this filtering process through the following:

1. the size, concentrated ownership, owner wealth, and profit orientation of the dominant mass media firms
2. advertising as the primary income source of the mass media
3. the dependence of the media on information provided by government, business, and "experts" funded and approved by these primary sources
4. "flak" as a means of disciplining the media
5. "anticommunism" as a national secular religion and ideological control mechanism

These elements interact with and reinforce one another. They fix the boundaries of media discourse and the definition of what is newsworthy, and they explain the origins and operations of propaganda campaigns.

SIZE AND OWNERSHIP OF THE
MASS MEDIA: THE FIRST FILTER

By 1850, improvements in technology and the drive to communicate with a mass audience that could be "sold" to advertisers had developed newspaper technology to a level that made entry into the business very difficult without substantial financial resources. Thus the first filter—the very large investment needed to own a major newspaper or other mass medium—was already in force over a century ago and has become increasingly effective since. In 1987 there were some 1,500 daily newspapers, 11,000 magazines, 10,000 radio and 1,500 TV stations, 2,400 book publishers, and 7 movie studios in the United States—some 25,000 media entities in all. But most of the news dispensers among this set were small and depended on the national media and wire services for all but very local news. Many more were part of multimedia chains.

In 1983, Ben Bagdikian reported in his book *The Media Monopoly* that by the beginning of the 1980s most U.S. mass media—newspapers, magazines, radio, television, books, and movies—were controlled by 50 corporations (pp. 4-5). Four years later, in his 1987 revision of the book, Bagdikian observed that 29 corporations now accounted for the same majority fraction as the 50 largest had controlled shortly before (p. xvi). These giants are also diversified into other fields, including insurance, banking, advertising, frozen foods, tobacco, weapons production, and nuclear energy.

The dominant media companies are large, profit-seeking corporations, owned and controlled by very wealthy boards and individuals. Many are run completely as moneymaking concerns, and for the others as well there are powerful pressures from stockholders, directors, and bankers to focus on the bottom line. These pressures intensified over the 1980s as media stocks became stock market favorites and actual or prospective owners of media properties were able to generate great wealth from increased audience size and advertising revenues (e.g., Rupert Murdoch, Time Warner, and many others). This encouraged the entry of speculators and takeovers, and increased the pressure and temptation to focus more intensively on profitability.

These trends accelerated when the rules were loosened limiting media monopolies, cross-ownership of media in the same area of the country, the number of TV and radio stations the networks could own, and media control by nonmedia companies (e.g., ABC, CBS, NBC). The Federal Communications Commission also abandoned many of its restrictions—which were not very strict anyway—on broadcast commercials, TV violence, and the "Fairness Doctrine" (which supported equal broadcasting time for opposing views), opening the door to purely moneymaking dictates over the use of the airwaves.

Those who control the media giants come into close relation with the corporate community through joint membership on boards of directors and business relations with commercial and investment bankers. These are their sources of credit, who help with banking services and advise both on opportunities to buy media firms and on takeover threats from other firms. Banks and similar "institutional" investors are also large owners of media stock. These holdings, individually and collectively, do not convey control on a daily basis, but if managers fail to pursue actions that favor shareholder returns, institutional investors will be inclined to sell the stock (depressing its price) or to listen sympathetically to outsiders contemplating takeovers.

These investors constitute a force that helps to integrate media companies into market strategies and away from responsibility to the democratic process. The large media companies have also diversified beyond the media field, and nonmedia companies have established a strong presence in the mass media. The most important cases of the latter are GE (General Electric), which owns the NBC network, and

Westinghouse, which owns major TV broadcasting stations, a cable network, and a radio station network. GE and Westinghouse are both huge, diversified, multinational companies heavily involved in the controversial areas of weapons production and nuclear power.

Another structural relationship of importance is the media companies' dependence on and ties with government. Apart from the issues raised in Chapters 6 and 7 of this volume, the major media also depend on the government for more general policy support. All business firms are interested in taxes, interest rates, labor policies, and the level of enforcement of the antitrust (anti-business monopoly) laws.

Thus during the 1980s the systematic reduction of business taxes, weakening of labor unions, and relaxation of antitrust law enforcement benefited media corporations as well as other members of the business community. GE and Westinghouse depend on the government to subsidize their expensive research and development of nuclear power and defense. *Reader's Digest, Time, Newsweek,* and movie and TV syndication sellers also depend on diplomatic support for their rights to penetrate foreign cultures with U.S. commercial and cultural messages. The media giants, advertising agencies, and great multinational corporations have a close interest in a favorable climate of investment in the Third World, and their relationships with the government in these policies are intimate.

THE ADVERTISING LICENSE
TO DO BUSINESS: THE SECOND FILTER

Newspapers obtain about 75% of their revenues from advertisers, general-circulation magazines about 50%, and broadcasters almost 100%. Before advertising became prominent, the price of a newspaper had to cover the costs of doing business. With the growth of advertising, papers that attracted ads could sell copies well below production costs. Papers without advertising faced a serious dilemma: to raise their prices or to have less surplus to invest in making the paper more salable (features, attractive format, promotion). An advertising-based media system will tend to drive out of existence or into marginality the media companies that depend on selling price alone. With advertising, the free market does not yield a neutral system in which the consumers decide which media will suit them best. The advertisers' choices heavily influence media prosperity—and survival (Barnouw, 1978).

Since the introduction of press advertising, working-class and radical papers have constantly been at a serious disadvantage, as their readers have tended to be of modest means, a factor that has always reduced advertiser interest in media they patronized. Working-class and radical media also suffer from more overt political discrimination by advertisers, as many firms refuse to patronize media they perceive as damaging to their interests. Advertisers also select among specific broadcasts on the basis of criteria that are culturally and politically conservative. Advertisers on national television are for the most part very large corporations, such as Philip Morris, Procter & Gamble, General Motors, Sears, and RJR Nabisco. These advertisers will rarely sponsor programs that seriously criticize sensitive corporate activities, such as ecological degradation, the workings of the military-industrial complex, or corporate support of and benefits from Third World tyrannies.

As advertising spots increase in price, broadcasters lose even more money on programs if advertisers shun them. For instance, ABC Television's once-in-a-blue-moon feature on the impact of nuclear war on the United States, *The Day After* (1983), had almost all advertisers canceling their options on spots during or around the program. So as the broadcasters come under (a) more pressure to behave as profit makers and (b) less pressure from the FCC to operate a public service, there is a strong tendency for them to eliminate programming that has significant public affairs content.

SOURCING MASS MEDIA NEWS:
THE THIRD FILTER

The mass media are drawn into an intimate relationship with the power structure, national and local, because of cost factors and mutual interests. Cost savings dictate that the media concentrate their reporters where significant news often occurs, where important rumors and leaks abound, and where regular press conferences are held. The White House, Pentagon, and State Department in Washington, D.C., and, on a local basis, city hall and the police department, are the subject of regular news "beats" for reporters. Business corporations and trade groups are also regular suppliers of stories deemed newsworthy. These organizations turn out a large volume of material that meets the demands of news organizations for reliable, scheduled input.

Government and corporate sources also have the credibility associated with their status. Partly to maintain the image of objectivity, but also to protect themselves from criticisms of bias and the increasingly serious threat of libel suits, the media need news that can be portrayed as accurate. Information from sources that may be presumed credible also reduces investigative expense, whereas material from sources that are not seemingly credible, or that will elicit criticism and threats, requires careful and costly checking.

Thus when President Reagan asserted in March 1986 that the Nicaraguan government was heavily involved in drug smuggling, this was immediately published without checking. (It was a false statement.) On the other hand, a steady stream of claims by imprisoned drug traders and even by U.S. intelligence and Drug Enforcement Administration personnel that the U.S.-backed Nicaraguan Contras were smuggling drugs into the United States, with official connivance (L. Cockburn, 1988), was treated much more cautiously, was held to require stringent checking, and received little media coverage (even though, in this case, the claims were true).

The information operations of the powerful government and corporate bureaucracies that constitute primary news sources are vast and skillful. They have special and unequal access to the media. Because they supply news, have continuous contact with the reporter on the beat, and can freeze reporters out of news stories if they are uncooperative, the powerful can use personal relationships, threats, and rewards to influence and coerce media personnel.

Perhaps more important, powerful sources regularly take advantage of reporters' routines and need for copy to "manage" the media, to manipulate them into following the agenda of one vector or another in the power structure. Part of this management process consists of showering the media with stories that serve to reinforce a particular framework by which to interpret events.

The relation between power and sourcing extends beyond providing continuing "news" to molding the supply of "experts." Official sources could be threatened by highly respectable alternative sources that offer dissident views with obvious knowledge. Energetic attempts are made to reduce this problem by "co-opting the experts" (that is, finding like-minded specialists, paying them as consultants, funding their research, and organizing think tanks that will hire them and help to publish their findings).

During the 1970s and early 1980s, a string of institutions were created and old ones were reactivated in order to propagandize the corporate viewpoint. Among the most important of these institutions were the Heritage Foundation, the American Enterprise Institute, and the Georgetown Center for Strategic and International Studies. Many hundreds of intellectuals were brought to these institutions, and their work was funded and disseminated to the media in a sophisticated program that can reasonably be defined as a propaganda effort.

FLAK AND THE ENFORCERS:
THE FOURTH FILTER

Flak here refers to negative responses to media statements or programs. It may take the form of letters to the media, telegrams, phone calls, petitions, lawsuits, speeches and bills before Congress, or other modes of complaint, threat, and punitive action. It may be organized centrally or locally, or it may consist of the entirely independent actions of individuals. For example, individuals may call in or write to protest the showing of a movie they regard as sacrilegious or subversive; or the gun lobby may mobilize its members to complain about a program that points up the hazards of private gun ownership.

If flak is produced on a large scale, it can be both uncomfortable and costly to the media. Positions have to be defended within the organization and without, sometimes before legislatures and possibly even in court. Advertisers may withdraw patronage. TV advertising is mainly of consumer goods that are readily subject to organized boycott. During the McCarthy years in the early 1950s (see below as well as Downing, Chapter 14), many advertisers and broadcasters were coerced into silence and the blacklisting of employees by organized and determined Red hunters' threats to organize consumer boycotts. Advertisers are still concerned about possibly offending constituencies that might produce flak, and demand for "suitable" programming is a continuing feature of the media environment.

The ability to produce flak, especially costly and threatening flak, is related to power. The 1967 CBS documentary *The Selling of the Pentagon*, which focused on armed services and military contractor propaganda designed to scare the public into believing that more weapons are always needed, aroused the ire of very substantial interests, and the negative feedback was great, even including congressional hearings.

Serious flak increased in close parallel with business's increased resentment of media criticism of its activities, and the corporate offensive of the 1970s and 1980s. Along with its other political investments of those years, the corporate community sponsored the growth of institutions such as the American Legal Foundation, Capital Legal Foundation, Accuracy in Media (AIM), the Center for Media and Public Affairs, and the Media Institute. These may be regarded as institutions organized for the specific purpose of producing flak. The function of AIM, for example, is to harass the media and put pressure on them to follow the corporate agenda and a hard-line rightist foreign policy. It conditions the media to expect trouble and cost increases for violating conservative standards.

ANTICOMMUNISM AS A CONTROL MECHANISM: THE FIFTH FILTER

The final filter is the ideology of anticommunism. The threat of social rather than business ownership has always been the specter haunting property owners, as it threatens the very root of their class position and superior status. The Soviet (1917), Chinese (1949), and Cuban (1959) revolutions were all traumas to U.S. elites. The ongoing conflicts and well-publicized abuses of communist states contributed for decades to elevating opposition to communism to a first principle of U.S. ideology and politics.

This ideology has helped mobilize the populace against an enemy, and because the concept of "communism" is fuzzy, it can be used against anybody advocating policies threatening property interests or supportive of accommodation with communist states, or any kind of radicalism. Being labeled communist has almost always unnerved the U.S. Left and labor movement and served to slow down radical opposition movements.

Liberals, often accused of being procommunist or insufficiently anticommunist, are kept continually on the defensive in a nation where anticommunism is like a dominant unifying religion. This generally causes liberals to behave very much like conservatives. In the cases of the U.S. subversion of Guatemala (1947-1954) and the military attacks on Nicaragua (1981-1987), allegations of communist links and a communist threat caused many liberals to support CIA intervention; others lapsed into silence, paralyzed by fear of being tarred with charges of disloyalty to the national religion. In the 1950s and 1960s, the FBI under J. Edgar Hoover defined support for African American civil rights as "communist," and even though this did not stop the movement, almost all felt compelled to take the charge seriously.

The anticommunist control mechanism penetrates the system to exercise a profound influence on the mass media. In normal times as well as in periods of "Red scares" (see below), issues tend to be framed in terms of a two-sided world of communist and anticommunist powers, with gains and losses allocated to one side or the other and rooting for "our side" considered entirely legitimate news practice.

It is a moot question how powerful anticommunism will be in the aftermath of the collapse of Soviet communism and disintegration of the Soviet bloc from 1989, and the retreat from communism elsewhere. It should be noted, however, that the fear of communism antedated the Russian revolution, and that inflated claims of a Red (anarchist, or communist) upheaval and "outside agitator" threat were a common characteristic of business, government, and media reactions to labor disputes in the late nineteenth century (Donner, 1990). In Latin America and in some U.S. business circles, communism has long been identified with any demands and challenges from below (Herman, 1982, pp. 33-36). The Western establishment will surely be subjected to such challenges in the "new world order," already under economic slowdown and strain, and it is possible that the traditional response will follow.

However, without a powerful and nuclear-armed Evil Empire (Reagan's term for the Soviet Union) in the wings, tying labor disputes to a foreign enemy may be more difficult, and antilabor propaganda may have to rely more on claims of violence and the damage to the community from work stoppages. As regards foreign policy, the U.S. invasion of Panama in 1989 and the assault on Iraq in 1991 show that demonization of a noncommunist enemy and alleged threats to oil supplies and international law, and from drug dealers, with full mass media cooperation, are a highly satisfactory substitute for anticommunism for U.S. leaders (Mowlana, Gerbner, & Schiller, 1992; Shalom, 1993).

Propaganda Campaigns and the Mass Media

The five filters discussed above narrow the range of news that passes through the gates, and even more sharply limit what can become "big news," that is, sustained news campaigns rather than occasional dissident reports ("little news"). By definition, news from leading establishment sources meets one major filter requirement and is readily used by the mass media.

Dissident voices, opposition to U.S. policies from poorly funded individuals and groups, domestic and foreign, are at a disadvantage as credible sources. They do not seem "serious" in terms of the way reality is perceived by the gatekeepers or other powerful parties who influence the filtering process. The mass media and government can therefore make an event "newsworthy" merely by giving it their sustained attention. By the same token, they can make another perfectly newsworthy event a nonhappening for the bulk of the population. The government and mass media can also make a story that serves their needs into a major propaganda campaign.

Major propaganda campaigns are not spontaneous. They tend to be well timed to provide the ideological mobilization sought by important domestic power groups. The Red scare of 1919-1920 took place at a time when labor organization was very active across the country, and when big business was alarmed at the challenge to its power in the factories. Many thousands of radicals of all sorts of views were arrested, violently hauled from their homes; many were imprisoned, and a number were deported (Kennedy, 1980, pp. 278-279, 288-292). It was claimed that they were plotting to overthrow the government.

A second example of a propaganda campaign is that of Senator Joseph McCarthy and the Red scare associated with his name (McCarthyism) in the late 1940s and early 1950s (Caute, 1978). Once again, the nation was said to be under dire threat of collapse from communist subversion, including 205 supposed Soviet agents in the State Department. This campaign served well to weaken the New Deal reform coalition that had formed under the Roosevelt presidency in 1933-1945, and replaced it with a Cold War/arms race/probusiness/labor-control policy alignment.

A third example is the alleged Bulgarian/KGB involvement in the 1981 shooting of Pope John Paul II. This factually flimsy claim was transformed into a major international propaganda campaign (Herman & Brodhead, 1986). It was a period of heightened tension between the Soviet Union and the United States—and its allies, including Italy—over the placement of advanced nuclear missiles in Western Europe. Antinuclear movements were becoming extremely active in both Western Europe and the United States, and the "news" of a sinister, callous plot to assassinate the most important leader of world Christendom was a potent way to revivify the communist specter.

News stories in this framework are selected on a highly politicized basis. In 1984, a respected and militant supporter of Polish Solidarity, Father Popieluszko, was kidnapped in Warsaw, beaten, and murdered by a cell of the Polish secret police. This ugly event was highlighted in U.S. media: The *New York Times* ran 78 articles and 3 editorials; *Time* and *Newsweek*, combined, ran 16 articles; and CBS News broadcast 46 news items. Yet the murders, sometimes even more hideous, of 100 clergy, nuns, and other religious workers by agents of U.S. client regimes in Latin America over the period 1964-1980 attracted far less media coverage. Only 57 *New York Times* articles (no editorials), 10 *Time* and *Newsweek* articles, and 37 CBS News items were allocated to their fates, indicating that "unworthy" victims in a friendly state were valued at less than one-hundredth of "worthy" victims in a communist state, as measured by media attention.

These split standards have great ideological significance. Continued emphasis on the real and alleged misdeeds of the enemy serves to convince people to feel seriously threatened by stop-at-nothing enemies and so of the need for new weapons, even though their research and development have usually been under way for years already. The playing down and rationalization of "own side" repression in friendly client states, such as Indonesia, Zaire, and Guatemala, allow us in the United States to hold on to our self-image as citizens of a beneficent and humane government, in contrast with the image of enemy countries, whose governments assassinate leaders and repress democratic movements.

The elite and the mass media, however, are not a solid monolith on all issues. Where the powerful are in disagreement with each other, the agents of power will reflect a certain diversity of tactical judgments on how to attain their shared overall aims. They will still exclude views and facts that challenge their aims.

Even when there is no internal elite dissent, there is still some slippage in the mass media, and information that tends to undermine the official line can be found, though rarely on the front page. This is one of the strengths of the U.S. system. The volume of inconvenient facts can expand, as it did during the Vietnam War in the period from 1963 to 1975, in response to the growth of a critical constituency. Even in this exceptional case, however, it was very rare for news and comment to find its way into the mass media unless it was inside the framework of established dogma (postulating benevolent U.S. aims, the United States responding to communist aggression and terror).

Apologists for U.S. policy in Southeast Asia at that time still point to "communist atrocities," periodic "pessimism" of media pundits over the war's winnability, and the debates over tactics as showing that the media were "adversarial" and even "lost" the war (Braestrup, 1977). The seeming "reasonableness" of the media process, with inconvenient facts allowed sparingly and within the official framework of assumptions, with fundamental dissent excluded altogether from "big news," and with small-scale alternative media harassed but not wiped out altogether, makes for a propaganda system far more credible and effective in putting over a patriotic agenda than one with official censorship.

Conclusions

The political economy of the U.S. mass media is dominated by communication gatekeepers who are not media professionals so much as large profit-making organizations with close ties to government and business. This network of the powerful provides news and entertainment filtered to meet elite demands and to avoid offending materials. The filtering process is imperfect, however. Although they agree on basic premises, the elite frequently disagree on tactics, and beyond this, normal news-making processes do not screen out all inconvenient facts and stories. It is extremely rare, however, for such dissonant items to graduate to act as a framework that questions generally accepted principles, or to be part of "big news." This presentation of dissident themes only episodically, within official frameworks, and implemented by free-market forces without state censorship, enhances the credibility of the dominant ideology and perspectives.

Further Questions

1. Who owns the controlling interest of the top U.S., British, French, Canadian, and Mexican media companies (TV networks, newspaper chains, national newsmagazines, large metropolitan dailies)? Are they individuals or corporations? What are their business, government, and social connections?

2. How can those who legally own a magazine or network control or influence its content if they do not manage it on a day-to-day basis and if interference in news decisions is considered bad practice? Can they influence the work of a reporter on their staff who covers Central America or South Africa or the Middle East? Or who covers poverty in the United States? Or the Pentagon?

3. Were the media adversarial during the Vietnam War? Study this question taking account of different periods of the war and the differences between criticisms of tactics and basic assumptions. Compare Peter Braestrup (1977) with Daniel Hallin (1989) and Herman and Chomsky (1988, chap. 5, app. 3). Were the media adversarial during the 1989 Panama invasion, where, it appears, several thousand people died (see Chomsky, 1991, pp. 149-173)? Were they adversarial during the Persian Gulf War of 1990-1991?

6 Mass Media and the U.S. Presidency

CEDRIC J. ROBINSON

Today many people complain about media blitzes during major election periods and the huge sums of money spent on campaigns by candidates with wealth behind them. The strategy model for such candidates in many parts of the world now is the campaign for U.S. president. People shake their heads in disbelief, point to all the glitzy nonsense—and yet back it comes at the next election. From the now well-known deceptive press photograph of President Woodrow Wilson taken in 1920, in which he appears fully in physical control with his wife at his side, when in reality she was holding his arm to stop it shaking as he appeared to sign a document, U.S. presidents and candidates for the presidency have used the media to buttress their power. Franklin D. Roosevelt's radio "fireside chats," the 1960 Kennedy-Nixon television debates, Nixon's scrupulously crafted media campaign for the presidency in 1968, and the 1980s Reagan administration's media management techniques are only some examples.

In this chapter, Robinson investigates a key dimension of the media and political power in the United States, namely, how media relate to the presidency, the nation's highest political office. Ever since Franklin Roosevelt used radio in the 1930s to broadcast his famous "fireside chats" to the nation, the media and the presidency have been intimately connected. From 1960 on, the relationship has become more and more problematic. *In that year, the narrow presidential victory of Kennedy over then Vice President Nixon was widely attributed to Kennedy's superior television image, for Nixon had done better when his message was carried by radio. When Nixon finally attained the White House in 1968, he did so after the first of the minutely crafted media campaigns that seem now to be taken as inevitable in a presidential election.*

Robinson discusses some of the key moments in the media-presidency relationship since, but takes the trouble to place this recent history in the longer perspective of the development of the U.S. presidency from the turn of the century. By doing this, he is able to direct our attention away from what might be called petty explanations of the cautious respect with which the media normally handle presidents—that is, in terms of how telegenic presidents are, or how successfully they get along with journalists—and focuses rather on both media and presidency as institutions of the same power structure.

It is important that you realize why Robinson and some of the other contributors to this volume focus so closely and critically on the period 1980-1988, the years of the Reagan administration. There are two issues at stake here. One is that the study of media cannot be undertaken seriously without the recognition that their role can change from time to time, sometimes quite sharply. The Reagan years were one such period, although, as Robinson points out, the change did not emerge out of the blue. The media are not unchanging institutions about which one can learn permanently true "facts."

The second issue is that the contributors are not motivated in their critiques by loyalty to the Republican Party's rival party. Their critiques are based on their independent analysis of the 1980s as a turning point for U.S. media, one that led in some very disquieting directions.

The presidency is the single most important subject reported by U.S. news media. The White House, together with a select group of agencies of the federal government, is routinely the focus of two-thirds of the news reported on the nightly news programs of the three major television networks, and news of Washington occupies 50% of airtime (Hertsgaard, 1988, p. 6). It is also the case that officials of the U.S. government serve as the primary sources for a third of the news stories appearing on the front pages of America's leading newspapers (Gans, 1979, pp. 15ff.). Not surprisingly, then, network news, news-magazines, and newspapers are rather uniform in both story content and news emphasis (Brown, Bybee, Wearden, & Straughan, 1987; Foote & Steele, 1986; Riffe, Ellis, Rogers, Van Ommeren, & Wood-man, 1986). It is just such news that constitutes an important part of the information environment for public opinion.

The dominance of the presidency prompts a number of questions about the relationship between the White House and news production. The most important is whether media coverage of the executive branch arises out of independent journalistic inquiry or from govern-ment manipulation of news production. In short, are the media functioning as free and, when need be, critical instruments of demo-cratic debate, or are they largely means of official manipulation of public opinion?

Traditionally the first, "adversarial," interpretation of the media was upheld by professors of journalism as well as by professional journalists themselves. But more recently, critics—journalists and researchers—have taken more seriously the second, "hegemonic," view (Altschull, 1986; Halberstam, 1979; Parenti, 1986). To under-stand these alternative perspectives, we should treat them not just as conflicting points on a continuum of debate but also as the products of particular historical and political events. Let us begin by looking at that background, which is essential if we are to understand the real nature of the U.S. presidency this century, rather than a rosy myth of the presidency. Once we understand the presidency itself better, we can assess its relation to the media more clearly.

The "American Century" and the Presidency

The strong presidency so frequently evoked by the Reagan and Bush administrations has its roots not in any vague tradition of U.S. leadership of the free and democratic nations, but in the colonies seized by the American state from the end of the nineteenth century (Drinnon, 1980; W. A. Williams, 1980, pp. 136ff.). Under the presi-dential leadership of McKinley, Roosevelt, Taft, and Wilson, the United States undertook military adventures and interventions with regularity between 1898 and 1920. These episodes are not generally focused on in high school or college classes on U.S. history, but that they occurred is not in dispute. Their frequency is astonishing, as the following list makes clear: In 1898, the United States sent troops to Nicaragua and China; in 1899, to Nicaragua, Samoa, and the Philippines; in 1900, again to China; in 1901, to Colombia; in 1902, again to Colombia; in 1903, to Honduras, the Dominican Republic, Panama (where they remained from 1903 to 1914), and Syria (now Lebanon); in 1904, to Korea and Morocco; in 1906, to Cuba (until 1909); in 1907, to Honduras; in 1910, to Nicaragua; in 1911, to Honduras and China; in 1912, to Honduras, Panama, Cuba, China, Turkey, and Nicaragua (1912-1925); in 1913, to Mexico; in 1914, to Haiti, the Dominican Republic, and Mexico (1914-1917); in 1915, to Haiti (occupied until 1934); in 1916, to the Dominican Republic (until 1924); in 1917, to Cuba (until 1933); in 1918, to Mexico and the Soviet Union; and in 1919, to Honduras.

These were not isolated episodes, but a continuous part of presidential decision-making in support of the global quest of U.S. business for commerce and empire. To understand the U.S. presidency, knowledge of these actions is central. The above list does not cover all such actions. In 1898, spurred on by the hysterical nationalism of the yellow press, led by William Randolph Hearst and Joseph Pulitzer, the Spanish-American War secured American control over sugar-producing Cuba and Puerto Rico, the labor-rich Philippines, and strategically located Guam. Hawaii was seized at the same time. This bounty would prove of great benefit to American businesses, not the least of which were the varied interests of National City Bank (a Rockefeller concern).

In 1900, this war—and its companion press—also produced the first imperial president, Theodore Roosevelt. Two years earlier it had been Roosevelt, as assistant secretary of the U.S. Navy, who had initiated the Philippines war by ordering the Pacific Squadron to Manila. Later, during Roosevelt's administration, in anticipation of the construction of the Panama Canal, a secessionist rebellion in what was then a northern province of Colombia was manufactured by the United States (four months before the fact the exact date for the revolution was published in the *New York World*—Pulitzer's paper). It was thus that Colombia lost a valuable part of its territory and the country of Panama was created.

The press scarcely missed a beat in supplying its readers with supposed justifications for these invasions. In domestic newspapers, nationalist resistance on the part of Filipinos, Haitians, Cubans, and others was characterized as savagery and banditry; American military repression of them, however, was costumed as "pacification." The seizure of their resources by American corporations and banks was claimed as amends for native misdeeds (i.e., rebellion) or as acceptable because the natives were not exploiting them commercially themselves. But General Smedley Darlington Butler, the Marine commander of many of these missions, put the objective more starkly:

> I spent most of my time being a high-class muscle man for Big Business, for Wall Street and for the bankers. . . . Thus I helped make Haiti and Cuba a decent place for the National City Bank to collect revenues in. . . . I helped purify Nicaragua for the international banking house of Brown Brothers in 1909-1912. I brought light to the Dominican Republic for American sugar interests in 1916. I helped make Honduras "right" for American fruit companies in 1903. (quoted in Pearce, 1982, p. 20)

As a consequence of similar observations, General Butler, for two whole decades one of the most celebrated military figures in the press, suddenly became a "nonperson" to American journalism and practically vanished from the press. The major media were rather consistent in their support of these foreign policies.

The presidency also developed in relation to domestic events in the period 1890-1920 (Zinn, 1980, chaps. 12-15), a period of mammoth industrial expansion fueled by vast labor immigration. At home, presidents, business, and the mainstream press assigned clear priority to commercial interests over social needs, a policy that was soon contested by the public. Large sectors of the American people—Blacks, women, socialists, labor, and the new immigrants—pressed for democratic reforms: desegregation and civil rights, votes for women, trade union rights, and anti-imperialism. An adversarial press was largely confined to alternative media such as magazines, foreign-language newspapers, and books (by authors such as Jack London, Theodore Dreiser, Frank Norris, Upton Sinclair, Sinclair Lewis, F. Scott Fitzgerald, John Steinbeck, and Ernest Hemingway), all with limited readership at the time.

During the 1920s and 1930s this growing political and economic instability escalated. The era was marked by bitter and often violent labor strikes, political marches, race riots and other civil disorders, lynchings of Blacks and immigrants, government corruption scandals, and, not least, the Great Depression. The growing disparities of income between the rich and the poor—between 1922 and 1929, one-tenth of 1% of the families at the top received as much income as 42% of the families in the nation (Zinn, 1980, p. 373)—gave new urgency to democratic demands.

Nevertheless, ordinary Americans had diminishing impact on the presidency and the selection of candidates for that office. The political system did not adapt to be more responsive. Instead, factions among the wealthy fought over control of the presidency and of the two major political parties, often making elections a mockery of democratic expression. Power continued to gravitate toward the center.

On the domestic front, the mainstream American press achieved an unenviable record of news distortion and the suppression of information about business and political elites. Examples are many. News of the Teapot Dome scandal (fraudulent leasing of naval oil reserves) was suppressed for nearly two years. In 1925, under pressure from none other than newspaper publishers, the Congress passed legislation forbidding the publication of income tax figures. In the 1920s the gathering depression and bank instability went unreported until the Great Crash of 1929. The magnitude of unemployment, layoffs, and farm and housing evictions was concealed until after the height of the Great Depression. In 1933, the press denounced the findings of the Senate Banking and Currency Committee that the J. P. Morgan banking interests "had given away valuable stock options to political, financial, journalistic and social leaders." In 1934, the press denounced the charges by General Butler that Morgan agents had conspired to organize a fascistic coup against President Franklin Roosevelt (Archer, 1973).

More than any other factor, World War II pulled the nation out of the Depression through massive industrial rearmament under government financing. The United States became the dominant economic and military power in the capitalist world-system. With this global prominence came policy responsibilities and obligations, political resources and opportunities that further contributed to centralizing the federal power structure away from Congress to the executive branch (the White House, the State Department, the Justice Department, the Defense Department, and so on). As defending the "national interest" had come to be defined as maintaining U.S. imperial power, so checks on executive action shrank in both foreign and domestic spheres. By the time of Eisenhower's presidency in the early 1950s, whole areas of national policy—nuclear policy (see Demac & Downing, Chapter 7), the CIA overthrow of the Iranian government (1953) and the Guatemalan government (1954)—were outside the sphere of public debate or beyond congressional scrutiny and accountability.

In other words, in the eighteenth and nineteenth centuries the U.S. presidency enjoyed an international image as a progressive institution, as a democratic alternative to hereditary monarchy and despotic rule. As the twentieth century gathered momentum, that tradition of the presidency was actually eroding rapidly under the pressures of U.S. development as a world power. The mainstream media were much more likely to be approving than to be critical of this world role. In practice, from very early on, this meant supporting presidential actions, especially overseas, and not being "adversarial" in foreign policy. Enthusiasm for "bipartisan" foreign policy in Congress underpinned this concentration of power.

The most frequent public defense of this centralization of decision-making has been managerial: The Constitution's separation of powers besets the presidency with "structural rigidities" or, as the Committee on the Constitutional System complained in 1988, it produces "confrontation, indecision and deadlock" (Moore, 1988, pp. 56-57). In other words, the Constitution's "checks and balances" are a practical nuisance in the eyes of supporters of the contemporary presidency.

In considering the relation of the media to the presidency, therefore, we must keep this twentieth-century accumulation of power in the executive branch and the reasons for it firmly in mind. Assessing how adversarial the media are means judging their performance not in the abstract but in relation to this centralization and its basic causes. Are the media a part of this process, or do they set themselves apart from it? If the latter, how and how much?

Commercial Modes of News Production

The commercial development of mass communications is itself an important source of change in U.S. politics (see Herman, Chapter 5). Presidents, as the ideological symbols of American power, the personification of the government, and the center of bureaucratic activity, have been the most natural focal point for journalists (Paletz & Entman, 1981, pp. 55ff.). Television has had the greatest influence of all media on the power of the presidency. As David Halberstam (1979) has observed, "The rising power of communications . . . loaded the institutional balance vastly toward the executive branch" (p. 693). It was precisely this supportive relationship between the presidency and mass media that was in evidence during much of the Vietnam War and the more recent American interventions in Grenada, Nicaragua, and the Middle East (Herman & Chomsky, 1988; Hertsgaard, 1988).

Television journalism has also contributed to the impoverishment of public debate. Television, with its 40-second scraps of news and its dependency on visual images, tends to diminish informative or investigative journalism to illustrated bite-size fast food. Thus in national elections catchy campaign slogans, percentage wobbles in opinion polls, and the minutely crafted images of candidates have displaced democracy, which requires an interrogation of party philosophy, in-depth discussions of policy priorities, and analyses of the social impact of economic policies. The government effort devoted to the manipulation of public opinion and information has supplanted the democratic principle of an educated citizenry.

Furthermore, as Herman (Chapter 5) and Demac and Downing (Chapter 7) note in their contributions to this volume, from the late 1940s onward the Cold War and McCarthyism established new limits, still rather effective to this day, on mainstream media debate—ideological limits. The elimination at that time from the American political spectrum of every view to the left of center in the name of "anticommunism" produced a major shift in the American political vocabulary: Centrists became liberals, conservatives became moderates, reactionaries became conservatives—and the Left became voiceless radicals (Jezer, 1982). This displacement of the center of political debate toward the conservative end of the spectrum still largely holds sway.

These ideological restrictions provided the conditions for a new relationship between the news media and the government and other official sources of news. According to one theory of news, "Government and other 'official' news sources [became] co-participants with the media in the creation of standard news themes" (Bennett, Gressett, & Haltom, 1985, p. 50). This raised major problems for the standard professional claim of journalists, that they report the news objectively. Normally they interpret this as giving balanced space to different perspectives. In response to the government-endorsed Cold War ideology, however, most mainstream media defined left-of-center perspectives—for example, in favor of civil rights and labor union freedoms, against invasions of other countries—as communist, hostile to freedom, disloyal to one's fellow citizens, and at best soft-headed. Yet unless the government is also to be defined as objective, media professionals certainly cannot pretend to be objective if they allow the government to make their news judgments for them. Bennett et al. (1985) maintain:

> In place of an operational definition of objectivity, mass media journal-ism . . . substituted the popular myth that the pronouncements of government officials and institutional elites somehow represent the reality in which the majority of people live. (p. 51)

Yet for a century and more, effective challenges have been mounted and important criticisms voiced about the everyday reality of this majority, mostly from one quarter: the left of center. In understanding the media and the presidency, then, we have to extend our historical vision. We need to acknowledge the long-term impact of omitting these perspectives from the mainstream media's list of views and policy options to be taken seriously. We also need to recognize the role of centralized power and the presidency in encouraging the mass communication of Cold War ideology over so many decades, and thus in encouraging this narrowing of acceptable political debate.

It is only from the vantage point of this history that we can begin to understand two of the crucial episodes in the more recent history of media coverage of the presidency, namely, the attempts by Presidents Johnson and Nixon to pursue the Southeast Asian war up to 1975 without the congressional oversight the Constitution requires, and the Watergate scandal that ultimately forced President Nixon to resign from office two years into his second term.

The Vietnam War, Watergate, and the Media

Though the news media are widely credited (or blamed) for ending American involvement in Vietnam, a more accurate construction would place greater emphasis on their role in encouraging public support for the war. For six years, from 1962 to 1967, with few exceptions the news media portrayed the war in terms faithful to "the framework of interpretation formulated by the state authorities" (Herman & Chomsky, 1988, p. 200). In painstaking detail, Hersh (1983), Halberstam (1979), Hallin (1989), and Herman and Chomsky (1988) have demolished the farcical claim of an independent American press during the Vietnam War. Throughout its duration, those who opposed the war remained "at the bottom of the media's hierarchy of legitimate political actors" (Hallin, 1989, p. 192). Thus, even in the final years of American military involvement, the press followed the Nixon administration into the empty slogans (Herman & Chomsky, 1988, pp. 193-206) of "pacification" (creating hamlets secure from guerrilla presence), "Vietnamization" (turning the fighting over to the unenthusiastic South Vietnamese army), and "peace with honor" (no humiliation for the United States, whatever the human cost).

The Watergate scandal had been the final and traumatic turning point for the Nixon administration. Watergate took its name from an apartment complex in Washington, D.C., where the Democratic Party had its national head office. During the period leading up to the 1972 presidential election, burglars were caught trying to raid the office. After a considerable period of media silence, it gradually began to trickle out in some media that the burglars had been sent by leading officials in the Nixon presidential cabinet. After sustained denials, some officials confessed their involvement, and the order was traced directly to President Nixon. Faced with an impeachment vote, he resigned in 1974. Most mainstream media were quiet on the subject until the final stages of the scandal. Rooted in Nixon's and Henry Kissinger's conduct of their Vietnam policy, the program of illegal wiretapping and domestic spying had led to the destruction of Nixon's presidency:

> It had come full circle. Nixon and Kissinger had designed a policy for Southeast Asia of secret threats and secret military activities. To protect those secrets they had resorted to illegalities. And then, years later, those illegalities had become a public issue just at a time when the administration was finally on the verge of achieving a stalemate in Vietnam. (Hersh, 1983, p. 637)

The trauma of Watergate and its parent, Vietnam, was not confined to those who had served Nixon and later served Reagan. It also took its toll on the media. Lessons learned in that crisis not only prepared Reagan's communication strategists for the task of news manipulation but also conditioned the media for subservience. The conventions of news production conspired against the emergence of an adversarial press during the Watergate scandal. Summarizing their analysis of the performance of the news media, Paletz and Entman (1981) observe:

They began by neglecting the scandals, calling them a caper. Then, when events were thrust into prominence by investigations and hearings, the bulk of the press cooperated with Nixon's strategy of laying the blame on his associates—thereby preserving the legitimacy of the president and the presidency. Then, as evidence of Nixon's guilt became overt, dramatic, and threatening, the media contributed to his downfall. But they then helped to resolve public disquiet without pursuing the underlying lessons of the corruption. (p. 158)

The "Adversarial" Press and the Presidency

The period 1973-1980 was one of considerable disarray among the country's economic and political policy makers. It had begun with the civil rights movement, opposition to the Vietnam War, and the Watergate crisis, and had been extended into activist consumer, women's, and environmental movements.

The Reagan presidency, Bagdikian (1987) argues, was the response of corporate power:

Corporate leaders counterattacked. . . . They raised large quantities of money to elect a government majority sympathetic to big business. They created a countrywide network of foundations and intellectual institutes to promote corporatism as a national philosophy. They achieved the repeal of laws and regulations that had been in place for decades. But they turned their most vituperative attacks upon the mass media. (p. 211)

As we have seen, these attacks coincided with a massive reorganization of media corporations. So when Ronald Reagan assumed the presidency in 1981, he was received by a compliant Washington press corps. For the most part during the next several years, following the lead of these correspondents, the national press would either ignore or misinterpret evidence of the public's lack of support for the president just as earlier it had ignored his campaign misrepresentations (Barber, 1987).

Within the Reagan administration itself, news managers such as James Baker, Michael Deaver, David Gergen, Larry Speakes, and Richard Darman were assembled in order to "package" the news.[1] Their job, as Hertsgaard (1988) documents, was deception, even down to the smallest detail:

> The extensive public relations apparatus assembled within the Reagan White House did most of its work out of sight: in private White House meetings each morning to set the "line of the day" that would later be fed to the press; in regular phone calls to the television networks intended to influence coverage of Reagan on the evening news; in quiet executive orders imposing extraordinary new government secrecy measures, including granting the FBI and CIA permission to infiltrate the press. (pp. 5-6)

Disingenuously, Larry Speakes kept a sign on his desk that read: "You don't tell us how to stage the news, we won't tell you how to cover it" (Hertsgaard, 1988, pp. 26-27). It was from their experiences of news production during Vietnam and Watergate that many in President Reagan's media team developed their confidence in "damage control" (acting quickly to isolate embarrassing news), the "line of the day," and "spin" (telling the truth, but with a particular edge or angle) as devices for the effective manipulation of news production. Some analysts have suggested alternative explanations for the failure of the press to give an accurate accounting to public opinion: Reagan's "genial relations . . . with the Washington political and media establishment" (in contrast to Carter's), Reagan's "large" electoral victory, Reagan's success with Congress, his "highly affluent and efficient right wing" support, or "an enormous subconscious desire in Washington for the president to succeed after a string of failed presidencies" (King & Schudson, 1987, p. 39).

Far more important than these factors, however, are the consequences of corporate ownership and control of the news media, the increasingly routine dependency of journalists on government officials for information, and the subsequent reluctance among media executives and managers to perform the role of an adversarial press. It was politics and organization, rather than psychological constraints, that provided Reagan's communication managers the leverage and opportunities to manufacture the image of the "Great Communicator" in the national media.

This was most effective in the Iran-Contra scandal of 1986 and the years following (Hertsgaard, 1988, chaps. 13-15). It transpired that Reagan—who had defined Iran as a "terrorist state" and had committed himself never to deal with terrorists—had not blocked his aides' sale of weapons to the Iranian government. Nor had he interfered with the profits on the sale being used to support the "Contras," a mercenary force supported and directed by the CIA as part of the Reagan administration quest to overthrow the Nicaraguan government by violence. This arms supply was illegal, because the United States was not at war with Nicaragua, and arms deliveries had been voted down by Congress. Despite a great deal of media comment, the media's considerable resources were never deployed to follow the story through to the end. It can only be speculated that none of the powers that be, including top media owners and executives, wanted a second, even more explosive, Watergate within 12 years of the first. The heat never got as far as Reagan or his vice president, George Bush.

The media mergers (e.g., Rupert Murdoch's acquisition of Walter Annenberg's publishing empire; the merger of Time, Inc., and Warner Communications, Inc.; and of Bell Atlantic and Telecommunications, Inc.) either completed or set in motion during the Reagan and Bush administrations significantly shifted the center of gravity in the relationship between the presidency and the mass media. With the increasing concentration of control over information and media industries, the presidency itself was reconstituted as a site for the convergence of corporate interests, national interests, and marketing strategies. The media apparatus and procedures developed in the Reagan White House by David Gergen, Michael Deaver, Roger Ailes, and Leslie Janka mirrored this altered political terrain. Within one year of Bush's election to the presidency, a dramatic instance demonstrated this new reality.

In December 1989 President Bush launched Operation Just Cause, the packaged-for-media designation for the invasion of Panama. The official rationales given for the invasion were the "inherent right" of the United States to "self-defense" and the right of the United States to "protect its citizens and military installations" and to pursue the drug lord Manuel Noriega, Panamanian military dictator. The authorizations cited were the Treaty of the Organization of American States (OAS) and the Panama Canal Treaty.

Cooper (1990), citing a Data Center analysis, identifies four failures in news media coverage of the invasion, at least until long after the event: the failure to examine these legal claims, the failure to examine the unstated reasons for the invasions, the failure to examine the character of the new Panamanian government installed by the United States, and the failure to note the U.S. government's long and close connections with Noriega.

In fact, ironically, Article 20 of the OAS Treaty forbids the use of force by its signatories "on any grounds whatsoever," and the Panama Canal Treaty explicitly bars intervention to change the Panamanian government. As regards unstated reasons for invading, the right wing of the Republican Party had continuously opposed the 1979 Canal Treaty that will hand the canal back to Panama in the year 2000, and indeed in 1988 had published a manifesto ("Santa Fe II: A Strategy for Latin America in the Nineties") that proposed invading Panama to take back the canal, to oust Noriega, and to change the Panamanian Constitution. The postinvasion Panamanian leaders installed by the United States (Endara, Ford, Calderon) were hardly heralds of democracy; they sprang from political parties with either an ultraconservative policy or one that strongly supported U.S. dominance in Panama. Finally, Noriega, now the demonized drug lord, had been for the previous 26 years a CIA agent; between 1979 and 1989, the agency had paid him $1.2 million.

News media performance during the U.S. war against Iraq (Operations Desert Shield and Desert Storm) was equally dismal (Jensen, 1992; Kellner, 1992; MacArthur, 1991). During the six months it took the Bush administration to get United Nations support for a military response to Saddam Hussein's occupation of Kuwait, the U.S. press largely ignored how Bush and his predecessors had built up Iraq's military despite Saddam Hussein's long and brutal rule, or the Pentagon's donation of military intelligence to Iraq during the 1980-1988 Iraq-Iran war, or Bush's opposition to attempts in Congress before August 1990 to wield sanctions against Iraq.

NBC and CBS refused to air videotape of Iraqi civilian casualties provided to them by Jon Alpert and Maryann DeLeo, Emmy Award winners and long-term contractual suppliers of independent news footage to the networks. The press and the networks squelched reports of "friendly fire" casualties on the U.S./U.N. side, and discarded reports casting doubt on the allied side's military effectiveness (of 88,500 tons of bombs delivered to Iraqi targets in Iraq and Kuwait, 70% missed, and the much-praised Patriot interception missiles hit just one incoming Iraqi Scud missile).

The media equally avoided detached commentary on allied military tactics, such as the use of napalm, the plowing under the sand of thousands of Iraqi troops in their trenches, or the infamous "Turkey Shoot," during which retreating Iraqi troops were strafed from the air as they fled north. Indeed, as in Grenada and Panama, the press voluntarily submitted to military censorship. Some reporters went so far as to inform on freelance colleagues who were avoiding contact with army "public affairs" officers. Finally, the news media blithely repeated over and over that the war was "to restore democracy" in Kuwait, regardless of the fact that the al-Saba royal family had always ruled the territory with the acquiescence of a puppet parliament.

These specifics are important: Every time there is a new U.S. military intervention abroad, the news media tend to treat it as though it had no precedents, and to blind us with authoritative-sounding statements—for example, about the Panama Canal Treaty (which none of us has read or has a copy of) or the superhuman technical brilliance of the U.S. military's weaponry. We need to learn to stand back and think, not just produce a knee-jerk "yes," as in the public okay given to the Korean and Vietnam Wars, in which, together, more than 100,000 Americans were killed and many more permanently maimed, not to mention the many more numerous Koreans and Vietnamese who suffered.

Some media critics (e.g., Hertsgaard, 1988) have proposed that journalists behaved this way because they had become the "stenographers of power," subject to "manipulation by inundation" and thus reduced to merely editing official copy. This view largely downplays the independent agency, corporate resources, and social influence of mass media themselves. This reality was much in evidence during the first year of the Clinton administration, where it became clear that government leaders now need to adjust their policy ambitions to what can be marketed over the screen or on the front page.

For Clinton perhaps the most telling (and painful) lesson in this reality was his June 1993 withdrawal of the nomination of Lani Guinier for the office of assistant attorney general for civil rights. Guinier had in the past forcefully argued that there is still no level playing field for African Americans, Latinos, and others in the United States, and that much more effective measures to achieve racial justice should therefore be explored.

There had been a buildup to this crisis. Clinton had been the object of a sustained hostile media campaign quite unparalleled in the Bush or Reagan presidencies, whatever their shortcomings. The attacks ranged very widely. They embraced his alleged lack of policy concerning Bosnia in southeastern Europe and Somalia in the Horn of Africa, veering from proposing military action to rejecting it in Bosnia, and from humanitarian objectives to military action and back again in the second case. They focused on his campaign rejection of Bush's deportation of Haitian refugees and subsequent adoption of the same policy, and on his campaign attacks on the North American Free Trade Agreement (NAFTA) followed by his all-out support for it; on his botched nominations for attorney general; even on the cost of one of his haircuts. In response, to help rescue the situation, Clinton fired his press secretary and appointed as the replacement none other than David Gergen.

However, upon assuming the presidency, Clinton had had reason to believe that the interconnected issues of civil rights and aid to the cities were high on the American public's agenda, following the extensive urban disturbances in Los Angeles and elsewhere in spring 1992. Hence his nomination of Lani Guinier for the civil rights position. But he was equally rebuffed on the plight of the cities. In February 1993, he had submitted legislation to Congress authorizing $16 billion in aid for the cities (less than one-fifteenth of that year's military budget, a twelfth of what is spent annually on advertising in the United States, and a quarter of what is spent on sports). The proposal was abandoned in the face of a Republican filibuster and news media indifference. Then, when he nominated Guinier in April 1993, the press largely followed the *Wall Street Journal* in labeling her "Quota Queen" and "extremist." In June 1993, he concluded by announcing his "reassessment" of Guinier's qualifications.[2]

From that point on, Clinton's capitulation to news media domination showed further signs of becoming standard practice. He ordered the bombing of Baghdad in response to reports of an unproven Iraqi plot to assassinate Bush on the latter's visit to Kuwait. His welfare reform proposal depended upon "workfare," a form of forced labor, and his health care reform proposal was reformulated to the dictates of the drug companies, the health insurance corporations, and the medical profession's elite. And he appointed David Gergen as director of communications.

These policies originated in the corporate imagination, that is, in the global firms that have come to dominate the mass media, as discussed in the contributions to this volume by Herman (Chapter 5), Rodríguez (Chapter 8), and McQuail (Chapter 9). In turn, as Bagdikian (1987) dramatically describes the production of information, the mass media serve to define the issues that acquire public attention:

> There are 50,000 print reporters and 50,000 broadcast reporters in the country; and each day they are pointed toward particular tasks, particular stories, particular personalities, particular government activities, particular foreign scenes, particular series. (p. 32)

And not toward others.

Conclusions

The claim to the existence of free, independent, and impartial media in the United States has come under increasing scrutiny and criticism. In large measure, the reason for this is the dismal and indifferent performance of the media themselves. And nowhere have they been more pathetic than in their reporting of the presidency. Given the spectacular technical advances in news production, it is ironic that the news media appear less competent today than ever before.

The character of American journalism has been traced to several causes, ranging from an organizational reliance on elite and official news sources ("objectivity" and "balance," in journalistic parlance) to the mass media's voracious appetite for a high volume of news matter. At root, however, is the continuing concentration of corporate ownership and control of news media organizations and the resultant subordination of news production to the interests of corporate capital. Equally, the electoral interests of presidential aspirants and the executive concerns of presidents make them hostage to the resources and interests of corporate capital. It is not too surprising, then, that the presidency, in seeking to fulfill these commitments, has set out to achieve substantial influence in the production of news.

Further Questions

1. Consider whether the cultural hegemony of the news media is eroding. One piece of evidence for this might be the decline in popular support for sitting presidents; another, the persistently lower turnouts for presidential elections. What might be the bases of that erosion? Perhaps what Ellen Wood (1988) has termed the "devaluation of democracy" (p. 14)—in other words, its reduction to the fanfare and procedures of elections rather than the extension of real power to the majority—is a factor. What do you think needs to be done?

2. Is it imaginable that increasing division between rich and poor in the United States and the nation's declining global power will converge with these other trends to produce social forces that will in turn compel the creation of a more responsible media, or social forces that will lead to even less responsible media?

Notes

1. James Baker was Reagan's chief of staff (1981-1985) and secretary of the treasury (1985-1988) and Bush's 1988 campaign director; in 1989 he was appointed secretary of state and continued in that role until resigning to manage Bush's 1992 reelection campaign. Deaver was Reagan's deputy chief of staff, 1981-1985. He subsequently joined the serried ranks of Reagan administration officials indicted in court, in his case accused of earning money shortly after leaving office by using his government connections to represent another government to the United States. Gergen was White House director of communications (1981-1984), later senior editor at *U.S. News & World Report,* and then came back to prominence as President Clinton's director of communications. Speakes was Reagan's press secretary (1981-1986), then briefly chief press spokesman at Merrill Lynch until forced to resign because of his public admission that he had concocted some of Reagan's official public statements without consultation with the president. Darman was Reagan's low-profile, high-influence presidential assistant (1981-1989), who monitored the entire paper flow in and out of Reagan's office. In 1989 Bush put him in charge of the extremely powerful Office of Management and Budget, where he stayed throughout the Bush presidency.

2. Incredibly, Clinton claimed he had not read Guinier's publications until the morning of June 3, 1993. They had been friends since attending Yale Law School together. Guinier and Hillary Rodham Clinton had served together for years on the board of the Children's Defense Fund.

7 The Tug-of-War Over the First Amendment

DONNA A. DEMAC

JOHN DOWNING

The First Amendment to the U.S. Constitution is for many media specialists the jewel in the crown of the U.S. media system. Demac and Downing examine its actual impact, along with laws such as the Freedom of Information Act and relevant presidential orders. They proceed to review the continual challenges to these protections of free speech and the right to know, particularly from government itself, by the FBI and the CIA, with their passion for secrecy and surveillance. Far from open information being an established fact, the battle for it is one that is constantly being fought and refought in the United States.

The history of the nuclear industry, both military and civilian, is an example the authors cite at some length in illustrating the practical problems of realizing free speech and information rights in the United States. From its very beginning, nuclear policy of all kinds has been shrouded in secrecy and public relations doublespeak ("nukespeak," as it has been termed). Through this focus, Demac and Downing emphasize that these freedoms are not just abstract liberal ideas, but go to the heart of our lives. Military confrontation with then Soviet Union and permanent nuclear poisoning of the environment were and are not abstract issues. They affect our future and that of our children and grandchildren. As has often been said, what we do not know can kill us. It is of little use celebrating democracy as a label to attach to the United States if it does not work properly in such crucial areas as these.

> Congress shall make no law respecting an establishment of religion, or prohibiting the free exercise thereof; or abridging the freedom of speech, or of the press; or the right of the people peaceably to assemble, and to petition the Government for a redress of grievances. (First Amendment to the U.S. Constitution, 1791)

More than 200 years ago, when these words were first voted into the U.S. Constitution, they were an extraordinary advance in political rights. Only in revolutionary France were the citizens of another country already possessors of such guarantees by the year 1791. Yet, only 7 years later, Congress passed the Sedition Act, which permitted prison sentences and heavy fines for anyone criticizing the president or the government. The act, which was aimed at suppressing the Republicans, met a wave of resistance from newspaper editors and publishers, despite prison sentences, that eventually led to its repeal in 1800.

The First Amendment is often trumpeted as an impregnable guarantee. However, the story of the Sedition Act suggests that the First Amendment actually resembles a battleground on which freedom of speech (and of the press, and of the right to follow one's religious beliefs or lack of them) must continually be fought for in the face of attempts by the state to punish those with dissident views.

In the pages that follow, we will argue in favor of this interpretation, basing our argument on more detailed presentations we have published elsewhere (Demac, 1985, 1988; Downing, 1986). The issue is not one for historians or lawyers only, however; if the "tug-of-war" view is correct, then we need always to be vigilant against attempts to reduce our rights to free speech and freedom of the press. If the opposing view is correct, no effort is needed on our part; the First Amendment will be respected automatically.

Those who think the First Amendment needs no defending need to give close attention to the role of the courts. U.S. law works a great deal from "precedent." This means that if, in a particular case, existing law is interpreted by the court more widely or more narrowly than had been done before, the new judgment can be used to argue in favor of other extensions or restrictions to the law. If, for example, pornographic magazines were to be banned, many people would not worry about freedom of speech, and some would think pornography is an abuse of free speech anyway. But legally, it is impossible to ban pornography without opening the door to the banning of other communications. For instance, if a pornographic magazine can be censored, then why not a sexually explicit novel by D. H. Lawrence, or pamphlets that explain clearly about contraception or AIDS? So being relaxed about First Amendment protections of our rights to free speech and information is more complicated than one might think. The danger does not arise only in a dramatic situation, such as if Congress were to consider abolishing the First Amendment. It typically arises in small ways, in areas where we are inclined to trust the good sense and decency of those in authority. Below, for example, we will examine the use of the doctrine of "national security" as it has been used to justify government secrecy and strict controls on access to classified and unclassified information. No one wishes the nation to be insecure, but under the banner of national security, exactly what needs to be classified as secret? And who decides?

Threats to freedom are typically small and gradual, but they accumulate. In countries such as Germany, Italy, Spain, and Portugal, all of which have had fascist governments within the past 50 years, the laws restricting freedom were put in place only a piece at a time, never all at once. The relaxed view needs to take this into account. Indeed, in our view, we all need to recognize that we have many tendencies toward censorship and self-censorship in any society, which can be allowed to expand or can be fought. The contributions in this book by Herman (Chapter 5), Robinson (Chapter 6), Rodríguez (Chapter 8), Corea (Chapter 20), Williams and Miller (Chapter 24), and Sreberny-Mohammadi (Chapter 25) all raise questions that show the practical complexities of the issue.

We should never lose sight of one key matter: Without free speech and information, democracy cannot function. People unjustly in prison cannot begin to communicate their cases. Governments that can keep their plans secret do not need to care what the people think. Public debate over alternative national policies could be suppressed; antiwar movements or campaigns for racial justice and environmental safety could be outlawed if there were no right to voice questions.

We will now examine other laws and presidential decrees that directly affect freedom of speech and information. We will then note the importance of the courts in enforcing (or not enforcing) certain laws. Finally, we will examine some major instances of U.S. institutions that have sought, and seek, to restrict public information in defiance of the spirit of the First Amendment.

Information Legislation and Orders
in the United States

THE FREEDOM OF INFORMATION ACT

Up to 1966, when the original version of the Freedom of Information Act (FOIA) was passed, federal officials could decide arbitrarily whether or not to release government information. The FOIA for the first time imposed an affirmative duty on federal agencies to make available information about their operations. The FOIA was strengthened in 1974 because of a series of revelations about government misbehavior, ranging from the Watergate affair (see Robinson, Chapter 6) to covert CIA and FBI harassment and break-ins against domestic political activists, and to assassination attempts against foreign leaders.

How does it work? Agencies are supposed to respond to FOIA requests within 10 working days, and to appeals against refusal of information within 20. These appeals may be taken to federal courts. In practice, the CIA often takes up to two years to respond. In its strengthened form, the FOIA declares firmly in favor of disclosure—but there are nine exemptions in the act, including classified documents and confidential business information. Others have been added every year; in 1985, for instance, the CIA's operational records were added. The tug-of-war continues, including at the state level, where each state has some version of such legislation.

Also, in practice, the attitude of each presidential administration directly affects the operation of FOIA. In 1982 the Reagan administration gave government agencies permission to classify information retroactively. It also eliminated an earlier requirement to balance the government's concern with secrecy against the public's right to information, so that "When in doubt, classify!" became the guiding principle of government. On top of this, the fees for FOIA use have continued to rise, and refusals have frequently been based upon an official's subjective interpretation of why the request was being made. On the credit side, the federal FOIA has enabled writers to document intense FBI harassment of Dr. Martin Luther King, Jr., safety problems at nuclear power plants, and sloppy federal enforcement of environmental and civil rights laws. One of the ironies of its operation, however, is that its most intensive users are corporations seeking to uncover information on their competitors.

THE SUNSHINE ACT

Passed in 1976, the Sunshine Act declared that "the public is entitled to the fullest practicable information regarding the decision-making processes of the Federal Government." It required that the public be allowed into the meetings of some 60 federal agencies. So far, so good—a clear application of the First Amendment. But a number of agencies fought back, especially the Nuclear Regulatory Commission, by redefining what a meeting was, by having its commissioners vote over the phone, or by "finding" wide-ranging uses of specific exemptions in the law.

WHISTLE-BLOWER LAWS

The First Amendment has never applied to the workplace. Employees' rights to free speech and information there have been subject to complete control by management, without any legal redress. Since the mid-1970s, however, the federal government has passed a dozen laws to protect employees who go public with information about improper or dangerous behavior by their employers, if this information serves the public interest. The dangers of nuclear and other forms of pollution are obvious cases in point. Nonetheless, both government and corporations often take strong action against whistle-blowers. As one writer observed:

> In [the former] Soviet Union, whistleblowers [were] sent directly to criminal psychiatric wards. In this country, we drive our whistleblowers to the borders of insanity and sometimes over the edge by humiliating them, taking their jobs, demoting them, or forcing them to do non-work; slander and character assassination are frequently used. (Ball, 1984, p. 307)

One such instance of such treatment was the case of Roger Boisjoly of Morton Thiokol, who warned his employers that the space shuttle *Challenger* might explode if launched under cold conditions. Interviewed on television, he said he had meant to act in the company's best interest. However, he was ostracized in the company, and he resigned. Another case was the mysterious road death of Karen Silkwood, the antinuclear campaigner whose story was dramatized in the film *Silkwood*, with Meryl Streep portraying the lead. It is important to remember that the law may at times be a very blunt and clumsy instrument for defending the freedom of speech and information in the workplace.

THE PAPERWORK REDUCTION ACT

Passed in 1980 with the ostensible purpose of reducing the volume of bureaucratic paper flow, the Paperwork Reduction Act was promptly used to curtail public access to government information. Under the guidance of the powerful Office of Management and Budget, government agencies used the act to transfer management of key information programs to the private sector. By 1985, one-fourth of all government publications had been dropped. In some cases, information was made available only on computer tapes, which put its utilization out of the financial and technical reach of the vast majority of citizens.

Among the government publications stopped as a result of the act were *Health Care Financial Trends, Analysis of Child Abuse and Neglect Research*, the *Civil Rights Directory*, and the *Conservation Yearbook*. Pamphlets on high blood pressure and prenatal care were cut, as was a series of booklets on daily living skills for the mentally retarded. Information about health, safety at work, and education was sharply reduced. No study was ever done to assess whether or not cutting particular publications would be damaging to the public interest. The application of the Paperwork Reduction Act tellingly illustrated how misleading the titles of laws can be, and how easily their objectives can be distorted by the agencies that implement them.

THE FEDERAL DEPOSITORY LIBRARY ACT

Passed in 1902 and administered by the U.S. Government Printing Office, the Federal Depository Library Act provides government publications free of charge to about 1,400 libraries, on condition that they in turn provide access to the public. It is one of the most practical ways of ensuring that citizens can obtain important information, and puts flesh on the bones of the First Amendment.

Yet here again, the forces discouraging the flow of information have been active, especially since the 1980s. The Reagan administration initiated a policy of leaving private agencies to supply information previously made available by the government. In other words, market forces were expected to respond to single out which forms of information were in demand, as measured by who would pay for them. Not only did private agencies not take up the slack, as the free-market doctrine asserted they surely would, but in the few cases where they did move into the information domain, libraries now had to pay for the information.

PRESIDENTIAL ORDERS

A major shift occurred with the arrival of the Reagan administration in 1981. Hertsgaard (1988) has suggested that the Reagan team and its influential backers were determined to recoup the ground lost in the 1970s for government and corporate freedom of maneuver, as a result of the Watergate scandal and the ensuing demand for open information. Indeed, the promised "Reagan revolution," rolling back social programs developed since the 1940s and hugely expanding military spending, made public information access potentially a source of greater opposition to the changes.

Certainly, new restrictions on information flow were put into effect almost immediately, with wide-ranging consequences. Government employees were required to sign "nondisclosure" contracts binding them for life—in other words, preventing them from publicizing any negative experience of government service. Some 300,000 had signed these contracts by 1988. A considerable amount of unclassified information became defined as "sensitive," thus barring widespread access to it. A number of scientists working on government contracts were prevented from publishing their results or communicating them at professional conventions, to the point at which distinguished university presidents and others warned of the dangers for productive scientific exchange of information.

As regards restrictions on freedom of speech, the FBI and the CIA—the latter supposedly a foreign affairs agency—were allowed to conduct surveillance of political opposition groups. The Sanctuary movement—a largely religious movement dedicated to enabling Salvadoran refugees to escape from their government's terrorism and avoid deportation back to El Salvador at the hands of the Immigration

Service—was infiltrated and spied upon, had its phones tapped and its offices raided. This was confirmed by a former FBI agent who had been involved in the agency's program, and by 1,000 pages of FBI files released by an FOIA court case.

Thus the Reagan administration took steps to make access to government information more difficult. The Bush administration did little to move away from these policies. After this 12-year reign of executive secrecy, many observers hoped that a Democratic Clinton administration would move in the direction of more open government. As of early 1994, however, it was clear that changing government executive orders and attitudes that focused on restricting access, rather than on maximizing disclosure, is a long process. Unfortunately, the Clinton compass had not moved toward openness in a definitive sense. To a significant extent, Clinton's hands were tied because of the discretion government agencies now possessed in deciding whether to disclose information. In addition, the case law in the 1980s and early 1990s had tilted considerably in favor of nondisclosure. What this meant in a practical sense was that agencies had less power of their own to decide whether to release requested information.

One illustration serves to highlight the problem. The FOIA's Exemption 3 required agencies to withhold information when another agency statute—for example, a tax law—prohibited disclosure. One such law was the Privacy Act, which forbade the release of personal information. Previously, a great deal of individual information was available so long as release would not constitute a clearly unwarranted invasion of privacy. The burden was on the agency to prove that disclosure was unwarranted. However, all this changed after the Supreme Court decided a case in 1989 in which it defined a new test for balancing privacy against public interests. The Court shifted the burden of proof to the requester and said that the only public interest in disclosure of personal information was the extent to which it shed light on government activities or operations. If disclosure would not do that, even a minimal privacy interest would be adequate to prevent personal information from being disclosed.

The Court's new standard quickly proved to be nearly impossible to meet. Records that might have been routinely released before were now considered "protected." Hence one can imagine the greater difficulty in investigating the "who" and "how" of government conduct concerning agencies such as the Department of Housing and Urban Development and "leads" in numerous other situations involving the federal government. As Harry Hammitt, the well-respected editor of *Access Reports*, a newsletter about the FOIA, has written: "The bottom line is that agencies are considerably more constrained in what they can do than they were several years ago."

On the positive side, Clinton administration Attorney General Janet Reno rescinded some policies adopted by the Reagan administration and indicated that it would be Justice Department policy to defend FOIA exemptions only in situations in which to do so would damage a specific concern explicitly protected by that exemption.

In 1994, Hazel O'Leary, Clinton administration Energy Department secretary, finally did what previous administrations, Republican and Democratic, had point-blank refused to do. She publicly acknowledged that from numerous nuclear tests conducted in the 1950s in Utah and Nevada, and from other experiments on humans at that time, many men, women, and small children had died, often slow and agonizing deaths. She also publicly spoke of her shame and revulsion at the consistent government lies, cover-ups, and denials in the face of many residents' protests and attempts to win compensation over the decades since.

There had indeed been a growing demand on the government to drop its secrecy concerning this Cold War nightmare (the public rationale offered at the time was that the United States had to have the best bomb or the Soviets would pull ahead in the arms race). Documentary films, including *Paul Jacobs and the Nuclear Gang* (1979) and *The Atomic Cafe* (1982), and books such as *Justice Downwind* (1986), by Utah University dean Howard Ball, and Carole Gallagher's *American Ground Zero: The Secret Nuclear War* (1993) were among alternative accounts of the truth that shredded successive administrations' callous denials. There had also been repeated FOIA requests to declassify the relevant documents. Justice, finally, was at hand, after more than 40 years. Yet many had died in the meantime, many of their families had also died without receiving the slightest compensation, and it remained to be seen whether Congress would make meaningful restitution to those still left.[1]

The First Amendment to the U.S. Constitution, as we have said, is not a magic talisman; it offers some support to the public in a continuous tug-of-war. The Clinton administration has also shown a preference for secrecy in some of its activities. For instance, at the end of 1993 a federal judge ruled that the White House was improperly keeping records of the National Health Care Reform task force from the public. Reporters had not been able to find out the names of those most closely involved, and thus whether they represented insurance company interests, American Medical Association interests, or other interested parties.

The point of the varying examples offered above is that it takes more than four years of a different presidency to change the direction of government policies. Public vigilance on First Amendment freedoms remains essential.

The Importance of the Courts

Above, we made reference to court enforcement of the laws and the Constitution. It is important to recall that both the Constitution and the country's laws depend entirely upon being enforced in practice. Ringing declarations of principle are powerless on their own. Let us examine two instances in order to illustrate this point as it applies to freedom of speech and information.

In the early 1960s, the movement for African American civil rights was spreading through the South—too slowly for those without civil rights, too quickly for the whites who were opposed to them. A number of state governments tried to stop the national media from reporting the brutal handling of peaceful protest. The mechanism they sought to use was libel law, arguing that the news media were damaging state officials' public reputations through their reporting on events and policies. The U.S. Supreme Court, adjudicating the initially successful case of Police Commissioner Sullivan in Montgomery, Alabama, against the *New York Times*, overturned his lawyers' argument. It required future plaintiffs to demonstrate "a reckless disregard for the truth" on the part of the media they were suing for libel. The national and international impact of press and TV coverage of the demonstrations was able to be sustained, and was vital in pushing the federal government to support civil rights more actively.

In 1988, 24 years later, the Supreme Court evinced a sharply different attitude toward freedom of speech. Three St. Louis high school students had appealed the fact that their school principal had cut two articles from the school magazine they edited. The topics were teen pregnancy and the impact of divorce on children. The Supreme Court, though not unanimously, argued that educators have the right to censor material in school-sponsored publications if it is out of line with "legitimate pedagogical concerns."

Perhaps high school publications do not seem very significant, but this is exactly the point at which the issue raised at the outset of this chapter begins to be important—namely, the question of precedent and its use in the legal system. Why should high school students not be encouraged to think about teen pregnancy and the impact of divorce on families? What kind of education is being offered that can rule these subjects out? These were the points raised about the case by a dissenting Supreme Court justice, and in turn they underline another important issue in this matter.

The composition of the Supreme Court makes a huge difference to the interpretation of laws and the Constitution, and one of the legacies of the 12 Reagan and Bush years was the packing of the Court with politically conservative members. There is a myth that the Court stands above politics, yet both of President Reagan's appointees, and President Roosevelt's unsuccessful attempt in the 1930s to expand the number of Supreme Court justices to sway a hitherto hostile conservative Court in favor of his New Deal policies, explode the myth. A whole layer of lower-level justices was also appointed during the Reagan years, so that it is certain that court judgments on information issues, not to mention many others, will be sharply influenced by these men and women well into the twenty-first century.

Subversion of Information Freedom: Some Examples

In this section, we propose to introduce some major cases in which the free speech and information principles of the First Amendment have been flouted. Other contributions to this volume, such as Downing's on alternative media (Chapter 14), cite further instances, especially the period of McCarthyism in the 1950s and the Iran-Contra conspiracy of the 1980s. The two examples we investigate here are secrecy about nuclear issues and the use of arguments centering on "national security" to justify government secrecy. These issues were very closely related in the Cold War era, and they continue to illustrate a U.S. government practice that is very far from extinct.

NUCLEAR SECRETS

From the very outset, nuclear weaponry was shrouded in the deepest secrecy (Hilgartner, Bell, & O'Connor, 1983; Morone & Woodhouse,

1989). President Roosevelt set up the Manhattan Project, which developed the atomic bomb, without notifying Congress, despite the fact that it employed tens of thousands of people and involved the construction of whole towns whose existence was kept off maps. It might be thought that wartime conditions justified this secrecy, but after the war, in 1946, the Atomic Energy Act classified as secret all material related to the design, manufacture, or utilization of atomic weapons; the production of special nuclear material; and the use of special nuclear material in the production of energy. This last restriction was very important, because it set the tone for nuclear power plants, nuclear waste disposal, the transport of nuclear waste, and safety standards at nuclear power plants, up to the time of this writing.

The same 1946 act created a special category of classified information, technically referred to as "restricted data," but more usually referred to as "born classified." Any information, idea, or concept in this category is automatically classified from the moment someone thinks it, unless it is specifically declassified by the Department of Energy. By contrast, other government information withheld on grounds of national security requires specific decisions to become classified. Hilgartner et al. (1983, pp. 63-64) cite the case of a journalist who wrote to his congressional representative and raised a series of questions about the costs of expanding production at the Savannah River and Hanford nuclear plants. His letter was forwarded to the Department of Energy by his representative and promptly declared classified. (Both plants were later proven to have flouted safety regulations repeatedly, and to be responsible for nuclear contamination on a scale yet to be assessed fully.)

One of the strangest but most revealing episodes in the saga of nuclear secrecy occurred in 1979. A small monthly magazine, *The Progressive*, was set to publish an article that the government claimed contained the formula for making a hydrogen bomb. The information was all derived from public sources, and of course it is much less plausible that someone could obtain the massive infrastructure to make an H-bomb than that he or she could learn how to do it in principle. Nonetheless, in the course of the government's campaign to stop the article's being published, a series of actions or propositions were advanced in court, each of which raises major questions about First Amendment rights to the freedom of information (Hilgartner et al., 1983, pp. 66-71).

First, a federal court imposed prior restraint, banning the magazine from publishing the article, and classifying it. The magazine's editors had to work very hard to find scientists with sufficient security clearance to be allowed to read it who would also be prepared to testify that its information was entirely and easily derived from the public domain. The scientists' affidavits, gathered by the editors, were themselves promptly classified by the government. The editors' lawyers had to obtain security clearance to be allowed to represent them.

Second, in the trial the government put forward the argument that it is legitimate to classify materials retroactively. Which materials? They included an article in an eighth-grade-level encyclopedia and the journalist's copy of his college physics text, because he had underlined parts of it. The Justice Department also asserted that arguments over whether these books contained secrets were also secret, and therefore the hearing could be held only in secret.

Third, when the case went to appeal, some fascinating responses made themselves evident. A researcher for the editors who was working at the Los Alamos library went out to lunch, only to find on his return that an unclassified document he had been consulting was missing, its card had vanished from the library card catalog, and that the librarian denied all knowledge of the matter. Shortly afterward the entire library was closed "for inventory and review." It was later moved in its entirety into a classified category.

Fourth, during the appeal the government argued that technical information was exempt from First Amendment coverage on the grounds that science has nothing to do with political debate, and that the courts were not sufficiently informed to make judgments on technical matters. The government then withdrew its case mid-appeal, because the material had by now been published by several other media in order to solidify the case against censorship. At the same time, no reform of the classification system was introduced. This saga indicates, perhaps more than anything else, that the secretive mindset that many people in the West attributed exclusively to communist bureaucracy and its clones was alive and well in the United States of America, at least in the nuclear policy area—which was hardly a trivial area for public concern.

THE NATIONAL SECURITY ARGUMENT

We have noted that although no one wishes the nation to be imperiled, this desire cannot reasonably be used to justify giving power to a small group of people to decide more or less in secret what the majority can be trusted to know. The terror of nuclear annihilation and the legitimate desire for national security are easily used by some against the public interest. The wider the security net, the less the powers that be need to be accountable to us, for it becomes easy for them to claim that we cannot be allowed to review the evidence for their actions. "Trust me!" they say. This trustful attitude is also worryingly common among journalists. As information professionals, they might be expected to cast a cautious eye on such claims. In practice, however, this is not so (for more discussion of this issue, see Rodríguez, Chapter 8).

The national security argument became very solidly established in the 1980s under the Reagan administration. A 1982 classification order listed the following government information as eligible for classification:

> (1) military plans, weapons or operations; (2) the vulnerabilities or capabilities of systems, installations, projects or plans relating to the national security; (3) foreign government information; (4) intelligence activities (including special activities, or intelligence sources or methods); (5) foreign relations or foreign activities of the United States; (6) scientific, technological or economic matters relating to the national security; (7) United States government programs for safeguarding nuclear materials or facilities; (8) cryptology [i.e., secret code construction or breaking]; (9) a confidential source; or (10) other categories of information that are related to the national security and that require protection against unauthorized disclosure as determined by the President or agency heads or other officials who have been delegated original classification authority by the President. (Executive Order 12356)

This statement is worth reading slowly, both for its catchall vague clauses (notably the last one), which could justify practically any classifying action, and for its seemingly more reasonable and understandable clauses. An example of the latter is the programs to safeguard nuclear materials and facilities (item 7). No one wants them to be vulnerable. Yet the very secrecy in which nuclear matters had been shrouded was precisely the factor that enabled so many of these facilities to operate unsafely, as a 1989 FBI investigation demonstrated.

A closer consideration of items 1 and 2 also raises questions about how far the public could be excluded from information about costly and ineffective weapons systems. In other words, our national security and well-being demand we know more, not less. Decisions must be broadly arrived at; they cannot be the private province of some appointed officials whose technical information might or might not be sufficient, never mind their capacity to reason in ways that represent the majority of the public. Some writers coined the term "national security state" to refer to the intensive and growing concentration of secrecy at the apex of government in the name of the public's security.

Conclusions

We have seen that freedom of information and of speech are principles enshrined at the highest level of the Constitution, but that in practice the issues are part of a continuous tug-of-war. In turn, the actual decisions that have to be made about information—such as decisions concerning national security or nuclear safety—are often clouded over by the claim that government experts know best what we should or should not be allowed to know.

No one would argue that each and every item of information should be automatically and instantly made public. There is, however, a very large area between that extreme position and the claims put forward by the U.S. government during the 1980s—the precedent for which in many ways was the 1946 Atomic Energy Act, which invented the concept of "born classified"—that huge discretion over secrecy and publication should be handed without further ado to what Hilgartner et al. (1983) describe as the "classification priesthood."

Further Questions

1. A further issue concerns the censorship of books to be used in schools and to be available in public libraries. At intervals throughout this century, fundamentalist religious groups have tried to get certain books banned from school use, and others removed from library shelves. The same groups have strived to make sure that only the biblical version of human origins—the Adam and Eve legend—should be taught in schools, or, if not that version alone, then with equal time to scientific accounts. Texts that have not done so have actually been excluded from classrooms in a number of schools and school districts. Teachers could not adopt them. In other communities, certain books have been banned from public libraries; the favorite, it seems, is the J. D. Salinger novel *The Catcher in the Rye*. Does this indicate that

censorship is not simply a government or corporate vice, but that there are powerful forces in society in general that are unhappy with the general application of the First Amendment? Does the existence of such forces represent the same danger as government censorship?

2. What do you think about the question of racist hate speech, on or off campus, and the First Amendment? For some, a parallel could be drawn with burning the U.S. flag in public (and every nation has its cherished symbols), which would deeply distress many U.S. citizens. If you ban racist hate speech, then you ban flag burning, and you are on the slippery slope with no means of stopping. An opposite view, taken by Matsuda, Lawrence, Delgado, and Crenshaw (1993), among others, is that the issue of racist hate speech should be examined first and foremost from the point of view of the target. For that person, such speech is very often just part of a systemic experience of hostility, discrimination, and violence or its threat, based on a continuous saga of 400 years or more. The sense of permanent vulnerability to attack, Matsuda et al. argue, must be taken into the equation, which it generally has not been by legislatures, courts, or university administrations. Harm, these authors assert, is done to hate speakers, if unsanctioned, because they learn they can get away with it. Harm is obviously done to the target, often part of racial groups tolerated at best on campus, with few faculty members actively supporting their rights. Harm is done, too, to the university's ideals of intelligent thought and ethical behavior, and its claim to be open to all without favor. What do you think is the most effective way of balancing these important issues?

3. What is the likelihood the federal government will make sure that electronically stored unclassified information is made easily accessible to the public? Soon, this will be the only form in which most government information will be available, and at present computer tapes are the typical mode of storage. These are beyond most people's technical and financial means to access. Ensuring access to the new technology for storing and disseminating information is a vital part of strengthening First Amendment freedoms in the information age.

Note

1. The same bomb testing was done on soldiers by Britain at the Woomera range in Australia, by France, and by the former USSR, accompanied by the same government secrecy and denials in each case.

8 Control Mechanisms of National News Making
Britain, Canada, Mexico, and the United States

AMÉRICA RODRÍGUEZ

There is one key set of questions that many critical media analysts leave out. What are the mechanisms by which journalists and other media employees are kept seemingly loyal to their editors, senior executives, publishers, and corporate boards? What are the intervening stages by which media employees are kept on track? Rodríguez explores the mechanisms of journalistic control and their effects in Britain, Canada, Mexico, and the United States by examining the countries' national news systems. Although there are differences in the economic structures and organization of these four countries' media systems, the chapter explores the similarities in their national news production processes, especially their dominance by political elites and the self-censorship mechanisms of journalists.

Rodríguez concludes that a mix of factors are at work in keeping journalists in line, ranging from their own comfort with the status quo to their desire for career advancement, to the normal requirement to follow orders. The rules of the news-making game are not written; they become clear in the day-to-day process of making news, but they always center on treating government officials as well as business and other societal leaders and the institutions they represent with cautious deference. Consequently, self-censoring journalists produce uncritical news that is supportive of the social and political status quo, and the mechanisms of control operate in very similar fashion in different countries. This argument tends to put a great deal of responsibility on the shoulders of journalists to develop a different practice—a difficult task, given the constraints outlined here and in other chapters.

This chapter attempts to explore the journalistic control mechanisms and their impacts in the news systems of the United States, Canada, Britain, and Mexico. Although the differences among these countries are many, the similarities in their national news production processes, especially their domination by the respective countries' political elites, are striking. National journalists, themselves the elite of their profession, are members of society's dominant elite. Their daily capsules of global reality tell us most of what we know of our fellow citizens and our government, and frame our understandings of the world. Their power to influence our thinking stems from their access to power—these journalists are positioned at the nexus of national political power, and not, as myth would have it, because they have a "ringside seat," but because they are an integral part of the process. This is not to say that national journalists play starring roles in their countries' political dramas, but rather to stress that they are not mere observers of power; the making of national news is purposeful social action.

In the United States, these reporters, editors, and producers work for nationally distributed newspapers and magazines such as the *New York Times, Wall Street Journal, Time,* and *Newsweek* or for national electronic media—that is, the three broadcast networks and CNN (Cable News Network). Increasingly, however, these journalists have less illustrious employers: the Gannett or Cox or Knight-Ridder news services. With the ongoing concentration of U.S. media ("Since 1983, the number of companies controlling most of the national daily circulation has shrunk from twenty to eleven"; Bagdikian, 1992, p. ix) and the subsequent shrinkage of the local press, these national wire services have taken the place of a Washington, D.C., bureau for those local newspapers that still exist. The reason is clear: It costs much less to subscribe to a "wire" than to maintain a branch office in the nation's capital.

CBS Headquarters, New York

Let me cite a personal experience of this concentration. In a recent move from Southern California to central Texas, I left behind palm trees and the Pacific, but the front page of my new hometown daily routinely carries stories with familiar bylines—courtesy of the *Los Angeles Times* news service. And, of course, I can still have the *New York Times* delivered to my doorstep; after all, one of its national editions is printed right here in Austin. I begin this chapter with a discussion of the centralization of U.S. news. Who are these influential journalists? Why do they present our national life to us in the way they do? The making of national news is not a completely closed system. To illustrate this point, I briefly discuss the *Noticiero Univisión,* the most important news source for the 23 million Latinos living in the United States. This U.S.-produced Spanish-language national newscast points up the limitations and possibilities of trying to expand the agenda of the U.S. national news system.

Talking to Themselves

U.S. national journalists spend most of the day talking to each other—literally and metaphorically. They watch CNN and the networks' news programs with their morning coffee, before turning to the *New York Times* and *Wall Street Journal*—regardless of whether their desks are in New York, Los Angeles, Miami, or Chicago. Once at the office, they scan other national news sources, such as the Associated Press. There are, to be sure, variations among the stories provided by national news services, but the topics chosen and their essential framing are more alike than not. This continuous one-dimensional professional conversation is reinforced by the daily routinized actions that make up the lives of national journalists. They attend the same news conferences and briefings, and ask questions of the same officials. Often these are people who are employed (by elected officials, lobbying organizations, or think tanks) for the sole purpose of talking to journalists, who then, through national media outlets (and over lunch, or at the gym), talk to other national journalists.

That journalists produce news with each other in mind is not a new research finding. For U.S. mainstream journalists actively to consider, say, the needs of their audience (in any way but as consumers) would be to breach the professional "objectivity" code, a self-justifying philosophy that claims to produce journalistic political neutrality. Continuously consulting (explicitly or tacitly) one's colleagues, in contrast, is considered, under this code, to be desirable professional behavior (see the discussion of self-censorship below). What is new is the proliferation and pervasiveness of national news. When Herbert Gans published his study of U.S. national news media, *Deciding What's News*, in 1979, there was no national delivery of the *New York Times* or the *Wall Street Journal*. CNN was still on Ted Turner's drawing board and (with the exception of the Associated Press and United Press International) other national news services (both video and print) were just beginning to garner subscribers. Today, the possibility of total dependence on the national news culture is perhaps the most salient aspect of how national news is made and diffused.

Today, among these few national news outlets, some news organizations have more power than others to make news. The *New York Times*, long considered the nation's "paper of record," retains its ability to set the national news media's, and so the nation's, agenda. Its feature stories put places and events on the national journalistic map; its "hard" news coverage validates certain topics; its analyses set the tone and often the content of national debates. To cite but one example, the *New York Times* played a major role in establishing the parameters of the national "debate" about health care reform in 1992-1993. It did not do this directly. Rather, the *Times*'s influence on other national media helped create the terms with which the national discussion of health care would be conducted.

Early on, public discussions about health care reform contained two broad options, "managed care" (a less drastic reform) and "single payer" (similar to the Canadian or British national insurance model). The Clinton administration, which had endorsed the managed care approach, favored the *Times* with leaks, and other journalists, not wanting to be left behind, followed the lead of the *Times* and wrote about managed care. After a couple of months, mention of a single-payer plan, whereby the federal government would provide universal health care, had all but disappeared from the *New York Times* and other national media—despite the fact that this form of plan had dozens of supporters (and potential supporters) in Congress (Lieberman, 1993).

These were not the sole factors at work, but the *Times*'s shunning of the single-payer option was pivotal in the establishment of the contours of the health care debate. Coverage in the national media shifted from a discussion of two significantly different approaches to health care reform to health policy horse-trading and backroom negotiations on Capitol Hill. A study conducted by the Kaiser Family Foundation of health care reform coverage in the *Los Angeles Times*, *New York Times*, *Washington Post*, *Wall Street Journal*, and *USA Today* found that the single largest topic reported on in the context of health care reform at that time was "politics" (see *Columbia Journalism Review*, November/December 1993).

This example of the relationship between the White House and the *New York Times* (and the *Times* and other national media) illustrates not coercion or corruption, but rather almost banal business as usual.

The Clinton administration, like others before it, used the mechanisms of the national journalistic culture for its own ends. At the same time, the *New York Times* was using the administration for its own ends. Put another way, the common interests of the administration (to gain approval for health care reform) and elite journalists (to keep abreast of a complex major story) coincided to frame public "debate."

What Does a Fish Know About Water?

The national journalistic map of the United States is skewed toward events that occur in the northeast corridor of the country, particularly those that happen in Washington, D.C. More national news is produced in the capital (with 1% of the population) than in any other U.S. city. This is not only predictable but, in one respect, appropriate. It is, after all, one of the central responsibilities of journalists to keep the public apprised of the federal government's actions. However, the media's focus on federal government news (or Beltway news, as it is called, after the interstate highway that encircles Washington) is often so tight that it threatens to exclude consideration of the rest of the country. (For a discussion of how this Washington, D.C., focus affects international news production, see Sreberny-Mohammadi, Chapter 25.)

To understand why this is so, think of Washington, D.C., as a company town. The "business" of Washington is the federal government. Its "employees" include lobbyists, public interest groups, members of Congress and cabinet officers and their staffs—and national journalists. These groups are linked by their interest in the national government. As the federal government has grown, so have the numbers of journalists working in Washington, D.C.: In 1961 there were some 1,500; by 1987 there were more than 5,300 (Hess, 1987, p. 13).

By and large, these men and women are at the peak of their careers; there are few assignments that are more prestigious. These journalists tend to be well educated, well paid, and, as Michael Kelly (1993) details in a startlingly candid *New York Times Magazine* article, well connected. Kelly counts among Washington "insiders" high-ranking government officials, political advisers, campaign consultants, and, not least, national journalists:

> They go to the same parties, send their children to the same schools, live in the same neighborhoods. They interview each other, argue with each

other, sleep with each other, marry each other, live and die by each other's judgement. . . . Not surprisingly they tend to believe the same things at the same time. (p. 64)

Among Washington's elite, professional lives are inseparable from private lives. A well-respected national correspondent is the daughter of a congressional representative and the sister of one of the capital's chief lawyer-lobbyists; another is married to the president of a major public interest group. Familial ties reinforce broader social and class loyalties, which are then reproduced in professional relationships. All concerned are, almost inevitably, heavily invested in maintaining this tightly interlocking system of personal and professional relationships.

It is no wonder, then, that distortions arise when Washington-based journalists report on the power dynamics of which they are an integral part. The challenge for national reporters or editors is somehow to see beyond this heady obsession with Washington politics and include in their news making the reality that most of the country lies beyond the Beltway. Most often, they do not meet that challenge. By and large, reporting about national politics is about one or another horse race— about instrumental, strategic displays of power, not about key social issues.

Another enduring consequence of Beltway myopia concerns a central image of Ronald Reagan's presidency. Throughout 1981-1983, the national press corps trumpeted Reagan as the "Great Communicator," routinely celebrating his "magnetism," charisma, and charm—this despite the fact that polls showed that in his first two years in office, Reagan was one of the least popular presidents in the post-World War II period. When this disparity between polls and punditry was pointed out, the journalists explained it away, pointing to a difference between the popularity of Reagan's policies and his personal popularity. This was no more true than the other claim.

How is it that the myth of the Great Communicator prospered when widely available polls flatly contradicted it? Robinson (Chapter 6) argues that corporate power over the media had a great deal to do with it. Another, complementary explanation focuses attention on face-to-face communication inside the Beltway. Reagan was extremely popular with politicians (and their staffs) on Capitol Hill, as well as with other Washington "insiders." They saw him as a welcome change from recent "failed presidencies" and, in particular, the strained press relations of the Nixon (1969-1974) and Carter (1977-1981) administrations. That was the "buzz" in Washington at the time—a perception that took root as it was repeated among those in the Washington power elite, "powerfully amplified by the news media," which "helped to establish myth as truth" (King & Schudson, 1987, p. 39).

This example, as well as the previous one about the coverage of health care reform, points up the overriding tendency in the U.S. national news culture to produce news that is supportive of the policies and points of view—market competition in health care, a strong presidency—embraced by the political elite, of which national journalists are members. In other words, the goal is to produce inoffensive, entertaining news that promotes mainstream societal values. The pressure that journalists feel to produce this kind of news emanates from ratings and advertising-conscious media owners as well as from within themselves.

Self-Censorship

Journalistic self-censorship involves not coercion, but compliance; it is an internal control mechanism. Journalists, like people in other lines of work, want to keep their jobs and advance their careers. Editors (who want to impress their bosses) watch and read other media to see if their reporters have "gotten it," that is, found out all the information about a given story, and analyzed it appropriately. If a reporter "misses" a story, or an angle of a story, that reporter loses favor with the editor. The editor conveys that loss of favor by not giving the errant journalist good assignments, or by publishing the reporter's stories on an obscure corner of page 27, or, in broadcasting, by bumping the reporter's stories to, say, the Saturday-evening broadcast.

Other indications to a journalist that he or she is not toeing the line come from sources. Government officials, particularly elected representatives, are not shy about complaining to an editor when they feel they have not been portrayed "fairly" in a news story. Furthermore, sources can restrict a journalist's access to the news by not granting interviews, by suggesting to associates that they not grant a particular journalist interviews, and by not returning phone calls. Without sources, a journalist cannot produce news.

In the cases of both the editor and the source, the journalist who wants to get ahead pulls punches, changes the offending behavior, and is rewarded, by being the recipient of a news "leak" or by having his or her stories given prominent play. The "rules" of the news-making game are unwritten and largely unacknowledged, but in the day-to-day process of making news they become clearly drawn. They center on treating government officials, business and other societal leaders, and the institutions they represent with cautious deference. The result? As the discussion above regarding the coverage of health care reform and the mythologizing of President Reagan's popularity illustrate, the result is largely uncritical news, supportive of the status quo, produced by self-congratulatory journalists.

Leaks in the System?

Efforts by media institutions to open up the nation's news systems, for example, by diversifying the gender, ethnic, and racial makeup of their employees, have generally failed, as industry leaders readily acknowledge. The American Association of Newspaper Editors (ASNE) reports that from 1977 to 1992 the number of ethnic minority newsroom employees increased from 4% to just over 10%, although ethnic minority groups constitute about 25% of the U.S. population (cited in Cose, 1993). Broadcast trade associations report similar figures.

Separate figures for the key nationally distributed media are not available, but anecdotal evidence suggests that although a few institutions have made significant efforts to diversify their staffs, generally speaking, national newsrooms remain predominantly white and male. National minority journalists report that the glass ceiling that limits their rise in their career is virtually shatterproof. We have done our part, editors reason; we have filled our "minority slot(s)."

When, in 1993, the *New York Times*, to its credit, increased the representation of African Americans in its newsroom and, perhaps more significantly, consciously broadened the point of view of many of its news stories to include previously ignored minority community perspectives, it met with dismissive responses from many within the journalistic profession. Citing a series of *Times* articles that included the perspectives of blacks, unauthorized immigrants, gay men, and lesbians, William McGowan (1993) wrote, in an editorial in the *Columbia Journalism Review*, "The search for minority points of view has opened up opportunities for racial and ethnic cheerleading" (p. 53). "Cheerleading," as used here, is a contemptuous dismissal of the ethnic and racial dilemma that pervades U.S. life, as if it were a trivial, nonnewsworthy topic.

The editorial questioned whether journalists of color can maintain their professional "objectivity" when reporting on minority communities; it equated efforts to broaden the conception of "news" to include long-disenfranchised communities with blind enthusiasm for "ethnic" viewpoints—as though the Anglo majority does not also constitute an ethnic group. *Times* publisher Arthur Ochs Sulzberger, Jr., responding to charges that his newspaper is soft on minorities, said, "First, you have to get them on the agenda" (quoted in McGowan, 1993, p. 54). In the years ahead, it will be interesting to see whether this reformist leadership by the *Times* will be followed in other areas of news policy.

The National News—in Spanish

Latinos are not on the U.S. national news agenda. A recent content analysis of *ABC World News Tonight with Peter Jennings* revealed that less than 1% of the most-watched nightly national newscast concerned U.S. Latinos (Rodríguez, 1993). Latino cabinet members are occasionally considered news makers, but Latino communities—which the U.S. Census Bureau predicts will make up the largest U.S. ethnic minority group in the year 2020—rarely are. However, outside the mainstream national media, Latinos do have an alternative resource for news.

The *Noticiero Univisión* is the nightly national newscast of Univisión, the largest Spanish-language television network in the United States, and itself the U.S. subsidiary of Televisa, the Mexican entertainment conglomerate. The *Noticiero* maintains editorial independence from the parent company. Visually, this newscast looks much like its mainstream counterparts: Its correspondents stand in front of important buildings as they conclude their 100-second reports; the cast of characters in its national political coverage is practically identical—the president, members of Congress, and so on.

While many Univisión journalists were born in Latin America, all were trained in the United States, in the same university journalism programs as their mainstream counterparts. They too wake up with CNN and the *New York Times*. They too are members of the elite, relative to both the U.S. Latino and general U.S. populations. Like journalists employed by other national news media, Univisión journalists are making news that affirms, rather than questions, U.S. political institutions and processes.

With the volume up and a closer look, however, one sees a distinctly different perspective on the *Noticiero* concerning what constitutes "news" in the United States and the world. The U.S. map that the *Noticiero Univisión* journalists employ includes communities along the U.S.-Mexico border and neighborhoods in U.S. cities where Spanish is the principal language spoken. While not neglecting Beltway news, this newscast enlarges traditional notions of who makes up the United States and what national news is. Similarly, although Univisión journalists report on the former Soviet republics and on Asian and European nations, most of their foreign resources are directed to the countries of Latin America. At the risk of restating the obvious, a final major difference between the *Noticiero Univisión* and mainstream national newscasts is the Spanish language and the largely working-class audience that language symbolically represents.

These Spanish-speaking journalists are, above all else, U.S. journalists, albeit Latinos. They wholly embrace U.S. journalistic ideology, positioning themselves as interpreters of U.S. political life for their largely immigrant audience. This regularly involves harsh criticism of anti-immigrant hostility. But overall, the *Noticiero Univisión* should be understood as a tiny, alternative slice of the U.S. national news system, evidence of both the national news culture's resilience and its willingness to incorporate difference—up to a point.

Canada

The Canadian and U.S. national news systems share two fundamental structural factors: (a) the journalists' adherence to the professional ideology commonly referred to as "objectivity" and (b) media ownership concentration and that ownership's interconnections with the country's political elite. These similarities follow from the two countries' closely interlocking economies and cultures. However, it is important to distinguish other elements of Canadian political life and gauge their expressions in the process of national news production. First, the economic similarities of their media systems.

Like its neighbor to the south, Canada's national news system is controlled by diversified media conglomerates. The largest of these is owned by Conrad Black. His media empire controls 325 newspapers on four continents, including London's *Daily Telegraph,* the *Jerusalem Post,* and Canada's largest newspaper chain, Southam Inc. Ken Thomason, the other major player in Canadian media, is the owner of the prestigious *Toronto Globe and Mail* and 37 other dailies. Two corporations control 59% of Canadian daily newspaper circulation, and they are corporations with extensive interests outside the newspaper industry run by the corporate elite. Is this alarming? American journalist and educator Ben Bagdikian (1992) raised eyebrows in the United States when he pointed out that "fourteen dominant companies have half or more of the newspaper business" in that country (Winter & Hassanpour, 1994, p. 7). Fourteen with half, versus two with 59%—hmmm.

Magazine, radio, and television ownership in Canada are similarly concentrated in a few hands. As in the United States, this degree of concentration has been accelerating in the past decade. The consequences for Canadian public life are at once obvious and subtle. Clearly, there are fewer media voices. Less apparent are the tight interrelations between the major media and the political elite.

Conrad Black is a longtime personal friend of former Prime Minister Brian Mulroney. Mulroney's closest political adviser is also a key business associate of Black's. Not surprisingly, Black's vast media empire reflects the same conservative politics that Mulroney champions. Journalists are clearly warned of the consequences should they challenge this political view. One of Black's senior media managers told an interviewer, "If editors disagree with us, they should disagree when they are no longer in our employ" (quoted in Winter & Hassanpour, 1994, p. 9). This blatant interference with editorial autonomy has "chilled" much Canadian journalistic initiative.

The tendency of Canadian newspapers to promote the neoconservative agenda in the past decade (another similarity with U.S. media) has been only partially offset by the alternative perspectives offered by a few of the programs produced by the publicly owned CBC (Canadian Broadcasting Corporation) television and radio networks. For instance, although in 1993 the CBC brought to the attention of the nation government abuses of Native peoples in the sparsely populated regions of northern Canada, its national political coverage is often indistinguishable from that of the profit-oriented media. In 1981, a Canadian government commission called this bland news coverage "Pablum Canada." Since then, Canadian critics agree, budget cutbacks at the CBC and the ongoing concentration of media ownership have contributed to a further homogenization of Canadian media.

Stephen Block (1992) illustrates how the interests of national Canadian television journalists converged with those of the nation's business and political leaders in the 1987-1988 debate over the Free Trade Agreement (FTA), a measure backed by the Reagan and Mulroney administrations that lowered tariff barriers between the United States and Canada. At the crux of Block's critique lies the key journalistic concept of "balance," the notion that in each story "both sides" must be represented. In covering the FTA, Canadian journalists were eager to support the government and to promote what they construed as a healthy economic future for Canada. In so doing, they violated this key (albeit usually illusory) tenet of objectivity and balance. This happened because of their deference toward, and uncritical use of, their sources. Government and business predictions of the likely effects of the FTA were repeated in interview after interview as assertions. These in turn were accepted as unquestionable truths by journalists, thereby obviating the need for "balanced," alternative voices—this despite the FTA's significant and debatable effects on Canada's environmental and industrial policies.

These dimensions are all reminiscent of the U.S. media situation. On the other hand, Quebec, Canada's French-speaking province, is a source of many of the country's alternative voices. Quebec residents' demands for autonomy have provoked a deep political crisis that questions fundamental notions of national identity and sovereignty. The ongoing question of Quebec has preempted formation of a national media consensus on a number of key issues in Canada. One sign of this is that Quebec's journalists (like U.S. ethnic minority journalists) are regularly accused of unprofessional partisanship by the country's majority English-language media. The coverage of the latest referenda about Quebec's future in 1992 in both English and French media led to intense national debate about the role of the media in Canadian political life (Taras, 1993). Whether this airing of the critical link between politics and media will have salutary effects in other areas of public life remains to be seen.

Britain

Britain has a peculiar status when it comes to media freedom and questions of control and censorship. On the one hand, the British system of government is known internationally as the "Mother of

Parliaments," which implies an exceptionally strong tradition of public debate and therefore of media freedom. On the other hand, it also has one of the strongest traditions of government secrecy, and some of the tightest laws and procedures controlling media, outside of dictatorial regimes (Downing, 1986; Schlesinger, 1988, pp. xi-xliv, 205-243). Britain also has, like the United States, Canada, and Mexico, very considerable concentration of ownership of major media (Curran & Seaton, 1985). Let us explore these paradoxes a little further, insofar as they affect the degree to which news professionals are able to do their reporting independently. We will do so with the help of two examples: the institution of the "Lobby correspondent" and the reporting of the Northern Ireland conflict.

The word *Lobby* in this context denotes from the entrance space just outside the House of Commons debating chamber, in which a select number of journalists are allowed to wait and intercept government ministers and other members of Parliament for interviews as they leave the chamber. From this privileged access to this particular space is derived the further sense of "the" Lobby correspondent, namely, one of a select corps of political correspondents who are given regular briefings by government ministers, on the understanding that the minister or source will not be named without that person's permission and that the briefing information will be released to the public only according to the time line set by the minister (Tunstall, 1977).

In other words, a bargain is set. For the privilege of getting news early, and without the stress of having to hunt it out, journalists and their editors voluntarily accept the restraints on its publication set by the government. A journalist who breaks this code may be deprived of Lobby privileges, which would effectively mean the job of political reporting would become impossible, because all the journalist's peers would have access to early information that she or he does not. Such a journalist's editor would not be pleased, either. Reassignment to a less prestigious position would almost certainly follow, or possibly firing. No case is known of a newspaper or broadcast station challenging the government by sending in a replacement journalist to repeat the behavior of a journalist who has lost Lobby privileges.

A still more stringent instance of this mechanism was put in place during the war between Britain and Argentina in 1982. Argentina's military dictatorship sought domestic popularity by reclaiming some tiny islands—called the Malvinas in Argentina, the Falklands in Britain—located in the bitterly cold South Atlantic Ocean and seized from Argentina by Britain's navy in the nineteenth century. When Britain sent a naval fleet to expel the Argentinian military, only a tiny number of journalists were allowed to accompany the fleet to report the war, and their reporting was subject to strict military censorship and time embargoes. This mechanism, referred to as "the pool," was adopted by the Reagan administration when the United States invaded the Caribbean island of Grenada the next year, 1983, and then again during the invasion of Panama in 1989 and the war against Iraq in 1990-1991 (see Robinson, Chapter 6).

The usual justification for these wartime controls is that lives may accidentally be lost by reporters who care only about deadlines and high audience or circulation figures. Yet it is equally likely that lives may be lost, and in much greater numbers, owing to the stupidity of military commanders and the folly of a pointless war. History is drenched with the blood of such disasters, and courageous independent reporting might help to check them. The British tradition of government secrecy, which has produced both Lobby correspondents and the pool, coexists in direct contradiction with Britain's democratic traditions.

The vital insight to be gained, however, is that the process works in large part through the degree to which media editors and owners, and therefore journalists, connive in it. Reporting on the Northern Ireland conflict (Schlesinger, 1988) also sheds light on the same mechanisms.

The military conflict in Northern Ireland since 1969 represented the legacy of British colonization more than 800 years ago. In the seventeenth century, as part of their continuing effort to control Ireland, the British gave farmers from Scotland land to settle in parts of the North. A further distinguishing mark of these settlers was their Protestant hostility to Catholicism, the faith of the vast majority in Ireland (though the original colonization of Ireland had been of Catholics by Catholics).

When, early in this century, the British government proposed limited independence for Ireland (home rule), along the same lines as for Australia and Canada, a number of these settlers' descendants plotted a rebellion. The government backed down and, in 1921, partitioned Ireland, with six counties in the northeast retained as a "province" of Britain. In these six counties was entrenched a Protestant majority that retained its power through systematic discrimination against the Catholics, now a permanently marooned minority. Many Protestants were as poor as the average Catholics, but had the gut feeling that their prospects were better being tied to the Protestant elite and to Britain than in a united country dominated by Catholics.

Thus the stage was set for the prolonged armed conflict that eventually erupted in 1969, with the British army sent in officially to restore public order, but quickly losing the respect and indeed earning the fear and detestation of many members of the Catholic public. Attempts to report this situation honestly in British media have repeatedly run into trouble. Successive British governments have threatened broadcasting organizations, especially the BBC, with methods varying from hostile campaigns in the mostly conservative press to legislation banning interviews with members of paramilitary organizations such as the Irish Republican Army (IRA). This reached a ludicrous point in late 1993 and early 1994, when the British government was offering to negotiate with the IRA and yet its spokespersons' responses could be read over the airwaves only by actors with Irish accents.

Two important points to recognize for present purposes are the immense difficulty faced by those few journalists who tried from time to time to report professionally on Northern Ireland, and the general readiness of most media organizations to serve government policy rather than "objectivity."

However, this generally accurate summary of the situation should not blind us to the extent to which at certain points it was possible for unofficial perspectives on certain issues in the Northern Ireland situation to surface and achieve prominence in the media. Examples are the pivotal 1974 Protestant Ulster Workers' strike and the false convictions and imprisonment of Irish men and women (the Guildford Four, the Birmingham Six). It has been argued that in those cases the threadbare evidence produced by the government and the availability of well-informed alternative sources for the news media combined to open up fissures in the media agenda set by the British power structure.

Mexico

Up to this point, I have discussed the national news systems of highly developed, postindustrial nations. Mexico, in contrast, is a developing nation—a member of what is sometimes called the Second World, a society where it is estimated that more than half the population lives in abject poverty. There is, however, a large working class in the cities, and smaller middle and professional classes. Mexico does not have the poorest economy in Latin America, and it is home to the man whom *Forbes* magazine in 1993 named the wealthiest Latin American, Emilio Azcárraga.

The cornerstone of Azcárraga's $3 billion personal fortune is Televisa, a virtual television monopoly in Mexico and the largest producer of Spanish-language television programming in the world. Azcárraga also owns or has controlling interest in Mexico's largest cable TV company; in Univisión, as noted above; in six of Mexico's top radio stations; in PanAmSat, a satellite; in two record companies; in a billboard advertising monopoly; in a movie studio and a publishing company; in Mexico City's largest sports stadium; and in sundry real estate. Together, Azcárraga companies take in an astonishing $4 out of every $5 spent on advertising in Mexico (Miller & Darling, 1991).

In other words, Azcárraga has an iron grip on Mexico's media, and he is not shy about using it. Advertisers are required to pay a year in advance or lose the chance of reaching the Mexican public with their messages. Entertainers and artists work exclusively for Azcárraga enterprises—transgressors are blackballed throughout Latin America, their careers ruined. But it is in the national political sphere that Azcárraga has left his largest mark on Mexico. It is estimated that more than half of the Mexican population is illiterate, making them dependent on the Azcárraga broadcasting empire for their political information.

Azcárraga (and before him his father Emilio, Sr., the founder of Televisa) has an intimate, mutually beneficial relationship with Mexico's ruling party, known by its Spanish initials, the PRI. Televisa journalists (both radio and TV) are effusive in their support of PRI government officials and candidates, and regularly misrepresent opposition candidates as violent and evil (Aguayo, 1992).

Furthermore, over the years, Televisa has blatantly censored news that is not flattering to the PRI. Examples abound. In 1968, no mention was made of the government massacre of hundreds of students in Tlatelolco square in the weeks preceding the Mexico City Olympics. In 1985, Televisa did not report on organized protests against the government's handling of the effects of the Mexico City earthquake. In the past decade, Televisa has not reported on the increasing number of charges of electoral fraud throughout the country.

For Televisa, the reward for its deceptive, fawning news coverage can be seen as narrowly economic, in that there has never been a government effort to curb Televisa's monopolies or otherwise regulate the entertainment conglomerate. But the rewards have also been broadly ideological. The Azcárraga family is both a primary creator and preserver of a political culture that has dominated the country virtually unchallenged for nearly 80 years.

Since 1988, and the election of President Carlos Salinas de Gortari, there have been a few cracks in the Mexican national news system. It is no longer commonplace for a journalist to arrive for, say, a luncheon with a government official and find an envelope full of cash on the assigned seat—payment for a favorable story. Media companies for the first time now pay the expenses of reporters traveling with the president when he leaves Mexico City. Before, expenses (usually lavish accommodations) were picked up by the presidency. The government's paper monopoly, which had kept Mexico's newspapers from publishing critical stories, has been broken, and livelier political dialogue can now be found in the Mexican press. In addition, with much fanfare, the government sold its national television network. Theoretically, Televisa now has competition, though it remains to be seen whether the new television network will develop a critical voice. Still, censorship of alternative voices continues—on Televisa and elsewhere.

Summary

The national news systems discussed in this chapter, for all their diversity and complexity, share two salient characteristics. Their economic structures are built on highly concentrated patterns of ownership. That is, the ownership of the national media system is centralized in very few hands. These owners, and the journalists they employ, in turn have close personal and professional relationships with the political elites of their respective nations. The interaction of these two factors—ownership concentration and the tight web of relations within the political elite—has created national news production processes intent on safeguarding privilege and status. They consequently stifle—though do not completely silence—the robust public debate central to genuine democracy.

Further Questions

1. Has media ownership concentration in each of the countries discussed created single "national conversations" in those countries? Compare and contrast your answers for each country.

2. How would you reconcile the often-proclaimed pursuit of "objectivity" by journalists with the questions raised in this chapter?

3. Is journalists' self-censorship different in kind, or in its impact on society, from employees' customary caution in challenging the boss?

4. What are the major intervening stages by which media employees are kept on track? Can you suggest a few examples?

5. What are some of the similarities of the media systems in the four countries discussed in this chapter? Explain in detail.

9 Western European Media
The Mixed Model Under Threat

DENIS McQUAIL

Western European nations have a long tradition of organizing broad-casting as a legal monopoly via a public corporation. To the American reader who knows only the U.S. free enterprise broadcasting system, where even the minority public channels are heavily sponsored by corporate advertising, such a situation may sound potentially fraught with danger. Who will be able to prevent the government from broad-casting only what it wants people to know?

It is true that, notably in France, governments up until the mid-1980s directly controlled broadcasting on issues it deemed sensitive, and that during the Fascist periods in Germany (1933-1945), Italy (1922-1944), and Spain (1939-1976), dictatorial government control was in force, but the usual pattern of state-sponsored broadcasting in Western Europe has been nowhere near as subservient to governments as the American reader might suppose.

Indeed, as McQuail points out, in many of these countries there has been a strong commitment among broadcasters to what is called "public service" broadcasting. Broadcasting has been defined not as a market commodity to be traded like any other product, but as a common valued resource, like clean air, that a democratic government should organize for the collective welfare of its citizens to ensure they are properly informed and educated, as well as entertained and amused.

Hence a public corporation at partial arm's length from the government has seemed the most viable way to provide this service.

Gradually since World War II, and with more momentum during the 1980s, these public broadcasting systems have encountered competition from newer, privately owned commercial networks almost everywhere in Western Europe. The effects have been mixed, and they are the subject of many disputes. However, the argument that publicly controlled networks of this kind automatically pave the way to dictatorship is rarely heard. Sometimes the networks have been described as stuffy or stick-in-the-mud, but not as antidemocratic.

If for no other reason than that you should be aware that it is perfectly possible to organize media systems in various ways, McQuail's account of the traditional broadcasting model in Western Europe and how it is changing is an important one for you to study. Like the next two chapters in this section, this chapter also presents you with a sense of the importance of different media "philosophies" in shaping media organization and output. The free-market model is dominant in the United States, but that does not automatically make it normal for the rest of the world. Are there not advantages to be considered in the "public service" approach?

The Old Order

There was a time when one could speak of broadcasting in Western Europe as having a similar pattern across most countries, with many features common to the different national systems. This model may be considered to represent the "old order," which held sway until the early 1980s. With some necessary oversimplification, this old order had the features described below.

Public service. There was a strong component of public service in the media goals. The main elements of cultural policy were that diverse tastes, interests and subcultures in the nation should be represented, along with different regions and minority languages. Public service philosophy also discriminated in favor of cultural and informative programming and special services for children and young people.

Public accountability. Public accountability was achieved mainly through regulatory bodies and parliaments that had ultimate control over most funding. The normal method of financing broadcasting in Europe was through annual license fees set by governments from time to time and collected from each household by the post office or similar agency.

Monopoly. Broadcasting was a monopoly, or almost so. One public body, such as the British Broadcasting Corporation, was licensed to broadcast by the government. Monopoly privilege was usually based on the argument that only a few channels were available, a pretext that concealed a determination not to let this potent communications medium slip out of government control. However, public broadcasting monopolies had a good deal of independence in overall editorial policy and day-to-day decisions, despite ultimate accountability to government and the general public. Government monopoly did not involve the close control of all media output that typified the USSR from 1930 to 1985 (see Downing, Chapter 11).

Politicization versus neutralization. Broadcasting was usually either highly politicized or politically neutralized. Broadcasting occupied a politically sensitive position and responded to the typical concerns of the elite of the political system. The forms of politicization or neutralization varied a good deal across Europe, depending on the local political culture and conventions. At one end, political parties and groups colonized broadcasting in proportion to their voting strength—though parties of the Left had to fight to be given proportional access. At the other end, the general aim was to keep parties at a distance and minimize the direct involvement of politicians in broadcasting. The former pattern was more typical of continental Europe, the latter of Britain and Scandinavia. A variation could be found in Italy and France, where conservative parties in government ran broadcasting more or less as their own property until other parties gradually achieved proportional access (from 1968 in Italy, from 1981 in France).

National scope. European broadcasting has generally had a national character. This has been shown by the legal requirement to serve the entire territory, the expectation that the national language and culture would be protected, the location of broadcasting headquarters in the capital, and the task of representing the country in international cultural events. There were cases that deviated from this national model, such as Germany, where provincial governments organize broadcasting; Holland, with its inclusion of religious and political organizations in broadcasting; and Belgium, with its division into French and Flemish communities.

Noncommercialism. Although there are many examples during the old order of significant funding from commercial sources—especially through charges for spot advertising—the balance of revenue in hardly any European country came from advertising. There was a widespread policy that broadcasting should not be dominated by the search for profit, but by the priorities of professional broadcasters and audiences. Where income from advertising was allowed, it was under strict conditions, designed to shield program making from the need to make money. This gave management and broadcasters considerable scope and created "space" in the system that could be used for cultural or social purposes that were not necessarily profitable.

The Mixed Model

It is clear from the preceding account why the typical European broadcasting system could be called a "mixed model": It had mixed sources of revenue, with advertising as well as license income from audiences, and it had mixed goals, some determined by governments and politicians, some by professionals, some by various interest groups, and some even by the audience, which could exert indirect political pressure.

This system rested on diverse supports within each society. The main interests that sustained it were as follows: (a) the political elite, which was able to achieve access or neutralization and still retained the right to intervene on particular issues, either in public or behind the scenes, and did not have to worry about broadcast challenges that it could not control; (b) the cultural elite (whether of the Right, favoring traditional values, or of the Left, disliking commercialism); (c) the public postal and telecommunications authorities, which generally also enjoyed a privileged position in supplying the hardware and controlling technical standards; (d) the press, which was protected from unsettling competition for advertising revenues; (e) the audience, which over the years in most countries seems to have been more appreciative than critical of a service that, although limited, was reasonably high in quality and low in cost, and fulfilled its expectations of a public service.

Before looking at the changes that affected the old order in the 1980s and subsequently, we must remember that this is a simplified model. There was much intercountry variation under the old order (Euromedia Research Group, 1992). This diversity is an important benefit of noncommercialism, because the logic of commerce is to standardize structures as well as profit-making goals. Most Western European broadcasting systems fit within three main groups of nations: four small Nordic countries—Denmark, Sweden, Norway, Finland; the big five—Britain, Germany, France, Italy, Spain; and several small countries left over—Holland, Belgium, Austria, Switzerland. The Nordic countries generally conformed very closely to the model of the old order and were strongly noncommercial. Of the big countries, Britain and

France were quite close to the model, as was Germany, apart from its federal structure. Italy deviated from the model after 1976, when private, commercial broadcasting at the local level proliferated outside the system of public control. Spain was both heavily dominated by the state and heavily dependent on commercial revenue—a different type of mixture. Generally, each small country created some variant of the model to suit its particular circumstances.

The Model Destabilized

The mixed model first came under considerable strains and pressures in the 1980s. These appeared to destabilize it, to present the old order as an anachronism, and to raise doubts about its survival (Dyson & Humphreys, 1986; Siune & Truetzschler, 1992). It is vital to understand the reason behind the changes if we are to be able to predict the longer-term development of broadcasting in Europe. The most fundamental reason for change appears to be the changing technologies of distribution (De Bens & Knoche, 1987). The widely accepted justification for monopoly rested on the argument that broadcasting channels and resources were scarce, and thus there was a need for close regulation. With cable and satellite able to distribute messages over much larger areas at relatively lower costs, promising an abundance that print media already enjoyed, the old argument for monopoly crumbled. New technologies offered greater freedom to send and receive, and a much greater potential for choice.

These technological changes coincided in Europe with another kind of change, in the political climate. These policy changes are complicated, and varied somewhat from nation to nation, but essentially they included (a) a trend toward limiting taxpayer support and greater reliance on market forces; (b) a widespread belief that the new communication and information technologies would underpin future economic growth and thus should be stimulated; (c) the ripple effects of U.S. deregulation; (d) the acceleration of plans to create a more integrated Europe, politically and socially as well as economically, which implied a convergence of broadcasting systems (European Economic Community, 1984); and, last but not least, (e) renewed pressure from old and new commercial operators, including individuals such as Rupert Murdoch and Sylvio Berlusconi and corporations such as

Hachette SA and Bertelsman AG, to open up European broadcasting to commercial competition.

Some of these pressures are clearly related or mutually reinforcing. Governments like to relax regulation and encourage expansion and innovation they do not have to pay for because financiers and media barons produce the investment money. The "Europeanization" of broadcasting policy supported the logic of commercial development as a way of fighting off the increased competition in both hardware and software markets from the United States and Japan.

So far, I have said nothing about the "consumer," the audience for broadcasting in whose interest, and at whose expense, the old order was supposedly run. It is hard to know how to assess the consumer's position, because so many self-interested parties claim to represent the consumer's point of view. The most obvious argument is that the public in general welcomes changes in the direction of more choice and variety in radio and television programming. The success of the VCR in many countries is one indication of this. But the evidence of strong demand for more television channels is not very clear, and it would be wrong to suggest that this revolution in European broadcasting was the result of unstoppable consumer demand for new suppliers or pent-up dissatisfaction with the old order.

Media Moguls of the 1990s

MEDIA MOGUL 1: RUPERT MURDOCH

Rupert Murdoch has been called the "Magellan of the Information Age," because he comes splashing down on one continent after another (Bagdikian, 1989).[1] He inherited an Australian newspaper, the *News*, in Adelaide from his father in 1954. In 1960, at the age of 29, he began to buy out papers in Sydney, Melbourne, and Brisbane, and established the first continental newspaper, the *Australian* in 1964. In 1969 he embarked on acquiring newspapers elsewhere, purchasing the British *News of the World* and the *Sun*; the latter became in 1977 the biggest-selling newspaper in the English-speaking world, with a circulation of 4 million, combining sexy pin-ups on page 3 with souped-up dramatic headlines. Murdoch acquired the establishment *Times* of London and *Sunday Times* and used them to support Margaret Thatcher into power, as he used the *New York Post* (which he resold in 1988) to support the Reagan administration. The U.S. Federal Communications Commission permitted him to do what no other broadcaster had been allowed, to acquire a television station in a city where he also owned a daily newspaper and to keep both of them. Indeed, Murdoch had to renounce his Australian nationality and become an American citizen in order to purchase seven U.S. TV stations. His launch of the Fox Broadcasting Company as a fourth network in 1985 permanently changed the face of American television.

Combined, Murdoch owns and controls two-thirds of newspaper circulation in Australia, almost half of New Zealand's press, and about a third of the British press, as well as a number of American newspapers, along with *TV Guide*, which enjoys a circulation of 17 million in the United States. He also has considerable stakes in book and magazine publishing companies in Britain. He owns the 20th Century Fox movie studio, the Sky Channel in Europe, and has controlling shares in Star Television, based in Hong Kong, whose satellite footprint reaches across Asia, making him one of the twentieth-century's richest and most global media moguls.

MEDIA MOGUL 2: REINHARD MOHN AND BERTELSMAN AG

Reinhard Mohn, a member of a long-established publishing family, presides over one of the largest media corporations in the world. In 1988, Bertelsman AG had 42,000 employees in 25 countries on four continents, with revenues of more than $6.5 billion and net profits of $230 million. The company has reached the limit of print market share permitted by West Germany's Federal Cartel Office, including the popular West German magazine *Stern*, and recently outbid two government public systems for the new TV satellite channel that will cover Germany. It also owns U.S. publishing firms Doubleday, Bantam, and Dell; the Literary Guild book club; and RCA and Arista Records. The family owns 89% of company stock, yet none of Mohn's sons is an heir to the fortune, control of which will go to a charitable foundation.

MEDIA MOGULS 3, 4, AND 5:
HENRY LUCE AND HARRY AND JACK WARNER

The Time Warner merger in 1988 created the largest media corporation in the world, with a total value of $18 billion, far more than a number of Third World countries combined, and a workforce of 335,460. This merged company has subsidiaries in Australia, Asia, Europe, and Latin America. The company now includes Warner Brothers film studios, publishing ventures (including Warner paperbacks; Scott Foresman; Little, Brown; Time-Life Books; and the Book-of-the-Month Club), record companies (such as WCI), and American cable television companies (including Home Box Office and Cinemax). It is the largest magazine publisher in the United States, with *Time, Life, Sports Illustrated, Fortune, People,* and others, with a worldwide readership estimated at 120 million.

Also worthy of note. Sylvio Berlusconi, the Italian media magnate and owner of Fininvest, won the Italian elections in the spring of 1994, using his many media channels to support his far-right candidacy. This is one of the most obvious examples to date of corporate media control being used to gain political power. In February 1994 one of the most expensive media takeovers of all time was concluded for $10 billion, as Viacom, chaired by Sumner Redstone, already owner of MTV, Showtime, and other cable channels in the United States, gained control of entertainment giant Paramount (owner of the Paramount film studio, Simon & Schuster publishing, Madison Square Garden, and the New York Knicks basketball team). Thus the new Viacom-Paramount blockbuster will cover the range of activities of the information age: cable TV, film, broadcast television, book publishing, theme parks, music retailing, and video rentals. Takeovers such as those described here, that bring about shrinkage in the number but expansion in the size of media corporations, are part of a process known as *conglomeratization.*

Assessing the Changes

This section summarizes the degree and kinds of change that have occurred in the various national broadcasting systems of Western Europe. Italy was the trailblazer: From 1976, Italy permitted private local broadcasting, and there was a mushrooming of commercial, unregulated, and mainly local television and radio stations. These have now been institutionalized into a set of advertising-supported commercial channels, dominated by the media magnate Berlusconi and his Fininvest Company, which competes with RAI's public broadcasting system, which is financed by both advertising and publicly collected receiver license revenue. The transition to a dual system of competing public and commercial television was confirmed by the new Broadcasting Law of 1990, which effectively legalized the fait accompli of 1976. The Italian changes had as much to do originally with the stifling dominance of political parties that had colonized the airwaves, especially the conservative Christian Democrats, as with the new technology, which has still not made a great impact on Italian broadcasting. A new chapter in the story appeared to open in 1994 with Berlusconi's entry into national politics, linked with conservative forces in the North of Italy and the neo-Fascist party in the South, dedicated to defeating the regrouped forces of the Left. His media empire generated a media blizzard in support of his candidacy.

Britain still has a closely regulated system, divided more or less equally between the BBC, funded solely by receiver license fees, and Independent Television (ITV), which is supported by advertising revenue. Both operate two national channels, but both now have increasing competition from a third force—Murdoch's British Sky Broadcasting, which, as of 1994, can reach about 10% of households via satellite or cable and will almost certainly grow as cabling develops more rapidly during the 1990s. It is this service that most truly represents the forces of commercialism, because ITV still carries significant public service obligations as a condition of the licenses that were sold to the operating companies under the Broadcasting Act of 1990.

Great efforts were made during the 1980s by Conservative administrations to encourage the growth of a new commercial sector based on cable and satellite, which would gradually outflank the BBC as the main public broadcaster. This process happened much more slowly than was expected, and the traditionalism of British political culture has, among other things, worked to the advantage of the BBC, which is likely to see its mandate confirmed for another period when its existing 12-year license comes up for renewal in 1996. The public service concept has proved capable of adaptation, and the BBC has been able to draw on a coalition of forces to ensure continuity. Nevertheless, there is a process of gradual change in the British media environment that keeps public broadcasting on the defensive and struggling to maintain its role.

The German government has similarly encouraged private competition by way of expanded cable systems served by satellite systems, without directly changing the position of public broadcasting. This operation has been much more successful than the comparable effort in Britain, but the result has been a somewhat similar mixed public and commercial system that is relatively stable. Attention has been diverted from the issue of public versus private competition by the drive to mold not only the former East German media system but also the radically democratic media structure hammered out in the first months of transition in eastern Germany into the pattern of the former West German system.

In France, Europe's most radical changes of the 1980s were implemented, including the sale of one public channel and the licensing of three or four new local or satellite-distributed channels, funded by subscription and advertising. Despite France's pioneer role in advancing the theory of new information technology and the success of videotex (Minitel), politics were a greater cause of change than was technology. The results are still unclear, although public broadcasting has been very much weakened and has declined to a subordinate position in audience terms, with doubts raised about its future viability.

Spain was rather late to follow the example of its neighbors, but it too developed a new commercial television sector alongside the old state system, although it is held back by economic problems and technological limitations.

The countries with the strongest traditions of public service broadcasting have generally been smaller nations that are concerned with protecting their national languages and cultures. Broadcasting in the Scandinavian countries has probably been least destabilized by new technological and commercial pressures, although all have been affected by cross-border reception of cable and satellite stations, and both Denmark and Norway have ended their public broadcasting monopolies and allowed a competing commercial channel within the national system. In the Low Countries, both Belgium and the Netherlands have paid for their very high degree of cabling by losing much of the audience for public service channels to commercial or foreign (sometimes both) competition. The Netherlands retains its unique system, in which broadcasting time is allocated to key social groups based on politics, religion, and way of life, but the system is ailing financially and even more commercialization is on the way. In Belgium, home-based commercial channels as well as cross-border flows have driven the public broadcasting system into an even tighter financial corner and into a minority audience status. In relatively rich small countries such as Austria and Switzerland, the public system has remained largely intact, but in other small and poorer countries, such as Ireland, Portugal, and Greece, adaptation has meant yet more commercialization and less public control.

Throughout Europe, the "communications revolution" has led to a greatly increased supply of television on new or expanded channels. The media consumer has more choices, although it is not certain that the range of programming has really widened, except where commercial television has become available for the first time and there is more popular, entertaining, and often imported content offered. Public broadcasting has everywhere been in relative decline, as measured by its share of the audience, and there is little doubt that nearly everywhere, public broadcasters have been obliged to think in more "commercial" terms (i.e., about attracting and pleasing the audience) in order to compete. There is much more emphasis within public broadcasting on efficiency in the use of resources and on market thinking. There is also much greater use of independent production companies, in the interests of efficiency and diversity. Governments have usually sponsored these changes, and few if any public broadcasting organizations have had the political will or strength to stand up against such pressures. Adaptation is regarded as inevitable; the only questions concern where it will end and just what role there will be for public service broadcasting at the end of it.

Commercialization and Transnationalization

Broadcasting has become more transnational as a result of new technology and of the efforts of new media conglomerates to develop transnational markets. Beginning in Western Europe, this process has spread to Eastern Europe, where there is less resistance from the poorly funded and sometimes delegitimated existing public broadcasting institutions. Two dominant trends now influence the direction of European broadcasting policy and reality, those of commercialization and transnationalization.

Commercialization refers to a process by which broadcasting comes increasingly to rely on revenue from advertisers, sponsors, or subscriptions, and changes accordingly. This means tending toward cut-throat competition, seeking to maximize profits, aiming for the largest possible audience, and neglecting unprofitable programming for minorities and for cultural purposes, the kind that public service broadcasting is supposed to provide. The process of commercialization takes many different forms, ranging from the sale of public assets (as in France) to an almost imperceptible change of cultural climate in which commercial values influence all aspects of programming.

Transnationalization (see Sepstrup, 1989) refers to the increasing transborder flow of services and programs and the increased exposure of audiences to an imported media culture. This trend is fueled in part by consumer demand, but mainly by the need to fill the proliferating channels from a limited supply of European programs. Although this may be considered a threat to national cultural identity, it is also an unstoppable process in the new, more integrated, Europe for which the slogan "Television Without Frontiers" has been coined. The European Community has also implemented regulations (the Television Directive of 1989) that require member states to allow access to television channels originating in other member states provided they meet some agreed-upon minimum content standards. In this context, the issue that remains most problematic is the relatively large import of non-European (especially American) programming. This has stimulated some countermeasures in the forms of quotas and production subsidies that have proved controversial in negotiations over global free trade; it is very difficult to disentangle the cultural interest from the economic. It is also the case that internationalization has been viewed with alarm in some circles, mainly because it is so closely associated with commercialization.

The New Entrepreneurship

There have been a variety of entrepreneurial strategies for penetrating the public service bastion of Western Europe, and the results have taken varied forms. The first model was to hire satellite transponder space to beam cheap bought-in material for transmission to (limited) cable systems in other countries in return for international advertising revenue. This is how Rupert Murdoch's Sky Channel venture began, and the example was followed by another operation (Super-Channel) that had several owners before becoming the property of NBC. The most successful cross-frontier satellite operations in Europe have developed on the basis of the Astra satellite program, run by the Luxembourg company CLT-SAS, which is still on course to open up a relatively new market for direct-to-household broadcasting. The single most successful example is Murdoch's Sky Broadcasting Channel, which targets Britain and Ireland in particular. This represents a general change of strategy in Europe, following the realization that particular national markets are more viable than transnational ones.

Other variants of this model have been developed on the Continent, especially by media magnates with extensive empires, such as Berlusconi and Mohn. Their aim has been to penetrate particular markets with advertising-supported content in the national language, especially German, Italian, French, and Spanish. This has proved more successful than the pan-European ventures and continues to produce new examples. One glowing instance of success is that of the Luxembourg company RTL, which in the space of two or three years took a 40% share of the Dutch television audience, helped by high cable distribution and the new European rules governing access. Most of these ventures are daring and unashamedly commercial, exploiting loopholes in the law and showing a readiness to spend (and lose) considerable amounts of venture capital in the hope of future profit in a more commercial environment. More often than not, risk taking has been rewarded, although there have also been a good many failures.

More limited commercial models include provision (sometimes via subscription cable) of specialized content such as films or sporting events. In general, where it succeeds, subscription income is rated more highly than advertising revenue and is a more certain source of revenue in an increasingly fragmented broadcasting situation. The spread of cable television has been slower than was anticipated, but it is gradually accelerating and is making greater diversity of distribution channels more viable. Direct-to-home satellite broadcasting has also made significant advances as the costs have gone down, but is still well behind cable in Europe as the main alternative to conventional terrestrial broadcasting transmission.

Because of the gradual enlarging of the available audience as a result of cable and satellite, there is still much jostling for position in the market for a transnational audience, especially in respect to news, business, and sports. In this context, CNN is only one of several competitors for the elusive pan-European audience market. The BBC is another would-be player with hopes of success in the international market, and is pressing to take a more competitive profile alongside its public service role.

The New Politics
of Broadcasting

It is not clear that the new order is any less politicized than the old, but the politics are different. First, the response to or engineering of change has generally been a matter of policy. Britain, Germany, and France quite deliberately set out to make their systems more commercial and to encourage the expansion of new technologies in this way. In many cases, socialist parties have been supportive of or reluctant to oppose change because they too recognize the possible economic benefits. Thus more or less conscious political decisions have been made to let commerce pay for risky innovation.

Second, European-level politics and the economic goals of the European Community as well as the more cultural goals of the broader Council of Europe have exerted strong influences on national broadcasting policy, especially in harmonizing and liberalizing regulations for commercialism and promoting the health of European media industries (European Institute for the Media, 1988). Third, politics has turned toward widespread reregulation, drafting new rules for new commercial operators and new remits for public broadcasting and telecommunications. Media policy is now an important part of the political agenda across Europe.

Over the decade of the 1980s, the European debate shifted from cultural and political issues to economic and industrial ones. There has been a shift in emphasis away from public service and the needs of citizens to the supposed interests of consumers and entrepreneurs. Media politics is no longer a solely national matter; transnational influences are recognized, and there is a more developed sense of the interdependence of various media, especially because cross-media ownership has become such a powerful commercial reality.

How Much Has Changed?

The legitimacy of the old order of European broadcasting has been severely challenged, and there have been considerable changes in climate, policy, and actual institutional arrangements. First of all, monopolistic structures have been dismantled in order to allow access for independent commercial competitors. Second, there is a much greater supply of channels and programs available to most European viewers and listeners. Third, there is less regulation and control of content and more freedom to earn money from advertising. Fourth, the "new media" of cable, satellite, and video have clearly had a dramatic impact on the media landscape in Europe, and the process is far from complete. There has been a significant development of new, interactive, media, although still with uncertain growth prospects. Perhaps teletext, generally provided free of charge and increasingly available to viewers, can be counted as the most innovative element in the European media experience, if one ignores the novelty of multiple channels and 24-hour viewing.

In general, adoption of innovations has been very much slower than predicted; this reflects not only economic circumstances but also the wide degree of popular contentment with the traditional arrangements. The biggest changes, of course, have been taking place in Eastern Europe, where old structures have been dismantled and many new commercial ventures have started up, often with the help of the media magnates of Western Europe. The results are dramatic in their local impact on public broadcasting, although in economic terms they are still marginal for the entrepreneurs.

Public service broadcasting remains, at first sight, largely intact. It is operated nearly everywhere by the same bodies and under similar terms to those that obtained under the old order. Only one public channel—TF1 in France—has been privatized, and at the other end of the spectrum we can still find a major public broadcaster—the BBC—that has successfully held out against pressures to carry commercial advertising.

Generally, public broadcasters have been fairly successful in dealing with increased competition, greatly helped by their relatively secure revenue base and other assets and privileges. They have often entered the audience market aggressively, seeking to attract large audiences by scheduling more popular programs at peak hours and copying some of the tactics of commercial broadcasters (see Siune & Truetzschler, 1992). This has been criticized as "backdoor commercialism," but there has been little alternative if the noncommercial public service goals are to be realized. Loss of the audience could mean all-around failure and loss of political support. In addition to their own efforts, barriers of language and national culture and the preference for domestic product have helped to protect many European public systems.

This picture of relative security is deceptive. It conceals a gradual erosion of public service broadcasting nearly everywhere, and in some instances a near-crisis situation (in France, Italy, and Belgium, for example). It also conceals a widespread loss of certainty about the future role for public service broadcasting in a competitive, multichannel environment. There are widespread fears for the increasing neglect of many values upheld by the older public service concept, not least because of the creeping commercialism entailed in competitive strategies (Blumler, 1992). At the same time, there is resistance by public broadcasters to becoming a cultural "ghetto," with only a symbolic and marginal task. This serves to highlight the dilemma in which public service broadcasting now finds itself.

Conclusions

Politically sponsored and technologically driven changes have not been powerful enough to destroy the old system, but they have modified it and left it vulnerable to future shifts of fortune. It is not easy to predict the future of public broadcasting, although the changes of the 1980s offer some lessons. The most important factor is political willingness to continue to sponsor and regulate broadcasting, whether for cultural, political, or economic reasons. If the will remains, then elements of the older European model will remain. Because politicians do not like to lose what they control, given the political sensitivity and utility of broadcasting, it is unlikely that broadcasting will be abandoned to the free market.

The "Europeanization" of media politics, which had brought a certain commercial "liberalization," still carries expectations of national performance and responsibility. There is still considerable nationalism in European countries that can be used to mobilize public opinion against foreign intervention, whether in the form of "Europe" (i.e., the central bureaucracy of the European Community is based in Brussels) or transnational media operators, with their foreign content and designs on the home market.

The technological environment is probably more uncertain than the political environment, yet new technologies alone are nothing without the institutional framework and public support to implement them. We are likely to see a decade of further testing of the viability and appeal of new broadcasting technologies, particularly DBS, but we may still end up with a more open, more diverse, more commercial, more populist, and more loosely regulated version of the old order. There are anxieties, particularly about the preservation of some space outside the market for other voices in society to communicate. The biggest danger lies in further surrender to the commercial imperative and in the loss of the inter- and intracountry diversity that has kept alive alternate possibilities to the monotony offered by capitalism and its market logic.

Further Questions

1. Compare the schedules of European television channels with American television schedules. Are there differences in the amount of news programming, entertainment, original drama, and so on over the course of one week?

2. The issue of "cultural identity" has been raised in Europe and in the Third World (see Mohammadi, Chapter 21). Explore the arguments made and the different solutions adopted. For whom is this a bigger issue, and why?

3. What are the benefits and the dangers of a media future dominated by such enormous cultural producers?

Note

1. This section and the one below on Henry Luce and Harry and Jack Warner are drawn from Bagdikian (1989).

10 Media in Multicultural Nations
Some Comparisons

ANDREW JAKUBOWICZ

Jakubowicz introduces two new and crucial concepts in this chapter: globalization and multiculturalism. Both terms have become a ready part of our current vocabulary, yet neither names a simple phenomenon. The phenomenon of globalization has been described as the "stretching" of social relations beyond our ordinary local lives, and the global media play a central part in that process of bringing other people's cultures and habits into our own living rooms (see the glossary for further clarification; see also Mohammadi, Chapter 21, and Sreberny-Mohammadi, Chapter 25). Such mediated encounters with other cultures may challenge our understanding of and identification with our own "nation" and encourage identification with transnational groups as well as subcultural groups.

It is the recognition of the existence of the latter, and ways of supporting minority cultural expression, that is the focus of policies of multiculturalism. Historically, different nation-states have had different orientations toward multiculturalism, depending on their media structures, on attitudes toward minority groups, and on the kinds of support available for cultural and media activities. Jakubowicz analyzes different approaches to multiculturalism and the media by examining the cases of the United States, the United Kingdom, and Australia, and how these policies can affect the very sense of nationhood in these countries.

Globalization and the Emergence of Multicultural Nations

In the last decade of the twentieth century, globalization has come to have a major impact on the politics and sociology of communication in modern nation-states. With the rapid acceleration in the movement of capital on an international scale, populations too have moved in unprecedented ways. The very idea of the "nation" has become problematized as a consequence of changes in the structure of large corporations and in the wake of the decay of the great nineteenth- and twentieth-century empires. Many large corporations have resources far greater than many nation-states, and within nations, many formed out of the breakup of the old empires and thus reflective of boundaries within those empires, ethnic communities find themselves in conflicts that have shattered the nations in which they were placed.

Many communication theorists have argued that the mass media and the communications infrastructure they utilize have been crucial in the creation of both the idea of the nation as an association of citizens with rights joined together by a common heritage and set of values and the possibility of that idea being realized. Just as newspapers and the telegraph in the nineteenth century allowed the emerging middle classes and intellectuals in many European societies to challenge the hegemonic power of autocratic rulers and imperial centers and to argue for democratic nations made up of national cultures (A. D. Smith, 1981), so radio became both an agency for the assertion of the nation and, in many places, a device to stimulate revolutionary liberation struggles against colonial rule in the early and middle parts of the twentieth century. The "imagined community" that underlies the cultural dimension of the contemporary nation owes an enormous debt to the stimulation to that imagination that radio and cinema have offered and continue to offer today (Anderson, 1983). In the contemporary world, cinema and, to a greater extent, television offer alternative imaginaries that escape the control of national governments.

For instance, in Warsaw, Poland, in June 1983, the Palace of Culture was screening *All That Jazz*, a film full of wonderful images of Park Avenue apartments, wealth, and style, an evocation of everything that was "Western" for Poles living under the "Eastern" regime in the wake of martial law and repression by the communist state. At the same time, state-run television was showing news programs of poverty, unemployment, and riots in Britain (taken off the satellite feed from the BBC or ITV news) that were scoffed at by dissident Poles as government propaganda against capitalism. West German television played a pivotal role in undermining the legitimacy of the East German regime by countering its government's political claims, but also, and more important, by revealing the consumer lifestyle that lay enticingly beyond the Berlin Wall.

One of the key dimensions of globalization lies then in the penetration of these images of desire, these attractions of the consumer lifestyle and their unfulfillable promises of mass consumption. And mass communication commodities lie at the heart of the consumer experience—televisions, radios, cassette and CD players, computers and video games become the very stuff of the new imaginary. This process of globalization does not create a single global culture, but rather challenges local identities and suggests new possibilities that existing political structures may be incapable of addressing.

As Anthony D. Smith (1990, pp. 179-180) has demonstrated, the nation is formed out of historic identities, where there is a sense of succession through generations, where there is a shared memory of key events and personages in the collective history, and where there is some sense of a common destiny on the part of those collectively sharing those experiences. National identity rests heavily on the communication and reiteration of these experiences and memories within the social collectivity to sustain the cohesion of the people and maintain the legitimacy of the state.

In the contemporary era, most nations are conglomerations of many cultural groups, with one group or coalition usually dominant, either as a consequence of previous aggressive conquest or slow migration or through the legacy of colonial decisions about administrative convenience. This suggests that within any modern nation the social order is undergoing strain from competing cultural experiences and perspectives, strains that are compounded by societies where cultural differences are reinforced or overlaid by economic and political differences.

Where a multiplicity of cultural groups exist, where there are core historical experiences or perspectives that are not shared throughout the society, we can talk of a multicultural society. The problem for the modern state then becomes how to hold together a culturally diverse society in such a way that the nation survives. Clearly there are many situations where nations are dissolving in conflict and vicious bloodshed, and where, in the gross words of the Yugoslav wars, the direction is one of "ethnic cleansing," where nation and some revised sense of a unique common culture are presented as identical. The situation has emerged in which the new nationalists argue that a multicultural nation is impossible.

Communication Policy Dilemmas 困境 in Multicultural Societies

Multicultural societies have developed across the world, particularly in the older metropolitan centers as the "empire strikes back," when residents of former colonial or quasi-colonial regions seek the economic opportunities they believe exist in the former imperial cities. Thus Britain first recruited and then sought to prevent the immigration of people from newly independent colonies in Africa, Asia, and Central America. France experienced immigration from the former colonies of Algeria, West Africa, and Indochina. Germany recruited "guestworkers" from southern Europe and then Turkey, under the illusion that the "guests" would be good enough to leave when they were no longer required by the "host" society.

In addition, colonial settler societies have evolved into complex multicultural communities, where the original colonizing powers have left their descendants, and often those of their imported slaves, but where also survive the remnants of indigenous populations, and where waves of later immigrants have arrived in the period of great industrial expansion after 1945.

Thus multicultural societies experience a number of communication flows. The dominant social order sustains its own imagined community and value system through mass media that it controls. In the main English-speaking countries discussed in this chapter, private corporations, community groups, and the state all operate electronic media, as in the cases of Australia and Great Britain, or the electronic media are either privately or communally owned, as in the United States. In all the cases examined, the state does not own any print media, most of which is concentrated in the hands of a few large multinational organizations, many with holdings in all the countries discussed.

Across the world, minority cultural groups experience a number of different situations, reflecting in the main the state ideology regarding policy in relation to both the regulation of the media and the management of minority participation in society. One extreme position decrees that minorities are denied any cultural expression, are forbidden to use their language, and are assumed to have a future incorporated into the dominant group. This position is usually described as *assimilation*. An example of such a position is found in Han Chinese policy in Tibet.

We also find situations in which minorities are given a certain freedom to express their own cultural preferences in language and behavior, but the dominant cultural institutions are not affected by these expressions. Minorities are expected to utilize "mainstream" institutions according to the cultural mores of the dominant community and to move between the two cultures, making their own accommodation as required. Minorities may establish their own communal institutions, including radio, television, and print outlets, and even community language and religious schools. This is a form of integration, and reflects a view of minority-majority relations in which the minority will gradually adapt to new social values over a period of a number of generations. This view prevailed in Australia from about 1950 until the mid-1970s, is reflected in contemporary American policy, and typifies French policy until recently.

Some multicultural societies have moved toward a position in which minority rights are articulated and protected, and in which the right to express cultural values within an overall commitment to the state as a core institution is highly valued. In such cases we find changes occurring within both the minority communities and the majority institutions, so that irrespective of cultural background the individual gains access to a similar quality of services and goods in a culturally sensitive and supportive framework. There is widespread state support for the expression of cultural difference and a sharing of cultural practices among communities where these are acceptable. Here social scientists talk of *culturally pluralist* society and social institutions. In various ways and to differing extents, Canada, Australia, and Great Britain present this picture.

The polar opposite to assimilation can be found in various forms of separate development within one nation. Here cultural collectivities develop their own institutions, and organize and manage most facets of life within their own communal boundaries. There may be territorial separation as well, so that the state becomes effectively a federation of different communities, sharing central resources and administration. The state either ostensibly guarantees certain common rights of legal, social, and economic citizenship, in the most egalitarian version of separate development (as to some extent with the Inuit in Canada and some remote Aboriginal communities in Australia), or works to suppress some groups to the benefit of others (as under apartheid in South Africa).

Patterns of Mass Media Development in Multicultural Societies

There are three main components that should be covered in any analysis of the media in multicultural societies, and there are a number of methods that can be used to get there. In simple terms, the components are (a) the ownership and organization of production, (b) the content of media and the representation of minorities and inter-group relations, and (c) the "uses" that audiences make of the media and the impacts those uses have on media production and content.

The methods that can be employed in examining these components include those drawn from radical political economy (e.g., the work of Herman & Chomsky, 1988, on the relationship between the commercial interests of media corporations and their reporting of news), from empirical organization studies (e.g., C. Cockburn, 1983, on technological change, gender relations, and the printing industry), from semiotics and cultural studies (e.g., Fiske, 1987; Seiter, 1987), from content analysis (e.g., Greenberg, 1980, in relation to life on American television dramas), from social psychology in relation to media effects on audiences (e.g., Cumberbatch & Howitt, 1989), and from ethnographic studies in relation to audience uses of media (e.g., Morley & Silverstone, 1991). In the following sections I will refer to each of the components and draw on relevant studies to demonstrate the sorts of questions that have been asked of the media in multicultural societies and the sorts of outcomes these questions have provided. I focus on three multicultural societies—the United States, the United Kingdom, and Australia—in order to explore the relationships under examination.

The United States

The United States was formed out of a number of invasions by European powers—the English in the East, the Spanish in the Southwest, and the French in the South. The descendants of the invaders fought for liberation against their own metropolitan powers, and then the ethnic minorities ∧ African, chinese, and many immigrants from other countries.

against each other, all the while seeking to subjugate the indigenous peoples. In addition, the European powers had imported African slave workers throughout the Americas. During the mid- and late nineteenth century, American capital imported workers from China to build the western railroads. In the late nineteenth and early twentieth centuries, the United States became for a period a haven of refuge for immigrants from central and eastern Europe, and then a focus for migration from southern Europe. After World War II, immigration increased from Latin America and from various parts of Asia.

By the end of the nineteenth century, the American state was actively involved in nation building, and communalizing the myriad collectivities that had settled there. The press became a crucial part of that process, beginning a tradition of supporting American imperial development in Central and South America. The press baron William Randolph Hearst was actively involved in promoting the interests of U.S. corporations in Central America, and his corporations and others sought intervention by the United States in countries such as Cuba, Nicaragua, and the Dominican Republic. One consequence of active U.S. involvement was that many residents of the new empire thus created sought refuge and opportunity on the U.S. mainland.

The concept of American or national interests depended on agreement about the constituency of the nation. Early ethnic communities had developed their own press, and strong ethnic communal cultural networks were created in cities such as New York and Chicago. However, after World War I, sentiment turned against immigrants as potential subversives and communists, with particular attacks made on the "foreign-language press," which was seen as un-American.

However, as the mainstream English-language media were unwilling to incorporate ethnic interests and did not engage at all with the needs of the Black or Native American communities, and there was no central government media involvement, minority community media continued to operate. With the advent of radio, some communities managed to gain access to outlets, but for the most part this was limited to a few big cities. It was only under rising political pressure in the 1970s that the U.S. government, through the Federal Communications Commission, allowed special provisions to be made to ease the entry of Hispanic broadcasters into a tightly Anglo marketplace (Zolf, 1989).

Thus the U.S. media environment is typified by private corporations, with ownership increasingly concentrated in fewer groups. This is as much a characteristic of ethnic communities as it is of the wider society. Zolf (1989) reports that in 1986 the Telemundo Group, which operates throughout South America and Central America, covered 57% of the TV and radio stations broadcasting in Spanish in the United States.

The content of media in the United States also reflects important structural issues in relations among cultural groups. In their review of studies on ethnic minorities and the media in the United States, Greenberg and Brand (1993) report on research spanning 20 years. They suggest that three types of approaches have been used in the study of the portrayal of ethnic minorities in the media: (a) comparison of the incidence of minorities in the media with their numbers in the wider population, (b) comparison of the significance of the roles played by minorities with the significance of those played by whites, and (c) comparison of majority and minority characters within given programs.

There is overwhelming evidence that ethnic minorities are substantially underrepresented in "entertainment programs" on American television. Where they do appear, there are many more men than women, and few appear in major roles. Latino men appear far less often than do African American men, and Native Americans almost never appear. The majority of nonwhite roles are "domestic," reflecting their concentration in situation comedies, whereas white males predominate in action/adventure programming. Nonwhites are more likely to be portrayed in lower-status jobs, to an even greater extent than their participation in the general population. When researchers have looked at where nonwhites tend to appear on television, they have discovered that the vast majority are on Black-dominated shows—particularly so in the case of Black women.

Whereas entertainment programming takes audiences into the realms of desire and imagination, news programs claim to report reality. What do they express about the multicultural reality of American society? The evidence suggests that Blacks are more likely to be shown in police custody than are whites, more likely to be presented anonymously, and less likely to be defended in the text, whereas Black politicians are presented more regularly as seeking to advance Black rather than wider community interests (Entman, 1992; cited in Greenberg & Brand, 1993).

Despite strong pressure from industry unions on broadcasters, and despite strong campaigns to encourage program executives to introduce nontraditional casting, minorities are consistently underrepresented on American television. Where they are represented, they possess significantly less power and status than do the whites on American TV. Where minorities appear, particularly those who are undifferentiated foreigners, they are very likely to be seen as villains and criminals.

Writing in 1993 for the Screen Actors Guild and the American Federation of Radio and Television Artists, veteran television researcher George Gerbner, who originated the Cultural Indicators project in 1969 at the behest of the National Commission on the Causes and Prevention of Violence, and who had undertaken wide-ranging studies of the media for a quarter of a century, was still forced to say:

> The world of television seems to be frozen in a time-warp of obsolete and damaging representations. . . . People of color, the vast majority of humankind, and estimated to reach a majority in America by the year 2000, are 13 percent of the major network prime-time and less than 5 percent of children's program casts. . . . A child viewer sees the fewest minorities. (pp. 11-12)

This overarching power of the dominant culture has had serious consequences for indigenous Americans, as can be seen in studies of Alaskan and Hawaiian media. Daley and James (1992) note in their analysis of rural Alaska as "the periphery of the periphery" that in 1970 most of the communities they studied had no television, telephones, or radio. Development took place very dramatically, so that by the end of the 1980s this situation had been reversed. In the process, Native Alaskans' attempts to develop a television service controlled by indigenous groups that could protect rural communities and cultures from the impact of sex and violence in commercial television and reflect the values of the local people was subordinated to the drive by government for technocratic efficiency and the push for product generated by the dominant culture.

Henningham (1992) sees Hawaiian Native media as suffering under the impact of political and cultural domination, in which the Hawaiian language was destroyed in the name of assimilation into the mainstream of Anglo-American society. In the period before the politics of biculturalism, government inertia and compliance with cultural suppression led to the erosion of the capacity of surviving Hawaiian communities to use their language. However, under the impact of the civil rights movement of the 1960s, an indigenous revival occurred that led to a resurgence of interest in language, supported finally by a state government institution, the Office of Hawaiian Affairs. Yet in the 1990s, domination by commercial broadcasting interests and dependency on the state limit radical Hawaiian cultural development to the use of restricted cable or public TV access. Even in the mainstream media white journalists predominate; more than 70% of print journalists are white, although whites' presence in the population at large is 25%.

The evidence suggests that in the American case, where government policy is accepting of cultural diversity and supports equal opportunity, but is reluctant to intrude into the freedoms of the media to behave as they wish, the multiculturalism of the society is not fully represented in its major communications media. This distortion may have significant implications for the capacity of the society to work effectively as a multicultural society based on mutual respect for and understanding of difference.

We turn now to the British context, where the state is more directly involved in media and has developed social institutions designed to combat discrimination, and yet where the diversity of the society also faces barriers to representation.

Great Britain

The United Kingdom is a title that embodies a useful fiction—that the various nations and communities that inhabit the British Isles form one society with shared values, traditions, and histories. For the purposes of this chapter, multiculturalism in the United Kingdom has to encompass the four nations of England, Scotland, Ireland, and Wales; a number of languages and regionalisms based on different cultures and histories, such as the people of Cornwall in the southwest; and the immigration of people from the Empire. For instance, well over 10% of the population of London is not British; in 1991, in one south London borough, interpreters were being sought who could speak Arabic (North African and Middle Eastern dialects), Bengali/Sylheti, Cantonese, Farsi, French African dialects, Greek, Kurdish Soproni dialect, Portuguese, Punjabi, Urdu, Somali, South American Spanish, Tamil, Tigrigna, Turkish, Twi, Vietnamese, Yoruba, and British Sign. The same area is also home to many people from the West Indies and their children, Black Britons.

This diversity suggests that some major policy issues are involved in relation to cultural pluralism in Britain. At the level of national integration, the relationships with Wales, Scotland, and Northern Ireland were heavily assimilationist until recently. With rising Scots and Welsh nationalism, the central government has developed policies that seek to recognize cultural differences to some extent, seeing in the acceptance of cultural pluralism the possibility of sustaining the union at the level of institutions and economy. Meanwhile, overt civil war in Northern Ireland and a culturally divided community there creates enormous problems for any clear communications and media policy, except those that prohibit public expressions by representatives of the Irish Republican Army.

Television is made up of the British Broadcasting Corporation (BBC), which is financed by license fees paid by audiences on their television sets, and the independent (or commercial) sector, which is made up of regional broadcasters linked together through the Independent Television network. The British environment is characterized by a strong "public service" orientation toward audiences in both state and private broadcasting, supported directly by and to some extent controlled by government bodies, and a diversity of privately operated press outlets that are not under government control but are industry self-regulated through the Press Council. Thus the limited access to broadcasting licenses involves the state in promoting diversity through regulation, whereas the "open market" in newspapers and magazines allows for the (often questioned) assumption that the market will deliver to specific consumers what they desire.

There has been significant research into the relationship between the British media and the issues of cultural pluralism, a relationship made more complex by a government policy on immigration that is increasingly restrictive and often described as racist and a government policy in broadcasting that in 1992 introduced the competitive market into commercial broadcasting. The commercial sector has handled the issues raised in relation to a multicultural society in two ways: through the creation of Channel Four, a national broadcaster, committed to the interests of minority groups—reflecting differences of culture, ethnicity, sexuality, age, region—and in a lesser extent through the employment of Black presenters and the occasional inclusion of Black or other minority characters.

Both Channel Four and the BBC offer programming in Welsh, and BBC local radio offers opportunities for community programs, which might be Gujerati in Leicester or Urdu in Bradford. The presence of minorities in Britain elicits a response within the media, but one that focuses on them within their differences. There is very little attempt to open up the majority of British media to reflect the multicultural society, nor is there much attempt to deflect the sustained racism of the popular tabloid press. In the wake of widespread pirate (unlicensed and illegal) community radio in the 1970s and 1980s that the government could not stop, there is now a range of government-sanctioned community controlled broadcasters, many of them Black or Asian.

Within mainstream programming, few programs incorporate ethnically diverse actors or roles. In the few more "socially aware" programs, such as the drama series *East Enders*, there are regular Black and Asian characters and story lines. However, some of the most popular TV soap operas, including shows from Australia such as *Neighbours* and *Home and Away*, are characterized by their lack of cultural diversity. In November 1993, Australian television senior manager and former London television manager Bruce Gyngell was reported in the Australian press as expressing the belief that the popularity of those programs in Britain is attributable to the fact that they reinforce British racist ideas of a white society. Yet these all-white programs can also be popular among Black and Asian communities. For example, research in the west of London among Jat Pathan (people from the Khyber Pass area of northwest Pakistan) suggests that teenagers from these communities see the open and free parent-child relations in the Australian suburbs portrayed in these programs as models for how they would like their parents to relate to them.

The most progressive engagement with multiculturalism in British media lies with the commercial Channel Four, which has specifically commissioned ethnic minority and national program makers to develop work that reflects British social diversity. Out of this investment has come features such as *My Beautiful Laundrette*, a story of cross-race homosexual love in the London suburbs. Channel Four also supports work by documentary makers such as Bandung Films and has been crucial, in conjunction with the British Film Institute, in the development of a Black British film culture, associated with such directors as Isaac Julien and John Akomphrah. Many of these films address the experience of the generation of 1981, youth caught up in the Brixton uprising and the urban clashes that set the cities of Britain alight that summer (Daniels & Gerson, 1989).

The margins address the challenge to British society from its multicultural population. The mainstream, what Dutch researcher Teun van Dijk (1991b) describes as the right-wing, press defends that sea of core values against what it sees not as a challenge but as a series of threats. The key newspapers involved include the tabloids the *Star*, the *Sun*, the *News of the World*, and the *Daily Mail* and, in a more conservative format of broadsheet, the *Times* of London (under the ownership of U.S.-based Murdoch's News Ltd., also owner of the *Sun* and *News of the World*) and the *Daily Telegraph* (owned by Conrad Black, a Canadian media mogul with interests in Australia's *Sydney Morning Herald*). Speaking of the tabloids, the National Union of Journalists' secretary has condemned them as "disgusting stuff" because of their racist headlines and stories, such as "Whites Flee School of Fear: Black Gangs Beat Us Up Say Pupils" (Black Rights [U.K.], 1988, p. 72).

Van Dijk (1991a) has argued that the racism of the right-wing press is consciously designed to sustain the subordination of ethnic minorities and to undermine the racial justice strategies of institutions such as the Council for Racial Equality (CRE). He argues that the "news report in the *Mail* may contribute to the legitimation and reproduction of anti-immigration ideologies and racism in British society" (p. 119).

If the United States reflects a media policy situation where government stands back almost completely from engagement with the media on behalf of minorities or in pursuit of a socially just multicultural society (in part as a consequence of the First Amendment to the Constitution, which guarantees free speech), and Britain reflects a policy situation where government acts on the margins but leaves the market and the industries to control the mainstream situation, Australia can be said to have developed a far more interventionist (and many would argue successful) multicultural media strategy.

Australia

Australia, with a population the size of Greater Los Angeles in a land mass about the size of the continental United States, excluding Alaska, offers a case study in planned social goals. The invasion and settlement of Australia by the British took place in 1788, about the time the United States was achieving independence from Britain, and within then living memory of the incorporation of Scotland into the union that became the United Kingdom.

The foundation myth of European Australia was that the land the British and their descendants settled belonged to no one before their arrival—it was *terra nullius*. The native peoples, now referred to as Aborigines and Torres Strait Islanders, were thought to be nomadic peoples who lived off the land but did not "own" it.

In 1992, after a decade of legal battles and 200 years of struggles by indigenous peoples for land rights, the Australian High Court ruled that native title had indeed existed on invasion day, and in many parts of Australia the title continued. Thus, at its heart, in much the same way as the United States or Canada, but very differently from Britain, Australia is a land peopled by two sorts of nations—the Aboriginal nations and the European/Asian nation formed in a federation of colonies in 1900.

Throughout the nineteenth century, Australia experienced rapid growth in non-Aboriginal population through massive immigration, from Europe and China. The Chinese migration came in the wake of the gold rushes of the 1850s and after; there were also indentured South Pacific Islanders brought to work the sugar cane fields. By the end of the nineteenth century, Australia was already a multicultural society, made up of English and Irish and Scots, Italians and Poles and Germans, Chinese and Afghans, Pacific Islanders and members of hundreds of Aboriginal tribes. The formation of the Commonwealth in 1901 produced racially focused legislation—non-European immigration was effectively banned, many of the South Pacific Islanders were repatriated, and priority given to British immigration. After World War II, the government implemented an immigration program that would bring 3 million immigrants in 50 years. Initially, the commitment was to British and Eastern and Western Europeans, but this gave way to Italians and Greeks, Turks and Lebanese. In the early 1970s the White Australia Policy was officially abandoned, and soon thereafter, with the end of the Vietnam War, thousands of Indochinese migrated, some as boat people.

During the White Australia period, government policy was firmly assimilationist. The media took little or no notice of the immigrants or of Aborigines. For the former, the major offering on radio was English-language programs, whereas the general attitude in the media was that Aborigines would die out in time, their descendants assimilating into the European population. Ethnic communities developed their own newspapers and flourishing cultural lives. The occasional commercial radio station offered programs in Italian, but government regulations required that translations be made into English.

With the late 1960s, the civil rights movements that were sweeping the Western world took hold in Australia as well. Aboriginal groups fought for recognition as citizens (achieved in only 1967), and ethnic groups developed the ethnic workers' movement and sought ethnic rights. By 1973 a progressive Labour government, the first since 1949, was elected and introduced some major changes. It abolished race as a basis for immigrant selection, reduced the waiting time for citizenship, supported the development of community-run and participative radio, granted the first Aboriginal land rights, and established the first ethnic-language radio programs. It adopted a policy of multiculturalism to replace assimilationism, committing Australia to a long-term program of cultural recognition of minorities and their integration into the mainstream of Australian life as equal participants.

By 1977, the Conservative government that followed Labour had agreed to continue with the ethnic broadcasting initiative, and established the Special Broadcasting Service (SBS) (to parallel the other national broadcaster,) the Australian Broadcasting Commission (after 1983, the Australian Broadcasting Corporation), the ABC. The SBS operated radio stations in Sydney and Melbourne, broadcasting in more than 50 languages and passing on its programs to community-controlled stations, including a number of ethnic stations, around the country (Jakubowicz, 1987, 1989).

The government then proceeded to use SBS as the vehicle for the development of what was initially ethnic but then became multicultural television. The policy as it began on radio was planned to help ethnic communities with low English skills and little access to mainstream media to understand various government programs such as health insurance, social security, and unemployment benefits. This settlement advice provided the rationale, but it developed into a commitment to the maintenance of language and culture as a policy goal. Although the effect of this was to reinforce very traditional values in the various communities, it did open up opportunities for ethnic broadcasters who had been totally excluded from the electronic media (Bell, 1993).

With television, the policy underwent a controversial transformation, to focus on nation building through the mutual understanding of diverse cultures. From the outset, all programs in languages other than English were to be subtitled in English. They were thus accessible to anyone literate in the language of the dominant culture. Although the organization was dominated by Anglo-Australian media professionals, it increasingly sought to be an "international" rather than a multicultural programmer; significant numbers of mainstream European films from countries with fairly small populations in Australia but highly valued film cultures began to appear. The aim became increasingly to show the world to Australia, so much so that the audience increasingly was made up of high-income and well-educated parts of the middle class as much as the mass of working-class immigrants (Coupe & Jakubowicz, 1993).

In the late 1980s there was considerable tension over the future of multicultural broadcasting. In 1986, the new Labour government tried to abolish SBS and amalgamate it into the ABC, an organization continually criticized by ethnic communities and Aboriginal groups for its failure to respond to its charter requirement to reflect the multicultural nature of Australian society. There was a huge political backlash from ethnic communities, and the government abandoned the idea. The attempt did, however, make it "possible" (read "necessary") for SBS to take advertising, which it has done since 1993.

The commercial television and radio sectors effectively avoided issues relating to multiculturalism. Although the ABC showed the occasional ethnic actor and its radio news programs in particular sought out "ethnic stories," the commercial sectors did almost nothing. An occasional experiment in the early 1980s with mixed language and subtitled dramas was abandoned as commercial channels all went into financial crisis in the late 1980s. The Media Alliance (the media industry trade union for actors, journalists, and so on) sought negotiations along the lines of the Guild and Equity in the United States with producers and broadcasters, to monitor and increase employment of ethnic and Aboriginal actors (Communications Law Centre, 1992). This met with no success, even though by 1994 there were two or three Aboriginal "stars" in commercial television.

The commercial electronic media had been regulated by a government agency, the Australian Broadcasting Tribunal, up until 1992. It had promulgated several guidelines prohibiting gratuitous racial vilification, and had launched some unsuccessful prosecutions against radio talk-show hosts for racist remarks. However, in late 1992 the Tribunal was abolished, replaced by the Australian Broadcasting Authority, which is modeled in part on the British Independent Television

Authority. The emphasis was to be on industry self-regulation. The first-draft industry guidelines released late in 1992 contained no reference to forbidding racism or promoting cultural pluralism. A sustained campaign by ethnic organizations and government bodies involved in multiculturalism resulted in amendments that banned racial vilification and committed the industry to the advancement of multiculturalism. Community groups continued to press the ABA for a more "proactive" policy that would ensure that the media would be reflective of the multicultural reality of Australian society. ABA and ABC reports and independent studies had demonstrated deeply entrenched racist stereotypes and the exclusion of Aborigines and immigrants from much of the Australian media (Australian Broadcasting Corporation, 1992; Bostock, 1993; Jakubowicz, 1994; Meadows, 1992; Nugent, Loncar, & Aisbett, 1993). However, the commercial channels resisted what they saw as demands for social engineering, and the ABA, still feeling its way in the deregulatory environment, was reluctant to intrude into the difficult territory of self-regulation on issues as controversial as ethnicity and race.

The Aboriginal involvement in Australian media reflects the three dimensions of media analysis. Aborigines have been involved in struggles with the media over negative and stereotypical representation (usually as violent, drunk, or dangerous); with media bureaucracies over their reluctance to employ Aborigines, particularly in creative roles (Langton, 1993); and with the wider communications environment as they have sought to bypass Anglo-Australian-controlled media through the creation of their own media for their own audiences (Meadows, 1992). In the last case, Aborigines in 1992 formed the National Indigenous Media Association, made up of broadcasters and journalists from community stations around the country, independent video production groups, Aborigines working in SBS and ABC, and people operating the BRACS program, a remote area scheme in which local communities control the distribution of signals from commercial broadcasters. (The main TV broadcast license for central Australia is also owned by a company with majority Aboriginal control.)

The Aboriginal experiences demonstrate how much the pattern of media production and distribution are the outcomes of political struggles to advance voices marginalized in the dominant media discourses. Even in a society where the espoused policy of government is that of multiculturalism, the pressure to ensure that the pluralism that exists in fact is heard and seen in practice has to be sustained.

Conclusion

The development of multicultural societies is not a recent phenomenon, but the extent and complexity that they now exhibit present major challenges for state policies concerned with creating and sustaining national cohesion. Mass media play a crucial role in this process of dreaming up the nation, and thus governments cannot avoid coming to terms with how communications policies affect their wider social goals. This chapter has explored three historically situated approaches to this issue, using the United States, the United Kingdom, and Australia as examples.

Despite its diversity and size, the United States has taken a pathway that is least effective in relation to multicultural outcomes. Despite decades of debate and argument, the increasing diversity of U.S. society has not intruded into the mainstream of American media in anything like its real-world scale, particularly in relation to smaller minorities. In the United Kingdom the focus has been on individual rights, and there has been a fundamental reticence by government to back agencies such as the CRE in moving the media into more active and positive engagement with minority groups. In the Australian context, the success of SBS as a separate development model has been seen by many as an opportunity for the Anglo-Australian media to justify their neglect of cultural pluralism.

In each of these countries, the press has been the most difficult area for government. The United States, in part because of its population density, has a diversity of newspapers and magazines serving minority communities (though in some areas, such as East Los Angeles, these communities are the majority). However, the impacts of minorities outside their own communities have been limited, with the press of the dominant culture still overwhelmingly employing its own people and telling its own stories. A similar picture holds in the United Kingdom, where the Press Council, a voluntary industry body, has little real effect on the racist discourses that litter the tabloid right-wing press. In Australia, a Press Council modeled on the British approach has shown a great deal of concern about freedom of the press to publish untrammeled by government interference, but has been reluctant to agree with Aboriginal or ethnic complaints against press accounts.

I would conclude, then, by noting that the media involvement in the processing of the narratives of the nation has extremely important wider social consequences. This relationship can be fashioned to have more socially just outcomes if the state is prepared to adopt clear policies that seek to create the conditions for cross-cultural communication and social justice. Where governments avoid these issues or allow for de facto separate development, the broader goals of social cohesion can face a major threat.

Further Questions

1. Map the ethnic and religious diversity of your locality and then map the diversity of the media channels available in that location. Who speaks and who is silent? Who views which channels? That is, is there any ethnic crossover in viewing habits and tastes?

2. With the rise of global communications as well as more local alternative cultural production, what is the future of national culture and nation-states? Is there an American or British or any other national culture? How is it manifest? Whose culture is it?

11 Media, Dictatorship, and the Reemergence of "Civil Society"

JOHN DOWNING

This chapter addresses the following question: What are the roles of media during the period of transition into a dictatorship, during a dictatorship, and in the transition toward a more democratic regime? The examples of media examined so far in this volume come mostly from the United States and similar political systems that, although some fall short of full, strong democracy, nonetheless are not dictatorships. Because it is generally agreed that a vigorous media system is essential to a democracy that is one in deed, not merely in name, it is vital to understand the potential roles of media during a descent into dictatorship, while under its heel, and in the process of dislodging it and re-creating what is sometimes called "civil society." What follows, then, consists of lessons of both warning and hope.

The example employed is the period of Communist rule in Russia from late 1917 to the early 1990s. This was one of the longest-lasting dictatorial regimes in the twentieth century, and so poses the most questions and offers the most facets for examination. Many of its media mechanisms have been seen elsewhere, justified sometimes in the name of anticommunism (e.g., Argentina, 1976-1983; Chile, 1973-1989; Indonesia, 1965 to the time of this writing) or of Christianity (e.g., the white supremacist regime in South Africa, 1948-1994) or of Islam (e.g., Iran, 1980 to the time of this writing). The Fascist regimes of Nazi Germany (1933-1945), Mussolini's Italy (1922-1944), Franco's Spain (1939-1976), and Salazar's Portugal (1926-1974) also employed many similar media policies.

Many people in the West used to assume confidently that they understood the Soviet media system. They saw it quite simply as the readiest illustration of a top-heavy government media monopoly that could manage to produce only boring propaganda. It was a convenient example that by contrast appeared to define the virtues of the U.S. system; supposedly, politics out, free enterprise in, everyone's happy.

In this chapter Downing attempts to describe how this dictatorial media system emerged and changed in character during the decades following the 1917 Bolshevik revolution. His analysis challenges the common assumption that Soviet media were frozen in a pattern begun abruptly in 1917 through to the arrival of Gorbachev as Soviet leader in 1985 and the beginnings of glasnost. Actually, the clampdown of Stalin's dictatorship took 21 years from the 1917 revolution to be complete, and the roots of Gorbachev's glasnost policies lay in the late 1950s. Downing also discusses how alternative underground media (samizdat) operated in Soviet Russia and in Soviet-controlled Poland, and the part these media played in the breakup of the Soviet bloc and the Soviet system itself.

It is important to recall that Soviet media were originally conceived according to yet another normative media theory, namely, that media exist for the purpose of developing political awareness and commitment to work for a just and fair society, that is, a socialist philosophy. One of the tragedies of the twentieth century is the process by which those ideals became perverted into their absolute opposite under the Stalin regime and at the hands of his successors at the helm of the Soviet state.

We should note that the socialist normative theory of the media in its original form was designed to avoid the tilt of free-market media toward the capitalist class, and to give voice to ordinary working men and women in their desire for a better world. It was thought that the most effective role of socialist media was either to help organize revolutionary activists, in the case of the Marxist party newspaper, or to mobilize the general public, in the case of other, more mass-based *media. There was never any wish or expectation that these media would depend upon advertising revenues, although for a while after 1917 some of them accepted advertisements. Politics was always the priority.*

To some degree, the philosophy of development media operated for quite a time as a cousin to this original perspective. The needs of nations in the Southern Hemisphere for effective communication about infant hygiene, literacy, nutrition, and agricultural techniques make media potentially valuable sources of information, perhaps marking the difference between life and death. If they fulfill this role, who could object? Yet, just as socialist media became instruments of uncontrolled state power, so too may "development" media. Who aside from the state elite has the right to define what is socialist media policy, or what is development media policy? That is a crucial question to consider, and yet the original media objectives cannot simply be junked because there are no easy answers.

This chapter sets out to convey four issues: (a) the basic history and character of media during the period of Soviet rule, (b) the way dictatorship began to operate piece by piece in and through the media system, (c) the "feel" of a dictatorial media system, and (d) the way some alternative media were used gradually to re-create "civil society." The beginning of wisdom in understanding media and dictatorship is to recognize that Soviet daily life was made up of the usual range of normal everyday activities, from working for a living to using the transport system, to spending time exposed to media, to falling in love. Although many such activities were framed differently in the Soviet Union compared with the United States, it was not "another planet."

An Outline History of the Soviet Media System to 1985

To understand some of the basic features of Soviet media in their heyday (Kagarlitsky, 1988; Remington, 1988) it is necessary to go back to the period before the 1917 revolution, when the founders of Soviet Communism were revolutionaries living mostly in hiding, banned not only in Russia but from many other countries as well. Russia was not a democracy then either; it knew only a few months of rather chaotic and limited wartime democracy in 1917 between the overthrow of the czars and the Bolshevik revolution. It was a heavily militarized, centralized government run by hereditary emperor-kings, the czars.

There were some who dreamed of replacing the czarist regime, not with one just a little more open, but with a dynamic new society where farmer and worker, thinker and government official would unite to break down privilege forever. One such group, a rather tiny one, were the so-called Bolsheviks.[1]

Under the czars, despite occasional letups, selling an opposition newspaper openly was to invite police raids on the press, the seizure of lists of activists, and their arrest and imprisonment. The Bolsheviks argued that only a secretive, tightly disciplined organization had any chance of survival. We must, argued Lenin, have our act together even better than the czar's secret police. The party newspaper, circulating underground, was the voice of the Bolshevik leadership: If the leaders voted to establish a policy, the paper would publish it and develop it—but not question it. It was out of this situation, then, that the Bolsheviks developed what became the hallmark of their media system, the tight relationship between the Communist Party and the media (although it is also true that for political parties to run newspapers directly was much more common then—today the art is for parties to try to manipulate favorable TV coverage).

The other early component of the Soviet media system was the Bolsheviks' view that media exist for the purpose of mobilizing the public for revolution. Before 1917, this meant they focused on the damage done under czarism and capitalism, and what might be done to overthrow both. During the war, in addressing often starving soldiers, workers, and farmers, they called for bread, peace, and land. Afterward, the media focused on defending the revolution, especially during the desperate years of the civil war, 1918-1920, and on the vision of creating a new type of human being appropriate for the new Communist era. Clearly, this was a radically different set of objectives to those typical of Western media—a socialist normative media theory rather than a free-market philosophy.

Once the Bolsheviks had seized power in 1917, they were faced within a few months with civil war, which at its height stretched over three fronts totaling 5,000 miles. Their opponents were armed by 14 Western nations, whereas their own resources had to come from inside the country, itself devastated after the 1914-1918 world war.

To begin with, most other political parties were allowed to publish their papers, even when they spoke out against the Bolshevik government's policies. However, not long after the civil war began, non-Bolshevik media were suppressed. Other nations at war have taken similar actions against the media and free expression, but the crucial difference here was that after the war the previous media were never restored.

Similarly, with disastrous implications for the future of open expression, after the civil war the Communist Party banned organized factions within its ranks. With the Communist Party by then the only legal political organization, people were denied the right to set up factions—semiparties—inside it that could push for varying policies and keep debate alive. For those who think Communists always had a uniform set of beliefs and therefore would have nothing to debate anyway, it comes as a major surprise to read about the fierce quarrels within the Soviet Communist Party during the 1920s concerning how best to develop the country's economy, whether slowly and cautiously or in an all-out rush. The ban on factions, therefore, sought to stop these disagreements from going fully public and thus from diluting the Party's capacity to speak with a single authoritative voice in a country where the majority regarded it with suspicion, and many with resentment.

Despite this, all the way through to the late 1920s there was an extraordinary blossoming of inventiveness and imagination in certain Soviet media, especially in film, photography, poster art, theater, poetry, literature, and the arts in general (Gleason, Kenez, & Stites, 1985). Some of the most advanced artistic work in Europe took place in the Soviet Union during those years. Some of it was very much public art, like the famous agit-trains—trains painted with portraits of revolutionary soldiers, workers, and farmers, and with Bolshevik slogans on them, that traveled through remote regions and thus communicated to distant areas and to the very large number of illiterate citizens the fact that there was a new and revolutionary government. Film and photography, generally despised as low culture by elites elsewhere, were encouraged in the USSR in part because of their mass appeal. Some of the works produced, however, were very much in the forefront of experimental and abstract art, with little or no such appeal.

It was during the 1920s that Stalin and his apparatus of clones were gradually establishing their extensive control over Soviet society. It would not be until 1938 that this control could be defined as total, but in the process of establishing it, the public sphere for debate—and therefore for open media and artistic expression—shrank to the vanishing point. Then, expression of alternative views, even painting in disapproved styles (such as abstract art), became not just disregarded by the public, but an activity for which one could be imprisoned and perhaps die in a labor camp. At the height of the Stalin era the great poet Anna Akhmatova committed to memory her long poem *Requiem*, which dealt with Stalin's repressions, and then had various friends memorize sections of it, so that the political police would never be able to find it written down.

Miserably, this straitjacketing process took place in the name of socialism and justice, not of the dictatorship that it actually was. Lenin's corpse was embalmed in 1924, and the regime began citing his phrases to sanctify each new turn of policy, rather in the way some people will quote little gobbets from religious texts to justify whatever they wish to do. It was an ironic as well as a tragic development, given that Lenin had spent his entire political career in heated debate with one or another political adversary, and had quite often been outvoted in the Bolshevik Party even after 1917.

This process of shrinking the public sphere and the right to public debate, it is important to understand, did not take place overnight. It was a piecemeal development that came about over more than 10 years. Each new restriction was justified in the name of a higher cause, whether defense against another Western invasion, the need to develop the country's industry as fast as possible so as to improve living standards, or—to the Party faithful—the need to protect the Party's prestige. It happened slowly, so there was never one moment when the people could wake up, be universally and instantaneously horrified, and mobilize quickly against the attempt to crush free expression.

In particular, the more open-minded wing of the Communist Party, led by Nikolai Bukharin, was very well represented among top media professionals. It was not until Bukharin was maneuvered out of the leadership by Stalin at the end of the 1920s, and his followers rapidly replaced in editorial offices, that the media came under Stalinist control. In 1938 Bukharin was executed, having first gotten his young wife secretly to commit to memory a statement denying the absurd charges of spying trumped up against him. This case, like the story of Akhmatova's poem related above, is reminiscent of the "culture of fear" found at certain periods in Argentina or El Salvador (see O'Connor & Downing, Chapter 1).

Many dictatorships are too busy establishing control overall and consolidating their power to bring in an immediate absolute blanket on media expression. One result is that many people wait to protest until it really is too late to change the direction of events.

The resulting Soviet media were indeed leaden, doctrinaire, given to effusive praise of Stalin and his favorites, and totally silent about the crushing grip of the secret police on the nation. You could have read Soviet media in the early 1930s, when literally millions of farmers were run out of their homes and deported with only the clothes they were wearing to the frozen north or far east, and many children and elderly people died in the process, and all you would have read would be accounts celebrating the exciting new organization of agriculture that was putting the Soviet Union at the forefront of the world.

At the same time, it is important to understand not only the role of censorship in squelching the truth, but also how a dictatorial regime, through its media, can actually stimulate some people to support what it is doing, not just frighten them or misinform them. How can this be?

First, there is no doubt that there was passionate enthusiasm for the regime's policies among a minority of Russians, especially young, educated city dwellers, both in the earliest phase of the revolution and from the end of the 1920s. Those who were committed really did feel that they were on the cutting edge of human history and world development—a frequent conviction of energetic youth—and that on their efforts and policies hung the successful future of the planet, leaving the miseries of earlier generations behind for good. One such was a young military engineer, Pyotr Grigorenko, later a famous dissident, whose heart swelled with pride when his technical expertise enabled him to blow up the ancient cathedral in Minsk without harming any surrounding buildings and with no loss of life. Another was Lev Kopelev, also a famous dissident and later to be jailed for many years, who went out to the countryside in 1930 with his comrades in a surge of political enthusiasm on a mission to clear out the reactionary farmers who—according to Soviet media at the time—were blocking their poorer fellow villagers' heartfelt desire to farm cooperatively.

For such as these—and sadly, these were decent and well-meaning people—Soviet media were generally convincing. We may wonder how this was possible, but if so, we need to step back and perhaps compare that mentality with passionately held attitudes elsewhere. One of the reasons, for instance, that nuclear bomb testing in Utah through the

1950s and 1960s received few complaints was that Mormon beliefs— very widely held in that state—encourage intense patriotism and trust in the government (see Ball, 1986; C. Gallagher, 1993, pp. xxvi-xxxi). Utah residents were consequently easily convinced that, for instance, the desert sun was more dangerous than the bomb. Women accepted claims that their "neurosis" about radiation was more likely to lead to cancer than was radiation itself.

In Britain, we might compare the frenzy of patriotism that was so rapidly mobilized in 1982 in favor of war with Argentina over some tiny South Atlantic islands (the Malvinas/Falkland Islands) that 98% of the public could not have found on a map before the crisis broke. Or the public anger over the 1993 film *In the Name of the Father*, which told the attested story of a group of Irish men, women, and children jailed, in some cases for 15 years, for a bombing they did not do or support, and of the police conspiracy to put them and keep them in jail. Unfortunately, some people—sometimes many—junk their ability to think critically and substitute the fake clarity and comfort of knee-jerk patriotism or "law-and-order" absolutism.

A second reason for loyalty and belief in Soviet media was as follows. A paradoxical advantage to the Soviet leadership of the Nazi invasion of 1941-1944 was that it confirmed the traditional Russian fear of being invaded and conquered. This fear was based on a real enough history, and when brought into the here-and-now with the 20 million or more Soviet citizens who died in World War II, and the decades of nuclear war threat that followed, the determination of the Soviet regime to be militarily strong and defend Mother Russia struck a deep nationalist chord that had little to do with Communism, but much to do with being Russian. A result often was that Russians totally distrusted their media when they trumpeted domestic economic progress (this they could dispute from direct experience), but would entirely believe them when they warned of external threats from the United States or Germany. We shall see below how this response began to crumble during the later 1980s, though it has still by no means disappeared.

Stalin died in 1953, and some small media changes began to be evident from 1954, with larger ones in 1956-1957. This period is often referred to as the "thaw." The premiership of Khrushchev in 1956-1964 saw the publication of some novels quite sharply critical of the Stalin era, such as Solzhenitsyn's famous *One Day in the Life of Ivan Denisovich*. Remember, novels that dealt in any fashion with the terrible atrocities of the Stalin era were not pulp spectaculars that people read to take their minds off things, but stories of recent suffering and political repression that were being allowed into public debate for the first time. Also remember that Russian culture has always promoted great respect for literature, and that by the early 1960s literacy rates in the Soviet Union were high. These novels' impact was enormous.

Certain publications, such as *Izvestiya* (the *News*), the main government daily, and the monthly literary magazine *Novy Mir* (*New World*), which serialized Solzhenitsyn and other critical voices, enjoyed Khrushchev's special patronage and acted as his mouthpieces in the struggles he had with Stalin's old guard. After Khrushchev was ousted in 1964, there was a landmark trial the following year of two writers named Sinyavsky and Daniel, who received long jail terms for writing critically for publication outside the USSR. This trial signaled the end of Khrushchev's thaw.

In 1968, major waves of political protest in neighboring Czechoslovakia and Poland, also Soviet bloc regimes, panicked the leadership into a systematic clampdown, and many critical writers began to be sent to jail or psychiatric wards. Only at the very end of the Brezhnev era, in the early 1980s, as a result of the gradual unwinding of the whole Soviet system, did critical voices begin to reassert themselves in any official media.

At the close of this chapter I will take up the story again from this point, namely, the reemergence of civil society and glasnost, and the transition to the contemporary Russian media system. However, to understand how that transition occurred, we need first to get a clearer picture of the Stalinist media system as a whole, and then to appreciate the slow-fuse operation of alternative media within it. Let us take each of these in turn.

Basic Aspects of Soviet Media Before the 1991 Transition

ORGANIZATION

Before anything else, the basic relation of the Communist Party to government and media has to be understood. The Communist Party in a Soviet-style society was not comparable to a conventional political party in the West. In the United States, for example, although both major parties have their devotees, the party organizations are primarily machines for getting presidential candidates, congressional representatives, governors, and mayors elected.

The Communist Party of the Soviet Union (CPSU), by contrast, was the sole political party. In theory, it contained within its ranks the cream of the Soviet working class, farmers, and thinkers. In practice, joining was often a necessary career move for promotion to high office, rather than an act of political commitment. The CPSU considered itself uniquely qualified to act as the leading institution in the nation's life, to propose policy to government that it was then the government's responsibility to legislate. It prodded compliance with its priorities through the network of Party cells organized in virtually every factory, farm, office, media institution, and school in the land. From a few years after the revolution, the CPSU developed a list (the *nomenklatura*) of appropriate individuals for high office in the Party or the state, rather like a directory of the Soviet power structure. The Party's ability to use this list, to handpick those it approved and to exclude those it disapproved, was perhaps the single greatest mechanism of its power—along with individuals' eagerness to be on the list.

Thus official media were all directly under the control of the government, with Party cells inside them, or under the Party's immediate control, as was *Pravda*. Radio and television were government run, with the State Committee for Radio and Television (Gosteleradio) formally in charge of their operation. All of the 100,000 or more journalists (as of 1989) were licensed through the Union of Journalists.

Until the Gorbachev era, there were three bodies specifically charged with operating media control. One was the Chief Board for the Preservation of State Secrets in the Press, known as Glavlit, which was the official censorship body, exercising both pre- and postpublication censorship. The second was more strategic, namely, the Propaganda Department of the CPSU Central Committee, whose task was to set out the fundamental guidelines that editors were to observe. The third was the State Security Committee (KGB), whose role enabled greater flexibility and promptness in dealing with problems than either of the other two. It could simply send its agents to editorial offices or call in editorial staff to account for their actions. From 1985 onward, all these agencies began to have smaller and smaller roles.

These, then, were the "gatekeepers" of the Soviet media system. However, the frequency with which they intervened in the media should not be overestimated. The chief way in which control was exerted was for journalists to censor themselves. Self-censorship is, as we saw in Chapter 7, a very widespread phenomenon. Its ultimate form in the USSR was to be seen in the person who opted not to become a journalist at all, because of the hopelessness of that position in such a situation. Journalism was not a respected profession. After 1985, however, with the glasnost era, it began to become much more so.

THE PARALLEL OFFICIAL COMMUNICATION SYSTEM

One feature of the Soviet system that differentiated it from other dictatorial media systems was its enormous lecture-circuit program. People in factories and offices, whether Party members or not, were required to attend political lectures and discussions every month in their workplaces, sometimes at the beginning of a shift, sometimes during the lunch break. The numbers varied from period to period. The lectures, usually 15-20 minutes in length, might be organized by the Party; by the so-called Knowledge Society, whose aim was to promote atheism; the national civil defense association; or the labor unions. The so-called Houses Of Culture (we might say Cultural Centers) were another location where lecture programs were frequent.

This system was used at certain points in time to communicate on topics not dealt with in the media. Most often, however, it was used for reinforcement, rather like the huge slogans attached to the sides of major buildings, such as "Communism Will Win" or "Forward With the Party." Some analysts have suggested that these constant reiterations were not delivered in the expectation of convincing people of their truth, but rather to remind them that they could not evade the regime and its priorities. Even if this is the case, it is important to note that people's overt alienation at having to attend these lectures was growing quickly throughout the 1980s.

READERS' LETTERS

No description of Soviet media would be complete without some mention of the importance of readers' letters to various publications. At *Pravda* alone there were 45 full-time staff members to handle readers' letters. The volume of mail received has been estimated at twice that received by U.S. newspapers. The process of selection for publication was shrouded in some mystery, but some surprisingly frank accounts of everyday problems and miseries were regularly printed. Those who wrote were overwhelmingly older people, and many more industrial workers or farmers than professionals or intellectuals. The rule was that every letter was to be answered, at least in some fashion.

Contrary to many people's beliefs that public criticism was totally banned in the Soviet Union, the opening of readers' letters was always quite widely used, though never, of course, to express total opposition to the regime. There were certain conventions in force, so that what was criticized was apparently a problem in just one factory or in just one city agency, not a problem with the system as a whole. Nonetheless, readers were likely to feel some resonance with their own experiences, and thus the institution did succeed in airing frequent grievances. Sometimes reporters were sent on special assignment to investigate particular letters, and major feature articles would appear. Soon afterward, the media would announce that the offenders had been disciplined or fired, a seeming sign that the regime was vigilant in guarding against abuses. Readers' letters, then, functioned as both a safety valve for the public and an early warning system for the Soviet authorities.

However, I should also note that the letters section of the newspaper had the lowest prestige of any department. Student journalists doing internships were often sent to the letters department, and usually complained bitterly about the assignment. In the initial years of the Gorbachev era, the use of the letters pages became even more widespread. When, however, the new Congress of Deputies was set up in 1988, letter writers began to send their communications directly to the deputies rather than to the press.

COMMUNICATION TECHNOLOGIES

The use of new technologies for media transmission in the Soviet Union deserves some mention. The expansion of television, to which great attention was given ever since the early 1960s, was made possible through the use of satellites (Downing, 1985). The costs of extending television service to the whole country by building booster relay stations would have been stupendous, so the development of satellite transmission was of the greatest importance. As a result, bored military conscripts in far-flung regions and sailors on icebreaker ships in the Arctic were no longer cut off from national TV. Likewise, *Pravda* was printed via satellite facsimile simultaneously across the country's 11 time zones.

Television (and film, when it was a new medium) was always a favored medium within the Soviet leadership, because it reproduced identical messages everywhere. There was no chance of variation or omission, as was always possible in the case of stage plays or even standard Communist Party lectures. Furthermore, television is a one-way medium: People might talk at the set, but it does not listen.

Other communication technologies were slower to take off. Personal telephones were very rare by comparison with the United States, and both switches and lines were of low quality. Telephones were mostly in government and industrial offices, and were used for relaying or receiving orders from above, not for chats between private individuals. Personal computers were very seldom in individual hands, with printers and modems hardly ever to be found outside official institutions. Photocopying machines were licensed by the state; individuals could not own them, and access to them was strictly controlled. Even typewriters were registered.

WHAT DID SOVIET MEDIA LOOK LIKE?

With a vast range of weekly and monthly magazines covering sports, science, ecology, literature of all kinds from the intense to the trivial, international current affairs, history, wildlife, architecture, fashion, and hobbies, it is hard to generalize accurately about Soviet print media. In 1989 there were about 8,000 daily newspapers in the Soviet Union, amounting to about 170 million copies a year, and another nearly 8,000 weeklies. All were subsidized, and so copies were very inexpensive. Admittedly, girlie magazines, violent and lurid comic strips, and trade magazines on fast-food franchises and endless other money-making projects were not available, so some of the variety to which Westerners are accustomed was missing.

Another difference between U.S. and Soviet media was that most Soviet newspapers had only four to six pages and hardly any advertisements. Also, with no commercials, there were four program channels for television and four for radio (though this small number was normal for Europe at that period). Only in the western, most highly populated, part of the country could all four TV channels be received, and even then only in certain regions. One of the channels was educational; another's programming was more regionally based.

The types of shots, editing cuts, and camera angles in Soviet film and television were often different from those common in Western visual media. Although some now-familiar devices were actually pioneered in the early Soviet Union—the split screen, for instance—the legacy of the Stalin era weighed heavily upon visual media as upon other areas of social life. The tradition of what was called "socialist realism" in art, which under Stalin was the only artistic style permitted, was long-lived. The typical socialist realist painting showed the good guys looking healthy, strong, purposeful, and smiling, and the bad guys looking perverted and loathsome, not unlike the white-hatted and black-hatted cowboys in many American westerns.

The suspenseful, fast-cutting, quick-paced style of most U.S. films and TV movies very gradually found its way onto Soviet screens during the 1980s. The use of young women's sexual allure as a major component of filmmaking began to surface only in the late 1980s. By the end of the 1980s, some TV programs were beginning to reflect the fast pace of TV formats in the West, and, indeed, explicit sex scenes seemed to become for a while almost a required element in new movies.

FILM

Movies have always been an important aspect of Soviet mass communication. Lenin defined cinema as "the most important art" because of its dramatic potential, its wide distribution capacity, and its uniformity of message across all copies. Some Soviet directors, such as Sergei Eisenstein, have been among the leading influences in world cinema. As well as documentaries of all kinds, the Soviet Union produced about 240 feature films a year. The majority came from the big studios in Leningrad and Moscow, but each of the 15 republics that made up the Soviet Union had its own studio. Interestingly, some of the smaller republics, such as Georgia in the south, managed to produce more original films than the leading centers. The contents of feature films fell into the following categories: contemporary, historical and about the revolution, World War II, historical/biographical, adaptations from literature, adventure, comedy, and musical.

Films about the "Great Patriotic War" (World War II) were made constantly after 1945. They reflected the horrifying wound dealt to Soviet society by the Nazi invasion. (The Americans, British, and Western Allies together lost fewer than 2 million.) This wound, as noted above, was utilized skillfully by the regime for decades to heighten public anxiety about the West's militarism, and so to help unify people around itself. (The Cold War paid off politically for the regimes of both superpowers.)

World War II films were as frequent in the Soviet Union as western adventure movies used to be in the United States, or as police series are today. All kept alive major cultural myths for their respective societies.

AUDIENCES

From the late 1960s, it became increasingly common in the Soviet Union to conduct opinion polls, including audience and readership surveys. As a result, we have come to know much more than we once did about Soviet preferences and habits in using media (Mickiewicz, 1981). Indeed, some surveys quickly showed that Soviet TV was rather ineffective in getting out its intended political messages. After the Gorbachev era, methods of systematic opinion polling were introduced to some degree in Russian media and elsewhere, although often the procedures were less rigorously followed than they should have been to guarantee reliable results. Other surveys indicated that the Soviet audience had a strong appetite for international news. Movies and musical variety shows appealed most of all. Sports programs and nature documentaries were also very popular. By contrast, programs about industry, poetry readings, and news analysis were well down the list of preferences. Adventure, comedy, musical, and World War II movies topped movie audiences' preference ratings.

However, as the decades lengthened away from World War II, as nuclear war did not materialize, as the majority of citizens were no longer illiterate or semiliterate inhabitants of remote villages, the public—especially the younger members of the public—began to be more and more alienated by official media. A litmus test of the change in audience attitudes was the way that increasing numbers of young people, the beneficiaries of these changes, began to express their chronic boredom with the mass of World War II movie spectaculars. This growing skepticism among the young, also expressed in their rock music preferences, their dress, and their graffiti, was the surest sign that the future was in the process of being lost to Soviet media. And beyond them, to the *nomenklatura*.

The Slow Fuse of Alternative Media and the Growth of Civil Society

Before Khrushchev, no one expected to be able to publish critical thoughts, and thus many writings were "for the drawer," as the expression went—typescripts hidden in drawers by authors in the hope that one day things would change and they could be published. Following the Brezhnev era clampdown, however, an alternative public sphere developed underground among writers who otherwise would have expressed themselves more publicly: the unofficial circulation of typescript books, poems, articles, and plays. This began before photocopying, so sheets of carbon paper were interleaved between sheets of typing paper to produce multiple copies. The further down the sheets were from the typewriter keys, the more blurred the text; furthermore, there were no margins, no graphics, no pictures. These were not good-looking documents, but they were in exceptionally high demand. The convention was that if you got to read one, you agreed to type more copies for further distribution. This was "self-published" (which is what the word *samizdat* means), as opposed to government-published under censorship.

The penalties for passing on samizdat publications were severe, though they no longer meant execution, which might easily have been the case in the Stalin era. Technically, making up to nine copies was legal, but in practice other laws were used to send those involved with samizdat to jail. Not only writing was circulated in this way, but also audiocassettes of songs (called *magnitizdat*) that sometimes directly, sometimes covertly, challenged the inherited political order. Some very famous writers and singers circulated their work in this way (G. S. Smith, 1984). Other people had books published by Soviet emigré presses in Paris and elsewhere, and then smuggled back into the Soviet Union. The videocassette recorder took this process an interesting stage further.

The contents of samizdat media varied considerably. Some were direct attacks on the Soviet regime, some were attempts to reform it; some were novels, short stories, and plays; some were religious (because religious expression was barely permitted); and some expressed the desire for national independence by one of the nations, such as Ukraine or Georgia, originally conquered by the Russian Empire and then "inherited" by the Soviet government in 1917.

The most impressive samizdat publications were in Poland rather than in Russia. Especially from 1976 onward, properly bound books and regularly appearing, well-printed magazines, in very considerable numbers, marked the Polish alternative public sphere. This was in large part a result of the rapid growth from 1980 of the political movement known as Solidarity. Step by step, Solidarity hacked out more space in Polish life. Initially, someone might put a samizdat book on a shelf at home, rather than hide it away out of fear that it might be seen by an informer or during a police visit. Later, someone might go openly to an apartment where such publications were sold, instead of secretively borrowing a copy from a friend. Finally, individuals would openly read samizdat works on the bus or the train, or in another public place. Even after Solidarity was banned and martial law was declared in December 1981, a flood of samizdat publications still continued to circulate. Increasingly, the situation in Poland both encouraged Russian dissidents and intimidated and nonplused the loyal members of the Soviet *nomenklatura*.

The picture of alternative media would not be complete without reference to foreign radio stations that broadcast into the Soviet bloc (Shanor, 1985), of which there were quite a number, from the relatively dispassionate BBC World Service, Voice of America, and Deutsche Welle to the much more truculent Radio Liberty (for the USSR) and Radio Free Europe (for East Central Europe). Sometimes their transmissions were jammed, so that it was virtually impossible to hear them in these countries. Sometimes vicious infighting about political priorities convulsed their internal organization, as departments became colonized by exponents of one or other viewpoint. But at their best, they amplified samizdat publications by rebroadcasting their contents to much wider audiences than might otherwise have had access to them. And they provided news about world events and alternative information about the Soviet bloc that was otherwise unavailable.

Thus, even though the circulation of samizdat works was relatively small (Medvedev, 1984), the creative development of alternative media was very important in the Soviet media situation. We see here a dismal paradox: Soviet media, themselves alternative media before the revolution, eventually sparked alternative media of their own. Kagarlitsky (1988) makes the important point that samizdat media were part of the long Russian tradition of dissident intellectual communication from the days of the czars' censorship, and thus retained a potency within that culture that dissident views rarely achieve in the West. Condee and Padunov (1989) provide an absorbing account of how developments in Moscow's semiofficial theater also began to pave the way for glasnost.

Other everyday responses to a media system that failed to give information on key issues, or that wrapped it up in officialese, include the following. Rumor, word-of-mouth communication, became a key alternative information source. This is very unusual in a more open media situation, though those who know from working in them how rumor works in bureaucracies may have pause to reflect at this point on the role of bureaucracy in our lives. Telling political jokes against the regime also became a major art form. One favorite Polish story had the economics minister buying an American computer, a Polish computer, and a Soviet computer. He asked each one to tell him why there were meat shortages in Poland. The U.S. computer flashed up on the screen, "Please define shortage." The Polish computer requested, "Define meat." The Soviet computer flashed, "What is your name and identity number? Show your permission to seek this information!" Graffiti, too, expressed the frustration of young people with official youth culture, and their longing for access to the latest in Western rock music (Bushnell, 1989). Quite often graffiti were in English, a way of disputing the Soviet elite's claim that Russian popular music was all young Russians needed.

Such cultural responses are well known from many different countries as grassroots reactions to highly controlled media systems. In their different ways, jokes, graffiti, samizdat, and foreign radio stations all played a part in the painfully slow development of a public sphere of dialogue and self-expression—in other words, civil society—that it became harder and harder for the regime to squelch or answer. One of reformer Gorbachev's prime aims upon assuming the reins of power in 1985 was precisely to overcome the huge gulf between what was pronounced officially in public and what citizens said about the country in private, including the very officials who earlier the same day might have been extolling the wonders of the regime and its progress at some official conference.

The Glasnost Era
and the Transition to the Present

Although in the next era of glasnost significant changes began to be seen, this inherited system would not vanish in a puff of smoke, given the many tens of thousands of media professionals who had been trained and had their careers within it. The word *glasnost* became the symbol of Gorbachev's intended restructuring of the Soviet system, and had a direct bearing on the media. Its original meaning signified publicity, the public sphere, and is derived from a word for "voice." In the new context it denoted the drive to voice endemic problems and embarrassing issues out in the open, instead of concealing them or cloaking them in officialese.

The first, rather mixed, signal that glasnost media policies were in operation followed the 1986 Chernobyl nuclear plant disaster. This might have been hushed up, as was a similar disaster in the Chelyabinsk area in the 1950s, if it had not been for the new policy. The fact that some Western media might have reported Chernobyl instantly, rather than 48 hours later, should not blind us to the sharp change in media policy evident from that point on (Mickiewicz, 1988, pp. 60-68). At the same time, media coverage of these issues in Western countries has scarcely been a model; witness the Hanford nuclear power station in the United States or the Windscale/Sellafield station in Britain. A different example is media treatment of the Soviet invasion of Afghanistan in 1979, which began by being automatically endorsed by the media, but then came to be more and more vigorously criticized once Gorbachev announced a policy review on the subject (Downing, 1988c).

One very evident feature of glasnost in the later 1980s was the open exploration of the regime's history, especially the huge network of slave-labor camps in the 1930s and 1940s and Stalin's systematic murder of potential rivals and opponents, Communist and non-Communist alike. Much of this was known in the West, but had never been published in Soviet media; even Solzhenitsyn's Denisovich had stopped short of that.

On the other hand, rehabilitating major architects of the revolution whom Stalin had denounced as traitors and had executed concerned a history now long past. This being so, after the initial flurry of tremendous excitement as to what would be published next, people quickly became used to the revelations of past horrors. Given the downward slide of an already poor economy, they began to be much more interested in bread-and-butter economic problems. During an extended period in Moscow in 1990, I found that a slogan drawn from a similar period in Portugal drew many smiles of recognition. Portugal's dictatorship collapsed in 1974, and there followed an explosion of media freedom. Yet severe economic problems continued. Workers in the city of Setubal coined this slogan in 1975: "Under the dictatorship we were hungry, but were forbidden to say so—now we can say so whenever we want!"

Much that was written at the time about Gorbachev's reforms and glasnost gave the impression that there had been a total overnight change in media policy, stretching the length and breadth of the country (almost mirroring the naive view of the "instantaneous" establishment of the Stalinist media system criticized above). Habits, procedures, and institutions formed over decades are not altered so readily. Gorbachev himself was certainly no "First Amendment campaigner," nor were the reformers around him. But even if they had been, the situation they inherited would not have simply clicked into place and changed at their command. Especially out in the many far-flung provinces, local Communist Party bosses were in no hurry to throw away their power. Media professionals who depended upon them for their jobs and careers were not likely to rush to challenge the *nomenklatura*, although some courageous ones did. Furthermore, journalists had been trained in a totally different mode. Self-censorship was bred into their bones; it could not be expelled overnight.

There followed, therefore, a protracted political stalemate among various wings of political opinion, a stalemate made the more difficult to resolve by the rapidly worsening economic situation. Some Russians wanted to turn the clock back to Brezhnev. Some wanted to turn it back to the czars and a new version of medieval Russia. Some wanted to turn Russia instantly into a get-rich-quick version of capitalist society. Some wanted to turn it into a moderate, stable democracy. Most felt humiliated by Russia's public misery.

Yet there were very few media professionals or media that could service this agonizing debate and help to move it forward. It was a rather chaotic media situation. Masses of new newspapers and magazines appeared and disappeared, how-to books flourished, pornography flourished, paper for publishing soared stratospherically in price, private radio stations opened up, two television services were established.

Those in power typically saw television as their rightful medium of communication: President Yeltsin, for example, fired and hired four directors of Ostankino Television over the period 1991-1994; and in their confrontation with Yeltsin in October 1993, parliamentary leaders sent their followers out on a march to seize control of Ostankino Television, a confrontation that ended in considerable bloodshed. Not only were pro-Communist newspapers banned after the siege of the Parliament building in October 1993, but the *Independent Newspaper* (*Nyezavisimaya Gazeta*), as independent as its name, was repeatedly threatened with being muzzled by members of President Yeltsin's team. No one in power seemed to value the notion of independent media—old traditions were clearly dying hard.

At the time of this writing, in early 1994, it makes little sense to offer predictions about how the media situation in Russia will eventually develop. Issues there are so complex and contested that forecasts are foolish. In other Eastern European countries formerly in the Soviet bloc, many similar problems are visible, including the ready assumption of those in power that television belongs rightfully to them to push their views of political issues. Nonetheless, it is my hope that this overview of eight decades of media, dictatorship, and change will help you to see the differences—and the similarities—in the relations between media and the power structures in democratic and dictatorial societies.

Further Questions

1. Do all forms of state try to control the media? How far do major media ever go to oppose this assault on their activities?

2. What importance do a country's history and culture have in shaping its media system?

3. What is the significance of self-censorship among journalists in any media system?

4. Do Western media, too, albeit without officially so acknowledging it as did Soviet media, serve as political mobilizers? (See Herman, Chapter 5; and Robinson, Chapter 6.)

Note

1. At the turn of the century, Communists were called Social Democrats, a term that has now come to be used to describe socialists who accept parliamentary democracy as the only major road to socialism. The Russian Social Democrats split in 1903 in a hotly contested party congress into majority and minority factions, the majority being termed (in Russian) *Bolsheviki*. This was Lenin's group.

PART III

Audiences and Users

The nature of the media audience is currently one of the most controversial areas of media analysis. It raises some questions about our models of human action, or why we think people act and believe as they do, and our models of media power, or the way we think the media exercise power in society. Although most of us think we choose media content and react "simply" as individuals, early media analysts used to describe us as the "mass" audience, rather uniform in our responses, passive, and manipulated by media content. Gradually, however, media analysts and professionals alike have come to see the audience as diverse, segmented by social background, including class and ethnic differences, by cultural taste, and by patterns of consumption, which implies different kinds of reactions to the same media content. Moreover, the old model of the passive audience, readily absorbing like hospital patients the hypodermic needle insertion of media values and attitudes, is challenged by arguments about the "active audience" creatively and critically interacting with media content. In Chapter 12, Ang takes us through these shifting concepts of the audience, which remind us that media effects cannot be read simply from media content, omitting the media audience. Of course, some would argue that the ever-changing, ever-present flow of media output is itself the addictive fix of the twentieth century. How many hours a day do you spend watching television? How many have you spent in the past?

Many still question the extent of audience activity, of "resistive" reactions to the media. The extent of this audience diversity is questioned by Thomas in her chapter on the educational functions of entertainment in the final section of the book. It is also challenged by the commercial dynamic of U.S. media, which themselves "package" audiences for advertisers and hence "package" specialized content for target audiences. As Gandy argues in Chapter 13, the monitoring of audiences is becoming ever more refined and pervasive. How far, and in what ways, we can resist these attempts to structure our media use and consumption habits and find new and resistive meanings is of crucial social significance.

One logic of the argument about the "active" and resistive audience is for ordinary people to become involved in the actual production of media texts. This frequently happens in processes of social change, as Downing explores in Chapter 14. More people producing more and increasingly diverse media would be a significant cultural and political change in and of itself.

12 The Nature of the Audience

IEN ANG

Most of us have heard and used the terms mass media and mass communication all our lives. Only one pair of eyes watches the screen or reads the newspaper at a time—even when surrounded by other pairs of eyes and ears—but apparently the media are believed to involve processes of mass communication. Where did this concept of "mass" come from, and does it make any sense?

Ang begins Part III by taking us on a tour of the history and meaning of some terms we have used all our lives without examination. By way of introducing the study of media audiences, she asks us to consider the ways we think the media exercise power in society. For citizens of the information age, the question is vital: What does it mean for us to live as audience members of the mass media?

The idea of the "masses," popular in social thought of the nineteenth century, was particularly influential during the first half of the twentieth century. During that time, new media such as movies and radio attracted millions of people, alarming many cultural observers and critics. Phrases such as mass society, mass culture, and mass audiences, created to describe the unprecedented numbers of participants

AUTHOR'S NOTE: I would like to thank James Lull for his comments on an earlier draft of this chapter.

in the new media, carried the idea that radio, movies, and television acted as hypodermic needles, injecting messages directly into the veins of a passive, mindless, mass audience. It was felt that all other social institutions between the growing media and the masses, such as community and religion, had collapsed.

The image of media audiences as passive, faceless people of low taste and intelligence, now ascribed largely to television's "couch potatoes," actually yields no understanding of media audiences themselves and is of only historical interest to contemporary analysts. In our affluent cultures, life without the media would be almost unthinkable anyway. In fact, given that 98% of American households now have at least one television set, we must all be "masses." Or, as the British cultural analyst Raymond Williams puts it, there are no masses, "only ways of seeing people as masses"—and those ways tend to be elitist and moralistic, often derived from a "high-culture" perspective.

This chapter presents a summary of past ways of looking at audiences and shows how audiences are being considered today. Ang's approach downplays the power of the media to create universally understood messages and emphasizes instead how people make meanings. "Watching television," or participating in any media event, is not a one-dimensional activity that has equivalent meanings or significance for all people at all times. Men and women, boys and girls, different ethnic groups and subcultures—all participate and perceive differently. For instance, adolescent girls may appreciate Madonna for her image of independence; men may appreciate her sexuality. The internationally popular television series Dallas was one thing for Americans, but something else again for Asian viewers.

Although the nature of the media "audience" is not very well understood, either by commercial concerns interested in creating audiences or by media analysts embroiled in professional controversy, the changing perspectives on this study and the promise of real information about our roles as media audiences are intriguing. Audiences are what we are.

Our everyday lives are permeated by the mass media. At home, you may casually watch TV together with your family, or listen to a CD you have just bought. Driving to school in your car, you may have the car radio on as you pass dozens of huge billboards along the road that are there to be seen but that you hardly notice. Or you may wear your Walkman headphones and listen to some music while waiting for the subway. During lunch hour, you may read today's newspaper or exchange the latest gossip about the love lives of the stars. Meanwhile, your VCR is taping your favorite soap opera so you can watch it after school. On the weekend, you go to a movie with a date, or you go dancing until late at night to the latest dance hits. Alternatively, you may decide to stay home and read an engrossing science fiction novel or browse through a stack of magazines. In all these activities, you are part of the media audience. Or, to put it more precisely, you are a member of many different media audiences at once. How can we make sense of this fact? What does it mean for us to live as audience members for the mass media?

These are interesting and important questions, but, strangely enough, communication scholars have not come up with too many satisfactory answers so far. Our knowledge about the nature of media audiences is thus rather limited. This is because the most influential conceptions of the audience are incapable of doing justice to the heterogeneous ways in which, as the summary above suggests, the media are used and take on meanings for people. In the next section, I describe two of these dominant conceptions: the audience as *mass* and the audience as *market*. In the past few decades, however, more and more communication scholars have realized the limitations of these conceptions and have attempted to develop new perspectives on media audiences. In a subsequent section, I will go into some of the more recent perspectives on media audiences. In these perspectives, theory and research are designed precisely to get a more nuanced picture of the specific social and cultural meanings of media use and reception for people in different contexts. I close the chapter with some concluding remarks.

Classic Conceptions: The Audience as Mass and Market

The term *mass audience* is easily associated with the media because the media are generally assumed to involve processes of mass communication. The concept of "mass" was especially influential in the first half of this century. At that time, media such as the cinema and radio made their entrance and rapidly gained a popularity that was unprecedented.

These media attracted millions of people, a startling development that concerned many cultural observers and critics. They saw these popular media as important constituents of what they called a "mass society," and perceived their audiences as "masses" who absorb "mass culture."

Sociologist Herbert Blumer (1950) describes "the mass" as follows:

> *First,* its membership may come from all walks of life, and from all distinguishable social strata; it may include people of different class position, of different vocation, of different cultural attainment, and of different wealth. One can recognize this in the case of the mass of people who follow a murder trial. *Secondly,* the mass is an anonymous group, or more exactly is composed of anonymous individuals. *Third,* there exists little interaction or change of experience between members of the mass. They are usually physically separated from one another, and, being anonymous, do not have the opportunity to mill as do members of the crowd. *Fourth,* the mass is very loosely organized and is not able to act with the concertedness or unity of a crowd.

The conception of media audiences as masses, then, emphasizes their large size and sees them as composed of isolated and unknown individuals. Although this conception was presented as a purely descriptive way of perceiving audiences, it is surrounded by many additional, evaluative meanings, which are usually very negative. Because the model held that community and religious organizations no longer helped people understand the world, the mass was often seen as individualized, essentially passive, and easily manipulated. It is therefore not surprising that a lot of early fears about the powers of the media were fed by the idea of the mass. Some early theorists were concerned that the media, and especially very popular media such as movies, radio, and later television, were acting like "hypodermic needles"—injecting messages directly into the veins of their completely defenseless viewers and listeners. More generally, the mass audience was often looked down on as made up of people with low taste and intelligence.

An early example of the condescending image of media audiences that was derived from the conception of mass is the following description of the "typical" radio listener. It comes from Roy Durstine, a very prominent advertising agency executive in the 1930s:

> The typical listening audience for a radio program is a tired, bored, middle-aged man and woman whose lives are empty and who have exhausted their sources of outside amusement when they have taken a quick look at an

evening paper. . . . Radio provides a vast source of delight and entertainment for the barren lives of the millions. (quoted in Stamps, 1979)

We should add that similar views can still be heard, but nowadays more often in relation to television than to radio. It is now the television audience that is still occasionally perceived as a huge mass of more or less passive, faceless viewers, as the expression *couch potatoes* suggests.

In sum, the concept of the mass can be criticized because it does not give us any understanding of the worlds of media audiences themselves. After all, would we see ourselves as passive, easily manipulated, and anonymous while we are watching television? As British cultural analyst Raymond Williams (1961) has put it, there are in fact no masses, but "only ways of seeing people as masses." And those ways of seeing tend to be elitist and moralistic.

Another influential way of perceiving media audiences comes from the commercial context in which media industries operate. In this, audiences are seen as potential "consumers" of media material, as "market." Furthermore, they are seen as potential consumers for the products offered for sale in advertising, which forms the financial source for the production of media material (see Gandy, Chapter 13). However, because market researchers are generally concerned merely with quantitative and "objective" information about numbers of viewers, listeners, readers, and so on, they do not give us insight into the more qualitative and more "subjective" aspects of media consumption. Thus looking at ratings and similar figures does not give us any sense of what the experience of television viewing, music listening, or book reading means to people. As Todd Gitlin (1983), a critical communication scholar, has remarked about the meaning of ratings, "The numbers only sample sets tuned in, not necessarily shows watched, let alone grasped, remembered, loved, learned from, deeply anticipated, or mildly tolerated" (p. 54). Media sociologist Denis McQuail (1987) puts it this way: "The market view is inevitably the view 'from the media.' We never conceive of ourselves as belonging to markets, rather we are placed in market categories or identified as part of a target group by others" (p. 221).

Changing Perspectives

Although the concepts of mass and market have very different origins, they also share some similar assumptions about the nature of media audiences, of which two are most important. First, they tend to ignore the fact that media audiences consist of human beings who do not merely more or less passively respond to media output, but are actively involved, both emotionally and intellectually, with particular forms of media material. Second, they do not take account of the fact that we do not consume media material as isolated and solitary individuals, but in particular social settings and within certain cultural frameworks. Some communication scholars have long challenged the dominant concepts of mass and market. They have attempted to develop alternative perspectives on media audiences that emphasize the study of the meaning of media consumption as a social and cultural activity. The earliest attempts to do this were undertaken by researchers of the "uses and gratifications" tradition. Their starting point was that the media are functional for people, that using media gratifies certain needs and wants. Another group of researchers interested in audience activity consists of those who study media reception. These researchers are concerned with the ways in which people interpret and make sense of media texts. Finally, a recent trend within academic audience research is the growing awareness of the need to understand how mass media fit into the context of everyday life.

USES AND GRATIFICATIONS

Uses and gratifications researchers assume that media audiences are active in their choices of media material. From this perspective, the use of media is a highly selective and motivated activity, not just a mindless pastime. In general, people use the media because they expect that doing so will give them some gratifications—hence the name of this research tradition. These gratifications are assumed to be related with the satisfaction of social and psychological needs experienced by the individual (Blumler & Katz, 1974; Rosengren, Palmgreen, & Wenner, 1985).

In typical empirical studies within this tradition, audience members are asked to fill out long questionnaires about why they watch certain television programs or pick out any other kind of media material. Over the years, responses gathered from these studies have shown a rather regular pattern. It turns out that the reasons repeatedly mentioned by people can be divided into the following categories (McQuail, 1987, p. 73):

- *information:* finding out about society and the world; seeking advice on practical matters; satisfying curiosity and interest; learning
- *personal identity:* finding reinforcement for personal values; finding models for behavior; identifying with valued others; gaining insight into oneself
- *integration and social interaction:* gaining insight into circumstances of others; gaining a sense of belonging; finding a basis for conversation; helping to carry out social roles
- *entertainment:* being diverted from problems; relaxation; getting cultural and aesthetic pleasure and enjoyment; filling time; emotional release; sexual arousal

Most people will be able to recognize themselves in many of the items mentioned, and it has been the merit of uses and gratifications researchers that they have provided sufficient empirical evidence for all of them. That is, people turn to the media and make use of them for a variety of reasons, not just one. Yet there are also problems with this approach. I will sum up only some of the most important criticisms here (Elliot, 1974).

First of all, the approach is individualistic: It takes into account only individual uses of the media and the psychological gratifications derived from them. The fact that people get in touch with media in particular social contexts tends to be ignored. As a result, the approach does not take into consideration that some uses of the media are not related to the pursuit of gratifications at all. For example, some media use may be forced upon people rather than freely chosen. Think about parents who have to endure the sound of loud rock music because their teenage kids have the volume turned up, or about the resentment of sexist advertising felt by feminists.

A second problem has to do with the lack of attention within the approach to the content of media output. In other words, uses and gratifications researchers attempt to find out why people use media, but forget to analyze exactly what people get out of a TV show, a book, or a pop song. What is overlooked here are the meanings that people give to media culture.

Finally, there is a political problem that stems from the general starting point of the uses and gratifications approach. By emphasizing the fact that using the media is always functional to people—that is, that uses are always related to gratifications—the approach may implicitly offer a justification for the existing ways in which the mass media are organized. If people always find some satisfaction in their media use, it could be argued, they must also be perfectly content with the material that is made available by the media. So we could all too easily conclude that because the media give us what we want, there is no reason whatsoever to change them. But this reasoning takes into account only what is actually available, ignoring the possibility that alternative kinds of media output (e.g., more documentaries or penetrating news reporting on television, or more programming for Blacks, gays, or other cultural and ethnic minorities) might be even more gratifying for many people.

RECEPTION ANALYSIS

Another group of researchers has taken up the task that was left aside by the uses and gratifications approach: They have started to examine how audiences construct meanings out of media offerings, generally called *texts*. This kind of research can be assembled under the heading of reception analysis.

The starting point here is the assumption that the meaning of media texts is not something fixed, or inherent within the text. Rather, media texts acquire meaning only at the moment of reception, that is, when they are read, viewed, listened to, and so on. In other words, audiences are seen as producers of meaning, not just consumers of media content: They decode or interpret media texts in ways that are related to their social and cultural circumstances and to the ways in which they subjectively experience those circumstances. From this perspective, reception researchers have begun to study the different ways diverse audience groups interpret the same media texts. Their interest is directed not to the individual ways in which people make sense of such texts, but to social meanings, that is, meanings that are culturally shared. Some reception researchers use the term "interpretive communities" to denote groups of people who make common interpretations of a text (Radway, 1987). We could also speak about "subcultures" (Hebdige, 1979) consisting of people who share a preference for a particular type of media material (e.g., soap opera lovers or heavy metal fans). Such communities or subcultures do not have to be physically united in one location; they can be geographically dispersed, and can consist of many different kinds of people who do not know each other, but are symbolically connected by their shared interest in a media product. In general, what reception researchers aim to uncover is how people in their own social and historical contexts make sense of all kinds of media texts in ways that are meaningful, suitable, and accessible to them.

For example, it is interesting to see how a massively popular TV show such as *Dallas* has been received and interpreted by different groups and peoples throughout the world. For most Americans, the fact that the city of Dallas is the center of the Texas oil industry must be quite familiar knowledge. However, many people who live in Europe or in Third World countries and who watch *Dallas* may not even be sure where Texas is. As a result, it is very likely that they will interpret the story differently from Americans. Several researchers, among them Tamar Liebes and Elihu Katz (1986) from Israel, have found that non-Americans are more ready to see in *Dallas* a "realistic" representation of America than are Americans themselves, who are more inclined to emphasize the showy aspects of the glamorous soap opera. Thus a viewer in a study conducted in Holland gave this comment about the Ewings of *Dallas*: "Actually they are all a bit stupid. And oversensational. Affected and genuinely American—money-appearance-relationship maniacs—family and nation, etc!" (Ang, 1985, p. 108). In short, although *Dallas* is an almost globally popular program, that does not mean that it is interpreted and made sense of in identical ways. *Dallas* is a different program in America than in Europe, and still different again in Nigeria or Japan.

However, this still does not mean that all Americans interpret *Dallas* or any other show in the same way. After all, there are many groups, communities, and subcultures within the United States, too, and according to reception researchers, each will "negotiate" the text in ways that make sense within its own social and cultural situation. For example, adolescent girl fans of Madonna (whose songs, films, performances, magazine interviews, and so on can be regarded as a set of texts) will interpret her in ways entirely different from those of male, middle-class readers of *Playboy*. The girls may adore and imitate her for her image of independence. As some girl fans say: "She's sexy but she doesn't need men. . . . She's kind of there all by herself" (quoted in Fiske, 1987). *Playboy* readers, on the other hand, may stress her sexual attractiveness to men in their reception.

Unlike uses and gratifications researchers, reception researchers do not usually use the standard questionnaire as a method of investigation. Instead, they use more small-scale, qualitative methods, such as group interviews and in-depth individual interviews, in which they try to unravel the interpretations made of certain media content by a small group of viewers or readers. Thus they generally do not construct a complete set of categories such as the list of gratifications mentioned above. This is because they think that reception and the production of meaning cannot be isolated from the specific contexts in which they take place, and can be understood only meaningfully. Thus Radway (1984) has examined the ways in which a group of avid readers interpret romance novels; Hobson (1982) and Seiter, Borchers, Kreutzner, and Warth (1991) have investigated how working-class women in England and the United States make sense of their favorite soap operas; and Peterson (1987) has studied the diverse meanings a group of college students attached to Cindy Lauper's pop song "Girls Just Want to Have Fun."

The perspective of reception analysis is not without its limitations, also. In their emphasis on interpretation and production of textual meaning, reception researchers still tend to isolate the text-audience relationship from the larger context in which the media are consumed by people. That context is everyday life, and it is to this important consideration that we now turn.

THE MEDIA IN EVERYDAY LIFE

Uses and gratifications researchers have attempted to answer the question of why people make use of media offerings. Reception researchers are interested in what people see in the media: which meanings they get out of it. The question being left out in both approaches, however, is the deceptively simple one of how people live with the media. In other words, How are the media integrated into our everyday lives?

One audience researcher who has begun to tackle this question is David Morley (1986), an Englishman. He remarks that when we examine what it means for people to watch television, it may be more important to look at the domestic context of family life in which people use television than to find out which interpretations people make of any particular type of programming. He is thus interested in the role of watching television in what he calls "the politics of the living room." The overall aim of Morley's research is to show that "watching television" cannot be assumed to be a one-dimensional activity that has equivalent meaning or significance at all times for all who perform it.

To illustrate this point, consider a woman saying the following: "Early in the evening we watch very little TV. Only when my husband is in a real rage. He comes home, hardly says anything, and switches on the TV." According to Herman Bausinger (1984), a German researcher, in this case turning on the TV set doesn't signify "I would like to watch this," but rather, "I would like to hear and see nothing." Bausinger also sums up some general points we need to keep in mind when we want to understand the place of the media in everyday life. Here are the most important ones:

- To make a meaningful study of the use of the media, it is necessary to take all the different media into consideration and to examine the "media ensemble" that everyone deals with today. Audiences integrate the contents of radio, TV, newspapers, and other print media.
- As a rule, the media are not used completely or with full concentration. We read parts of sports reviews, skim through magazines, and zap from channel to channel when we don't like what's on TV.
- The media are an integral part of the routines and rituals of everyday life. Thus media use cannot be isolated, because it is constantly interrelated with other activities, such as talking or doing housework. In other words, "mass" communication and "interpersonal" communication cannot be separated.
- Media use is not an isolated, individual process, but a collective process. Even when reading the newspaper one is often not truly alone, but interacting with family, friends, colleagues.

In a study of the place of television viewing in family life, Morley (1986) interviewed 18 working-class families in London. Among the most interesting results of his study are the gender differences found in viewing preferences and styles. For example, the men in Morley's sample preferred to watch factual programs (news and sports), whereas the women preferred fiction (soap operas and other drama series). Furthermore, the men favored watching programs attentively ("in order not to miss anything"), whereas the women tended to combine their viewing with other activities, such as knitting, talking, and doing household chores. Indeed, many of the women felt that just watching television without doing anything else would be a waste of time. As one woman said: "You've got things to do, you know, and you can't keep watching television. You think, 'Oh my God, I should have done this or that.'" Another general conclusion Morley draws is that when the family is together, men are usually in control of the selection of programs. He remarks: "Masculine power is evident in a number of the families as the ultimate determinant on occasions of conflict over viewing choices." He quotes one man as saying: "We discuss what we all want to watch and the biggest wins. That's me. I'm the biggest." Symbolic for the power exerted by the man in the house is his control over the remote control device, both for the TV set and for the VCR. One daughter in Morley's study said: "Dad keeps both the automatic controls—one on each side of the chair." This does not mean that women do not get the chance to watch their favorite programs, but more often than not they have to do it when they are alone, when other members of the family are "out of the way."

Of course, such gender-related patterns of viewing do not occur in all families. The situation may be different in families of different classes and ethnic backgrounds, in single-parent or two-career families, and so on. Still, that this is a predominant pattern in the United States has been confirmed by the work of several American researchers (e.g., Lindlof, Shatzer, & Wilkinson, 1988; Lull, 1982).

It is important to note that these patterns are not based either on differences between women and men or on a natural authority possessed by men. Rather, they are products of the particular social roles that men and women occupy within the American home. For men, the home is primarily defined as a place to rest from a hard day's work. Therefore, they tend to consider watching television as something they have naturally earned. Women, however, are usually the ones who are responsible for the well-being and care of family members and for running the household—even though today most women work outside the home as well. As a result, their television viewing is often interrupted by a continuing sense of domestic responsibility, and they often give up their own preferences in the service of others.

Research such as Morley's is beginning to map the intricate social circumstances in which patterns of media consumption are organized in people's day-to-day routines. Those relationships are shot through not only with pleasure and gratifications, but also with power and conflict. But much remains unknown about the place of the media in our everyday lives. Most of the research done so far has been limited to television, perhaps because it is the most widely used medium. Furthermore, it would be interesting to look not only at male-female relationships in terms of patterns of media consumption, but also at the relationships between children and parents, between siblings, between friends, colleagues, and so on—both at home and outside the home.

Even more than reception analysis, the study of media in everyday life depends on methods that are capable of capturing the fine-grained details in which the media are part of our routine activities. It is for this reason that "ethnographic" approaches to the study of media audiences have recently gained interest among communication scholars. In such approaches, researchers attempt to come to culturally sensitive understandings of the complex subjective worlds of media audiences by using a variety of methods of investigation, such as depth interviewing and spending time with their subjects in participant observation.

Concluding Remarks

Media audiences are not "masses"—anonymous and passive aggregates of people without identity. Nor are they merely "markets"—the target groups of the media industries. This chapter has indicated how media audiences are active in the ways in which they use, interpret, and take pleasure in media products. That is to say, there are many different ways in which, and why, different people engage with different media. We cannot say in advance which meanings and effects media content will have on audiences. It will depend on who these people are (e.g., in terms of class, gender, race, religious conviction, regional or national background) and the specific social and cultural contexts in which these media are embedded when they "reach" their audiences. Furthermore, we have seen how the media have come to play a central role in the shaping and arrangement of our everyday lives and social relationships. That is, the media are now so pervasive—all around us, everywhere, all the time—that they virtually have become a natural part of our environment. For most of us who live in advanced capitalist industrial societies, life without media has become utterly unimaginable. It is this all-pervasiveness of media presence with which research into media audiences still has to come to terms.

A good example is the rise of CNN, the 24-hour cable news channel. For those who can receive it, CNN has made television news instantly available at all times of the day. This means that we no longer have to switch on at a particular time to catch the news; we can now watch anytime we want. In addition, CNN has also gained much success in covering the news "as it happens," for example, during the Gulf War and other world events. This means that we are now given the illusion that we can be direct witnesses to important things happening in distant parts of the world from the safety of our living rooms—the world of the 1990s has become what Canadian media theorist Marshall McLuhan, back in the 1960s, called a "global village."

Finally, it is important to realize that we cannot examine the "nature" of audiences without considering the corporate strategies aimed at turning us into audiences. That is to say, we must realize that audiences are made, not naturally given. Take CNN again. Before this channel was available, few of us would have missed the opportunity to go "around the world in 30 minutes" (as one CNN slogan goes) at virtually any time of the day. Once the opportunity was there, however, some of us developed a "need" for it, just as people who never had television before the 1950s quickly got used to it and would have missed it if it had been taken away. In this respect, we must not forget that CNN is now also available in many parts of the world outside the United States. Yet the news put out by CNN remains distinctively American in terms of point of view, news values, ideological biases, language use, communication style, and so on. What are audiences outside of the United States to make of CNN's presentation of "world news"? Do they accept it as neutral and internationally valid, or recognize it—and perhaps discard it—as "typically American" in both content and form? We need to ask such questions if we are to understand the nature of media audiences throughout the world in the 1990s and beyond.

Further Questions

1. How might our patterns of consumption be influenced by the growing importance of new multimedia technologies?

2. How has CNN influenced Americans' news viewing habits? Who is most interested in watching CNN, and why? Has the availability of instant world news through CNN changed people's awareness of world events? If so, how?

13 Tracking the Audience
Personal Information and Privacy

OSCAR H. GANDY, Jr.

Since the end of World War II, our technology has given us many boons, but it has clearly also given us the potential for previously unimagined control over personal freedom. The recent explosion of computer technology has turned Orwell's "Big Brother" into a potential everyday reality. Anyone who has ever used a credit card or subscribed to a magazine has probably received solicitations targeted specifically to his or her socioeconomic status. This means that the subscriber has become a "profile" constructed from past purchases and interests. If Big Brother isn't watching, corporate interests surely are.

In this chapter Gandy, taking a tack very different from Ang's in Chapter 12, explores the current status of personal information and privacy from the perspective of audience analysis and political economy. He especially examines the close relationship between media industries and the consumption promoted by advertisers (compare Chapter 19, by Douglas Kellner). He points out that media industries consider the attention a person pays to a TV screen during the few seconds of an ad to be a "product" sold by the broadcasting company to advertisers. He also argues that the time the audience spends viewing commercials is its "labor." He then reviews the different means of monitoring audiences, including the increasingly precise ways advertisers target audiences, and describes the effect this capitalistic "logic" has on democracy and personal freedom.

In the United States, audiences—especially television audiences—are monitored to a very high degree. The industry view of audience as product explains the mundane paradox of why popular programs with respectable ratings sometimes disappear: Despite their size, the audiences are not the ones advertisers want. On the other hand, networks may continue to air programs that generate smaller-than-average audiences if those audiences are the kinds that advertisers covet.

Audience measurement, a form of surveillance in the pursuit of expanded profits, takes place electronically and continuously. The goal is to fine-tune the mechanisms of "audience production." Computer technology makes it easy to match viewing behaviors with other consumer information, such as food purchases, and consumer behavior can be linked to a household's viewing patterns. Cereal advertisers can learn whether children who like comedy shows prefer crunchiness more than kids who like action/adventure programs. Improvements in the technology of "addressability" permit advertisers to reach target audiences with ever-increasing accuracy.

How concerned we should be about the movement toward greater control and management of audiences depends upon our expectations of a democratic society. Computer-based systems of audience assessment weaken the balance of power between individuals and business or government organizations. Now that both government and corporate bureaucracies collect and share information about people in ways we seem powerless to control, our social security numbers have become universal identifiers capable of linking virtually all records of our interactions with the commercial system. The only way to escape the information net is to give up credit cards and buy goods and services under aliases—to become a nonperson.

Although one of a capitalist system's vaunted merits is supposedly its encouragement of risk-taking by capitalists, Gandy demonstrates that contemporary capitalism is intensely preoccupied with reducing risk, if not canceling it altogether. It is chilling to consider what this could mean for the U.S. system of government. We may not yet have reached the point where television looks at us the way we look at it, but infrared set-top "peoplemeters" will soon have the capacity to monitor num-

bers, ages, and family affiliations of viewers, to tell what shows they are watching, and to feed this information to computers, where it can be matched with other kinds of information and then used, often without our knowledge, and perhaps against us.

Crises of Control in the Information Age

Computers, and the telecommunications networks that carry information among them, are said to be the harbingers of the latest industrial revolution. Computers have changed the ways we work, play, understand, and relate to our environments (see Sinha & Stone, Chapter 15). As devices for storing, processing, and exchanging information, computers greatly amplify and extend the power of those who control their use. It is essential to understand that the growing importance of computer-based information systems does not rest in the technology itself, but in the continually changing interactions among technologies, the economic and social conditions that characterize their primary uses, and the cultural practices, including the systems of laws, regulations, and regulatory institutions, that govern us. This chapter examines some of these complex interactions through an exploration of the role of computers and telecommunications networks in the audience assessment process.

The use of computers and the intellectual technology of management planning and marketing research are all part of a process of rationalization. *Rationalization* refers to the pursuit of efficiency in the production, distribution, and sale of goods and services. Rationalization can also be applied to the business of government through its role in the collection and redistribution of wealth or in the performance of its police function. Rationalization is an information-dependent process, requiring more and more workers who are producing information and analysis or utilizing information technology to store and transmit this information. Thus, for some analysts, the transformation of industrial economies into "information economies" is primarily a reflection of the increased need to rationalize complex, interdependent systems, rather than a decision to produce information instead of material goods.

Surveillance and rationalization also imply an increase in the ability of capitalists to exercise control over individuals in their roles as

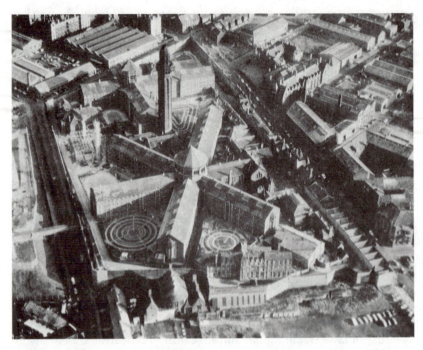

Panopticon-Shaped Prison, Britain

employees, consumers, and citizens. Their control is increased to the extent that the initiative, independence, and autonomy of the individual is reduced or transferred to other people. Surveillance provides the information necessary for greater control.

The kind of control that surveillance provides is not absolute. Social control under democratic social organization can be as subtle as the distinction between discipline and punishment. Discipline in individuals and society is maintained by virtue of a continual threat of punishment. Discipline also involves people's accepting for themselves the belief that the behaviors maintained by the threat of punishment are in fact correct, rational, or moral behaviors. Once accepted, or internalized, those beliefs and values provide the basis for self-control, the most efficient form of discipline.

An early-nineteenth-century design for a prison was named the *panopticon*. This prison was designed in an octopus shape so as to provide the guards at the center with continuous and unobstructed views of all the prisoners. Prisoners would never know for sure who was watching or if they were actually being watched at any particular moment. This design for a prison was thought to be particularly efficient because it also allowed the guards to isolate prisoners and to locate them in special wings or areas on the basis of their past behavior, their degree of rehabilitation, or their particular tendencies and habits.

Many critical communications scholars see the panopticon as a useful metaphor. They see contemporary society as developing into a panoptic system with similar forms of isolation, grouping, and surveillance, organized for the purposes of discipline and control. Such perspectives may be also applied to the study of audiences.

Rationalization in the information economy involves increased, almost continuous, surveillance of individuals in all those areas of existence that have been or are being brought under the control of capitalist logic. That is, surveillance is necessary for rationalizing human behavior, for making it more efficient and profitable in all conceivable activities. More generally, we can recognize tendencies toward increased surveillance of individuals for the purposes of rationalizing their behavior in the spheres of employment, consumer behavior, and citizenship. The analysis of audiences has relevance for each and every one of these spheres. I commence this discussion with two new alternative ways of understanding audiences: as products and as labor.

Perspectives on Audiences

AUDIENCES AS PRODUCTS

Although it is not a universal or even the dominant view within traditional discussions of mass media, many critical observers see audiences as the products of an industrial or manufacturing process. The notion of audience as product provides a particularly insightful perspective from which to understand mass media in general, and advertiser-supported media in particular. The focus here will be on commercial television as the premier advertising mass medium.

There is no direct economic relationship between the broadcaster and the audience in the United States. Commercial broadcasters "produce audiences" or, more precisely, blocks of time during which it is possible to communicate with audiences, which they then sell to advertisers. The market that exists is between broadcasters and advertisers or their agents. When we talk of "selling time," the reference is to the unit of time, the "spot" during which the advertiser is free to make a pitch to the audience that the broadcaster has promised to produce and deliver. The rates the broadcaster is able to charge these advertisers depend upon the size and income level of audience. The broadcaster realizes profits when the costs of producing promised audiences are substantially less than the advertising fees the broadcaster is able to charge for access. Not all audiences, even audiences of equal size, are of equal value to advertisers in general, or to advertisers of particular products. Part of audiences' value is associated with the amount of their spendable income and their propensity to spend it for particular goods and services. Advertisers of expensive "big ticket" items are unwilling to pay very much at all for an audience that is unemployed, retired, or for some other reason falls into the low-income category. Thus the broadcaster, or any other producer of audiences for sale at a profit, is sensitive to demands for particular audience attributes.

The size and quality of the audience produced is also the result of the technologies and raw materials used in their production. Just as one might produce a variety of cakes with different combinations of flour, sugar, and spices, the same is true of the audience product. Because of different tastes for violence, "action," sexual explicitness, comedy, and music, different combinations of these qualities in programs will attract different audiences.

If we also consider the potential audience member as an input into the eventual "product," the availability of some of those inputs will vary across times of day and across days of the week. Now that many women work outside the home, the proportion of women available to be sold as audience members during the day is smaller than it once was. Still fewer men are available for "sale" during those hours, and the scarcity of males makes it costly to attempt their production as audience members during weekday hours. Socially active teenagers also tend not to be available on Saturday evenings, and a review of the television schedule will reveal that network programmers have generally taken that fact into account.

As with other products, the cost of input is governed by the nature of competitive demands. "Audience producers" are essentially in competition with each other for the attention of potential audience members. However, some analysts would suggest that there has been an unspoken agreement among the major competitors (the networks) that their mutual interests are best served by each programmer's specializing in the production of a specific audience type during a particular day part. This "counterprogramming" strategy would operate to divide the audience members up without blurring objectives among the dominant audience producers.

Such specialization is more clearly the case with radio, where programming style is fairly uniform across the program schedule and stations can be easily classed into types on the basis of their formats and the audiences they traditionally produce. This specialization, which is also increasingly characteristic of cable television networks, is referred to as the *magazine model* or *narrowcasting*. Over the years, especially since the emergence of television as the principal mass medium, general-interest magazines have likewise given way to targeted advertising vehicles that treat quite narrow ranges of topics and appeal to specialized audience interests.

It is this view of audience as product that explains why popular programs may be dropped from the broadcast schedule. Not just any audience will do. If a program fails to produce or "attract" an audience with a realizable market value exceeding the cost of producing it, it will not be renewed. Thus programs that might have respectable ratings in terms of audience size are dropped from the schedule because the audiences produced are not valued by advertisers. In those markets where Black people make up a large share of the primary audience base, high local ratings have not generated corresponding support. This is attributable to low estimates of Black people's purchasing powers as well as to conventional racist assumptions.

This perspective also makes clear the tendency of networks to keep programs on their schedules that generate smaller-than-average audiences, if these particular audiences have attributes that are in great demand. This is the character of certain programs (the yuppie-centered *thirtysomething* was one such show) that have been identified as "cable proof." That is, the upscale audiences that have been increasingly turning away from the networks to view premium cable fare will return to the networks to view certain shows. Because of this, networks have been assured that higher-than-normal fees will be paid for these audiences because of their relative value as consumers.

AUDIENCES AS LABOR

Thinking of the audience as labor takes a bit more work. Communication theorist Dallas Smythe (1981) is credited with early attempts to specify the nature of the work that audiences do. Smythe introduced this concept in the context of a critique of capitalism that suggested that under advanced capitalism, we have less leisure time than we once assumed. Time away from work is the time when workers must regenerate their energies in order to return to the factories and offices the next day. Unfortunately, Smythe argued, when the workers sat down to relax, to watch a little television, their viewing is not entirely recreation; rather, it is, in part, exploitative labor. Television viewers work as audiences.

The work of audiences, in Smythe's initial formulation, is the work of watching commercials, making sense of them, and ultimately behaving as consumers appropriate to their social position. The payment for this work is the pleasure, stimulation, or entertainment derived from consuming the material that appears between the commercial messages.

More recently, Sut Jhally and Bill Livant (1986) have sharpened Smythe's analysis and attempted to extend the metaphor further. Their task was to describe how broadcasters captured the profits produced by these audience workers, and how they utilized improved technology to increase the rate of exploitation of this labor. In their analysis, audiences are made to work harder by having to view more individual commercials for each minute of entertainment. Thus we have seen the 1-minute commercial give way to 30-, 15-, and 10-second spots, increasing the amount that programmers can charge for the same minutes of audience access. This increase in productivity does increase broadcasters' profits.

Another way audience workers may be made to work more efficiently is by being exposed only to those messages for which they are best suited by virtue of lifestyle, income, or other measures of consumer potential. Thus the messages are tailored more closely for the tastes, preferences, experiences, and resources of the audience working for a particular broadcaster at a particular point in time. Audience research, within this model, is similar to the kind of management research that seeks to inform employers how to select the best workers for their factories or organizations—in audience research, the best consumers are chosen.

Many examples of this effort to improve the productivity of the audience worker can be found in those advertiser-dependent media not subject to strict government or industry regulation. Popular magazines, such as those for hobbyists interested in photography, are filled with commercials. It is impossible to turn a page without meeting an ad, or brushing aside an insert, or picking up a reader response card that has fallen to the floor. And, as one might expect, the ads are clearly linked to the editorial focus of the periodical, offering cameras, film, processing services, and so on. Some cable television programs are advertisements disguised as documentaries. These "program-length commercials" seek to increase the efficiency of the audience workforce by avoiding the tendency of some laborers to goof off, sleep, talk to each other, read the paper, "zap" commercials, "graze" between programs, or even leave the room during clearly identifiable commercials.

Audience Measurement as Surveillance: New Developments

Audience measurement is surveillance. It is performed for the same reasons as surveillance of workers in the factories, or in the secretarial pool. In the pursuit of expanded profits, the surveillance of audiences seeks to fine-tune the main mechanisms of "audience production." Gary Marx (1988) identifies several attributes of the new surveillance environment that have clear reflections in the technology and practice of audience assessment. It is clear, for example, that the new surveillance technologies transcend time, distance, darkness, and other physical barriers. Audiences are measured electronically and continuously. The records of audience behavior can be stored electronically and transmitted instantaneously to remote sites upon request. Audience viewing behaviors can be combined easily with other information about individuals or groups. Increasingly, audience assessment technology is becoming automatic, "passive" (no action, such as filling out a viewing diary, is needed), and relatively unobtrusive. People are less and less aware that their behavior as audiences is being measured. Indeed, as Marx (1988) reminds us, the new surveillance is frequently involuntary—there are no simple ways to avoid being counted.

The growth in surveillance accelerates because the process is increasingly technology-intensive, that is, dependent more upon machines, essentially computers, that operate more efficiently than humans and are capable of monitoring multiple sites at the same time. The declining costs of surveillance mean that more and more firms in the audience business will consider its use to be essential. The new surveillance is both more intensive and more extensive. It measures more attributes and behaviors of more people across more aspects of their lives.

Increasingly, the surveillance of audiences resembles police surveillance of suspected criminals. It has become interventive and preventive, rather than reactive and investigative. Specials and "made-for-television movies" are audience "stings," pretested to see if audiences will be attracted (usually by new variants on old themes). Fringe time periods and fringe programmers test limits of public acceptability to see how many and what kinds of folk will be tempted by unusual or more "adult" content. Such a role in pushing the limits of mainstream tastes has been played by Rupert Murdoch's Fox network in reaching new depths of violence and sexual explicitness.

Rather than pursuing particular individuals or suspects, the new audience surveillance approaches focus on categories, groups, or "types" of individuals. Just as "terrorist" or "drug smuggler" profiles are used to select travelers who are subjected to more intensive customs searches, similar profiles are used to target messages to audiences likely to respond or to avoid those for whom particular messages or programs will have little appeal. "Two-car pet owners" would be an example of a consumer category.

PEOPLEMETERS

Peoplemeters are merely the latest in a continuing string of improvements in the technology of broadcast audience measurement. This search for increasing accuracy and precision in "audience ratings" has been described in fine detail by Hugh Beville (1985). From the beginnings of the industry in 1928, when market researchers relied upon costly personal interviews to determine how many American households actually owned radios, to the development of passive infrared detectors that take note of which household members are in front of the television set, the goal has been the same—rationalization. Technical developments in statistical sampling that increase the accuracy of estimates of audience behavior have been pursued with dedication. Similar efforts have been directed at increasing the scope of the data gathered from those sampled.

Personal recall of television programs watched has always been seen as unreliable. Ratings specialists and their clients have recognized that diaries tended to be completed from memory, often on the day before they were to be returned, rather than being filled in on an hourly or daily basis. In addition, most diaries tended to be filled in by one member of the household who served as the unreliable recorder of family viewing. Telephone coincidentals, in which a sample of respondents were asked to identify what programs they were viewing when the phone rang, had long been the method used for quality control of the diary method. However, their use was severely restricted in practice by the cost of employing telephone interviewers, people's objections to intrusion, and associated problems of administration.

Automatic, passive devices have improved significantly from the time of the Nielsen audiometer, first installed in test markets in 1935. This primitive device involved a mechanical stylus inscribing a waxed-paper tape in response to the location of the broadcast tuning dial. In a creative portent of contemporary audience measurement, the early A. C. Nielsen market research services included gathering data about what kinds of consumer goods households had in their pantries at the times when their agents went to collect the audiometer tape. Although these meters were eventually improved to the extent that they could be read automatically and continuously from Nielsen's remote data-processing center, meters were still limited by the fact that they measured only the use of the household set at a time when advertisers were interested in more detailed demographics and personal viewing patterns.

The peoplemeter, introduced into the United States by AGB Research in 1982, represented a significant improvement in individual audience assessment. Although still plagued by problems of sampling and concerns about the validity of estimates of viewing by youngsters who rapidly tired of "tapping in" to note the beginning and end of their viewing periods, by 1987 the technology was firmly established. Improvements in peoplemeters can be expected in the direction of greater "passivity." Heat sources (body temperature), heart rates, and body size (adults or children) can be registered, and passive set-top devices can record when known individuals (members of the household) enter or leave the viewing environment and whether or not their eyes are open.

The presence of guests is likely to be queried with an on-screen display, and encoding devices will allow households to record relevant demographic data about guests for the duration of their stay.

ADDRESSABILITY

The peoplemeters in use, or on the drawing board, even those that now measure exposure to commercials and provide ratings for commercials, rather than programs, do not, however, provide the most valued information about audience exposure—whether audiences are paying attention to, and being influenced by, the commercial message (see Ang, Chapter 12).

Addressability refers to the ability of advanced telecommunications systems to direct a message stream to a particular device (e.g., a TV set or a mainframe computer) with a digitally encoded address. *Verifiability* refers to the ability of advanced systems to note the status of tuners, decoders, and response devices to "verify" the status of information systems, to note whether messages have been received, and at what time. *Segmentation* and *targeting* refer to the classification of audiences into groups on the basis of information provided in response to questions, or on the basis of past performance as consumers or viewers. The qualities of addressability and verifiability make it much easier to segment audiences into different types. Then these segmented audiences may be subsequently targeted with specialized messages previously determined to be highly effective in reaching similar segments. Addressability allows targeted messages to be sent to particular segments.

Thus, in test-market communities, individuals are recruited to be part of programs with informative titles such as Behaviorscan or ScanAmerica. In return for small payments and the opportunity to participate in pools for larger prizes, families agree to provide detailed personal, social, and demographic information about themselves. They also agree to utilize a special identification card when they make purchases at selected stores in the community. The UPC (universal product code) or bar code scanners in the checkout counters link the consumer purchases with the viewing behavior of the particular household. In some other systems, family members are paid to run an electronic scanner along the UPC stripes of all purchases the family makes. It thus becomes possible to establish the correlation between the commercials family members are exposed to and the purchases they make.

Where more advanced dual-cable, or addressable, systems allow different commercials to be sent to different households, it is possible to achieve true laboratory control over the presentation of this commercial stimulus, and even to select the editorial environment in which it will be viewed. Thus marketers are able to determine whether ads for cookies that emphasize the crunch work better with youngsters than with adults. More than that, such systems provide information to advertisers about whether youngsters who like comedy shows prefer crunchiness more than youngsters who like action/adventure programs.

The goals of social management through these home networking systems have been described in careful detail by Kevin G. Wilson (1988). Advanced telecommunications systems will present more and more information to individuals in their homes through high-capacity cables. As the nation's cable systems are updated to provide more sophisticated systems capable of digital addressability of programs and messages (see Demac, Chapter 16), it will be more common for individuals to be charged directly for the material they receive; some projections call for pay-per-view TV in 40 million households by 1996. It is the blending of commercial and pay-per-view or cost-per-unit/page/screen systems that will delink advertising from generalized-appeal TV ads and will spread its reach to the entire realm of individual and family information processing. Reading, viewing, listening, banking, communication, and shopping activities will increasingly display the same quality of commercial transactions. As such, those transactions will provide the surveillance information necessary for the efficient operation of capitalism as its reach is extended into all aspects of daily life.

TRACKING THE AUDIENCE WHEREVER IT CAN BE FOUND

Tracking audiences is not limited to the volunteers who participate in paid research programs. A great many of us are part of experiments and market tests that are conducted without the courtesy of requesting our informed consent. Magazines and discount coupons are frequently utilized in efforts to link editorial content to commercial appeals. Advances in printing and binding make it possible for marketers to insert coupons in magazines that are code marked with the identification of the household or address where it was sent. Thus when an individual decides to use one of these coupons to purchase some item, the advertiser soon knows not only what kind of person responds to which kind of appeal, but to which store, with which prices or advertising pressure. Such coupon marking also allows market researchers to determine how many miles people are willing to drive from their homes in pursuit of apparent bargains.

Even general-interest magazines are being produced in specialized regional, neighborhood, or ZIP code-specific editions. The coming years will see magazines that are subscriber specific in terms of the advertisements they contain. Because of advances in ZIP code analysis, led by the Claritas Corporation, magazines have become highly competitive vehicles for targeted appeals, and the lists of their subscribers represent valuable data resources that may be sold at varying costs per thousand to advertisers who want them. Indeed, there is a large and growing industry in consumer lists. Each week, a newsletter serving the direct marketing industry describes new lists that have just come on the market, with prices ranging from $40 to $90 per thousand names for one-time-only commercial use. There are lists of magazine subscribers that might provide information about individuals' hobbies and recreational interests, political orientations, levels of education or sophistication, even degrees of ethnic identification. Other lists are easily developed from computerized records of sales and other transactions. Even calls to 800 numbers for information contribute to the growth of marketable lists. Commercially available telephone services automatically provide the firm with the name, address and phone number of the inquiring party. All of these lists provide the possibility for developing rather comprehensive profiles of individuals.

Advances in computer software have lowered the costs involved in simultaneous comparison of two or more lists. This procedure, called *matching*, has been used extensively by government agencies at the federal and state levels to identify individuals who, for one reason or another, would be considered ineligible for some public service. Thus matches of lists of bank accounts with requests for welfare or public assistance might turn up a "good hit": the name of an individual who appears on both lists. For marketing purposes, a good hit might involve a person turning up on a list of buyers of quality chocolates who is also on a list of participants in weight-control programs. Individuals so identified might become the prime targets for discount coupons for some new designer chocolates that will be inserted in their next issue of *Time* or *People*.

The Realm of Social Consequences

Why should we be concerned about this movement toward greater control or management of the behavior of audiences? Clearly, one's answer depends on one's expectations of a democratic society. From a critical perspective, one that recognizes the contradictions and conflicts between the logic of capitalism and the values of freedom and equality that are part of the democratic ideal, it becomes important to identify the consequences that flow from the uncontrolled and unchallenged extension of that logic to greater and greater areas of our daily lives.

One critique of the application of computer-based systems to the rationalization of audience production is that this technology deskills and devalues the contribution of labor. Where formerly skilled workers are unemployed and newly hired workers are reduced to button pushers, there is no pride in or attachment to the products of their labor. There is irony and danger in these developments. The irony is that one of the merits of a capitalist economy is supposed to be its encouragement of risk taking by capitalists. Yet the developments discussed above demonstrate an intense preoccupation with reducing risk for advertisers and their business clients—even, if possible, canceling risk altogether. It is the same logic that has led to clone products on TV and that could reduce our skills as consumers, packaging our likes and dislikes until we begin to lose the talent to make our own choices among goods and services, to use our own imagination to plan our daily consumption. And what future is there for low-income consumers when all these ads are targeted to the supposed needs of the wealthy?

Privacy and the Control of Personal Information

Perhaps the greatest threat these computer-based systems for audience assessment represent is their potential to worsen the balance of power between individuals and bureaucratic organizations. Personal information streams out of the lives of individuals much like blood out of an open wound, and it collects in pools in the computers of corporations and government bureaucracies. Public access to similar data about the firms and organizations that increasingly structure our options and opportunities is more costly to obtain and impossible to access.

Personal privacy, as currently conceived, concerns the right to control the collection, distribution, and use of information about oneself. The courts and legislatures have come to define the limits of that right in terms of what society agrees is a "reasonable expectation" of privacy. To the extent that we accept the rationale of market efficiency, and that sophisticated marketing is progress, most business and government uses of personal information can be justified in those terms. Rather than considering the overall implications of a loss of individual power and control, protective legislation focuses on restricting a specific information practice that has been identified as an abuse. Thus, rather than an absolute limit on the collection or use of personal information, we have a flexible limit that contracts each time some abuse becomes routinized by bureaucratic practice. The social security number has, through routine use, become the universal identifier capable of linking virtually all records of our interaction with the commercial system. Its collection has become so commonplace that the courts will likely assert before too long that there is no longer any reasonable expectation of privacy with regard to it.

There is fairly widespread concern that our personal privacy rights have come under attack. People know that government and corporate bureaucracies can and do collect and share information about them in ways that they are powerless to control and that will not return to benefit them. Surveys suggest that there is a glimmer of understanding about the nature and use of profiles based on the compilation of personal details. But resistance is almost nonexistent, and what little there is may be seen as passive and defeatist. Marketing and public opinion researchers are reporting more refusals and survey terminations than at any time in the past. A few individuals refuse to apply for services or opportunities because they would rather not provide the information such applications would require. A nearly invisible minority simply refuses to enter the system of records, giving up the convenience of credit cards and acquiring goods and services under assumed names or aliases. Escaping the information net means becoming a nonperson. One maintains privacy through the loss of all else.

Information Grazing and Zapping

A good many of those who still view broadcast fare have videotaped it; they are screening programs at times other than their actual broadcast and, more important from the advertiser's standpoint, fast-forwarding through or zapping the commercials with their remote control units. This workers' revolt is taking place in the homes of relatively high-income, technologically advanced families, who are also highly valued by advertisers. Many others switch frequently among channels (grazing), which means neither advertisers nor broadcasters can rely on their being exposed to the commercials. These are all signs of dissatisfaction on a wide scale, but it is atomized, not yet a rebellion with a voice and articulated demands. What the prospects are for an increase in organized opposition is a major question to be considered.

Further Questions

1. How do you relate individuals' attempts at control with the degree to which audiences may be "active"?

2. How can we organize to protect our privacy from information surveillance?

3. What kinds of consumer education movements exist, and how important are they or could they be in developing public awareness?

14 Alternative Media and the Boston Tea Party

JOHN DOWNING

As Gandy suggests in Chapter 13, Big Brother may be breathing down our necks, but audiences are not powerless to resist the onslaught of mainstream media. In this last chapter on the study of audiences, Downing responds to concerns about the limits the media set on public discourse by reviewing the long tradition of alternative media that have sprung up especially in times of political and economic turmoil and have exercised powerful effects in determining the course of events.

The communications media are not only products of society; they also help mobilize social movements (see Chapter 21, by Ali Mohammadi). In fact, whenever mainstream media choose not to represent important facets of social or political reality, alternative media flourish. A poorly photocopied sheet of paper may be seized upon and shared by many people if the need is real. But regardless of what form they take, the essence of alternative media is their creation of horizontal links for the public's own communication and empowerment. This contrasts radically with the vertical or one-way flow of communication from the mainstream media, which, with their government and corporate links, are not nearly democratic enough for a democratic society.

Beginning with the pamphleteers and the Boston Gazette of the American Revolutionary period, Downing takes us on a brief tour of the history of radical alternative media in the United States. Despite their small size and general absence from histories of journalism, alternative media have played significant roles in the country's history, airing views on feminism, labor, abolition, socialism, civil rights, pacifism, and free speech.

The alternative tradition continues in the 1990s. PeaceNet uses the computer and the modem to connect social activists here and abroad. Broadcasting out of New York, the Deep Dish TV Satellite Network disseminates community programming that highlights many of the issues the mainstream media handle poorly or not at all.

In showing us a tradition that stretches from 1760 to the present, Downing demonstrates that "active" audiences—as opposed to the passive masses of conventional wisdom—not only exist, they can and do produce diverse media. Alternative media result when audiences think about who they are in relation to their political context and take their lives into their own hands. Given the power of media outside the mainstream to create new opinion centers that can ripen into social change, thinking about the audience is one of the most important subjects raised in this book.

The label of *alternative media* can be applied to a host of different cultural activities. Clearly, they must be alternative to the mainstream media, including the big broadcasting and cable companies or newspapers of record, such as the *Washington Post* or the *Wall Street Journal*. But that still leaves a great deal of space for variety. Within the United States alone there is a gigantic mass of small-scale publications for particular audiences. These range from the specialized bulletins of different branches of industry that circulate to select executives and have subscription rates of $1,500 per year and up to little parochial newsletters that cost pennies or are entirely subsidized. In between there are endless specialist magazines for cycling, cooking, cat, and computer enthusiasts, to name but a few. Ethnic media that cater to the many different groups in the United States are yet another important category of alternative media. These take various forms. In Chapter 8, Rodríguez notes how U.S. Spanish-language television news differs rather little from mainstream media, whereas other ethnic media may have much more antagonistic attitudes toward the power structure. Still others, such as Turkish films on video in Germany or Indian films in Britain, may simply offer continued access to entertainment from immigrants' countries of birth. In this chapter, the term *alternative media* is reserved for certain categories not so far mentioned: politically dissident media that offer radical alternatives to mainstream debate.[1]

It must be said immediately that the political mainstream in the United States is a rather thin stream compared with political debate in many other countries. Politicians get very heated, and debate can be quite rowdy and rude, but in terms of real issues the mainstream politics in the United States, essentially between Democrats and Republicans, is like a media circus in a porkbarrel. The issue is pork—What goodies can come the way of our congressional district, our sector of the economy?—and the circus is television performance aided by megabuck campaign funds. Real public issues—homelessness, poverty, racism, AIDS, ecology, military support for despotic foreign governments—are mostly on the margins of mainstream political debate. So "alternative" is quite an extensive zone for serious political debate in the United States, not to mention Britain and a number of other countries. Nonetheless, a frequent reaction to small-scale radical media is, What good are they? How can they possibly make a dent? Who reads them or watches them? How many even know they exist?

That is where this chapter's title reference to the Boston Tea Party comes in. For some years now, a replica of the original sailing ship that brought the tea cargo to Boston has been moored in Boston Harbor as a floating museum. The replica actually made the Atlantic crossing, yet it is such a minute vessel compared with the size of ships today, it looks so flimsy, that it is hard to believe it could survive the Atlantic Ocean. Yet from such a tiny vessel were tipped the tea chests in the American revolt against British tyranny. That action, minuscule as it was, captured the imagination of the rebels and played a vital part in galvanizing resistance to the British crown. Not everyone became a rebel; George Washington had to draft people to fight. All the same, size alone was no index of the impact of the Boston Tea Party. And that is the beginning of wisdom in thinking about radical alternative media.

Another consideration is important. In Chapters 12 and 13, we have been examining the work that audiences do in reinterpreting the TV programs they watch, or in absorbing commercials. The notion of the "active" audience is an important one, to get away from the rather contemptuous attitude that says the audience is passive, inert, the model of the couch potato. But active audiences are but one step away from being media creators and producers themselves. In the earliest days of radio broadcasting in Germany in the 1920s, the great dramatist Bertolt Brecht (1983) wrote:

> Radio should be converted from a distribution system to a communication system. Radio could be the most wonderful public communication system imaginable, a gigantic system of channels—could be, that is, if it were capable not only of transmitting but of receiving, of making the listener not only hear but also speak, not of isolating him but of connecting him. This means that radio would have to give up being a purveyor and organize the listener as purveyor. (pp. 169-172)

What Brecht said sums up the essence of the alternative media idea, namely, the creation of *horizontal* linkages for the public's own communication networks, to assist in its empowerment. Such linkages contrast sharply with the *vertical* communication flows of the mainstream media, owned by giant corporations and basically sharing an entertainment-oriented, mainstream angle of vision on the issues that concern ordinary people. In a democratic society, such media are not nearly democratic enough. To be precise, their communication flows are not simply vertical, but top-down, from them to us. The only flow in the opposite direction that is genuinely ours, not just part of one of the commercial audience surveys Gandy discusses in Chapter 13, occurs when we write them letters—hardly an evenly balanced communication interaction.

Let us now move to an outline of the history of radical alternative media in the United States, to give a sense of the quite significant roles they have played in the country's history—despite their absence from many journalism histories.

Alternative Media
in the United States, 1760-1993

In Chapter 2, Sreberny-Mohammadi noted how the use of the vernacular in books and pamphlets encouraged the ferment of ideas and rebellious political movements in Europe at the time of the Reformation. By the time of the American War of Independence, literacy had increased further in the Colonies, with the result that many flyers, pamphlets, newspapers, and books circulated as part of the buildup to the armed struggle, and during it, to support the campaign. Prominent among such revolutionary writers was Tom Paine, whose pamphlet *Common Sense* (1776) went through numerous printings and was very widely read. Here is an excerpt:

> This is supposing the present race of kings in the world to have had an honorable origin: whereas it is more than probable, that, could we take off the dark covering of antiquity and trace them to their first rise, we should find the first of them nothing better than the principal ruffian of some restless gang, whose savage manners or pre-eminence in subtility obtained him the title of chief among the plunderers; and who by increasing in power and extending his depredations, overawed the quiet and defenceless to purchase their safety by frequent contributions. . . . But it is not so much the absurdity as the evil of hereditary succession which concerns mankind. . . . Men who look upon themselves as born to reign, and others to obey, soon grow insolent. Selected from the rest of mankind, their minds are early poisoned by importance. . . . But where, say some, is the King of America? I'll tell you, friend, he reigns above, and doth not make havoc of mankind like the Royal Brute of Great Britain. (in Conway, 1967, pp. 80-81, 99)

Paine later went on to publish in favor of the 1789 French Revolution. Along with Paine were no less than Samuel and John Adams, who worked for the weekly *Boston Gazette* from the 1760s onward. And there were many, many more.

In the nineteenth century a labor press began to develop, representing the growing body of workers that was beginning to build the industrial might of the United States. Concentrated in the 1830s and 1840s in cities such as Philadelphia, New York, and Boston, these working-class newspapers strove to bring about changes in the wages and conditions in American factories. The first ethnic press also began about this time, with the Black newspaper *Freedom's Journal* starting in New York in 1827, the *Cherokee Phoenix* in the South in 1828, and the Chinese-language *Golden Hills News* in San Francisco in the 1850s.

Perhaps the most striking example of alternative media in the first two-thirds of the century was the abolitionist press, which urged the ending of slavery in the United States. Of the many campaigners, preeminent was Frederick Douglass, himself born into slavery, largely self-educated, and then, as a freedman, a tireless campaigner and writer against the barbarism of racism and enslavement. This is an excerpt from one of his articles, originally printed in his newspaper, *North Star*:

> I have been made to feel keenly that I am in an enemy's land—surrounded on all sides by hardships, difficulties and dangers—that on the side of the oppressor there is power, and that there are few to take up the cause of my deeply injured and down-trodden people. These things grieve, but do not appal me. Not an inch will I retreat—not one jot of zeal will I abate—not one word will I retract; and, in the strength of God, while the red current of life flows through my veins, I will continue to labor for the downfall of slavery and the freedom of my race. I am denounced as an offender. I am not ignorant of my offences. I plead guilty to the worst of those laid to my charge. Amplified as they have been, enormous as they are alleged to be, I do not shrink from looking them full in the face, and glorying in having committed them. My crime is, that I have assumed to be a man, entitled to all the rights, privileges and dignity, which belong to human nature—that color is no crime, and that all men are brothers. I have acted on this presumption. (in Foner, 1950, p. 126)

As the century moved on, women too began to organize, in support of their right to vote, and they too began to publish newspapers and pamphlets. Among the newspapers were *Lily* and *Revolution*, edited, respectively, by Amelia Bloomer and by Elizabeth Cady Stanton and Susan B. Anthony. *Lily* lasted 10 years, *Revolution* for 4, and both contributed to the slow groundswell in women's consciousness and organization. Equally important was the growth in the numbers of women writing novels and short stories that contributed to the expression of women's perspectives and sensibilities.

With the tremendous upsurge of labor immigration from the 1880s on, much of it from southern and eastern Europe, the American labor movement took on a new character. Until then, the political perspectives of American workers had largely been confined to demands for a better deal at work. The new arrivals brought with them wider perspectives on social and political change, derived from socialist, Marxist, and anarchist philosophies that sought to understand society as a whole. Such perspectives tried to point out the interconnections between exploitation in the workplace and slum housing, between industrial accidents and poor health care, between factory discipline and the police force.

Many publications reflected this new flowering of political debate, such as the Socialist Party's Kansas-printed but nationally distributed *Appeal to Reason*, which ran from 1895 to 1917, and at its high watermark in 1912 sold three-quarters of a million copies. Less widely circulated, but still influential, was *Mother Earth*, a magazine published by the anarchist and feminist Emma Goldman, whose parents had fled Russia in the 1880s to escape anti-Semitic persecution, and who herself became a byword for militant campaigns for peace, birth control rights for women, prisoners' rights, and many other movements. Here is a sample of the spirited writing she produced:

> The State is commonly regarded as the highest form of organization. But is it in reality a true organization? Is it not rather a sample of the kind of arbitrary institution, cunningly imposed upon the masses?
>
> Industry, too, is called an organization; yet nothing is farther from the truth. Industry is the ceaseless piracy of the rich against the poor.
>
> We are asked to believe that the Army is an organization, but a close investigation will show that it is nothing else than a cruel instrument of blind force.
>
> The Public School! The colleges and other institutions of learning, are they not models of organization, offering the people fine opportunities for instruction? Far from it. The school, more than any other institution, is a veritable barrack, where the human mind is drilled and manipulated into submission to various social and moral spooks, and thus fitted to continue our system of exploitation and oppression.
>
> Organization, as we [anarchists] understand it, however, is a different thing. It is based, primarily, on freedom. It is a natural and voluntary grouping of energies to secure results beneficial to humanity. (Goldman, 1969, p. 35)

Another very lively socialist newspaper in the early twentieth century was *The Masses*, edited by Max Eastman, who later switched his social and political views almost totally and ended up editing the cozy, conservative monthly, *Reader's Digest*. *The Masses*, however, was irreverent, imaginative, and unorthodox. It also carried some of the most exciting and challenging feminist writing of the day, as Margaret Jones has documented in her book *Heretics and Hellraisers* (1993).

Until the 1930s, African Americans had been alone in developing film as an alternative medium (Nesteby, 1982, chaps. 5-6). In the 1930s Depression decade, however, the joblessness and poverty familiar to many African Americans suddenly became a reality to white America as well. Between a quarter and a third of all Americans were thrown out of work, and until U.S. entry into World War II in 1941 at last fired up the industrial machine, there seemed no hope of economic or social improvement for millions upon millions of families.

Hollywood films mostly sought to entertain, to give people something to take their minds off the situation, but small groups of alternative filmmakers set out to provide something more constructive. They wanted to use film to communicate as vividly as possible the true scale of the economic disaster and the efforts of people across the country to fight back against the callous imposition of poverty and hunger. They also wanted their films to be discussed locally after they were shown—quite unlike the Hollywood theatrical system, where audience members go their separate ways as soon as the credits roll. In other words, they wanted to foster an active audience that could use film to discuss the practical options open to unemployed workers to fight for justice and social change. Units such as the Workers' Film and Photo League, and later Nykino (Alexander, 1981), joined the marches of the unemployed. From inside demonstrations they would film the police clubbing the marchers, rather than keep to the safe and implicitly biased position behind the police lines that most news camera operators preferred (and still prefer).

After the war there was an explosion of militant labor activism in the 15-month strike wave of 1945 and 1946. This resurgence was also fueled by the political optimism generated by having won the war, having crushed Fascism in Europe and Japan, having said farewell to the Depression, and having both Americans and Soviets working together to defeat the Nazis.

Almost immediately, however, the first Cold War between the United States and the Soviet Union began, generally dated from March 1946 (the second Cold War was in 1980-1986, in the early part of the Reagan presidency). Following the Communist-led revolution in China in 1949 and the Korean War of 1950-1953, during which Korea was partitioned between a Communist North and a pro-West South, the political leadership in the United States moved from strongly anticommunist to hysterically anticommunist. China was widely declared to have been "lost," and when it joined in the Korean War on the other side, the military repeatedly urged Presidents Truman and Eisenhower to use nuclear bombs against it.

In this tense and overheated climate emerged a senator from Wisconsin, Joseph McCarthy, who would spearhead a four-year reign of fear inside the United States, causing teachers, film directors, screenwriters, State Department officials, labor activists, and a host of others to be dismissed from their work and to be effectively unemployable—often simply on the *accusation* of being traitors to their country, that is, communists or "fellow travelers." The definitions were pretty loose. To be, or to have been, active in working for Black civil rights; to have known some communists during the Depression decade and to refuse to name them to the FBI; to be an ad production director who employed a suspected "Red" actor in a TV commercial; to be a labor union activist; to be a university instructor who tried to analyze the reality of China, rather than simply condemning it—any of these could get an individual into deep trouble.

Alternative media during McCarthyism faced enormous problems. The response of many political dissidents was to keep their heads down and hope the storm would pass. Let us consider two cases of media that fought back. One was the weekly newspaper the *National Guardian* (from 1967, the *Guardian*). The other was KPFA, a listener-supported radio station in Berkeley, California, which eventually led to the foundation of four other similar stations in Los Angeles, New York, Houston, and Washington, D.C. (the Pacifica stations). These cases are interesting; they illustrate the special importance of alternative media in periods of political suppression, and they continued in existence for more than 40 years. KPFA is the first major example of alternative radio in the United States.

Until it closed in 1993, the *Guardian* was edited in New York City. It nearly always took a very independent line both in relation to the U.S. government and in relation to revolutions abroad. Whereas newspapers belonging to political sects would always trot out the sect's current "line," the *Guardian* generally retained a distance from all ready-made political positions. In the 1950s, when Yugoslavia was pursuing an independent path, aligned with neither Moscow nor Washington, the newspaper supported it. In periods when mainstream media reporting of ongoing political struggles in Latin America and Africa was sketchy, to say the least, the *Guardian* would include reports from people on the front lines. In the civil rights struggles in the South in the late 1950s and early 1960s, the paper was passed from hand to hand at marches and rallies as practically the only source that would cover the situation fully and honestly. It was read not just by big-city political activists, but by citizens scattered the length and breadth of the country, in remote villages and towns. It never achieved the circulation of, say, *Appeal to Reason*, but in the frightened days of McCarthyism, it was one of the few media beacons of sanity and fearlessness.

KPFA was founded to be a public forum for a variety of views, but with special emphasis on pacifist perspectives, some Quakers having been active in setting it up. During McCarthyism, the continued existence of a radio station in which a full spectrum of views could be expressed was a major achievement. In the early years, the political spectrum included Caspar Weinberger, who would eventually (as President Reagan's defense secretary) force through the largest military budgets in U.S. history, communist activist Dorothy Healy, and people of all persuasions.

The achievement was fragile, however. Both the *Guardian* and KPFA received their share of unwelcome attention from the government during McCarthyism and afterward. It seems strange that small-scale media of this ilk should attract repeated attempts to squelch them, but as the account of Soviet underground (samizdat) media in Chapter 11 indicates, size alone does not indicate significance. Even if some observers are inclined to dismiss alternative media skeptically as of no account, neither the U.S. nor the Soviet government has agreed.

The ways in which the government tried to shut them down, without taking the provocative step of officially censoring them, were various. In the case of the *Guardian*, pressure was put on news vendors not to put it on sale or they would face FBI inquiries themselves. Subscribers in some parts of the country received visits from local FBI agents, asking them whether they approved of what they were reading—which could in turn lead to their encountering all kinds of problems from antileftist zealots in their local communities. Every time the *Guardian* presses were about to print the paper, the staff meticulously checked for foreign objects that would wreck the machinery. From time to time such sabotage was avoided. Cedric Belfrage, one of the paper's three founders (along with James Aronson and John MacManus), was imprisoned and deported, albeit on no criminal charge. This was possible because of his British citizenship, although he had lived in the United States for 20 years and had an American family.

In the case of KPFA, there were repeated threats to have its license to broadcast suspended by the Federal Communications Commission, and it was also once subjected to review by the Senate Internal Security Subcommittee. Not only was this unnerving and dispiriting, but, in the FCC cases, it meant spending a considerable amount of extremely scarce funds on hiring lawyers to represent the station. Other tactics used to close down alternative media have included IRS tax audits (which mean engaging the costly services of accountants for audits that might drag on for a year or more) and government pressure on landlords not to renew leases on premises occupied by alternative media projects. These methods fall well short of the savage repression practiced in some countries, but they are completely disloyal to the spirit of the First Amendment.

The four major political movements of the 1960s—the continuing civil rights movement, the student movement against the Vietnam War, the movements of ethnic and racial protest in the inner cities, and the revived women's movement—proved to be highly fertile ground for new alternative media. KPFA was deeply involved in the pitched confrontations between students and police in the Berkeley free speech movement of 1964, and the *National Guardian* very early on identified the Vietnam War as an unjust and barbarous crusade, long before mainstream media began to criticize it. Many other media projects, mostly print—such as *Rat, Seed,* and *Liberation News Service*—sprang up and played a key part in the movements, and later folded. Some continued, such as *Report on the Americas,* from the North American Congress on Latin America, and *Akwesasne Notes,* a Native American publication based in the Mohawk nation. During the 1960s, 16-millimeter film began to be used again, following the precedent of the 1930s, and a number of documentaries were produced on the Black struggle and the antiwar movement. One, made in 1974 and titled *Hearts and Minds,* exposed the real character of the Vietnam War as opposed to its TV news presentation, and went on to win an Academy Award.

Indeed, one of the most absorbing alternative media sagas of that period was the alternative media explosion inside the armed forces, examples being the *Bond,* published by the American Servicemen's Union, and *Ally.* Try as they would to stamp these publications out, the Army top brass faced such powerful interest among GIs in these underground papers that arrests for distributing them dropped away. The generals feared further alienating their unwilling troops by creating martyrs to censorship. An example of writing that appeared in the *Bond* follows:

> I was an apathetic person without any strong views on subjects dealing with peace, war, oppression, rights, etc., until I was sent to Vietnam in January of '69. While "serving" my country in that crime of illegal involvement, I saw the people of Vietnam degraded, cursed and humiliated almost daily. I saw the way North Vietnamese prisoners were treated

by our "wholesome" American soldiers. . . . Most of all I talked with the people of Vietnam and heard what THEY wanted and how they felt about U.S. involvement.

I came back a changed person, no longer apathetic, sickened by the war and what it was doing.

At the present time I am on the editorial staff of a recently started underground newspaper and I am very interested in starting a chapter of the American Serviceman's Union here. (in Aronson, 1972, p. 214)

Current Initiatives

To bring the story more or less up to the present, the discussion now moves to some more contemporary alternative media projects that have used electronic technologies for their work. The two selected are PeaceNet and Deep Dish TV Satellite Network.

PeaceNet, based in Berkeley, California, since 1985, uses the power of the computer and the modem order to link up various peace activists with others across the United States, within Western European countries, and in some other countries, such as Kenya and Costa Rica. For a relatively small monthly fee, users can hook into continuing messages and debates and current information about a whole variety of issues, including peace and disarmament strictly defined, environmental issues, Native American struggles, Central America and Southern Africa support groups, and many other matters. The isolation often experienced by small groups working on particular issues in this vast country can be quite quickly broken down by this means, and up-to-the-minute information can be made available much more readily than by newspapers or mail. Indeed, groups working with each other across substantial distances can send documents back and forth much more cheaply and quickly than they could by mail. Given the tiny budgets of many alternative projects, this is a major consideration.

Deep Dish TV Satellite Network first transmitted in New York in 1986. Using satellite communication technology and hooking up with 300 public-access channels on cable stations across the United States, it offered 10 one-hour programs a week for 10 weeks in that year, and in 1988 expanded to 20 weeks. Its objective is to make community TV programming, estimated by Deep Dish at more than 16,000 hours produced each year, more widely available, so that all the effort and creativity involved are not limited to a single cable channel. The programs transmitted have been compilations of locally produced TV, on many issues: Latino images, young people, aging, homelessness, AIDS, a four-part rapidly compiled series on the 1991 war against Iraq, a multipart critique timed for the quincentenary observance of Columbus's arrival in the Americas. The types of issues that mainstream media deal with so rarely and poorly, with their vertical communication flows, are substituted in the Deep Dish project by people—old, young, Latino, the homeless, workers, gays—speaking for themselves and producing media coverage about their own concerns.

In other words, the tradition of Sam and John Adams, of Tom Paine and Frederick Douglass, of Emma Goldman and countless others, continues. It is a tradition alive and well in most countries of the world, in one form or another, although there is no space to review those experiences here. What we must now do is stand back for a moment from this information about alternative media and assess what can be said about alternative media impact in general.

Conclusions: The Alternative Forum of Political Movements

There is little doubt that alternative media flourish most vigorously in the wastelands left by mainstream media. When the latter, because of the biases of their owners, editors, and, often, journalists, choose not to represent important slices of social and political reality, then the public becomes increasingly hungry for honest and comprehensive information about those issues. When the mainstream media misrepresent social and political realities, then, again, alternative media come into their own. They provide an alternative public forum—sometimes referred to as the "public sphere" or "public realm"—to the official forum and the official story (Downing, 1988a). They meet a heartfelt need for both information and the opportunity to share experiences and strategies, mistakes and successes.

These media have a much harder road to walk when they appear to be voices crying in a wilderness, when only a dedicated minority seems to listen, like the *Guardian* and KPFA in the McCarthy years. Without a vigorous political movement to feed into their columns or wavebands, and to be fed and stimulated in turn by what they produce, it takes tremendous commitment to sustain the effort and the creativity needed. In crisis situations, a poorly photocopied typed sheet of paper will be seized upon and shared by many people because its contents are in demand. In more normal situations, questions of presentation, style, format, wit, imagination, and—not least—finance require sustained attention.

There is a vital interaction between political movements and media (see Mohammadi, Chapter 21): Without their own media, political movements are stymied. Communication from above, the vertical communication criticized earlier on, will fill the gap left open. The powers that be will have a free run. Equally, however, whether or not political movements come to maturity has a great deal to do with the prior existence of opinion centers, media that have begun to arouse people's awareness of the scope and source of the problems they face on a daily basis.

Further Questions

1. What is the relation between ethnic media and alternative media? What is the significance of the facts that the history of African American media is mostly one of challenge to the status quo and the history of Latino media (admittedly often owned by Anglos) is mostly one of compliance (Downing, 1992)?

2. What are the practicalities of alternative media? These can vary from the most immediate, such as how to meet the bills and organize distribution, to the tougher still, such as how democratic the organization of the newspaper or video production team should be. If media are to promote democracy, should not their own organizations be democratic? And if this is agreed, then what kind of democracy works best in the media (Downing, 1984)?

3. What is the comparative international experience of alternative media? This can be very illuminating in regard to many such questions, as also in regard to the relations between such media and political movements. Political cinema in the Third World (Downing, 1987), clandestine radio stations and guerrilla movements, samizdat works in Eastern Europe, and audiocassettes in the Iranian revolution (Sreberny-Mohammadi & Mohammadi, 1994) are only some of the international examples that repay careful study.

Note

1. Some people would include extreme rightist alternative media, such as the computer bulletin board networks used by white supremacist groups (Kay, 1988) or their

cable TV programs. In my view, these groups are not disconnected from the mainstream cultural reality of white racism in the United States (see Chapter 20), even if their love of violence seems to set them apart.

PART IV

Information Technologies

In this section we introduce you to some of the new technologies of communication that have rapidly made their mark on the way we live. A great deal has been written about these technologies and their impacts, whether within rich countries or on poorer countries' prospects for economic development. In our view, what has been written has often consisted of hype and speculation, much of which is conveyed by the phrase "the information society." This phrase is used to conjure a future when seemingly all that happens will be computerized and a present in which suddenly almost every one has been transformed into an "information worker." Municipal bureaucrats and their secretaries, telephone switch operators, research scientists, journalists, economists, microchip circuit assemblers, TV repair technicians, entertainers—all are redefined and lumped together and somehow trimmed into "the future," a clean, efficient twenty-first century laden with technological marvels and no pain. All we will want to know, all we will need to live, will be at our fingertips with a few keystrokes, summoned via satellite and flashing along the fiber optics, or so the mythmakers would have us believe.

However, in the real world, the situation can be interpreted as being a good deal more somber. Governments and corporations are restricting the flow of information they value, pumping out the perspectives and "facts" they would have us value, and gathering more and more information about our activities for their own purposes. Microcircuit assemblers are contracting a variety of industrial diseases, and the circuits they make are being installed in missile nose cones.

253

Which of these perspectives is more valid? What evidence would you cite in support of one position or the other? The three chapters that follow provide basic information that can feed into your thinking on the subject. Those who already have substantial technical knowledge may want to skip some of these pages; others will find them a necessary basic introduction to the world of new communications technology. Remember the arguments of Sreberny-Mohammadi (Chapter 2) and Winston (Chapter 4) in Part I, especially their combined insistence on the interaction in earlier history between social and cultural forces and new communications technologies. As Winston proposes, the technology always offers opportunities, it always has a radical potential, but whether that is realized depends on the pressures exerted by different groups within society. Media by themselves do not make anything happen; how new technologies are put to use, for socially benign or politically nefarious tasks, is a critical issue as we approach the twenty-first century.

15 Computers and Communication

NIKHIL SINHA

ALLUCQUÉRE ROSANNE STONE

A necessary first step in media studies today is to recognize that the distribution and processing of data are forms of communication, just as media and interpersonal communications are. Even if no human being specifically originates or receives the information, and even if a computer automatically processes the data without a specific instruction to do so in each case, communication is still taking place through the medium of the computer. As Gandy (Chapter 13) points out, the interface between data communication and media communication is developing extremely quickly, and the old boundaries between media industries and telecommunications industries have been eroded. Computerization and digitalization of information have been key to that process.

Sinha and Stone review some of the major computer hardware and software developments over the past hundred years. Computers now affect many aspects of the ways we work and live. They are currently used in many different forms of communication, especially in electronic mail (e-mail) and teleconferencing, and in databases of various kinds, and these applications raise questions of surveillance and privacy. Computers affect how the military prepares and wages war, as in the Persian Gulf War, which graphically showed how computer applications are transforming military weaponry and tactics with missiles and precision bombs guided to their targets by tiny on-board computers. Computers also, however, provide a medium through which we can foster strategies for peace, as in the PeaceNet organization (see Downing, Chapter 14). Sinha and Stone conclude that as ordinary citizens we live in a world that for the most part is not of our making, but the computer has the potential to provide ordinary people with the ability to use technology for our own ends and take some control over our own lives.

> A Computer is a universal machine. . . . it can perform any task that can be described in symbols.
>
> ALAN TURING

When the history of the twentieth century is written there is little doubt that future historians will recognize the computer as one of the most remarkable inventions of the century. The computer is the first machine ever invented whose uses are not confined by the purposes for which it was invented. The uses of a computer, the functions it can perform, are limited mainly by our ability to communicate to it a set of instructions. A computer consists of three main parts: hardware, the physical part; software, the instructions that tell the computer what to do; and interfaces, which communicate between machines and humans. As the British mathematician Alan Turing pointed out, the computer is truly a universal machine—that is, able to manipulate any information whatsoever, as long as the information can be expressed in symbolic form. Most communication involves the creation and sharing of meaning through the exchange of symbols. Human language is a symbolic system in which words represent things and ideas; mathematics and musical scales, in which notes on paper represent certain sounds, are two more examples. These symbolic systems are translatable into a special binary symbolic system of 0s and 1s that the computer uses to communicate. Hence we are able to use this remarkable machine to calculate the trajectory of *Apollo 11*, play chess, compose music, write poetry, draw pictures, design cars, simulate the hole in the ozone layer, predict the weather, and do a multitude of other things, some we cannot yet imagine.

Although its name, *computer*, is a function of the first purpose for which it was developed (to calculate with numbers), in terms of what it can do its name could as easily be painter, writer, or musician. It is this versatility of the computer, this universality, that has enabled it to permeate every aspect of modern life, affect every social institution, and change virtually every human activity. The computer is unlike any other technology yet developed. Whereas other technologies have extended human physical abilities or allowed us to overcome our physical limitations, the computer has extended our mental faculties, enhanced our intellectual capabilities in ways previously unimaginable. In this chapter we will explore the ways in which computers are dramatically changing human society and consider the promises and threats of computer-based communication.

Origins of the Computer

The earliest ancestors of modern computers were machines or instruments designed to perform arithmetical tasks, such as the abacus, developed in China 2,000 years ago. Later forerunners include instruments developed by the French philosopher Blaise Pascal, who is widely credited with building the first "digital calculating machine" in 1642, and the German philosopher Gottfried Wilhelm von Leibniz, who invented an instrument that could add and multiply. By the eighteenth century, the Jacquard textile loom had been developed in France. The loom's "software" consisted of cards punched with holes that represented the fabric design, and the "hardware," made of mechanical rods and levers, read the pattern of holes and controlled the actual motions of the shuttle and thread. During the first half of the nineteenth century, Charles Babbage, an English mathematician, designed an automatic mechanical calculating machine that he called a "difference engine." Babbage then moved on to the construction of what today would be described as a general-purpose, fully programmable, automatic mechanical computer that he called an "analytical engine." Some researchers believe that many of the ideas for its construction were suggested by Babbage's close friend Ada Lovelace, who also designed its software and has thereby come to be known as the first computer programmer. The U.S. Defense Department's official programming language is named Ada, in her honor.

The analytical engine was to operate automatically, by steam power, and would require only one attendant. The operating characteristics that Babbage wanted—full programmability and user-determined applications—foreshadowed the design of the modern computer. But few people in the mid-1800s saw the need for such a device, the British government withdrew its support, and a hundred years passed before Babbage's dream was realized. As Winston (see Chapter 4) would argue, there was no "supervening social necessity" at this point in history to foster the development of such a revolutionary machine.

Development of the Modern Computer

It took the outbreak of World War II to revive interest in the development of automatic digital computers. Three developments during the war laid the groundwork for modern computing. In Germany, a young civil engineer, Konrad Zuse, was put to work to develop a computer to aid the German war machine, and in 1941 he developed the first mechanical, general-purpose digital computer using electromagnetic relays. It was slow and cumbersome, but it worked. In England, Alan Turing, a brilliant young mathematician, was recruited by British Intelligence to help crack German spy codes. His work led to the development of Colossus, the first computer designed not to do calculations but to manipulate letters and symbols. In spite of his brilliant work, Turing was viciously persecuted for his homosexuality. Driven to despair, he committed suicide by eating a poisoned apple—a fact that may have found its way into the naming of the first successful personal computer company, Apple Computer.

In the United States there was a desperate need to develop firing tables to help artillery gunners determine the correct firing trajectory for their guns. The necessary calculations were slow and complicated work. In 1942, the Defense Department commissioned engineers at the University of Pennsylvania to design a machine that could compute firing tables automatically. Their machine, an "electrical numerical integrator and calculator," or ENIAC, was not completed in time to help the war effort, but it became the prototype of the modern computer. Instead of using electromagnetic relays, it used vacuum tubes, which could perform calculations about 1,000 times faster.

In all three instances, the role of the military was pivotal in the development of the first generation of computers. This trend continues today, with military needs driving the development of a number of computer advances. The Cold War between the West and the former Soviet bloc from 1946 to 1991 triggered the development of a new generation of weapons designed to deliver nuclear warheads across the globe. These missile systems, based on land, sea, and air, required sophisticated computers to guide and control their trajectories. Additionally, the rapid growth of nuclear arsenals required the development of command-and-control systems that could coordinate a nuclear war should it break out. Computers were at the heart of such systems. The merging of computers with laser weapons technology was also at the core of the so-called Star Wars systems developed during the Reagan administration. The earliest computer network, ARPANET, and what was later to become the world's largest computer network, Internet, were both developed for military purposes.

More recently, the 1991 war in the Persian Gulf, between the United States and Iraq, graphically showed how computer applications are transforming military weapons and tactics. Cruise missiles and precision bombs were guided to their targets by tiny on-board computers that contained detailed information of the topography of the areas over which they traveled. U.S. pilots rehearsed their missions using flight simulators that surrounded them with realistic images of the terrain over which they would pass. During the actual missions, the pilots sometimes saw their targets only as computerized cockpit displays rather than as actual buildings or aircraft (hence the nickname the "Nintendo war"). Many of them then flew home to watch their missions replayed on the CNN cable network.

The development of computers was also boosted by the space race, which in the 1960s was a key issue of the Cold War. President Kennedy's challenge to put a man on the moon in a decade could be fulfilled only with the development of an on-board computer system powerful enough to guide a spacecraft during the final phases of its trip to the moon. The development of integrated circuits (ICs) and later of very-large-scale integrated circuits (VLSIs) began the process of the miniaturization of the computer that continued with the development of the microprocessor and resulted eventually in the creation of the revolutionary machine that today sits atop millions of desks—the personal computer. In the mid-1970s the Altair, the first commercial "home computer" (the term *personal computer* was not yet in use), was marketed by a small company in Austin, Texas. The surprising demand for the Altair triggered the development of smaller and more user-friendly computers by a host of small companies. At that time the computer industry was dominated by the giant International Business Machines (IBM), which specialized in building huge mainframe computers for large corporations and institutions, based on the philosophy that data processing should be centralized in one machine to which access could be carefully controlled. A single mainframe was meant to service the needs of hundreds of users, but only one user at a time. IBM predicted that no more than five mainframes would be sufficient to handle the computing needs of the entire world. The idea that many people could share a mainframe at the same time, a process called *multitasking*, was still in the laboratory stage.

The personal computer revolution that was triggered by Altair found a home in California's Silicon Valley, named after the mineral used to manufacture the integrated circuits, or chips, that are the building blocks of computers. In this climate, Steve Jobs and Steve Wozniak, two young men working out of a garage in Palo Alto, began making a computer they called the Apple, based on one of the first commercial microprocessors. Almost simultaneously, the Commodore Corporation announced the Pet, based on the same microprocessor. The Apple and the Pet were different from the Altair in a major and critical way. Information was entered into the Altair in digital form, by means of switches on its front panel. This meant that use of the Altair was restricted to experimenters with the patience to master a thorough understanding of the binary language of computers. Both the Apple and the Pet, in contrast, used typewriterlike keyboards to enter information, and the translation of that information into the digital language the microprocessor could understand was carried out by a software program called an *interpreter*. The interpreter was written by a young programmer named Bill Gates, who had formed a small software company named Microsoft to market it. Gates named the interpreter program BASIC, partly as a tip of the hat to an imaginary and hopeful "universal language" popular in science fiction. The development of the interpreter moved the personal computer out of the small and specialized experimenters' market and made it accessible to anyone who could operate a keyboard. A few years later, IBM moved into the home computer market and announced its Personal Computer (PC). IBM's business clout and huge advertising budget assured that the name would stick, and it has come to refer to any small computer—not just one made by IBM.

IBM's marketing strategy for its PC was quite different from Apple's. Although there was a brief time early in Apple's career when cheap copies ("clones") of the Apple made in East Asia were widely available, Apple pursued a vigorous campaign to keep its technology proprietary. It was only in 1993 that Apple, pressed by financial needs, finally licensed another manufacturer to use Apple technology in a product. IBM, however, not only encouraged other companies to manufacture PCs using IBM technology, but also published the PC's specifications. In a short time thousands of manufacturers were producing PC clones or add-on accessories for them. Competition was fierce, and prices dropped. It appears to have been this move on IBM's part that made the personal computer cheap and plentiful on a scale that Apple was at that time reluctant to match.

In the 1980s, Xerox developed the Alto, which used a graphical user interface (GUI), in which files were represented not by words but by small drawings of objects normally found on a desk. The researchers called these drawings *icons*. The Alto had other advanced features as well, such as a mouse, which meant that the user could move objects around on the screen with a natural hand movement; and windows, which meant that the computer could display more than one task at a time. In addition, the Alto was a radical departure from mainframe philosophy. Instead of centralizing processing power in a single computer, to which would be connected a large number of input/output devices or terminals, the Alto made each terminal a small independent processor that shared information with all the other terminals, a system that the Xerox researchers called *distributed processing*.

The advantages of distributed processing—such as eliminating the disruption caused by failures in the mainframe, immediate processing of individual jobs, and intercommunication between workers via their computers—completely escaped both Xerox's and IBM's management and marketing departments. Nor did Xerox want to market the Alto, so Apple Computer developed its own version and marketed it as the Apple Macintosh. With the commercial reality of an inexpensive computer with a simple intuitive graphic interface, mouse, and windows, the PC revolution had finally arrived.

Computers in the Economy

Although computers, both mainframes and PCs, are now commonplace in the business environment, the civilian spread of computing after World War II was much slower in developing than were the military and space applications. Remember that as late as 1958 IBM had predicted that only five computers would be sufficient to meet worldwide data processing needs. It took the economic crises of the second half of the 1970s to create conditions under which the potential of computers could be realized.

The late 1970s saw the worst recession the industrialized world had encountered since World War II, characterized by high unemployment, low profitability of corporations, and rising prices. Corporations turned to computers to boost the productivity of their workers, thereby lowering costs and raising profits. In 1982, U.S. companies were investing about $10 billion a year in computing technologies; by 1992 they were investing about $80 billion, more than in any other technology. Thus industry's need to increase efficiency was a large factor in the development and spread of computers.

Computers have now permeated all aspects of business and the economy. Computers control almost all stages of the manufacturing process, from the design of products with the help of computer-aided design (CAD) programs to the manufacturing of products through control of assembly lines. They are also used to boost the efficiency of payroll, accounting, inventory, and other "back-office" operations, and can boost competitiveness by aiding in the development of innovative products and services and by improving the ways in which they are marketed. Computers have played a significant role in the coordination of global economic activities. The internationalization of business has led to the extensive use of computers by transnational corporations (TNCs) to keep track of their far-flung operations. The control of TNCs depends on the rapid and secure processing and transfer of information across the world. The merging of computer and telecommunication technologies, which is at the heart of the information revolution, has made both possible.

The impact of computers has been deeply felt in the financial sector. Banking and stock and currency markets depend heavily on computers to process transactions around the world. These sectors are less financial than information industries—information that is stored and processed by computers. Similarly, insurance and credit industries rely on computers for the evaluation of risk and the acceptance or rejection of customer applications. The development of so-called expert systems—computer programs designed to replicate human decision-making processes—have greatly enhanced the role of computers in these areas. For a time, researchers believed that expert systems would eventually take over many tasks currently performed by humans. It was also believed that artificial intelligence, the development of truly intelligent computers that could understand human speech and perform humanlike reasoning, would not be long in arriving. However, both of these problems have proved far more intractable than early researchers anticipated. The process of creating an expert system— capturing the knowledge and skills of a human expert in the form of a computer program—did not take into consideration how much of human skill is tacit, or below the conscious level. Similarly, in artificial intelligence systems the most basic element, recognition of natural human speech in context, has proved impossibly complex. In addition, some philosophers argue that human intelligence itself can arise only in social interactions; thus a computer, which is not raised or nurtured but built, can never become truly intelligent. The debate continues to the present day.

Computers and Social Surveillance

Although computers have done much to enhance business productivity, their impacts on workers have only recently begun to be manifest. During the recession of the late 1980s and early 1990s, the largest number of layoffs took place among white-collar workers, those who work most closely with computers. Although it is difficult to say that these retrenchments are a direct outcome of the introduction of computers, there is considerable evidence that computers are changing the ways in which work has traditionally been performed. Computers have raised fears of a two-tiered workforce—the top tier characterized by a minority of highly skilled, highly educated, and highly paid information workers, and the lower tier characterized by low-paid, less-educated service and manufacturing workers.

Allied to this is the impact of computers on the monitoring of workers. Corporate and office networks provide managers and supervisors with the ability to eavesdrop on virtually every aspect of a networked computing environment, with or without the approval or knowledge of the workers. Supervisors can view the contents of data files and electronic messages, audit time and usage, delete and alter messages, and overwrite private passwords. Network-monitoring programs and specially designed surveillance programs for mainframe computers can log every detail of every computer transaction. There is mounting evidence that the potential to eavesdrop is being swiftly transformed into the actuality of privacy invasion as corporations strive to maximize worker productivity. Some surveys indicate that nearly 80% of workers in the telecommunications, insurance, and banking industries are subject to some form of computer surveillance.

The impact of computers on individual privacy is not confined to the workplace; it is commonplace in the everyday activities we engage in as members of a modern complex society—obtaining credit, going to the doctor, renting a movie, getting a driver's license, using the phone, applying for benefits and entitlements, and, most frequently, purchasing consumer goods and services. So deep and widespread are the possibilities of using computers to monitor citizens that some have called this the biggest threat to democracy in industrialized countries (Burnham, 1983).

Democratic societies protect the privacy of individuals, groups, and associations by limiting the power of government agencies and corporations to collect and disseminate information about them. The computer provides public and private agencies with new means of collecting and storing information about individuals, thus eroding or bypassing established legal protections. Access to the total computerized profile of an individual means that (a) very little privacy remains, for it is hard to know how to prevent abuse of the knowledge, and (b) computer errors can seriously affect an individual's life, as in the case of incorrect credit ratings. (For a treatment of this danger at the hands of a police state, see the movie *Brazil*.)

For instance, both state and federal governments are increasingly using computer "matching" programs that search through welfare, employment, and other social service data banks to detect and "kick out" what appear to be instances of fraud. Corporations use information gathered through credit card and other consumer transactions to build up extensive computer files of individuals. These profiles are used to develop credit reports and to produce profiles of "attractive consumers" for direct marketing activities. Some public disclosure of personal information is necessary for government and corporate agencies to provide services to citizens and consumers, but computers have contributed to the blurring of the boundaries between what is necessary disclosure and what is invasion of privacy. As computer technology and its applications grow, the proper balances among individual privacy, public disclosure, and government and corporate surveillance will continue to be a major social issue.

The Social Impact of Computers

Computers have permeated almost every aspect of society. *Time* magazine declared the computer "Machine of the Year" in 1982, and by the mid-1980s the personal computer had invaded the home. Its uses range from managing family accounts to storing recipes; from giving children an educational "head start" to playing computer games. By the early 1990s, computer-based information systems such as videotex were providing information and electronic mail services to millions of homes. Through these systems users can purchase products; make airline, hotel, and car rental reservations; book theater tickets; check the weather, stock market quotes, or the latest sports results; and communicate through e-mail with thousands of people around the world.

These computer applications initially raised great expectations of a future society characterized by high-paying information jobs, increased leisure and entertainment time, and the development of what the popular writer Alvin Toffler has called the "electronic cottage." The electronic cottage is made possible by the development of telework, work performed outside the normal organizational limits of space and time, and telecommuting, the use of computers and telecommunications to transmit work to the worker, rather than having workers commute to the workplace. But in the 1980s it became evident that if there were such benefits to be had from computers, they would be unevenly distributed among different groups in society.

There were great hopes that the widespread introduction of computers would enhance employment opportunities for women in the workforce, but trends in the 1980s were not very encouraging. Statistics from the U.S. Department of Labor Women's Bureau reveal that while the number of women in computer-related occupations increased by 245,000 between 1985 and 1990, most of them were in low-paying, nonmanagement jobs. And although the number of computer managers more than doubled between 1980 and 1990, the proportion of women in these jobs increased slowly, from 18% to 25%. The situation is even worse for minorities as whole and minority women in particular. About 92% of computer managers in 1990 were white—the same proportion as in 1980 (Johnson, 1990).

The seeds of this lower participation are sown in the educational system. Although the numbers of women receiving bachelor's, master's, and doctoral degrees in computer science increased from 1980 to 1986, they decreased in 1987 and 1988. Women continue to be dramatically underrepresented on the faculties of computer science and computer engineering departments; in 1988-1989, only 6.5% of such faculty members were women. The lack of adequate role models may discourage women from entering these fields. The situation is not very encouraging at the school level, either. Although there is now considerable evidence that girls are as adept and accomplished in computer-related activities as boys, schools continue to encourage boys to study computer-related subjects and simultaneously discourage girls from acquiring computer skills (Rosenberg, 1992). Under conditions of limited computer resources and time, this has resulted in boys outnumbering girls in every computer-related activity—computer courses, computer-aided instruction, and computer games. The corresponding male gendering of computer-associated culture may well lead to a highly skewed acquisition of computer skills and computer literacy.

The idea that people should be computer literate hardly seems controversial in the 1990s. However, there remains considerable disagreement over the definition, importance, and relevance of computer literacy. Should it include such knowledge as programming? What about issues relating to the historical, social, or economic impacts of computers? Even more contentious is the relationship between computer literacy and traditional literacy. Computers designed to be used by illiterate workers in low-end service sector occupations raise fears that they might encourage illiteracy and school dropouts. What is clear is that the impacts of computers are not universal or uniform. It is likely that the impacts of computers are conditioned by such social and economic characteristics as class, race, gender, and geographic location.

Computer Networks

Computers are increasingly being linked together in various ways through networks. Small local area networks (LANs) allow computer users within a limited range to share documents and software, whereas larger networks, such as the Internet, link millions of personal and mainframe computers across the world—a sort of network of networks. Public networks are publicly owned, and any person willing to pay the cost can join; semipublic networks are privately owned but are used for public purposes. For instance, airline reservation systems—such as APOLLO and SABRE, owned by United and American Airlines, respectively—are owned by airlines but are used by travel agents the world over to make public reservations. Networks can be private if their ownership and use is restricted, for instance, inter- and intracorporate networks, as well as those of the Defense Department, NASA, and universities.

The Internet is the most remarkable network. Consisting of public, semipublic, and private networks, it may become the foundation of the so-called information superhighway. The Internet grew out of the Defense Department's need to develop a command-and-control system that could be used to issue orders to the armed forces in the event of a nuclear war. Existing information channels, such as the telephone system, relied on switching technology, a kind of electronic crossroads. If the switches are knocked out, so is the system. The solution was to develop an interconnected network in which there were no preferred pathways from one user to another. All users would be linked independently to every other user, and information could be sent by many different routes to the final destination. The spread of this idea to computer networks in universities and research labs in the 1960s and 1970s laid the foundation for the Internet. In the mid-1980s the National Science Foundation underwrote the installation of a nationwide system of high-speed data-transmission lines, and these now form the backbone of the Internet's U.S. section.

The Internet is far-flung, however, linking computers in dozens of countries, and is neither owned nor controlled by any single organization. The costs of the network are borne by its main users—universities, national labs, high-tech corporations, and national governments. Millions of people around the world access the Internet to send and receive electronic messages, participate in discussion groups of all kinds, share data files, download free computer programs (called "freeware" or "shareware"), access libraries, and more. The Internet is capable of carrying data, text, sound, and video, limited only by the capacity of the cables through which the information is sent. In many ways the Internet presents a vision of the emerging computer-based communications environment: a decentralized, even anarchic, electronic freeway, providing a vast social space within which people can meet, talk, exchange, share—in short, communicate. In his novel *Neuromancer*, William Gibson (1984) dubbed this new social space, partly real and partly imaginary, *cyberspace*; that name has been popularized by the International Conferences on Cyberspace, and it has stuck.

Financial and logistical pressures on the Internet are beginning to mount. Throughout 1992 and 1993, the Internet was estimated to be growing at the rate of 15%-25% a month, and the growth rate may be accelerating. The effects of such explosive change on the system are uncertain.

One of the most urgent debates concerning an (inter)national "information highway" concerns issues of copyright. Who owns the information in the Internet, and how can that ownership be protected? When a book is published, the author's right to be paid for the work used to be enforced by the physical necessity of manufacturing and selling the book itself, with the selling price including royalties for the author as well as profit for the publisher. During the late 1980s, inexpensive copying became widely available, making it possible in many cases to photocopy a book for less than its purchase price. Copyright laws forbid the copying of a book without the publisher's permission, but this part of the law had previously been largely a formality, because it had been cheaper to buy a book than to copy it. In the early 1990s, an association of publishers brought suit against one of the major copying chains to prevent the copying of books unless the copier pays a fee for each copy. The publishers claimed that the copyright inheres not in the physical book but in the information it contains, regardless of the medium through which that information is published. This idea, formalized in law, is called *intellectual property.*

How to manage the rights to intellectual property is one of the key problems to be worked out before authors and publishers will be willing to upload copyrighted material to the Internet. Before issues of privatization and pay per use were raised in the early 1990s, theorists such as Theodor Holm Nelson, who coined the term *hypertext,* believed that eventually the entire world would be connected by one vast network, accessible to all. In such a situation the key problem is how to make information universally accessible while at the same time protecting authors' rights to their work. As early as the 1960s, Nelson theorized a system that allowed information to be searched and retrieved from a database of any arbitrarily large size, and that would automatically bill the retriever (see T. H. Nelson, 1974, 1980). Nelson reasoned that in a worldwide system the per word cost would be so low that anyone could afford to pay, and the authors would be able to make a comfortable living. The task of actually designing a working system of such size took more than 30 years, and by the time Nelson had finally produced a working prototype of the system, called Xanadu, the character of the coming information superhighway had changed. Instead of a single worldwide net to which everyone would be connected, with money being exchanged directly between user and individual provider, large communications conglomerates were already jockeying for position to provide the services and collect the fees. In other words, the system they proposed would resemble something like cable TV or telephone service, in which a single provider acts as distributor and control point.

During the Reagan and Bush administrations, the U.S. federal government began quietly selling off rights to certain databases that contain such information as court decisions and committee proceedings. These databases, formerly available to the public at no charge, are now sold by private corporations on a pay-per-access basis. Even the government itself pays fees to use its own information contained in these databases.

The controversy is quite similar to the arguments surrounding each new communication medium. Will access be universal and free, or restricted and costly? Will the medium be a public utility or privately owned? What is the best compromise? Current debates over ownership of and access to the information superhighway may well put an end to the anarchic and free-wheeling growth of the Internet, as well as to any prospect of a truly "public" network.

Virtual Communities

Bulletin board services (BBSs) and graphics-based virtual communities are other instances of emerging electronic environments that simulate and model human societies. The first virtual communities based on communication technology were the on-line BBSs of the mid-1970s. These were not dependent upon the widespread ownership of computers, but of terminals; however, even a used terminal cost several hundred dollars, so that access to the first bulletin boards was mainly limited to electronics experimenters, ham radio operators, and the early computer builders—that is, white Western males.

BBSs were named after their perceived function—virtual places, conceived to be like physical bulletin boards, where people could post notes for general reading. The first successful BBS programs were primitive, usually allowing the user to search for messages alphabetically, or simply to read messages in the order in which they were posted. These programs were sold by their authors for very little or were given away as shareware—part of the early utopian ethic of electronic virtual communities. The idea of shareware was that the computer was a passage point for circulating concepts of community. The important thing about shareware was that, rather than making an immediate profit for the producer, it would nourish the community in expectation that such nourishment would in time come back around to the nourisher.

Within a few months of the first BBS's appearance, three San Francisco computer programmers developed a revolutionary kind of BBS, one that allowed messages to be attached to each other by topics and branching subtopics in a treelike structure. The CommuniTree Group, as they called themselves, saw their BBS as transformative because of the structure it presupposed and simultaneously created— the mode of tree-structured discourse and the community that would speak it—and because it was another order of "extension," a kind of prosthesis. The BBS that the CommuniTree Group envisioned was not merely a virtual location, but an extension of the participants' instrumentality into a virtual social space.

By using the word *tree*, the group managed to invoke a kind of organic flavor to their project that fit easily into the "posthippie" Northern Californian discourse of the 1970s. Each branch of the tree was to be a separate conference that grew naturally out of its root message by virtue of each subsequent message that was attached to it. The continuity between messages grew from whatever thread of thought each reader found interesting. Conferences that lacked participation would cease to grow, but would remain on-line as archives of failed discourse and as potential sources of inspiration for other, more flourishing conferences.

The group was acutely aware that the networks and computer systems within which their utopian project was embedded were not simply controlled by, but owed their very existence to, the military-industrial-government complex to whose agendas CommuniTree was radically opposed. The group was not daunted by this knowledge. Rather, members believed that their approach, with its emphasis on smallness and multiplicity, decentered command structures, and relatively low-tech components, could exist within or even infect the larger, totalizing communication structures that they shared with such formidable monoliths as the Defense Advanced Research Products Agency, or DARPA.

CommuniTree 1 went on-line in May 1978 in the San Francisco Bay Area, one year after the introduction of the Apple II computer and its first typewritten and hand-drawn operating manual. CommuniTree 2 followed quickly. The opening sentence of the prospectus for the first conference was "We are as gods and might as well get good at it." This technospiritual bumptiousness characterized the early conferences. The conferencees saw themselves not primarily as readers of bulletin boards or as participants in a novel discourse, but rather as agents of a new kind of social experiment. They saw the terminal or personal computer as a tool for social transformation by the ways it refigured social interaction. BBS conversations were like a kind of public letter writing or posting of broadsides. They were meant to be read and replied to some time later than they were posted. But their participants saw them as conversations nonetheless, as social acts, and as a kind of play.

Events in the marketplace were conspiring to bring trouble to the new communities, however. In 1982, Apple Computer entered into the first of a series of agreements with the IRS in which Apple was permitted to give computers away to public schools in lieu of paying part of its federal taxes. Within a fairly short time, there were significant numbers of personal computers accessible to students of grammar school and high school age, and some had modems.

Students discovered the CommuniTree's phone number and wasted no time in logging on to the conferences. They appeared uninspired by the relatively intellectual and spiritual air of the ongoing debates, and proceeded to jam the Tree with obscene messages. Other young hackers enjoyed the sport of attempting to "crash" the system by discovering bugs in the system commands. It seems clear that there was tremendous excitement in the technokids' newfound power to destroy things at a distance, anonymously and at no risk to themselves—and this point should not be lost on those who study the conduct of war in the age of intelligent machines.

After a few months of continual assault, the Tree expired, choked to death by "the consequences of freedom of expression," as one participant put it. Yet within a few years there was a proliferation of on-line virtual communities, with perhaps less visionary character but with vastly superior message-handling capability, and with enhancements that allowed monitoring and disconnection of "troublesome" participants. The age of surveillance and social control had arrived for the virtual communities.

A second form of virtual community involves graphics-based systems. The first of these is Habitat, designed by Chip Morningstar and Randall Farmer as a large-scale, for-profit social experiment running on a mainframe in Tokyo. Similar systems are available in the United States. Habitat is inhabitable in that, when the user logs on, he or she operates a cartoon figure, called an *avatar*, that can walk around in the environment and participate in the ongoing social life of the Habitat community. The look of the Habitat space is cartoonlike, so the computer can draw it quickly. When the user wants his or her character to speak, he or she types out the words on the Commodore's keyboard, and these appear in a cartoonlike speech balloon over the head of the user's character. The speech balloon is visible to any other user nearby in the virtual space. The user sees whatever other people are in the immediate vicinity in the form of other cartoonlike figures.

The term *nearby* has idiosyncratic and local meaning in cyberspace. In the case of Habitat, it means that two avatars occupy space that looks the same on both users' screens. Avatars can change clothes and body parts. Within the simulation, the terms used to describe the framework for these changes are worth remarking: An avatar goes to the "spray shop" to buy body colors or clothes (the Japanese description is ambiguous as to which) and to the "head shop" to buy a new head, but to the "sex change clinic" to change sex. Changing heads is a commercial transaction, but changing sex is a medical one, a different register of social order, even when what is being changed is just a cartoon created with computer code.

Of the people who sign up for Habitat, the ratio of men to women is four to one. However, inside Habitat the ratio of self-defined men to self-defined women is three to one. This means that roughly 150,000 men are cross-dressing as women in Habitat. The same thing happens in text-based virtual communities. On-line, women (or people who say they are women) attract more interest and get more attention. In Habitat men enjoy the pleasurable qualities of being women without having to experience the oppression that goes with that attractiveness. Should any unpleasant event occur, such as someone harassing them, they can simply log out—an option not available to women in real life.

In Habitat, as in all the virtual communities, a person may have as many avatars as he or she can afford. This allows many people to play out different personalities in a safe atmosphere. Once an inhabitant of a virtual community understands that the person he or she is talking to may be completely different off-line than he or she seems on-line, social interactions proceed in much the same ways they do in face-to-face situations.

Habitat's economic dimension makes monetary exchanges possible, and in any money economy it is likely that sex will be one of the items for sale. Sex workers exist in Habitat, in an environment where sexual play is free of disease—although your computer can still catch a virus! Many everyday social formations spring up spontaneously in Habitat. There are marriages and divorces, churches, a criminal underworld, law enforcers, newspapers, and many other quite ordinary activities analogous to those in real life.

Lessons of the Virtual Communities

The participants of electronically mediated virtual communities acquire skills that are useful for the virtual social environments developing in late-twentieth-century technologized nations. The participants learn to delegate their agencies to body representatives that exist in cyberspaces, but the interactions they have in those spaces are much like interactions in the real world. Shy children develop useful social skills on-line that they are then able to apply to face-to-face interactions with "real" playmates. Virtual social interactions also make heavy use of reading skills, because many of the virtual communities are text based; even in graphics-based communities, speech is still in text form.

Virtual communities, however, raise problems of "whereness." In cyberspace you are everywhere and somewhere and nowhere, but almost never "here" in the physical sense. In everyday life, the governmental and regulatory structures of city, state, and nation tend to increase the specificity of whereness. Things like phone numbers, addresses, and social security numbers increase whereness. Governmental and regulatory bodies use such location technologies to halt or reverse the gradual and pervasive disappearance of the socially and legally defined individual in an age in which the meanings of terms such as *distance* and *direction* are subject to increasing slippage. Virtual communities are characteristic of our creative use of communication technology to create new social opportunities in a time when physical communities are fragmenting or absent. In the near future there will be tremendous increases in their popularity and diversity.

Computer Games

The first computer game, Spacewar, was written in 1960, symbolizing the close linkages between the military and the development of computers, and also pointed up the intricate linkages among computers, gender, and violence. Even in the 1990s, computer games are almost exclusively about violence—killing opponents and destroying mission objectives. They are overwhelmingly written by males, and the women in them, when there are women in them, are generally restricted to the roles of sex kittens or helpless victims to be saved.

Continuing efforts to reduce the sexism and violence in computer games have had little effect. Programmers are almost all young men in their late teens and 20s, and few have highly developed reading skills. A high percentage of these programmers have poorly developed social skills, and they tend to see the women in their lives, when there are such, in much the same way they see the women in their games. When pressed, they claim quite firmly that there is no sexism in their games, just as they perceive no sexism in their lives (Stone, 1991, 1993).

Issues of ethics and social responsibility, combined with market pressures, have led two major game companies, Sega and Electronic Arts, to commission studies of women and computer games. If the market penetration of game hardware and software continues at the present rate, within a few years a majority of children and teenagers will spend more time playing computer games than they spend watching television. Educators have begun to experiment with writing educational games that take advantage of the huge data storage capacity of multimedia CDs. The use of interactive multimedia technology and computer games as educational tools collapses the boundaries between learning and play, and suggests that the meaning of education might undergo a change with the coming of the information age. Correctly perceiving and interpreting this change and seizing the advantages for new kinds of education that interactive gaming may promise may well be the greatest challenge of the new media.

Conclusions

How will the "information age" of computers affect social, political, and economic institutions? Most writers either project a society in which the quality of life will be considerably enhanced for all members of society or paint a grim picture of a surveillance society, in which everyday life will be controlled and monitored by governments and corporations. The reality will probably lie somewhere in between. For some groups and institutions, computers may well improve the conditions under which they learn, work, communicate, and buy, sell, or access goods and services. But these basic opportunities may remain out of the reach of individuals and groups who either cannot afford them or are discriminated against because of race, age, or gender.

Computers are still shrinking in both size and cost. As early as the 1970s, Nicholas Negroponte, the founder of the MIT Media Lab, predicted that by 1990 the computer in a microwave oven would be more powerful than the one on an office desk in 1975—a prediction that is rapidly becoming reality. When computers become sufficiently small and inexpensive that it is feasible to put extremely powerful ones in such likely and unlikely items as bathroom shower stalls, TV sets, light switches, jewelry, walls, windows, toys, garbage cans, and lawn mowers, the idea of what a computer is will undergo a change. Computers will cease to be large desktop objects. Their uses and even their meaning will diffuse, literally fade into the woodwork or landscape. To a certain extent their functions will become invisible, and we will stop noticing or thinking about them. They will just be there, like our internal organs—a circumstance that has been called *ubiquitous computing*. Some of these tiny computers will be implanted inside humans, as pacemakers are now, to correct physical problems such as heart impairments and hearing loss; but perhaps also to enhance our lives in as-yet unknown ways. Such electronically enhanced humans already have a name: cyborgs, or *cybernetic organisms* (Haraway, 1985/1991). How computers will affect our lives in such a world, how they will change the meanings that life has for us, remains to be seen. We cannot know what, for example, "human" means when one is surrounded by—or permeated by—invisible computers that respond to light, voice, or movement in instant interaction.

As with most technological innovations, the choices of where computers will be introduced, what they will be used for, and who will benefit from their deployment are not within the control of individual members of society. Governments and corporations usually have the power and resources to make such determinations. As ordinary citizens we live in a world that for the most part is not of our making. But the computer also has the potential to provide ordinary citizens with the ability to use technology for their own ends—to set up alternative modes of communication, to establish new types of communities, and even to subvert the socially dominant uses and applications of computers. In the 1990s, the computer represents the main technological site in which the struggles to define the "information society" are being played out. On the outcome of these struggles may well hinge the shape, substance, and meaning of democratic life, community, and even the meaning of humanity well into the next century.

Further Questions

1. Survey your class. How many people have microcomputers at home? What are they used for, beyond game playing and writing student papers? What could they be used for?

2. Monitor debate about the information superhighway and the concerns that are voiced. What are the most pressing issues and how can they be addressed in national policy making?

3. Learn how to surf the Internet and send an e-mail message to one of the editors of this book.

16 New Communication Technologies and Deregulation

DONNA A. DEMAC

with LICHING SUNG

The birth of each new communication technology promises vast new potential for good—but does "new" always equal "good"? In this chapter Demac counters the constant bombardment of rosy propaganda we hear about the joys of the "information age" with a sober look at some of the most promising new transmission technologies and the ways they are being implemented. If their bright side is shining potential, their dark side is their preemption by forces that do not necessarily have the welfare of all of humankind at heart.

The transmission technologies developed in recent decades—satellites, computers, fiber optics, cable television, mobile telephony, high-definition television, broadband technologies—all share striking ambiguities of application. Satellites are wonderful for beaming education programs to thinly populated areas in Alaska, but they are also used for military reconnaissance. Computers may be incredible labor savers, but secretaries now work on machines that monitor when they begin work, when they take breaks, how many keystrokes they type, and if they meet their quotas: That is, they work on machines that turn people into machines. Average Americans are slowly but surely acquiescing to the electronic mapping of their whole existence.

Since the massive deregulation of telecommunications and broadcasting that took place during the 1980s, government policy for important aspects of nationwide communications is nearly nonexistent. Safeguards for communities, individuals, and free speech have been scrapped wholesale in favor of blind faith in market forces. How well these forces can be expected to operate is illustrated by the recent experience in cable television. After the deregulated industry became the playground of corporate monopolies and a thorn in the side of consumers, it had its prices reregulated by Congress in 1993. Meanwhile, as the channels of communication multiply, the scarcity of good television programming becomes all the more striking.

The transmission technologies that bring us so much pleasure also enable governments and corporations to restrict the flow of information, distribute their own propaganda, and gather increasing amounts of information about their citizens. A growing gap exists between the potential of technology to give people better control over their lives and the drive by others to use it for profit and centralizing control. Just one of the high social costs associated with the information society, as Sinha and Stone equally emphasize in Chapter 15, is the pervasive involvement of the military in the development of new technology. If we believe that new technologies automatically equal progress, this fact should give us pause to think more soberly.

Technologies by themselves, as Winston argues in Chapter 4, do nothing and make nothing happen. Their net effects are the result of how they are used, and how they are used depends upon the cultural dynamics of the societies in which they are deployed.

On June 11, 1979, Walter Wriston, then chair of Citicorp, gave a speech titled "Information, Electronics and Gold," in which he described how computers, satellites, electronic funds transfer, and high-speed fiber-optic telephone lines were eliminating the problems of space and time. "Whether we like it or not," Wriston said, "mankind now has a completely integrated, international financial and informational marketplace capable of moving money and ideas to any place on this planet within minutes." As the head of a multinational corporation with more than 1,000 offices worldwide, Wriston argued that nothing should stand in the way of "an integrated economic and financial marketplace which government," and all of us, "must learn to live with."

Not everyone is as ready as Wriston to embrace a world of advanced technology. There is no doubt that computers, satellites, and the other technologies discussed in this chapter are having dramatic impacts on our lives. Homes, offices, hospitals, and schools fill up each year with more gadgets that people can plug in and play. In 1993 the plans for huge expansions in channel capacity were becoming part of a new preoccupation with interactive television services. Companies began to talk of an electronic superhighway that would deliver not only a vast array of cable channels but also video on demand, computer games, and information services (see the section on broadband technologies, below).

As of 1994, the Clinton/Gore administration was urging that new policies suited to the so-called information superhighway be adopted, with cooperation between government and private industry, on a national and international scale. Such policies should facilitate the development of nationwide broadband (i.e., high-capacity) networks, but at the same time continue a policy of universal access to telephone and related information services. "Universal access" meant that people with low incomes or who live in remote areas should not be priced out of these communications.

Yet some argue that it is people, as much as the new gadgets, that are being "plugged and played." Siegel and Markoff (1986) warn:

> If Silicon Valley represents the promise of a technological utopia, it also epitomizes the peril of an Orwellian world out of control. Slowly but surely the average American has unknowingly accepted the electronic mapping of his or her entire existence. (p. 7)

Others argue that computerized networks are intensifying society's more serious problems, including class divisions, threats to civil and human rights, and global warfare.

Where do you stand in this debate? Do you tend to equate new technologies with progress, or do you agree that people should be wary of being "plugged in and played"? The perspective taken in this chapter is that in order for society to reap the greatest benefit from the new technologies, we must look beneath the surface and acknowledge their dark side.

Background: Deregulation of Telecommunications and Broadcasting

To understand the new transmission technologies, we need to understand (a) the transnational corporate economy as it is has developed over the past 40 years and penetrated almost every corner of the planet and (b) the technical possibilities opened up to corporations by merging with these new telecommunications channels (satellites, fiber optics, and so on) the computer's capacity to transform all video, data, and voice information into electronic pulses. It is against this dual background—the transnational economy and the computer-telecommunications hookup—that we need to understand U.S. policy on new information technology.

A third element is the revival in corporate and government circles of the belief that market forces must know best, and, notably, what is the best national communications policy. A key agent in the deregulation of telecommunications and broadcasting has been the Federal Communications Commission, which was set the task—especially in the 1980s under the Reagan administration, but even before then—of cutting back its own powers of intervention in U.S. communications policy, leaving it to be dominated by market forces.

A historic event occurred in U.S. communications policy in 1981, when the federal government and AT&T reached an agreement that allowed the long-established phone monopoly to enter the computer field, then dominated by IBM. In exchange, AT&T gave up its monopoly over nationwide telephone service, spinning off its local subsidiaries into seven giant regional monopolies. These soon became powerful, profitable firms in their own right.

One consequence of the 1981 agreement, which went into effect in 1984, was the announcement of the interest of the United States in the global expansion of the telecommunications hardware and software industries. Once AT&T was unleashed to compete internationally, a shake-up in the equipment markets and regulatory customs of other countries was sure to follow (see McQuail, Chapter 9).

In the United States, the breakup of AT&T began a long period of constantly changing rates for telephone service. Between 1934 and 1984, AT&T had held a monopoly in this sector and was required under the Communications Act of 1934 to offer reliable, affordable telephone service to all. After 1984, competition in the delivery of long-distance service among firms such as AT&T, MCI, and Sprint brought down the cost of long-distance calls, but the savings to individuals were often canceled out by hefty increases in the costs of local service.

A second major change in communications policy involved the deregulation of broadcasting. Policies of the Federal Communications Commission that had limited amounts of advertising, required stations to assess community needs on a regular basis, and set minimum standards for public affairs, news, and local programs were repealed or amended. Faith in the infallible wisdom of market forces gave full priority to corporate rights to advertise over these other "public service" objectives. From 1981 to 1984, the following changes were made:

- *Radio* (January 1981): Deregulation eliminated ascertainment of community programming needs; limits on advertising time; guidelines on minimum hours of news, public affairs, and local programming; and requirements that stations keep program logs open for public inspection.
- *Television* (June 1984): Deregulation had the same effects as on radio.
- *Children's television* (December 1983): Recommendations that broadcasters schedule children's programs throughout the week, develop more educational programs, and schedule programs for specific age groups were eliminated.
- *Fairness Doctrine* (repealed, 1987): This requirement that stations provide programs on controversial issues of public concern and do so in a balanced fashion was eliminated.
- *Multiple ownership rules* (amended, August 1984): This change increased from 7 to 12 the number of AM and FM radio stations a company could own (from 7 AM and 7 FM to 12 of each); similar action was taken for television. In 1988 the ceiling was raised again, with certain limitations, to 18 AM, 18 FM, and 18 broadcast stations.
- *Sale of broadcast stations* (amended, 1984): This amendment changed the length of time an owner had to hold on to a station from three years to one year. The objective of the old policy was to encourage continuity in attention to community interests; the new rule has resulted in rapid turnover and has enabled the concentration of media ownership.

As of 1994, there is little government policy for nationwide communications. Though the Communications Act of 1934 is still in effect, the earlier regulations have been repealed and few new policies have been established for computers, satellites, fiber optics, or other advanced technology systems. Market forces are expected to construct policy by themselves.

Profiles of the New
Transmission Technologies

This section provides brief descriptions of cable television, satellites, fiber optics, broadband technologies, high-definition television (HDTV), and mobile telephony. Though the technologies are treated separately here, it should be noted that they are often used in combination with one another, and especially with computers. This is especially true when it comes to the information and communication networks of transnational corporations. Indeed, high-speed, high-tech systems that facilitate the movement of goods, services, and information are at the center of today's transnational economy. The fax machine is not included for specific comment because its operation is easy to understand and it has very quickly become commonplace, but it is one more example of this trend.

COMPUTERS

Sinha and Stone have introduced a number of major computer communications uses in Chapter 15; here we need to begin by examining some further aspects related to labor and the economy. At the workplace, computer technologies have contributed to the plugged-in labor force. Secretaries now work on machines that monitor when they begin work, when they take breaks, how many keystrokes they type, and whether or not they meet their quotas. Telephone operators have been required to complete a phone call every 26 seconds. Supermarket checkout clerks work with optical character readers that compute the number of purchases they ring up in a given time period. In addition, computer technology has allowed companies to automate many jobs, deskilling and cheapening their value as many thousands of people a year have been replaced by machines.

One consequence of the reductions in the labor force is that consumers are often required to do more work to get the services they need. They go to phone stores to pick up phones that were once installed at their homes. They take their phones out to be repaired. They punch numbers in on their telephone keypads in response to automated recordings that replace human telephone salespeople. A computer error originating at a company or a bank often takes endless letters and calls to clear up.

The future factory will be dominated by computer data communication in many directions. *Robotics* is the term for computerized manufacture, which in today's factory has islands of computerized machines that make other machines. Soon we will see these islands linked up into an archipelago of intercommunicating producing agents. A microcircuit can register that the cutting edge on a robot's machine tool is wearing out and summon up a replacement just before it is needed. Indeed, "just-in-time" computerized parts delivery is already saving corporations very large sums indeed, by cutting out downtime spent waiting for replacements and materials to arrive. The very design of the product itself, once the specialized domain of the drafting office's skill, has now been wrenched away and is part of computer-aided design and manufacture (CadCam). All these data communications can cross oceans and continents as easily as they can cross a factory floor.

CABLE TELEVISION

Cable television started out in the late 1940s as a technique for delivering broadcast signals to remote or mountainous areas that could not be reached by the existing broadcast stations. A powerful antenna would receive the broadcast signal and relay it to households via cable. By the late 1980s, most cities and towns across the country had cable systems that carried the regular broadcast channels in addition to more than 150 cable program services. With cable, TV has moved from a time when most television viewers paid for television indirectly, through the costs of the products advertised, to direct payment of a monthly cable charge or pay-per-view channel.

Cable TV differs from broadcast television in that it provides a much greater number of channels. All cable subscribers receive a basic level of service that includes the broadcast channels, "direct-access" cable channels that are often made available through provisions in the local cable franchise, and additional channels that require no extra payment by the subscriber. After signing on to receive the basic tier, cable subscribers have the option of receiving "pay TV" channels for which they pay additional sums.

In 1984, Congress passed the Cable Communications Policy Act, which divided up authority over cable systems between the federal and state or local governments. Specifically, it recognized the right of local governments to franchise cable systems. In addition, Congress said that local authorities could arrange for citizens to have direct access to putting out programs over one or more channels in the cable system, stating that this would further the goal of program diversity. Most access centers, of which there are now about 2,000, offer video training to citizens as well as subsequent use of the facility's equipment to make and screen their programs over access channels. (See also Downing's discussion of Deep Dish TV in Chapter 14.)

The endorsement of a public-access channel in each cable system is considered one of the few distinguishing aspects of this service. Cable generally provides old movies, sports, music videos, and news. In other words, it has not lived up to its original promise of expanding the range of programs available to the public. More channels have generally not meant more diversity. System owners have quite often been less than cooperative in developing their public-access channels.

However, cable also raises the danger of a local information monopoly. As stated above, when it comes to broadcast stations, a single company is not allowed to own more than 36 radio and 18 television stations across the nation. In contrast, the owner of a cable system may control 30 or more channels in one community, and with the advent of important new technologies for compressing multiple signals so they can be carried over a single cable, this number of channels could rise as high as 500. And because, in virtually all places, there is only one cable system operating in a given community, that company effectively controls all the TV programs entering its community's homes.

This situation becomes far more severe when one looks at the power of multiple system operators (MSOs). One of the biggest, Time Warner, Inc., owns hundreds of cable systems nationwide, as well as a number of pay-cable services. The latter gives it strong motivation to exclude other pay-TV companies' products. The viewing choices available to many millions of Americans are thus determined by this one corporate conglomerate.

In 1993 Congress overturned former President Bush's veto and passed a new cable act that reestablished regulation of cable service prices. This was in part a response to widespread public complaints against cable companies for poor servicing of faults and rising monthly rates. The new law changed cable operators' obligation to carry local broadcast signals on their channels (the "must-carry" rule) and gave broadcasters instead the option of negotiating fees (royalties) with cable companies to permit the cable companies to retransmit broadcasts. In cases where no agreement can be reached, the cable company cannot retransmit the broadcast station's output.

COMMUNICATION SATELLITES

The idea of using satellites to transmit information dates back to an article published by British physicist Arthur C. Clarke in 1945. Clarke saw that a satellite parked in one particular orbit, called the geostationary orbit (GSO), 22,300 miles above the equator, could transmit to up to a third of the earth's surface. Three satellites would cover the entire globe.

It is generally acknowledged that the majority of satellites in orbit are used for military rather than civilian purposes. The so-called Star Wars program (the Strategic Defense Initiative), for example, attracted much public attention for its plan to take the arms race in space a major step ahead by developing ultra-high-speed satellite-carried weaponry (Manno, 1984).

Today in many affluent nations the use of satellites for long-distance telephone calls, weather forecasting, and broadcast transmission (e.g., for international sports events and "hot" news) is taken for granted. In addition, hospitals, universities, farmers, large and small businesses, and the government depend upon satellites on a daily basis for the information they need. Also, satellites linked to computers and telephone lines have transformed global trade and finance. IBM's network, for example, reaches its 400,000 employees in 145 countries with a combination of satellites and telephone lines. Motorola Corporation, at the time of this writing, has advanced plans for a worldwide satellite/mobile telephone system.

One of the most remarkable features of satellite communications is the possibility of direct TV communication across vast distances. Journalists, rock musicians, and high school choral singers have engaged in live meetings transmitted via satellite. In 1985, musicians in several countries joined together to stage the globally transmitted Live Aid concert to raise funds to address starvation in Africa. This program was so successful that, soon after, Farm Aid (a benefit concert to help small U.S. farmers) was transmitted via satellite from the United States. Corporations such as CNN and Star TV present live images from around the world, not only of such events as the Olympic Games, but also of crises and upheavals, often as they unfold.

During the 1960s, the United States committed itself to ensuring that as many countries as possible benefited from this powerful new technology. For the next decade, NASA made satellite time available to other countries on an experimental basis. One such project involved the Indian government's use of a NASA satellite in the 1970s to experiment with the transmission of educational television to hundreds of impoverished villages. This project was a success, and, from 1983, India had its own Insat satellite series, used for weather forecasting, data transmission, and education. In 1994, the following countries own satellites: the United States, Russia, France, Germany, Italy, the People's Republic of China, India, Brazil, Indonesia, Japan, Canada, Mexico, and the United Kingdom.

In 1964 the International Telecommunications Satellite Organization (INTELSAT) was founded in order to coordinate satellite communication use across its member and user nations (in 1989 totaling, respectively, 110 and 165). In 1971 the Intersputnik organization was founded to fulfill much the same purposes for the then Soviet bloc nations, though mostly with emphasis on television and primarily serving the Soviet Union and its allies. Inmarsat organizes international satellite communication for merchant ships, and Cospas-Sarsat does the same for distress and rescue messages on the high seas.

Many developing nations have been concerned that the orbit used for satellite communications would be filled up by a handful of countries by the time Third World countries were in a position to launch satellites. In 1979, the largest international conference ever held took place under the auspices of the International Telecommunication Union in Geneva, Switzerland. Representatives of 145 countries attended, the majority from developing nations, although Western industrialized countries sent much larger contingents. The developing nations demanded that the rule of "first come, first served" be changed to provide equitable access to the orbit for all countries.

In the 1980s, two more ITU conferences took place, each involving a month or more of intense negotiation. At the end, it was agreed that the "first come, first served" procedure would be altered to a scheme in which one slot would be reserved for every nation on the globe. Although this is a victory in principle for equity, as Hamelink shows in Chapter 17, many more policies need to be altered before there is true equity in world communication and information.

Many industrialized and developing countries use data provided by "remote sensing" satellites to obtain images of the earth, for pinpointing oil and mineral deposits, for mapping, for monitoring crops, and for disaster relief. Although most of this information is purchased from a few countries, during the next 20 years it is likely that an increasing number of countries will own their own remote sensing satellites.

This technology was originally developed for military surveillance, to observe troop movements and to photograph military installations. Then, in 1972, the United States launched LandSat, the first civilian remote sensing satellite. In the 1980s, LandSat's ownership was switched over to a private company (EoSat). In France, a company called Spot Image took the lead in turning remote sensing data into a profitable commodity. The Soviet Union too began to market some of its remote sensing images. Both the French and Soviet systems produced very high-definition images. This intensified the efforts of developing nations to get involved, because of their concern that if they did not own remote sensing satellites they would be at the mercy of foreign companies for information about their own countries.

This technology is also being used by the media for coverage of major international events. However, the sale of remote sensing images prompted objections from the U.S. government, which claims that national security would be threatened if the media could provide pictures of its military installations in other countries.

FIBER OPTICS

As with other communication systems, a fiber-optic link includes a transmitter, a transmission medium, and a receiver. Fiber-optic cables consist of extremely pure, thin strands of glass through which voice, data, facsimile, and video transmissions are sent over beams of laser light. Compared with typical copper telephone wires, optical cable is lighter, takes up much less space, and can carry more than 800 times as many phone calls. Fiber-optic cables also compete with satellites. The main advantages of fiber-optic cable over a satellite are that it is less affected by weather conditions and can relay a far greater volume of information. On the other hand, cable is a point-to-point mode. It does not have the satellite's point-to-multipoint capacity to link many locations simultaneously.

The development of fiber optics has led to still more competition among U.S. firms. The telephone companies want to be able to use their lines to carry television signals and information services into homes (sometimes referred to as the "video dial-tone" approach). The cable companies have fought back, vowing to enter the telephone business. Meanwhile, electricity supply corporations see a possible opening for themselves, in that they too have electric power lines running into homes and offices all across the country. In 1994, the

Clinton administration announced its intention to open up competition among all these potential suppliers.

BROADBAND TECHNOLOGIES

Broadband technologies, from time to time referred to by the name of one of their projected forms as Integrated Services Digital Network (ISDN), are already in the planning stages. Broadband technologies involve a single telecommunications system capable of transmitting voice, data, and video, including HDTV (see below). All of these formats would be merged into a digital format at one end for purposes of transit and then decoded again at the other end. The main benefit of this would be extremely fast rates of transmission—as much as 128,000 or more bits of information a second.

ISDN has been discussed in public mostly in terms of home installations. It is much more likely that it would initially be used by central business district office blocks. Some U.S. telecommunications corporations have invested very heavily in the development of these technologies, so in some shape or form they will probably be in operation before long. Yet the search for ways of sending more and more information of different sorts at faster and faster speeds will also intensify problems of privacy invasion, monitoring at the workplace, and the treatment of more kinds of information as commodities.

HIGH-DEFINITION TELEVISION

By the late 1980s there was already considerable discussion of the potential for high-definition television. U.S. television sets offer a 525-line picture, but HDTV would provide 1,125 lines and a more realistic screen aspect ratio (5:3 instead of the current 4:3). The image would be much clearer, the colors better, the depth greater, the shape of people's faces more like their real shape. It would be like having a Cinemascope picture on a TV screen, except that the blurring of rapid sideways movements would probably continue as now.

Japanese and European engineers were initially much closer to producing a workable HDTV system than were U.S. engineers, except that the latter have focused on developing a digital system that will also be compatible with the lower resolution of current TV sets. Thus the issue has also become one of catching up in the technology race. Still other methods of achieving similar results, known collectively as advanced compatible television (ACTV), have been investigated as well. Meanwhile, the familiar competition is in full swing between different technical standards, an operation of the free market that is wonderful for the corporations that produce sets, but extremely tiresome and expensive for the consumer on a shrinking planet.

The original applications of any of these systems were not primarily entertainment based. HDTV cameras might, it is argued, save Hollywood productions a lot of money, because direct video shooting and editing are much less costly than film or film-to-video editing. Nonetheless, and more intriguing, the Pentagon has been very interested in developing HDTV's military uses, most likely in remote sensing and missile guidance—so much so that it successfully lobbied for antitrust laws to be suspended so that AT&T, IBM, and Motorola could do joint HDTV research. ARPA, the Advanced Research Projects Agency—which before the end of the Cold War was run directly from the Pentagon, and was known as DARPA (the D standing for Defense)—has also spent many millions of dollars funding HDTV development.

MOBILE PERSONAL COMMUNICATION[1]

Mobile telephony, the use of radio for voice communications, is the fastest-growing sector in telecommunications and one of the most important innovations in telecommunications history. Modern mobile communications have the potential to liberate us from the physical constraints of a wholly wired telecommunications network. Their advent will redefine our expectations about what telecommunications can do.

Mobile telephony has existed side by side with traditional wire-based telephone service for decades. However, it was not until the introduction of the cellular telephone in the early 1980s that it became popular. The slow development of mobile telephony vis-à-vis its fixed counterpart is largely the result of earlier technological and regulatory constraints.

Unlike the previous mobile telephone, which used a high-power transmitter/receiver to cover an entire service area, cellular radio divides areas into small regions called cells that each have a radius of 2 to 10 miles. Each cell is equipped with a low-power base station that transmits and receives signals. Instead of spreading its signal over the entire service area, a cellular base station sends its signal out only as far as the particular cell extends. Hence calls in cells not adjacent to one another can use the same channel, or frequency, without interfering with each other. The ability to use the same channel simultaneously for several calls, or frequency reuse, is what makes cellular telephone significantly more efficient than the conventional systems it replaced. A powerful computer that serves as the central switch "hands off" the signal from one cell to another as the user moves about, and interconnects calls made to and from the mobile unit with the public wired network. Although cellular radio represents a significant improvement over its predecessor, it would not have been possible without the growth in digital switching systems and rapid developments in microprocessors. Government's allocation of more radio spectrum also helped ease the channel capacity problem that had inhibited the growth of mobile telephony previously.

Because the cost of constructing a cellular telephone system is lower than the cost of a wire-based system, cellular telephone is being touted as a cost-efficient way to improve telecommunications services in countries where such services are scarce or inadequate. In several former Soviet bloc countries, such as eastern Germany, Hungary, and Russia, the construction of cellular systems has received priority over fixed networks in the modernization of telecommunications infrastructure. Developing countries in Africa, Latin American, and Asia have also begun to install cellular telephone systems, in part to bypass the inadequacies of their fixed telecommunications systems. In many of these countries, cellular telephone has brought electronic voice communications to some people for the first time in history.

As cellular telephone services have become more pervasive in industrialized countries, cellular systems designed originally mainly for moving vehicles have come to be used more and more for personal communications. It has become clear that people covet the freedom of being able to communicate anywhere, anytime, not only from their vehicles. At the time of this writing, a new generation of mobile communications, under the name Personal Communications Services (PCS), is being researched and developed. PCS would allow a user to access a wide range of services—from paging, voice telephony, and digital data services to audio and visual communications—by using a pocket-size portable set. These services would be available in all situations in which the user may be found, indoor or outdoor, and ranging from dense urban centers to rural and remote areas. In addition to land-based mobile services, several satellite-based systems are also being proposed to provide global personal communication services. Dick Tracy's watch-telephone is no longer pure fantasy.

One of the most critical issues affecting the expansion of mobile telephony concerns—yet again—competing technical standards. At present, there are about 10 different cellular standards in the world, mainly because of some countries' determination to have protected markets for their own telecommunications industries. The absence of a common standard has contributed to the relatively slow introduction of cellular telephone services in developing countries. However, as mobile telephony has become an integral part of the global telecommunications network, there is a pressing need for compatibility and interconnectivity among these new communications systems. To avoid repeating the balkanization of standards for the next generation of mobile communications systems, and to rectify the patchy and chaotic situation created by multiple cellular networks, the International Telecommunication Union has launched a program to develop a single global standard for the next generation of mobile systems, scheduled to be introduced around the year 2000. The success of this effort, however, will depend on major nations' willingness to cooperate.

The coming of modern mobile telephony relates directly to the coming of an information-oriented economy in which almost all forms of economic activity have become increasingly information-intensive. The need to access information from anywhere, anytime, demanded a communications infrastructure with capabilities much more flexible than those of the fixed-wire telephone network. Cellular telephony and its successors emerged in response to the pressing communications needs of the modern workforce.

Conclusions

The pervasive involvement of the military in the development of much new technology is one example of the high social costs associated with the world of advanced communications technology. In general, there is a growing gap between the potential of technology to give people better control over their lives and the drive by others to use it for profit and centralizing control. This gap makes it all the more difficult to know if the introduction of new technology equals progress.

The risks associated with advanced technologies should lead more people to seek out information about how various technologies are applied in their own environments. Developments should be followed closely for the ways they affect the operations of government, the national economy and employment trends, and the standard of living throughout society.

Further Questions

1. Which people cannot easily gain admission to the "information age"? What can be done for such people?

2. Will there be a deepening division between skilled and unskilled workforces? Will we see the emergence of a high-tech minority and a mass of people whose work is drastically changed as a result of automation and deskilling?

3. What is involved in designing appropriate, socially beneficial uses for new communication technologies? What types of organizations should be involved? What is the government's responsibility?

Note

1. This subsection was written by Liching Sung.

17 Information Imbalance Across the Globe

CEES J. HAMELINK

In this chapter, Hamelink sharply reminds us that debate about new communication technologies tends to be a luxury that can be enjoyed in affluent countries of the West, or of East Asia—but rarely in the South. He provides us with figures that relentlessly hammer home the truth that the planet is in desperate need of a new information and communication order, that communications hardware and software are primarily to be found in the Northern Hemisphere; that attempts to challenge this imbalance, such as the UNESCO policies of the 1970s and 1980s, which reflected Third World nations' demands for equity in communications, have been for the most part harshly rebuffed.

When there are more telephones in Japan than in the whole of the continent of Africa, when the French government can give away computer terminals (the Minitel) to 4 million of its citizens, yet Brazil could be assailed in the 1980s by the U.S. government for trying to develop its own computer industry through government regulations forbidding computer imports, then global communication inequity has clearly become an issue that demands a response from reasonable people and a farsighted resolution. The question remains open as to whether or not such a resolution is within the vision of the transnational communications corporations.

These issues of equity are also posed to some degree within the rich nations: As communications corporations in country after country are

293

increasingly freed from government oversight, will they not move to skim the cream from the communications market and leave the poor, especially the elderly, to wonder how to afford telephone service? As databases become more and more expensive to use, what prospect is there for critical—and generally underfunded—researchers to work with them to provide information of service to the public rather than to corporate capital?

All in all, the gulf between rich and poor in information and communication has rapidly become a reality; it is no longer only a prediction. This intensification of social divisions in the world as well as at home cannot but signal serious conflicts ahead.

In studies of international communication, a great deal of attention has been paid to the global imbalances between rich and poor countries in terms of flows of media products, such as news, television programs, and films (International Commission for the Study of Communication Problems, 1980; A. Smith, 1984). Far less attention has been paid to the overall imbalances in *information* that exist in the world economy between core and peripheral nations. *Core* nations are the rich, industrialized countries: the United States, Canada, Western Europe, Japan, Australia. The economic *periphery* consists of the poorer, predominantly rural countries of Africa, Asia, and Latin America, countries that are often referred to as the South or the Third World. The term *peripheral* as used here is not intended to imply that these nations are culturally peripheral or of peripheral human value; it merely indicates that they are economically peripheral within the global power that exists at present. This chapter will address three main questions: What do we mean by *information imbalance*? How did the information imbalance between the core and the periphery develop? How does this information imbalance affect the prospects for development in the periphery?

Information Imbalance in the World

Let us begin with some basic definitions: (a) *Information imbalance* essentially means that some countries have a great deal more useful information than others. (b) It also means that some countries have

better information capacities—the ability to produce, record, process, and distribute information—than others. (c) This capacity is dependent upon access to information hardware processors, such as computers, and carriers, such as books. (d) It is equally dependent upon information software—the contents of information. (e) There are also many different forms of information. Such categories of information may include scientific and technical information, financial and trading information, resource information, military information, and political and current affairs information.

Let us look at the *information hardware* question first. Most of the world's hardware processors and carriers are installed in the core countries, and the technology that is basic to their manufacture and upgrading is designed, developed, and controlled by and in the core. In the international trading of information hardware, the United States and Western Europe have been the largest exporters, but they are now powerfully challenged by Japan and other Asian producers.

A few figures can vividly show the differential distribution of information hardware around the world. The data listed below were gathered by UNESCO (1989); the base year for these figures is 1984:

- Together, all the peripheral countries own only 4% of the world's computer hardware.
- Of the world's 700 million telephones, 75% can be found in the 9 richest countries. The poor countries possess less than 10%, and in most rural areas there is less than 1 telephone for every 1,000 people. There are more telephones in Japan alone (with a 1988 population of 121 million) than in the 50 nations of Africa combined (with a 1988 population 4 times that of Japan and a land mass more than 80 times greater).
- In 39 peripheral countries there are no newspapers, and in 30 others there is only one. By contrast, Japan has 125 dailies and the United States has 168.
- In the United States a daily newspaper enjoys a circulation of about 268 copies per 1,000 people; in Japan the comparable figure is 562. The African average is 16.5 copies per 1,000.
- Europe produces an average of 12,000 new book titles every year. African nations produce fewer than 350. Europe has an average of 1,400 public libraries per country where the public has free access to information. African countries have an average of 18 libraries per country.
- The world average for radio set ownership is 330 per 1,000. In the core countries, the average is 990 (2,100 in the United States), whereas in the periphery it is 142. In 34 peripheral countries there is no television. The world average for television set ownership is 137 per 1,000, but the gap between rich countries and poor countries is wide: 447 sets per 1,000 for the former and 36 per 1,000 for the latter.

The periphery countries are extremely interested in improving their manufacturing capacity to produce information hardware themselves. China is currently one of the largest producers of television receivers. Increasingly, poor countries see information processors and carriers such as computers and satellites as instruments to promote economic and social development, as factors of progress. African leaders in 1985 issued the Yamousoukrou declaration, which states: "One of the main keys to solving Africa's development problems lies in mastering the rational management of information in all its forms. This is therefore not only a positive force for regional and continental integration but also an essential condition for the survival of Africa within the community of nations in the 21st century" (from a 1986 report by the International Bureau of Infomatics).

There is already a considerable spread of capacity in information hardware manufacturing in a number of countries, including Brazil, India, South Korea, and Malaysia. India has achieved significant growth in the domestic manufacturing of information hardware, estimating in its 1986-1990 technology development plan that the growth in computer demand would reach U.S. $862.5 million. India aims to export advanced computer technology as well as to improving its telecommunications capacity.

The periphery is also becoming more important as an import market for information hardware, with Brazil, Mexico, Venezuela, Argentina, the People's Republic of China, Saudi Arabia, Hong Kong, and Thailand among the largest importers. But this importation is not without problems, because the international market for information hardware is tightly controlled by a very few suppliers on whom importing countries have to depend. As they often lack the necessary expertise to assess the hardware they require, they are often sold obsolete products.

The periphery also has problems in producing information hardware, which is usually based on a very narrow range of specialized goods. Investment in this production, moreover, comes mainly from large transnational companies, which target certain peripheral countries because of their authoritarian governments; economic incentives, such as tax privileges and low wages; and knowledge of English among the elites. Exports are mainly products made by transnational manufacturers in offshore production and assembly operations by their subsidiaries. A large proportion of this trade, in reality, consists of transactions inside a company, between its subsidiaries and its headquarters.

The result of this process is that the core of the technical know-how remains under the control of the transnational company, and the peripheral country plays a minor role just in assembly. Thus, all in all, there is stark international inequality in information hardware production.

For *information software*, we can look at the volume and direction of information flows and the possibilities of generating, distributing, or accessing relevant information. International information flows are imbalanced, given that most of the world's information moves among the core countries and less between the core and the periphery; very little flows among the countries of the periphery. Less than 10% of all telephone, telex, and telegraph traffic takes place between peripheral countries. Flows between the core and periphery tend to be one-way.

Estimates suggest that the flow of news from core to periphery is 100 times more than the flow in the opposite direction. Thus in the mid-1980s in international broadcasting, Europe broadcast 855 hours yearly to Africa, whereas Africa broadcast only 70 hours back. Imbalances are evident in television importation also, so that Western European countries import on average 33% of their programs, whereas African countries import 55% of total TV programs (UNESCO, 1989).

If we look at different kinds of information, we find other hidden kinds of imbalances. For the most part, the flow between core and periphery consists of "raw," unprocessed information coming from the periphery, whereas the core provides ready-made information packages, and—as with manufactured goods—the considerable value added by processing translates into higher costs for the periphery if it wants to buy its own information back in processed form. One example would be remote sensing by satellites that digitally encode images of, say, the shoals of tuna off the coast of Nigeria. The image is free, but it requires sophisticated computer processing to be intelligible, and thus the processed information has to be bought at a high price.

In the field of *scientific and technical information* the imbalance exists also; only 3% of the world's research and development takes place in peripheral countries (National Science Foundation, 1984). Only 1% of the world's patent grants are held by nationals of peripheral countries, because in most of those countries the technology patents are held by a small number of transnational corporations. Most of the world's scientific and technical information is produced and owned by individuals and companies in the core.

Full access to *financial and trading information* is the privileged property of a few private enterprises in the core. Most of this information flows as computer data through the communications networks of large banks and as economic data through news agencies and newspapers. There are also the specialized financial database services, such as AP/Dow Jones, Chase Econometrics, and Reuters. Poor countries (like most ordinary individuals) are handicapped in accessing information about the complex and rapidly changing international finance system, are late in receiving information about rates of exchange and interest, and have little access to the international brokerage circuit or to the vast and expensive systems for distributing this information. Western industrialized countries, on the other hand, enjoy rapid access to financial and trading information. This means that in trade negotiations, for example, the peripheral nation is at a considerable disadvantage when bargaining, often having fewer skilled negotiators and less useful information.

Resource information is another area where the core has enormous advantages, mainly through data collection about global natural resources through remote sensing via satellites. This can be used to monitor harvests and for mineral exploitation with obvious benefits; for example, New York commodity traders can know more about imminent Brazilian coffee harvests than do the Brazilian coffee producers, and so can determine prices on the commodities markets. Similarly, international fishing companies know more about the whereabouts of tuna shoals than do the local fishermen off the west coast of Africa, and use this information to land the best catches.

In the field of *military intelligence* it is obvious that poor countries cannot hope to compete with the extensive and very sophisticated surveillance networks that the major powers have developed. The Gulf War of 1991 clearly demonstrated the advantages of U.S. access to spy satellites and computer systems that collect and process billions of bits of information. The United States and other major powers can monitor, record, and identify thousands of private conversations, and can collect such seemingly trivial bits of information as the laundry lists of other countries' submarine crews. Satellite photography now allows the identification of objects just 12 inches in diameter from an altitude of 150 miles. U.S. spy satellites include the IMEWS and Keyhole 11, which have provided very precise information about tests of strategic and tactical nuclear weapons in the former Soviet Union.

Increasingly, outer space has become a militarized zone; it is estimated that about 75% of satellites launched over the past decade have been for military use. Listening posts also collect valuable military information. NATO posts in Turkey monitor armed forces' broadcasts, collect seismographic evidence on subterranean nuclear explosions, and monitor the movement of Russian satellites via radar; at the world's largest listening post in Menwith Hill, United Kingdom, the American National Security Agency monitors all transoceanic telephone and telex traffic to and from Eastern Europe.

Rich countries also have great advantages in the field of *political information*, particularly in areas of psychological warfare, propaganda, and disinformation. The 1991 Gulf War provides again the most recent illustration. The allied forces used smart missiles but also employed public relations agencies, orchestrated the international press, and fabricated and distorted information to delegitimate the enemy and mislead the public. Peripheral countries have little chance to correct or counter such propaganda campaigns. As I noted in previous work: "Both the CIA and the KGB have elaborate networks for deliberate distortion of political information. Disinformation employs the fabrication and distortion of information to legitimate one's own operations and to delegitimate and mislead the enemy. The CIA has a lengthy history of disinformation activity, on which it is estimated that the agency spends $1 billion annually" (Hamelink, 1986).

There are also severe international imbalances in a more public form of information, *news*. For printed news there are on the world market, since the sale of United Press International (UPI) to Middle East Broadcasting, only the Associated Press (AP), Reuters, and Agence France Presse (AFP). For visual news there are two leading agencies, the former Visnews, now Reuters Television, and the ABC-affiliated World Television Network (WTN). Reuters TV supplies TV news to more than 40 broadcasters in 85 countries, reaching almost half a billion households. WTN provides news to 100 broadcasters in some 90 countries and reaches an audience of more than 3 billion people.

In 1993 there was speculation that Reuters was planning to acquire WTN, thus reducing the major players to one market leader. Second in line for international TV news are the BBC World Service and CNN. CNN distributes around the clock to more than 200 subscribers and is available in more than 700 million households. In 1993, the Associated Press announced that it was ready to enter the TV news market. APTV will be a serious competitor for Reuters TV and WTN.

The average daily news production of the world agencies ranges from an output of 17 million words a day by AP to 3.3 million words by Agence France Presse (Mowlana, 1986). By contrast, the only international news agency with a particular interest in covering developments in the poor countries is InterPress Service, which puts out 150,000 words a day. World news is predominantly about events in the core. When the periphery is covered, there are usually some other news pegs at work, such as a link to some superpower conflict (Afghanistan/Nicaragua), a threat to core interests (Iran-Iraq War), a sensational drama (floods in Bangladesh, murder in Sri Lanka, famine in Ethiopia), a postcolonial relationship (news about ex-colonies), or some exotic sexual dimension. Thus much of the time the periphery is invisible, or it is presented in a distorted form. (For further discussion of news coverage of the Third World, see Sreberny-Mohammadi, Chapter 25.)

Thus, overall, information flows across the world are imbalanced in terms of their direction, their volume, and their quality. The capacity to produce, distribute, and access pertinent information is very unequally distributed among the world's countries, and the core countries have infinitely more control over the software of the world's information than do the peripheral countries.

How Did Information Imbalance Develop?

A central factor that explains these global imbalances is the history of colonial expansion by European nations into the rest of the world. Before the fifteenth century, when European colonial expansion began, the countries of the periphery possessed elaborate trade and information networks. These routes originated in the ancient empires of Egypt, China, India, and Mesopotamia (more or less modern Iraq), and connected Asia, Africa, the Mediterranean, and the Pacific. The spice and silk routes linked Mesopotamia and Iran with India and China. Gold was extracted in West Africa and transported across the Sahara to North Africa and the Middle East by Tuareg tradesmen who possessed vast knowledge about the desert. Before Vasco da Gama's travels from Portugal in the fifteenth century, trading took place between what is now Zimbabwe and China (for Chinese pottery) and India (for gold and ivory). Before Captain Cook traveled to the South Seas, Melanesian and Polynesian seafarers had developed sufficient geographic information to make long voyages. While Europeans painstakingly charted Australia, the native Aborigines already possessed extensive knowledge of the territories they had inhabited since ancient times. Although European historians often suggested (and still sometimes do) that indigenous peoples lacked useful information, extensive evidence points in the opposite direction.

By the mid-eighteenth century, however, an international colonial economy had materialized. Gradually, trade and information traffic was rerouted from exchanges among the periphery to flows between the core—Britain, France, Spain, Holland, Portugal, and so on—and the periphery. For example, the North African trade routes became obsolete as a result of the slave trade across the Atlantic. This pattern is still reflected in contemporary communications, so that telephone calls between East and West Africa are routed via European capitals. Beyond the rerouting of trade and information, new values and ideas— a new culture—were introduced to the periphery. Alongside the colonial traders and gunboats came missionaries intent on saving "primitive" souls and expanding God's kingdom on earth. In turn, they often set up the first foreign schools, in which the language, religion, and general culture of the European colonizers were taught to a small, select group of the colonized—by definition, those prepared to compromise with colonial rule sufficiently to allow them to enter such institutions.

Not everyone who passed through such schools precisely mimicked the colonists, but nonetheless these schools served to generate a whole new set of perspectives among the indigenous elites of the colonies. As generation succeeded generation, and a few individuals began to make their way to France and England and the Netherlands to study at universities there, graduation from such places became a mark of distinction acknowledged by many who had not achieved it. Graduates had played the Europeans at their own game and won. But in the process, European culture was coming to be prized, for many purposes, above the national culture or cultures. The well-worn path of Latin American students to U.S. or French universities tells the same story. Military education was also significant—at St. Cyr in France, at Sandhurst in England, and at numerous U.S. establishments. Many of the military takeovers of governments in periphery countries have been led by graduates of military academies in the core countries.

Whether by the military path, the business path, or the government route, the people running the affairs of peripheral countries after independence were overwhelmingly drawn from the ranks of those who had passed through core educational systems. Indeed, the expansion of university education in the peripheral nations has mostly been based on models copied from core countries, the cultures of which have thus been perpetuated, in differing degrees, despite demands for authentic local models of education (see Mohammadi, Chapter 21).

Once the colonial powers ceased to exert direct administrative control, beginning with Irish independence in 1920 and gaining momentum with Philippine and Indian independence in 1945 and 1947, this educational and cultural tradition became more important than ever. There was no longer a colonial governor, no longer a detachment of the army, no longer a white government administration to secure by force the continued economic profitability of the former colonies for business interests in the core countries. There was instead a cultural apparatus and inheritance that at some level kept most of the former colonies, through their own new rulers, within the ambit of their old masters.

Thus in the search for economic development, both the products and the new development models of the West were generally sought after by the new rulers. Equally, consumer products were sought after by the new elite, who could afford to buy them—from Mercedes Benz cars to Swiss perfumes to Scotch whiskey to French fashions. Media imports, especially television and film, were generic advertisements for Western consumerism, even if not a single commercial was included (Mohammadi investigates this process in detail in Chapter 21).

The transfer of technology itself created similar problems. Information technology, for instance, was introduced not primarily to meet basic needs, but to support the expansion of transnational business. Studies on the deployment of telephony, educational television, and satellite communication suggest that although peoples in the periphery do benefit from the introduction of such technologies, the primary beneficiaries are the foreign and national elites; frequently, also, the intended development objectives are not achieved, and serious balance-of-payments problems occur, as the hardware has to be paid for regardless (Clippinger, 1976).

Importing information hardware also has consequences for software. Many foreign companies insist on "turnkey" projects that tie the delivery of the hardware (such as a television station) to the purchase of certain software (such as foreign television programming). This undercuts the local production of necessary software. The international information market is dominated by fewer than 100 transnational companies that control more than three-quarters of all the world's information hardware and software. These companies are interlocked and share financial interests (Hamelink, 1983). For example, General Electric, the fifth-largest industrial company in the United States, with $49 billion in revenue and $3.4 billion in profit in 1988, has strong links with Citibank and Morgan Guaranty Trust, is interlocked with Honeywell as well as the Japanese electronics firm Toshiba, and now owns RCA and NBC.

With such a power base, the companies in the international "information-industrial complex" leave little or no space for peripheral countries to participate in these markets. This has important consequences for information imbalance. On the one hand, much information is produced for domestic markets, so that the Associated Press essentially produces news for the U.S. market, and that production is guided by the market's news demands. On the other hand, whenever the domestic market does not yield sufficient revenues, the information industry distributes internationally, as with the sale of television programs. For example, although the costs of producing a program such as *Dallas* may be covered by domestic sales, profit may come only with international sales.

Thus overseas markets are important for generating profit, but have no say about content. International pricing of television programs and other cultural products can also vary greatly, so that the price can be as high as the market will bear or less than the competitive price of a local production, flooding the local market and undermining local production. However, a few periphery countries are important cultural producers: India and Egypt produce films that are in demand, and Brazil produces successful soap operas.

All these processes mean that, despite their formal political independence, most periphery countries still experience neocolonial relationships. The flow of cultural products, the transfer of technology, the role of national elites tied to core centers, and the mechanisms of the international market all work to maintain the advantage that the core countries already possess.

Does Information Imbalance Matter?

Information imbalance does matter, in a number of ways crucial both to the poor nations themselves and to the whole international system. First, the inadequate information capacities of most peripheral countries are a serious obstacle to their own efforts to combat poverty and other deprivations. Their capacity to provide warnings about dramatic weather conditions or to communicate about health and hygiene practices or the benefits of a new development program requires an extensive information system. The peripheral countries must be able to discuss their own priorities and provide their own information about raw material requirements, import/export relations, and technological and labor needs. Without information about resources, finance, and trade, periphery countries are continuously at a disadvantage in negotiations with core countries, and this jeopardizes their survival as independent nations.

Second, the national sovereignty of periphery countries is threatened when so much information about them is stored in data banks in other countries. If a country lacks information about itself, it is limited in the decisions it can make about its own future. If a foreign country possesses such information, as when a mineral-exploiting corporation holds information about mineral-rich periphery countries, it means that decision making has been exported and national independence is undermined.

Third, information imbalance leads to the cultural integration of the periphery countries in the culture promoted by the core. Imported cultural programming encourages consumerism and individualism, and diverts attention from any regard for the long-term needs of the country. Internal rifts develop as urban elites become part of the international economy while the rural poor get left behind. A nation needs cultural independence to develop its own language, forms of musical expression, literature, theater, educational system, suitable technologies, and what it chooses to preserve from its cultural heritage. Information imbalance thus undermines cultural self-determination.

Improving the Imbalance: What Can Be Done?

How can the international information imbalance be improved? There are three major approaches. One stresses the interdependence of the world's nations and suggests that peripheral countries should be better integrated into the international economy so that they can then catch up through international transfers of finance, knowledge, and technology. The basic problem with this approach is that such international transfers and modernization policies often increase the dependence of poor countries and do not help them to resolve their basic problems of deprivation and poverty. This approach suggests that the core and periphery share mutual interests.

A second approach suggests that peripheral countries need greater bargaining power. They could pressure the core for fairer schemes and terms of trade, for cheaper transfers of technology, and for solutions to massive external debt problems. Bargaining strength can be developed if the periphery pools resources and energy, such as raw materials. But these bargaining chips may be undermined by changes in the core countries, such as replacing human labor with robots and the production of synthetic products instead of products requiring natural raw materials. The third approach suggests radical self-reliance (Hamelink, 1983). It suggests that poor countries disassociate themselves—delink—from international networks that hamper their development. Because isolated efforts by individual countries are doomed to failure, this kind of strategy demands collective effort across the periphery, which in itself requires the solving of many old and difficult conflicts among the poor countries themselves. It also requires a visionary leadership willing to forgo the immediate benefits of links with the core.

Conclusion

Information imbalance takes many forms, as has been discussed above. It is especially entrenched in the differential capacities for collecting, processing, and utilizing information between the core and the periphery. Redressing this imbalance cannot mean that all countries must end up with equally sophisticated levels of information processing, but it would mean that each country develops the level necessary for its independent survival as a sovereign nation. Information imbalance is a crucial part of international relations in the postcolonial world. Because so many vested interests are involved in this unequal situation, it will be a long time before it is resolved.

Further Questions

1. Do the kinds of information imbalances described in this chapter exist within the domestic information situation inside the United States?

2. Identify some major transnational corporations and map out their patterns of ownership and corporate linkages. Explore further the political and cultural implications of this international trend.

3. Would it be a solution to the problems of information imbalance if the periphery countries were to delink from the international information market and develop their own alternative information resources? Apart from delinking, what other kinds of interactions between the core and the periphery would counteract the existing information imbalance?

PART V

Mass Media
and Popular Culture

In this final section of the book, we introduce you to a series of studies written largely from cultural studies perspectives. From reading earlier contributions by O'Connor and Downing (Chapter 1), Ang (Chapter 12), and Downing (Chapter 14), you know that the area of cultural studies entails approaches to media that stress both the variety of influences upon communication and the interactive nature of the communication process. In other words, the concept of communication as an individualized, one-way transmission (Who says what to whom with what effect?) is rejected.

Instead, communication is argued to be a collective, two-way, and multiply determined process. Cultural studies analysts focus on how the elements of national and international culture are generated and developed, on the "culture industry," on active audiences, and most of all on the mutual influences between a nation's cultures and its media institutions. Culture is seen as constantly developing and conflictual, not as static or seamless. Cultural products are analyzed for the excitement and pleasure they evoke, for their reflection of our dreams and hopes, not only as sources of political confusion and control.

These last two ways of seeing culture do not exclude each other. A widely popular film that encourages racism needs to be understood not just for the ways it cues into those forces in our culture, but for the attractiveness of its total message. Contradictory elements in its

309

message also need to be perceived, along with contradictory responses in its audiences. Only thus can we grasp the combination of factors that enable such a media text to reinforce the repression of people of color.

Finally, for U.S. readers, who are often barely aware of the cultural impact the United States has across the globe or of the cultural backdrop of other nations' responses to its planetary power, the international dimensions of cultural studies analysis are especially important. We begin, however, with a focus that strikes a sensitive nerve in every culture, but that promises to extend everyone's frontiers of awareness and enrich their understanding of communication and culture: the question of gender.

18 Gender, Representation, and the Media

LIESBET VAN ZOONEN

Arguably, there have been three stages in recent times in the thinking about women. The first was the era of women's suffrage, the demand for the right to vote, a demand that in the United States can be dated back to a famous conference at Seneca Falls in New York State in 1845. In many countries women's right to vote was finally conceded during the 1920s, though in France not until after World War II.

The second phase was that of social movements for women's liberation, emerging in the United States and other countries during the 1960s. These movements took on a much larger agenda than the right to vote. Their targets ranged from sexist images of women in advertising and media to women's confinement to domestic chores, to the unequal salaries and career opportunities (the "glass ceiling") women experience—in other words, the entire spectrum of women's existence, the whole complex array of social and cultural mechanisms that reduce women's freedom in comparison with men's.

The third and most recent phase has been to move beyond focusing simply and solely upon women and their treatment as a way of understanding the issue, to an examination of the whole question of gender in culture and society. What is it that makes males men? Testosterone? Shaving? A passion for competitive sports? Dress? Power

positions? What is it that makes females women? A uterus? Hairstyle?
Affection for babies? Dress? Lower pay?

Van Zoonen argues that media play a particularly significant role in
confirming and making apparently natural the division between the
genders. However, she also argues that in sometimes very subtle ways,
and at other times very directly, contemporary media raise questions
about our sexual identities in ways that are much closer to how many
people privately feel. In other words, simultaneous with an official,
"normal," gender-divided culture coexist media texts that echo our
frequent real feelings of gender confusion, of which "gender-bending"
is one manifestation.

Much of this book is about political and economic power. This chapter
addresses an important issue by focusing on the power of gender in
media and culture. Further, Van Zoonen introduces the French ana-
lyst Jean Baudrillard's argument that media do not so much distort
reality as create it for us.

In the early 1980s, when I had just moved from a small town in the
north of the Netherlands to the capital, Amsterdam, to study
political science, one of my friends took me to a bar called Madame
Arthur in the red light district. It was a small and crowded place, with
a minute stage in the back. If the name didn't ring a bell in my still
naive provincial mind, the clientele certainly did; the bar was a
hangout for male-to-female transvestites. I was confused and excited.
Although I knew about the phenomenon from television, I had never
seen real transvestites before, and certainly not from the close distance
enforced by the dimensions of Madame Arthur. These men were not
men, but they were not like the women I knew either. What where
they? Soon the excitement and the spectacle superseded my confusion
and I stopped worrying. After all, this was a weekend in Amsterdam,
time for enjoyment. It gave me a good story to go home with, so why
worry about existential questions?

A few years later, another friend took me to a lesbian dance night.
This time, my confusion was not so easily suspended. I knew it was
a women-only night, but I saw many women about whom I was rather
confused. Menswear, angular body movements, and macho behavior
made me wonder, What made these women women? Still, they were

not like the men I knew either. In a way I was envious; they made me feel terribly mainstream and dull, longing for the audacity to transgress the conventional codes of femininity the way they did. I was even more bewildered to find out I felt attracted to some of the women who were really gorgeous men, hoping and at the same time fearing to be noticed by them. The spectacle of it all didn't ease my worries. If their gender was hard to identify, what did my simultaneous jealousy and attraction make me? It was a much more unsettling experience than the night at Madame Arthur, and I left early. Dancing with an acute crisis of gender identity is not much fun, and it doesn't make a good story to go home with.

These two experiences made me realize how important the (re)presentation of one's gender—in the form of body language, dress, makeup, hairstyle, use of language, jewelry, and so on—is for the identification of one's "real" gender, both by others and by oneself. One may even wonder, as I will ask in this chapter, whether there is a fundamental difference between the representation and the "real" thing. As soon as the representational codes are seriously subverted, it becomes difficult, if not impossible, to identify human beings as either women or men.

In a less salient and more modest way, I had experienced the importance of the representation of one's gender in high school. I needed very strong glasses, was tall and muscular for my age, and my hair would never take shape of the pictures at the hairdresser. Moreover, I had a preference for strong language. To the boys, these traits made me a great pal, one of the guys almost—but not a nice girl to go out with. Smaller and more amiable girls without glasses made more desirable dates. As Dorothy Parker says, "Men don't make passes at girls who wear glasses." My attractiveness as a woman and as a date began right after I got contact lenses, to my delight and annoyance. The contacts didn't make me another person, or did they? Obviously, to others (men and women), the change in appearance made me more of a woman than I was before, and I noticed my own behavior and reactions changing too. It seemed as if looking more like a "true" woman made it easier for me to feel and act like one too, signaling that the representation of my femininity may have been as important as my "real" gender identity.

It is precisely this (lack of) distinction between the representation of gender and gender itself that I want to explore in this chapter.[1] To do so, I shall focus not only on individual representations of gender, as I have done until now, but also on the collectively produced and received gender representations of the mass media. Using cross-dressing, heavy metal music, films such as *Tootsie* and *Gentlemen Prefer Blondes,* Madonna, and soap operas as examples, I shall first ask what "gender" actually is. I shall then consider how gender is represented in the media, and finally I shall discuss how these representations are articulated in the gendered subjectivities of daily life. Postmodernism will be an inevitable part of this discussion, because of its denial of a distinction between representation and reality.

What Is Gender?
Popular Music and Cross-Dressing

For many of us, gender may seem the most self-evident part of our identities. We know which box to check off when asked about our gender in questionnaires; we hardly ever doubt which door to take when going into a public restroom; when engaging in team sports, we know whether to sign up for the men's or women's teams. Very seldom do we explicitly question our own gender except maybe for some turbulent periods and moments in our lives, such as in adolescence or at transvestites' balls. Yet being men and women is not as obvious as it seems, as is shown, for instance, in the realms of popular music, the women's and gay rights movements, and cross-dressing.

Popular music, and MTV in particular, presents on a regular basis performers whose gender identities are unclear, often deliberately construed to bend the traditional conventions of gender. David Bowie and Grace Jones were the "gender-benders" of my generation, succeeded by a range of others such as Freddie Mercury, Boy George, Prince, Madonna, and, more recently, k. d. lang. In fact, notwithstanding the stereotypical portrayal of women and men in music videos (Vincent, Davis, & Boruszkowski, 1987), MTV seems to be the only part of mainstream culture in which subversions of gender are no exception or a sign of marginality. MTV, however, is firmly located in the sphere of the performing arts, in which disrupting conventions of gender, and a series of other norms, is not uncommon and in fact is often perceived as an ordinary ingredient of extravagant lifestyles supposedly common to artists. The performing arts are thus construed as such an exceptional sphere of life, a realm of fantasy, that the gender-bending taking place there does not necessarily or always undermine prevailing notions of gender.

If we look, for example, at the elements of femininity incorporated in the performances of many heavy metal bands, this point is paramount. Denski and Sholle (1992) argue that heavy metal music, despite its aggressive macho style, is heavily marked with feminine elements. Long, often curly, hair, makeup, hairless bodies, soft velvet clothing, and excessive jewelry all contradict the almost caricatured masculine language, movements, behavior, and aggressive heterosexuality of heavy metal performers. Two factors convince Denski and Sholle that the blurred gender codes in heavy metal cannot be seen as a subversion of traditional masculinity, but instead offer "a thinly disguised reproduction of traditional masculine roles of power and domination" (p. 59). First, heavy metal is also loaded with signs of aggressive male heterosexuality. One obvious sign of the "bad behavior" expected and required of heavy metal bands is to dominate and use women, as expressed, for instance, in lyrics, album covers, and offstage conduct. Second, in the reception of heavy metal there is no indication of any subversion of gender identities. On the contrary, heavy metal fans are found to detest more obvious gender-benders, such as Boy George, for their alleged lack of authenticity and their confused gender identities. The signs of femininity in heavy metal, then, are used to signify a rebellion against authority and dominant culture in general, rather than to show a dissatisfaction with gender dichotomies as we know them. Denski and Sholle conclude that the feminine elements in heavy metal function "as another sign of 'outrageousness' connected to the general theme of decadence ('sex, drugs and rock 'n' roll') prevalent to hard rock performance, rather than a serious challenge to established gender binaries" (p. 58).

Gender has been much more seriously contested by the women's and gay rights movements and the theories emerging from these contexts. Although some feminist theories assume an essential gender identity, construing women and men as innately and essentially different, the majority assume gender to be a social and cultural construction, something built on biological differences. In the words of the famous French feminist Simone de Beauvoir, "One is not born a woman, one is made a woman."[2] Thus our gender, like other aspects of our identity, is a product of circumstances, opportunities, and limitations, and is therefore instable.

There are several approaches to theorizing the construction of gender. Poststructuralist thinkers, who I find most helpful to my argument and who explain the ambiguities in gender discussed above quite adequately, consider gender to be a discursive construct. In order to understand this notion properly we need to realize, following the French psychoanalytic theory of Jacques Lacan, that we become subjects through the acquisition of language. In other words, as we are born and raised into this world we learn to think, feel, and express ourselves with the linguistic means our society provides us. Of course, we can invent our own words and symbols, but nobody would understand us. Thus language sets sometimes powerful limits to our experiences of ourselves, others, and our surroundings. This is very important in thinking about how we communicate gender to each other, inside or outside of the the media.

A different example of how gender is constructed rather than natural is shown by cross-dressing, which—contrary to the popular stereotype—is practiced more by heterosexual men than by homosexual men; a cross-dresser is not the same as a drag queen. Cross-dressing is actually such a widespread phenomenon that there are special clubs, groups, and magazines that offer opportunities for showing oneself, for mutual support, and for exchange of information and experiences.[3] Although it may seem that cross-dressing is simply a way of dressing up, a temporary performance, an outward appearance, it also involves a change of behavior and in many cases a transformation of subjectivity. According to Garber (1992), there are hundreds of stories of lifelong cross-dressers who were only "found out" after their deaths, leaving their relatives with the question of who they "really" were—an irrelevant question, as I shall explain shortly. Garber recounts the example of jazz musician Billy Tipton, who was married and had three adopted sons, and who was discovered after his death in the late 1980s to have been a woman. Whereas his wife and children went on thinking of him as their husband and father, the media considered him to be a woman and kept speaking of "she" and "her," trying to pin Tipton's "true" gender down on the basis of his bodily features. What we see happening here, Garber claims, is that binary gender discourse is so powerful that it succeeds in overriding and denying identities that do not fit the dichotomy. The particular subjectivity of Billy Tipton and his counterparts, which cannot be defined as "man" or "woman" but rather constitutes a third space, is dismissed in favor of dominant gender discourse.

Stories like these may tell us several other things about the nature of gender, for instance, that the representation of gender may be more decisive than the "real" thing. In fact, in Billy Tipton's and other similar cases the whole idea that a "true" or "real" gender exists is being undermined. (Re)presenting oneself as a woman or a man, regardless of one's body, apparently makes one into a woman or a man. As Judith Butler (1990) argues, "If a true gender is a fantasy instituted and inscribed on the surface of bodies, then it seems that genders can be neither true nor false, but are only produced as the truth effects of a discourse" (p. 136). *Representation* may therefore be a misleading term, because it still suggests that there is some reality or truth to be represented. Although it may be less misleading to think of gender as an "appearance" instead, this ignores the relation between the appearance or representation and subjectivity. The emphasis in this chapter on appearances, on performance and pretending, may falsely suggest that gender is just a role we play, as if we are continuously on stage creating and holding up a gender image, an image or role we can throw off as soon as we are offstage. But what are we left with then? Is there actually an offstage when it comes to gender?

The crucial question to ask, then, concerns the relation between gender as a product of discourse and human subjectivity, our sense of self. In the 1982 movie *Tootsie*, starring Dustin Hoffman as a cross-dressing actor, we can see quite literally how the two interact. Hoffman plays an unemployed actor, Michael Dorsey, who is desperate for work and decides to try his luck dressed as a middle-aged woman, Dorothy Michaels. Dorothy auditions for the role of hospital secretary in a daytime series and is at first turned down because the part requires a tough and aggressive woman, whereas Michael's impersonation is soft-spoken and gentle. At the snap of a finger Michael turns into a more forceful woman and is hired for the part. Until then, Dorothy is still a conscious creation of Michael, but slowly Dorothy becomes a true persona, not Michael or an impersonation of Michael but a new human being whose ideas, feelings, behaviors, and experiences have been formed in interaction with her social position as a woman and her surroundings, which—of course—treat her as a woman. We see Dorothy's subjectivity slowly evolving from the discourse in which she is caught. At the end of the film, when Dorothy has fallen in love with one of her co-actresses, whose father in turn has fallen in love with Dorothy, she decides she cannot bear fooling them anymore. Dorothy exposes Michael or Michael exposes Dorothy; at this point in the film the revelation can be seen as coming from both persons. By then, Dorothy has become a separate person to whom Michael is of little importance. She is missed by her friends and by the audience.

My brief excursions into cross-dressing and *Tootsie* are meant to illustrate the more abstract notions of poststructural gender theory, which states that true or essential identities do not exist but are the products of a discourse that makes us believe in them. The cross-dresser is the visible sign of the failure of that system, suggesting that gender is an act—performed not only by cross-dressers, but put up continuously by us all—albeit one with very real consequences. Whereas the metaphors of acting and appearance suggest that gender is something we can play or struggle with at will, which more and more people do, for that matter, it is also something that is ingrained in our sense of self, in our subjectivity. Our subjectivities are, after all, constituted—however fragmentary and temporary—in the discursive and symbolic realms of our lives.

At the level of individual gender identities we can thus consider the distinction between "real" gender and its representations an illusion, a result of dominant gender discourse in which most of us have come to identify ourself within the binary opposition of being either man or woman. I shall now turn to the question of whether the collapse of a distinction between reality and representation also holds for the collective representations of gender in the mass media. If there is no reality of gender to represent, what is it that we see when we see gender in the media?

Media and Representation: Confirming and Undermining Gender Discourse

The representation of women and men in the media is often discussed in relation to its adequate reflection of reality. It is often said that women are underrepresented in media content compared with the 50% of the population they constitute. Alternatively, it is argued that in reality many more women work than we get to see or read about in media content. Likewise, men are overrepresented in the media and are rarely shown in home environments. Another argument deals with the definitions of femininity and masculinity presented to us in media content: For women, submissiveness, availability, and compliance are held up as ideals, and consumption is presented as the road to self-fulfillment; men, on the other hand, are presented as dominant, violent, and powerful. Thus many authors complain that the portrayals of gender in the media are not representative of the positions of women and men in current societies (e.g., Cantor, 1978; Lazier-Smith, 1989). Apparently, those who make such statements conceive of gender as a more or less stable and easily identifiable distinction between women and men that ought to be represented correctly. As the above discussion on the unstable character of gender discourse shows, this is a problematic assumption. If a reality of gender does not exist, either at a subjective level or at a collective level, and we acknowledge only multiple and unstable representatives, it is impossible to conclude that media produce a "distorted" picture of gender. What, then, is it we see when we see gender in the media? Is it a representation without any relation to reality? Does it represent only itself, as would be argued by postmodernists such as Jean Baudrillard (1988)? Or is it a representation of something that has an existence outside of the media, maybe not a literal reflection of women's and men's lives and identities but maybe of modes of thinking and sets of norms and values, of current discourses, in other words? And how do media representations of gender relate to the gendered subjectivities and the representational practices of human beings in their daily lives?

Looking at the media representations of gender as expressions of dominant gender discourse—defined by its binary and hierarchical character—the abundance of research carried out in this area in the past decades suggests that gender is both confirmed and undermined by media texts. The research on stereotypes of women in the media (the portrayal of men has hardly been examined), for instance, can be interpreted not as evidence of a distorted picture of reality, but as support for two other hypotheses: that media confirm dominant gender discourse by presenting gender as a dichotomous phenomenon in which men are more important and powerful than women, and that research on stereotypes itself confirms dominant gender discourse as well by overlooking the inconsistencies and disruptions in the portrayal of gender. Let me elaborate this by briefly reviewing the results of research on stereotypes, drawing from summaries provided by M. Gallagher (1980) and Fejes (1992). Gallagher found depressing similarities between Western industrialized, Eastern communist, and Southern developing countries: Women are underrepresented in the media, in production as well as in content. They are shown in their roles in the family and rarely in the workplace. If they work, they work in low-status jobs without much power or authority. They tend to be young and conventionally pretty, defined in relation to their husbands, fathers, sons, bosses, or other men, and portrayed as passive, indecisive, submissive, dependent, and so on. Fejes (1992) summarizes the rare examinations that have been made of the portrayals of men in the media and reports that the representations of men can be characterized as the opposite of the portrayals of women. From his and Gallagher's summaries we can concoct the dichotomy of gender as represented in the media:

women	men
underrepresentation	overrepresentation
family context	work context
low-status jobs	high-status positions
no authority	authority
no power	powerful
related to others	individual
passive	active
emotional	rational
dependent	independent
submissive	resistant
indecisive	resolute

This list could go on. Fejes (1992) concludes, "Based on these empirical studies, it is evident that men, as portrayed on adult television, do not deviate much from the traditional patriarchal notion of men and masculinity" (p. 12). Neither do women seem to be portrayed outside the discursive realm of patriarchy, supporting the hypothesis suggested earlier that media portrayals represent a dichotomous and hierarchical definition of gender.

We can all mention exceptions to the dichotomies presented above. Indeed, the 1980s and 1990s have confronted American television viewers with an unprecedented number of working women and mothering fathers (Cantor & Cantor, 1991), although a backlash has been noted more recently too (Faludi, 1991). Moreover, one wonders how ambivalent gender portrayals are registered in research projects like these. Would Freddie Mercury performing as a vacuum-cleaning housewife in Queen's video for the song "I Want to Break Free" be listed as a man or a woman? Either way, the researchers would miss the point of his/her character. Research on stereotypes rarely acknowledges such divergences and ambivalences; it represents gender discourse in the media as if it is as solid and impervious as a concrete wall, and therewith reproduces the very phenomenon it wants to question—the dichotomous and hierarchical nature of gender. Other researchers have found it more useful to focus on the cracks in the wall, highlighting the contradictions in gender discourse to the extent that it seems to have become impossible to think of it as impervious and solid. Rather, it resembles an edifice that could come down any minute.

Feminist film scholar Jacky Byars (1991) has called such an approach an attempt at "recuperation," in which one examines media texts "looking for their internal contradictions and for the (potential) presence of strong feminine voices that resist patriarchal dominance" (p. 20). Thus one examines the struggles inherent to gender discourse in the media rather than the consensus, the negotiations rather than the agreement. Consider, for example, the classic 1953 Hollywood movie *Gentlemen Prefer Blondes*, starring Jane Russell and Marilyn Monroe. Although a product of popular culture that often presents dominant gender discourse, *Gentlemen Prefer Blondes* can be seen as subversive text (Arbuthnot & Seneca, 1982/1990). The two actresses portray strong, independent women who have ventured jointly on a boat trip to seek husbands. The heterosexual quest for romance might be the manifest narrative of the film, but underneath it is a story of resistance to male objectification and female love and friendship. There is a continuous tension between the romantic text and the feminist "subtext." Monroe and Russell are constructed as objects for the male gaze, but they always return the look, scanning their surroundings for appropriate husband material. In their dress and stature they resist sexual objectification, which is furthermore prevented by particular camera angles and lighting. The more important source of resistant pleasure, however, involves the friendship of the two women, which entails a genuine affection for each other despite displays of feelings of competition and jealousy over male courting; the women often look at each other lovingly, and frequently touch and caress one another. When they have finally succeeded in finding husbands, their double wedding scene can be seen as evidence that their matrimonial commitments are only superficial, and do not endanger the endurance of their friendship. Arbuthnot and Seneca (1982/1990) note: "It is the tension between male objectification and women's resistance to that objectification that opens *Gentlemen Prefer Blondes* to a feminist reading. It is the clear and celebrated connection between Marilyn Monroe and Jane Russell that, for us, transforms *Gentlemen Prefer Blondes* into a profoundly feminist text" (p. 123).

In fact, any media text, regardless of its manifest stereotypical character, can be interpreted against the grain of its dominant discourse. Media texts are *polysemic*, that is, they carry multiple meanings that do not produce a single, dominant discourse. Even blatant gender stereotypes may not be what they seem, as is tellingly illustrated by the American television comedy series *Married . . . with Children*. The series features a white, working-class nuclear family consisting of a husband, wife, daughter, and son. Peggy Bundy, the mother, is portrayed as the ever-consuming housewife, interested in her nail polish and her husband's paycheck only. Al portrays the quintessential lazy, good-for-nothing husband, a lousy provider who hates work, dislikes his family, and prefers watching television over almost anything. Sex is never on his mind, to the enormous frustration of his wife. Their teenage daughter is a proverbial sexy dumb blonde, their son a foul-mouthed adolescent with no respect for his parents. Gender and family stereotypes are taken to extremes in *Married . . . with Children* and become sources of laughter that expose and undermine dominant gender discourse instead of confirming and strengthening them.

Yet not every parody on gender, not every instance of gender-bending, necessarily has a subversive nature, as indicated by the analysis of heavy metal music mentioned earlier. The feminine elements in heavy metal performances are primarily used as easily manageable signs of rebellion against society in general, not as expressions of dissatisfaction with dominant gender discourse.

The relation between media representations of gender and the "reality" of gender does not concern an articulation with the material reality of gender roles and positions, as the research on stereotypes suggests. The issue is an articulation with the discursive reality of gender ranging from confirmation to subversion, none of them ever uncontested. Taking this one step further, radical postmodern thinkers would argue that the distinction between gender discourse in the media and gender discourse outside of the media is an artificial one, and that we are actually dealing with one inseparable, self-contained discursive realm. Reality and the media representation of gender have collapsed into a world of simulations or *simulacra*, as Baudrillard calls them. There are many easily understandable concrete phenomena that can be considered perfect examples of these simulacra. Let's look, for instance, at *Truth or Dare*, Madonna's autobiographical documentary of her Blonde Ambition Tour.

The film presents the performance of Madonna's show in a number of cities throughout the world, shows what is going on backstage, and reveals parts of Madonna's life offstage. The backstage and offstage scenes are in black and white and the show elements are in color, suggesting a clear distinction between Madonna's public performance and her private life. However, the differences between the color and black-and-white scenes gradually lose importance, and by the end of the film we are not so sure anymore of any relevant distinctions among onstage, backstage, and offstage (Pribram, 1993).

The question of whether Madonna really shows her true self to the audience has dominated popular and critical reception of the film. The most widespread conclusion seems to be that *Truth or Dare* is just another example of Madonna's capacity to control her image, that it does not tell us anything about her real self. In such comments the implicit assumption is, again, that there is a fundamental difference between representation and reality, that there is a true, core identity to be found and revealed after all the masks and disguises have been peeled away. The more postmodern interpretation, that there is no fundamental distinction between representation and reality, that "what you see is what you get," that there is nothing beyond the appearance, is made—although unwillingly—in the movie by Warren Beatty, Madonna's lover at the time. At some point, Madonna is checked by a doctor because of problems with her voice. While the doctor is examining her throat, the camera keeps rolling, and Beatty wonders aloud whether this should be filmed too. In a scene often commented on, Beatty then exclaims, both desperately and critically: "Turn the camera off? She doesn't want to live off camera, much less talk. There is nothing to say off camera. Why would you say something if it's off camera? What point is there of existing?" Even Beatty, who would be one of the few to know, cannot find another—supposedly more authentic—Madonna than the public person.

The unsuccessful attempts of fans, critics, and other parties to pin down the "genuine" Madonna resemble the confusion incited by cross-dressers, who also cannot be defined in terms of an "authentic" identity and also pose the question of the relation between the appearance and the "real." As in the cross-dressers' case, to maintain the illusion that there is something more important beyond the appearance is to deny the relevance and the value of the appearance itself. Whereas cross-dressers undermine the dichotomy of gender—one is either man or woman—and present us with a third possibility, the

Madonna phenomenon undermines another dichotomy—between reality and representation—and suggests a third option: reality as representation or appearance; a simulation or "simulacrum," as Baudrillard has called it.

> If one sees her in this way, she can then be received at surface value, confusions and contradictions intact. That is, there is no definitive "real," no authentic Madonna, beyond the person(a) we already know through her various incarnations, guises, and forms. Following Baudrillard, if there is no authentic, then the appearances themselves, by displacing the authentic, become real (or, to use his term, the hyperreal). (Pribram, 1993, p. 202)

The "hyperreal" has become a much more ordinary phenomenon than we may think at first sight. The Madonna phenomenon is not the only easily available example of a simulacrum. In the world of politics and journalism, simulacra also exist abundantly in the form of "pseudoevents," events especially set up for media coverage and meaningless without coverage. The many contradictions and uncertainties in contemporary gender discourse in the media may also suggest that there is no definite relation to "real" gender discourse anymore, that the multifaceted appearance of gender is the relevant phenomenon instead. Advertising, for instance, is a genre that has begun to explore the ambivalence of gender. Wernick (1991) contends that whereas the appearances of women and men in advertising used to signify dominant dichotomous gender discourse, more and more these appearances have been exploited to signify unexpected themes. Male bodies, for instance, are often constructed as passive objects of the gaze of heterosexual (and homosexual) audiences. Female bodies may be used to point at power, authority, and control. Wernick contends that the ultimate consequence of this interchangeability is that gender has become an arbitrary sign in advertising, without any direct relation to its referent in real life, although, as we have seen, this referent is not an unproblematic stable phenomenon either.

One may conclude, then, that the representation of gender in the media is not a representation at all, for there is no reality to which it refers—or rather this reality is so contradictory and ambiguous that any attempt to pin it down is futile. Gender discourse in the media, then, should be thought of in postmodern terms of appearance rather than representation. It is a separate phenomenon that calls for attention to itself rather than to the alleged but nonexistent truth behind it. This is not to say that gender as appearance in the media has nothing to do with reality, only that we should look for its articulation on a different plane. The question is not how gender in the media represents reality, but how it functions in reality, in particular, how it is articulated with the gendered subjectivities of human beings in their daily lives. Given that, as I have argued above, our subjectivity is constituted in language, the hyperreal of the media is an inevitable part of the discursive realm of gender in which we are taken up, interacting not only with other discourses such as those of sexuality and ethnicity but also with the social and material conditions of daily life. Postmodernism that follows Baudrillard has little to say about such issues and is, according to its critics, little more than an elitist analysis of aesthetic forms denying the "social materialism" of the hyperreal, that is, the question of how it is part of everyday life (Fiske, 1991).

Media, Gender, and Everyday Life

Most research on the use and interpretation of media in everyday life suffers from the same dichotomization of gender as the research on stereotypes and dominant gender discourse in general. Take, for example, research on the popularity of television soap operas. Much of it is inspired by the quantitative fact that women are the most avid viewers of soaps; this fact is seen to originate in soap operas' centrality of themes and values associated with the private sphere. The focus on women as protagonists, on their rational and calculated actions, and on their mischievous attitudes toward male power form some of the sources of pleasure for the female audience. Further pleasures stem from the ability of soaps to evoke a mode of reception that is simultaneously critical and involved. The particular scheduling of daytime soaps ensures that the audience will consist of housewives and others working outside of the mainstream daytime labor market (e.g., Brown, 1990; Seiter, Borchers, Kreutzner, & Warth, 1991).

Concealed but straightforward causal models are thus employed; researchers assume that the identifications enabled by the female characters of soaps are important reasons for their popularity among women. In other words, most reception analysts assume that first you are a woman or a man, and then you like soaps and romances or sports and documentaries. Such a notion of gender construes the concept again as a relatively constant and consistent feature of human identity. However, as discussed earlier, being a "woman" or a "man" only *seems* to provide a stable and uncontested identity. Even within dominant gender discourse, there are still many distinct and contradictory subject positions to take up. It may even seem as if in each social situation an appropriate gender identity has to be established and expressed anew. As I have noted, in adolescence gender insecurity may be most salient and painful, and in this respect gender discourse in the media, as presented by Madonna, among others, may be most relevant: "Adolescents are themselves trying out various identities, and Madonna's constant alteration may well satisfy deep needs for self-experimentation, deep needs to move beyond the constraints of given gender sign systems" (Kaplan, 1993, p. 158).

Ien Ang's (1990) essay about the "feminization" pleasures of soaps can serve as a further illustration. She argues that in the never-ending process of feminization—constructing the appropriate feminine identity—the female characters of soap operas offer fantasy modes of femininity that enable viewers to try out different subjectivities without the risks involved in real life. "In fantasy and fiction, however, there is no punishment for whatever identity one takes up, no matter how headstrong or destructive: there will be no retribution, no defeat will ensue" (p. 86). Thus possibilities for identification do not form the source of female pleasure in soaps, but precisely the opposite: The options for experimenting with unknown and extreme identities make soaps enjoyable. Gender does not precede media reception and genre preference, but almost the reverse. A particular mode of reception is part of the ongoing construction of gender. In other words, "gender identities—feminine and masculine subjectivities—are constructed in the practices of everyday life in which media consumption is subsumed" (Ang & Hermes, 1991, p. 308).

Despite its potential status as hyperreal, media representations of gender discourse are relevant to the realities of daily life because they have become part of our subjectivity by offering modes of understanding and representing ourselves. They enable us to explore our multiple subjectivities and the differential investments we may have in several gendered subject positions, an investment being "something between emotional commitment and a vested interest, in the relative power (satisfaction, reward, payoff) which that position promises (but does not necessarily fulfill)" (De Lauretis, 1987, p. 16). It is precisely because of these differential investments that apparently subversive

elements of gender-bending—as present, for instance, in the performance of heavy metal bands—do not produce a subversion of dominant
gender discourse. Heavy metal fans, being primarily insecure adolescent boys, have too much to lose by admitting insecurities of gender
(Denski & Sholle, 1992, p. 53). Thus, whereas the articulation of
gender discourse in the media with the formation of subjectivity in
everyday life may take on a subversive character, it may just as well
confirm the dominant modes of thinking about gender as dichotomous
and hierarchical. As Jake Hermes (1993) suggests, popular culture
"may be used to realign oneself with dominant identities" (p. 209).

Having come to the end of this chapter, it seems as if we are left
with more questions and uncertainties than answers. To summarize
somewhat crudely: Gender appears to be an unstable phenomenon
only ostensibly pinned down in the dominant discourse of binary and
hierarchical gender relations, but in fact continuously escaping cate-
gorization and definition. Media representations seem to miss direct
referents in reality and represent not much more than themselves.
The articulation of these representations with gendered subjectivities
in daily life may amount to different things depending on people's
differential investments in gender identities, resulting in the subversion as well as the confirmation of dominant gender discourse. The
emphasis on the unstable character of gender and the continuous
negotiation taking place in and with media texts may suggest that it
is a volatile, almost meaningless category that can be filled with
meaning according to individual preferences, social conditions, cultural peculiarities, or historical contingencies. It may obscure the
power relations in which gender is embedded, and the very terminology of "gender" may conceal that "masculinity" often implies a discourse of power and centrality, whereas "femininity" is more commonly related to powerlessness and marginality. Looking at gender
from this perspective, the instabilities noted in this chapter are marginal phenomena only, a long way from the situation in which it would
be impossible to speak of "gender" at all. That would possibly qualify
as a postculturalist utopia in which "freedom lies in our capacity to
discover the historical links between certain modes of self-understanding and modes of domination, and to resist the ways in which
we have already been classified and identified by dominant discourses"
(Sawicki, 1991, p. 43). After all, wouldn't it be wonderful if life was
one big transvestites' ball?

Further Questions

1. Do media programs push boys and men to think they should be tough and always in control of their feelings? If so, are the media effective in this, and in which ways?

2. How do you rate the impacts of children's toys on the way boys and girls begin to understand the social meanings of their genders? Do boys always play with imitation guns and girls with dolls?

3. In which sectors of the media industry are women most likely to be employed? At which levels of authority? If women had more power within the media industry, would it change the industry's gender portrayals?

Notes

1. In this chapter I draw on some ideas and phrases from my book *Feminist Media Studies* (Zoonen, 1994).

2. It is an interesting example of gender difference to notice the change in meaning when applying De Beauvoir's (1972, p. 295) statement to the male case: "One is not born a man, one is made a man." Associations of the army and other places where "men are made" come to mind, suggesting that being made into a woman is a very different process from being made into a man.

3. Indicative of current gender relations is that the male-to-female cross-dresser is not only a more common phenomenon, but also much better served by support groups, shops, magazines, and so on.

19 Advertising and Consumer Culture

DOUGLAS KELLNER

Some critical analysts focus mainly on the political economy of media, as discussed in Chapters 5 and 6 of this volume. Others concentrate overwhelmingly on cultural studies, as in this section. Kellner tries to fuse these perspectives together, examining not just the economic basis of U.S. broadcasting and the press—advertising—but also advertising's impact in creating a consumerist culture that seems at times to envelop us all.

The intellectual source of much of his critique is a group of German intellectuals who were forced into exile, mainly to the United States, by the Nazis' accession to power in 1933. Based originally at a short-lived research institute at Frankfurt University, they are the founders of what has become known as the Frankfurt school of critical theory. Their view of contemporary mass culture has been highly influential since. They are noted for their insistence on how mass-produced contemporary culture provides us with substitutes for genuine experience, for love, for curiosity of the mind; on how it manipulates our anxieties about ourselves; and on how it caters to a fraction of our intelligence and effectively sells us short as human beings.

AUTHOR'S NOTE: I would like to thank the editors as well as Steve Best, John Harms, and Robert Goldman.

Perhaps nowhere is this argument more plausible than in mass adver-tising. Kellner mercilessly dissects the ridiculous—but still potent—advertising messages that play upon our fears and uncertainties about how to present ourselves socially, how to behave in public and in private. Kellner also analyzes the fashion industry, which is advertis-ing's principal commercial bedfellow. These are pervasive compo-nents of our everyday cultural lives, of how we are pulled and tugged about by these corporate forces, unless we live as hermits in the wilderness. Even when we refuse to conform to the dictates of fashion and advertising, we are aware at the same time that we have resisted their pressure.

Furthermore, in sustaining an ongoing pattern of high spending and consumer debt, two economic objectives are realized. One is that mass-produced items always find buyers, which means the economy is less prone to crisis and collapse, in contrast to the 1930s, when between a third and a quarter of Americans were out of work. No one wants that experience repeated, but at the same time, the consumer products that have been sold most intensively are often dangerous and polluting, namely, cars and cigarettes. Auto and road construction, oil, and tobacco corporations improve their balance sheets, the economy seems stable—but what about our lungs, our limbs, our lives, the balance sheet of our physical and social health?

The second economic objective realized is work discipline. A currently popular bumper sticker says, "I owe, I owe, so off to work I go." People moonlight to meet their consumer debt payments. Few people really relish Monday mornings. Yet our culture tells us we can enjoy our-selves to the limit—of our ability to work.

According to figures published in the September 1992 issue of the *Journal of Advertising,* in the early 1990s in the United States more than $130 billion, or roughly 2% of the gross national product, was spent annually on advertising (p. 130). When one considers that an ever larger amount of money is also spent on design, packaging, marketing, and product display, one sees just what is squandered on advertising and marketing. Only 8 cents of the cosmetics sales dollar goes to pay for ingredients; the rest goes to packaging, promotion, and marketing (R. Goldman, 1987, p. 697). Advertising commands a tremendous amount of resources and talent and is a crucial component of the capitalist economic system.

The expansion of marketing and advertising was originally the result of mass production. By the early years of the twentieth century, industrial capitalism had perfected techniques of mass production. The assembly line, scientific management of the labor process, and the emergence of the modern corporation revolutionized production and made possible the creation of new mass consumer goods. New modes of advertising, marketing, packaging, and design helped produce the mass consumption necessary for the purchase of all these new commodities. By the 1920s, corporations, advertising agencies, and market research organizations began planning ways to "produce" consumers (see Gandy, Chapter 11) and to promote consumption as a way of life in the United States (Ewen, 1976, 1988). Individual resistance to new products had to be broken down, and individuals had to be convinced that it was acceptable to purchase goods they had previously produced themselves and that it was morally justifiable to consume, to spend money, and to gratify desires.

Previously, puritan work and savings ethics and a morality of delayed gratification prevailed, so advertising had to convince individuals that consumption was now a morally acceptable route to happiness and satisfaction. Advertising also attempted to create problems and fears to which commodities were a solution; thus, for instance, unless individuals bought products to combat their bad breath or body odor, they would not be socially acceptable. In this way, a "commodity self" emerged in which different products allowed individuals to communicate different aspects of "their" personalities that could be shaped by using the right products and producing the right images. Advertising tells us that new commodities will make us happier, more popular, and successful. Fashion in turn provides the constant cycle of new products, styles, and images that keep consumer demand at a high level. Advertising tells us that to be up-to-date we must be fashionable; we must buy and exhibit all the latest products and fashions. Advertising and fashion also promote a worldview complete with ethics, politics, gender role models, and a sense of appropriate and inappropriate daily social behavior.

These two industries thus have crucial economic and socializing functions in creating consumer demand, shaping behavior, and inducing people to participate in and thus reproduce consumer society. In this chapter I will examine some "mainstream" approaches to advertising as information and then present critical theories of advertising and fashion that provide more complete analysis as to how these two processes function to produce consumers and to integrate individuals within the consumer society. I will show how broader social values can be "read" from advertising content, and conclude with some criticisms of consumer culture and some proposals concerning how to minimize manipulation by the advertising and fashion industries.

Advertising: Information or Persuasion?

Mainstream writers essentially defend the institutions, lifestyles, and values of consumer capitalism, and apologists for the advertising industry interpret it as a form of information that provides consumers with up-to-date news concerning commodities and the impetus necessary to maintain a high level of production and affluence (Konig, 1973, p. 29). Likewise, defenders of the fashion industry claim that it, too, merely provides a constant turnover of new products and styles that meet consumer needs for novelty, change, and desire for style. They argue that fashion "opens up, with all its new developments, new horizons, enriches and diversifies life and makes it more attractive; it also acts as a powerful stimulus to the economy" (McClure & Fulton, 1964, p. 21).

In most standard textbooks and theories, fashion and advertising are therefore presented as beneficial aspects of an innovative and dynamic consumer society that provides individuals with the goods and styles that they themselves desire. Thus in "A Statement of Advertising Principles" defined by the Advertising Federation of America, one reads, "Good advertising aims to inform the consumer and help him to buy more intelligently" (Ulanoff, 1977, p. 22). Another defender of the industry takes the same position: "Advertising is an integral part of business. Its primary function is to sell products, services, and ideas by informing the public of their good points and their availability" (quoted in Harms, 1989).

Yet advertisers also admit that they are attempting to persuade buyers to purchase certain products, and divide buying motivations into "rational" and "irrational" behaviors (Switkin, 1981, p. 66). In the words of one mainstream theorist, whereas informative advertising aims to appeal to reason and provides "reasons why" individuals should purchase products, by contrast, "advertising that addresses itself chiefly to the emotions, rather than to reason or intellect, is called human interest copy. This kind of advertising is based on appeals to . . . emotions to which the average person reacts" (Switkin, 1981, p. 4). Little advertising is purely "informative." There are informative ads in the classified sections of newspapers, but television ads are mainly image based, creating associations between products and desired conditions, such as happiness and success. Advertising is persuasive, relying on emotional appeals, dramatic or comic images, and manipulation of basic fears and desire.

Michael Schudson (1984) has compiled a great deal of evidence indicating that advertising has limited effects, and he cites a large number of unsuccessful advertising campaigns. Deeply suspicious of the view that advertising automatically has an impact on people, Schudson claims that ads have "only the most happenstance and eclectic theoretical foundation; they are not based on any serious understanding of people's attitudes about worldly goods" (p. 63). He claims that few people actually believe in advertising and that there is little compelling evidence that it actually persuades or manipulates consumers into buying.

Recent empirical research into advertising effectiveness tends to confirm Schudson's suspicions: According to statistics published in the September 1992 issue of the *Journal of Advertising*, advertising produced an increase in sales in less than half of the cases studied; indeed, advertising had little or no effect on product sales in more than three-quarters of the cases studied. Yet such dismissal of the effects of advertising covers over the fact that there is evidence that much advertising does work and that, moreover, advertising is part of a climate that promotes consumption, along with marketing, promotion, telecommunications, packaging and display, and an environment of stores, malls, and shopping. In this context, advertising helps shape values, thoughts, fantasies, and behavior.

Thus defining the impact of advertising purely in terms of its success in pushing specific products skates right past the wider question of how advertising forms part of a whole promotional culture that shapes citizens into consumers, transmitting endlessly the message that buying and consuming will solve problems and bring about happiness, social and sexual. It provides lifestyle models to emulate— or to avoid, because of their body odor, poor and outdated dress, or (for women only) lack of sufficient slenderness. Thus ads are important cultural texts that should be subjected to cultural criticism.

Reading Advertisements Critically

Learning how to read advertising critically thus provides individuals with important tools for interpreting contemporary American culture and avoiding manipulation. Ads are complex texts, the images, words, framing devices, and structures of which attempt to influence individuals into accepting certain values and role models and into adopting certain lifestyles.

In order to sell their products, corporations undertake campaigns to associate them with positive and desirable images. Thus in the 1950s, Marlboro undertook a campaign to associate its cigarette with masculinity and with being a "true man." Previously, Marlboro had been packaged as a mild, women's cigarette, and the "Marlboro man" campaign attempted to capture the male market with images of archetypal and culturally familiar characters such as the cowboy, with its connotations of masculinity, independence, and ruggedness. Thus consumption of the product was associated with socially desirable traits, here masculinity. For decades, the Marlboro cowboy has been the central symbol in Marlboro ads. Yet in the 1990s the cowboy has become a relatively small figure, overshadowed by images of snow, trees, and sky. Why this shift from masculine cowboy to images of nature?

All ads are social texts that respond to key developments during the period in which they appear. As the health hazards of smoking became more widely known, a mandatory health warning appeared on all packaging and advertising. "Light" and low-tar cigarettes are also responses to the health concern, so too Marlboro ads now feature images of clean, pure, wholesome nature, as if it were "normal" to smoke cigarettes and as if cigarettes were a healthy, "natural" product. The imagery is itself "light," white, green, snowy, and airy, often showing horses gamboling in snow or water, trying to associate cigarettes through the process of "metonymy," or contiguous association, with these natural elements. This glosses over the fact that cigarettes are an artificial, synthetic product, full of dangerous pesticides, preservatives, and other chemicals.

The Marlboro ads also draw on images of tradition (the cowboy), hard work, domesticating animals, and other values, as if smoking were a noble activity sanctioned by tradition. The images and text create a symbolic construct that tries to camouflage the contradictions between the "heavy" work and the "light" cigarette, between the "natural" scene and the "artificial" product, and between the rugged masculinity of the Marlboro man and the "light" cigarette. In fact, this latter contradiction can be explained by the marketing ploy of suggesting to men that they can both be highly masculine and smoke a (supposedly) "healthier" cigarette, while also appealing to "independent-minded" women who might enjoy smoking a "man's" cigarette that is also "lighter" and "healthier."

A 1989 Marlboro ad featured the gnarled hands of an old cowboy holding a lighted cigarette. The subliminal message is that you too can smoke and live to a ripe old age (whereas the "real" person who played the Marlboro cowboy for many years had just died of cancer after giving many interviews warning of the dangers of smoking). It thus invites the consumer to a pleasurable experience and subliminally tries to allay fears that the experience is a dangerous one that might actually be life threatening.

Thus ads offer symbolic gratifications to consumers and try to associate their products with socially desired values. The well-known Virginia Slims advertising campaign, with its slogan, "You've come a long way, baby," tries to denote social progress for women, associating this progress with the right to smoke. Many of these ads try to visualize the positive change for women. They often depict the bad old days when, for example, a working woman lights up a cigarette and angers her boss, contrasted with the modern beautiful Virginia Slims woman confidently and happily holding a cigarette in her hand. The ads connote a message of progress, linking Virginia Slims to the "modern woman" who has progressed from oppressed servant of men to independent subject of her own life. The appearance of the 1989 Virginia Slims woman contributed to this message; for example, her hair was teased, her makeup perfect, her smile dazzling, and her clothes flamboyant, with mismatched earrings, connoting independence, style, and nonconformity. A red hat, carelessly tossed back over her shoulder, a gold bracelet, an exotic short shirt, all were carefully contrived to effect an image of individuality, daring, and sexuality.

It is interesting to compare contemporary Virginia Slims women with earlier images. As recently as 1983, the Virginia Slims woman was much more conventionally pretty, more conservatively attired, and less flamboyant and sexy. The shift in image reflects changes in cultural ideals and a "yuppie" emphasis on high fashion and individuality, as well as the collapse of moral taboos about women's sexuality. Also, during the Reagan 1980s there was increased emphasis on wealth and luxury, which is still reflected in the current image. Thus ads sell not only products but social values and ideals.

The Virginia Slims woman is very slim, like her brand name, maintaining the powerful cultural pressure on women to achieve this socially desirable trait. In fact, Lucky Strike carried out a successful advertising campaign in the 1930s that associated smoking with weight reduction, and Virginia Slims plays on this tradition. The connection of smoking and slimness is far from innocent and has contributed to eating disorders, faddish diets and exercise programs, and a dramatic increase in anorexia among young women, as well as rising cancer rates. As Judith Williamson (1978) points out, advertising "addresses" individuals and invites them to identify with certain products, images, and behavior, and this is most powerful for women.

Advertising sells its products and view of the world through visual and verbal rhetorics, design, and layout, to which tremendous psychological research, artistic resources, and marketing strategies are devoted. Advertising, fashion, and consumerism are of crucial importance in producing the needs, values, and daily behavior that dominate our lives in contemporary capitalist economies.

Fashion and the Manufacture of Image

To keep a high level of consumer demand in place, the advertising and fashion industries have to persuade consumers to change deep-rooted habits, to throw away old products and buy new ones continually. Advertising and the fashion industry thus combine individuality and conformity in curious ways. Individuals consume and pursue fashion to individuate themselves, yet do so in order to be socially accepted—to fit in and be popular. Moreover, mass-produced goods and fashion are used to produce a fake individuality, a "commodity self," an "image."

In today's society, corporations, politicians, and individuals are all obsessed with image (Boorstin, 1962). Much magazine advertising is therefore devoted to stylish images, whether of clothes, cosmetics, automobiles, or liquor. Clothing ads show the "proper" image for specific social groups and classes. Upscale magazines directed toward the upper class and the upwardly mobile feature luxury items and high fashion as an essential part of a successful lifestyle. General-readership magazines and some specialty magazines sell less-expensive mass-produced products that are promoted as magical roads to romance and popularity for middle- and working-class audiences.

The two ads reproduced here provide examples. The first projects to upscale male readers that they must have a variety of fashionable clothes in order to be popular and sexually successful. The sexist caption at the top, "So Many Women / So Little Time," appeals to the busy young man on the make. The nine images of different clothes and different women equates the two, projecting the idea that women are available for "consumption" in the same way new jackets are. The second ad highlights the message that in a competitive world a man must be well dressed and fashionable. The motto at the top, "The Survival of the Trimmest" plays on the Darwinian thesis of the survival of the fittest in a dangerous and violent world. The menacing talons of the eagle at the top of the picture reinforce the image of danger. The young man in the center is coded as a hunter with a lethal crossbow and arrow, ready for the kill. The color of the exotic background of the desert and animals is a golden hue that provides a surrealistic aura to the scene. It signals to the attentive reader that the ad is an allegory of life in a competitive capitalist society, the jungle in which only the fittest survive, and it is the clothes that are the young man's "weapon." The sensual language and the phallic bow make it unclear exactly what the man's prey is. Indeed, despite their careful crafting, ads remain minitexts open to different critical readings if closely examined.

Television, Advertising, and Fashion

Television is one of the most ubiquitous and influential promoters of advertising and fashion. TV advertising is expensive, sophisticated, and ever more frequent during an era in which the deregulation of television allows the networks to show as many ads as they desire during a given time period. Television ads are typically 60-, 30-, 15-, or even 10-second dramatizations of the value of consumerism as a way of life and the joys and benefits of the consumer society. TV ads frequently adopt the conflict-resolution structure of television programming. Situation comedies and action/adventure programs present problems and conflicts and then offer solutions that celebrate traditional values, institutions, and authority figures. Similarly, in advertising a problem is shown, the commodity is offered as a solution, and happiness is the outcome.

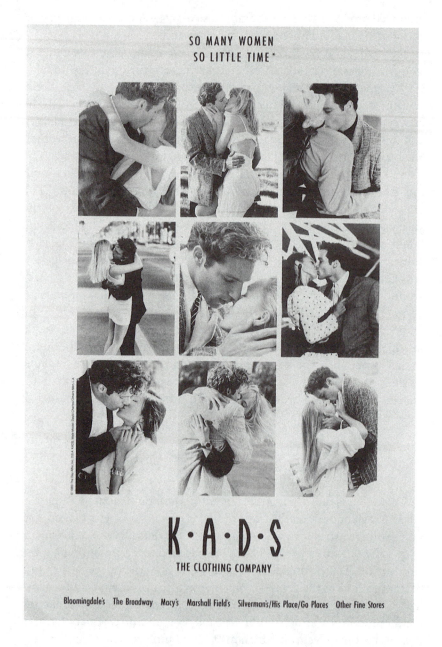

SO MANY WOMEN
SO LITTLE TIME*

K·A·D·S
THE CLOTHING COMPANY

Bloomingdale's   The Broadway   Macy's   Marshall Field's   Silverman's/His Place/Go Places   Other Fine Stores

Classic television ads presented problems like "ring around the collar" and "tired blood" and commodities that would solve these problems. They portrayed numerous sagas of young men or women

The Survival of the Trimmest.

The look of success today is trim, lean, lithe. Fioravanti has captured it brilliantly. In his masterfully tailored suits and sportcoats of superlative fabrics. At fine stores everywhere or write: 135 West 50th Street, New York, NY 10020, Suite 1925. The Trim Collection.

unable to get dates because of bad breath or unappetizing hair, magically transformed into highly attractive and successful sex objects through the mouthwash or shampoo advertised. Television advertising is especially suitable for portraying such magical transformation and metamorphosis, building on fantasy imagery borrowed from myths, fairy tales, or contemporary media. Television is our primary storytelling medium, and ads provide brief narrative dramas that vividly present the agonies and ecstasies of life in the consumer culture.

Television stands at the center of our symbol system and provides mythic and ritualistic celebrations of dominant values and institutions (Kellner, 1982). Thus ads can be read as capitalist morality plays that celebrate dominant values, specific modes of action, and the "good life," much as medieval morality plays celebrated Christianity. Anheuser-Busch's "The night belongs to Michelob" ads of the late 1980s used high-tech, fast-paced imagery to associate the beer with a modern consumer lifestyle of cars, dance clubs, bars, and urban street culture. The images were dazzling, the editing was fast, and the pictures were tracked with loud music and Michelob slogans. The ads thus sold both beer and the fast life in the fast lane, linking Michelob to the paradise of consumer capitalism. During the late 1980s we were also treated to nightly incantations that "the heartbeat of America [is] today's Chevrolet." The cars sped through attractive landscapes and showed individuals, couples, and families enjoying the mobile and fun-filled life made possible by their cars. These ads equated owning and driving a car with being a real American, and used patriotism to try to persuade U.S. citizens to buy "American" cars rather than "foreign" models (as if the two were clearly distinguishable any longer).

TV ads are highly sophisticated, highly creative, and produced with the newest high-tech instruments and aesthetic strategies. Tremendous amounts of time, talent, and resources are devoted to producing such images, which are typically more expensive than programming. Networks receive up to half a million dollars and more for each prime-time ad spot. Indeed, television programming itself is little more than bait for viewers who are sold to advertisers. One of the gigantic swindles perpetrated on the public today is that commercial television is free, that advertising pays for network television. In fact, consumers pay for the programming through higher prices for the goods they purchase. Many television series are themselves advertisements for wealth, luxury, fashion, and a high-consumption lifestyle (an argument developed by Sari Thomas in Chapter 26).

In a way, advertising is the art form of consumer capitalism, and it runs the gamut of aesthetic forms, from nitty-gritty realism to fantastic surrealism. As Robert Goldman (1984) has argued, certain ads promote an idealized version of American history and the institutions and values of corporate capitalism as they try to huckster their products. For instance, McDonald's ads frequently contain images of small-town America, family life, middle-class affluence, and integrated Americana that surround the images of the Big Macs and Macmuffins they are trying to sell. Other ads promote American ideology by equating consumerism with "freedom of choice" (e.g., between light and regular beer) or tell you to be an "individual" by buying this or that product. Note that individuality and freedom are here defined in terms of possession, consumption, and style, as opposed to thought, action, dissent, rational behavior, and autonomy, which were the basis of previous definitions of individualism promoted by the U.S. Founding Fathers and nineteenth-century individualists such as Thoreau, Emerson, and Whitman.

Critical Perspectives on Consumer Culture

Threats to individuality, democracy, and community from consumer culture were a primary focus of a group of critical social theorists known today as the Frankfurt school. These social theorists, who included Max Horkheimer, Erich Fromm, Theodor Adorno, Leo Lowenthal, and Herbert Marcuse, were forced in the early 1930s to flee Nazi Germany and emigrated to the United States (Kellner, 1989). While in exile, they developed one of the first systematic critical perspectives on advertising, fashion, and the consumer society. In a 1938 article, "On the Fetish Character of Music and the Regression of Hearing," Adorno (1938/1980) offers some critical perceptions on the newly emerging consumer culture in the United States, written in powerfully condensed language:

> The couple out driving who spend their time identifying every passing car and being happy if they recognize the trademarks speeding by, the girl whose satisfaction consists solely in the fact that she and her boyfriend "look good"; . . . before the theological caprices of commodities, the consumers become temple slaves.

For all the couple's apparent freedom and enjoyment, Adorno argues, they are actually slaves to the ever-changing demands of the fashion industry's new commodities, which act like a capricious and tyrannical deity of old.

In a later work by Adorno and Horkheimer, *The Dialectic of Enlightenment*, written in 1947, the authors analyze the way that mass culture and communication produce consumers for the "culture industries" (see Adorno & Horkheimer, 1947/1972). Their experiences in Europe sensitized them to the danger that the manipulative techniques of advertising and propaganda in the consumer society could be developed to usher in some version of Fascism in the political sphere:

> The ruthless unity in the culture industry is evidence of what will happen in politics. Marked differentiations such as . . . magazines in different price ranges, depend not so much on subject matter as on classifying,

organizing, and labelling consumers. Something is provided for all so that none may escape; the distinctions are emphasized and extended. The public is catered for with a hierarchical range of mass-produced products of varying quality. . . . Everybody must behave (as if spontaneously) in accordance with his previously determined and indexed level, and choose the category of mass product turned out for his type. Consumers appear as statistics on research organization charts, and are divided by income groups into red, green, and blue areas; the technique is that used for any type of propaganda.

Culture was no longer a form of creative expression but a standardized manufactured product, almost indistinguishable from the advertising that surrounded it:

The assembly-line character of the culture industry, the synthetic, planned method of turning out its products (factory-like not only in the studio but, more or less, in the compilation of cheap biographies, pseudo-documentary novels, and hit songs) is very suited to advertising. The effect, the trick, the isolated repeatable device, have always been used to exhibit goods for advertising purposes. . . . Advertising and the culture industry merge technically as well as economically. In both cases the same thing can be seen in innumerable places, and the mechanical repetition of the same cultural product has come to be the same as that of the propaganda slogan. In both cases the insistent demand for effectiveness makes technology into psycho-technology, into a procedure for manipulating men. In both cases the standards are striking yet familiar, the easy yet catchy, the skillful yet simple; the object is to overpower the customer, who is conceived as absent-minded or resistant. (p. 123)

Twenty years later, Marcuse (1964) argued that consumer culture produced "false needs" that induced individuals to buy into a consumer lifestyle. He was among the first to argue, as I have above, that the individuality offered by consumer culture is a pseudoindividuality, constructed and promoted for purposes of manipulation and social control. Thus to be genuinely free and individual, one must free oneself from a whole system of pleasures, consumption, and entertainment administered by the power structure. According to Marcuse:

Political freedom would mean liberation of individuals from politics over which they have no effective control. Similarly, intellectual freedom would mean the restoration of individual thought now absorbed by mass communication.

Not only is the consumer society based on a tremendous waste of resources and talents, but corporate control of the economy has made the United States look alike all over: Drive down any street in the United States and you will see generic America in the form of filling stations selling the same brands of gas, fast-food chains selling the same junk food, video stores renting the same (quite small) selection of films, and chains of other types selling the same goods everywhere. Through quasi-monopolies, advertising, price fixing, mergers, and other corporate developments, giant corporations have come to dominate economy and society in the United States. While enjoying less variety and diversity of goods, the consumer must pay for the entire corporate infrastructure and advertising and packaging, actually subsidizing the very industries that indoctrinate and exploit us.

Conclusion

Manipulation by the advertising and fashion industries can be avoided. Generally, generic products of the same or better quality can be had, and at lower prices. We can resist the machinations of fashion, choosing our clothes and other products on grounds of usefulness, durability, value, and actual need, instead of allowing ourselves to be manipulated by advertising. We must also learn to read and decipher advertising, to see through the hype so that we can analyze and criticize advertising's persuasive techniques. Corporate propaganda aside, advertising is a parasitic industry and a tremendous social drain. By the early 1990s, as noted at the outset of this chapter, $130 billion was spent annually in the United States on advertising—far more money than was spent on schooling. Advertising is a disgraceful waste of resources, talent, and time. Eventually, citizens of the United States and similarly advertising-saturated nations are going to have to question seriously the priorities, values, and institutions of consumer capitalism if we wish to preserve the democracy, freedom, health rights, and individuality to which we pay lip service.

Further Questions

1. How has the advertising industry used images of women's and men's bodies? What do you think of some critics' claim that advertis-

ing constantly promotes an ideal of woman as a slender, youthful sex object for men to enjoy and for women to measure themselves against? Is there truth in this claim? If so, what are the implications for the ways we understand ourselves as male and female, and the ways we behave?

2. How can we better educate consumers? What alternatives to current advertising could be developed that would provide reliable information without the hard sell?

3. In recent years, advertising has emphasized more and more strongly the importance of targeting very specific audiences, especially consumers with deep pockets. This has meant that popular TV programs have sometimes been dropped because their audiences have not been sufficiently affluent. What implications does this have for the frequent claim by spokespersons of the television industry that they simply give the public what it wants?

20 Racism and the American Way of Media

ASH COREA

Racism is as integral a dimension of U.S. culture as advertising, and it has even deeper roots. There is a curious view that racism more or less vanished with the success of the civil rights struggles against segregation and for voting rights of the 1950s and 1960s. This claim lies somewhere between hypocrisy and willful blindness to everyday realities. It is not only in the United States that white people exclude Black people from opportunity, but the American dream of a fair deal for all citizens is exposed as a cynical myth given that discrimination and disadvantage assigned by skin color are so systematic. Native Americans, African Americans, Asian Americans, and Latinos have current experiences of racism to relate, not just stories from bygone years, even though these experiences also have a continuity with the years of slavery and colonial subjugation.

Communicating racism, both in mass media and in the everyday conversations fed by the mass media, sustains it as an active cultural, and therefore political, force. Corea examines the way media, especially television, continue to stereotype both majority and minority, by means of some thought-provoking contrasts. She proceeds to summarize both the history of media portrayal of African Americans and their very limited presence in positions of influence in media institutions. At the close of her argument, she addresses the significance of

*the widely popular Black-cast Cosby Show to ask whether U.S. televi-
sion, unlike the leopard, has changed its spots.*

*Although Corea's analysis focuses on African American experience, a
considerable amount of what she points out can be applied to the
experiences of other so-called minorities in the United States, such as
Latinos. One of the problems with the term minority is that it lumps
together people of widely differing backgrounds and cultures because
of one factor: the readiness of white people to discriminate against
them. And because they are labeled minorities, they are effectively
marginalized and set apart from mainstream social life. The fact
remains that collectively we are speaking of up to a quarter of the U.S.
population, more than 60 million human beings, whose origins in
Africa, Latin America, and Asia make them part of the nonwhite
majority of the planet.*

*For the twenty-first century, how we communicate concerning this
issue and how quickly U.S. mass culture adapts to this reality are of
pressing importance. Where do U.S. media stand?*

Many writers argue that the media merely reflect what is happening out there. What is more, on television African Americans,
women, and white men seem to have the same opportunities that exist
in the society. Eddie Murphy and *In Living Color* can mock Stevie
Wonder and other African American celebrities, Arsenio Hall can have
a long-running and successful TV talk show, Bill Cosby can make it
to the top of the ratings, Geraldo Rivera can make headlines, Connie
Chung can draw a top news anchor salary. So it must be true: Everyone
has the same opportunities.

However, in the United States the overwhelming factor that defines
the position a group will occupy is color. Education, wealth, occupation, gender, and religion are also part of the picture, but, nevertheless,
being African American normally means occupying the bottom stra-
tum. This in turn limits access to the benefits produced within the
society. As a group, African Americans compete with other groups who
are discriminated against, such as Hispanics and Native Americans,
for the honor of being at the bottom. Gender does intervene in this
matrix: Women occupy lower positions when compared with men.

USA, anno 1957

In the complex array of factors at work, four clear points emerge. First, white men occupy the apex of the hierarchy in the United States, in terms of both power and status. Second, white women earn lower salaries (on average, two-thirds those of white men) and have much less political influence. Third, African American men have less political influence still and are paid substantially less than white men. Finally, African American women earn less than the other three groups, although they have greater access than African American men to very low-paying jobs such as babysitting, fast-food restaurant work, and cleaning. They have the very least political power. For those citizens of the United States who have difficulty believing the evidence before their own eyes, seemingly endless studies have documented this pattern in detail, from Gunnar Myrdal's *An American Dilemma* (1944) through the series of reports issued in 1989 by the Special Committee on Children, Youth and the Family of the U.S. House of Representatives.

So far, then, it has been suggested that there is in reality, if not in TV reality, a distinct relationship between color and access to wealth and power by members of certain groups. These groups are further subdivided by gender, with white men at the apex, followed by white women and then African American men. At the very bottom are African American women. A similar analysis would generally be valid for Latinos, Native Americans, and Asian Americans.

As the discussion now moves to a consideration of how media, in particular television, relate to this reality, the following three questions should be kept in mind:

1. Do African Americans and white Americans occupy the same positions within the controlling structures of the media?
2. Does television portray African Americans and white Americans as being equal to each other and as coexisting in a multiracial environment?
3. What factors are there that could militate against African Americans and white Americans receiving equal treatment on television?

African Americans and Employment in Media

Consider the following statement by an African American TV executive who was asked about the operation of power in the television industry:

> Positions of real power have been in the past, and continue to be, reserved for a network of white males who all know each other, run the industry, and occasionally allow a token number of White women to preside with them over the decision making process. (Massing, 1982, p. 44)

One could dismiss this TV executive's statement as sour grapes. However, in 1986 a report titled *Minority Broadcasting Facts* was released by the National Association of Broadcasters, and in it were the following figures on the numbers of general managers of commercial TV stations who were nonwhite: 9 African Americans and 5 Latinos. There were also 4 African American TV station managers. Yet in the United States there are nearly 1,300 commercial TV stations. Clearly, then, African Americans are not overwhelmingly represented in the controlling structures of television.

The Federal Communications Commission also released an equal opportunity trend report in 1988 that outlined ethnic minority employment in television and cable over the period 1983-1987. Ethnic groups were subdivided between males and females, and also between categories of employment. During 1987 the overall number of people employed was 176,159, compared with 160,967 for 1983. The proportion of minority professionals increased a little, from 15.3% in 1983 to 16.2% in 1987, or 28,590 in all, mainly owing to the presence of a few more Latino professionals. The 1987 percentages for minorities subdivided by gender were as follows: 4.2% African American women; 4.7% African American men; 2.2% Latinas; 3.4% Latinos.

However, the figures also showed that ethnic minorities were underrepresented in the top four groups, which jointly account for about 85% of all positions: officials and managers, 10.6% (3,832); professionals, 14.7% (8,006); technicians, 19.8% (6,345); sales workers, 10.0% (2,391). According to Dr. Edward Wachtel (1986), if we were to look more closely at these categories we would see that they serve to mask the real underrepresentation of African Americans in the power structure of the electronic media. Wachtel suggests that a more adequate picture of the real situation would be given if we were to match minority employment with salary. Is a sales worker, for example, an executive who sells ad spots to corporations, or that executive's typist?

So in answer to the first question posed, we can draw the following conclusion. Ethnic minorities such as African Americans exhibit a minimal presence in the upper echelons of influence in television, especially in the three big networks.

A 1993 report published by the National Association of Black Journalists Print Task Force shows that a significant number of African Americans leave the print media within five years of taking their first jobs. The Black journalists surveyed expressed the following typical concerns: (a) Newsroom managers are not committed to retaining or promoting Black journalists; (b) Black journalists spend longer than non-Black journalists in entry-level positions; and (c) Black journalists are not kept informed, as non-Black journalists are, about seminars and other opportunities to advance their careers. The surveyed journalists also felt that raising these issues would damage their chances for advancement: First Amendment or no First Amendment, their experience of the newsroom atmosphere was that it actively discouraged them from even voicing the issue.

There seems no reason, given these realities, why the number or proportion of ethnic minority journalists should ever see improvement. Although overall from 1991 to 1993 there was a slight rise, from 9.39% to 10.25%, in the proportion of all print journalists who were from ethnic minorities, 45% of daily newspapers still employed no minorities at all. Black journalists' belief that management generally is not committed to their hiring, retention, or promotion is certainly supported by these data. At the same time, print media executives cite the dearth of Black journalists and editors as the reason they cannot find qualified Black candidates for promotion to executive levels. (For data concerning ethnic minority presence, or absence, in other areas of the U.S. communication industry, see Downing, 1994.)

Jill Nelson, in her book *Volunteer Slavery* (1993), confirms that the milieu of the newspaper militates against the promotion and retention of African American journalists. Invariably, if African American journalists are hired, their managers either do not expect them to be well prepared for the craft or have unrealistic expectations of their performance. The tiny number of Black people in management positions often means that Black journalists do not get the level of mentoring support that other journalists get. One well-known white American TV journalist gave a presentation at a seminar in 1993 in which he recounted how he had been mentored when he was totally unknown and poorly prepared, and how his mentor had been instrumental in getting the inexperienced journalist's inevitable initial bloopers excused. Sadly, the same journalist was able to say later the same day, without any apparent awareness of his contradictory stance, that there are simply no qualified ethnic minority candidates for the top jobs in TV news. This was a classic illustration of the gulf between ethnic minority and white perceptions inside the media.

TV and African Americans: Hostility, Segregation, or Avoidance

Looking back over the social development of audiences for public entertainment or sports in the United States, it is clear that, historically, public entertainment has always been organized with African Americans absent from or segregated in the theater or stadium, in most places in the North and in all of the South (Nasaw, 1993). Differences of social class, of white ethnicity, of gender, and of religious belief were minimized, but only at the cost of firmly drawing a color line that materially contributed to the white U.S. public's definition of normal, full Americans as white people.

In keeping with this tradition, television, argues Michael Winston (1982), from its early stages, either was directly hostile to African Americans or ignored them: "It was to be 'white' not simply, as newspapers were, in its employment practices, but in its projection of American life—insofar as it reflected American reality at all" (p. 177).

In spite of the civil rights movements of the 1940s, 1950s, and 1960s, in spite of the Black power movements of the 1960s and 1970s, there still exists among many white people an underlying belief in and image of the United States as essentially a white country. African Americans are seen as peripheral to the growth and development of the United States. Essentially, African Americans are stereotyped as a problem in an otherwise harmonious country. For example, in urban America being a mugger is synonymous with being African American or Hispanic. The immediate image we accept as the norm is that of whites being mugged by African Americans and Hispanics.

How did this belief that all African Americans are potential muggers originate and become so embedded in the culture? Leading Black communication scholars in Britain have traced out the genesis of this image in British media (see Hall, Critcher, Jefferson, Clarke, & Roberts, 1978), but the full story has yet to be told for the United States. Let us, however, refresh our memories about how television handled the 1989 incident in which a jogger was raped and viciously beaten in Central Park. By contrast, let us consider the media treatment of the so-called preppie murder, which occurred in the same park in 1987.

In the television news coverage of the former incident, viewers were informed that the jogger was an investment banker, which immediately set the tone that she was a worthy person. Next, they were informed that the attack occurred in the part of Central Park that borders Harlem, a predominantly poor African American and Latino district. Viewers were bombarded with details about how the woman was brutally beaten, raped, and left to die by these cruel African American and Hispanic young thugs. One particular young man charged with involvement was singled out as being from a good family;

he was doing well in school and should have been looking forward to a bright future. There was in general, however, little information given about the conditions and environments of these young African Americans, whereas there was an implied and shared assumption that all African American men are liable to be violent, cruel, and vicious muggers, the kind of people who would predictably perpetrate such a crime on decent white women.

We should pause, however, to ask about the young white man who, in 1987, raped and murdered a white woman in Central Park—an incident the press labeled the "preppie murder." He was portrayed as a fine, upstanding young man who, under the influence of drugs and alcohol, coupled with sexy provocation from the young woman, lost his head and accidentally strangled her. Television reports did not dwell on this victim with the same intense attention given the Central Park jogger, or on the barbarism of this act. Instead, they presented viewers with extenuating circumstances that would enable them to understand that this was not a premeditated crime, but just an unforeseen accident. (If only the dead girl's body could itself become an accident.)

By contrast, no extenuating circumstances were offered to explain the barbarous behavior of the young men who raped and beat the jogger (who narrowly survived the incident). No attention was focused, justifiably or not, on the harsh poverty of much of Harlem as an extenuating factor, nor—more to the point—did the media trouble to ask the basic question of what kinds of individuals most of the young men were. The television coverage did not dwell on how some of these young men had been terrorizing the residents in their apartment buildings for months on end. It was not until the white woman jogger was mugged that these residents experienced some respite from the terror and harassment they had endured without any police protection or interest. Only white victims seemed to count.

Why were these two incidents treated so differently by television, especially given that in the preppie case the white woman was dead, whereas the jogger survived? Color. In the Central Park incident it was African Americans attacking fine, respectable whites, not a preppie behaving out of character. Television viewers were presented with well-established categories that they took for granted and accepted as real.

On the other hand, the Central Park preppie murder was unreal. Young, wealthy white men do not murder respectable white women.

Therefore, the woman was at fault. She must have been a quasi-prostitute, loose, asking for it, deserving of what happened to her. Otherwise she would not have been killed by a white man in Central Park.

Public outrage against the attackers of the Central Park jogger was phenomenal. There were suggestions that they should be castrated, locked up and the keys thrown away, given the death sentence. The preppie murder did not evoke such intense responses. That situation was presented as unclear, as if there were doubt as to whether the suspect actually committed the murder. On television he was shown leaving court with his parents and his lawyer. A Catholic bishop was wheeled out as a character reference. Indeed, the whole tone of the proceedings on television lacked the "hang 'em high" lynching response meted out to the attackers of the Central Park jogger.

Were these two incidents treated the same by television? No. Both crimes were hideous, and the attackers should be punished. However, one victim was dead, whereas the other, though badly beaten and raped, was alive and recovering. Why are the African Americans more deserving of punishment than a white murderer? We can subscribe to that position only if we accept the established belief that African Americans are violent, uncontrollable, and uncivilized, or if we consider it obvious that they require more punishment regardless of whatever crimes they have committed.

These two violent incidents are important because they illustrate that African American and white American offenders are not portrayed as equally deserving of punishment. The television treatments of both events were presented within a context that relied on accepted racial belief about African Americans. That belief can be stated as follows: African Americans have an inherent tendency to mug, rape, murder, and otherwise disrupt the normal orderly processes characteristic of white society in the United States of America (the preppie murder notwithstanding).

To move to more everyday TV, let us examine the virtual apartheid that exists in most television situation comedies. African Americans and white Americans are not portrayed as living or interacting harmoniously. Sitcoms are either African American or white American (rarely the former, until the success of *The Jeffersons* and later *The Cosby Show*). Also, as Gray (1986) observes, many all-Black sitcoms have not stirred from stereotyped and demeaning portrayals. He comments on the patronizing, even contemptuous, assumptions behind a series such as *Diff'rent Strokes*, which was integrated in the formal sense but centered on a white man's adoption of two Black boys. In fact, television has invariably followed the successful formula of the radio programs that preceded it, which presented African Americans in a demeaning manner. Television, according to Professor J. Fred MacDonald (1983), became "visualized radio: the enactment for viewers of story lines and stereotypes that had proven successful for decades on radio" (p. 7). The influence of film and its generally racist portrayals was also of considerable importance (Nesteby, 1982).

In general, as television developed, either African Americans were portrayed as simple, happy, uneducable buffoons or they were ignored. A classic example of their being ignored is the fact that many Vietnam War documentaries scarcely included or mentioned them, even though African Americans were greatly overrepresented in the fighting compared with their numbers in the general population.

A different but very important example can be seen in the development of art in the United States, especially music, where African Americans have played a central creative role. Television, radio, and the music industry have managed to take over the cultural forms produced by African Americans, such as blues, jazz, and swing, without their actual participation. The original swing bands were those of Duke Ellington and Count Basie, yet it was bands such as Glen Miller's and the Dorsey Brothers' that were dubbed the "Kings of Swing." Some readers might argue that Duke Ellington and Count Basie were recognized by TV as being talented and great musicians, but was it just coincidental that the Glenn Miller Band and the Dorsey Brothers Band received much more time on radio, television, and film?

If it was coincidental, why has there never been an African American musical star with his or her own musical television series, with national syndication and a national advertising sponsor? In 1956, *The Nat "King" Cole Show* premiered on NBC, but in spite of NBC's efforts and the show's popularity, the show never found a national sponsor and was canceled in 1957. None of the conglomerates wanted to be closely identified with a "Negro program." Cole himself wrote after this experience that "racial prejudice is more finance than romance" (see MacDonald, 1983, p. 62).

Thus regardless of whether we are discussing the presentation of African Americans in a barbaric situation such as the crime committed against the Central Park jogger, or in sitcoms, or in TV documentaries about the Vietnam War, or the cultural appreciation of music in this society, there is one compelling factor that we cannot ignore: the presentation of African Americans as marginal in this society. There is no parity between African Americans and whites on television. Apart from some TV commercials full of instant cheerfulness around food or drink, African Americans and white Americans are not shown as living in an integrated society where they interact as friendly equals, respectful of each other's needs and tolerant of each other's differences.

Racist Stereotyping on TV: From Amos 'n' Andy to Cosby

To understand the long roots of these problems in U.S. television, we have to begin with *Amos 'n' Andy*, which was initially a very popular radio show and then was transferred to television. The *Amos 'n' Andy* radio formula originated with racial stereotypes derived from white vaudeville entertainers performing in "blackface," that is, with their faces painted with caricatural African features. According to Barlow (in press), the blackface characters that white comedians Freeman Gosden and Charles Correll developed for their characters in radio's *Amos 'n' Andy* were fairly typical of the prevailing minstrel stereotypes in white popular culture. Amos was the classic "Uncle Tom" stereotype; Andy was the "coon." These figures were easily recognizable in white popular culture, and had been since well before the Civil War (Lott, 1993). Gosden, who was from southern Virginia, attributed his mastering of "Negro dialect" to having been raised by an African American housekeeper. He also had from childhood a close friend called Snowball, who lived in his household as the boys grew up. According to Gosden, Snowball was the source of his humor for the show.

The stereotypes that Gosden and Correll portrayed on radio in the 1920s and 1930s served a variety of purposes in the social and political arena of the epoch. The characters of Amos and Andy were identified as having no education and, by definition, no intelligence. African Americans in the South mostly did not have the vote in 1938, when this radio program was at its zenith. The implication that white Americans derived from this program was very crude: African Americans are grossly ignorant and uneducated. Therefore, to give them the vote, decent jobs, political power, would be tantamount to reducing American democracy to a racial injustice—to whites.

In 1951 *Amos 'n' Andy* premiered on television, with African American actors instead of whites in blackface. How did African Americans respond to this presentation of themselves on white television? This episode is important, not only in the development of the racial politics of American television, but also in the acknowledgment that audiences can be active, not merely passive, in their responses to media. The National Association for the Advancement of Colored People (NAACP) sought an injunction to prevent CBS from putting the program on television. Several groups sensitive to the African American struggle for civil rights condemned *Amos 'n' Andy* as an affront to social achievement. The Michigan Federation of Teachers called the TV series "a gross and vulgar caricature of fifteen million Negro citizens of our country" (MacDonald, 1983, p. 27). Several eminent African Americans blasted the show, describing it as the slow and steady poison of 20 years on radio now being transferred to TV. The African American *Pittsburgh Courier* led a successful campaign to have the show pulled.

One question that must not be avoided is why African Americans agreed to portray themselves and their race in such a demeaning manner. The answer is simple: job opportunities. African American actors were overwhelmingly excluded from TV and film except as infrequent guest stars on variety shows or as "walk-ons" (usually in the roles of house servants); very rarely were they stars in filmed or live drama. Examples of this exclusion are legion. The great singer Lena Horne was originally allowed only as far as a film soundtrack, while a white actress mouthed the words she sang on camera. Paul Robeson, the distinguished actor, thinker, and political campaigner, appeared as co-lead in a film glorifying British colonialism in Africa (*Sanders of the River*). Hattie McDaniel, attacked by some African Americans for her role as maid to Scarlett in *Gone with the Wind*, snapped that she would rather earn $7,000 a week acting a maid than $7 being one. *Amos 'n' Andy* provided regular employment for 142 African Americans who were paid handsome salaries and had a chance to develop their careers.

However, the purpose of this discussion is to demonstrate that the television industry quite consciously developed a program written, produced, and directed by white men that broadcast a stereotypical projection of African American life. Has there been a radical change in the media industry since then as far as African Americans are concerned? Quite frankly, no, despite appearances that might seem to be to the contrary.

During the 1970s, African Americans achieved increasing visibility in news coverage because of the political events of that era. Although the political upheavals of the 1960s and 1970s resulted in a few more African Americans being able to participate in TV, the overall numbers in any part of the production process—as actors, producers, camera operators, or executives—have not risen significantly. Contributions of African Americans to television since the 1970s should not be casually dismissed. However, the manner in which they have been treated on TV despite their contributions has been very dishonorable and disrespectful of their sensibilities.

It should be noted that African Americans have gained a significant market as actors and actresses in TV commercials and also public service announcements. But major producers continue to avoid employing the many talented African Americans outside the advertising sphere. Some of the stereotypes that are still very active in producers' minds are depicted in Robert Townsend's comic yet serious 1987 feature film *Hollywood Shuffle*.

The issue is how to interpret greater visibility. African Americans are more visible on television today, and they are not as subjugated as they were in the *Amos 'n' Andy* era. Since 1988, one of television's top four White House journalists has been Cable News Network's Bernard Shaw, an African American. Nevertheless, despite individual gains, African Americans as a group do not have the same degree of opportunity as do white people as a group in the television industry. The key example that might be cited against this interpretation of the trends is *The Cosby Show*, which was immensely popular during the late 1980s and is still widely syndicated, nationally and internationally, but has an all-African American cast. We turn now to a presentation of two contrary positions on whether this show has reversed the image of African Americans on television.

Professor Marc Crispin Miller (1988) argues that *The Cosby Show* owes much of its immense success to advertising, because the Huxtables' milieu is "upbeat and as well stocked as a window display at Bloomingdales" (p. 69). The Huxtables are successful, wealthy, comfortable, and African Americans. Within their environment the atmosphere is comfortable, without any serious discord, a far cry from the racial caricatures of *Amos 'n' Andy*—maybe. According to Miller, Cliff Huxtable's image represents a threat combined with a reassurance. In spite of his dark skin and physically imposing stature, he has an agreeable persona that should alleviate the fears of whites. Nevertheless, says Miller, many whites continue to have the mugging nightmare, and are terrified that one day African Americans will steal their worldly possessions. Therefore, *The Cosby Show* has renovated the image so that there appear to be no feelings of animosity toward whites from African Americans, and so that all the old injustices seem to have been rectified. This type of reassurance, Miller states, is needed by white Americans because they are both spatially and psychologically removed from the masses of poor African Americans. In other words, *The Cosby Show* offers white Americans a view of reality that is reassuring and acceptable, just the way they want it to be—no guilt, no fears.

However, let us also consider Downing's (1988b) contrary analysis of *The Cosby Show*, in which he argues that the reasons for its popularity cannot be reduced to one variable only, such as its soothing effect on white America. His position is that it has a different function for African American audiences from its function for white audiences, and also that its positive effects for white audiences are related to its mixing together multiple strands of professional achievement, family life, antisexist positions, and humor, together with an attack on racism that is not preachy. Be that as it may, the TV reality of *The Cosby Show* is not the norm for most African Americans in this society. On the other hand, it does portray African Americans with dignity in a medium that has generally failed to do so.

At the same time, it has to be acknowledged that *The Cosby Show* is a celebration of the virtues of the upper-middle-class lifestyle that can be achieved through the education system (to which Bill Cosby himself feels a strong commitment; in 1989 he gave $20 million from his earnings to a college for African American women). Both parents in the show are professionals: He is an obstetrician; she is a lawyer. This has to be placed in a sobering context: Data from the late 1980s indicate that the number of African Americans enrolling in colleges had dropped significantly. At the upper end, the number of African Americans earning doctorates had also declined. Given the limited scope for African Americans on television, *The Cosby Show* represents a refreshing though limited change of pace.

More recent studies of *The Cosby's Show*'s U.S. reception argue that the show's popularity among all audiences is a result of their different perceptions of reality. African Americans, Jhally and Lewis (1992) argue, see the show as portraying a Black family in harmony. Conflicts over male and female roles or sibling rivalries are resolved in a supportive and loving environment. This Black family is not depicted as dysfunctional, stereotypical, violent, drug addicted, or a problem to the rest of society, the usual media fare. White audiences identify with it because this Black family is shown as made up of pleasant, decent human beings, "successful and attractive black people whom white people can respect, admire, and even identify with" (p. 5).

The show's critics continue to argue that it lets racism off the hook, and that the level of wealth and comfort attained by this Black family does not reflect the lives of the vast majority of African Americans in the United States. During the Reagan and Bush administrations, the social and economic conditions of Black people in the United States deteriorated significantly, even though white Americans were simultaneously discovering through *The Cosby Show* that African Americans are human beings. The implications of this contradiction are twofold. First, affluent African Americans may be seen as human beings, and the less affluent as less human. Second, *The Cosby Show* gives justification to the American illusion that anyone can make it, so that less advantaged African Americans have only themselves to blame for their poverty.

Jhally and Lewis (1992) found that class and color together are factors in terms of audience identification with *The Cosby Show*. Members of the white working class tend to identify with the family, whereas white upper-middle-class viewers are more skeptical about the parents' ability to be so available and even-tempered with the four children. The professions of medicine and law invariably cause parents to experience generally high stress levels and to have relatively little time for their children, two factors never in evidence in the show. African American working-class families in Jhally and Lewis's study tended to feel that the show does not reflect their own lived experience, but nonetheless they could relate to the individual characters' behavior as being more believable than that of the usual African American family on TV.

Finally, Jhally and Lewis (1992) present an analysis of the content of prime-time U.S. television over the periods 1971-1976, the pre-Cosby era, and 1984-1989, the Cosby era, in order to establish which characters could be defined as upper-middle-class, which as working-class, and which as ethnic minority. They found that 16% of Black characters in the pre-Cosby era were working-class, but that there were none at all in the Cosby period (pp. 58-59). In other words, in contradiction to the reality of deteriorating conditions for African Americans during those years, they were presented, if at all, as occupying positions at the higher and more successful end of the social scale.

However, as against this focus in TV, in cinema the years 1989-1993 saw a sudden explosion of Black-directed movies focused on the other end of the social scale. Some of the best known, and most insightful on certain levels, were Spike Lee's *Do the Right Thing* and John Singleton's *Boyz N the Hood*. Many of the creative teams producing these films were also largely African American, which was definitely a forward move. Still, looking back on these films collectively (e.g., *New Jack City, Juice, Straight Out of Brooklyn, Rage in Harlem, Menace II Society*), their almost uniform stress on crime, extreme violence, marauding youth gangs, drug dependency, and the impossibility of escape from or constructive action in poor African American neighborhoods represents yet again only a single dimension of everyday Black existence in the United States. That dimension is indeed more frightening in certain Black areas or subareas than in white areas, for the former are where the toll is taken. Yet considered together, these movies have done nothing to dislodge white stereotypes about the threat represented by African Americans. More reflective films that came out during the same period, such as Charles Burnett's *To Sleep With Anger*, Julie Dash's *Daughters of the Dust*, and Neil Jimenez's *The Waterdance*, had minimal advertising budgets, short runs, and as a result, very poor exposure. Formula was all.

Conclusions

Throughout this discussion, I have examined aspects of how television portrays reality while making African Americans invisible, or segregating them. The U.S. version of apartheid is as evident in TV as it is in city neighborhoods. At the same time, when African Americans do appear, their presentation generally fits the racist culture of this society like a glove. It is especially the case that the absence of African Americans from positions of authority in the television industry has contributed to their lack of influence over media roles and portrayals.

Further Questions

1. How have other groups been portrayed in the media, such as Latinos, Native Americans, Asian Americans, Arabs, Jews? What are the similarities of the portrayals of these groups to those of African Americans? What are the differences?

2. To what would you attribute the success of African American women writers, such as Toni Morrison, Maya Angelou, and Alice Walker, in having their voices heard and their stories published? Are African American women seen as less threatening by the white majority than African American men? Does their success herald a breakthrough to be followed by others?

3. What are the lessons of the protests against *Amos 'n' Andy* for the active audience in its relation to media authorities? Do you know of other protests against racial stereotyping in the media?

21 Cultural Imperialism and Cultural Identity

ALI MOHAMMADI

Just as cultural studies and political economy are two approaches to media studies that often seem to be pulling in opposite directions, so, too, international communication frequently seems to be off on its own. This chapter offers important insights into the way culture and communication operate internationally, not just within the space of one country. In doing so, it brings together the approaches of international communication, political economy, and cultural studies.

The first reality that demands attention is that this planet's history since about 1500 is marked by the way certain countries—such as Spain, Britain, France, Russia, the United States, and Japan—have invaded and dominated other nations in pursuit of profit and power. Other empires have done the same, but not on the unprecedented scale of these countries. That is the core of today's international relations (see Hamelink, Chapter 17).

In turn, a significant part of those international relations consists of cultural and communication relations. Some critical researchers have argued that the national cultures of the Third World are virtually on the way to extinction as a result of Western, especially U.S., cultural imperialism, with media influence at the cutting edge of the process. Others have attacked this view as overly conspiratorial, as though the Western countries were plotting to sabotage the independence of these nations, and have stressed that cheap TV series from the United States, for example, may be the only way an impoverished nation can fill its television schedules. They also accuse the critics of being too snobbish in their tastes, noting that many U.S. television series are enormously popular outside as well as inside the United States.

Mohammadi seeks to move beyond these generalized positions to identify both the influence of Western culture and the birth of its counterpart, cultural resistance and the communication of cultural identity. He does so by examining Iran. Throughout the decade of the 1980s, as Sreberny-Mohammadi shows in Chapter 25, Iran was portrayed in U.S. media as an enemy nation, as was the United States in Iranian media. In the decades before that, ironically, the governments and media of both nations were extremely positive about each other. These stereotypes have left many Americans confused and bitter, with no understanding of the seemingly sudden switch in Iranian attitudes from 1979.

Mohammadi explains the effect on Iranians of many decades of systematic Western cultural influence, a process actively supported by the shah's government up until 1979. In turn, he underlines the active cultural resistance this process provoked among many Iranians. He also analyzes the colossal impact of alternative media in developing this cultural resistance, while at the same time acknowledging how for some groups this resistance fused with religious fundamentalism, which tragically left Iranians in general subjected to the obscurantist version of Islamic belief of the Khomeini regime. This outcome was specific to Iran, but in other ways Iran serves as a very clear case study for the cultural dynamics in many other Third World nations.

International Powers and National Cultures: An Uneven Contest

One description of the world we live in is "postimperialist." Much of world history from 1945 has centered on the struggles of subjugated peoples to extricate themselves from the European empires of the nineteenth century and to create the newly independent nations of Africa, the Middle East, and Asia. But despite the demise of political imperialism, the economic dominance of the West has meant that many nations of the Third World find themselves still tied in very complex ways to the dynamics of Western industrial societies. Hence these Third World nations find it very difficult to pursue their own definitions of, and paths to, independent development. These new ties are different from the older ties of imperialism. The new kinds of ties are often referred to as ties of *dependency*, and "cultural imperialism" has been analyzed as one major form of dependency. The purpose of this chapter is to analyze this new cultural imperialism and to show the vitally important role that communications technologies and flows of cultural products have in keeping planetary ties of dependency alive.

This process will be illustrated through a detailed examination of one Third World country, Iran. Although at the turn of the twentieth century the British and the Russians competed for influence in Iran, and the United States played a major role in Iranian affairs, helping to reinstate the shah in 1953, Iran was never directly colonized. Iran tried very deliberately to use communications for a particular development strategy, one strongly supported by the West, but found that the costs were greater than the benefits. This is a case study with powerful implications for other Third World nations and for mainstream—noncritical—communications analysis.

What Is Imperialism?

The essence of imperialism is domination by one nation over another. That relationship might be direct or indirect, and might be based on a mixture of military, political, and economic controls. There have been many different forms of imperial relations throughout world history, from the Greek and Roman empires to the Persian, Moghul, Chinese, Ottoman, and many others. But the forms of empire that have had the greatest impact on our contemporary world are the European, American, and Japanese forms of empire that prevailed through the nineteenth century into the twentieth century. Even European domination went through various stages. There were relationships that were more purely economic or "mercantilist," as in the early Portuguese empire, where the European power essentially extracted the resources it required, whether gold or ivory or slaves, from the dominated territory. Often such relations required military conquest at the outset and a continued military presence to enforce the economic exploitation.

By the end of the nineteenth century, a new form of relation had been developed that was based on the formal conquest, annexation,

Iran and Its Neighbors

and administration of territories by the imperial powers. As Hobsbawm (1989) summarizes the process:

> Between 1880 and 1914 . . . most of the world outside Europe and the Americas was formally partitioned into territories under the formal rule or informal political domination of one or the other of a handful of states: mainly Great Britain, France, Germany, Italy, the Netherlands, Belgium, the USA and Japan. (p. 57)

About one-quarter of the globe's land surface was distributed or redistributed among a half dozen states, ushering in the age of imperialism based on colonial rule. This form of direct political and administrative domination helped to create a truly planetary capitalist economy in which economic transactions and flows of goods, capital, and people now penetrated into the most remote regions. The world was fundamentally divided into strong and weak, advanced and backward areas (Hobsbawm, 1989).

There were many different reactions to and consequences of imperialism, both within the "mother" power, such as movements for democracy, for socialism, and for women's rights, and also within the Third World, where revolution—as in Mexico between 1910 and 1920 or in China toward the end of the nineteenth century—or growing anticolonial movements for liberation—as in India—began to develop. Since 1945, the "postwar world" has been defined by these struggles against imperial domination and the success of independence movements in the creation of "new," independent political nations in Africa, Asia, and the Middle East. Thus, for example, India freed itself from the British in 1947, Indonesia liberated itself from the Dutch in 1960, Zaire was freed from Belgian domination in 1960, and Algeria became independent from the French in 1962 (Harris, 1987).

This process of political independence might appear to be the end of the story, but in fact it is only the start of a new global dynamic that we might label the process of *cultural imperialism* or *cultural dependency*. When the colonial powers packed their bags and removed their nationals from administrative positions directly running the government and the economy, that was not the end of their influence. Often they left behind a European language, as the "lingua franca" of the country's new governing classes. They left behind European values and attitudes, including religion, ways of organizing public life, styles of politics, forms of education, and professional training, clothing styles, and many other cultural habits, none of which had existed prior to colonial domination. All of these phenomena continued to have effects long after the formal, direct, political rule of the colonies was ended, and have created a new kind of model of domination called *neocolonialism*. In turn, neocolonialism has sparked new kinds of struggles to eradicate this enduring cultural influence in the Third World. Let us look at the constitution of this Third World and then examine how cultural issues came to be such a central focus in current international politics.

Where Is the Third World?

The term *Third World* is also a phenomenon of the divisions in the world since World War II. The United States and the Soviet Union were allies against Fascism during the war, but immediately after its conclusion the realignment of "democratic countries" versus "communist countries" took place. Then the Cold War, which is still in a process of thawing, divided the world into two camps, the First World and the Second World, each of which had its own sphere of economic relations, political influence, and military arrangements (NATO versus Warsaw Pact). Rivalry and competition between the two superpowers have brought the whole world to the edge of war on certain occasions, as in the 1950-1953 Korean War, the 1962 Cuban missile crisis, and the 1973 Arab-Israeli war.

Third World is a label applied to the new independent countries of the South, many of which are among the *nonaligned* nations, countries that were not interested in supporting either of the superpowers in their regional or international conflicts. The nonaligned movement was started at a huge international convention of the nations of the South in Bandung, Indonesia, in 1955 and is a formal organization of independent nation-states. *Third World* is a much looser term, and actually covers over a great deal of difference in levels of economic development and political outlooks among the nations of the South. With the demise of the Soviet Union in 1991, the Second World has disappeared, and with the rise of the rapidly developing countries of Southeast Asia, for example, some have seen the growth of a "fourth world." With the increasing globalization of markets, technology, and information, the end of the twentieth century may witness the emergence of new, more regional alliances, such as the economic groupings of the EEC, NAFTA, and ASEAN. Thus our terminology is currently in some confusion. However, *Third World* for now remains a useful shorthand, and we will continue to use it here (Harris, 1987).

Cultural Identity in the Third World

It was the independence movements in the developing world that made many people aware of the cultural dimensions of colonial domination. Many leaders in the Third World have paid serious and continuing attention to the issue of cultural freedom. For example, one of Gandhi's major concerns while he led India's independence movement was how to create an independent national identity that could unite the Indian people, who were scattered over 750,000 villages and spoke many different languages. Concerned about how to foster national unity in the face of the legacy of British cultural domination, Gandhi once proclaimed:

> I do not want my house to be walled on all sides and my windows to be stuffed. I want the culture of all lands to be blown about my house as freely as possible but I refuse to be blown off my feet by any one of them. (quoted in Hamelink, 1983, p. 26)

In a major echo of Gandhi's concern, at a key 1973 meeting of the heads of states of the nonaligned nations there was a formal joint declaration that the activities of imperialism were not limited to the economic and political domains, but encompassed social and cultural areas as well, imposing a foreign ideological domination on the peoples of the developing world. Many Third World nations were becoming aware of the superiority of the advanced world, in communications technologies but also in communications software, the news, entertainment, and other cultural products that the technologies transmitted, and that, as a result, their own national cultures and identities had become threatened (Harris, 1987).

It is not very hard to recognize that the continuance of Western dominance over Third World nations, even after their formal independence, was based partly on advanced technologies, including communication technologies. But it was also based on an ideology, accepted in many parts of the Third World, that there was only one path to economic development, which was to emulate the process of development of Western industrial capitalist societies.

In the 1960s, when certain Third World nations did not appear to be developing economically as fast as they had been expected to, Western analysts began to develop models and theories of development and to explain the "blockages" to development that they thought prevented Third World countries from developing like Western ones. One of their arguments was that Third World countries lacked investment capital, so the World Bank was established. Some argued that Third World countries lacked skilled entrepreneurs and professionals, so various educational scholarships, exchanges, and training programs were established to bring the necessary expertise to developing countries. But one of the most powerful models, widely adopted in Third World societies, dealt with the role of communications in development, as propounded by U.S. theorists Daniel Lerner and Wilbur Schramm (see, e.g., their chapters in Pye, 1963).

Modernization Theory: Development as Westernization

"Modernization" theory held that underdeveloped nations had not yet experienced an industrial revolution, but through proper savings and investment a "takeoff" into industrial growth could take place. For this investment process to work, the right attitudes were very important; for the right attitudes to develop, there needed to be the same mix of political and economic structures that had worked in Western industrialization. Prominent among these structures were said to be mass media (Mohammadi, 1976).

In the early 1950s, Daniel Lerner conducted a study in various Middle Eastern countries, including Turkey, Lebanon, and Iran. He argued that the growth of literacy and the operation of electronic media both played decisive roles in the modernization process. The media were multipliers of the "mobile personality," a frame of mind that was no longer mired in village traditions but was open to new influences and insights—even, without specifying the matter, to U.S. influences and perspectives. He recommended a basic minimum media infrastructure for all developing countries. Media would convey the appropriate contents to promote economic consumption and political participation among hitherto static and traditionalist peoples in supposedly stagnant and disconnected rural communities (Lerner, 1958).

The changes in attitudes, expectations, and values proposed would create a welcoming rather than a suspicious response to U.S. and other Western encroachments on traditional cultures. Investment in development, including communications infrastructure, would have to include external as well as internal sources, and that investment required the right kind of political and cultural climate, with a welcoming government, welcoming businessmen, and congenial cultural forms.

What was valuable in the traditional culture was defined, effectively, as anything that did not impede the growth of Western capitalist endeavors; what had to change culturally was anything that interfered with this process. Clearly, Lerner never defined the issue as cultural imperialism sabotaging cultural identity. For him, mass media were automatically progressive. We, however, have to stand back from his policy-oriented studies and face that very question.

To begin to draw attention to some of these issues, it is instructive to examine a major Middle Eastern nation at the heart of the U.S. and Western oil-related strategy in the region, namely, Iran. Despite or perhaps even because of its contentious relations with the United States since 1979, Iran particularly merits study—not least because Lerner's theories were put into practice there in a more thorough way than perhaps in any other Third World nation, as part and parcel of the last shah's strategy of pro-Western modernization. Iran is also an instructive case study because it was never directly colonized, so an examination of the impact of Western culture in Iran shows vividly how neocolonial subordination and cultural inferiority can be fostered from a distance, without the elaborate machinery of colonial rule.

The Case of Iran

Iran is located on the southern border of Central Asia and stretches south to the Persian Gulf. It borders Turkey to the northwest and Afghanistan and Pakistan to the east. In 1994 it had a population of more than 60 million. From a geopolitical viewpoint, the strategic location of Iran between East and West is very crucial. Iran's political system up to 1979 was monarchical dictatorship, but then 2,500 years of kingship were terminated by the Iranian revolution under the leadership of the Ayatollah Khomeini (see also Sreberny-Mohammadi, Chapter 25).

MEDIA AND DEVELOPMENT IN IRAN

Through a close look at the process of development in Iran we can see a clear pattern of dependent economic development that was centrally based on the export of crude oil and raw materials, with expansion linked to foreign investment. This economic dependence provided the basis for political and military dependence in both technological and human expertise. In the 1970s businessmen from all over the world waited in Tehran hotels to clinch multimillion-dollar deals of all kinds. Slowly, too, the media in Iran tried to convince people of the benefits of modernity and created new needs that consumer durables could satisfy.

Prior to World War II, Iran did not have a national broadcasting system. Iran's first radio transmitter went on the air in 1940. Radio programs were limited to evening broadcasts that consisted of the national anthem, major messages from government, news, and some Persian and Western music. In the early days of radio, loudspeakers and radio receivers were hooked up in various parts of Tehran, the capital, and people were very excited by this unprecedented form of communication. When the national anthem was played, people would rise and stand still. This was one of the first modern symbols of Iranian nationhood, broadcast over electronic media imported from the advanced world. Slowly, radio was used to maintain political control, to spread the ideological rhetoric of modernization, and to prepare Iranians for the neocolonial relationship that would strengthen after World War II.

In 1959, the last shah of Iran was persuaded by an imaginative urban entrepreneur to allow the establishment of commercial television. The entrepreneur was the son of a rich businessman whose wealth was based on importing Pepsi Cola from the United States. This first television station was allowed to operate tax free for five years while it developed commercial television and promoted the expansion of a consumer market, as in the United States. The family who controlled the television monopoly also controlled the importation of most television receivers, possessing the franchise for RCA products in Iran.

Television became a multiplier of Western and consumption values. These were overtly displayed in advertisements for new consumer products and were also embedded in the depiction of Western lifestyles carried by American films and television series such as *I Love Lucy* and *Bonanza*. Private television supported the monarchy's strategy of capitalist development. After some studies were undertaken, and worried that the Baha'i religious sect was monopolizing television, the shah decided to take over private television and transform it into a government-financed and -operated service. In 1966 National Iranian

Television started broadcasting (its first message was from the shah, of course), and among the first test week's programming was the broadcast of the shah's birthday celebration. Soon radio was amalgamated with television to create National Iranian Radio and Television (NIRT). Consumerism was still encouraged through advertising, but, more important, NIRT tried to foster support for the regime through the glorification of the monarchy and support for modernization, maintaining the state ideology. Every royal activity was broadcast, and the glorious history of 2,500 years of Persian monarchy was celebrated wherever possible, but the media also propagated the idea that the shah's major concern was to modernize Iran along the lines of the countries of Western Europe; television nightly news began with images of dams and new buildings, the physical symbols of development.

Radio and television were given substantial government budgets, so that coverage expanded rapidly. From 2 television transmitters in 1966, the number rose to 88 by 1974, and coverage increased from 2.1 million people to 15 million of both urban and rural populations, more than half the country; radio coverage was almost universal (Mohammadi, 1976). By the mid-1970s, NIRT had became the second-largest broadcasting network in Asia, after NHK of Japan. Thus most of the nation was connected through broadcasting, linking small villages with major urban centers and creating a novel national audience.

Yet, at the same time, literacy levels remained low, particularly for women, and there were not enough primary schools to accommodate all children of school age. Publishing and the press were strictly censored, so there was little choice among the dull daily newspapers, which thus had very low circulations. One commentator noted that "if Iran continues on its present path, it will be the first nation in the world to have nationally spread television before a nationally spread press." Thus Iran seemed to leap over the stage of literacy and print development, moving almost directly from a traditional oral culture to an electronic one.

Even a brief glance at Iranian mass media in the mid-1970s would have indicated that the broadcast or published materials were not designed to preserve national culture or to raise the level of public education. Rather, they promoted the alluring manifestations of Western culture, with little consideration of the urgent needs and demands of Iranian society; they did little more than amuse and entertain their audience. One international study made in 1975 revealed that of 11 developing countries studied, NIRT had one of the highest levels of imported television programming, including Western feature films—78% of all television content—and broadcast the lowest proportion of serious programs—only 22% of total broadcast time. Typical imported programs were *Baretta, Star Trek, Marcus Welby, MD, Tarzan,* and the soap opera *Days of Our Lives.* When homemade programs were aired they became extremely popular, but much domestic programming was rather anemic because of actual and self-censorship. The prevailing policy seemed to disregard the cultural implications of importing so much Western media content, which carried Western lifestyles, gender roles, consumption values, and so on. And whereas, for many developing countries, the economic argument that it is much cheaper to buy foreign programming than to produce your own had some justification, NIRT's large budgets did not support such an argument. It seemed to be safer for the regime to allow a lot of Western entertainment to be imported than allow possibly critical homemade programs to appear (Motamed-Nejad, 1976).

The rapid expansion of broadcasting was a central element of the shah's ambitious development project, as he tried to use the communications media to help bring about the change from a traditional to a modern society. But it failed because the modernization process did not go far enough; indeed, the strategy has been described as "pseudo-modernization," a desire for the superficial style of modernity without the deeper structural changes that true development requires. For example, the government, through the mass media, talked about modernization but failed to provide adequate and coherent national health care or education. It spent millions in developing NIRT, but failed to electrify large areas, so many rural people ran their televisions and lighting from small portable generators. It talked about improving working conditions, but would not allow labor unions to operate. It established many universities, but would not allow the free exchange of ideas or free access to written materials. Iranian writers, artists, and broadcasters all had to fit in with the prevailing rhetoric of modernization, and no criticism was allowed. The security system of SAVAK (the shah's secret police) was waiting for any oppositional voices to be raised. Severe political repression thus blocked popular participation and discussion of social needs, the heart of political development.

Those in the educated middle class felt frustrated about the lack of political participation and the lack of cultural freedom, which allowed importation of American television but blocked the production of good, critical, indigenous programs. They felt frustrated as the political concerns of the state interfered in the legal system, the educational system, and the broadcasting system, undermining professional practices and independence. They felt the pinch of rampant inflation in the 1970s, with house and car prices rocketing, and watched as foreign "experts" were favored over Iranians with comparable skills.

The traditional middle classes, particularly the bazaar merchants and the clergy, were threatened by this Westernized mode of development. The economic position of the bazaaris was being undermined by large multinational corporations and agribusiness, and the social authority of the clergy was threatened by secular education and the media. They were also horrified at the effects Western values were having on the fabric of Iranian society. For example, the system of dating and marriage shown in the imported Western programming was totally in contradiction with the Islamic tradition of marriage, in which parents play a very significant role in selecting a suitable spouses and dating of any sort without the presence of a relative is not allowed. Khomeini had been speaking out since the 1940s about the negative impact of Western values, and warned that the media were propaganda vehicles for Western imperialists who were trying to undermine Iran. Some religious authorities publicly denounced watching television, and others declared that having a television was a sinful act. The city of Qum, which is the equivalent of the Vatican for Iranian Shi'ite Muslims, actually banned television during the shah's reign.

From 1976, helped by Jimmy Carter's human rights policy, both the secular opposition and the religious opposition began to use a variety of small media to voice their objections to the regime. Professional groups such as lawyers and writers wrote "open letters" to the shah, demanding an end to regime intervention in the process of law and greater freedom of expression. The religious opposition also began to mobilize, and developed a communications system quite independent from the big media of the state to politicize the people. The leaders used the national network of mosques and bazaars to preach their Islamic identity against the dependent Westernization of the shah. When Khomeini left his isolated place of exile in a small village in Iraq for the outskirts of Paris in 1977, he became the focus of much Western media attention. Also, the religious network transmitted his speeches across the international telephone lines to Tehran, and within hours thousands of audiocassettes of his voice were available on the streets of the capital and were carried to other cities and villages for all to hear—a new international electronic pulpit. In a still very oral culture, where the clergy have great social authority and are used to addressing ordinary people at the mosques, this was very powerful (Sreberny-Mohammadi & Mohammadi, 1994).

A popular movement against the shah began to grow, and when demonstrators were killed through regime violence, the Islamic mourning pattern of the seventh and fortieth days gave the demonstrations a religious rhythm. Gradually, political groups—communist, socialist, nationalist, democratic—banned by the regime resurfaced and countless photocopied leaflets began to circulate, setting out analyses, making political demands, organizing demonstrations. Thus certain small media, particularly audiocassettes and leaflets, were used very effectively in the Iranian popular mobilization, another example of alternative media use described by Downing in Chapter 14. These small media are interesting because they are so easily reproduced, making it extremely difficult for any regime to block their circulation. When the military tried to maintain order and took over NIRT in November 1978, the personnel went on strike, so for three months radio and television were run by the military while the professionals produced underground newspapers debunking the regime news.

Thus a combination of religious authority and small media mobilized some of the largest demonstrations in recent history, bringing together modern and traditional groups united in hostility to the pattern of Westernized development of the shah, combining a mixture of economic discontents, political frustrations, and cultural concerns into a single slogan, "Down with the shah." In January 1979, the shah left "on holiday," never to return, and in February, the Ayatollah Khomeini established the Islamic Republic of Iran.

Conclusion

The communication and development model failed to understand the historically different cultural contexts of Third World societies; as applied to Iran, it served to bring the West into Iranian living rooms and allowed Iranians to compare themselves with Westerners, exacerbating existing economic, political, and cultural frustrations. The

model failed to pay attention to political development or less quantifiable aspirations such as equality, justice, freedom, identity, and even
happiness. In the context of Iran, the communications and development process seemed to suggest that Western patterns of life and
attitudes were the only ones of value, to be imitated by Iranians, and
that indigenous Iranian culture had little to offer. The process created
not only great gaps of wealth between urban elites and the rural poor
but also a deep sense of cultural inferiority, which the clergy effectively
used to mobilize people against the regime.

Frantz Fanon (1967) presents a vivid image of the effects of Western
cultural products on the people of the Third World:

> Young people have at their disposition leisure occupations designed for
> the youth of capitalist countries: detective novels, penny-in-the-slot ma-
> chines, sexy photographs, pornographic literature, films banned to those
> under sixteen, and above all alcohol. In the West the family circle, the
> effects of education and the relatively high standard of living of the
> working classes provide a more or less efficient protection against the
> harmful action of these pastimes. But in an African country, where mental
> development is uneven, where the violent collision of two worlds has
> considerably shaken old traditions and thrown the universe of the percep-
> tions out of focus, the impressionability and sensibility of the young
> Africans are at the mercy of the various assaults made upon them by the
> very nature of Western culture. (pp. 157-158)

Although written about a different cultural context, these words could
also be applied to Iran. The development strategy in Iran was undermining the very basis of cultural identity and the traditional values of Iranian
society. The rapid change from small-scale self-sufficiency to commodity
production for the markets, the neglect of channels for political participation, and the blocking of self-expression and indigenous cultural
development undermined the harmony and tranquility of cultural life.
The process of development, by definition, upsets the pattern of life that
went before, but in the West that process went hand in hand with the
basic values and cultural patterns of those societies. In Iran, as in much
of the developing world, development was replaced by a mimetic Westernization, a copying of the superficial elements of the modern West
without the fundamental political and social changes required. Economic
dependency, as in the spread of montage industries, which merely
assemble consumer technologies developed elsewhere (thus not helping
an independent economic sector to grow), was supported by cultural

dependency, in which mass media broadcast news and cultural entertainment programs more attuned to the markets of industrial nations or regime needs than the cultural habits of the Iranian people.

Iran is a unique example of a Third World country that implemented the communication and development model to accelerate the process of modernization, and the model failed dramatically. Communications can help people find new norms and harmony in a period of transition, but in the Iranian case, the effect was totally the reverse.

The Iranian experience makes us question the powerful media/powerful effects model of communication. The shah could control all the media, but he could not produce political legitimacy. And Iranians could watch a lot of American programming and still prefer their own values. Thus both the communications and development model—which suggested that media could play such an important, positive, role in economic and political development—*and* the cultural imperialism model—which said that media were carriers of Western values that would swamp Third World cultures—are too one-dimensional, as the Iranian movement has shown.

The rhetoric of revolution included slogans against Westernization, consumerism, and the idea of self-determination, expressed in the slogan of "Not East, nor West, only Islam." The tragedy of Iran is that although cultural identity may be an important appeal against the forces of Westernization, it alone does not guarantee broader progressive social values such as freedom and justice, which were fundamental demands of the popular movement. Also, many felt that their religious identity was their cultural identity, not anticipating the rigid fundamentalism that ensued; currently, many Iranians are concerned that their traditional Iranian culture and its music and dance are being suppressed. Many have been killed or imprisoned, and many others have left Iran. The Islamic Republic has thus bitterly disappointed many hopes, and has inherited many of the old problems that the shah did not solve. Analyzing the global context in which Iranian modernization and then popular resistance took place helps to explain the deep dilemmas of political, economic, and cultural development that confront Third World nations.

Further Questions

1. What is it that is attractive to many Third World viewers about U.S. television programs and films? How is it that the frequent

violence in such media does not necessarily seem to give the United States a negative and unattractive image?

2. How might television help to preserve and reenergize cultural traditions? Are cultural traditions always worth preserving? How would you judge?

3. How do you evaluate the rapid growth in television exports from some Third World nations, especially Mexican and Brazilian *telenovelas* (soap operas), or the longer-established export of Indian films? How would you compare their impacts on cultural identity with the impact of U.S. media exports?

22 Popular Music
Between Celebration and Despair

KEITH NEGUS

Popular music is one of the most important components of mass communications. But is "popular" music really popular—does it really represent the people—or is it merely a commercial emanation of big business concerns that produce and disseminate it?

In this chapter, Negus reviews the ways media analysts have considered this problem and offers a new perspective of his own. What he has to say relates strongly to the audience analyses presented by Ang (Chapter 12) and Gandy (Chapter 13) as well as the discussion of culture presented by O'Connor and Downing (Chapter 1).

Questions about popular music take us to the front lines of media analysis. Beginning at the "despair" end of the scale, adherents of the influential Frankfurt school pessimistically view popular music as the product of a "culture industry" designed to numb the minds and facilitate the domination and manipulation of the "masses." A similar view is held by others who harbor a more populist belief in the potential of popular music, but who despair that this creative and cultural potential is inevitably corrupted by the entertainment industry.

At the other end of the spectrum, those who "celebrate" popular music argue that audiences are not passive "masses," but active entities able to transform and reclaim commercially produced music for their own use.

These polar views of despair and celebration give all the power in popular music either to commercial interests or to audiences, respectively.

One way out of lending extreme emphasis to either music listeners or the music business is to see how the various elements of popular music—performers, texts, audiences, industry, and their symbols— "articulate" with one another. For Negus, articulation means the way that the many aspects of producing and listening to music link up with the background culture. Articulation joins together elements that are not necessarily related, but that can and do affect each other profoundly. During the 1960s, for instance, popular music was used at festivals, demonstrations, "be-ins," and "happenings" for antiauthoritarian, political, and blissful purposes that were radically at odds with the ideology and motivations of the commercial sources that produced the music. Similarly, in the 1980s and 1990s, hip-hop and rap styles have deconstructed musical forms, intents, and artifacts to create a vital new synthesis characterized both by high artistry and unusually incisive social commentary. In both cases, radical, subversive, and antiestablishment forms have been extruded out of the commercial establishment's own product.

Negus refers to the career of popular singer/songwriter Sinéad O'Connor as an instance of how images and intent can articulate with both industry and audiences to create new meanings. Is O'Connor's bald head a protest against sexism, a gesture of solidarity with Fascist skinheads, an expression of outrage at the world's injustice, or a valuable logo co-opted by the entertainment media? Negus concludes that O'Connor's identity—and popular music—cannot be comprehended by reference to the recording industry, the audience, or the artist alone. Neither despair nor celebration is conceptually comprehensive enough to avoid pitfalls in cultural analysis. The concept of articulation, linking artist, industry, texts, and audience, promises fruitful routes for meaningful research and analysis.

When we study popular music, it is often hard to separate our own musical tastes, aesthetic judgments, and political commitments from our arguments. Rhythms, lyrics, and melodies not only move us physically and emotionally, but may evoke a sense of belonging to or solidarity with particular communities. We may identify strongly with certain performers and musical sounds, and may make "academic" arguments that directly connect with our own and many other people's experiences as fans. We may listen to some music and despair at the repetition and banality of a standardized formula and declare that the audiences for such music are merely being manipulated by advertising and marketing. In contrast, we may engage with the activities of musicians on the street or participate in an event in a concealed basement club and delight in the spontaneous and imaginative creation of an alternative to Top 40 pop. Such everyday musical experiences and judgments connect directly to enduring intellectual questions about popular music as a form of culture and as a medium of communication.

I take as my theme for this chapter the idea of celebration and despair that I have just evoked, as arguments about popular music often lead to such conclusions. There are two basic variations on the theme of despair. One is derived from the "mass culture" critique that emerged in the 1930s and 1940s and, as applied to popular music, is strongly associated with the writings of Theodor Adorno. This is, in many ways, the pessimistic lament of the cultural elitist, dismayed at the homogeneity and vulgarity of mass taste, concerned that production has become standardized and consumption passive. The other version, which shares a number of assumptions with this position, comes from writers who have more populist beliefs in the potential of popular music. However, such writers, employing arguments from the theoretical tradition of political economy, often end up despairing that any creative or cultural possibilities have been corrupted by the corporate entertainment industry.

There are many versions of celebration (one only has to look at the numerous biographies of musicians that fill the shelves of bookstores, for example), but the theory that has become most prominent in media and cultural studies concerns the audience. It is an argument about how consumers are able to reclaim and transform the products that have been produced by a commercial industry: Audiences are not passive; rather, they engage in vibrant, creative, and diverse forms of cultural activity.

In this chapter I shall briefly set out these positions and argue that they tend to privilege either production or consumption. I will then introduce the concept of *articulation* and argue for an approach that attempts to overcome this division by studying the connections between production and consumption. I will illustrate this with reference to the performer Sinéad O'Connor, and in doing so raise some questions about the "mediations" that connect the industry, artists, audiences, and texts of popular music.

The Route to Despair:
The Mass Culture Argument

One of the most significant and influential accounts of how culture, and particularly popular music, is produced and consumed was developed by Theodor Adorno and Max Horkheimer. These two theorists were members of a group of predominantly German-Jewish intellectuals who have become widely known as the Frankfurt school and who produced a substantial body of analysis between the 1930s and the 1960s. To understand why Adorno and Horkheimer reached such pessimistic conclusions about culture, and to appreciate the context in which they were writing, a bit of background detail is necessary. Both writers had lived through the futile bloodshed of World War I in Europe. Both had also observed the failure of the working-class revolutions that had spread across Europe after the Russian Revolution of 1917 and were questioning the potential of working-class movements to bring about progressive social change (as anticipated by Marx). While Stalin was starting to twist Marx's utopian ideas into a dogmatic orthodoxy that supported an authoritarian dictatorship, Adorno and Horkheimer were also acutely aware that Fascism was spreading throughout Europe. In 1933 Hitler and the Nazis seized power in Germany. Being both Jewish and Marxist, Adorno and Horkheimer had to flee from Germany and eventually relocated in the United States.

This historical context is very important for how Adorno and Horkheimer's cultural theory developed. As they observed what was occurring across Europe, Adorno and Horkheimer asked how the development of modern European thought, instead of progressing toward a more human and liberated society, was leading to "a new kind of barbarism"; the cold rational logic of totalitarianism and Fascism.

Adorno and Horkheimer were not only attempting to understand how this was occurring in Europe. When forced into exile, they were dismayed by the "vulgarity" of the commercial culture they found in the United States: Movies, jazz music, inexpensive high-circulation magazines, dance crazes, and radio were far more widespread in their new home than they had been in Europe. This seemed a stark contrast with the high cultural tradition that they had left behind. Adorno and Horkheimer considered that this "mass culture" had emerged as a result of processes similar to those that had given rise to Fascist totalitarianism in Europe. Hence they were explicitly concerned with how forms of culture could contribute to authoritarian forms of domination. So, in their argument, the domination and manipulation of the "masses" becomes explicitly connected to the production and dissemination of a particular form of "mass culture."

It is in this context that Adorno and Horkheimer, in collaboration, and Adorno individually, developed an argument about popular music. Writing against those who believed that the arts were somehow independent of industry and commerce, Adorno and Horkheimer (1947/1979) asserted that popular music was produced by a "culture industry" that was no different from the industries that manufactured vast quantities of consumer goods. All products were made and distributed according to rationalized organizational procedures and for the purpose of profit maximization. The culture industry was nothing more than an "assembly line" producing standardized products (as also discussed by Kellner in Chapter 19). Key terms that recur continuously throughout their work are *standardization, repetition,* and *pseudoindividuality.* For Adorno and Horkheimer (1947/1979), the concept of pseudoindividuality means that everything produced by the culture industry is the same; it only *appears* to be different. They argue, "Pseudo individuality is rife: from the standardised jazz improvisation to the exceptional film star whose hair curls over her eye to demonstrate her originality" (p. 154).

All individuality is an illusion that is actively fostered by the culture industry to provide diversion from the drudgery of working life and the exploitative conditions created by the capitalist system. By making this argument, Adorno and Horkheimer explicitly link a political and economical analysis of standardized production to a social psychological theory of the experience of consumption. As mass culture, popular music requires the listener to make very little effort. Indeed, popular music actually causes the "regression of listening." In one of his characteristically despairing condemnations of popular music, Adorno (1991) asserts that "there is a neurotic mechanism of stupidity in listening; the arrogantly ignorant rejection of everything unfamiliar is its sure sign. Regressive listeners behave like children" (pp. 44-45).

Adorno castigates those who like to hear familiar harmonies, rhythms, and melodies. Good music must be difficult and demanding. It must challenge us and demand complete attention. There is no place in Adorno's scheme for entertainment; popular music merely provides a form of diversion and prepares workers for the next working day of drudgery. (In some of his writings Adorno attempts to make a direct connection between the rhythms of jazz and the operations of machinery in factories.) Popular music as "mass culture" and entertainment leads to passivity; it makes people accept the status quo and engenders obedience toward authoritarianism. Adorno (1976) seems quite certain of this when he asserts that "popular music constitutes the dregs of musical history. . . . it sets up a system of conditioned reflexes in its victim" (p. 29).

Adorno and Horkheimer present a powerful argument about what happens to music when it is subject to industrial capitalist production. Music becomes merely a standardized and repetitive element of "mass culture." It has no aesthetic value whatsoever and leads to a very specific type of consumption that is passive, obedient, and easily manipulated. Does this type of argument sound familiar? Have you ever defended your own music as complex and demanding and criticized other forms of music as standardized and repetitive? Have you heard people explain the worldwide popularity of performers such as Michael Jackson or Madonna by arguing that the audiences are being manipulated by the record industry? Such everyday arguments are common and indicate how residues of the "mass culture" argument still permeate discussions of popular music, both inside and outside the academy.

Partial Despair:
Co-Optation by the Corporations

Steve Chapple and Reebee Garofalo (1977) have similar things to say about how capitalist corporations turn popular music into a commodity. However, unlike Adorno, who can see no value in popular music as a cultural form, these writers do wish to claim some value for it. Like many intellectuals who have written about popular music since the late 1960s, Chapple and Garofalo are members of a generation that grew up with rock and roll and developed a belief in the radical social potential of rock music when connected to youthful rebellion against authoritarianism or when harnessed to political campaigns (such as the civil rights movement and the protest movement against U.S. involvement in Vietnam). Popular music thus does provide numerous possibilities for individual or collective expression and for communicating and engendering political solidarity. However, such possibilities are either not realized or severely restricted because of the impact of the music industry.

In an extensive historical account of the record industry in the United States, Chapple and Garofalo (1977) argue that the concentration of ownership among a few major companies that control access to the means of recording and reproducing pop music has enabled capitalist corporations to "colonize leisure." Performers and recording industry personnel have become absorbed into an entertainment business that is an integral component of the corporate structure. The prospects for creative artists or politically radical performers are bleak. Any possibilities that might arise in the production of popular music are absorbed and "co-opted" by a ruthless and exploitative commercial system.

A similar argument has been made by Nelson George (1988) concerning the impact of the record industry on the music and cultural identities of Black performers. For George, the white-dominated industry has been directly responsible for transforming Black forms of expression into a commodity and for contributing to "the death of rhythm and blues." Tracing the appropriation of rhythm and blues styles by white performers and the commercial packaging and promotion of Black artists throughout the twentieth century, George reaches similar conclusions about the ways in which cultural and political possibilities are destroyed when subject to the corporate system. Like Chapple and Garofalo, he is particularly concerned about the rationalization and restructuring of the record industry that gained momentum during the late 1960s. This has been decisive. It has ripped apart the connections established among Black musicians, independent Black and white businesses, and the Black community. In their place it has instituted the "conglomerate control of black music." According to George, commercial imperatives and corporate domination have forced Black artists to adopt a "crossover mentality" if they are to reach a mass white audience. In doing so, Black musicians have often reneged on their previous political commitments and altered both their music and their appearance. In the process, they have compromised their cultural identity.

George's argument raises important questions about the connections between popular music and issues of race and racism. Just what does it mean if Black performers appear, over time, with lighter skin tones? (George gives the examples of Michael Jackson and George Benson.) Is "crossover" (music that moves across different categories, but specifically in this case from the rhythm and blues/urban charts into the Top 40) simply about trying to appear more acceptable to white audiences? Are performers diluting or denying their racial identities? Are Michael Jackson and Prince, with their "disquieting androgyny," presenting "alarmingly un-black and unmasculine figure[s]," as George suggests (p. 174)? Or are these artists, in their songs and images, challenging the racial, sexual, and ethnic categories that have become associated with musical expression? Such questions are by no means straightforward, and they connect directly with issues of race and gender discussed elsewhere in this book.

Apart from these specific questions that arise from George's argument, do you find the general perspective presented here a useful explanation of the impact of the music industry on popular music? Does corporate ownership directly determine the way in which popular music is produced? Is it simply a tale of compromise and co-optation— the "sellout" to the system? This type of argument seems to suggest that the working practices of thousands of people employed in the record industry, the sounds of musicians, and ultimately the activities of audiences become little more than responses to the commercial power of corporations.

Celebrations of Consumption: Fans and Active Audiences

Rejecting the despair of such conclusions, writers such as Iain Chambers and Lisa Lewis have attempted to shift the focus away from the corporations and onto the audiences, emphasizing how popular music is actively used. From this alternative perspective, audiences are not the passive victims suggested by previous theorists.

Chambers (1985) proposes that although record companies might control how music is produced, they are unable to control the way it is used or the meanings invested in its texts and technologies by audiences. He asserts that the commodities of the music industry are transformed as they are "appropriated" by various groups and individuals and used for the expression of individual identities, symbolic resistance, leisure pursuits, and forms of collective and democratic musical creativity in everyday life. Drawing examples from the 1960s, when hippies used music at festivals, demonstrations, and various "happenings," to the reuse of vinyl records, turntables, tape machines, and mixers in rap and hip-hop in the 1980s, Chambers emphasizes the diversity of pop music styles. Throughout these changes, popular music has been central to audiences' and listeners' lives, and often has had direct impacts on the surrounding society and culture (the Woodstock festival of 1969, the punk period of 1976-1979, and the activity that became focused on the Nelson Mandela Concert in 1988 are just a few examples). This is the complete opposite of Adorno's model of standardization, repetition, and passivity. It is an account in which the texts and technologies of popular music continually provide opportunities for a wider range of people to participate in aesthetic, political, and cultural activity.

Like Chambers, Lewis (1990, 1992) emphasizes the activity of audiences by focusing on the viewers of MTV and the activities of fans at concerts and various other public events. Against writers such as Adorno, she argues that fans are not regressive obsessed individuals, nor are they a manipulated "mass." Instead, fans are imaginative, discriminating people who are capable of making a number of fine distinctions and who actively participate in creating the meanings that become associated with popular music. Fans contribute an integral element to our understanding of popular music and particular artists. Lewis suggests that fans create communities with collective, shared senses of identity built around their appreciation of particular performers. Such groups produce important "reservoirs of knowledge" that directly contribute to the meanings attributed to performers. (How could we understand the enduring popularity of Bob Dylan, for example, without reference to the legions of highly intelligent people who have followed him around for years and who have continued to find profound meanings in even his most banal utterances?)

Lewis shares Chambers's emphasis on the way popular music is "polysemic"; despite the corporations' best efforts, it cannot simply have one meaning. Many possible meanings are made available at the same time, and it is ultimately audience members who are able to "appropriate" these and determine which meanings will predominate. Not only is this a more optimistic theory, it provides important insights into how people receive music in different ways. In doing so, it challenges the idea that audiences are passive. From this perspective audiences are very active. But where does such a theory lead us? Is the music industry producing so much choice? Are we all sovereign consumers, free and spontaneously creative? The problem here is that the impact of the corporations and the production and marketing methods of the music industry seems to disappear from view. Such a perspective completely avoids the issue of how the activities of consumption might be shaped by the recording industry. It ignores how musical products are made available for "appropriation" in the first place, and the connections that are established with specific audiences.

Between Production and Consumption: Mediations and Articulations

A number of writers have attempted to steer a course between these positions, most notably Simon Frith in Britain and Larry Grossberg in the United States. In a prolific body of work that is difficult to summarize or condense into a single argument, Frith has emphasized how production tends to predominate and has argued that it is the corporations that, ultimately, provide the sounds we hear and the products we consume (see, e.g., Frith, 1988b). However, the corporations cannot "control" popular music in any simple way; artists and audiences frequently play important roles in shaping how music is both produced and consumed (see Frith, 1986). Frith has written extensively about performers, industries, and audiences (see Frith, 1983, 1988a), and has highlighted the different values, beliefs, terminologies, and judgments that are made by performers, by those within the corporations, and by audiences (and, incidentally, by academics). Much of his work points to the distinctive breaks that seem to appear in the experience of music among the fan, the performer, and the record industry worker. Frith contends that we cannot simply read off, deduce, or understand one from another.

The implication of Frith's work is that there is no *necessary* connection between a form of production and a way of consuming music. A connection has to be created; production is not simply standardized and dominating, but neither are audiences passive or always spontaneously creative. This is a theme that has been pursued, albeit in a different way, by Grossberg (1992), who has also produced a sophisticated theory about the position of music within North

American culture. Grossberg argues that studying popular music does not simply involve following the linear communication of musical messages from producers to consumers. Instead, it requires the examination of processes of "articulation" in which particular sounds have to seek out, be sought by, and connect with particular audiences. During such a complex social process, the meaning of music and any social effects it may generate arise out of a process in which performer, industry, text, and audience "articulate" with each other and with the surrounding culture and social-political system.

The concept of *articulation*, which is useful for raising questions about the relationship between production and consumption, has two senses. First, we articulate to communicate. We always express ourselves by articulating to some person or group (using language, but also employing other cultural codes—nonlinguistic expressions, bodily gestures, and so on). Our articulations are directed toward others; we do not articulate in a vacuum. When applying this concept to popular music, we can argue that an artist is always articulating, through various intermediaries, to audiences who are always part of the process of articulating cultural meaning.

The second aspect of articulation derives from the general definition of the term as involving the linking together of two elements. For example, an articulated truck is made of two separate sections: a tractor and a trailer connected by a pivot bar. The act of articulation involves a process of bringing together. As Grossberg (1992) points out, articulation involves "the practice of linking together elements which have no necessary relation to each other" (p. 397).

By adopting the concept of articulation, we can start to examine how the meanings of popular music arise not only out of how artists and audiences articulate, but out of the various audio, visual, and verbal elements that are combined and connected at the same time. Think of rap and hip-hop, for example. These styles of music involve the combining and connecting of a number of elements that do not have any necessary connection with each other until they are combined into these forms of music. These styles involve particular ways of using technology: scratching and mixing, using turntables to create new sounds from elements taken from existing recordings. This is combined with a particular way of using language that draws on the traditions of "toasting" in African American and Caribbean culture and fuses this with contemporary street slang and the rejuvenated clichés of pop. This is combined further with specific ways of transforming sports clothing (reversed baseball caps, oversized pants and sweat-shirts, and so on) and very specific ways of using the body. Perform-ances by both producers and their audiences bring together elements from dancing to soul music with traces of robotic mime and ironic (and not so ironic) gestures of macho male prowess. Further elements include the specific subjects of songs, which often have social mes-sages, and the ways in which particular samples are used (James Brown, for example) to articulate particular senses of history.

I want to conclude by illustrating the process of articulation in slightly more detail by reference to the performer Sinéad O'Connor. My argument is that focusing on processes of articulation and the mediations that link production and consumption can help us to raise critical questions about popular music. Meanings are not simply imposed by production or appropriated in the act of consumption. Meanings are created, constraints are imposed, and possibilities are continually opened up through the processes that connect artists, industry, audiences, and texts.

Sinéad O'Connor: The Articulation, Mediation, and Interpretation of Musical Meaning

Sinéad O'Connor enjoyed considerable celebrity toward the end of the 1980s and beginning of the 1990s. Through three intense, emo-tional albums, a series of equally passionate stage performances, and some controversial media appearances, she provoked strong reactions of both support and condemnation. In her sounds, words, and images she continually drew attention to instances of social injustice and raised questions about Irishness, sexuality, childhood and mother-hood, religion, and racism.

Our understanding of Sinéad O'Connor and her music and the ways these themes are communicated is derived from our engagement with how she "performs" (and is reported to perform) across the range of media texts that contribute to our knowledge of her identity. Such performative texts include interviews, personal appearances, public activities, music videos, and all the public communicative actions that contribute to how we understand and interpret her music. We can rarely know any artist directly. The relationship between artist and audience is always mediated by the gatekeepers and intermediaries of the music and entertainment industries, and I want to give just a brief indication of this process here.

As fans, our first contact with a new singer or band may be with the music alone, or perhaps with the music as it accompanies the iconography of a video. Frequently, however, our first contact is with an image: on a poster, album cover, or magazine cover, or in a photo within the print media. We often see the face and body before we listen to the sounds and read the words. These images are carefully put together. Their construction involves the artist's collaboration with a range of personnel, such as publicists, marketing staff, photographers, stylists, and video directors (Negus, 1992). The image defines an artist in a specific way, as a particular type of human being and as a product placed within the genre categories of the music industry. The image also helps to explain how an artist's music should be understood.

The initial visual image of any recording artist is therefore crucial to the production and consumption of popular music. The visual image connotes a type of music, an attitude toward life, and a lifestyle; it denotes the artist as a particular type. One of the reasons Sinéad O'Connor was so immediately recognizable and a focus of attention was that she had shaved her head. She was a *bald woman*. This was immediately visible as an act of choice. Women do not usually go bald; O'Connor had chosen to make herself bald. Whether or not she realized the effect that this would have is hard to tell, but she was certainly called upon continually to explain it. In 1991 she told a rock newspaper that she had adopted the hairstyle in a fit of temper because the directors of her record company had asked her to wear high-heel boots and tight jeans, and to grow her hair. Two years later, while commenting on the abuse of children, she told a journalist that she had shaved her head as an expression of her anger and outrage at injustice in the world.

O'Connor's head became a focus of attention and was subject to various interpretations (see Hayes, 1991). Its associations with Fascism and the British youth cult of the skinhead was noted, as was its connection with the adoption of this style by lesbians as a refusal of male definitions of beauty and femininity. When trying to find meaning in O'Connor's music, some journalists connected the confessional nature of many of her songs to the shaving of the head by religious groups as an act of penance or contrition. Others referred to the shaved heads of asylum inmates and prisoners (society's victims) when describing the anger vented in much of her music. The image was actively used as a guide and articulated with the meanings of the music, particularly on the albums *The Lion and the Cobra* (1988) and *I Do Not Want What I Haven't Got* (1990).

My point in mentioning these connections and attempts at interpretation is not to try to identify whether any particular explanation
is true or false. It is to highlight how the reason for the shaved head
became an integral part of the articulation of O'Connor's identity. She
was continually called upon to explain this act to various journalists,
who then interpreted and mediated the information to audiences. It
became part of how her music was understood (confessional, angry,
narrating the victim, refusal, and so on).

As I have mentioned, O'Connor publicly declared that her hairstyle
was partly an oppositional gesture against record company executives
who wanted her to adopt a more conventionally feminine image.
However, in rejecting this she then frequently had to confront media
representatives who made this very act a central issue. In trying to
negate a gender stereotype, she emphasized her deviation from the
conventional, and this became part of the way in which her gender
identity was often reinforced in the mainstream media. There are
important questions here about the different ways in which male and
female performers are presented and promoted. Female performers
tend to be asked far more questions about their appearance than do
male artists. As a consequence, this becomes part of the way in which
their identity is articulated and their intentions are understood by
their audiences.

The bald head became an instantly identifiable sign of Sinéad
O'Connor, and was marketed by the recording industry as a "brand
image," placed across the music-related entertainment media. However, it did not become just a commodity; O'Connor was not simply
co-opted by the corporations. This style was simultaneously adopted
and imitated by audiences and used as a sign of identification and
expression of solidarity by fans attending concerts. It was used to
signify identification with the performer, but also to create and communicate affiliations with other fans sharing in the music and its
associated values and beliefs. The meanings adopted by fans did not
coincide with those of the industry, but neither were they spontaneously created. A process of articulation occurred that linked together
artist, industry, and audience.

I have concentrated on the head in this discussion because it has
been the most consistent, conspicuous, and commented upon element
of O'Connor's visual image, and it was integral to the way she was
marketed and mediated during the promotion of her first two albums.
My comments here are intended as a brief and partial illustration of

how a performer's identity cannot be understood simply by reference to the industry, the audience, or the artist alone; rather, it must be understood through a process in which the artist's identity is articulated across a web of mediations that link the conventionally separated spheres of production and consumption. Such an approach, pursuing the connections between the artists and audiences for popular music, may provide routes for further research and analysis that can weave between the twin pitfalls of despairing at the power of corporations and celebrating the joy of consumers.

Further Questions

1. What are the communication differences between attending a rock concert and listening to the same concert by yourself on headphones?

2. What does it mean for our understanding of music and communication that American popular music, currently very influential in many parts of the world, has very strong African and African American roots and fertilization?

3. Why is it that some of the most vital popular music often has to fight to be aired by mainstream radio and recording companies, and usually begins in small alternative media?

23 Cinema and Communication

MARY DESJARDINS

Cinema has historically been the only mass medium that has managed to "make it" into the realm of high culture, to join opera, ballet, painting, and sculpture. Desjardins points out, however, that as in so many other spheres of life, both the mass and popular cultural dimensions of cinema have to be foregrounded if we are to be able to understand it as a form of communication. In making this argument, she addresses some of the same concerns that animate Negus's discussion of popular music in Chapter 22, Kellner's analysis of advertising in Chapter 19, and Ang's review of the television audience in Chapter 12.

Desjardins begins by reviewing the contested early history of American cinema and its transition to the Hollywood "dream factory"—as sociologist Hortense Powdermaker (1950/1979) once termed it—that began to turn out the immense volume of films, year after year, that still dominate the planet's screens. She shows the important role that was played by immigrant worker audiences in the 1910s and 1920s, and by the rise to prominence of the advertising industry. At the same time, she notes the importance of the cult of individual identity in twentieth-century U.S. culture and its links to the Hollywood star cult.

Desjardins also explores further the issues of the "mass" and the "popular," and suggests that in practice Hollywood films quite often

show a tension between the dictates of corporate profit-and-loss con-
siderations involved in financing a film and the need to appeal to a
public engaged in debating issues of social equity, whether in terms of
class or gender or racism. She concludes the chapter with introduc-
tions to the notion of film "language," to types of film (feature,
documentary, experimental), and to the global film dominance of
Hollywood, and she raises some questions about the future of cinema
in an era when interactive media are much debated.

A common lament of the contemporary film lover is that most films
today are made with more emphasis on "high concept" than on
character or story development. *High concept* is the current term used
to describe a film based on an idea that can be summed up in a sentence
or two, and that can be packaged as a total commercial onslaught,
including ancillary products such as toys and T-shirts, and amazing
special effects. On top of this, film viewing is most often experienced
in small, cramped theaters in the company of noisy viewers accustomed to talking across the TV. However, the days when film was a
pure and simple experience, when films were watched in hushed
reverence, may have been just one moment—a blip, as it were—in the
history of motion pictures.

A hundred years ago, in the first decade of film production, the film
industries of the United States, Britain, France, and Germany were more
concerned with the technology of film than with the films themselves.
The Edison Company in the United States and Pathé Company in
France, for example, made—or felt they could make—most of their profits
from developing movie cameras and projectors and securing (and eventually litigating for) their patents and royalties (Elsaesser, 1990). These
companies manufactured equipment to be incompatible with that of
other companies, just like TV sets, computers, and mobile phones in a
later period, so they made films to help market their technology, selling
them by quantity (in feet of film) rather than by quality. During this
period, films were exhibited in many different locations (vaudeville
houses, storefront theaters, converted saloons, churches, lecture halls)
and under many conditions, from middle-class decorous to loose and
rowdy; audiences were made up of people from diverse ethnic and class
backgrounds (Hansen, 1991).

It is important to understand that the current forms of film production and exhibition—which some may feel trash their ideal cinematic

experience—are as much tied to historical shifts in technology, industrialized capitalism, and the consumer and leisure habits of film audiences as they were almost a hundred years ago. Of course, film audiences were attentive to films' meanings even in historical periods when technological and screening practices seemed to define so much of the cinematic experience. Despite valuable studies that examine cinema as "art," films have a longer and more pervasive existence as popular culture, the products of the beliefs, practices, and fantasies of ordinary people.

This chapter looks at cinema as popular culture, with special attention to the implications of its emergence in a historical moment when a number of industrialized countries were establishing mass consumption patterns. Films and filmmaking in industrialized countries are part of a popular culture that is, above all, a mass culture. Historians studying the technological development of motion pictures or their historical content (re-creations of the Spanish-American War, or footage of the bombing of Hiroshima or President Kennedy's assassination, for instance) like to point out that the history of cinema is also the history of the twentieth century. This is equally true if we think of cinema in terms of its mass production by giant corporations and its consumption by a mass audience. Once these corporations realized the profitable worth of the film product itself, they worked very hard to consolidate their "vertical integration" of the total cinema process (owning and/or controlling production, distribution, and exhibition) and so creating all the conditions for a truly mass cinema audience (Elsaesser, 1990; Musser, 1990).

The Beginnings of Mass Cinema and Mass Audiences

What was this environment and how has it been sustained? This question has to be answered differently according to the specific national context in which cinema has flourished, even though striking similarities exist among the earliest movie industries and products of industrialized Europe and the United States. The American context is especially interesting in the early years of the motion picture industry, however, because mass reception had to be organized among a population that then too was very diverse in terms of ethnicity and race (because of the immense wave of labor immigration from eastern and southern Europe in the years 1880-1920) and in which a number of individuals could improve their social and economic status more quickly than in Europe. In other words, the creation of a mass audience, meaning a relatively homogeneous public for a new cultural product, was a major challenge for an industry still creating and litigating technological devices, yet embedded in a rapidly changing and diversifying nation (Elsaesser, 1990).

This pre-World War I period of U.S. film history is one of the most widely studied and hotly debated among current film historians. All seem to agree, however, that securing the mass audience was related to a confluence of factors, including the industry's moves toward the use of straightforward plots, establishment of business practices that would ensure a steady flow of film product and standardized movie theater practices, and the publicizing of filmgoing as superior to other forms of popular entertainment, giving it more respectability (El-saesser, 1990, pp. 153-168). I will elaborate on the first of these factors later in the chapter; but first, regarding the industry's business practices and the boosting of filmgoing as socially acceptable, several points may be made.

The increasing vertical integration (i.e., the increasingly corporate organization) of the film industry was the necessary practical foundation for what it provided, namely, fantasy scenarios. In a consumer society that appealed through advertising and product design to new U.S. citizens' supposed desires for individuality and modernity, while still staying safely within the bounds of middle-class morality, these scenarios enabled the film industry to unify (some might say homogenize) a large and diverse population. Consumption of films and other products enhancing one's self-identification as an "individual" and "modern" united this population. Even if the working class could not afford all consumer products, buying on credit and the dreams evoked by advertising sustained desire for middle-class lifestyles while smoothing out previous class and ethnic loyalties.

The film industry contributed to this new environment in ways that resulted in cinema's ascendancy over most other popular public entertainments. By 1915, several picture palaces—large, grandiosely ornamented movie theaters—had opened in urban areas, and even the smaller cities and towns had theaters just for movies, separate from the venues for live entertainment and more stable financially—and architecturally!—than the theaters built during the nickelodeon boom that began in 1905 (Musser, 1990).

Significantly, most movie theaters shifted business sense and sensibility from that typical of the wandering showman to one that emphasized predictable experiences for employees and audiences. Norms of behavior familiar to middle-class venues were imposed—silence during the movie, clean and tidy surroundings, and, in the South, audience segregation, with Blacks in the balconies or in separate theaters altogether. In other words, the cinematic experience was understood by producers and exhibitors as socially appropriate for the middle class, and it was advertised as such, just as other industries were promoting the social legitimacy of their products—from deodorant to how-to books—on the basis of their therapeutic qualities (Marchand, 1985).

One of the most significant appeals to the filmgoing public as consumers, not only on the level of products and dramatic experiences, but also on the level of notions of modernity and unique personal identity, was the industry's development of a star system. The cultivation of stars for audience identification and adulation is still one of the most important cultural activities of cinema worldwide (an activity it shares with the television and recording industries), and has proven to be one of its most financially stable ways of funding and promoting films, even amid enormous changes in star-industry relations. In the late 1910s and early 1920s, the industry's promotion of films through the promotion of stars was part of a larger cultural trend; the industry utilized not only stage-star discourses available since at least the nineteenth century, but also new definitions of the individual as a unique personality.

This new understanding of the self was different (though never completely separate) from the individual as a moral character, a notion that had driven the farmer- and factory-oriented culture of America's past. This individual-as-personality was unique, yet could continually transform or update him- or herself by keeping pace with the changes of modernity, which meant, in practice, changing through the acquisition of material goods and style. Stars were the new gods of the personality, as they fulfilled notions of modern transformation not only through acting parts but by living myths of success. They were (and are) at once ordinary and extraordinary (de Cordova, 1990; Dyer, 1979).

Yet stars had to live up to middle-class standards of propriety and morality, even as they enjoyed spectacular wealth and some intangible appeal, which some might call charisma or simply "It" (as novelist and tastemaker Elinor Glynn dubbed silent-era star Clara Bow's defining quality). After a number of sex scandals involving stars in the 1920s, the American film industry actually took control over their behavior, which it successfully maintained (with the occasional exceptions, as when Ingrid Bergman became pregnant during an adulterous affair with Italian director Roberto Rossellini in 1949) until the 1950s, when changing norms of moral behavior and the studios' waning economic power combined to give stars more autonomy in the creation of their public selves (today's supermarket tabloids show how far we have traveled since then). Until this point, however, star images needed tending because of the continual importance to the consumer industries of stars' films balancing out unruly sexual desires with middle-class morality.

As noted, the films themselves were created within, and helped to sustain, a consumer culture that was also a popular culture for a mass audience. Even though now many advertisers and film companies define audiences as "segmented" (see, e.g., Ang, Chapter 12, and Gandy, Chapter 13)—by income, age, gender, and ethnic status—and even though film must now compete economically with video, this generalized consumer culture still holds sway (see also Kellner, Chapter 19).

One indication of the sustained place for films in popular culture today is their position as targets of commentary and critique. Many of the social critiques of films today are motivated by the same or similar concerns as in the past: the negative effects of sex and violence on the youth audience, stereotypical depictions of race and gender, escapist and predictable plot formulas, and spin-off purchases, such as toys, that "sucker" audiences at home and abroad. Whether centering on their encouragement of immoral behavior or their implicit endorsement of authoritarian government, the social criticism of films in past and present has arisen largely because of the discomfort many critics have as they observe a supposedly authentic popular culture seemingly drowned out by a shoddy, dollar-conscious, corporate-driven mass culture (see O'Connor and Downing, Chapter 1).

Popular social commentators and special interest groups of the 1930s, like those in the 1990s, were understandably concerned about increased violence in civil society and looked to movies as a possible cause, because of their seductive power to provide fantasy scenarios of power and freedom. The intellectual historians and critical thinkers of the 1920s-1930s known as the Frankfurt school were painfully aware of the power of the mass media (in their experience, film and radio) to manipulate audiences and to encourage uncritical thinking, whether to serve the aims of Nazi propaganda or simply for escapism. They were responding not only to the commercial motives behind the media industries' reach to the masses in the United States and industrialized Europe, but also to the annexation of the German film industry to Hitler's Fascist regime in 1933-1945. The Nazi leadership not only could force the film industry into service of their political party through an organizational takeover, but knew how to use the powers of the media in terms of their forms of expression.

Likewise, thinkers and film scholars of the 1970s and 1980s were rightfully concerned about the legacy of U.S. domination of the world film market (see Mohammadi, Chapter 21) and the reproduction of class and gender inequities when they analyzed how Hollywood films "position" film spectators as upper-status white males—in other words, how these films address spectators as if that were what they all were, and thus steer them into viewing their lives through that narrow lens. However, it is important to sustain a notion of films' political impact without also idealizing supposedly "authentic" popular culture forms from a precapitalist past, like the carnival (Russo, 1986; Stallybrass & White, 1986), or overestimating films' power to unify the diverse desires and temporary or partial identifications of their audiences with the action or the characters (compare, again, Ang, Chapter 12).

Cultural Studies and Understanding Cinema

A cultural studies model for understanding films, the film industry, and audiences is helpful in this regard because it examines films in terms of both their mass, consumer appeal (which benefits corporate capitalism) and their roots in popular culture. In turn, popular culture potentially expresses desires and fantasies deeply important to many social groups and definitions of ourselves that can be at odds with the logic of consumerism, and not fully held in check by it.

For example, in the popular 1955 American melodrama *All That Heaven Allows*, the female protagonist ultimately opts out of the consumerist lifestyle that has her "keeping up with the Joneses" in purchases and propriety for a "simple" life with a younger man in the country. Similarly, perhaps some of the appeal of the surprisingly popular *The Piano* (1993), directed by Jane Campion, is in its female lead's rejection of a life that would deny creative expression and female sexual desire in order to build instead a repressive and imperialist middle-class society in the wilds of nineteenth-century New Zealand.

To look at films in terms of the distinctions between, as well as the similarities among, the "mass" and the "popular" is to see them as products of competing and overlapping priorities among and within the industry, culture, and the stories the films tell. Even if we understand the industry as having a profit-driven agenda (or a propagandistic one in cases where film industries serve this function for the government), to be able to attract audiences' attention repeatedly, it has had to adjust its story codes to conform to "ever shifting criteria of relevance and credibility" (Gledhill, 1988, p. 76). This means that the industry, in the name of short-term profit, may produce some films that question the long-term goals of capitalism and/or male dominance, and/or white dominance.

The 1991 film *Thelma & Louise*, directed by Ridley Scott, is a good example of this process. Attempting to solicit the female audience, which many critics suggested it had been losing since the 1960s, the American film industry was willing to take a chance on producing a film written by a woman who was "fed up with the passive role of women" in American movies (Callie Khouri, quoted in Schickel, 1991, p. 55). The film is about two women friends on the run after one has shot dead a man who was attempting to rape the other. In other words, the industry had to acknowledge and incorporate a feminist critique of their own product in order to produce films of continuing relevance and credibility to (at least a portion of) their audience.

But in hiring Ridley Scott, who reportedly added more violent imagery and cut some scenes between the two women characters, to direct the movie, the industry created a tension within the production, revealing the extent to which competing agendas exist within the industry itself. Also, the movie probably would not have been produced in the first place if it had not fit into familiar U.S. film genres—the outlaw/gangster film and the "road" film. Another level of dissonance in meaning, then, existed within the text, as it carried a "feminist critique"—men's readiness to rape, women's right to self-defense—within historically developed genres and iconography (the visual landscape) that historically had connoted expression of the individual's will through (a) violence and (b) travel at will.

Furthermore, the film text was released, promoted, and discussed in U.S. culture, where not only gender roles are in a process of revision owing to feminist movements, but where there are very contradictory notions of feminism itself and of "progressive" versus "regressive" media representations of women. Consequently, a variety of passionate debates were carried on in other popular media (radio, television, and mass publications) concerning the status of the characters of Thelma and Louise as feminist heroines.

The preceding discussion suggests that one task of the film scholar or critic is to investigate the conditions under which audiences read and understand those film worlds constructed by an industry trying to adjust textual codes to changing cultural notions of relevance (Gledhill, 1988; Staiger, 1992). But an associated task is to understand the language of film itself, how it operates as what some critics call a "textual system." A number of theories have been developed over the years to explain how film communicates by functioning like a language, but semiotics, which is concerned with the composition of signs and sign systems, is probably the most thoroughly argued theory.

The Language of Film

The sign, which is the smallest unit of meaning in semiotics, is composed of the *signifier* (in the case of sound films, the image and sound) and the *signified* (the concept that the signifier represents). Ferdinand de Saussure (1966), one of the founding theorists of semiotics, argues that the relation between the signifier and the signified is arbitrary, so that the word *dog* (or the letters *d, o, g*) have no natural relationship to the four-legged domesticated mammal that barks and wags its tail.

But what is complicated when we talk about signs in cinema is that the photographic image does have an indexical relation to the object photographed. This means that the photographed object was once present in front of a camera containing raw film stock and, through a chemical process, left its "imprint" on the celluloid. Consequently, many theorists have discussed the *reality effect* of film—how much more it seems like a recording of "real life" than does written language. Furthermore, the object photographed and the way it is photographed (including camera angles and distance from the camera) "signify" jointly, as a total package, so it is almost impossible to say filmic signs are simply *denotative*, that is, that film images have a single, obvious content.

Filmic signs seem highly *connotative*: Their formal arrangements use mise-en-scène (i.e., composition of shot and frame), lighting, camera movement, acting styles, editing, and so on. This suggests that filmic sign(s), unlike some others, offer a second level of meaning linked to our feelings, dreams, and desires (Stam, Burgoyne, & Flitterman-Lewis, 1992, p. 195). Much semiotic analysis stresses the difficulty of exhausting the possible meanings of signs and signifying systems, and the above discussion of *Thelma & Louise* suggests that signs (such as of two women on the road) are in any case interpreted by readers in light of their own experiences, of the point in history at which they see the film, and of the circumstances in which the film is produced and watched.

Types of Film: The Documentary, the Experimental, the Feature

Although all modes of filmmaking—the documentary, the avant-garde or experimental film, and the fictional narrative (the feature)—use the properties of the filmic medium, such as mise-en-scène, camera movement or position, and editing, they have different approaches toward the profilmic event (the action unfolding in front of the camera at the moment of shooting) and toward addressing the audience. The documentary tends to respect the profilmic event—that is, it claims to document what goes on before the camera, with a minimum of manipulation. Yet there is more than one school of thought on how much a documentary filmmaker should manipulate the results of capturing the profilmic. Early Soviet filmmaker Dziga Vertov argued for the heavy manipulation (through editing) of "fragments" of reality caught on film. His *Man With a Movie Camera* (1929) tried to capture the fast-changing reality of postrevolutionary Soviet society by juxtaposing images of Moscow citizens engaged in ordinary activities with images of the making of a film. In this way he tried to suggest a parallel and a solidarity between his own work as a filmmaker for the new society and the work of every Soviet citizen to the same end.

By contrast, the "direct cinema" school of documentary filmmaking favors keeping the integrity of the profilmic event apparent after the postproduction of the film, so that viewers see pretty much what they would have seen if they had been present on the scene of filming. For example, Frederick Wiseman's *High School* (1968) documents daily life in an American high school by having the camera follow students through their activities of the day, including club meetings, hallway high jinks, and confrontations with teachers. Wiseman tried to "respect" the events recorded by not having a voice-over narration and by using a minimum of editing within scenes.

The documentary concern with recording reality is usually connected to the director's or the funder's desire to change some aspect of that reality for the better. This is true even of "found footage" films (which juxtapose fragments of already shot footage), such as Cuban filmmaker Santiago Álvarez's *Now!* (1965), an edited collection of images of the American civil rights struggle with African American singer-activist Lena Horne singing "Now" on the sound track. Sometimes a documentary will try to re-create a past event according to eyewitness accounts by staging scenes with actors. For *The Thin Blue Line* (1988), director Errol Morris used the lighting and camera angles of a film noir fictional crime story—a film style that dwells on the harsh and sometimes grotesque aspects of human behavior (the word *noir*, black, being used in the sense of an all-pervasive corruption) to try to show how difficult it is to know the truth. Paradoxically, Morris became convinced while shooting his film that his subject—a man on death row—was innocent of the crime of which he had been convicted. The success of the film and the issues it raised prompted the alleged murderer to get a new trial, and his sentence was eventually overturned. These examples raise complex questions about the relations between media and reality that have yet to receive any definitive answers.

Documentaries were probably the first films exhibited for paying audiences. The form originated in France with the Lumière Brothers' series of films, known as *actualités*, that recorded ordinary events, such as workers leaving a factory, trains arriving in stations, and parents (one of the brothers and his wife) feeding their baby. From the time of their appearance in 1895, documentaries have served as both information and entertainment for the mass film audience. The documentary "urge" has also been present in many fictional film movements and styles, such as Italian neorealism, which sought a new fictional style to represent social issues in Italy in the period after World War II, and postrevolution Cuban film, which was not only made by directors schooled in documentary film and Italian neorealism, but had the specific tasks of educating the audience in Cuban history as part of a nationwide literacy campaign. Although films that were primarily documentary in style were very popular and visible in theaters worldwide in the first two decades of film production, they are now seen mostly on television (with the occasional exception, such as *The Thin Blue Line*, discussed above).

The avant-garde or experimental film is also rarely seen in theaters. Museums, classrooms, art galleries, and specialized television channels (in the United States, public television channels or "art" cable channels) are the most likely venues for films that take as their subject and agenda the exploration of the film medium itself. The properties of film technology and film language are often explored in the avant-garde film in the effort to understand more precisely how cinema is distinguished from other art forms. In the 1960s and 1970s, the avant-garde film tended to be the preferred medium and mode for artists with political messages who felt the conventional narrative codes of commercial cinema "naturalized"—took for granted and communicated as obvious, beyond question by sensible people—the political agendas of capitalist, patriarchal culture. However, throughout the history of avant-garde cinema—from the French surrealists' play with the erotic fantasies of Hollywood in *Smiling Madame Beudet* (1923) to American filmmaker Maya Deren's film-noirish exploration of her subjectivity in *Meshes of the Afternoon* (1943) to Cecile Barriga's *Meeting of Two Queens* (1991), a found-footage film in which images of Greta Garbo and Marlene Dietrich are edited together to suggest a romantic relationship between the two—avant-garde films have displayed a fascination with and exploration of popular culture and its pleasures.

Fictional narrative film is undoubtedly the most popular mode of filmmaking in the world, and yet, as I have suggested, it was probably not the first kind of film exhibited, nor was it immediately dominant when it appeared shortly after the Lumière Brothers showed their *actualités*. Early movie audiences were fascinated by many aspects of the film product and the filmgoing experience. Fictional films were one kind of filmic entertainment, albeit one that was related to other popular forms of entertainment, such as the comic strip, vaudeville, stage theater, the short story, and the novel.

Ultimately, fictional features best suited the vertically integrated film industry, which developed its power on the basis of its ability to produce regular product for a growing number of theaters serving diverse audiences. The production of regular film product was dependent on efficient procedures. Fictional narratives could be produced more quickly and predictably than documentaries because they were made in the controlled environments of studios or production companies, with a labor system increasingly modeled on the factory and the conveyor belt, and employing a stock company of actors. Documentaries, in contrast, depended upon actual events and specific individuals, and if any of these failed to turn out as predicted, or the necessary light and sound conditions could not be met, then the financial schedule of production, distribution, and exhibition would be in disarray.

By the early 1910s, fictional narratives were the dominant products of most film companies in industrialized nations. This does not mean, however, that fictional narratives as we know them today—whether products of Hollywood or of European industries—sprang up fully accessible to all audiences. Some theorists have suggested that "intertextual" relations were crucial to audience comprehension of early narrative films—films that to modern viewers may seem to be lacking in basic narrative information or causal links, because they are not aware of the other, nonfilm, texts to which the films allude. Film texts that could be understood in and of themselves without reference to any other text (because continuity editing constructed "realistic" space and action, and because simplified plot organization ensured cause-and-effect relations) developed only when the film industry moved to secure a truly mass audience. As noted above, audience members of certain classes, educational levels, and, perhaps, ethnic status might not have had access to all the appropriate intertextual allusions of the earlier films appealing to a middle-class, educated audience (Musser, 1990; Staiger, 1992).

The Growth of U.S. Cinema to Global Preeminence

It was on the basis of this guaranteed mass audience—through continuity-based fictional narratives and attractive exhibition and viewing practices—that the U.S. film industry secured a strong home market. This alone did not cause the further eventual domination of the world market by American films, but it poised the industry to take advantage of the right circumstances—which presented themselves at the outbreak of World War I in 1914, when many European industries shifted to war production and competition among those nations' films was stalled by closed borders. The American film industry began its domination of the world market at that point, and it has remained remarkably viable despite changes in global capitalism and the necessity of making adjustments to closed markets in such periods as World War II in 1939-1945 (which it was able to make up for from 1945 onward by reorganizing the postwar German and Japanese film industries in ways that benefited the importation of American film product).

It is unfair and reductive to suggest that the rest of the world's cinema is "alien" to the American industry, not only because the traditions established by American cinema in its earliest incarnations were actively imbibed from the French, Italian, British, and German products, but because these other industrialized European countries were, as are now much of Asia and Latin America and the newly "independent" Eastern European countries, organized in terms of a consumer culture. The fantasy scenarios of American film narratives and star discourses appealed then and now, in part, in many different cultural contexts because of this common economic and psychological organization and orientation of twentieth-century culture (for a different view, see Mohammadi, Chapter 21).

Some of the best international cinema has responded to this fact, such as the tragedies and satires by Germany's Rainer Werner Fassbinder, who wrote and directed films dealing not only with the legacy of Fascism in contemporary Germany, but with the alienation between people and within the individual's own self-awareness because of the lures and desires of consumer culture. Yet Fassbinder's films also show a love for the Hollywood melodrama of Minnelli and Sirk (the latter an émigré from Nazi Germany). Wim Wenders, Fassbinder's colleague, has almost obsessively "rewritten" the American western and melodrama genres—even making films in the United States—while benefiting from the looser, more open narrative form of contemporary German cinema. This has allowed him to make films that "play" with American genres rather than embody them and to meditate on the political implications of these popular cultural forms for modern Germany.

German feminist filmmaker Ulrike Ottinger has done something similar with the pirate-film genre in her *Madame X* (1977). Like Wenders, who in his film *Until the End of the World* (1991) turned to Japanese and Eastern cultures to find the future of cinema (and video), Ottinger has explored non-Western realms as visual landscapes for her meditations on cinema and the representation of women. In her almost three-hour long *Joanna d'Arc of Mongolia* (1988), several European women are captured by a Mongolian and her Amazon warriors. On the Mongolian steppes—a place that takes on metaphoric as well as literal meaning—the European women free themselves of their past identities, which Ottinger uses as an occasion to fantasize about a world without patriarchy and a cinema not bound by typical iconography or conventional structures of time.

New German Cinema was preceded by the French New Wave, among the first post-World War II film movements and directors to understand, love, and simultaneously hate American dominance of the film market. Films that came out of these movements were generated by this ambivalence. Godard, one of more than a hundred directors who made their feature film debuts in France in 1959, was probably the first director to understand how American films had "colonized" the unconscious desires of consumer culture with their seductive images of individual freedom and power. He not only ruthlessly analyzed this process in many of his films, he paid homage to the immensely powerful desires released by American film genres (from the musical to the gangster film to the western) and consumer culture.

After making films to support the student leftist movements of the 1960s, he eventually returned to a more artisanal mode of image making with partner Ann-Marie Mieville. Together they made two stunning video series, *France/Tour/Détour* and *Six Fois Deux*, profound and complex explorations of the different ways in which television and film address their viewing subjects, and the relations of these media to contemporary European culture.

The Future of Cinema

The directions taken by Wenders and Godard suggest that the future of cinema may lie in video or television. This observation may work itself out on many levels. Film may disappear, although its superior image resolution still affords great creativity and viewing pleasure. The way we view films may change to approximate the television experience and the viewing citizen it produces, which is more than likely a viewer in some kind of family context who interacts with video games, computers, and television. Although it is likely that many will still seek out the viewing experience in public movie houses, no matter how far from ideal they may be in some regards, television, video, and computer/CD-ROM delivery of film images are likely to be the dominant delivery systems in the future.

This shift could transform the place of film in consumer culture. Viewers who tape and watch films on video already zap through the commercials that interrupt broadcast films. Yet films, from *E.T.* to *Pretty Woman*, are still produced with consumer messages inscribed within the text. Time will tell if the newly forecast "interactive" movies, which allow individual spectators to change or direct narrative activity, will translate into media use that emphasizes more of the popular and less of the mass, consumer orientation of film culture.

Appendix: Select Filmography

EARLY FILMS IN EUROPE AND THE UNITED STATES

Workers Leaving the Factory (Lumière Bros., France, 1895)

Arrival of Express at Lyons (Lumière Bros., France, 1895)

A Trip to the Moon (Méliès, France, 1902)

The Life of an American Fireman (Porter for Edison Co., United States, 1903)

Rescued by Rover (Hepworth, England, 1905)

The Lonedale Operator (Griffith, United States, 1911)

Cabiria (Pastrone, Italy, 1914)

The Birth of a Nation (Griffith, United States, 1915)

The Cabinet of Dr. Caligari (Wiene, Germany, 1919)

Madame Du Barry (Lubitsch, France, 1919)

Male and Female (De Mille, United States, 1919)

Smiling Madame Beudet (Dulac, France, 1923)

Sherlock, Jr. (Keaton, United States, 1924)

The Crowd (Vidor, United States, 1928)

Battleship Potemkin (Eisenstein, Soviet Union, 1925)

Man With a Movie Camera (Vertov, Soviet Union, 1929)

ITALIAN NEOREALISM

Rome—Open City (Rossellini, Italy, 1945)

The Bicycle Thief (De Sica, Italy, 1949)

FRENCH NEW WAVE

Breathless (Godard, France, 1959)

The Four Hundred Blows (Truffaut, France, 1959)

EUROPEAN AND AMERICAN AVANT-GARDE AND DOCUMENTARY

Meshes of the Afternoon (Deren, United States, 1943)
The Thin Blue Line (Morris, United States, 1988)
Night and Fog (Resnais, France, 1955)
Sans Soleil (Marker, France, 1984)
Meeting of Two Queens (Barriga, Spain, 1991)

CUBAN FILM

Now! (Álvarez, Cuba, 1965)
LBJ (Álvarez, Cuba, 1968)
Lucía (Solas, Cuba, 1969)
Memories of Underdevelopment (Gutiérrez Alea, Cuba, 1968)

NEW GERMAN CINEMA

Ali—Fear Eats the Soul (Fassbinder, Germany, 1974)
Joanna d'Arc of Mongolia (Ottinger, Germany, 1988)
Kings of the Road (Wenders, Germany, 1976)
Madame X (Ottinger, Germany, 1977)
Until the End of the World (Wenders, Germany, 1991)

Further Questions

1. Consider the various differences between watching a film in a movie theater and watching it on video at home. How important is each in affecting the communication process of appreciating a movie? Would high-definition television (see Demac, Chapter 16) cancel out the differences?

2. In the United States, *film* is often sharply separated from *television* by media critics, and in turn *television* is often sharply distinguished from *video*. Why do you think these distinctions are made? Do they apply in other countries as well?

3. Documentary films are viewed much more commonly in Europe, Japan, Russia, Australia, and other countries than in the United States. Is this important for understanding the differences in media use and impact among these countries?

4. Film industries have often played important roles in promoting national imagery and myths. Immerse yourself in a set of films from one foreign country and try to identify the signifiers of national culture used in the films.

24 AIDS News and News Cultures

KEVIN WILLIAMS

DAVID MILLER

What does television news really tell us? Does it mirror reality? Does it provide a "window on the world"? Or does it display a particular version of reality? Television news has a seductive, naturalistic quality that encourages us to see it as somehow more reliable and satisfactory than news accounts in the print media. But television news does not simply report events or reflect what is happening; it actively constructs a representation of reality.

Most news is not observed by reporters. Information about events is obtained by reporters from others; news is not what happened, but what someone says happened or will happen. Therefore, the people who act as sources of information play a vital role in the news production process. What appears on television news programs is in

AUTHORS' NOTE: The study discussed here is part of the AIDS Media Research Project, a three-year project set up to examine the production of media messages about AIDS, the content of those messages, and their impact on the audience. We gratefully acknowledge the support of the Economic and Social Research Council (award XA 44250006), as well as that provided by our colleagues Jenny Kitzinger, Peter Beharrell, John Eldridge, Sally Macintyre, Mick Bloor, and Greg Philo.

413

the end largely the outcome of processes of negotiation between reporters and their sources.

The provocative study Williams and Miller discuss in this chapter suggests that only by understanding the process of negotiation between sources of information, within news organizations, and between sources and journalists can we make sense of how issues are reported by television news.

Some contrasts between the United States and Britain with regard to media coverage of HIV/AIDS are worth pointing out. Public communication on the subject during the 1980s and the early 1990s in the United States has pivoted on sexual ethics, because the disease has been overwhelmingly linked in media coverage with male homosexual lovemaking. Those terrified and scandalized by this age-old behavior have often been prone to define HIV/AIDS as just punishment for it. As a consequence, it has often been hushed up as shameful. A study of obituaries carried in the media trade magazine Variety showed that obituaries of those whose deaths resulted from AIDS often would say they had died of pneumonia or cancer or "a lengthy illness," and would avoid mentioning the names of the deceased persons' same-sex lovers (whereas widowed spouses would always be named) (Nardi, 1990). And this in a professional community where being gay is somewhat more accepted than in many other spheres of life, and at a time (i.e., after their deaths) when the individuals involved had nothing further to fear from discrimination.

Indeed, as U.S. news coverage has developed, HIV/AIDS has been linked in the media with what Sander L. Gilman (1988) calls "the four H's": homosexuality, hemophiliacs, heroin, and Haitians. Hemophiliacs have been considered "tragic victims" of contaminated blood transfusions, a definition that simultaneously implies that other persons with AIDS (PWAs) are getting what they deserve, and that PWAs are all marginal and pathetic members of society. The heroin connection with contaminated needles implies another appalling "lifestyle choice" by discarded members of society, but it conveniently glosses over the fact that yuppie substance abusers who have made the same choice can afford sterile needles; it also obscures the fact that the American dream does not seem to be working for either group. The "Haitian connection"—eventually found to be scientifically spurious—*tapped into racist images of Haitians as sexually licentious, as unwanted refugees on U.S. shores, and as ignorant citizens of "the poorest country in the hemisphere"—an image totally belied in reality by the extraordinary pride, courage, and history of the common Haitian people. Media coverage depicted AIDS as the property of the extruded. It did not come from "us," yet it could threaten "us." People started panicking about "getting" HIV in ways in which it was impossible to contract the virus, such as by simply being near someone who has it.*

The quality of U.S. media coverage of HIV/AIDS has not been improved by the more general puritan prudery endemic in U.S. public culture, which discourages any explicit discussion of sexual activity while at the same time permitting a vast pornography industry to flourish "under the counter." Hypocrisy appears to rule. One result is that many AIDS activists have adopted very confrontational media-related tactics, such as disrupting a cathedral service conducted by the cardinal of New York City, who had repeatedly denounced homosexual behavior. Such alternative media activists have noted that they feel the lid of this hypocritical consensus must be forced off the pot (S. Epstein, 1991). They want to be a truly active, articulate audience, not just mute, suffering objects of pity.

Mainstream and Alternative Perspectives on HIV/AIDS

The first reported death from AIDS in Britain occurred in 1982. The government, however, took very little action to prevent the spread of the disease before 1986, when, under pressure from gay activists, scientists, and clinicians involved with the disease, it launched a public health education campaign warning of the dangers of the spread of the disease to the heterosexual population. Between 1986 and 1987 there was a period of "national wartime emergency" when AIDS was a political priority at the highest level (Berridge & Strong, 1991). From 1988 onward, there was a "normalization" of the disease. AIDS treatment became a normal part of British health service provision, with information about the disease directed at specific target groups within the British population.

Television was at the heart of the government's effort to educate and inform the British public of AIDS and HIV, the virus that is believed to lead to the disease. TV advertisements were used to warn of the dangers of AIDS, and in March 1987 there was an unprecedented degree of cooperation among the BBC, ITV, and the government during "AIDS Week" on British television. The main message of the campaign was that the disease poses a threat to everyone, heterosexuals as well as gay men and drug users. To prevent the transmission of the virus, the campaign promoted "safer sex," particularly the use of condoms. There was no overt message about sexual ethics or orientation, although "sticking to one partner" was recommended. Compulsory testing for the virus was rejected. This was the basis of the official British perspective on AIDS.

Alternative perspectives in other media, some more traditional in outlook, challenged this orthodoxy. Some groups argued that AIDS health education was nothing more than "propaganda" aimed at heterosexuals. They asserted that the threat to heterosexuals was a myth, and that measures should be taken to segregate people with AIDS from the general population. Others argued that the official response was "homophobic" and ignored the problems of "persons with AIDS" or PWAs—a term that avoids defining those with AIDS as either just medical objects ("AIDS victims") or somehow blameworthy (e.g., gay men and intravenous drug users).

The importance of information and education in the fight against AIDS has led to considerable commentary on news coverage of the disease, including media coverage in the United States, Western Europe, Australia, Zambia, and Zimbabwe, and to representations of AIDS in films, newsmagazines, and broadcasting. Despite cultural differences regarding the language and imagery used to describe and discuss sex, sexual health, and sexuality, media coverage has been characterized mostly by blame, denial, fear, and prejudice. As Lupton (1994) states, "AIDS reporting in western nations has involved imagery associated with homophobia, fear, violence, contamination, invasion, vilification, racism, sexism, deviance, heroicism and xenophobia" (p. 21). The relationship between news coverage and government policy about AIDS has also been questioned, because news coverage of AIDS has seemed to rise and fall in Britain, the United States, and France parallel with the development of government interest and concern in the disease.

Despite the fact that most people in Western countries identify television news as their main source of AIDS information, there has been a surprising lack of systematic research into the content of TV news coverage of AIDS. One recent study of U.S. network news was conducted by Cook and Colby (1992), who found that "the networks attempted to reassure at least as much as they played up the story." The attention paid to AIDS by TV network news did not correspond with the development of the severity of the epidemic or the growth of medical interest. According to Cook and Colby, the coverage had more to do with the institutional dynamics of journalism than with the nature of the AIDS epidemic. As the epidemic developed, the TV news organizations took their cue from "authoritative scientific sources and political officials to let them know when news on AIDS would happen" (Cook & Colby, 1992, p. 102). Thus the decline of AIDS coverage on U.S. TV news at different times in the 1980s can be largely attributed to government inactivity. Gay men "were shown more often as carriers than as victims," but as the story developed "gay spokespersons were identified occasionally as authoritative sources" alongside doctors, government officials, and research scientists.

TV News Leads the Way

In our sample of British TV News we found that the most common type of "AIDS story" concerned the government's AIDS campaign. This constituted the largest group of news stories, ranging from items on the latest phase of the advertising campaign to announcements of policy on anonymized testing. Another significant category of news story concerned the activities of nongovernment bodies. This included the British Medical Association's training video for doctors, a Birmingham City Council scheme to involve prostitutes in AIDS education, and Football Association guidelines to players for safety.

A large number of news stories were about AIDS in other countries. Half of these stories were from the United States, and a further quarter concerned African countries. Less predictable stories, such as those about a patient being infected by HIV following a skin graft and about protests over the siting of a hospice, we assigned to a category labeled "other events and happenings." However, the most striking aspect of

TV news coverage during this period was the number of stories on the situations of people living with AIDS and HIV—the second largest number of stories in our sample. These varied considerably in the ways in which they were covered, but, most important, PWAs were given the opportunity on a number of occasions to speak for themselves and their own experiences.

Who Got on TV News

The range and frequency of interviews presented on television news provides one crude but important indicator of the sources used in the presentation of news events. In our sample of TV news coverage of AIDS we identified a total of 363 people who appeared in 611 interviews. The majority of these people, 70%, appeared only once and exclusively on one TV news channel. Only a small group of interviewees appeared regularly on all channels and in the contexts of a number of different stories.

The most common types of interviewees were medical and scientific experts. Other experts and professionals were also well represented: nursing staff, lawyers, counselors, caregivers, and spokespersons of organizations for people with AIDS and HIV, such as the Terrence Higgins Trust (THT), Britain's biggest AIDS charity, Body Positive, and Frontliners. However, few of these appeared more than once; the overwhelming majority (92%) appeared just once. The main exception was the leading spokesperson for the THT.

There were relatively large numbers of interviews with PWAs, but the people who appeared most regularly across the whole range of AIDS stories in our sample were government ministers. Nearly 50% of the interviews were conducted with the different ministers of health in this period. These were the central figures in the AIDS story on TV news. Most of their appearances were in news events such as press conferences. The regularity of appearance of government ministers indicates the orientation of TV news to the rhythms of political life and government activity. It is not simply a question of who gets on, however; it is also a question of how they are used in TV news stories.

Supporting the Official Line?

In the period 1986-1987, the British government's response to HIV/AIDS created a sense of national emergency that was reflected in the TV news coverage. Television news programs stressed official concern about the spread of AIDS.

> The government is setting up a top-level committee to warn that there is a danger of an AIDS epidemic sweeping the country. . . . There have been warnings from health experts for some time that the deadly disease could get out of hand. It is the speed with which it can spread that is so worrying. . . . effectively the government is declaring war on AIDS. (BBC1, 9:00 p.m. newscast, November 3, 1986)

TV news bulletins closely identified themselves with the government perspective and explicitly endorsed the view of the Department of Health and Social Security. Clear and unequivocal support was given by TV news to official warnings about the spread of the disease to the heterosexual population. Although there was much debate in sections of the British print media about the threat AIDS poses to heterosexuals (Beharrell, 1993), TV news dismissed such doubts and embraced the scientific and medical consensus that was established between 1987 and 1990. Expert opinion was used to support the official line. As TV news stated in 1986: "The experts agree that everyone is at risk and it is vital to find out about AIDS and how to protect ourselves from it" (ITN, 10:00 p.m. newscast, December 1, 1986). TV news bulletins were organized around the official perspective on AIDS, and medical, scientific, and expert opinion was used in support. Standard phrases such as "doctors say" or "experts now believe" were used to legitimate statements.

The close ties between TV news and medical/scientific opinion on AIDS were apparent in the early days of news coverage of the disease. Medical and science correspondents shared their main sources' concerns about the government's initial reluctance to address the disease. The correspondents often endorsed the pressure on government to act; the BBC's science correspondent commented on the announcement of the establishment of the government's AIDS Committee in 1986:

AIDS first appeared in Britain in 1979. Since the early 1980s specialists in the disease have been pleading for more to be done to stop it from spreading. Now it seems at last they are being listened to. (BBC1, 6:00 p.m. newscast, November 10, 1986)

TV news supported the government's campaign when it was launched and agreed with the official contention that there was the potential of an epidemic among heterosexuals. However, criticisms of the campaign centered on its lack of explicitness. As an ITN reporter stated at the outset of TV advertisements in 1986:

The ads on television, however, will not be explicit, for example, about the use of condoms and the help some people think they will give in preventing the spread of AIDS . . . and that will, perhaps, raise questions in some people's minds about how effective the whole campaign is going to be. . . . Previous government advertising has been criticized as being too bland when compared with some private campaigns containing very explicit advice run, for example, by one of the main charities involved, the Terrence Higgins Trust. (ITN, 10:00 p.m. newscast, November 11, 1986)

TV news marginalized other kinds of criticisms of the campaign. Voluntary organizations questioned the government's information-giving approach, but little notice was paid to them. There was no coherent strand of opposition to the campaign on moral grounds in the TV news. Even when spokespersons for this perspective were interviewed, the context was usually critical of their claims. TV news coverage was firmly wedded to the medical/scientific orthodoxy, and the criticisms of the details of the government's campaign reflected concerns that the campaign failed to live up to the expectations of this group.

The TV news reporting of AIDS conformed to the ways other diseases have been covered. On health matters, doctors and scientists have a higher credibility for journalists than do other sources of information. However, within the official perspective on AIDS there were differences, and these were reflected in the TV news coverage. Thus in the TV news coverage of HIV/AIDS there were criticisms of the government campaign, but they tended to be within the bounds of the official perspective on the disease. TV news thus did report differences of opinion on the AIDS campaign, but the disagreements aired were in general within the boundaries of "appropriate and responsible" debate, always defined in practice on TV as debate between official sources.

Medical/Scientific Sources and TV News

Access to TV news coverage of AIDS was dominated by medical and scientific experts. Of the 80 different scientists and doctors who appeared on TV news, 52 appeared on one occasion only. There were, however, a small number to whom the reporters returned regularly. In particular, the stories on medical and scientific research on AIDS were dominated by a small number of sources. The relationship between TV news and one of these scientific sources shows the problems inherent in such relationships.

Medical and scientific sources have a high degree of credibility in the eyes of television news personnel. Karpf (1988) points out that "being part of the scientifico-medical establishment is in itself sufficient in the media's eyes to make you a medical expert, even on an issue on which you have no specialist knowledge" (pp. 111-112). However, it is not a simple task for reporters to verify what scientific or medical sources tell them. Some journalists do not have the inclination or the knowledge to assess the quality of such information. In the absence of an objective standard by which to verify what they are told, journalists often value status and authority over other criteria in assessing the reliability of information. Eminent scientists and doctors can be excellent publicists whose opinions the media all too readily accept (Check, 1987). TV news has its own criteria for a source's worth. The visual and verbal requirements of the medium often outweigh concerns about the nature of what is said.

For example, the most interviewed scientist in our sample was described by the BBC's science correspondent as "one of Britain's leading experts on AIDS research" (BBC1, 6:00 p.m. newscast, September 10, 1987). In the same news story, it was reported that "a new vaccine against AIDS which is being developed in Britain may be tried out on humans within the next year." This was the same story that ITN had carried the previous February, when it reported on the work of this scientist in developing an AIDS vaccine. "Medical scientists . . . say they are hoping to start testing a vaccine on patients within 1 to 2 months" (ITN, 10:00 p.m. newscast, February 19, 1987). Yet up to the end of the 1980s this scientist had never even begun testing a vaccine, and had never published a single scientific paper on HIV or AIDS (Campbell, 1992).

Alternative Sources

Despite the dominance of official sources in the form of government ministers and doctors and scientists in the TV coverage of HIV/AIDS, other nonofficial sources did gain some access to the airwaves. The best example of such source coverage was the Terrence Higgins Trust, a charity set up to represent the interests of PWAs. The main spokesperson of the THT was interviewed on 16 news broadcasts in our sample. This was second only to the minister who held the health portfolio for the longest time during our sample, Norman Fowler. The THT established itself as a source of expert information about AIDS for the media.

> The Terrence Higgins Trust, set up in memory of the first British man to die of AIDS, pioneered public awareness of the threat. (ITN, 10:00 p.m. newscast, December 4, 1986)

By 1989, TV news had accepted the expert status of the THT to the extent that it no longer introduced or described the organization on screen other than by name caption.

The ability of the THT to overcome the lack of authoritativeness of other sources outside the medical establishment came in part because of the quality of information it provided, but also because of the image it promoted. Crucial to this image was the fact that its main spokesperson conformed to the needs and perceptions of TV news organizations. As the spokesperson told us:

> I am not threatening. I am 35. I am middle class. I speak BBC-type English. I am very acceptable. I am the kind of homosexual you can take home to your mother and it is a great relief to them.

Thus through its information strategy the THT was able to influence TV news coverage of HIV/AIDS. One of the organization's achievements was the replacement of the typical two-sided TV news discussion between a doctor and an interviewer with three-way discussions that included someone affected by HIV/AIDS.

Covering People With AIDS

People living with HIV or AIDS were featured prominently on TV news. Issues such as discrimination, prejudice, ignorance, and fear as well as medical and financial problems were reported. In very sharp contrast to the coverage in the British print media, many of the TV news reports attempted to inform and educate about the situation of PWAs.

The largest group of TV news interviewees was made up of PWAs, whose sources of HIV transmission or sexual orientation were nowhere specified. Only 4 interviews in our sample were with PWAs who were introduced as gay, in contrast with 16 hemophiliacs, a dramatic reversal of the actual proportion of gay men and hemophiliacs with HIV or AIDS. Interviews were also broadcast with the children, partners, families, and friends of PWAs. However, in the three and a half years studied, TV news never once carried an interview with the partner or lover of a gay man or with any members of a gay man's family. Such domestic settings were used only for heterosexuals, giving a quite erroneous representation that gay men do not have long-term committed relationships.

TV news did make distinctions between "guilty" and "innocent" victims. This surfaced explicitly in the coverage of HIV and hemophiliacs. One ITN headline referred to this group as the "innocent victims of AIDS" (ITN, 5:45 p.m. newscast, October 12, 1987). Meanwhile, the BBC reported on a "plea from people who got the AIDS virus by accident." The news reader explained that hemophiliacs face the threat of AIDS "through no fault of their own" (BBC1, 6:00 p.m. newscast, October 12, 1987). The obvious implication of such reporting is that gay men and drug users are to blame if they contract the virus, and are thus unworthy of our concern.

Such reporting became less apparent as groups such as the THT managed to put pressure on the TV news organizations. The labeling of "innocent" and "guilty" victims was even taken up as a news story. For instance, one ITN report began with the comment that "some believe it is wrong to discriminate between different categories of victim" (ITN, 10:00 p.m. newscast, November 16, 1987). The story included an interview with a member of the THT who stated that "immaterial of how a person contracted the disease, once they've got full-blown AIDS their needs are all very much the same and they [the government] should be catering now towards those needs."

In the coverage of PWAs, television news often made comparisons between people's physical appearance before and after they contracted the disease. The image of AIDS was one of decline, decay, and wasting.

> A self-portrait on the wall constantly reminds 37-year-old Gerry of how he used to be before he was infected with AIDS. Now this talented and trained artist is living in a hospice for dying AIDS patients in Kansas City. He used to be a body builder. (ITN *Channel Four News*, 7:00 p.m., November 12, 1986)

The painfully thin, haggard young man lying alone in a hospital bed came to represent the image of AIDS in the West in the early years of the disease.

However, TV news later came to carry reports that presented a different image of PWAs. A BBC report on the activities of the London Lighthouse Hospice, an organization that cares for people with AIDS, is illustrative of the attempts made to redefine the familiar image of PWAs. The news story was structured around the perspective of those living with AIDS. As one of the interviewees said in the story, "It sets a wonderful example, to see the smiling faces here and realize that AIDS in the end is not about death, it's about life and the liveliness of people here, people who have AIDS and the people who are helping them" (BBC1, 6:00 p.m. newscast, September 22, 1988).

TV news coverage of PWAs varied, sometimes in coverage of the same event by different channels. For example, the BBC reported on a visit by the British minister of health to a San Francisco hospital that included, according to the BBC, "his first-ever meeting with a hospitalized AIDS patient" (BBC1, 9:00 p.m. newscast, January 21, 1987). The patient was described as "a homosexual and a former drug user," and the report went on to say that "many of his friends have died of the disease. He now has it himself." The patient talked of his earlier life, saying, "It was a good time and we thought nothing of having casual sex or using recreational drugs." The story concluded with the stark comment, "By statistical averages of these cases, he has about one year to live." The narrative of this news story was constructed solely around the use of a PWA to warn others, with no concern for the subject of the report.

A radically different view of the minister's visit appeared on ITN that same night. The ITN news report was structured around the indifference shown to PWAs. The TV reporter commented that the patient "is angered by people who say it is just a homosexual disease and AIDS isn't their concern" (ITN, 10:00 p.m. newscast, January 21, 1987). The patient stated: "I wish I could tell all the straight people that, look, it's a virus, it's not running around checking sexual preference or race or class or anything, you know. It is just making people sick."

These two news accounts show that once an event is defined as newsworthy it can still be covered in very different ways. A number of factors can shape the coverage, including the information available, the reporter's own views, the journalistic strategies used to gain information, the journalist's sense of news values, and the influence of sources. The TV news coverage of PWAs shows the key role that sources can play in the construction of news accounts.

Conclusion

British TV news coverage of HIV/AIDS in the period discussed above was openly supportive of the government campaign and its key message about the threat of the virus to heterosexuals. Criticisms that were broadcast focused on the details of the campaign, in particular the lack of clarity and explicit language surrounding the campaign. Such criticisms reflected the view of the medical/scientific consensus established around the disease in the 1980s. Government and medical/scientific sources dominated TV news output on HIV/AIDS. Critical coverage of the government campaign reflected the concerns of the British medical/scientific orthodoxy, and the debate about HIV/AIDS on TV news primarily took place between official sources.

However, alternative sources were able to gain some access to TV news. An example is that the THT was able to establish itself as an "expert source" on problems of AIDS policy. TV news organizations, like the rest of the British media, initially went through a period of denial and victim blaming in their reporting on PWAs. In our sample there were examples of the "guilty victims" labeling that was very frequent in British print media reporting. But as the story progressed,

TV news began to challenge preconceptions of PWAs and to broadcast stories that portrayed the positive struggle of PWAs, as well as to endorse efforts to combat discrimination and increase funding for care. This was the result of the activities of alternative sources such as the THT and other gay and AIDS activist groups. The other important factors in shaping coverage of AIDS over this period were (a) the medical/scientific consensus concerning the adoption of a medical rather than a moral approach to the disease—often at odds with the government's pronouncements—and (b) broadcasters' notion of "social responsibility," embodied in the noncommercial culture that historically molded the development of British broadcasting, whether public service or advertising based (see McQuail, Chapter 9, and Jakubowicz, Chapter 10).

TV news coverage of AIDS in Britain has not, therefore, been neutral or objective. It has followed particular ways of understanding the disease and its consequences. Like news accounts elsewhere, these ways of understanding have been shaped by the official perspective on HIV/AIDS. However, TV news has not been uniform in the reporting of the disease, and as the AIDS story developed other sources of information were able to gain access to TV news and influence the coverage. Alternative sources of information on HIV and AIDS have been able to gain much more access to TV news in Britain than in the United States. This can be explained by the ability of AIDS organizations in Britain to build alliances with other sources and to influence the news media. Only by understanding the process of negotiation that takes place between sources of information, within news media organizations, and between sources and journalists can we make sense of how issues are reported by the news media.

Further Questions

1. How would you link up the perspective on news in this chapter with the chapters by Herman, Robinson, and Rodríguez in Part II? Do the views of these authors conflict at certain points? If you think they do—or if they don't—what do you think is the most accurate way to understand how news media put "reality" together (Schlesinger, 1988)?

2. This chapter notes in passing how different British TV coverage of AIDS has been from British print media coverage of the topic, which has fed much more on stereotypes about homosexuality and on public

fears. The authors argue that the difference may be explained especially by the "public service" operating philosophy of British broadcast news, as opposed to the much more commercial impulse of the print press (compare McQuail, Chapter 9). Can you think of any other possible explanations?

3. Monitor news coverage of other controversial issues, such as juvenile crime, environmental pollution, violence on the screen, immigration, or labor strikes, and try to find some alternative news source on that topic that is contrary to your present viewpoint. Then ask yourself how your understanding of the issue has been shaped by its news coverage.

25 Global News Media Cover the World

ANNABELLE SREBERNY-MOHAMMADI

For many years, most Americans were used to thinking of themselves as mercifully detached from the rest of the world and its conflicts. The United States joined in World War I reluctantly in 1917, three years after its beginning, and joined World War II equally reluctantly in 1941, two years after the war had commenced in Europe and Asia. Staying away from the battlefield is not irrational in itself on most occasions, but the issue for our purposes is that insularity—often termed isolationism—has been a marked feature of U.S. popular culture. One of the many reasons for the Vietnamese victory over the United States in 1975 was the widespread feeling in the United States that Americans were getting killed for no good purpose thousands of miles from home. The cruel irony is that, as Robinson notes in Chapter 6, American elites have rather consistently intervened on the world stage, sometimes, as in the case of Vietnam, dragging a largely unwilling public along.

Yet the United States is less and less able to pretend that it is an independent actor on the world stage, despite its enormous military might and technical advantages. It is part of a web of rich nations that have their own priorities, and it has an extensive series of client nations in the Third World, most of which are anxious to assert their own independence, at least from time to time. The lives of Americans cannot escape these developments, and they will increase as time goes on.

For this reason, international news is of the highest importance. If it is well constructed, it can help us adjust intelligently to the new position of the United States and, indeed, to anticipate likely changes in the world. In particular, it might help the American public to outgrow its habit of allowing Washington and Wall Street to make foreign policy, and may increase the number of independent commentators and critics in that area of life. The tragedy of lives lost in the Vietnam War—55,000 Americans and a million Vietnamese, not to speak of the maimed—is but one illustration of why this awareness matters.

In this chapter, Sreberny-Mohammadi traces out a number of the problems in conventional international news presentation in U.S. media. She shows us other dimensions of the communications imbalance between North and South already explored by Hamelink in Chapter 17, here contrasting the considerable quantity of information available in the affluent United States with its frequently poor quality of news presentation. As a case study of the processes in question, she selects Iran, a nation that from 1979 on has stirred passionate anger inside the United States and that therefore constitutes a particularly illuminating example of the negative impact of international news coverage, and of the ways it has typically failed to inform us adequately.

It was McLuhan who claimed that developments in electronic media and telecommunications have made the world into a "global village" (see McLuhan & Fiore, 1968). Yet whereas birthday cards from faraway aunties and phone calls from holiday boyfriends provide intimate ways of keeping in touch with other countries, for most people across the United States and in much of the industrialized world the domestic mass media—especially television—are the major source of information about international events in far-off places. The ways in which the media, particularly television, select and interpret events, what they focus on and what they omit, help to define public knowledge and construct public opinion. This public opinion may be educated—not only knowledgeable about the sequence of events but also fully informed about the reasons events occurred, the goals of national and world leaders, and the domestic and global implications of events—or it may be poorly informed, invited to see only dramatic moments rather then long-term processes and encouraged to develop a gung ho mentality toward the "national interest" rather than to appreciate the intricate interactions of most foreign policy issues.

International news coverage is a controversial and contested area of media production. Almost all Western professional journalists and many media analysts claim that international news coverage, like its domestic equivalent, is objective, truthful, and unbiased, and that what they report is "the way it really is." It is argued that if there is more news about one area than another, it is because the Americans or the British are more interested in certain places than others, it is easier and safer to report from some parts of the world than others, and if certain developing countries want better press, they should hire Madison Avenue public relations firms to improve their images abroad.

Many critical news analysts have argued, on the other hand, that U.S. media coverage of international issues in particular tends to focus on sensational, negative news of the "coup and catastrophe" kind; that there is an unbalanced focus on Western industrialized nations and Japan (and, once upon a time, the Soviet Union), while whole continents remain invisible if not in crisis; that international news tends to be shallow and oversimplified, concentrating on personalities and pronouncements of governments rather than exploring how issues affect ordinary people; and that coverage fragments complex problems into isolated events without providing explanations for and analyses of their causes. International news coverage in other Western democracies, such as Britain and France, operates within a different tradition of public service broadcasting and seems sometimes to offer a slightly more diverse news focus, but not much. In fact, there is a problem of actually defining what constitutes "international" news and separates it from "domestic" news coverage. The bulk of U.S. international news reporting actually concerns U.S. relations with other nations, and it is generally true that international news is most often defined in terms of the interests of the broadcasting nation, not the "intrinsic" importance or interest of the issue.

It is useful to explore international news reporting further by examining the U.S. coverage of one region of the world, familiarly called the Middle East, itself a name that is redolent of the map of the world as defined by the triumphant British and French powers in the period after World War I. (Presumably, if you live in that region, you would think a "middle east" is located somewhere else, perhaps in the Pacific?)

In the West, one familiar icon of Middle Eastern cultures is the veil, often used to represent cultural difference, if not backwardness. However, it is interesting to note that many linguistic terms that surround the veil are also used to describe news media. Both the veil and the media "cover" bodies/stories; both the veil and the media can also "uncover" what is hidden from view, although both can also "cover up"; indeed, both can be turned from nouns to verbs, and take over each other's roles: The media can veil issues, and the veil can mediate social reality. Both terms usefully suggest the various kinds of screens that exist at many different levels of our social life; the more familiar we are with cultural patterns and "screens" (such as what different dress codes mean in our own societies), the easier they are to interpret, and to see beyond. But the less we know about another culture, the harder it becomes to interpret how the media screen veils that reality, to know how the story has been constructed, to know what has been omitted, to see beyond. I hope that at this point you begin to appreciate the slipperiness of the linguistic terms *media* and *mediation,* and the problem of covering/uncovering/covering up that the media present to critical analysts.

Only very few nations are regularly covered in international news reporting. A study of the most frequently mentioned nations in U.S. network news coverage in the period 1972-1979 (Larson, 1982) found that only 20 nations were mentioned in more than 2% of international news stories, hardly extensive coverage. Most of those countries were the politically or economically powerful nations, such as the Soviet Union, Great Britain, France, the People's Republic of China, Japan, and Germany. Most of the rest were countries involved in wars or major conflicts, so that South Vietnam was the single most frequently mentioned nation from 1972 to 1975 and Middle Eastern nations such as Israel, Egypt, Lebanon, and Iran received substantial television news focus especially from 1976 to 1979. This means that much of the world remains invisible to us if it is not involved in some "newsworthy" and telegenic conflict.

Because the 1979 Islamic Revolution in Iran and the subsequent seizure of hostages in the U.S. embassy in Tehran captured overwhelming media attention, and because there was such an intimate relationship between U.S. government policy on Iran and U.S. media coverage, it is a highly instructive case study for pinpointing some typical problems in U.S. foreign news reporting, and thus for raising some general questions about the dilemmas of international news coverage in the West.

A Brief Profile of Iran

Iran has been a national entity and a monarchy for more than 2,500 years, dating back to the empire of Cyrus. It lies at the crossroads of Europe and Asia, and has suffered numerous invasions: by Greeks, Mongols, and Arabs. Despite these invasions, Iran has retained a strong sense of national identity and cultural tradition. Although historically Zoroastrianism was the prevailing religion, Islam came to Iran at the time of Mohammad, and a Shi'ite version of Islam has become the dominant religion, shared by 98% of the population from the sixteenth century on.

At the beginning of the twentieth century, Iran underwent a constitutional revolution, pressured by a new secularly educated middle class and sections of the clergy, which tried to limit the powers of the shahs (the monarchs) and to develop a framework for democratic participation, without much success. Reza Shah, who took the throne in 1925, wanted to modernize Iran along Western lines, including dress and other cultural patterns, and allowed the British to supervise the development of the oil industry.

His son, Mohammad Reza Shah, was forced into exile by a popular movement in the early 1950s, led by Mossadeq, that wanted both to nationalize the oil industry and to ensure the democratic process as guaranteed by the Constitution. The shah was returned through a coup in 1953, orchestrated by the British and Americans, and became a royal despot, controlling political and cultural life, imposing censorship, and organizing a secret police.

It was not until the 1970s that a real mass movement grew again against political repression, rapid Westernization, and lopsided economic development. This movement involved many sectors of the Iranian population, such as university professors and students, the professional middle class, traditional bazaar merchants, and the urban poor. Gradually, however, religious slogans overtook secular demands and the Ayatollah Khomeini became the charismatic figure to bind such a mass movement together (Sreberny-Mohammadi & Mohammadi, 1994). The shah was overthrown in January 1979 and an Islamic Republic was established in February of that year.

Like many Third World countries, Iran's economy was dominated by a single export product—in its case, oil. Because of its rich oil deposits and its key strategic location, the United States and other Western powers, together with the Soviet Union, were very closely concerned with Iranian affairs, and had been throughout the twentieth century.

U.S. Television Coverage of Iran

Iran enjoyed very good relations with the United States after the coup of 1953, received substantial military aid from the United States, and began to play a crucial role as a regional power in U.S. strategy in the Middle East. Thus Iran might have been expected to receive considerable media attention, but that was not the case. Until the end of the 1970s, Iran received a remarkably low level of news time, just over 5 minutes a year on weekly network newscasts, and the coverage was correspondingly narrow in perspective. The focus was either on the persona of the shah, exemplified by the pomp and splendor of his lavish coronation in 1971, or on oil, which fueled the rapid economic modernization the shah was trying to impose on Iran. The shah was portrayed as an insightful monarch who was trying to drag his backward population into the twentieth century, and in any brief attention to the repressive political system, the shah's dictatorship was justified as necessary for economic development to take place.

Almost no attention was paid to the living conditions of ordinary rural people, the bulk of Iran's population, whose conditions hardly improved—except for the addition of television run on generators!—and even declined, as self-sufficient agriculture gave way to international agribusiness. Almost no attention was paid to the fast and ungainly growth of Tehran, its traffic, pollution, and inflation, and the rapidly increasing divide between the conspicuous consumption of the urban rich and the lack of electricity, medical care, and schooling for the illiterate rural poor. Almost no attention was paid to human rights abuses, such as the absence of free speech, the impossibility of free political organization and debate, the control of trade unions, and the torture and murder of political opponents. Almost no attention was paid to the universities, or to the plight of academics, intellectuals, artists, and writers who were unable to practice their professions or lead their creative lives under the prevailing political conditions.

Why was this the case? Essentially, these conditions existed because U.S. government and corporations supported the shah, maintained only narrow channels of communication with Iranian government sources and supporters, and ignored the signs of looming political trouble even when they became pronounced. As late as December 1978, with millions of demonstrators on the streets of Iranian cities, President Carter was still calling the shah "an island of tranquility in a sea of troubles."

The media followed the lead of the political system. International news coverage is the area where political influence in news presentation is the strongest and where the adversary relationship between media and government and any notion of "fairness" are at their weakest (see also Robinson, Chapter 6). In their coverage of international events, the news media are more likely to present the perspectives current in the State Department and/or National Security Council than any other interpretation, and the "national interest" operates as an important criterion in selecting, and a crucial value in interpreting, events as news. This means that the question, How does this event affect the United States? blots out any independent attempt to understand the internal dynamics of a situation, the main actors, and their motivations.

Thus the U.S. media were blind to numerous signs of dissatisfaction and lacked the sources to explore any signs they may have detected. Like the State Department and the National Security Council, the media had not cultivated sources among crucial social sectors, such as bazaar merchants, university professors, or oil workers, who would have provided very different interpretations of what was happening in Iranian society. The narrow network of government sources created an illusion that the shah might be facing some temporary difficulties but enjoyed an essential stability, and they succeeded in so persuading and thus blinkering both U.S. politicians and the major mass media.

Alternate views and analyses of the popular movement were available, however. There were the reports of Amnesty International and PEN International; lengthy articles in Le Monde by Maxime Rodinson, long a scholar of the Middle East; articles in MERIP Reports, an alternative magazine on Middle East affairs; and reports on the BBC World Service, whose correspondent lived in Iran and had built up an extensive and varied network of contacts. Alternate sources of information and interpretation are almost always available to those who are interested enough and know where to look to find them. The media pay limited attention to mainstream academic journals such as Foreign Policy and Foreign Affairs, but almost never examine radical periodicals or the reports of small research institutes, whose alternate perspectives thus rarely penetrate into mainstream media coverage.

A lack of independent analysis, the acceptance of prevailing government views on foreign policy issues, and the ignoring of other sources of information color international news coverage, but production and economic pressures compound the process. International news coverage is increasingly expensive, and it does not regularly attract enormous audiences. In fact, were it not for FCC stipulations about "social responsibility" and the necessity for a minimum level of such news coverage, it is possible that for financial reasons international news coverage would disappear from general broadcasting and become the province of specialized news channels such as CNN on cable television. Economic pressures and audience priorities have steadily depleted the number of correspondents based abroad. This has implications for the ability of a correspondent to cover an international issue adequately. A correspondent might cover a Latin American economic issue one week and then fly to the Middle East to cover a military story the next, preparing for the assignment by reading what competing media have written. The correspondent is unlikely to be fluent in the relevant languages and so will be totally reliant on interpreters; he or she will lack a network of sources built up over time and so will be reliant upon officials and public figures and their perspectives; he or she will not be familiar with operating in highly policed societies to build access to and trust with alternative sources.

The damaging implications of such limited coverage of Iran came when the popular revolutionary movement burgeoned rapidly in 1977-1978 into some of the biggest mass demonstrations in Iranian history. U.S. government officials and major media were at a loss for explanations, hence their recourse to the easiest one, that the stubborn and backward Iranians were rebelling at being thrust into the twentieth century and that the protests were a reactionary movement against progress. U.S. media reports spoke of mobs running riot, as though there were no legitimate political reasons for action, and the shah was never referred to as a dictator or despot. Thus, far from objective reporting of "both sides," the media in the main adopted the political perspective of the shah, the U.S. proxy in the Gulf region and a major player in U.S. foreign policy.

But beyond the political blinkers manifested by the media lurks a deeper cultural mythology and ethnocentrism, displayed in the detail and nuance of the verbal and visual languages of television. Cultural mythologies can be found in all media systems and are often at their most pronounced in international news reporting; U.S. coverage of Iran is merely one vivid case of a very widespread phenomenon. News language, whether international or domestic, supplies subtle and not-so-subtle value-laden terms that constitute an interpretive framework for the audience. Thus it is important to examine media use of such terms as *terrorist, fanaticism,* and *crisis,* which can be contrasted with *freedom fighter, commitment,* and *conflict.* The terminology often derives from the prevailing political atlas, especially as articulated by the president of the day (for more on this issue, see Robinson, Chapter 6). Thus, for example, "terrorists" are always by definition tiny groups or individuals acting by themselves without popular support—never governments, whether Iranian, Israeli, or other.

In the Iran coverage, media language helped to stress cultural differences. Iranians were described in highly colored terms—"black-robed mullahs" (are we ever told of "black-robed bishops"?), the "turbaned" Khomeini, the "veiled" women—so that the indigenous cultural habits and religious practices were presented as bizarre, alien, and clearly reactionary, whereas the "modernizer" shah was portrayed as a strong ruler who had to be tough to develop such a backward people. The verbal code was supported by an even more effective visual code. It was common for references to Iran to be supported visually by pictures of either Royalist soldiers sporting weaponry or citizens marching in demonstrations, which served to suggest metonymically that the entire population was in a constant state of extreme political mobilization. Thus the ever-mobilized Iranian demonstrators in a news photograph came to stand for the whole population of Iran.

What was revealed in the coverage as the greatest omission of U.S. political and media analyses was any understanding of Shi'ism as the religious practice and cultural worldview of most Iranians. Nor was any sense provided of the loss of cultural identity precipitated by the pattern of modernization under the shah (see Mohammadi, Chapter 21). Hence the very superficial labeling of Khomeini and the religious perspective that developed as "fanatical" and "reactionary" rather than as revolutionary and courageous—which the demonstrators undoubtedly were in their unarmed opposition to the shah and his huge secret police and army. The inability to see the Iranian revolution as a popular movement uniting many different sectors of Iranian society mobilized for a number of political, economic, and cultural reasons is exemplified by the dominant media question in the postmortem on the Iranian revolution, which was "Who lost Iran?" The assumption was that Iran was a quasi-colony, a possession to be "lost" by the United States, rather than an independent nation in the midst of a painful and violent process of social change.

The Hostage Crisis

This narrow ethnocentrism was highlighted further in 1980 through-out the 444 days of the "hostage crisis," when the Iran story became the single most intensively covered story on all three television net-works and in the print media. Indeed, nightly coverage of this crisis, involving 53 American hostages, equaled and even surpassed average nightly coverage of the Vietnam War, which at one point involved more than 500,000 U.S. troops. Watergate and presidential campaigns are the only other contenders for such intensive yet long-term focus. Media coverage, especially when the leading U.S. newscaster, Walter Cronkite, counted each day in his nightly newscast, became a collec-tive public ritual.

It is important to ask why this was the case: Why did this particular event qualify for such massive media attention (Adams & Heyl, 1981)? There was the obvious "newsworthiness" of the event— a "crisis," a highly unusual set of events, relevant to a large audience—and there was a strong "human interest" angle. But there were other factors besides. It was an almost perfect televisual drama (Altheide, 1981), with all the necessary ingredients of a cultural and media myth. It offered a simple plot with two opposing sides, the "good guys" and "bad guys" readily visualized through images of blindfolded hostages and concerned families who were contrasted to the turbaned mullahs and angry crowds. It also directly involved the president of the United States, responsible both for U.S. policy vis-à-vis Iran and for allowing the fallen shah to enter the United States for medical treatment.

The coverage would undoubtedly have been very different if Iran had not permitted, rather than fostered, media attention. As it was, Iran somewhat effectively managed to use the media to speak directly to the American people, creating a new debate that "media diplomacy" was taking the place of more formal diplomatic channels, which had actually been broken. Within the "news as entertainment" mold the hostage crisis provided a political soap opera that occasioned collective national outrage, frustration, unity, nationalism, and, finally, with the safe return of the hostages, euphoria. The net effect was the creation and maintenance of a public perception of a menacing world in which the United States must stand tough and where America's allies welcomed Reagan's reassertion of America's prestige.

You might ask, So what is wrong with this coverage? Isn't that what really happened? To answer this, we need to look not only at what was presented and how it was constructed, but also at what was *not* said. First, the hostages were immediately presented as innocent individual victims rather than as U.S. government officials in military or foreign service positions, who could be viewed as representatives of relations between the United States and the shah. Iranian accusations about espionage out of the embassy were not responded to. Similarly, little attention was paid to Iranian demands for the return of the shah and his wealth to Iran (in marked contrast to the critical attention given to demands for return of the wealth of Ferdinand and Imelda Marcos to the Philippines). The shah was generally portrayed as a sick and harassed man, and little attention was paid to the history of political repression and growing economic inequality under his rule. Again, there was little attention to the role of religion in Iran, although religious leaders and religious rhetoric were by then dominant, and little attempt to explain why Iranians followed Khomeini, who was presented as an aged fanatic.

Thus any historical and political reasons that Iranians had for their actions were ignored, and the entire chain of events was labeled as the work of fanatical and lawless Muslims. As Altheide (1981) summarizes, "The Iranian situation was reduced to one story—the freeing of the hostages rather than coverage of its background and context, of the complexities of Iran, of alternative American policies, and of contemporary parochial politics in a world dominated by superpowers" (p. 155).

Although many Americans do not understand why there was a revolution or why the hostages were taken, they did come to "know" that Iran was an "enemy" of the United States, a "terrorist" state filled with Muslim fanatics. Thus news helps to create and perpetuate cultural myths about other peoples, labeling friends and naming enemies (Keen, 1987). Through the denial of legitimacy to any Iranian position, any basis for negotiation or solution was denied; foreign policy making was and remains stalled.

Some of the ironies and disturbing political consequences of this lack of independent media coverage have subsequently come to light. We now know that in U.S.-Iran relations during this period there was much more direct contact and double-dealing than the public was led to believe at the time. "Irangate," when it finally broke in the United States, revealed that the Reagan government—which had said it would never deal with terrorists—had, in fact, entered into direct deals with the Iranians to free hostages, even providing the Iranians with weaponry.

In what we should call the first Gulf War, the one fought between Iran and Iraq between 1980 and 1988, there was comparatively little media coverage, because the West did not want either side—neither the "Islamic fundamentalists" nor the autocratic Iraqis—to triumph, adopting a "plague on both your houses" attitude and providing media coverage only when one side seemed to be in danger of winning, which in the end neither side did. The media actually labeled this the "forgotten war," when they decided to remember it was happening, despite the fact that it was a war that killed hundreds of thousands of people, destroyed complete cities, saw probably the first modern missile attacks on heavily populated cities since the firebombing of Dresden, and involved the use of chemical weapons.

The "real," second, Gulf War took place in 1991, a seven-day wonder played out Nintendo-style between the liberation forces of the West and the new Hitler-incarnate, Saddam Hussein. The coverage of the Gulf War was a masterful propaganda operation, quickly stage-managed by the Pentagon, which operated news pools, orchestrated the information flow, and provided hyperreal pictures of "smart bombs" cleanly taking out the buildings of the enemy. The language of "surgical strikes" also cut at the truth, both omitting coverage of the actual human costs of the war and overlooking the many critical voices that remained opposed to the entire military adventure. A considerable critical literature on the media coverage of the Gulf War is now available (Kellner, 1992; Mowlana, Gerbner, & Schiller, 1992; Taylor, 1992). Again, one of the tragic ironies is that subsequently we have again learned that both the United States and the United Kingdom sold massive amounts of weapons to Saddam right up to the outbreak of war, actually helping him to construct the massive military machine that they then helped to destroy. Indeed, in Britain, the Scott Inquiry is still trying, in 1994, to uncover how "lapses" in government policy actually allowed military producers to sell weapons to Saddam in contravention of stated policy. In both Irangate and "Iraqscam," political leaders showed their talent for media manipulation and strategic forgetting—the pity is that the lack of independent media coverage cannot help to jog their memories.

The twists and turns of Western policy vis-à-vis both Iran and Iraq are the subject of much historical, political, and international relations analysis, which you could dip into for further detail. What is significant from a media perspective is to ask the crucial question: Why do the media fall so readily into line with government on foreign policy matters, rather than try to maintain a critical, independent stance?

The point of this analysis is *not* to condone Iranian government actions or to support the Islamic Republic. Nor is it to wave the flag for the antidemocratic Saddam Hussein. The point is to show that the news media's basic desire for dramatic and visual stories with readily comprehensible plots and identifiable actors leads them to create stereotypes, labels, and impressions that remain long after particular events have ended. There is currently growing interest in how the media and our culture depict and define "others," and there is considerable evidence of the very limited, narrow, and stereotypical image of the Middle East as the West's "Oriental" other that runs through Western literature, film, and news (see, e.g., Said, 1979, 1981; Shaheen, 1984). Not only has the term *fundamentalism* slipped easily into everyday vocabulary—almost invariably prefixed with *Islamic*—but we also increasingly hear of groups labeled with religious, rather than political, descriptions. Indeed, as ethnic conflict and racist sentiment appear to be on the rise across Europe, the political rhetoric of states increasingly stresses the Christian roots and cultural identities of the West. Thus the negative connotations attached to Middle Eastern political actors in international news coverage not only supported the easy slide into military action of the second Gulf War, but even after the cessation of military hostilities these discourses play a role in the ways we are invited to think about, and act toward, minorities in our midst—indeed, in the way we think about who "we" are. (It is instructive to compare Western debates about "multiculturalism" and cultural identity [see Jakubowicz, Chapter 10] with debates that come from the Third World [see Mohammadi, Chapter 21].)

Conclusion

The issues discussed here are relevant not only to U.S. media but to international news coverage in much of the world. There appears to be a worldwide skewing in the pattern of international news reporting, no doubt partly influenced by the structure of news materials available from the big international news agencies, such as the Associated Press and Reuters. Every national audience receives mostly news about its local region, so that Africans read most about Africa, Latin Americans about Latin America, and so on. A second tier of "consistent newsmakers," essentially North America and Europe, regularly receive considerable news media attention across most media systems, deemed newsworthy by dint of their power, not crisis. The third tier is made up of the current "hot spots," those areas of the Third World that are currently enduring some kind of crisis. There remain important "areas of invisibility" in many media systems, usually the areas of the Third World where no major "crisis" is supposedly unfolding, and Eastern Europe, until glasnost (Sreberny-Mohammadi, Nordenstreng, Stevenson, & Ugboajah, 1984). There has been little research since the breakup of the Soviet Union to show the new maps of regional/cultural attention that international media provide—something that needs to be done. The old pattern meant very unequal news attention to different parts of the world, an apparent disinterestedness in more positive news of development or the slow processes of social change, and an inability to explain most crises in relation to their causes, none of which seems to have changed in the so-called new world order.

One significant outcome of the second Gulf war was the emergence of CNN as a worldwide provider of television news. Again, in somewhat contradictory fashion, CNN reporters filed some of the few independent stories out of Baghdad before they had to leave, yet ultimately their role as sole source and their continuing prominence heralds a kind of international news product that compares with a Big Mac, a single homogeneous commodity divorced from the political realities, social concerns, and information needs of different polities and peoples. In the media's global rush for instant coverage and the best pictures, we stand to see a further erosion of independent, critical news coverage and analysis from reporters who know something about the places and issues they are covering—unless audiences demand better information and multiple perspectives in international news coverage, as they should in their domestic news coverage.

That superficiality and sensationalism suit the U.S. networks better than in-depth reporting and analysis is shown by a final example. In the summer of 1985 there was considerable network coverage of a skyjacking in which a TWA plane was taken to Beirut. When the skyjackers organized press conferences, audience ratings increased and the networks garnered increased revenues. The ABC crew members on the story had been based in Lebanon for some time, and had built up a network of contacts and information sources, and also spoke Arabic. They were thus privileged to special interviews and generally provided the best coverage of the tense and complex set of events, which included historical and political analyses of the ongoing conflicts in Lebanon and the wider Middle East. When the story ended, ABC, instead of commending the crew members for their excellent coverage, removed them from Beirut and assigned them to other duties, because the corporation felt they had become "too involved" with the situation they were covering.

Negative media stereotypes may be pernicious at a domestic level, maintaining unequal relations of race and gender, but they can be partially interpreted against everyday realities and often encounter strong opposing attitudes. Such media stereotypes can become globally dangerous at an international level, fueling cross-national misunderstanding, mistrust, and conflict. As the ties between nations become more complex and multifaceted, and when many apparently domestic problems turn out to have international dimensions, informed public opinion can help to create rational and peaceful foreign policy. Public opinion based on stereotypes and prejudices, without access to other sources of information and direct experience to temper the mediated messages, is more likely to support hostile relations, as with Iran and Iraq, rather than peaceful coexistence.

One problem is that no news coverage, however technologically sophisticated, can give equal weight to events in all of the 180 nations now recognized by the United Nations. Indeed, one of the central problems in news coverage is its very event-centeredness; news organizations jump instantly to cover each breaking story rather than stop to analyze the processes and structures behind the surface changes. On the one hand, we might say that that is the nature of news, and demand better documentaries and news analysis programming to fill in the analytic and information gaps; on the other hand, we could still argue for a different conception of news along the lines of the demands for a "new international information order" made by Third World nations in the late 1970s. Another issue that arises out of the coverage of such stories as the conflict in Bosnia and the famine in Angola concerns what Western viewers are supposed to do with the information carried in international news coverage—should they feel superior, guilty, compassionate, frustrated, or moved to act? If they should be moved to act, what kinds of actions are possible? Given the lack of political will and imagination in the particular cases of Bosnia and Angola, it is hard for the ordinary viewer to know what he or she can do. Considerable amounts of money have been collected by charities, and many groups have organized creative ways of collecting money, foodstuffs, clothing, and so on, for various crises as the media highlights them. But there are all sorts of limitations to such activities. Here the more relevant focus is the need to explore further the relationships among the information that news provides, public understanding and "global" awareness, and political and social action.

It seems that what we need is not more "good news," as British broadcaster Martyn Lewis wants, but more debate about what "good news coverage" is. In a global media environment, where distance has been reduced to seconds and other people's news is also our own, it is harder and harder to define what that can and should be. What could thinking *and* acting globally be?

Further Questions

1. Construct a "news map" of the world from a week of current news coverage in the quality press, or television. Does it fit the model presented here, or has the news map of the world altered? What is different, and why?

2. Identify some critical and alternative news channels and compare their coverage of a selected international news issue with that of the dominant television networks. Pinpoint the areas of omission and commission in both kinds of media. Find a native from the country in question, or an "expert" on the area, to give an analysis of the nature of the news coverage.

3. Compare U.S. news geography with the "worlds" of Russian, British, French, or other national news systems by comparing newspaper or television international news coverage for a week. Do we inhabit the same mediated world? If not, why not? What is the impact of the history of different colonial annexations on which Third World countries usually get covered?

26 Myths In and About Television
Entertainment and Economics

SARI THOMAS

In this chapter, Thomas sets out to puncture a series of popular propositions about television and U.S. culture. Some of these are widely accepted definitions of the function of television; others are commonly expressed judgments of the messages of television.

To begin with, she attacks the notion that television is simply entertainment and therefore of no particular consequence one way or the other. Against that view, she argues that TV is a powerful educational force, a significant source of orientation. She further proposes that television does not communicate commercial messages in advertisements alone, but that its entire output is saturated by economically oriented messages in favor of the status quo. This first section of her argument should be read in close conjunction with Chapters 12 and 13, on media audiences, for it presents a third angle of vision on the difficult problems of interpreting audience responses to media, and of relating media content to the political economy.

In the second part of her argument, Thomas proposes that far from TV being antibusiness, as some have claimed (for example, in its portrayal of corrupt businessmen in such series as Dallas *and* Dynasty*), the medium actually provides potent support for certain myths that sus-*

tain the business order. *Her argument here supports Kellner's analysis of advertising and consumerism in Chapter 19, with the difference that she locates consumerist pressures squarely within the entertainment/ education diet of television, not simply in the advertisements.*

Beyond the myths of consumer culture, however, are other myths of social mobility: that all individuals can advance as far as they want up the economic ladder if they work hard. This "American dream" is a source of continuing inspiration to many who migrate here. Simultaneously, it is a message to the majority still at the foot of the ladder that they have not exercised sufficient ingenuity to make use of the opportunities presented them, that they are lacking in drive. In reality, people achieve very little upward mobility compared with their parents, with the exception of a few sports and entertainment stars, and even these stars' careers usually last only a few years. But the notion that the dream can become real nourishes positive feelings about the nature of the society and self-blame if, despite one's efforts, one does not achieve it. The dream is a source of political and social stability.

The Myths About Television

For decades, critics have bemoaned the state of commercial U.S. television. In general, they say that programming is low-level, unimaginative pabulum. They argue that it serves only two purposes: to entertain a mindless audience and to create a marketing forum through advertisements in which to sell products and services to that mindless mass. It is assumed that these two functions, in combination, are the key mechanisms by which the sellers—network, corporation, and agency executives—get rich.

Although everyone might not hold such a harsh view of television, the two assumptions underlying this view are pretty much taken for granted by most members of our society. These assumptions can be spelled out as follows: (a) Television is an "entertainment medium," and (b) television's primary mechanism for economically supporting the established elite is through "audience commodification." Audiences are thought to be "commodified" through a multistep process: First, they are provided with "free entertainment" (the programming) and, next, research is conducted to find out what programs are watched by whom. Advertisers are then sold time slots within appropriate entertainment periods, where they, in turn, sell products and services to targeted audiences. Thus TV viewers become packaged commodities purchased by advertisers (Smythe, 1981).

In this chapter I refer to the two assumptions stated above as the primary myths *about* television. I use the term **myth** to represent any belief in a culture that is so ingrained in and pervasive among members of the society that, for the most part, what the belief asserts goes without question. In other words, the accuracy of the information contained in a myth is not, on an everyday level, very important. A myth is accepted *as a given*. Thus these two interrelated assumptions are understood as "the way things are" about television. Clearly, if you are a network executive, advertising executive, or sponsor, you will probably approve of the system as a positive example of capitalism at work. If you are a parent, educator, or political activist, you might be antagonized by the "mindless entertainment," the corporate greed you think is behind it, or both. Nevertheless, whether you approve or disapprove of the system on these terms, you also ultimately accept the above-mentioned myths about television: that it is mindless entertainment that supports capitalism by packaging audiences.

This chapter represents an attempt to clean the slate somewhat. Rather than argue for or against the system represented in the two myths, I will question the validity of the myths themselves. Is TV primarily an "entertainment" system? Is television's major contribution to capitalist economy made primarily through selling audiences to advertisers and, in turn, products to audiences?

The Myth About Entertainment

Whatever "entertainment" is—apparently the same phenomenon that induces people to cringe eagerly while watching slasher films, weep while reading romance stories, or cheer as they watch boxers inflicting brain damage on each other—television seemingly does provide it. But when people watch TV, is "entertainment" the only or even the major result of the viewing experience? Let us assume, instead, that TV provides the primary adult *educational* experience.

Statistics show that sleeping is the only activity in which the average American indulges more than television viewing (let alone combined media use). It is ironic that these two most popular activities—sleeping and TV—are commonly viewed as being similar in nature and effect. That is, we are led to believe that at least two-thirds of the average American day is spent in one form or another of vegetation. Whereas it is probably true that the average person *believes* that most viewing time is spent in the pursuit of entertainment, relaxation, or escape, perhaps there is actually a lot more going on during those thousands upon thousands of viewing hours.

Whatever their conscious motivation, when people watch television, they watch stories (drama or news) showing how "things" work. Television especially provides a window on many matters with which most of us have relatively little or no real-life experience. How police or lawyers operate; what life is like in New York, Miami, Shanghai; what rich people do at the dinner table; and thousands of other pieces of information come to us almost exclusively from television and, to a lesser extent, other popular media. When we are confronted with this information, it is very unlikely that we regard the information as "education"; we would hardly equate TV viewing with listening to a lecture in a classroom. Yet the two experiences may not be that far apart. In fact, the "educational" material coming from television stories probably has more to do with the business of ordinary life—values and ideas involved in our everyday judgments— than does the educational material in most formal classroom situations. Moreover, we may be more receptive to TV information than to that from classroom lectures precisely because we do not view TV stories as education. Indeed, it is unlikely that we would acknowledge or even recognize the source of much TV-gained information because its entrance into our store of knowledge is so subtle. This is why so much mass communication research on the effects of TV is very problematic; researchers often interview people in the mistaken assumption that people can articulate the full meaning of their viewing experiences.

This picture of "TV as education" is not a popular one. When the "educational" component of television is introduced into the debate, it typically appears in only three contexts: discussions of children, violent crime, and concerned or curious citizens. That is to say, "learning" from television is predicted for innocents, sociopaths, and those adults deliberately choosing to be informed through news, public affairs, and documentary programming. In terms of the third group, the fact that we persist in drawing a line between so-called information and entertainment programming attests to this assessed division in function; that is, we assume "entertainment" programming is *not* informative.

Within the discipline of communication, the early hypodermic model suggested "strong" media effects, whereas later models such as "uses and gratifications" theory suggested "weaker" effects (for more about these models, see Ang, Chapter 12). Although there are swings between strong and weak effects models, overall those theories arguing against powerful effects and for weaker ones have been the most popular among both scholars and the general public. Because weak effects theories stress individual differences in media use, they are highly compatible with the meritocratic philosophy of American capitalism, which holds that an individual's choices and actions will supposedly yield his or her status in the overall social structure, the concept of *autonomous individualism* (Elliot, 1974; Messaris, 1977). In the United States we like theories that stress our individual differences and emphasize the control we have over our own destinies.

But although there is considerable evidence to show that different people indeed do interact differently with the mass media, it is premature—in fact a leap in logic—to conclude that people walk away from the mass media with unique, individualized knowledge. Rather, a very limited number of preferences, identifications and, most important, interpretations arise, regardless of how many individual "interpreters" have been studied. These variations in media interaction can generally be linked to broad sociodemographic differences rather than to unique psychological distinctions.

Widespread belief in meaningful uniqueness and self-control helps keep the economic system going, but it does not necessarily mean that the belief is correct. We should also see that the myth of television "entertainment" serves this larger orientation very well. It is a myth that allows us to believe that we are in control of what we learn and know.

The Myth About Where the "Business" of Television Is Located

From a psychological perspective, it is generally believed that people use television to fulfill their own individual needs and that these needs lie largely within the realm of entertainment and relaxation. From an economic perspective, it is generally believed that although this source of entertainment is ostensibly free, its hidden costs are great, charging for that "free entertainment" in the everyday marketplace. Both these perspectives, the psychological and the economic, separate "entertainment" from some other commodity. From a psychological viewpoint, the distinction is between "entertainment" and "information," whereas in terms of economics, "entertainment" is made separate from "advertising." Economic interpretations typically relegate the "business" part of television to advertising (see Kellner, Chapter 19), and it is rare that the "entertainment" itself is understood to be commercially effective and a major component in the economics of both television and the larger world. More liberal economic interpretations acknowledge that the content of the "free lunch" (the "entertainment" programming) tends to reinforce the status quo so that it complements the audience-commodification process. However, this complementariness is traditionally viewed as indirect and vague with regard to the creation of bourgeois consumerism and the maintenance of social order.

It would be intellectually pointless to discount the importance of advertising and corporate structure in television's contribution to capitalism. My argument here is twofold: First, I suggest that "cultural reproduction"—the continuing attempt to reproduce the existing society—is the primary industry of all human societies. All social institutions, including the mass media industry, are but subsidiary firms for the "parent corporation" of culture production. What this means is that popular creations (whether material or symbolic) will generally reinforce the rules and values of the overall system. Put another way, we must look for the possibility that all major cultural artifacts and activities contribute, at different levels and in different ways, to the coordination and sustenance of the established system.

Second, the mythology in television programming reinforces American corporate structure as powerfully as, if not more powerfully than, the more obvious mechanisms of packaging audiences and selling commodities. Whereas television commercials largely sell specific products to a commodified audience, television "entertainment" serves, in part, to sell the audience on the general process of capitalism. Therefore, the teaching of this general process (of earning, buying, and selling) is a prerequisite of audience commodification and an essential contribution to the preservation of American capitalism.

To speak of the mythology *in* U.S. television is to speak of many things. This is not to suggest that the views and values represented on TV are various and conflicting, but rather that, like Proteus, they take many mutually reinforcing forms. Given the discussion thus far, there are two sets of myths *in* television "entertainment" that are most relevant: myths of labor and consumption and myths of social mobility.

The first set includes direct lessons about commercial issues, and the second provides the broader, stage-setting material for life in a commercialized system. Taken together, this mythology is instrumental in creating economic sensibilities that neatly serve the interests of the corporate elite and its reigning social structure.

Labor and Consumption in Television

Theberge (1981) argues that businessmen on American television come in one of three categories: crooks, con men, or clowns. He asserts that "business" is represented negatively to the American viewing public, but there are three problems with this conclusion. First, it can be argued that negative images of businesspeople on TV can be confused with negative images of *rich* businesspeople, and that it is wealth, not business per se, that is stigmatized (Thomas & Leshay, 1992). (Negative images of wealth are discussed below.) Second, it is also important to suggest that television's portrayal of businesspeople represents idiosyncratic images of individuals rather than a systemic characterization of business. That is to say, bad businesspeople on TV are typically shown to be uniformly bad people. J. R. Ewing of *Dallas*, for example, is not simply an evil businessman, but an evil person in all facets of his life, including business. Of course, it would be telling if TV businesspeople were malicious and unlawful at work and yet loving and honest family members, friends, and lovers, but this is not the case—at least not on TV. Thus it is difficult, again, to claim that business in particular is under indictment. Third, the specific TV portrayals of businesspeople are not necessarily the only, or the most important, means by which social messages about labor and consumption are conveyed. If we turn our attention to the seemingly mundane filler of TV drama—those trivial or background events that permeate "entertainment" programming—we see a number of things happening that very much contradict the supposedly negative images of business, commercial transaction, and so forth. These events may be accounted for, at least partially, in the nine myths described below.

MYTH 1: THE INCONSEQUENCE AND
INVISIBILITY OF EVERYDAY SPENDING

The world of U.S. television is pretty moneyless. Of course, characters engage in activities that require money in real life, but on television, the monetary transactions are rarely included, and when they are, payment is typically a fleeting and unconscious gesture. Every night on television dozens of scenes are played out in restaurants, nightclubs, taxicabs, and so forth, but the fact that these things cost money invariably becomes an issue only when comedy or crime is involved. A man, for example, may do some serious gulping (accompanied by an uproarious laugh track) when he discovers his date has chosen a restaurant where he can barely afford a salad. The neglect of everyday spending on TV would probably be dismissed by writers as necessary editing of irrelevant material; however, given that there are many other trivial events dramatized, one might question the function of this particular omission. It might be interpreted that viewers are being shown the pointlessness of seriously considering what is part and parcel of everyday costs. Like the spending of TV characters, our spending should remain unconscious, invisible, and inconsequential. If spending is not invisible, it is probably a laughing matter.

MYTH 2: EXCESS MONEY IS TO BE SPENT

The invisibility of spending on TV refers to money and credit card handling, the normal, everyday transactions requiring payment that are typically overlooked in the television world. Thus the act that for many is problematic, if not painful, is often ignored. However, that money is spent by television characters—especially regular folk—is often implied. What we often see on television are the results of spending—the products bought, the consumerism. Moreover, except for special instances that I will detail below, the purchase of products usually occurs in dramatic contexts where a working- or middle-class character accumulates some extra cash. For example, when Roxanne, a secretary on *L.A. Law*, makes a sizable sum on stock deals, she is immediately seen sporting new, expensive clothes and driving a new car. Indeed, when the money, obtained through insider trading tips, is confiscated, we find that she is dead broke. In a made-for-TV movie, a previously poor writer hired at high salary by a scandal tabloid immediately exchanges her new (and projected) bank balance for luxurious home and fur; an alternative, such as depositing her money in a college account for her young son, is not a choice written into the script. In almost all cases of this type, if and when the character runs short of funds, the plot text usually addresses this problem as new and totally separate from the character's failure to save.

In general, what we see on television are otherwise normal characters living to the ends of, or beyond, their means. Security savings do not seem to be a part of most fictional game plans. When characters do save, it is typically with a future purchase in mind. In fact, the portrayal of the relationship between children/teenagers and money is especially poignant in this regard. When younger characters need funds, it is invariably shown that their savings are close to nonexistent. For instance, almost every show featuring children has produced one or more episodes in which the children must jointly collect their funds to accomplish something important, such as replacing a broken household valuable before the parents return from a trip. Typically, the "wealthiest" of the children can contribute something on the order of $1.06. Moreover, on most shows featuring children and teens, grandmother's birthday check is usually committed to a future purchase before it even arrives. I do not mean to suggest that one should expect children (or adults) to have huge sums of cash on hand, but rather that the television message suggests total and constant moneylessness among the working and middle classes as a standard state, as well as the acceptability of credit debt.

MYTH 3: THE DESIRE FOR EXCESS ACCUMULATION OF CAPITAL AS DEVIANCE

No discussion of a "money is to be spent" theme would be complete without the mention of that myth's corollary: There is something wrong with those individuals bent upon accumulation rather than expenditure. On television, this moral bears most heavily on those characters who are currently without considerable wealth (although Western culture also tells comparable stories in relation to the materially endowed, e.g., stories of Scrooge and Midas). Moreover, television speaks to other problems endemic to wealth, as will be discussed later.

This myth is most typically manifested in comedy programs featuring characters whose deep interest in making and accumulating money is supposed to appear as obsessive and, thus, becomes the butt of jokes. The character of Alex Keaton in the situation comedy *Family Ties* is a clear incarnation of this myth. Alex is hardworking, intelligent, and reasonably moral in his choices, yet his profound interest in accumulating capital is portrayed as both strange and comic. *Murphy Brown*'s Miles Silverberg is a softer rendering of such a character; in addition to providing ethnic stereotype, Silverberg's character combines a high-ranking Harvard MBA with social gracelessness, immaturity, and more-than-occasional geekiness.

MYTH 4: CELEBRATION IS A MATERIAL EVENT

A lot of the time, TV characters have special reasons to be happy. There are classic causes of celebration (birthdays, anniversaries, and so on) and less classic ones (solving a crime case, reconciling interpersonal differences, exceptionally nice weather). When TV characters celebrate anything, the revelry inevitably involves spending money, so that celebration becomes operationally defined as a commercial event. In fact, characters' happiness with something seems to be directly proportional to the money that will be spent in its honor. If the celebration involves reconciliation—"making it up" to someone—then the character's sincerity can be measured by how much the "making up" will cost. As the first myth would suggest, celebration spending is typically done unflinchingly. For example, without careful deliberation, *L.A. Law's* Ann Kelsey purchases a tremendously expensive wristwatch for her fiance, with whom she has been fighting. But the story is old: In many *I Love Lucy* episodes, for instance, Ricky guiltily relents and allows Lucy to purchase the expensive hairdo and dress. As might be expected, such grandiose gestures are typically shown to achieve the desired effect; on television, this is one context in which good characters can be "bought." We are shown an equation where spending equals love and respect.

MYTH 5: SPENDING DEFEATS DEPRESSION

There may be a gender-coded corollary to the "celebration as material event" myth: Spending is antidepressive. Whereas male characters usually turn to their work when saddened (a relationship discussed below), depressed TV women often go shopping. Although television may not be the primary forum promulgating the notion that commercial consumption helps beat the blues, many incidents in fictional programming certainly reinforce this line of action. In an episode of *Cagney & Lacey*, for instance, Mary Beth Lacey, in a context of feeling inadequate, chooses to buy herself a "smart" hat to help alleviate her insecurities. While such feel-good spending may be thought a marker of women from earlier generations, one need only to observe the young women of *Beverly Hills 90210* or *Melrose Place* to see that the image is young and contemporary.

MYTH 6: MORE CONSUMPTION YIELDS BETTER TREATMENT

In TV contexts where spending is expected (restaurants, shops, hotels, and the like), those characters (presumably) spending a great deal receive excellent treatment. This is not to say that those who refrain from spending a lot are invariably mistreated or that the excellent treatment afforded big spenders is never given begrudgingly or with scorn. The staff in the series *Hotel*, for example, is incredibly pleasant to all guests. Of course, just staying at this luxury-class establishment would usually involve considerable expenditure. The point here is that on TV, spending demands at least superficial respect.

In a society characterized by its size and impersonality, television shows offer what appears to be a certain route for acquiring respect. Rich gangsters and corporate potentates may ultimately be shown to suffer in other ways, but one thing they usually do not suffer is lack of eager subordinates. Moreover, although it may not always be the case that TV's small tippers, cheapskates, and nonspenders are harassed, it is not uncommon to find them reviled or the butt of jokes. Disrespect (e.g., haughty insolence from a salesclerk) meets TV's nonspenders often enough to create a standard of expectation. Thus viewers are shown that "good" treatment might be directly proportional to the money they give.

MYTH 7: CHEAP IS VULGAR

Although homespun philosophy may argue that the simple things in life are what count, and TV characters may even mouth such sentiments, the portrayal of vulgarity is, more often than not, characterized by cheapness in deed or demeanor. An episode of *Dynasty*, for example, shows the then semivillainous Sammy Jo eating corn dogs (and other fast food) in an impromptu "picnic" in the Carrington mansion. Although the tone of such a scene could be endearing or charming, this one is not. Sammy Jo is characterized as vulgar; the "ladies" of the show dine on respectable food at elegantly set tables.

Ironically, television does sometimes indicate the vulgarity of spending, but it is important to realize that such dramatizations are usually confined to spending by the rich. It may be shown, for example, when a typically evil or buffoonish rich character flaunts his or her wealth through lavish tipping. Good rich characters (the few there are) are rarely portrayed as ostentatious; these may be the only characters for whom the "less is more" doctrine is shown to work positively. When lavishness is enacted by middle- and working-class persons on television, these acts are generally shown as kind and generous behavior.

The myths articulated above are omnipresent foliage in the scenery of U.S. programming. Myths concerning work and consumption also abound in typical stories. To recite each fully would require a much longer text, but the two myths that follow should adequately suggest the pattern to which the general ideology subscribes.

MYTH 8: SATISFACTION MUST BE EARNED

This myth mutates in a variety of social contexts. It may emerge, for example, as "Idle wealth breeds evil" or "Easy money is dangerous," but, collectively, such myths proclaim that hard work is the only key to understanding and appreciating the meaning and marvel of money. Thus in the older *Hill Street Blues*, for example, a young police officer wins substantial money in a lottery and then encounters many more (serious) problems than those existing in his life prior to this "run of luck." Similarly, after inheriting vast wealth in *Beverly Hills 90210*, Dylan encounters corruption, bad luck, and other misery. The philosophy also extends to nonmaterial issues. A TV romance plagued with difficulties in its early stages has better chances for meaningful survival than one that seems smooth sailing from the start. Actually, such "nonmaterial" parables can be interpreted as metaphors for the fundamental money-earning lesson. In any case, that satisfaction must be earned teaches workers to appreciate the current fruits of their labors and to feel assured that they have properly paved the way to appreciate riches that might accumulate. However, because it is all too possible that, in real life, labor will largely beget more labor, another lesson typically accompanies the one teaching that "satisfaction must be earned," as the next myth shows.

MYTH 9: WORK IS INHERENTLY SATISFYING
(ESPECIALLY REAL WORK)

When one examines the major differences between "good" and "bad" characters on TV, proportionally a higher number of "good" characters hold legitimate jobs. Moreover, of all working characters, the "good" ones are more likely to find satisfaction in their professions beyond the acquisition of money and power. The contrast between the 1980s serial *Falcon Crest*'s Angela Channing (a not-nice character who is forever scheming and making new power plays in the wine business) and Chase Gioberti (a decent character who is continually concerned about his vineyards) exemplifies this division. On *Melrose Place*, the good, working-class mechanic Jake even breaks off a romance with the scheming entrepreneur, Amanda, thus demonstrating this correlation between positive work ethic and moral rectitude. It is, of course, eminently important to teach "labor as its own reward" to a real world of inequitable compensation and false meritocracy. Indeed, this lesson is most powerfully conveyed by portraying already-wealthy characters driven to experience the reality of their ownership, as shown, for instance, in *Dynasty*'s very rich Dex Dexter, clad in work clothes and hard hat, laying oil pipeline. From the other side, several television plots per season revolve around a middle- or working-class character willingly foregoing "promotion" or job advancement involving more money but less "honest" work. Both Steven Keaton of *Family Ties* and Kate of *Kate & Allie*, for example, rejected job advancement for the sake of honorable considerations. More recently, *Beverly Hills 90210*'s Mr. Walsh, a good husband and parent, has on more than one occasion put his family before his job. In fact, basically good characters are often moved to give away ill-gotten riches (as when the very poor janitor in *Frank's Place* anonymously leaves thousands of criminally obtained dollars at an orphanage and thankfully resumes his post as janitor). Even the not-spotless *Roseanne* has quit a needed factory job when it meant compromising her ideals. These types of portrayals suggest that the value of work is not ultimately to be measured in the material payment received.

The above nine myths are among the many specific lessons on television encouraging the precise kind of work and spending habits benefiting the U.S. economic structure as it is currently calibrated. The myths of social mobility that follow are geared to a broader understanding and rationalization of the worker's place within that system.

Social Mobility in Television

In the United States, wealth and power are not evenly distributed, yet the relatively impoverished masses work very hard keeping the system afloat. Three interrelated messages regularly dramatized in U.S. television serve to make this system of imbalanced conditions acceptable to those who might otherwise find cause to object.

MYTH 1: THERE'S ROOM AT THE TOP

This first message emerges in television's distorted portrayal of the socioeconomic structure; that is, real-life statistics are distorted. Content-analysis research has borne out time and time again that the world of television is dominated much more by middle- to upper-class people than is American real life. Poorer people are simply not represented too often. Similarly, the occupations of television characters tend to lean far more to the professional, if not glamorous, side of the employment spectrum, whereas the masses of everyday workers who are needed for the overall real-life system are not proportionally portrayed. Although such "misrepresentations" might be "explained away" in a variety of ways (Thomas,

1986), it can be argued that the relatively heavy-viewing American public is being taught indirectly that wealth is more plentiful than it really is. High school seniors might be more inclined to apply to Harvard if they believe there are 5,000 openings rather than 800. In the maintenance of the social order, widespread belief in a roomier upper echelon might also suggest that the possibilities of upward social mobility are good. This sort of message, then, sets the stage for social mobility myth 2.

MYTH 2: ANYONE CAN ACHIEVE

Another theme popular in U.S. television is that, given the wide-open arena suggested in social mobility myth 1, anyone has a decent chance of accomplishing upward social mobility. Considering the continuing characters of U.S. TV drama, the majority of those who are wealthy or "better off" are portrayed as not having been born that way. Some have worked their way up (e.g., George Jefferson, Jonathan Hart, the Huxtables), some have married money (e.g., Krystle Carrington of *Dynasty* or Suzanne Sugarbaker of *Designing Women* and *Women of the House*), and some have vastly compounded a smaller fortune (e.g., Blake Carrington). TV news and interview programming similarly recounts such stories by chronicling the climbs to fame of celebrities such as Sylvester Stallone and Roseanne, and by publicizing the awarding of grand sums to formerly poor lottery winners.

In all, television may give us the decided impression that upward social mobility is quite feasible; however, this is not where television's ideological "story" ends. The ending is not always a happy one, and characters most definitely fall. The third social mobility myth makes the equation complete by indicating where trouble may be found.

MYTH 3: IT'S NOT SO GREAT AT THE TOP

As described, television suggests that there is a wide-open area for upward mobility to which everyone has a decent chance to ascend. These myths provide hope for the future, but they are not necessarily sufficient for the present. A message that can temper immediate hostility is dramatized in the third myth—that it's not so great at the top. This message may be translated in several ways, such as "Money doesn't buy happiness," "You can live on love," or "Wealth/power corrupts."

In daytime-television serials, the poorer families usually display a loving harmony that is in stark contrast to the interpersonal conflicts found within the very wealthy families. During prime time, misery and constant trauma await the Ewings of *Dallas*, the Carringtons of *Dynasty*, and so on, but the Waltons, the Ingallses, Dr. Quinn and her family, and others of their ilk are essentially at peace (Thomas & Callahan, 1982). Indeed, one of the reasons that nighttime serials may concentrate on the rich is that serialization requires "running" problems—serious complications—that can continue from episode to episode. Such problems on television are largely confined to the wealthy. Poorer or middle-class people are usually placed in contexts (often comedic) in which their problems can be resolved in half an hour. Still, even in comedy, the distinction between the evil rich and the decent poor can sustain as in, for instance, the contrast between the Simpson family and their show's Mr. Burns.

Made-for-TV movies also keep this myth alive by presenting many sentimental stories of poor people surviving in loving harmony. Similarly, many scenarios—particularly in docudramas—show characters who cannot find happiness in supposed wealth and success (e.g., variations on the "poor little rich girl" theme). Often these movies take viewers into the world of glamour, power, and wealth, and portray that terrain as insidiously treacherous. It seems that the only happy wealthy characters on TV are those who live below their means while doing good deeds (e.g., *Diff'rent Strokes's* Mr. Drummond or Commissioner McMillan of *McMillan and Wife*) and/or those who enrich their lives by risking death weekly (e.g., Jonathan and Jennifer Hart).

Again, the message in question is not limited to TV fiction, but appears quite regularly in news and documentary programming. Sonny Von Bülow is still technically alive in a coma, but this high-society matron's sad destruction received coverage hundreds of times more powerful and lengthy than that given to the numerous other victims of violent crime. The murder of the wealthy "Scarsdale Diet doctor," Herman Tarnower, by the headmistress of a private school was one of the few stories that competed with the Von Bülow saga. Barbara Walters interviewed all the relevant players; the network news took viewers into the very exclusive Newport, Rhode Island, and Scarsdale, New York, estates to query neighbors and show the "trouble in paradise." Most recently, the O.J. Simpson murder trial is frequently understood to portray the dark and downside of the fast-and-loose life that follows great and celebrated wealth. Clearly, it is not that we are taught especially to mourn Sonny Von Bülow or Herman Tarnower, or people like them; rather, the lesson is that wealth has an unseemly side, no matter how atypical the object lesson may be.

Collectively, what the three myths of social mobility provide is a rationalization for lives that are less than glamorous, powerful, or wealthy. Although viewers are taught to have hope if wealth and its concomitants are what they really desire, they are simultaneously instructed to be grateful for the prices they don't have to pay.

A Final Note

In recent years, much attention has been paid to the problems involved with pay television and VCRs. What is happening, it is asked, to the "business of television" when viewers can watch for hours without being confronted with advertisements, or when they can electronically zap the commercials? Clearly, if the concern is with the selling of specific products and/or the welfare of specific companies, such questions are pertinent. However, to the extent the concern is with a general decommercialized broadcasting system—a concern with the possible elimination of bourgeois consumerism—such worries would seem to be unfounded. American "entertainment" television, with or without commercials, contains a very rich economic lesson plan, as has been detailed in the list of myths presented here.

In a sense, the myths *about* television—that it is mindless entertainment, the only persuasive moments of which occur in advertisements and candidate debates—conspire with the myths *in* television. Capitalism is sold in our living rooms on a daily basis. However, in a society long wary of the hard sell, the most persuasive educational forum is probably one that seemingly offers only relaxation and choice.

Further Questions

1. Are some groups in the audience—such as men or women, recent immigrants or long-term citizens—more likely than others to accept the myths discussed in this chapter?

2. What, if any, experiences have you had that contradict these myths? How do people you know deal with the conflicts between their lives and television's "reality"?

3. Are these myths stable over time? Are there any new or alternative myths emerging?

27 Sport and the Spectacle

MICHAEL REAL

With Real's analysis of sport and media in the United States, we reach the final insights of this volume—last, but not least, for sports are of passionate concern to vast numbers of people, and are followed these days more through television than in personal attendance. Along with music, sport engages the great majority of the public. Understanding mass communication without attention to sports coverage is practically impossible. Many popular newspapers, whose readership is often despised by elitist cultural critics, are bought for the sports coverage much more than for the news pages, which are hardly glanced at most days.

Real analyzes the appeal of media sports and of sport in popular culture overall in terms of certain myths. His use of the term myth is different from that of Sari Thomas in Chapter 26. Thomas uses it to denote a popular belief based on weak or nonexistent foundations in reality. Real uses the term to denote the power of certain beliefs in our imagination and daily lives. Thomas uses myth in the sense of an unfounded viewpoint; Real uses it in the sense of a culturally established belief. Both use the word to pinpoint a strong formative influence.

Real distinguishes between conventional cultural analyses of sport, which see it simply as a good training in how to behave properly in life in general, and critical approaches that stress the conflict expressed in sport, whether between the management and the players, in the endorsement of violent behavior, or through the near exclusion of women. Most of his argument, however, is devoted to exploring the excitement and pleasure that sport offers its audiences. Real proposes that, whether in the process of identifying with a player or a team or in the enjoyment of suspense and tension ("liminality"), competitive sport is a mixed form of communication, like so many others commented upon in this volume. It offers release at the same time it provides confirmation about the status quo, a fantasy of achievement against the odds as well as an acknowledgment of the conflicts built into everyday social relations.

Mass-mediated sporting events often echo the various themes discussed in the pages of this volume. They are popular cultural products somewhat reflective of the dominant political economy, technologically transmitted, and received by active audiences. The high holidays of our culture are celebrated in the spectacles of media sports.

Why are mediated sports so popular? "The thrill of victory—the agony of defeat." Few experiences in life are sweeter than the taste of a well-earned victory in a sporting event. Even vicarious participation in a great victory can bring incredible exhilaration. Through the mass media, millions and even billions of viewers, listeners, and readers are brought immediately into the experience of a great sports performance. Many read the sports pages of the newspaper first—indeed, many read no other part of the paper. Diego Maradona and Michael Jordan, Monica Seles, announcers, agents, sponsors, networks—the ensemble of all media link mass communication with personal experience and bring us into a collective process. In that process, the emotional power of the gymnastic perfection of an Olga Korbut, Nadia Comaneci, or Mary Lou Retton, especially as enhanced by slow-motion video and musical sound track, can take your breath away or bring tears to your eyes. The fans of the New York "Miracle Mets" baseball franchise in 1969, through a decade of intense suffering with the sport's most miserable team, knew what it meant to feel a triumph was "earned." The feelings of sheer joy, of energy and control, of disciplined performance and expressiveness can carry immense power, even to a spectator at home. Of course, the more negative feelings of defeat, of having a victory snatched away, of performing poorly under pressure, the feelings of rejection and dejection, come along with the games as well.

What has critical communication research taught us of the central meaning and value of these experiences of a sports event received through the media of mass communication? What are some of the contending positions on how media and sport relate to the broader society? What kind of critical concepts does cultural studies analysis bring to the study of the sports media phenomenon? How does "mythic analysis" take us inside the social experiences and internal meaning of these ritual experiences of sport spectacles on media? "Stay tuned, sports fans, for answers to these and other exciting questions right after these commercial announcements."

Contending Positions:
Critical Versus Conventional

Cultural studies analysis generally regards the media experience as a text to be analyzed, whether a Shakespearean stage production, an episode of a TV series, or a major ball game. When a cultural studies approach is used to examine the topic of sports and media, it takes the subject apart as if it were an exotic and previously unknown tribal ritual in a foreign land. Rich in myth and ritual, the sports media wonderland provides a revealing text for cultural studies analysis. Myths and rituals take the dominant tendencies in a culture and sacralize them in a popular and repeatable form through which members of the culture can celebrate their common values. Shaquille O'Neal mythically represents superhero achievement, and a First Division or National Basketball Association game ritually celebrates such ideals and more.

In contrast to the cultural studies approach, conventional media theory approaches the issue of sports and media primarily in terms of quantifiable data. The basic questions of conventional theory concern phenomena, especially behavior changes, that are measurable. How many individuals viewed one television program? Is the cost of 30 seconds of advertising time justified by resulting changes in consumer behavior? What were the payments from networks to teams? These are more administrative (Lazarsfeld, 1941) and conventional (Smythe, 1981) styles of media research. This mainstream tradition of American behavioral science and ideology has generally dominated media studies in the United States for the past half century. Conventional research asks these smaller questions of more limited significance and answers them very precisely. Critical research, such as cultural studies analysis, asks larger questions that are answerable only through careful use of data, observation, reasoning, analysis, and criticism. Why do so many watch? Who profits from media sports? What values are reinforced or suppressed?

Theories of sport and society parallel the above distinctions between conventional and critical theory. Conventional theories of the relation-

ship between sports and the social order avoid criticism. They emphasize instead the usefulness of sport in integrating youth into the
cultural value of sports interests as recreational and entertainment
outlets. An extreme form of this theory appears in the gentlemanly
mythology to which Pierre de Coubertin, founder of the modern
Olympic Games, and others have subscribed. In this view, sports
teaches manly virtues and provides general vigor among the populace,
useful in work, school, business—and warfare.

Critical cultural theories of sport and society emphasize more the
conflict side of sport competition within the power relationships in
society. Whatever positive social integration sports accomplish, they
also injure people, create antagonisms among fans, encourage passive
consumption, pit owners against players, endorse male domination,
and in some cases encourage violence. The pressure to win has
abolished the traditional Grantland Rice stanza, "It matters not if you
win or lose, but how you play the game." Instead, coaches admonish
players, "Show me a good loser and I'll show you a loser" or "Nice guys
finish last."

In the following analysis, I draw data from conventional theory but
then utilize a cultural studies approach to attempt to define and
explain the fundamental dimensions of human experience and culture
at work in mass-mediated sports events. Cultural studies analysis
explores sports media in terms of its cultural importance, personal and
collective identity, archetypes, liminality, and related mythic and
ideological dimensions.

Ritual and Ideology in Media Sports

The massive spectacles of the World Cup, the Super Bowl, the
World Series, the NBA Play-Offs, the Olympics, college football, and
Wimbledon tennis all comprise texts replete with signs, codes, myths,
and ideology. Each takes in hundreds of millions of dollars from
television revenues and dominates national sports news for days or
weeks. These dominating cultural celebrations, and their numerous
lesser counterparts, are central expressions and forces in our society.

Media sports provide dominant myths in modern culture. In any
culture, myths first provide a perceptual system that produces the
common social understandings; media sports concretize the "common
sense" of our culture. Second, myths present exemplary models that

present a single life history as an "archetype" and pattern for imitation; media sports provide heroes. Third, myths present binary oppositions and conflict negotiation as they reduce history to intelligible patterns; media sports locate us in space and time through whichever teams we cheer on. Media analysts Breen and Corcoran (1982) conclude, "The analysis of the mythical dimension of telemediated messages allows us to more fully appreciate how we are shaped into what our culture considers to be moral creatures by both the form and content of television programming" (p. 133).

Media sports rituals are building blocks in larger cultural and ideological orientations. As O'Connor and Downing indicate in Chapter 1, one view of **culture** sees it as playing a role as social cement, helping to maintain the boundaries and definition of a group; culture is thus connected to the maintenance of social order and political power. In its mythic ritual configurations, sport is one part of the cultural whole. In performing cultural functions, sport also reflects and influences at least indirectly individuals' "ideologies," or systematic sets of ideas and priorities. Media sports tend to be conservative in nature, usually accepting rather than questioning the status quo. Today, major sports reproduce many of society's dominant cultural tendencies and are relayed through technologies developed in specific contexts. Filtered by a series of control mechanisms, major media sports today often foreground particular representations of gender, race, commerce, and transnationalization. Media experiences channel us, and mass-mediated sports play a role in this process alongside music, film, TV news, computers, and other media described in this book.

CULTURAL IMPORTANCE

The first noteworthy feature of the text of media sports is the obvious importance that we "natives" place on this ritual activity. Rituals are the repeated activities that act out myths. Just as important native rituals come to dominate for a few hours or days or weeks the life of a traditional village, so the televised football, baseball, basketball, hockey, or other major games take on central importance for whole communities and regions during specific periods. Fans schedule their lives on certain days, especially Saturdays and Sundays, around televised sports. They wear team colors when feelings are intense, at home as well as in the stadium. They spend valuable time and money reading sports pages to stay informed and in touch with their teams and stars. As U.S. radio commentator Bob Edwards (1987) has noted: "Many Americans are obsessed with sports. They follow their favorite team with racing hearts and trembling wallets."

The economics of media sports also illustrates the central importance of these mythic rituals to our culture. Samuelson (1989) estimates that Americans spend more than $60 billion annually on sports. That figure includes spectator sports that we watch ($7.2-$8.2 billion), recreational sports that we play ($46-$48 billion), and sports gambling ($7.4 billion lost on $56 billion bet). Media access to and promotion of sports is central to all those figures. One television network, CBS-TV, entered the 1990s with $2.2 billion worth of rights contracts to major sporting events; this included $1.1 billion for four years of major league baseball, $543 million for the 1992 and 1994 Winter Olympics, $450 million for three years of professional football, and $50 million and $56 million, respectively, for a year of professional and college basketball. Being a star in media sports in the United States means receiving an income in six or seven figures. A vast amount of resources, technology, money, energy, and time in America is given over to mediated sports.

PERSONAL IDENTIFICATION WITH COMPETITORS

Sports fans invariably root for one side in any competition. They identify with teams, players, regions, or whatever, so that outcomes take on personal significance for them. Mythic rituals in tribal and ancient cultures played this same role. The individual joining in the chant and dance around the ritual fire was united with the entire history and identity of this group of people. Social psychology has pointed out how personal identification with a group occurs when the self-identity of a person takes on the ideas and attitudes of the larger group. This "generalized other" of group identity then becomes the norm for social activity. Thus when a fan cheers the Chicago Bears or Toronto Blue Jays or Liverpool, that person takes on an additional identity and frame of reference beyond her or his immediate physical existence. A "fan" identifies with a competitor and cares about the outcome; the result is "us against them." Sports fans identify with "their" teams or stars and, through media, acquire information and understanding about them and feel emotional identification with them.

HEROIC ARCHETYPES AND EXEMPLARY MODELS

Media sports center attention on specific individuals who, through this process, become larger-than-life heroes and models for successful conduct. Just as in ancient Greece Theseus conquered the Minotaur and became a hero to all Athens, so Joe DiMaggio, a famous baseball player, not only set a record for the major leagues by hitting safely in 56 straight games, he also went on to marry (however briefly) another media legend, Marilyn Monroe, and even took on iconic significance with a mention in Paul Simon's song "Mrs. Robinson" and with appearances in Mr. Coffee television ads.

Carl Jung (1968) examined in detail the power of archetypes to reveal and control human psychology and life. Archetypes, in his argument, are idealized heroes or themes handed down through the collective unconscious of the human race. Sports today, in our mass-mediated culture, provide superstar archetypes to spur the imagination and dominate the ideals of youth and adult alike. In a media-saturated age, celebrity is not always a positive experience. At times these sports heroes seem to feel like Prometheus, chained to a high, craggy rock for having brought the gods' fire down to humans. Sports lets fans see not only great deeds but also the deflation of heroes in their bad moments, the failure of authority in crisis—reassuring experiences for common people all too aware of their own limitations. Subconsciously we may reflect, "If Diego Maradona or Mike Tyson or Pete Rose cannot control his personal life, perhaps my life is not so bad." Sports pages today examine the heroes in minute detail, warts and all, outlining details of greedy contracts, after-hours drug abuse, gambling, and energetic sex lives, but sports heroes and their motivating power over others live on.

Issues of feminism are especially obvious in mediated sports. Far fewer female than male heroes are held up for emulation, though women have received increasing coverage in sports media and have won some well-publicized competitions. The famous "battle of the sexes" in 1973 pitted a mouthy 55-year-old ex-Wimbledon champion and tennis hustler, Bobby Riggs, against female tennis champion Billie Jean King. Riggs had publicly charged that women tennis players were inferior and overpaid and that, even at his age, he could beat the best of them. On Mother's Day, he had managed to triumph over Margaret Court. King then accepted his challenge and, in front of the largest live audience ever to attend a tennis match and a vast television audience in 36 nations, resoundingly defeated Riggs 6-4, 6-3, 6-3. In so doing, mythically King became a modern Atalanta, able to compete with men in their own games, as had that fleet-footed maiden of ancient Greece. Princess Atalanta had been promised by her father as a bride to the winner of a lengthy footrace, but Atalanta herself entered the race and won, retaining her independence. Also following Atalanta, King was forced later to endure widely reported criticisms without once retreating in embarrassment.

In general, women have been largely excluded from the spotlight of modern sports media, and have often been stereotyped when represented, but they have been making substantial progress in recent years despite numerous continuing obstacles. Whatever the representation, fans become one in spirit with the great warriors of sports and rise with them to unimagined heights or fall tragically, dashed on the rocks. In either case, they are taken far beyond the desultory limits of routine, everyday life.

THE ADVENTUROUS QUEST

The great quest of Jason for the Golden Fleece and the wanderings of Odysseus for 20 years provide prototypes for the adventurous quest of athletes for the laurel wreath of victory. Predictable, easy victories carry little impact, but true struggle and deserved success have epic power. When Roger Bannister in 1954 became the first runner to break the once thought unreachable goal of a four-minute mile, millions felt as one with him as they heard of it on the radio or read it in the newspaper. Humans can overcome limits. Our seemingly fantastic quests can come to fruition.

Sports' privileged position as seemingly disconnected with the everyday world is both essential to its attraction and a source of danger. The quest can take on a negative side. Advertising and consumer culture, for example, has thoroughly infiltrated sports and can turn the stereotypical sports couch potato into a largely passive consumer of games, contests, and products (see also Kellner, Chapter 19). Similarly, although the world of sports seems to favor African American athletes, such publicity can set thousands of youths on an unrealistic search for the Holy Grail of professional athletics at the expense of every other career goal they might consider. As Ash Corea describes in Chapter 20, racism remains deep in the structure of power and control of media, despite the outward successes of many minority entertainers and athletes. The influence wielded by successful sports adventures can thus have both positive and negative cultural consequences.

At a distance, through the media, the sports fan shares the athlete's quest to overcome personal limits, to perform flawlessly, to defeat the opponent, to achieve the trophy. A Joe Carter World Series-winning home run, a Steffi Graf final service ace, a World Cup-winning goal—each can inspire wild cheering and remain etched in memory. The adventurous quest for achievement is basic to the human search for meaning, and media sports can carry us off on that quest each season, each day, each hour.

MARKING SPACE AND TIME

Who we are is intrinsically wrapped up with where we sense we are and with the point in history at which we see ourselves living. Traditionally, myth and ritual have played central roles in defining human place and time. The "sacred" places and times of tribes in Australia defined a most important sense of identity for members of Aboriginal society. Olympus was where the Greek gods dwelled, Mecca is the pilgrimage center of Islam, and the Vatican is the home of worldwide Roman Catholicism. In terms of time, the sabbath marks a day of worship and withdrawal from normal activities of work, Ramadan and Lent designate periods of commemorative observances during which fasting takes precedence over feasting, and worship sets aside certain moments and hours of the day as sacred.

In a secular culture, "special" times and places are increasingly marked off by media. The ritual darkness and popcorn of the movie theater, the exuberance of the rock concert, the intimacy of romantic music in the car, the togetherness of family television viewing—these become the special times and places where routine, regularized human existence is broken into by a higher power.

Media sports provide spatial orientation. Today the sources of geographic pride in a school, a city, or a country are often found in sports teams and events. Romanian gymnasts and Ethiopian runners mark the identity of those countries. Chicago is the Bears, Bulls, Hawks, Sox, and Cubs; Pittsburgh is the Pirates and Steelers; Boston is the Celtics and Red Sox. UCLA will forever be the school where John Wooden won nine NCAA basketball titles. Nebraska and Oklahoma would secede from the union if college football were abolished. Try to imagine Notre Dame University without football. Citizens may not take pride in their political representatives, their educational systems, their business communities, their transportation or public services, but insult their sports franchises and you may well have a fight on your hands. The stadium, field house, and whatever-dome are the sacred destiny of pilgrims and the center of public attention for quasi-holy rituals.

Time is similarly marked off by sports events. The high holiday of American media is the Super Bowl, followed by comparable secular holy days for the World Series, NBA and NCAA finals, Stanley Cup, Triple Crown, Masters' tournament, championship fights, and others. In Britain it is the Cup Final, the Test series, and Wimbledon. *Seasons* refers as much to sports seasons as annual weather cycles in contemporary discourse. "Sacred time" is the season, day, or hour when our team is playing, whether or not we also go to church or temple or mosque for more traditionally sacred observances. Media-distributed sports have become psychosocial centers of gravity, the fulcrums around which other aspects of our social and personal lives are organized.

BINARY OPPOSITIONS

The influential French anthropologist Claude Lévi-Strauss (1967) argued for the importance of identifying the fundamental two-sided conflicts, or binary oppositions, in traditional folktales and primitive ritual. In competitive sport there is one fundamental binary opposition, that between winning and losing. All competitive athletic preparation, strategy, and effort rises from that fundamental dichotomy.

There is an overlapping binary distinction between individual and team sports and typical gender patterns in sport. Female sports have traditionally been individual. Tennis, swimming, ice skating, golf, and gymnastics come to mind. But the dominant media sports in the United States have been team sports—baseball, basketball, football, and hockey, among others. This distinction directly correlates with the obvious underrepresentation of women in media sports. Women participate in individual sports that are less dominant in male-managed American media. And women are partially excluded from the "team" experience and connections in college sports that, according to Hennig and Jardin (1977), become an ingredient in success in later business careers and corporate boardrooms.

Another binary distinction, moving right from classical Marxism onto the sports pages, is the conflict between owners and workers, between management and labor. Who should receive the greater rewards and how much greater—those who risk the capital in the business side of sports or those who supply the labor in the manual side of sports? With television dollars creating inflation, both sides can become absurdly wealthy. Player strikes in major sports have made the sports pages read like financial pages. NFL owners cite the hefty $120,000 average annual salary of players, whereas the players' union notes the short average career in the league of only three and a half years. Sport mythology attempts at times to "transcend" this conflict by claiming "the game and the fans shouldn't suffer" because of labor-management disputes, as if the sport event itself were a fiction without real people making it work. The material reality is that one group labors and one group invests capital, and the interests of the two conflict.

A less obvious binary opposition in media sports distinguishes between playing and spectating. Once, sports were heralded for all their benefits of health and fitness to participants. But in the twentieth century, media have made access to sports at a distance the more customary and accessible form of involvement. This arms-length involvement in sports eliminates for spectators the benefits to physical health and reduces the benefits in general to psychic, emotional, and social ones. Although these benefits exist, they leave the possibility of fans' leading objectively passive and unhealthy lifestyles while fantasizing themselves into false self-images of action, vigor, and victory. Alas, the sports couch potato does exist.

Another distinction can be made between live attendance in the arena and media participation from another location. Arena attendance carries with it an environment of crowds, expressive behavior of cheering and booing, physical movement to and at the game, and other traditional experiences of the classic sports spectator. Media participation, however, isolates the fan from the event and its crowd. The media fan may share viewing with a small social group and cheer a bit but, for him or her, the event comes packaged with announcers, on-screen statistics, replays, and other "enhancements" of the arena experience. The two experiences are different, each with its own assets and liabilities. Fans sometimes make efforts to combine them. At games, for example, one can find spectators with radio earplugs, binoculars, and mini-TV sets to add on the media experience to the arena. Television viewing can take place in large social establishments, such as sports bars, where fan behavior and crowd interaction begin to resemble the arena environment.

Another valuable distinction that might be mentioned in this context is the clarification of differences between print and electronic forms of communication media. Electronic media allow instantaneous, real-time participation in a sport through television or radio. Print media—newspapers, magazines, and books—allow delayed re-presentation of sports events and facts. The latter excel at providing digests of highlights, standings, averages, schedules, and similar data and features. But electronic media capture the narrative sequence and dramatic tension of the actual sporting event while it happens. The differences among media described by Annabelle Sreberny-Moham-madi in Chapter 2 help to clarify this. The purposeful information seeker is best served by daily newspapers and *Sports Illustrated,* but the flexible thrill seeker will likely prefer ABC and ESPN. Rader (1984), in his otherwise excellent history of sports and television, argues that television, with its abundance and commercialism, has reduced and trivialized the earlier richness of the sports experience. In fact, the various media mutually support each other in sports coverage, and fans usually follow a mixture of electronic and print media. As Ien Ang explains in Chapter 12, our use of media includes all the different media, the "media ensemble" of radio, TV, newspapers, and other technologies that bring us together in this collective process.

EXPERIENCING LIMINALITY IN MEDIA SPORTS

Like traditional myths and rituals, media sports play a role in defining status and negotiating differences among people. Tribal leaders, ritual priests, initiated adolescents, prominent warriors, women elders, protected young—these and other categories of tribal society have their status ritualized and reinforced in the special festivals and celebrations of the village, which may also mark changes from one status to another.

According to anthropologist Victor Turner (1969), "liminality" is the crucial transition stage during ritual. During liminality (a word derived from the Latin for "threshold"), participants are in limbo, being neither what they were before nor what they will be afterward. The liminal stage thus provides a sense of possibility and magic and power unavailable anywhere else in social life. For example, when an adolescent is initiated into adulthood, there is often a ceremony of transition during which a group of initiates are isolated in a remote spot, are stripped of childish accouterments and made naked, are scarred or painted, and undergo trials and tests, existing for a time as no longer children but not yet adults. It is a time of heightened awe and emotional intensity from which participants will emerge permanently changed into their new social selves.

The media experience in general, and mediated sports in particular, possesses some of these qualities of liminality. The sports fan can achieve this state, this experience, either meagerly and on a trivial level in undisciplined chasing after games, or powerfully and consummately in entering knowingly and totally into the sequence of a powerful sporting event.

Imagine the transcendent power experienced by a New York Giants fan in the storybook 1951 saga of the finals. The hated cross-town rival Brooklyn Dodgers led by 13½ games on August 11. Suddenly the Giants put together winning streaks of 16 and 10 games. They managed to win their final 4 games, while the Dodgers were struggling to win only 3 of their last 7. The two teams ended the season tied. The Giants and Dodgers then split the first 2 out of 3 play-off games. Finally, in the third and final game, it was the last half of the ninth inning and the Dodgers led 4 to 1. With one out, one run in, and two men on, Bobby Thomson came to bat. The Dodgers brought in bullpen ace Ralph Branca. On his second pitch, Thomson homered into the lower left field seats of the Polo Grounds, giving the Giants a tumultuous 5 to 4 victory with his "shot heard 'round the world." Thomson's hit was the fantasy of every youthful sandlot player. The Giants' victory was the magical dream experience of every team locked in near-hopeless do-or-die travail. From the liminal insecurity of the pennant race, the Giant fan emerged transformed and transcendent, never again to lose that unparalleled memory.

The well-prepared and attentive sports fan can savor in varying degrees many such moments. The "miracle on ice" of the 1980 U.S. hockey team in the Lake Placid Winter Olympic Games was a classic. The underdog, inexperienced American team pulled off a series of last-second victories culminating in the wild final game triumph that left Al Michaels screaming, "Do you believe in miracles?" and a joyous nation limp with incredulous exhaustion. Bob Beamon's miracle long jump in the 1968 Olympics impossibly broke the world record by more than two full feet. Secretariat won the Triple Crown in horse racing with a decisiveness and grace never to be forgotten.

Unfortunately, the immature and unbalanced sports fan may emerge from the liminal experience a dangerous, even psychotic, individual, as soccer deaths and grandstand fistfighting constantly remind us. The liminal experience is powerful, a trial as well as a transformation, and not all emerge transcendent.

Sports, Power, and Ideology

Do media sports today collectively exercise hegemony favoring a particular ideology, as one might suspect from the chapters in this book on ideology, cultural determinism, media filters, control mechanisms over media professionals, TV news standardization, and other discussions of social power and representation? In many ways, often subtle, they do. The eminent Scandinavian social analyst Johan Galtung (1982) argues that big-time sports today have negative consequences in their "deep structure." He argues that, whatever its professed ideals, sport competition serves to impose Western cultural structures and standards of space, time, knowledge, nature, and competitive relationships. Cohesive, less differentiated, traditional societies learn from televised sports the more aggressive, competitive, fragmented, instrumental, exploitative style of modern sports provided by mass media. Everything is measured quantitatively and compared against absolutes. In Galtung's view, modern sports in their deep structure are not value-free recreation but a training field for Westernized lifestyles and value systems, sometimes even promoting aggressive nationalism and militarism.

Internationally, developing countries have far fewer possibilities for creating televised sports than do industrialized countries (see Hamelink, Chapter 17), just as there is less access to new technologies on the part of the information poor (see Demac, Chapter 16). The technology is operated by professional routines and codes in set narrative formats (see Rodríguez, Chapter 8; Williams & Miller, Chapter 24). The result is increasingly a transnationalized commercial product, as described by Denis McQuail (Chapter 9) and Douglas Kellner (Chapter 19). And this is important: As Sari Thomas argues in Chapter 26, media experience educates as well as entertains; because of this, media sports have real consequences.

Like religion, sports have often been used for political purposes, to prepare nations for war rather than to prevent warfare and other destructive behavior. Sports can be no more healthy than the general culture and ideology of which they form a part, and as a form of mythic and ritual behavior, must also be controlled by our reason. Critical thinking through cultural studies and mythic analysis opens up many of the inner dimensions of the experience of sports and media. Conventional research and data provide a shell of information that is necessary but somewhat rudimentary. Understanding sports, media, and spectacle can allow us to reveal both details and generalizations about our specific culture and our general humanity. This can protect us from damage and excess as well as enhance and extend our appreciation.

Further Questions

1. How does media packaging of sports, with technical devices such as multiple camera angles and slow-motion instant replays and "expert" commentary, change spectators' experience of sporting events?

2. What is the economic power of television in the Olympics and other sporting events? Why do some sports receive intensive coverage and others not? Is it simply a matter of the level of public interest in certain sports?

3. Why do sports commentators and others often identify success in international sporting contests with success for a nation, rather than success for the individual or the team? Why is national pride so strongly bound up with sporting prowess? Does it need to be?

Epilogue

Our essential tasks in compiling this reader have been to select areas of current communications research and inquiry and to present each as an arena of debate, not of fixed knowledge. In each chapter different perspectives and problems about some area of media have been raised. In a sense, the more we know, the more there is to explore and question.

We also hope that you now have some sense of why a critical, questioning stance is necessary, and of the importance of some of the problems that need to be posed. While we have mapped out many major issues, there are many other areas we have not addressed and questions we have not raised. You can develop your own agenda of issues and research projects, using the suggestions at the end of each chapter and developing your own.

One last comment: It is also important to think about what it is you are invited to think about and know while in college. What counts as the "curriculum," what subjects can you study, what perspectives are you introduced to? And, by implication, what subjects do not count, what topics do not appear in your syllabi, what perspectives are rarely discussed? Why is this? You should remember that the university also reflects interests and positions of different groups in society, and what they have come to value over time. But what is useful or important knowledge in a society also alters, and is often the subject of debate and controversy. Currently at many colleges debates are taking place about integrating more materials written by women and people of color, and cross-cultural perspectives, into different areas of the curriculum. Knowledge is not of a fixed truth, nor is it neutral.

What is defined as "knowledge," as established fact, often tends to support particular interests, and so it is always important to ask, *Why should we know this, and whom does such knowledge serve?*

We could ask, Who benefits from communications research? Does academic research "help" the industry, the audience, or no one at all except the academics themselves? Does this matter? We are not arguing that all knowledge must be directly practical, or even that all perspectives are equally valid and important. We are inviting you to think and talk about how universities package knowledge and the relationship of different groups to that knowledge, especially in the field that we are most interested in, media studies. Even think about how publishers package knowledge, what a textbook means by way of fixing in students' minds what is "reasonable" to say, and what "unreasonable," and whether in this book we have covered the most important and relevant issues. We obviously think so, but that is a valid topic of critical debate!

Now perhaps you understand better how the media are connected with economic forces, political processes, and cultural values and products in our society. We hope that this book will be the beginning of debates for you, not the end.

Glossary

affiliate: In this context, an affiliate is a local television station that contracts with one of the networks to take its programs plus the commercials the network has attached to them. An affiliate is not necessarily bound, as are a network's own stations, to use a network's entire programming. In the 1980s, certain major cable operators, such as Cable News Network and Turner Network Television, began to develop similar network-affiliate relationships with cable stations across the United States. These businesses are called *multiple system operators* (MSOs). See also Chapter 16, on new communication technologies.

agenda-setting: In general usage, an agenda is the list of items, usually in order of priority, to be discussed at a committee meeting. It is also any list of topics to be addressed. The agenda-setting approach sees news media as powerful because of their ability to define for us which events are most important and are therefore news, and which are not. Are women's rights important? Is the environment important? Are traffic fatalities or the love life of a TV star more important? Which gets prominence in news media coverage? People who see the media as having an agenda-setting function say this: News media power is based not so much on how the media interpret events to us as it is on the sheer fact that they can set our agenda of things to think about in the first place. See also **gatekeepers** and Chapters 5 and 25.

anarchism: This is a political philosophy and also a type of political activism, the modern origins of which lie in mid-nineteenth-century Europe. Anarchists typically believe that power should be decentralized so that government can be close enough to people for them to exercise effective control over their representatives. They do not, in spite of what is often claimed, advocate anarchy in the sense of chaos. Socialist anarchists are opposed both to the capitalist economic system and to centrally organized government, including communist government. Many anarchists are not socialists. There is not a great deal of uniformity of belief among anarchists. See also **communism, Marxism,** and **socialism,** and Chapter 14.

audience: The audience has been defined four ways: (a) as a mass, (b) passively, (c) actively, and (d) economically. (a) As a mass, the audience is understood as a collection of individuals whose primary connection is to the media, not to each other by way of friendship, family, or work ties (see mass). (b) The passive sense, rather close to the mass sense, indicates that people simply soak up whatever the media offer them. In strong versions of this view, the media are seen as all-powerful over the audience. (c) The active sense indicates that people make up their own minds about what the media present them with, often generating their own interpretations of the media text. In strong versions, the audience is seen as able to bend the media text to its own outlooks and concerns. (d) The economic definition sees the audience simply as consumers, people whose attention the media "delivers" over to advertisers so that corporations can make their sales pitches. See also **negotiation, reception theory,** and **uses and gratifications,** and Chapters 12, 13, 19, 21, and 26.

cable: (a) Cable is a communication transmission technology that uses primarily land lines, thus improving the quality of TV reception. Cable stations increasingly use fiber-optic cables, which are highly accurate and very fast, and can deal with very large volumes of traffic at a time. This makes them invaluable for any form of computerized transmission. Cable can also link up with satellites. (b) This term is also used to refer to the corporations and stations that are in the business of cable transmission to the 57%, of U.S. homes that, as of 1989, were cabled. See also **affiliate** and **network,** and Chapter 16.

capital: In economic analysis, capital may mean (a) savings, of a firm or individuals; (b) a sum of money invested; (c) the wealth of a corporation in money, machines, property, land, shares, or bonds (all bar labor power); (d) the value that labor produces on behalf of the corporation; (e) the long-term economic and political strategy (i.e., over decades and even centuries) of capital owners taken as a class, whether in a nation or among transnational corporations. The first three uses of the term are common in conventional economics; the latter two are used in critical and Marxist political economy. See also

capitalism, corporation, and **cultural capital,** and Chapters 5, 6, 13, and 19.

capitalism: This term is defined in several ways: (a) an economic system distinguished from feudalism and slavery by the fact that those who work are legally entitled to walk off the job when they choose (even though immediate financial hardship often keeps them from doing so); (b) an economic system defined by its competitive and efficient nature, which pushes each corporation to reinvest part of its profits in developing new methods of production and new products; (c) an economic system defined by its combination of innovation, expansion, and skillful but often merciless exploitation of labor; (d) the general way of life and cultural patterns of a capitalist society, such as the reduction of all aspects of living—health care, wildlife, creativity, information—to the prices they can fetch. Definitions a and b are most common in writing favorable to capitalism; definitions c and d, in writing critical of it. Today capitalism is overwhelmingly a global economic system. See also **corporation** and **transnational**.

censorship: This is the practice of forbidding publication or broadcast of certain views, words, and/or images. The source may be governments or other agencies, such as religious authorities, workplace managements, or school boards. Censorship may operate through the vetting of a text before it goes out ("prior restraint") or through various forms of punishment after the fact (threats, demotion, firing, fines, imprisonment, closing the newspaper or broadcast station, execution). See also **self-censorship** and Chapters 5 and 7.

class: This term describes a group of people defined in one of two ways: (a) by their similar social and financial standing (as in *middle class*) or (b) by their mutual relationship in the economic process (e.g., whether they plan manufacturing and banking and direct the economic process or carry out the process). The latter sense is integral to Marxist approaches, where the relation between the corporate classes and the working classes is seen as influencing all spheres of society, including culture and communication. Some analysts have seen this influence as very tight, others as much looser. See Chapters 1, 5, 6, 13, 17, 19, 22, and 26.

commodity: Anything that becomes an object to be sold, be it food, sex, recreation, cars, or drama, is a commodity. Some critical analysts (e.g., Kellner, Chapter 19; Gandy, Chapter 13) argue that modern capitalism reduces all aspects of life to commodities to be bought and sold, the process of "commodification."

communication: (a) A classical model of communication is that of the transmission process, using the analogy of the electrical circuit. "Who says what by which channel to whom?" is a standard version, which tends to imply that communication is individualized and one-way, that is, not interactive. (b) A second model defines communication as a sharing process, necessarily based upon a common culture and its codes if it is to take place at all. (c) A third model focuses upon the processes and institutions—mainstream and alternative—by which communication is produced, which stresses the cultural production of mass communications.

communism: This term can be used to refer to (a) the political belief in the practical possibility of moving toward a fair and equitable economic and political system, originally based on the analyses of Marx and Engels; (b) the political and economic institutions of the former Soviet Union and nations strongly influenced by that model; or (c) the varying left-wing political parties and movements in favor of either of the above in countries without Soviet-type institutions. See also **anarchism, capital, capitalism, Marxism,** and **socialism,** and Chapters 5 and 11.

community: A community may be formed by (a) a group of people defined by their common recognition of their mutual geographic bonds (e.g., a village or city neighborhood) or by their professional or cultural interests (e.g., journalists, computer hackers, sports fans); or by (b) a group of people perceived to have mutual bonds (e.g., "the international community," "the financial community") who are in fact generally in some form of conflict with one another. This use of the term often masks, deliberately or unthinkingly, these conflicts.

consumer society/consumerism: People who buy products are consumers. Some critical analysts have argued that modern capitalist economics is powered by the attempt to get us to consume more and more, whether we really need to or not, and that both advertising and consumer credit (e.g., use of credit cards) are part and parcel of the same drive. See Chapters 19 and 26.

copyright: This is the legal right of the creator to control who makes money out of his or her cultural invention—a TV series idea, a computer program, a book, a song—by copying it. As more and more cultural products are stored digitally in computers, and as more and more photocopy machines are available, policing this right has become extremely difficult.

corporation/corporate: A corporation is a firm, usually a giant firm, sometimes producing many different things, sometimes almost monopolizing one product area. Many media corporations are also involved in other areas, such as General Electric, which owns NBC and its affiliate TV and radio stations along with many other firms in other sectors. For a long time in the United States, AT&T monopolized telephones and IBM monopolized computers, and both are still dominant forces in these areas. The term *corporate* is often used to distinguish between nineteenth-century capitalism, when there were many small firms competing with each other, and twentieth-century capitalism, which has been dominated by giant firms. See also **transnational** and Chapters 5 and 6.

critical: As used here, this refers to questioning established opinion, querying both knowledge and the sources of knowledge, and refusing to take "authoritative views" as the last word. See also **critical theory** and the Preface.

critical theory: As used in this volume, this term refers to the perspectives associated with writers Theodor Adorno, Max Horkheimer, Herbert Marcuse, and others (sometimes known as the Frankfurt school). They tried to blend Freudian and Marxist perspectives into a critical analysis of contemporary capitalism, especially of its tendency to encourage conformist, bland communication and thinking in society at large. See Chapter 19.

cultural capital: This is a term coined by French sociologist Pierre Bourdieu to describe the cultural resources of the middle class, such as effective schooling, artistic taste, and knowledge. See Chapter 1.

cultural imperialism: Imperialism is the conquest and control of one country by a more powerful one. *Cultural imperialism* signifies the dimensions of the process that go beyond economic exploitation or military force. In the history of colonialism (i.e., the form of imperialism in which the government of the colony is run directly by foreigners), the educational and media systems of many Third World countries have been set up as replicas of those in Britain, France, or the United States and carry their values. Western advertising has made further inroads, as have architectural and fashion styles. Subtly but powerfully, the message has often been insinuated that Western cultures are superior to the cultures of the Third World. See also **identity** and Chapters 17 and 21.

cultural studies: Developed by Stuart Hall in Britain and James Carey in the United States, this critical approach to communication analysis argues that culture is an all-embracing dimension of communication, but retains major interconnections with political and economic forces. See also Chapter 1 and all chapters in Part V.

culture: This term is used in a series of different senses, for which see Chapter 1.

dependency: This is the state of many developing countries according to the argument that even after former colonies became politically independent in the middle decades of the twentieth century, they continued to be economically and culturally dependent on the Western powers and therefore heavily under the latter's influence, not least in media and communications hardware and software. See Chapters 17 and 21.

deregulation: This is the process by which governments reduce controls over broadcasting and telecommunications, whether by relaxing restrictions on broadcast station ownership, compelling monopoly communications institutions (e.g., the old AT&T telephone monopoly or French state broadcasting) to break up into separate firms, or yet other measures. The term does not mean that government stops regulation altogether. See Chapter 16.

determination/to determine: This is the process in which one event is caused by, or significantly influenced by, another. For example, in Chapter 5, Herman asks whether the ownership pattern of the U.S. media "determines" how they present the news.

discourse/discursive: This can be (a) a speech or (b) an argument or position, logical or otherwise, that has a number of interconnected views and assumptions built into it. Examples include religious discourse, engineering discourse, and sports discourse. The term focuses especially on the verbal expression of a particular position or argument. As used by French analyst Michel Foucault, it also signifies the public mode of talking about an issue (e.g., crime or sexuality), which also tends to change over time. See also **ideology** and **text**.

disinformation: This term is used to describe communication that purports to be accurate and truthful, but is in fact constructed to mislead. See also **information, propaganda, persuasion,** and **manipulation**.

elite/elitist: The elite is a small group of people in control of society as a whole, or of one segment of it. The term implies more homogeneity of outlook and policies than does the term *class*. The adjective implies the snobbish lifestyle and arrogant attitudes common within an elite.

empirical: This word describes any analysis carried out on actual situations, past or present. Critical researchers require this analysis to be shaped by an explicitly stated theory or theories; this is one of the factors that differentiates their approach from that of empiricist researchers, whose theoretical assumptions are sometimes implied rather than carefully worked out.

empiricist: Not to be confused with *empirical,* this term describes a very common approach to the study of human society in U.S. universities, so much so that other approaches often seem rather offbeat by comparison. In its simplest forms, the empiricist approach proceeds by (a) setting up certain categories of media output or audience reaction, and taking them as fixed; (b) counting how many items can be reckoned as falling within these categories; and then (c) drawing conclusions from the figures. The model for this procedure is drawn from a popular image of what physicists or chemists do in their scientific research, with the aim of making social research less subjective and more reliable—although that image has often been challenged as untrue to actual procedures in the physical sciences. A brief though oversimplified illustration would be if some members of the TV audience were to be asked, "Did you like this program a lot, a little, not at all, don't know, no response?" and their answers were then to be counted up, put in percentages, and taken as straightforward fact. Critical scholars usually argue that this kind of research tends to avoid deeper issues and complexity, and produces only superficial and trivial results.

ethnography: This is a research method, used mainly in anthropology, that is increasingly being used in communication research to study and map other cultures in detail. It usually involves a researcher's living with another cultural community over a period of time and systematically observing its way of life. People working in the cultural studies tradition consider a very important problem to be how we can properly know other cultures. See also Chapter 12.

Federal Communications Commission (FCC): This agency was originally founded as the Federal Radio Commission in 1927; its present title dates from 1934. It is the U.S. government's primary body through which to establish communications policy.

feminism: This is a social philosophy, and also a type of political activism, with its modern roots in the women's voting rights movements of the nineteenth century. Its contemporary roots in the United States are in both the women's liberation movements of the 1960s and the massive involvement of women in the workforce since 1950. Feminists are committed not only to equal rights for women in all spheres of life, private and public, but also to developing and communicating women's perspectives on all issues against male-dominated understanding of life—for example, on war and militarism, or on the value of sensitivity and nurturing in everyday relations. One does not have to be a woman to be a feminist.

gatekeeping/gatekeepers: This approach to news media sees editors in particular, and journalists in general, as deciding what is newsworthy and what is not, controlling the flow of news, selecting its priorities (agenda-setting), and rejecting news issues they do not rate as significant. As Herman notes in Chapter 5, this approach—while pointing us to many important aspects of journalistic training and decision making—generally omits the analysis of media ownership and how this may affect news output. See Chapters 5, 6, and 25.

globalization: This has become one of the key words of the 1990s. It has many connotations, among which the most significant are the following: (a) The idea of the world as a single place; Robertson (1992) suggests that we live at a time when more people have a sense of living on and sharing the planet with others (Gaia awareness) and an understanding that our local actions (e.g., environmental destruction) have consequences for distant, global, others. (b) The idea that Western modernity has extended globally; Giddens (1990) describes a fourfold structure of modernity that consists of a system of nation-states, global capitalist expansion, global media and information networks, and a system of military alliances, each of which now has a global reach. (c) The fear that global media networks and capitalist consumerism are producing a homogeneous global culture (the "McDonaldization" of the world), sometimes counterbalanced by arguments about increasing heterogeneity and difference. (d) A notion of a global civil society; this is perhaps more a hope than a reality, but it hinges on the possibility of building global solidarity for certain causes and ideas (environmentalism, human rights, feminism, and so on) and the use of global media forms (including the Internet) to build such transnational progressive social movements.

hardware: This is a general term that covers all physical communications equipment, from earphones to mainframe computers, from satellites in space to TV sets. Its corollary is software.

hegemony: A general term for dominance or control, *hegemony* has also been used more specifically by Italian social theorist Antonio Gramsci, who has been influential in critical cultural studies. As used by Gramsci, it signifies all the means of ideological leadership and dominance that a capitalist class and its allied classes, such as major landowners or professional and managerial classes, exert over wage workers. It operates together with the coercive controls of the police and military, which are deployed at those points where ideological hegemony breaks down and political movements erupt into rebellious activity. This hegemony operates through such institutions as education, religion, and the media, but not with any absolute or permanent force. See also **state** and Chapter 1.

identity: Two types of identity are of concern here: personal, psychological identity—the bundle of factors that make up an individual—and cultural identity. Cultural identity generally rests upon a common language, a shared history, a series of values or principles that are generally held to be important in living one's life, and some major symbols (e.g., the U.S. flag, the Japanese emperor system, the French Revolution) that are seen as expressing all these factors in a condensed form. However, cultural identity need not be national; also common are regional cultural identities (e.g. the U.S. South or Midwest, or Quebec in Canada), ethnic minority cultural identities, and social class cultural identities. These different identities can intersect in complicated ways. Furthermore, to add to the complexity, some scholars have argued that identity, personal or cultural, does not mean a single unified awareness of oneself or one's culture. Indeed, these varied identities are not mutually exclusive, but may all be valued in different contexts. See also Chapters 1 and 21.

ideology: This term has been used to connote both (a) a clearly defined and somewhat obnoxious and irrational viewpoint, tenaciously held by its proponents, and (b) the complex of ideas in society and their expression in social institutions, whether the military or the arts or the courts, which in turn dominate the way we live and how we understand the world around us. See also Chapter 1.

imperialism: See **cultural imperialism**.

informatics: This is a term used more in Europe than in the United States to refer to information policy and information technology; see both below.

information: As used here, this term refers to (a) a set of data or (b) electrical signals sent along a cable or through the air. See also **disinformation, information policy,** and **information technology**.

information policy: Policy regarding information is made up of government rules on (a) how open or secretive government should be with the public and (b) access to information hardware and its applications, including such issues as privacy from computerized surveillance and selling sophisticated hardware to other competitor nations.

information technology: This is a general term for computer-based communications technology, involving computer capacity for memory storage, data processing, and communication. See also Chapter 16.

Marxism: This term refers to the version of critical social analysis pioneered in the nineteenth century by Karl Marx and Friedrich Engels. It emphasizes the relations between social classes in the economic sphere as highly influential in all other social and cultural processes. Some of Marx and Engels's most famous followers pushed their argument much further, to claim economic forces as the sole determining factor in human history. Marx himself is famous for having declared that he was not a Marxist. The term also refers more generally to the state philosophy of communist countries. See also **anarchism, communism,** and **socialism.**

mass culture: This is a term used to refer to the general public's culture; it is often used with contempt. See also Chapter 1.

mass media: This term refers to media that reach many people, or the masses (also called mass communication); it may be thought of as the opposite of interpersonal communication.

mass society: Although it refers simply to the whole of a society, this term usually signifies that citizens have been reduced to separate individuals, "atomized," so to speak, and subjected to centralized one-way mass communication without the ability to communicate or organize with other people. Fascism is the clearest example, but some writers have pointed to the period of regimented political and commercial ideology during the first Cold War and the McCarthy era in the United States as an instance as well. See also Chapters 5 and 14.

media: This term, which is the plural of *medium*, has come to mean communications media specifically in many contexts: press, broadcasting, cinema, photography, video, satellites, cable, computers, photocopiers, fliers, billboards, and so on—both the physical objects and the organizations that activate them. It can also refer to virtually any object or activity as long as it carries some kind of symbolic meaning: children's toys, a wrestling match, a mathematical equation, a building, a flower. This much wider sense of the term is especially associated with French semiotician Roland Barthes.

myth: Two meanings of this term are relevant here: (a) a religious and/or heroic story expressing deeply held beliefs and emotions (see Chapter 27) and (b) an unfounded but widely accepted account of social, economic, or political reality (see Chapter 26).

negotiation: In communications analysis, this means that different understandings of reality are haggled over between different sets of people. The intended message of a TV situation comedy might be to encourage people to laugh at prejudice and bigotry as outmoded and foolish, as in the TV classics *All in the Family* with Archie Bunker (United States) or its British original *Till Death Do Us Part* with Alf Garnett. In fact, many audience members in both countries took these series as giving the green light to their own bigotry. They negotiated its officially intended meaning, in this case drastically. See also Chapter 12.

network: This term refers to a group of radio or television stations linked together; in the United States, ABC, CBS, and NBC are the three major broadcast networks, although Rupert Murdoch's Fox Broadcasting Company is a contending fourth, and various cable operators have also been endeavoring to establish effective networks. See also **affiliate** and **telecommunications network**.

orality: This term refers to the phase in the development of human communication before the full development of writing systems, when only a tiny handful of people, usually in royal courts, communicated through writing. Cultural history was therefore dependent upon the memorization of myths, poetry, and legends rather than upon being able to check written data. During this time almost all communication was conducted face-to-face.

patriarchy: This refers to the routines and mechanisms of power that males have deployed against females in the realms of ideas, everyday habits, social customs, religion, and laws, and have sustained through violence or its threat since time immemorial.

persuasion: This is the process of trying to influence other people in a particular direction, by using words, images, sounds, or their combination. The lines separating persuasion, propaganda, and information are often set by the person using the term, rather than by some absolute, generally agreed-upon criterion. This is because persuasion is thought to be acceptable, whereas propaganda and disinformation are thought to be unethical. Propaganda is something other people engage in producing, not something one admits to creating. See also **disinformation** and **propaganda**.

political economy analysis: This is an approach to social and communications analysis that stresses the interaction of political factors and economic institutions in determining communications or other processes. In critical communications research this approach is often set up as an opposing approach to cultural studies, although in this reader we have representatives of both positions, as in Chapters 1 and 5. See also **cultural studies**.

propaganda: This is the attempt to convince other people through the systematic packaging of information and manipulation of emotions, often in a form that intelligent audiences may find rather crude and unconvincing. In fact, this common definition masks the difference between crude and sophisticated propaganda, the latter sometimes referred to as *persuasion*. The dividing line is often hard to draw. See also **persuasion** and **disinformation**.

public service broadcasting: In a number of countries (e.g., Britain and Canada), broadcasting has been organized through a government corporation. In turn, this corporation has been set up at partial arm's length from the government's control of its output. The broadcasters are supposed, as professionals, to maintain independence from the government and other powerful interests, and to provide the public with a balanced diet of news, culture, education, and entertainment. This was defined as "public service" broadcasting and is the opposite of commercially based broadcasting as in the United States, where profit making determines programming and policy. According to the public service philosophy, broadcasting is a unique national resource that cannot be deployed in the nation's best interests simply by market forces. Under pressure from corporate media interests, however, this broadcasting philosophy has been under increasing attack. See also Chapter 9.

qualitative research: As applied to communications studies, this is research that concentrates on analyzing how meanings are conveyed or not, or how power operates in communication, without any attempt to study these with the aid of mathematics or statistics.

quantitative research: This is research that uses mathematics or statistics to pursue analysis. In fact, some communications research is conducted using a combination of quantitative and qualitative approaches; one need not exclude the other. See also **empiricist** and **ethnography**.

rationalization: This is the attempt to impose some rational order on a disordered situation. As used by the adherents of the Frankfurt school, this term signifies the unstoppable tendency of capitalism to blot out any human values save those of the economic market and the priorities of the power structure. Thus for Marcuse, Nazi death camps were the ultimate example of this negative rationality, with their efficient, scientific gas chambers and ovens to annihilate millions of human beings.

reception theory: This is a position that holds that the audience is active, bringing its own values and experiences to the viewing of television or reading. Thus women may react more negatively than men to TV portrayals of women, and minority ethnic group members may be angrier than members of the ethnic majority about the ways newspapers represent minorities. Variations, of course, are also very much in evidence within these groupings, not just between them. The emphasis in reception theory on what the audience does with media output sets it in direct opposition to the mass society approach. See also **audience, negotiation,** and **uses and gratifications,** and Chapter 12.

representation: This refers to the processes by which reality is conveyed in communication, through words, sounds, images, or their combination. Many critical scholars in cultural studies will argue that in fact the representation is the reality for all practical purposes. Many in the political economy mold will argue that reality cannot be simply in the mind, but makes its presence felt upon us in differential access to wealth, health care, power, and other areas of life, whether we are ready to acknowledge it or not. This is yet another round in a familiar battle among Western philosophers that has been going on since Plato and Aristotle, about how we can or do understand reality. Rather than dismiss it as pointless abstraction, you should try to think through each position carefully and why it is that people often adhere to one or the other: What are the advantages in insight that each brings?

rhetoric: In modern everyday use, this term refers to the persuasive and sometimes empty language of politicians, official spokespersons, advertising, and other communication sources. It is also the name of the study of persuasive language, dating back to Aristotle and ancient Greece. See also Chapter 2.

self-censorship: This takes place when media employees anticipate what the government, the authorities, or their editors will not wish to have communicated to the general public and decide to keep silent themselves to avoid making waves. Even in countries with censorship agencies, self-censorship is the most effective mechanism through which media output is censored on a daily basis. See also **censorship** and Chapters 6, 7, 11, and 25.

semiotics/semiology: This is the study of how signs of any kind work in society to communicate meanings. There are American, French, Italian, and Russian traditions of semiotic analysis, which do not always overlap. An important point of difference among semioticians is whether they focus strictly on dissecting the signs within a particular text, perhaps of a film or TV show, or whether they take the cultural codes of the film's context into account as well. See also Chapters 1 and 23.

socialism/socialist: This is a general term for the movement since the late 1800s for a more just and humane social order, and the different arguments and policies framed to that end. It is also used to describe political parties, in or out of government, that adopt this social order as their official goal but submit themselves to elections rather than establishing themselves by armed mass revolution (the classical credo of communists). See also **anarchism, communism,** and **Marxism**.

software: This term refers to the creative products in communications, such as computer programs, TV series, and film scripts. Its corollary is hardware.

South: This is a general term for the less economically developed countries of the planet, from their location in the Southern Hemisphere. It was coined to avoid some of the often negative connotations of the term *Third World.*

state: This term has several meanings: (a) one of the constituent units of a system having a federal government (e.g., the United States, Brazil, India, Mexico, Nigeria); (b) an independent nation; (c) the armed forces, judiciary, police forces, courts, and prisons that collectively maintain order in favor of the capitalist class (from classical Marxism). A theoretical use of the term in later Marxism, especially following Gramsci, includes communication institutions, such as the media and education, and government intervention in the capitalist economy (e.g., via the FCC) as part of the definition. This use tends to blur the distinction between public/governmental and private/business, perhaps reflecting the tendency of governments to intervene more and more in society during the twentieth century.

structure: This is a very common term in social science. Sometimes a society or an organization (e.g., a newspaper) is compared to the structure of the body—bones, veins, nerves, muscles, organs, skin. The interdependence of all the parts and their interrelated growth are therefore what is emphasized. Less frequently, the image of a bridge is used; a combination of opposing forces keeps the structure from collapsing. One way or another, the term prompts us to ask what the main elements or forces are that keep a particular society or communication institution in operation, and how they combine with each other. Alternatively, what are the elements at war with each other? See also **culture** and **system**.

subculture: This term applies to a group that represents a variant on a mainstream culture, whether merely a modified version, an opposed version, or one with little connection to the mainstream at all.

system: This is a very common term in social science. It signifies structure, but usually with the added implication that the structure is one that is functioning smoothly, not one that generates conflict. Sometimes this term is also used to alert our attention to the interaction between a social institution, such as a telecommunications corporation, and its environment of other corporations, customers, the government.

telecommunications: This includes any form of electronic information transmission using computers, telephone, telegraph, fax, cable, satellite, or microwave. The term is often reserved for nonbroadcast transmission, but it does not have to be.

telecommunications network: This is a system that links two or more points for electronic information transmission, usually involving the use of computers and telephone lines and/or satellites. See also Chapter 16.

text: This term often refers specifically to written communication, but it is also a general term for any communication, written or visual. This second meaning is used by researchers who focus upon texts' numerous strands of meaning and implied meaning. The Latin word for "woven together" is its origin.

theory: This term refers to a body of principles that attempt to develop clear, logical explanations for things. For example, a theory of media impact on the audience should try to define as clearly as possible which type of media output and which types of audiences (young, older, men, women) are involved. In the study of communications there are often competing theories, so that part of learning the subject means learning how to evaluate the strengths and weaknesses of a particular theory or theories. The everyday sense of the term involves abstract and irrelevant speculation about things, but that is not the sense intended here. There is no substitute, in the serious study of communication, for the careful theoretical analysis of communication processes. Deeper understanding is otherwise impossible.

Third World: This term was originally developed to signify (a) the less economically developed nations, and (b) the irrelevance of the Cold War between the West (the First World) and the Soviet bloc (the

Second World) to their development needs. Often today this is considered a negative term in the West because of what is seen as implied contempt for these nations' problems of poverty and instability, supposedly their own fault entirely. It also blurs the enormous variety of cultures in the Third World. See also **South**.

transnational: This term describes a giant corporation that is based in one country (typically the United States, Japan, or a Western European nation) but operates in many others. There are many such in the latter part of the twentieth century, and quite a number of them are media transnationals. Major examples at the time of this writing are Rupert Murdoch's News Corporation, AT&T, IBM, Saatchi & Saatchi Advertising, General Electric, and Sony. See also Chapter 9.

uses and gratifications: This is a term used to denote a type of media research very common in the United States in the 1950s and 1960s, and very influential since, which stressed the audience's views and preferences as determining what impact broadcasting had on them (and, by implication, on other media as well). The research methods used to study the uses made of broadcasting, and the gratifications audiences received from it, were largely empiricist. See also **audience** and **reception theory,** and Chapters 12 and 26.

References

Adams, W. C., & Heyl, P. (1981). From Cairo to Kabul with the networks, 1972-1980. In W. C. Adams (Ed.), *Television coverage of the Middle East*. Norwood, NJ: Ablex.

Adorno, T. W. (1976). *Introduction to the sociology of music*. New York: Seabury.

Adorno, T. W. (1980). On the fetish character of music and the regression of hearing. In A. Arato & E. Gebhardt (Eds.), *The essential Frankfurt school reader*. New York: Continuum. (Original work published 1938)

Adorno, T. W. (1991). *The cultural industry: Selected essays on mass culture* (J. Bernstein, Ed.). London: Routledge.

Adorno, T. W., & Horkheimer, M. (1972). *The dialectic of enlightenment*. New York: Continuum. (Original work published 1947)

Adorno, T. W., & Horkheimer, M. (1979). *The dialectic of enlightenment*. London: Verso. (Original work published 1947)

Aguayo, S. (1992, October). *Mexican human rights and electoral fraud*. Paper presented at the Center for U.S.-Mexican Studies, University of California, San Diego.

Alexander, W. (1981). *Film on the left: American documentary film from 1931 to 1942*. Princeton, NJ: Princeton University Press.

Allen, R., & Gomery, D. (1985). *Film history: Theory and practice*. New York: Knopf.

Altheide, D. (1981). Iran vs. U.S. TV news: The hostage story out of context. In W. C. Adams (Ed.), *Television coverage of the Middle East*. Norwood, NJ: Ablex.

Altschull, J. H. (1986). *Agents of power*. New York: Longman.

Anderson, B. (1983). *Imagined communities: Reflections on the origin and spread of nationalism*. London: Verso.

Ang, I. (1985). *Watching Dallas: Soap opera and the melodramatic imagination*. New York: Methuen.

Ang, I. (1990). Melodramatic identifications: Television and women's fantasy. In M. E. Brown (Ed.), *Television and women's culture: The politics of the popular* (pp. 75-88). London: Sage.

Ang, I., & Hermes, J. (1991). Gender and/in media consumption. In J. Curran & M. Gurevitch (Eds.), *Mass media and society* (pp. 307-329). London: Edward Arnold.

Arbuthnot, L., & Seneca, G. (1990). Pretext and text in *Gentlemen prefer blondes*. In P. Ehrens (Ed.), *Issues in feminist criticism*. Bloomington: Indiana University Press. (Original work published 1982)

Archer, J. (1973). *The plot to seize the White House*. New York: Hawthorne.

Ariès, P. (1962). *Centuries of childhood: A social history of family life* (R. Baldick, Trans.). New York: Vintage. (Original work published 1952)

Aronson, J. (1972). *Deadline for the media.* New York: Bobbs Merrill.

Aristotle. (1967). *The art of rhetoric* (J. H. Freese, Trans.). Cambridge, MA: Harvard University Press.

Australian Broadcasting Corporation. (1992). *Becoming Australian: A report on progress toward further representation of Australia's cultural diversity on ABC television.* Sydney: Author.

Bagdikian, B. (1983). *The media monopoly.* Boston: Beacon.

Bagdikian, B. (1987). *The media monopoly* (2nd ed.). Boston: Beacon.

Bagdikian, B. (1989). The lords of the global village. *The Nation, 248,* 805-820.

Bagdikian, B. (1992). *The media monopoly* (4th ed.). Boston: Beacon.

Ball, H. (Ed.). (1984). *Federal administrative agencies: Essays on power and politics.* Englewood Cliffs, NJ: Prentice Hall.

Ball, H. (1986). *Justice downwind: America's atomic testing program in the 1950s.* New York: Oxford University Press.

Barber, J. D. (1987, November-December). Candidate Reagan and "the sucker generation." *Columbia Journalism Review,* pp. 33-36.

Barlow, W. (in press). *Sounding out racism: The radio industry.* Washington, DC: Howard University Press.

Barnouw, E. (1978). *The sponsor.* New York: Oxford University Press.

Barthes, R. (1973). *Mythologies.* New York: Hill & Wang.

Baudrillard, J. (1988). *Selected writings.* (M. Poster, Ed.). Stanford: Stanford University Press.

Bausinger, H. (1984). Media, technology and daily life. *Media, Culture & Society, 6,* 343-351.

Beaver, F. (1983). *A history of the motion picture.* New York: McGraw-Hill.

Beharrell, P. (1993). AIDS and the British press. In Glasgow University Media Group, *Getting the message.* London: Routledge.

Bell, P. (1993). *Multicultural Australia in the media.* Canberra: Office of Multicultural Affairs.

Bennett, T. (1992). Putting policy into cultural studies. In L. Grossberg, C. Nelson, & P. A. Treichler (Eds.), *Cultural studies* (pp. 23-34). New York: Routledge.

Bennett, W. L., Gressett, L., & Haltom, W. (1985). Repairing the news. *Journal of Communication, 35,* 50-68.

Berger, A. A. (1991). *Media analysis techniques* (rev. ed.). Newbury Park, CA: Sage.

Berridge, V., & Strong, P. (1991). AIDS in the UK: Contemporary history and the study of policy. *Twentieth Century British History, 2*(2).

Beville, H. M., Jr. (1985). *Audience ratings: Radio, television and cable.* Hillsdale, NJ: Lawrence Erlbaum.

Black Rights (U.K.). (1988). *Black people, human rights and the media.* London: Author.

Block, S. (1992). Free trade on television: The triumph of business rhetoric. *Canadian Journal of Communication, 17,* 75-94.

Blumer, H. (1950). The mass, the public, and public opinion. In B. Berelson & M. Janowitz (Eds.), *Reader in public opinion and communication.* Glencoe, IL: Free Press.

Blumler, J. G. (Ed.). (1992). *Television and the public interest.* Newbury Park, CA: Sage.

Blumler, J. G., & Katz, E. (Eds.). (1974). *The uses of mass communications: Current perspectives on gratifications research.* Beverly Hills, CA: Sage.

Boorstin, D. (1962). *The image.* New York: Atheneum.

Bostock, L. (1993). *From the dark side: Survey of the portrayal of Aborigines and Torres Strait Islanders on commercial television* (Supplement to Monograph 3). North Sydney: Australian Broadcasting Authority.

Bourdieu, P. (1984). *Distinction: A social critique of the judgment of taste* (R. Nice, Trans.). Cambridge, MA: Harvard University Press.

Braestrup, P. (1977). *Big story*. Boulder, CO: Westview.

Brecht, B. (1983). Notes on the use of radio. In A. Mattelart & S. Siegelaub (Eds.), *Communication and class struggle* (Vol. 2). New York: International General.

Breen, M., & Corcoran, F. (1982). Myth in the television discourse. *Communication Monographs, 49*, 133.

Brown, J. D., Bybee, C., Wearden, S., & Straughan, D. M. (1987). Invisible power: Newspaper news sources and the limits of diversity. *Journalism Quarterly, 64*, 45-54.

Brown, M. E. (Ed.). (1990). *Television and women's culture: The politics of the popular*. London: Sage.

Burnham, D. (1983). *The rise of the computer state*. New York: Random House.

Bushnell, J. (1989). *Moscow graffiti: Language and subculture*. Winchester, MA: Unwin Hyman.

Butler, J. (1990). *Gender trouble: Feminism and the subversion of identity*. London: Routledge.

Byars, J. (1991). *All that Hollywood allows: Re-reading gender in 1950s melodrama*. Chapel Hill, NC: University of North Carolina Press.

Campbell, D. (1992, March 1). AIDS messiah with feet of clay. *Scotland on Sunday*.

Cantor, M. (1978). Where are the women in public broadcasting? In G. Tuchman (Ed.), *Hearth and home: Images of women and men in the media* (pp. 78-90). New York: Oxford University Press.

Cantor, M., & Cantor, J. (1991). *Prime time television: Content and control*. London: Sage.

Caute, D. (1978). *The great fear*. New York: Simon & Schuster.

Chambers, I. (1985). *Urban rhythms: Pop music and popular culture*. New York: Macmillan.

Chapple, S., & Garofalo, R. (1977). *Rock 'n' roll is here to pay*. Chicago: Nelson-Hall.

Check, W. (1987). Beyond the political model of reporting: nonspecific symptoms in media communication about AIDS. *Review of Infectious Diseases, 9*(5).

Chomsky, N. (1991). *Deterring democracy*. London: Verso.

Clippinger, J. H. (1976). *Who gains by communications development studies of information technologies in developing countries*. Cambridge, MA: Harvard University, Program on Information Technologies and Public Policy.

Cockburn, C. (1983). *Brothers: Male dominance and technological change*. London: Pluto.

Cockburn, L. (1988). *Out of control*. New York: Atlantic Monthly Press.

Communications Law Centre. (1992). *The representation of non-English speaking background people in Australian television drama*. Kensington, NSW: Author.

Condee, N., & Padunov, V. (1989). The Soviet cultural underground in the 1980s. In S. Siegelaub & A. Mattelart (Eds.), *Communication and class struggle* (Vol. 3). New York: International General.

Conway, M. D. (Ed.). (1967). *The writings of Thomas Paine* (Vol. 1). New York: AMS.

Cook, T., & Corby, D. E. (1992). *The mass mediated epidemic: The politics of AIDS on the nightly network news*.

Cooper, M. (1990, June 18). The press and the Panama invasion. *The Nation*, pp. 850-854.

Cose, E. (1993, October 4). A city room of many colors. *Newsweek*, p. 82.

Coupe, B., & Jakubowicz, A., with Randall L. (1993). *Next door neighbours: A report for the Office of Multicultural Affairs on ethnic group discussions of the Australian media*. Canberra: Office of Multicultural Affairs.

Cumberbatch, G., & Howitt, D. (1989). *A measure of uncertainty: The effects of mass media* (Broadcasting Standards Council Research Monograph No. 1). London: John Libbey.

Curran, J., & Seaton, J. (1985). *Power without responsibility: The press and broadcasting in Britain.* London: Methuen.

Daley, P., & James, B. (1992). Ethnic broadcasting in Alaska: The failure of a participatory model. In S. H. Riggins (Ed.), *Ethnic minority media: An international perspective.* Newbury Park, CA: Sage.

Daniels, T., & Gerson, J. (Eds.). (1989). *The colour black: Black images in British television.* London: British Film Institute Press.

De Beauvoir, S. (1972). *The second sex.* London: Penguin Books.

De Bens, E., & Knoche, M. (Eds.). (1987). *Electronic mass media in Western Europe: Prospects for development* (Report of the FAST Programme for the EC). Brussels: D. Reidel.

de Cordova, R. (1990). *Picture personalities: The emergence of the star system in America.* Urbana: University of Illinois Press.

De Lauretis, T. (1987). *Technologies of gender: Essays on theory, film and fiction.* London: Macmillan.

De Lauretis, T., & Heath, S. (Eds.). (1980). *The cinematic apparatus.* New York: St. Martin's.

Demac, D. (1985). *Keeping America uninformed.* New York: Pilgrim.

Demac, D. (1988). *Liberty denied: The current rise of censorship in America.* New York: Pen International Center.

Denski, S., & Sholle, D. (1992). Metal men and glamour boys: Gender performance in heavy metal. In S. Craig (Ed.), *Men, masculinity and the media* (pp. 41-60). London: Sage.

DiMaggio, P. (1982). Cultural capital and school success: The impact of status culture participation on the grades of U.S. high school students. *American Sociological Review, 47,* 189-201.

DiMaggio, P., & Useem, M. (1978). Cultural democracy in a period of cultural expansion: The social composition of arts audiences in the United States. *Social Problems, 26,* 180-197.

Donner, F. (1990). *Protectors of privilege: Red squads and police repression in urban America.* Berkeley: University of California Press.

Downing, J. (1984). *Radical media.* Boston: South End.

Downing, J. (1985). The Intersputnik system and Soviet television. *Soviet Studies, 37,* 465-483.

Downing, J. (1986). Government secrecy and the media in the United States and Britain. In P. Golding, G. Murdock, & P. Schlesinger (Eds.), *Communicating politics: Mass communications and the political process.* New York: Holmes & Meier.

Downing, J. (Ed.). (1987). *Film and politics in the Third World.* New York: Praeger/Autonomedia.

Downing, J. (1988a). The alternative public realm: The 1980s anti-nuclear press in West Germany and Britain. *Media, Culture & Society, 10,* 163-181.

Downing, J. (1988b). *The Cosby show* and American racial discourse. In G. Smitherman-Donaldson & T. A. van Dijk (Eds.), *Discourse and discrimination* (pp. 46-74). Detroit: Wayne State University Press.

Downing, J. (1988c). Soviet media coverage of Afghanistan. *Journal of Communication, 38*(4), 5-32.

Downing, J. (1992). Latino media in the Greater New York region. In S. H. Riggins (Ed.), *Ethnic minority media: An international perspective* (pp. 256-275). Newbury Park, CA: Sage.

Downing, J. (1994). Communications training programmes for members of ethnic minority groups in the United States of America: An overview. In C. Husband (Ed.),

A richer vision: The development of ethnic minority media in Western democracies (pp. 20-37). Paris/London: UNESCO/John Libbey.

Drinnon, R. (1980). *Facing west.* New York: Meridian.

Dyer, R. (1979). *Stars.* London: British Film Institute Press.

Dyson, K., & Humphreys, P. (1986). *The politics of the communication revolution in West Europe.* London: Frank Cass.

Edwards, B. (1987, November 10). *The morning edition* [Radio program]. National Public Radio.

Ehrenreich, B., & English, D. (1978). *For her own good: 150 years of the experts' advice to women.* Garden City, NY: Anchor.

Eisenstein, E. (1979). *The printing press as an agent of change: Communications and cultural transformations in early modern Europe* (2 vols.). New York: Cambridge University Press.

Elliot, P. (1974). Uses and gratifications research: A critique and a sociological alternative. In J. G. Blumler & E. Katz (Eds.), *The uses of mass communications: Current perspectives on gratifications research* (pp. 249-268). Beverly Hills, CA: Sage.

Elsaesser, T. (Ed.). (1990). *Early cinema: Space, frame, narrative.* London: British Film Institute Press.

Entman, R. M. (1992). Blacks in the news: Television, modern racism and cultural change. *Journalism Quarterly, 69,* 341-361.

Epstein, E. J. (1973). *News from nowhere.* New York: Random House.

Epstein, S. (1991). Democratic science? AIDS activism and the contested construction of knowledge. *Socialist Review, 21*(2), 35-65.

Euromedia Research Group. (1992). *The media in Western Europe.* London: Sage.

European Economic Community. (1984). *Television without frontiers: EEC green book.* Brussels: Commission of the European Communities.

European Institute for the Media. (1988). *Europe 2000.* Paris: Author.

Ewen, S. (1976). *Captains of consciousness.* New York: McGraw-Hill.

Ewen, S. (1988). *All consuming images.* New York: Basic Books.

Fabre, M. (1963). *A history of communications.* New York: Hawthorne.

Faludi, S. (1991). *Backlash: The undeclared war against American women.* New York: Crown.

Fanon, F. (1967). *The wretched of the earth.* Middlesex: Penguin.

Federal Communications Commission. (1988). *Broadcast and cable employment trend report 1987.* Washington, DC: Author.

Fejes, F. J. (1992). Masculinity as fact. In S. Craig (Ed.), *Men, masculinity and the media* (pp. 9-22). London: Sage.

Fiske, J. (1987). British cultural studies and television. In R. C. Allen (Ed.), *Channels of discourse.* Chapel Hill: University of North Carolina Press.

Fiske, J. (1991). Postmodernism and television. In J. Curran & M. Gurevitch (Eds.), *Mass media and society* (pp. 55-67). London: Edward Arnold.

Foner, P. (Ed.). (1950). *The life and writings of Frederick Douglass* (Vol. 2). New York: International.

Foote, J. S., & Steele, M. E. (1986, Spring). Degree of conformity in lead stories in early evening network newscasts. *Journalism Quarterly, 64,* 19-23.

Forgacs, D. (1989). *A Gramsci reader.* Cambridge, MA: Belknap.

Friedan, B. (1977). *The feminine mystique.* New York: Dell. (Original work published 1963)

Frith, S. (1983). *Sound effects: Youth, leisure and the politics of rock 'n' roll.* New York: Pantheon.

Frith, S. (1986). Art versus technology: The strange case of popular music. *Media, Culture & Society, 8,* 263-279.

Frith, S. (1988a). *Music for pleasure.* Cambridge: Polity.

Frith, S. (1988b). Video pop: Picking up the pieces. In S. Frith (Ed.), *Facing the music.* New York: Pantheon.

Gallagher, C. (1993). *American ground zero: The secret nuclear war.* Cambridge: MIT Press.

Gallagher, M. (1980). *Unequal opportunities: The case of women and the media.* Paris: UNESCO.

Galtung, J. (1982). Sport as carrier of deep culture and structure. *Current Research on Peace and Violence, 5,* 2-3.

Gans, H. (1979). *Deciding what's news: A study of* CBS Evening News, NBC Nightly News, Newsweek *and* Time. New York: Vintage.

Garber, M. (1992). *Vested interests: Cross-dressing and cultural anxiety.* London: Routledge.

George, N. (1988). *The death of rhythm and blues.* New York: Pantheon.

Gerbner, G. (1993, June 15). *Women and minorities on television: A study in casting and fate.* Report to the Screen Actors Guild and the American Federation of Radio and Television Artists, University of Pennsylvania, Annenberg School for Communication.

Gibson, W. (1984). *Neuromancer.* New York: Ace.

Giddens, A. (1990). *The consequences of modernity.* Stanford, CA: Stanford University Press.

Gilman, S. (1988). *Disease and representation.* Ithaca, NY: Cornell University Press.

Gitlin, T. (1983). *Inside prime time.* New York: Pantheon.

Gleason, A., Kenez, P., & Stites, R. (Eds.). (1985). *Bolshevik culture.* Bloomington: Indiana University Press.

Gledhill, C. (1988). Pleasurable negotiations. In E. D. Pribram (Ed.), *Female spectators: Looking at film and television.* London: Verso.

Goldman, E. (1969). *Anarchism and other essays.* New York: Dover.

Goldman, R. (1984). We make weekends: Leisure and the commodity form. *Social Text, 8,* 84-103.

Goldman, R. (1987). Marketing fragrances: Advertising and the production of commodity signs. *Theory, Culture and Society, 4,* 691-725.

Gouldner, A. (1976). *Dialectic of ideology and technology.* New York: Seabury.

Gramsci, A. (1971). *Selections from the prison notebooks* (Q. Hoare & G. Nowell-Smith, Trans.). New York: International.

Gray, H. (1986). Television and the new Black man: Black male images in prime-time situation comedy. *Media, Culture & Society, 8,* 223-242.

Greenberg, B. (1980). *Life on television: Content analyses of U.S. TV drama.* Norwood, NJ: Ablex.

Greenberg, B., & Brand, J. (1993). Minorities and the mass media: 1970s to 1990s. In J. Bryant & D. Zillmann (Eds.), *Media effects: Advances in theory and research.* Hillsdale, NJ: Lawrence Erlbaum.

Grossberg, L. (1992). *We gotta get out of this place: Popular conservatism and postmodern culture.* New York: Routledge.

Grossberg, L., Nelson, C., & Treichler, P. A. (Eds.). (1992). *Cultural studies.* New York: Routledge.

Habermas, J. (1979). The public sphere. In A. Mattelart & S. Siegelaub (Eds.), *Communication and class struggle* (Vol. 1, pp. 198-201). New York: International General.

Halberstam, D. (1979). *The powers that be.* New York: Knopf.

Hall, S. (1980). Cultural studies: Two paradigms. *Media, Culture & Society, 2*(1).

Hall, S., Critcher, C., Jefferson, T., Clarke, J., & Roberts, B. (1978). *Policing the crisis: Mugging, the state, and law and order.* London: Macmillan.

Hallin, D. (1989). *The "uncensored war": The media and Vietnam* (2nd ed.). New York: Oxford University Press.

Hamelink, C. J. (1983). *Finance and information*. Norwood, NJ: Ablex.

Hamelink, C. J. (1986). *Militarization in the information age*. World Council of Churches.

Hansen, M. (1991). *Babel and Babylon: Spectatorship in American silent film*. Cambridge, MA: Harvard University Press.

Haraway, D. J. (1991). A manifesto for cyborgs. In D. J. Haraway, *Simians, cyborgs, and women: The reinvention of nature*. New York: Routledge. (Original work published 1985)

Harms, J. (1989). *Advertising and the forms of mass communications: An immanent critique*. Unpublished manuscript.

Harris, N. (1987). *The end of the Third World*. Middlesex: Penguin.

Havelock, E. (1963). *Preface to Plato*. Cambridge, MA: Belknap.

Havelock, E. (1986). *The muse learns to write*. New Haven, CT: Yale University Press.

Hayes, D. (1991). *Sinéad O'Connor: So different*. New York: Omnibus.

Hebdige, D. (1979). *Subculture: The meaning of style*. London: Methuen.

Hendricks, G. (1961). *The Edison motion picture myth*. Berkeley: University of California Press.

Hennig, M., & Jardin, A. (1977). *The managerial woman*. Garden City, NY: Anchor.

Henningham, J. (1992). Flaws in the melting pot: Hawaiian media. In S. H. Riggins (Ed.), *Ethnic minority media: An international perspective* (pp. 149-161). Newbury Park, CA: Sage.

Herman, E. S. (1982). *The real terror network: Terrorism in fact and propaganda*. Boston: South End.

Herman, E. S., & Brodhead, F. (1986). *The rise and fall of the Bulgarian connection*. New York: Sheridan Square.

Herman, E. S., & Chomsky, N. (1988). *Manufacturing consent: The political economy of the mass media*. New York: Pantheon.

Hermes, J. (1993). *Easily put down: Women's magazines, readers, reporters and everyday life*. Unpublished doctoral thesis, University of Amsterdam.

Hersh, S. (1983). *The price of power*. New York: Summit.

Hertsgaard, M. (1988). *On bended knee: The press and the Reagan presidency*. New York: Farrar, Straus & Giroux.

Hess, S. (1987). *The Washington reporters*. Washington, DC: Brookings Institution.

Hilgartner, S., Bell, R. C., & O'Connor, R. (1983). *Nukespeak: The selling of nuclear technology in America*. New York: Penguin.

Hobsbawm, E. (1989). *Age of empire*. New York: Vintage.

Hobson, D. (1982). *Crossroads: The drama of a soap-opera*. London: Methuen.

International Commission for the Study of Communication Problems. (1980). *Many voices, one world*. Paris: UNESCO.

Jakubowicz, A. (1987). Days of our lives: Multiculturalism, mainstreaming and the "special" broadcasting service. *Media Information Australia, 45*, 18-32.

Jakubowicz, A. (1989). Speaking in tongues: Multicultural media and the constitution of the socially homogeneous Australian. In M. Wilson (Ed.), *Australian communications and the public sphere* (pp. 105-127). Sydney: Macmillan.

Jakubowicz, A. (1994). *Ethnicity, race and the media: Under pressure*. Sydney: Allen & Unwin.

Janeway, E. (1974). *Between myth and morning: Women awakening*. New York: William Morrow.

Jensen, C. (1992, February). The most underreported stories of 1991. *St. Louis Journalism Review*, pp. 10-11, 19.

Jezer, M. (1982). *The dark ages*. Boston: South End.

Jhally, S., & Lewis, J. (1992). *Enlightened racism*. Boulder, CO: Westview.

Jhally, S., & Livant, B. (1986). Watching as working: The valorization of audience consciousness. *Journal of Communication, 36*(3).

Johnson, M. (1990, December 3). Women under glass. *Computerworld*, p. 93.

Jones, M. C. (1993). *Heretics and hellraisers: Women contributors to "The masses," 1911-1917*. Austin: University of Texas Press.

Jung, C. (Ed.). (1968). *Man and his symbols*. New York: Dell.

Kagarlitsky, B. (1988). *The thinking reed*. New York: Verso.

Kaplan, E. A. (1993). Madonna's politics: Perversion, repression, or subversion? Or masks and/as mastery. In C. Schwichtenberg (Ed.), *The Madonna connection: Representational politics, subcultural identity, and cultural theory* (pp. 149-166). Boulder, CO: Westview.

Karpf, A. (1988). *Doctoring the media*. London: Routledge.

Kay, J. (1988). *Communicating through electronic bulletin boards in the white supremacy movement: Creating culture via computer* (Laase Communication Research Center Report 88-7). Lincoln: University of Nebraska.

Keen, S. (1987). *Faces of the enemy*. New York: Harper & Row.

Kellner, D. (1982). Television, mythology and ritual. *Praxis, 6*, 133-155.

Kellner, D. (1989). *Critical theory, Marxism and modernity*. Cambridge: Polity.

Kellner, D. (1992). *The Persian Gulf TV war*. Boulder, CO: Westview.

Kelly, M. (1993, October 31). David Gergen, master of the game. *New York Times Magazine*, pp. 64-71, 80, 94, 103.

Kennedy, D. M. (1980). *Over here: The First World War and American society*. New York: Oxford University Press.

King, E., & Schudson, M. (1987, November-December). The myth of the great communicator. *Columbia Journalism Review*, pp. 37-39.

Klapper, J. T. (1960). *The effects of mass communication*. New York: Free Press.

Konig, R. (1973). *A la mode*. New York: Seabury.

Langton, M. (1993). *Well I heard it on the radio and I saw it on television: An essay for the Australian Film Commission on the politics and aesthetics of filmmaking by and about Aboriginal people and things*. North Sydney: Australian Film Commission.

Larson, J. F. (1982). International affairs coverage on U.S. evening network news, 1972-1978. In W. C. Adams (Ed.), *Television coverage of international affairs*. Norwood, NJ: Ablex.

Lazarsfeld, P. (1941). Remarks on critical and administrative communication research. *Studies in Philosophy and Social Science, 9*, 2-16.

Lazier-Smith, L. (1989). A new "generation" of images of women. In P. Creedon (Ed.), *Women in mass communication: Challenging gender values* (pp. 247-260). Newbury Park, CA: Sage.

Lerner, D. (1958). *The passing of traditional society*. New York: Free Press.

Lévi-Strauss, C. (1967). *Structural anthropology*. Garden City, NY: Doubleday.

Lewis, L. (1990). *Gender politics and MTV: Voicing the difference*. Philadelphia: Temple University Press.

Lewis, L. (Ed.). (1992). *The adoring audience: Fan culture and popular media*. New York: Routledge.

Lichter, S. R., Rothman, S., & Lichter, L. (1986). *The media elite*. Bethesda, MD: Adler & Adler.

Lieberman, T. (1993, September-October). Health care coverage: Round one. *Columbia Journalism Review*, pp. 42-47.

Liebes, T., & Katz, E. (1986). Patterns of involvement in television fiction: A comparative analysis. *European Journal of Communication, 1*, 151-171.

Lindlof, T. R., Shatzer, M. J., & Wilkinson, D. (1988). Accommodation of video and television in the American family. In J. Lull (Ed.), *World families watch television.* Newbury Park, CA: Sage.

Logan, R. K. (1986). *The alphabet effect.* New York: William Morrow.

Lott, E. (1993). *Love and theft: Blackface minstrelsy and the American working class.* New York: Oxford University Press.

Lull, J. (1982). How families select television programs: A mass-observational study. *Journal of Broadcasting, 26,* 801-813.

Lupton, D. (1994). *Moral threats and dangerous desires: AIDS in the news media.* London: Taylor & Francis.

MacArthur, J. R. (1991). *Second front: Censorship and propaganda in the Gulf War.* Berkeley: University of California Press.

MacDonald, J. F. (1983). *Blacks and white TV: Afro-Americans in television since 1948.* Chicago: Nelson-Hall.

Manno, J. (1984). *Arming the heavens: The hidden military agenda for space, 1945-1995.* New York: Dodd, Mead.

Marchand, R. (1985). *Advertising the American dream: Making way for modernity, 1920-1940.* Berkeley: University of California Press.

Marcuse, H. (1964). *One dimensional man.* Boston: Beacon.

Marx, G. (1988). *Undercover: Police surveillance in America.* Berkeley: University of California Press.

Massing, M. (1982, November-December). Black-out in television. *Columbia Journalism Review,* pp. 38-44.

Mast, G. (1981). *A short history of the movies* (3rd ed.). New York: Bobbs Merrill.

Matsuda, M. J., Lawrence, C. R., III, Delgado, R., & Crenshaw, K. W. (1993). *Words that wound: Critical race theory, assaultive speech, and the First Amendment.* Boulder, CO: Westview.

McClure, L. W., & Fulton, P. C. (1964). *Advertising in the printed media.* New York: Macmillan.

McGowan, W. (1993, November-December). The other side of the rainbow. *Columbia Journalism Review,* pp. 53-57.

McLuhan, M. (1964). *Understanding media.* London: Methuen.

McLuhan, M., & Fiore, Q. (1968). *War and peace in the global village.* New York: McGraw-Hill.

McQuail, D. (1987). *Mass communication theory: An introduction.* London: Sage.

Meadows, M. (1992). Broadcasting in Aboriginal Australia: One mob, one voice, one land. In S. H. Riggins (Ed.), *Ethnic minority media: An international perspective* (pp. 82-101). Newbury Park, CA: Sage.

Medvedev, R. (Ed.). (1984). *Samizdat' register I.* New York: Pathfinder.

Messaris, P. (1977). Biases of self-reported "functions and gratifications" of mass media use. *Et Cetera, 34.*

Meyrowitz, J. (1985). *No sense of place: The impact of electronic media on social behavior.* New York: Oxford University Press.

Meyrowitz, J. (in press). Visible and invisible candidates: A case study in competing logic of campaign coverage. *Political Communication.*

Mickiewicz, E. P. (1981). *Media and the Russian public.* New York: Praeger.

Mickiewicz, E. P. (1988). *Split signals: Television and politics in the Soviet Union.* New York: Oxford University Press.

Miller, M., & Darling, J. (1991, November 10). El tigre. *Los Angeles Times Magazine,* pp. 24-29, 51.

Miller, M. C. (1988). Cosby knows best. In M. C. Miller, *Boxed-in: The culture of TV* (pp. 69-78). Evanston, IL: Northwestern University Press.

Mohammadi, A. (1976). *Development-support communication and instructional learning centers for rural areas in Iran.* Unpublished doctoral dissertation, Columbia University.

Moore, R. (1988). The Constitution, the presidency and 1988. *Presidential Studies Quarterly, 18*(1).

Morley, D. (1986). *Family television: Cultural power and domestic leisure.* London: Comedia.

Morley, D., & Silverstone, R. (1991). Communication and context: Ethnographic perspectives on the media audience. In K. Jensen & N. Jankowski (Eds.), *A handbook of qualitative methodologies for mass communication research* (pp. 149-162). London: Routledge.

Morone, J. G., & Woodhouse, E. J. (1989). *The demise of nuclear energy? Lessons for democratic control of technology.* New Haven, CT: Yale University Press.

Motamed-Nejad, K. (1976). *Communication and Westernization.* Tehran: College of Mass Communication.

Mowlana, H. (1986). *Global information and world communication.* New York: Longman.

Mowlana, H., Gerbner, G., & Schiller, H. (1992). *Triumph of the image.* Boulder, CO: Westview.

Musser, C. (1990). The nickelodeon era begins: Establishing the framework for Hollywood's mode of representation. In T. Elsaesser (Ed.), *Early cinema: Space, frame, narrative.* London: Verso.

Myrdal, G., with Sterner, R., & Rose, A. (1944). *An American dilemma: The Negro problem and modern democracy.* New York: Harper & Row.

Nardi, P. M. (1990). AIDS and obituaries: The perpetuation of stigma in the press. In D. Feldman (Ed.), *Culture and AIDS* (pp. 159-168). New York: Praeger.

Nasaw, D. (1993). *Going out: The rise and fall of public amusements.* New York: Basic Books.

National Association of Black Journalists Print Task Force. (1993). *Muted voices: Frustration and fear in the newsroom.* Reston, VA: National Association of Black Journalists.

National Association of Broadcasters. (1986). *Minority broadcasting facts.* Washington, DC: Author.

National Science Foundation. (1984). *Communications technology and economic development.* Washington, DC: Author.

Negus, K. (1992). *Producing pop: Culture and conflict in the popular music industry.* London: Edward Arnold.

Nelson, J. (1993). *Volunteer slavery: My authentic Negro experience.* Chicago: Noble.

Nelson, T. H. (1974). *Computer lib.* Redmond, WA: Microsoft Press.

Nelson, T. H. (1980). *Literary machines.* Mindful Press.

Nesteby, J. R. (1982). *Black images and American films, 1896-1954: The interplay between civil rights and film culture.* Lanham, MD: University Press of America.

Niane, D. T. (1965). *Sundiata* (G. Pickett, Trans.). London: Longman.

Nugent, S., Loncar, M., & Aisbett, K. (1993). *The people we see on TV: Cultural diversity on television* (Monograph 3). North Sydney: Australian Broadcasting Authority.

O'Connor, A. (1991). The emergence of cultural studies in Latin America. *Critical Studies in Mass Communication, 8*(1), 60-74.

Ogle, P. (1977, January 2). Development of sound systems: The commercial era. *Film Reader.*

Ong, W. (1982). *Orality and literacy.* New York: Methuen.

Paletz, D. L., & Entman, R. M. (1981). *Media power politics.* New York: Free Press.

Parenti, M. (1986). *Inventing reality: The politics of the mass media.* New York: St. Martin's.

Pearce, J. (1982). *Under the eagle*. Boston: South End.

Perry, L. (1984). *Intellectual life in America: A history*. New York: Franklin Watts.

Peterson, E. E. (1987). Media consumption and girls who want to have fun. *Critical Studies in Mass Communication, 4*(1), 37-50.

Postman, N. (1984). *Amusing ourselves to death: Public discourse in the age of show business*. New York: Viking Penguin.

Powdermaker, H. (1979). *Hollywood: The dream factory; an anthropologist looks at the movie-makers* (L. A. Coser & W. W. Powell, Eds.). Salem, NH: Ayer. (Original work published 1950)

Pribram, E. D. (1993). Seduction, control and the search for authenticity: Madonna's *Truth or Dare*. In C. Schwichtenberg (Ed.), *The Madonna connection: Representational politics, subcultural identity and cultural theory* (pp. 189-212). Boulder, CO: Westview.

Propp, V. (1968). *The morphology of the folktale* (2nd ed.). Austin: University of Texas Press. (Original work published 1928)

Pye, L. (Ed.). (1963). *Communications and political development*. Princeton, NJ: Princeton University Press.

Rader, B. (1984). *In its own image: How television has transformed sports*. New York: Free Press.

Radway, J. A. (1984). *Reading the romance: Women, patriarchy and popular literature*. Chapel Hill: University of North Carolina Press.

Radway, J. A. (1987). Interpretive communities and variable literacies (commentary on T. Lindlof, Media audiences as interpretive communities). In J. A. Anderson (Ed.), *Communication yearbook 11*. Newbury Park, CA: Sage.

Ramsaye, T. (1926). *A million and one nights*. New York: Simon & Schuster.

Rêgo, C. (1993). On readers and texts: Tracking the routes of cultural studies. In J. M. de Melo (Ed.), *Communication for a new world: Brazilian perspectives* (pp. 87-108). São Paulo: Universidade de São Paulo, School of Communication and the Arts.

Remington, T. (1988). *The truth of authority*. Pittsburgh: Pittsburgh University Press.

Riffe, D., Ellis, B., Rogers, M. K., Van Ommeren, R. L., & Woodman, K. A. (1986). Gatekeeping and the network news mix. *Journalism Quarterly, 63*, 315-321.

Robertson, R. (1992). *Globalization: Social theory and global culture*. Newbury Park, CA: Sage.

Rodríguez, A. (1993). *Made in the USA: The constructions of Univisión news*. Unpublished doctoral dissertation, University of California, San Diego, Department of Communication.

Rosenberg, R. S. (1992). *The social impact of computers*. Boston: Academic Press.

Rosengren, K. E., Palmgreen, P., & Wenner, L. (Eds.). (1985). *Media gratifications research: Current perspectives*. Beverly Hills, CA: Sage.

Russo, M. (1986). Female grotesques: Carnival and theory. In T. De Lauretis (Ed.), *Feminist studies, critical studies*. Bloomington: Indiana University Press.

Said, E. (1979). *Orientalism*. New York: Random House.

Said, E. (1981). *Covering Islam*. London: Routledge & Kegan Paul.

Samuelson, R. (1989, September 4). The American sports mania. *Newsweek*, p. 49.

Saussure, F. de. (1966). *A course in general linguistics* (W. Baskin, Trans.). New York: McGraw-Hill.

Sawicki, J. (1991). *Disciplining Foucault: Feminism, power and the body*. London: Routledge.

Schickel, R. (1991, June 24). Gender bender. *Time*.

Schlesinger, P. (1988). *Putting "reality" together* (2nd ed.). London: Methuen.

Schramm, W. (1988). *The story of human communication*. New York: Harper & Row.

Schudson, M. (1984). *Advertising, the uneasy persuasion*. New York: Basic Books.

Seiter, E. (1987). Semiotics and television. In R. Allen (Ed.), *Channels of discourse: Television and contemporary criticism* (pp. 17-44). London: Methuen.

Seiter, E., Borchers, H., Kreutzner, G., & Warth, E. M. (Eds.). (1991). *Remote control: Television, audiences and cultural power.* London: Routledge.

Sepstrup, P. (1989). Research into international television flows. *European Journal of Communication, 4*(4).

Shaheen, J. (1984). *The TV Arab.* Bowling Green, OH: Popular Press.

Shalom, S. R. (1993). *Imperial alibis: Rationalizing U.S. intervention after the Cold War.* Boston: South End.

Shanor, D. (1985). *Behind the lines.* New York: St. Martin's.

Siegel, L., & Markoff, J. (1986). *The high cost of high tech.* New York: Harper & Row.

Sigal, L. (1973). *Reporters and officials.* Lexington: D. C. Heath.

Siune, K., & Truetzschler, W. (Eds.). (1992). *Dynamics of media politics.* London: Sage.

Smith, A. (1984). *The geopolitics of information.* London: Faber & Faber.

Smith, A. D. (1981). *The ethnic revival in the modern world.* Cambridge: Cambridge University Press.

Smith, A. D. (1990). Towards a global culture? In M. Featherstone (Ed.), *Global culture: Nationalism, globalization and modernity* (pp. 179-192). London: Sage.

Smith, G. S. (1984). *Songs to seven strings.* Bloomington: Indiana University Press.

Smythe, D. (1981). *Dependency road: Communications, capitalism, consciousness, and Canada.* Norwood, NJ: Ablex.

Sreberny-Mohammadi, A., Nordenstreng, K., Stevenson, R., & Ugboajah, F. (1984). *Foreign news in the media: International reporting in 29 countries* (Reports and Papers on Mass Communication No. 93). Paris: UNESCO.

Sreberny-Mohammadi, A., & Mohammadi, A. (1994). *Small media, big revolution: Communications, culture and the Iranian revolution.* Minneapolis: University of Minnesota.

Staiger, J. (1992). *Interpreting films: Studies in the historical reception of American cinema.* Princeton, NJ: Princeton University Press.

Stallybrass, P., & White, A. (1986). *The politics and poetics of transgression.* Ithaca, NY: Cornell University Press.

Stam, R., Burgoyne, R., & Flitterman-Lewis, S. (1992). *New vocabularies in film semiotics: Structuralism, poststructuralism and beyond.* New York: Routledge.

Stamps, C. H. (1979). *The concept of the mass audience in American broadcasting.* New York: Arno.

Steinem, G. (1980). Introduction. In S. Levine & H. Lyons (Eds.), *Decade of women: A Ms. history of the seventies in words and pictures.* New York: Paragon.

Stone, A. R. (1991). Will the real body please stand up? Boundary stories about virtual cultures. In M. L. Benedikt (Ed.), *Cyberspace: First steps.* Cambridge: MIT Press.

Stone, A. R. (1993, December 3). Sex, death, and architecture. *ANY*, pp. 34-39.

Switkin, A. (1981). *Ads: Design and make your own car.* New York: Van Nostrand Reinhold.

Taras, D. (1993). The mass media and political crisis: Reporting Canada's constitutional struggles. *Canadian Journal of Communication, 18*, 75-94.

Taylor, P. (1992). *War and the media: Propaganda and persuasion in the Gulf War.* New York: St. Martin's.

Temple, R. (1986). *The genius of China.* New York: Simon & Schuster.

Theberge, L. J. (Ed.). (1981). *Crooks, conmen and clowns: Businessmen in TV entertainment.* Washington, DC: Media Institute.

Thomas, S. (1986). Mass media and social order. In G. Gumpert & R. Cathcart (Eds.), *Inter/media.* New York: Oxford University Press.

Thomas, S., & Callahan, B. P. (1982). Allocating happiness: Television families and social class. *Journal of Communication, 32.*

Thomas, S., & Leshay, S. V. (1992). Bad business? A reassessment of television's portrayal of businesspersons. *Journal of Communication, 42*(1), 95-105.

Tuchman, G. (1978). *Making news.* New York: Free Press.

Tunstall, J. (1977). *The media are American.* New York: Columbia University Press.

Turner, V. (1969). *The ritual process: Structure and anti-structure.* Ithaca, NY: Cornell University Press.

Ulanoff, S. (1977). *Advertising in America: An introduction to persuasive communication.* New York: Hastings.

UNESCO. (1989). *World communication report.* Paris: Author.

van Dijk, T. A. (1991a). The interdisciplinary study of news as discourse. In K. Jensen & N. Jankowski (Eds.), *A handbook of qualitative methodologies for mass communication research* (pp. 108-120). London: Routledge.

van Dijk, T. A. (1991b). *Racism and the press.* London: Routledge.

Vincent, R. C., Davis, D. K., & Boruzkowski, L. A. (1987). Sexism on MTV: The portrayal of women in rock videos. *Journalism Quarterly, 64,* 750-755.

Wachtel, E. (1986) *Television hiring practices.* New York: United Church of Christ, Office of Communication.

Wernick, A. (1991). *Promotional culture: Advertising, ideology and symbolic expression.* London: Sage.

Williams, F. (1982). *The communications revolution.* Beverly Hills, CA: Sage.

Williams, R. (1961). *The long revolution.* Harmondsworth: Penguin.

Williams, R. (1974). *Television: Technology and cultural form.* London: Fontana.

Williams, R. (1977). *Marxism and literature.* New York: Oxford University Press.

Williams, W. A. (1980). *Empire as a way of life.* New York: Oxford University Press.

Williamson, J. (1978). *Decoding advertisements.* London: Marion Boyars.

Wilson, K. G. (1988). *Technologies of control.* Madison: University of Wisconsin Press.

Winston, B. (1985). A whole technology of dyeing: A note on ideology and the apparatus of the chromatic moving image. *Daedelus, 114* (4).

Winston, B. (1986). *Misunderstanding media.* Cambridge, MA: Harvard University Press.

Winston, B. (1987). A mirror for Brunelleschi. *Daedelus, 116*(3).

Winston, M. R. (1982). Racial consciousness and the evolution of mass communication in the United States. *Daedelus, 111*(4), 171-182.

Winter, J., & Hassanpour, A. (1994, January-February). Canada's Jurassic media. *Canadian Forum,* pp. 1-12.

Wood, E. M. (1988, January-February). Capitalism and human emancipation. *New Left Review, 167.*

Zinn, H. (1980). *A people's history of the United States.* New York: Harper & Row.

Zolf, D. (1989). Comparisons of multicultural broadcasting in Canada and four other countries. *Canadian Ethnic Studies, 31*(2), 13-26.

Zoonen, L. van. (1994). *Feminist media studies.* London: Sage.

About the Authors

Ien Ang teaches in the Communication Department at Murdoch University, Perth, Australia. She is the author of *Watching* Dallas: *Soap Opera and the Melodramatic Imagination* and *Desperately Seeking the Audience.*

Ash Corea has taught at North London University and the College of New Rochelle, and has a master's degree in media studies from the New School for Social Research. She has produced alternative radio programs for women and teenagers and recently readopted her initial profession, as chef and joint owner of the Empanada Parlour in Austin, Texas.

Donna A. Demac is a lawyer and teaches at Columbia University Teachers College. She is the author of *Keeping America Uninformed* and *Liberty Denied: The Current Rise of Censorship in America,* and editor of *Tracing New Orbits.*

Mary Desjardins teaches in the Department of Radio-Television-Film at the University of Texas at Austin. She has published on women and cinema and on British cinema.

John Downing is John T. Jones Jr. Centennial Professor of Communication and Chair of the Department of Radio-Television-Film, College of Communication, University of Texas at Austin. He is the author of *The Media Machine* and *Radical Media,* a revised edition of which is in preparation, and editor of *Film and Politics in the Third*

World. He has also published numerous articles in such journals as *Media, Culture & Society, Journal of Communication, European Journal of Communication,* and *Critical Studies in Mass Communication,* and he serves on the editorial boards of *Discourse & Society* and *Javnost/Public Sphere* (Slovenia). He is currently working on a book about the implications for media communication theory of regime and media transitions in Eastern Europe and elsewhere.

Oscar H. Gandy, Jr., teaches in the Annenberg School for Communication at the University of Pennsylvania. He is the author of *Beyond Agenda-Setting* and coeditor of *Proceedings From the Tenth Annual Telecommunications Policy Research Conference.*

Cees J. Hamelink is Professor of International Communication at the University of Amsterdam and the immediate past president of the International Association for Mass Communication Research. His major publications include *Cultural Autonomy in Global Communications, The Technology Gamble, Trends in World Communication,* and *The Politics of World Communication.* His current research focuses on human rights aspects of world communication.

Edward Herman is Professor Emeritus of the Annenberg School for Communication and of the Wharton School of Finance, University of Pennsylvania. He is the author of *The Real Terror Network* and coauthor of *The Washington Connection* (with Noam Chomsky), *Manufacturing Consent* (with Noam Chomsky), *The Rise and Fall of the Bulgarian Connection* (with Frank Broderick), and *The "Terrorism" Industry* (with Gerry O'Sullivan). He is coeditor of *Lies of the Times.*

Andrew Jakubowicz teaches in the Humanities Department of Sydney University of Technology, Sydney, Australia. He is the author of *Ethnicity, Race and the Media: Under Pressure.*

Douglas Kellner teaches in the Philosophy Department at the University of Texas at Austin. He is the author of numerous books, including *The Persian Gulf TV War, Television and the Crisis of Democracy,* and *Critical Theory, Marxism and Modernity,* and is coauthor, with Michael Ryan, of *Camera Politica: The Politics and Ideology of Contemporary Hollywood Film.*

Denis McQuail is Professor of Mass Communication at the University of Amsterdam. His recent publications include *Media Performance, Introduction to Mass Communication Theory* (3rd edition), and *Communication Models,* with Sven Windhal. He has long been associated with the work of the Euromedia Research Group, and his current research interests center on communication theory, mass media policy, and audience research.

Joshua Meyrowitz teaches in the Communication Department at the University of New Hampshire. He is the author of *No Sense of Place: The Impact of Electronic Media on Social Behavior.*

David Miller is a member of the Stirling Media Research Institute at Stirling University in Scotland. His recent publications include *Don't Mention the War: Northern Ireland, Propaganda and the Media* and *Dying of Ignorance? AIDS, the Media and Public Belief* (with the Glasgow University Media Group). His research interests include the sociology of public relations and propaganda and the impact of media reporting on public opinion and society more generally. He is currently collaborating with Kevin Williams on a forthcoming book titled *Media Sources.*

Ali Mohammadi is Reader in the Department of English, Media, and Cultural Studies, Nottingham Trent University. He is coauthor, with Annabelle Sreberny-Mohammadi, of *Small Media, Big Revolution: Communications, Culture, and the Iranian Revolution.* His current research interests center on international communication as it relates to development and cultural policy, with a special interest in the Persian Gulf region and Central Asia.

Keith Negus is based at the Centre for Mass Communication Research, Leicester University. He entered higher education as a mature student in 1983, having previously performed with a number of professional and semiprofessional pop and rock groups. His doctoral study of the music industry was published as *Producing Pop: Culture and Conflict in the Popular Music Industry.* His current research interests include popular music as a medium of political communication and the connections and convergences between different media texts and technologies that are shaping the emerging "global" entertainment industry.

Alan O'Connor teaches in the Department of Cultural Studies at Trent University, Peterborough, Canada. He is the author of *Raymond Williams: Writing, Culture, Politics* and editor of *Raymond Williams on Television*. He serves on the editorial board of *Borderlines* (Toronto).

Michael Real teaches in the Department of Telecommunications and Film, San Diego State University. He is author of *Mass-Mediated Cultural Realities* and *SuperMedia*.

Cedric J. Robinson teaches in the Black Studies Department and the Political Science Department at the University of California at Santa Barbara. He is the author of *The Terms of Order* and *Black Marxism*. He serves on the editorial board of *Race and Class*.

América Rodríguez teaches in the Department of Radio-Television-Film at the University of Texas at Austin. She was previously Los Angeles correspondent for National Public Radio, and is the author of the forthcoming *Noticiero Univisión*.

Nikhil Sinha teaches in the Department of Radio-Television-Film at the University of Texas at Austin. He is a former Associate Editor at All-India Radio News, and has written on the political economy of telecommunications and development. He won the annual Pacific Telecommunications Council Award for best article in 1994.

Annabelle Sreberny-Mohammadi is Professor and Director of the Centre for Mass Communication Research, University of Leicester. She is coauthor, with Ali Mohammadi, of *Small Media, Big Revolution: Communications, Culture, and the Iranian Revolution* and coeditor, with S. Braman, of a forthcoming volume on *Globalization, Communication, and Transnational Civil Society*. Her most recent work includes a report for UNESCO on women, media, and development in a global context, as well as research on media policy in the Middle East, especially as it pertains to gender and representation.

Allucquére Rosanne Stone teaches in the Department of Radio-Television-Film at the University of Texas at Austin. She coorganized the founding series of International Cyberspace Conferences, and is author of the forthcoming *Technology and Desire*.

Liching Sung is a doctoral candidate in the Department of Radio-Television-Film at the University of Texas at Austin. She has published on international mobile telephony developments and policy, and won the international 1993 Communications Policy Research Award.

Sari Thomas teaches in the Department of Radio-Television-Film at Temple University. She has edited *Critical Studies in Mass Communication* as well as the Ablex book series Studies in Communication.

Kevin Williams is Senior Lecturer at Sheffield Hallam University. He was formerly Lecturer at the Centre for Journalism Studies, University of Wales Cardiff and Senior Research Fellow at the Mass Media Unit, Glasgow University. He has written a number of books and articles on communication and war, the latest of which was "The Ethics of War Reporting" in R. Chadwick and A. Belsey, eds., *Ethical Issues in Journalism and the Media*, 1992. His work on AIDS is about to be published as *AIDS, the Media and Public Opinion: Dying of Ignorance?*

Brian Winston is Professor and Director of the Centre for Journalism Studies at the University of Wales Cardiff. He is the author of a book on documentary film titled *Claiming the Real*, and of a revisionist history of media technologies titled *Misunderstanding Media*. He is currently working on a collection of his essays on media technologies.

Liesbet van Zoonen is Associate Professor in the Department of Communication of the University of Amsterdam. She is the author of *Feminist Media Studies* and has published on that subject in several international journals. She is currently working on the representation of politics in popular culture.